Transnational Legal Processes

Law in Context

Below is a listing of the more recent publications in the Law in Context Series

Editors: William Twining (University College, London) and
Christopher McCrudden (Lincoln College, Oxford)

Ashworth: *Sentencing and Criminal Justice*
Bell: *French Legal Cultures*
Bercusson: *European Labour Law*
Birkinshaw: *Freedom of Information: The Law, the Practice and the Ideal*
Cane: *Atiyah's Accidents Compensation and the Law*
Collins: *The Law of Contract*
Elworthy and Holder: *Environmental Protection: Text and Materials*
Fortin: *Children's Rights and the Developing Law*
Harlow and Rawlings: *Law and Administration: Text and Materials*
Harris: *An Introduction to Law*
Harris, Campbell & Halson: *Remedies in Contract and Tort*
Harvey: *Seeking Asylum in the UK: Problems and Prospects*
Lacey and Wells: *Reconstructing Criminal Law*
Likosky: *Transnational Legal Processes*
Moffat: *Trusts Trusts Law- Text and Materials*
Norrie: *Crime, Reason and History*
O'Dair: *Legal Ethics Text and Materials*
Oliver and Drewry: *The Law and Parliament*
Oliver: *Common Values and the Public- Private Divide*
Palmer and Roberts: *Dispute Processes: ADR and the Primary Forms of
        Decision Making*
Reed: *Internet Law: Text and Materials*
Scott and Black: *Cranston's Consumers and the Law*
Turpin: *British Government and the Constitution: Text, Cases and Materials*
Twining and Miers: *How to Do Things with Rules*
Twining: *Globalisation and Legal Theory*
Ward: *Shakespeare and the Legal Imagination*
Zander: *Cases and Materials on the English Legal System*
Zander: *The Law Making Process*

Transnational Legal Processes

Edited by

Michael Likosky

Wolfson College, University of Oxford

With a Foreword by

A Vaughan Lowe

Chichele Professor of Public International Law and Fellow,
All Souls College, University of Oxford

DAMAGED

Butterworths
LexisNexis™

Members of the LexisNexis Group worldwide

United Kingdom	Butterworths Tolley, a Division of Reed Elsevier (UK) Ltd, Halsbury House, 35 Chancery Lane, LONDON, WC2A 1EL, and 4 Hill Street, EDINBURGH EH2 3JZ
Argentina	Abeledo Perrot, Jurisprudencia Argentina and Depalma, BUENOS AIRES
Australia	Butterworths, a Division of Reed International Books Australia Pty Ltd, CHATSWOOD, New South Wales
Austria	ARD Betriebsdienst and Verlag Orac, VIENNA
Canada	Butterworths Canada Ltd, MARKHAM, Ontario
Chile	Publitecsa and Conosur Ltda, SANTIAGO DE CHILE
Czech Republic	Orac sro, PRAGUE
France	Editions du Juris-Classeur SA, PARIS
Hong Kong	Butterworths Asia (Hong Kong), HONG KONG
Hungary	Hvg Orac, BUDAPEST
India	Butterworths India, NEW DELHI
Ireland	Butterworths (Ireland) Ltd, DUBLIN
Italy	Giuffré, MILAN
Malaysia	Malayan Law Journal Sdn Bhd, KUALA LUMPUR
New Zealand	Butterworths of New Zealand, WELLINGTON
Poland	Wydawnictwa Prawnicze PWN, WARSAW
Singapore	Butterworths Asia, SINGAPORE
South Africa	Butterworths Publishers (Pty) Ltd, DURBAN
Switzerland	Stämpfli Verlag AG, BERNE
USA	LexisNexis, DAYTON, Ohio

A CIP Catalogue record for this book is available from the British Library.

ISBN 0 406 94674 4

Typeset by Doyle & Co, Colchester
Printed and bound in Great Britain by Cromwell Press, Trowbridge, Wilts

Visit Butterworths LexisNexis *direct* at www.butterworths.com

Foreword

Innovative world-views generally mutate from paradox to platitude.[1] They begin with paradoxes, with assertions or 'explanations' that the world we think we know is quite different from our understanding of it. Where we see freedom, in truth there is compulsion; where we see benevolence, in truth there is oppression; and so on. They end as commonplaces. Almost no one now regards the 'freedom' of the employee, or the drug addict, or the marketplace as being of itself a sufficient reason for non-intervention by the state, for example, although a century or so ago things were viewed differently. We have recognised (and re-cognition is the perfect term to describe what has occurred) the supposed 'freedom' to be partial, both permitting and perhaps even requiring intervention in order that it be truly realised. The examples are manifold and obvious.

Indeed, the point might be pushed further. It sometimes seems that the greater the paradox the greater the pull it exercises on our minds. At different ends of the political spectrum, the beliefs that Stalin liberated Russians and that wholesale privatisation of the welfare state leaves all people better off have both captured the imaginations (and, again, that term describes perfectly the process in question) of millions of people. The tale of the Emperor's new clothes illustrates a central truth concerning human understanding.

The idea of globalisation has mutated from paradox to platitude in just this way. It is difficult now to imagine how we saw the world before Marshal McLuhan's declaration in 1967 that 'the new electronic interdependence recreates the world in the image of the global village'. But it is worth trying. Great ideas that begin as paradoxes are noteworthy not merely because they alter the way in which we see the world, but also because they alter it in a way which, at least from certain points of view, appears to contradict common experience.

We now assume that we live in a world of global interdependence. But is that true? Certainly, international networks are a common phenomenon. The formal relations of inter-state diplomacy are mirrored in relations between businesses, academic institutions and military establishments, for example, that freely span international boundaries. Large numbers of people are involved, in their professional lives, in these networks; and the writers and likely readers of this book are, of course, among them. But is global interdependence really the new reality? Is this phenomenon either novel or an accurate reflection of the state of the world?

It is a constant surprise to realise how much our forebears travelled: Jefferson in Paris; McCartney in Beijing; Cortés in Mexico. More significant, perhaps, is

---

1   The observation was made by Isaiah Berlin in his essay 'Does Political Theory Still Exist?' (1962).

the remarkable scale and efficiency of the great trading empires – European, Arab, Chinese, Ottoman, and the rest. Trade and political relations between communities around the world proceeded routinely, on a global basis, supported by dispersed bureaucracies and pervasive legal systems, centuries ago. The idea that industrial or governmental action in one state can affect plant growers on the other side of the world and vice versa is hardly new.

It is of course true that certain incidents of these global relationships have changed significantly. Texts can move around the world at the speed of light – a fact that induces a particular frisson in those who see texts as the primary stuff of reality. Travel is faster and easier. Multinational brands are displacing local manufacturers. The scale of interdependence has become greater as the processes of specialisation have unfolded. But these changes must not be overstated. A McDonald's restaurant in Beijing has a different place in the social fabric from that of a McDonald's in downtown Houma, Louisiana, however much they might look alike. And even in terms of the undeniable differences in the speed and scale of international dealings, it is easy to overestimate the significance of the change. It is by no means clear, for example, that the processes of decision-making and implementation have accelerated in line with the increased speed of communication. That there are substantial changes underlying the 'globalisation' process cannot be denied; but on close inspection they may appear less marked, and less novel, than is often thought.

Does globalisation reflect the state of the world? It is undeniable that there is a part of society that is internationalised. But how typical is that part? Or to put what is essentially the same question in a different way, how much of the reality of life on this planet is accommodated within the perspective of globalisation? Not, I suspect, very much.

While there have been substantial improvements in certain areas during the thirty-odd years of the 'global village', recent World Bank figures estimate that over one thousand million people still live on less than one dollar a day. In many regions the number is increasing: in Eastern Europe and Central Asia, for example, the number of people living on less than a dollar a day is estimated to have increased from 1.1 million in 1987 to 24 million in 1998. More than half the world's population lives on less than two dollars a day. What does it mean to say that these people, the majority of the inhabitants of the planet, are residents in a 'global village'? How can those enlightened residents of the global village who live in affluent, caring, liberal democratic communities explain the co-existence of their – I should say, our – comfortable lives with the misery of the millions of other residents, particularly in Africa and Asia, who are constantly faced by poverty, disease and death? The wealth and technology exist to help the victims. The moral codes that are the orthodoxy of the rich nations purport to promote equality, minimum entitlements to basic human rights and the responsibility of the community to support its weakest members if they are unable to support themselves. How, then, can the co-existence of great wealth and abject poverty be explained? Surely the truth is that in practice these poor are precisely *not* seen as a part of our own community. This alone seems to me to divest the concept of 'globalisation' of most of its supposed significance. Can there really be a village, a community, without a sense of shared moral responsibility and shared destiny?

This is not simply a question of geographical distance. On inner-city estates in the UK, or in the rural south in the US, for example, one can find in the richest nations of the world many communities where the majority of people live unemployed, often in single-parent families, often living close to the poverty line. And in a paradox that perhaps heralds a new, post-globalisation, perspective, it is widely observed that as the old extended families and other traditional social groups fragment, many such people are practically house-bound and socially isolated, connected to the outside world only through the deforming links of television. Are they, too, to be counted as residents in the global village? Can a single perspective satisfactorily embrace the views both of those who are actors in the transnational system and also of those of the growing underclass who have no active role in the system, but are simply acted upon by it? Is the idea of the 'global village' any more than a banal acknowledgement that we all live on the same planet?

Despite the commonplace insistence on the shrinking world, the fact is that for most people and for most of the time, horizons are as resolutely local as they were decades, or even centuries, ago. When people look for help with their problems or for those to blame for them, or for those to whom to give help, they tend to look to those close to them. What matters is what is local. Even jet setting international lawyers are likely to be at least as much concerned by their own families and careers, by local weather, traffic conditions and the crashing of their computer programs, as they are by seismic political developments across the world. (Try to reckon honestly the time that you spend thinking or reading about yourself and your geographical and social locality, compared with the time spent on 'global' issues.) The preoccupations of the professional, public persona of the urbane internationalist are unlikely to match his or her private preoccupations. We talk in global terms; but we live locally. And yet globalisation is readily accepted as a central part of the world-view of the writing and reading classes. How is this?

Law, as an intellectual discipline, has as its characteristic mode of thought the 'as if' move. We treat complex relationships between individuals as if they were elegant bilateral contracts; compulsive shoplifters as if they deliberately formed the mens rea of theft; corporations as if they were individual persons undertaking legal obligations, and so on. International law is the same. Explicitly or implicitly it treats states as if they were persons; treaties as if they were contracts; questions of international responsibility as if they were questions of the law of tort or obligations; the list is endless. It has to be so: use of metaphor, fitting new situations into old forms, is the only practical alternative to the infinite effort of constantly re-engaging directly with reality. And globalisation ranks high in the list of our currently favoured metaphors.

In some respects at least, many of us in our professional lives do indeed think and act *as if* the world were a global village. Bond issues and investments are arranged with transactions hopping across state boundaries as if they were no more than dividers in a ring file. Litigation moves backwards and forwards across jurisdictions, as if between adjacent courtrooms. Rules and standards, applicable to everything from the design of electric plugs to ethical business standards and national constitutions, are developed and applied to countries around the world as if they were counties within a single country.

This is not to be condemned, even if there were a point in condemning the inevitable. Far from it. It is, in practice, the only hope for those whose lives rarely offer relief from the relentless struggle merely to survive. The networks that link governments, scientists, businesses and others around the world are the paths along which relief and assistance must travel from the rich to the poor and needy.

And the peculiar role of law is to clear those paths and make that movement of resources, wealth and knowledge possible.

As Michael Likosky points out in his introduction, whatever hope their might have been in 1945 that there would be a new world of co-equal sovereign states, neatly arranged in symmetrical relationships with each other like houses on the grid-plan streets of a prairie town, the reality is utterly different. There is no equality. There are no straight roads. The international landscape looks more like a maze of sheep tracks criss-crossing over a mountain range, half-hidden in the undergrowth and interrupted by streams and rocks, linking high peaks and barely known valleys.[2] The central concern uniting the chapters in this volume is the exploration of these pathways, mapping the disparities in power and patiently tracing the often elusive tracks and the synaptic breaks across which the cargo they carry must jump.

Over the past 30 years there has been much concern to demonstrate that Law is not a merely professional training but a vibrant field of intellectual inquiry in its own right, holding its own with philosophy, linguistics and the like. The idea that Law matters in the real world sometimes seems to have moved from centre stage. But there is still room for the view that the point of analysis and philosophising must not be merely to interpret the world, but to change it. Change is not the result of grand theories: it is the result of day-to-day implementation of theories, great or small. It succeeds or founders most often not because of the lack of originality or cohesion or insight in the Grand Theory, but because the theory is, to borrow Frances Cornford's words, magnificently unprepared for the long littleness of life. It is the particular merit of the chapters in this volume that their focus is precisely upon the little things, upon specific practical insights into the actual operation of Law in the world. The careful, objective analysis of the way the Law operates, rather than sweeping suppositions about the way in which it should operate, is the indispensable foundation upon which attempts to use the law to improve the quality of the lives of those with whom we share this planet must be built.

It is an honour to have been invited to contribute the Foreword to this volume, for which I thank Michael Likosky and the remarkable galaxy of distinguished and original thinkers into whose company I have intruded. The chapters are polished and engrossing, as one might hope. But more than that, they are important. Chapter after chapter of incisive analysis pinpoints the practical complexities of the transnational system and draws from the analyses some of the many lessons that must be learned if the world is develop into a truly global community.

AVL
All Souls College, Oxford

2   An image I owe to the artist R L Burns, whose paintings for the National Trust in Shropshire have drawn on the similarity of rural tracks and neural pathways.

Preface

This book began its life as a Trinity Term 1999 bi-weekly seminar series, 'The Globalisation Challenge to Transnational Law?', at the Centre for Socio-Legal Studies, University of Oxford. Since then, the roster of participants has changed and expanded considerably. Audience feedback, a well-received 2000 Law and Society Association Annual Meeting entitled 'Millennial Accidents: On the Road with the Rule of Law' and also a survey of the courses and literature on law and globalisation suggested a need for a reader on the topic.

To meet this need, the book is organised around four overlapping themes. Part I of the book presents frameworks for understanding the field writ large. Parts II and III look at particular subject areas, transnational commerce and processes of state change, respectively. And, as one of the most implicated areas of law by globalisation processes is public international law, Part IV looks at the relationship between public international law and the context in which it emerges and operates.

The transnational legal processes described in the four parts are often far-reaching; however, contributors generally pursue a sociolegal approach. Thus, a specific set of questions associated with the sociolegal approach is asked of transnational legal processes. These questions include: Why do parties pursue law to achieve their goals? What legal strategies do they undertake? How do these legal strategies operate in practice? Do they achieve their intended results? What are the unintended effects of these strategies?

One constant throughout the book is a preoccupation with power disparities. This is true whether the topic under study is global capital markets or immigration restrictions or conditionalities placed upon international financial aid. Disagreement exists about the nature and extent of disparities with some thinking them on the wane and others finding them intractable. Also, contributors employ different and often contested methodologies to uncover how these disparities function and the interests which legal processes serve. Part of what makes the book useful as a reader is this divergence regarding the state of power disparities and the methodological eclecticism in measuring them.

In putting together a book of this size, I have incurred many debts. I would like to thank my seminar series co-convenor, Joseph Perkovich, for his influence at the nascent stages of the project. I am indebted to Bryant Garth, Philip Lewis, Sally Falk Moore and William Twining who provided much appreciated encouragement throughout. I would like to express my gratitude to the publishers for their thoughtful guidance throughout the editing process. I would also like to thank the anonymous readers for what have proved to be valuable insights. A great debt is also owed to Bill and Marilyn Likosky. I am deeply thankful to Shelagh Mooberry for, among other things, her editorial skills, which were crucial for keeping the life of this project a manageable length. I thank Joy Mooberry who inspires my work and love.

MBL
March 2002

Contents

Editor's introduction: transnational law in the context of power disparities

M B LIKOSKY*

'I would not say how we plan. I would not say publicly how I plan to do anything.'[1]

'to look at law and records of legal activity is to look at the tracks left by combatants and their allies.'[2]

INTRODUCTION

As I write this introduction, the Italian government is deciding how to handle the stream of anti-globalisation activists entering into the country to protest the Group of Eight (G8) Summit in the port city of Genoa. Initially formed to deal with the oil crisis in the late 1970s as the G6, comprising France, Western Germany, Italy, Japan, the UK and the US, with time the issue agenda has broadened and the membership expanded to include Canada and Russia. Every year the leaders of these countries meet to explore the possibility of finding common solutions to pressing transnational social problems such as structural challenges posed by the globalisation of the economy and the threats posed by cross-border criminal cartels. Given the geopolitical power of the G8 governments and the economic strength of their corporate nationals, many argue that the policies emerging from the Summit will have far-reaching implications for the lives of persons throughout the world. Some go on to claim that the solutions to the transnational social problems will benefit a wealthy set of interests within the G8 countries and that the burdens will be unevenly distributed among the remainder of the world's population. Thus, given these pandemic implications, critics of the G8 urge that such decisions should be taken in a more democratically accountable forum. At present, many wonder whether the Genoa Summit will resemble the turbulent gatherings of recent years at the 1999 G8 meeting in Cologne, the 1999 World Trade Organization meeting in Seattle, the 2000 International Monetary Fund and World Bank meeting in Prague, and the EU meetings in Nice and Gothenburg in 2000 and 2001.

* mbl@calculus.wolf.ox.ac.uk. I would like to thank Sally Falk Moore for her helpful comments on this introduction.
1 Malcolm X (1998) p 143.
2 Kidder (1979) p 300.

xvii

On 13 July 2001, to stem the tide of anti-Summit activists, the Italian government announced the suspension of its adherence to the 1995 Schengen Agreement. Under this Agreement, the 11 contracting parties – Austria, Belgium, France, Italy, Germany, Greece, Luxembourg, the Netherlands, Portugal, Sweden and Spain – agreed to remove all common border controls for the purpose of facilitating the free movement of persons and goods in line with the tenets of liberalisation. The 1990 Convention Implementing the Schengen Agreement eliminated common border checks, allowing persons to move freely within the Schengen zone without showing their passports at national borders. The Amsterdam Treaty of the European Union incorporates the Schengen Agreement into the institutional framework of the EU. All EU member states, with the exception of the UK, Ireland and Denmark, are now contracting parties to the Agreement. Contracting parties may suspend the Agreement where 'public policy or national security so require'. The Italian government availed itself to this clause.

Several weeks ago, the Austrian government also suspended its adherence to the Schengen Agreement to dissuade activists from journeying through the country on their way to Genoa. Similarly, last year the French government suspended the Agreement in the context of a fiftieth anniversary celebration of the EU in Nice. Are we witnessing a trend towards the strategic use of treaty suspension as a tactic to counter political protests? Do these protests threaten national security? Do the suspensions impinge upon the fundamental rights of freedom of expression and association?

Regardless of whether the Italian government's suspension was legally justifiable or politically advisable, the champions of liberalisation found themselves ensnared in a paradox. On the one hand, they had vociferously claimed that liberalisation requires the free movement of people and goods. On the other hand, the free movement of people was here seen as an imminent threat to this meeting devoted to promoting liberalisation. It seemed that the once politically insulated field of meeting diplomacy has become increasingly transparent and open to political scrutiny due to the strategies of activists.

Importantly, these clashes at the inter-governmental meetings of the EU, the G8 and the International Monetary Fund and the World Bank indicate that disagreement exists over whether liberalisation will steadily improve the living standards of rich and poor alike. It also points to the ability of anti-globalisation activists to have their messages heard despite a lack of hierarchical organisation and in the face of relatively poor financial resources. For the time being, despite some violent factions, anti-globalisation activists seem to have a wellspring of normative capital. Meeting diplomacy has become a battle between globalisers from above – powerful governments and transnational corporations – and those from below – community groups and international non-governmental organisations. The battle between David and Goliath is being re-enacted on prime time.

However compelling, this is not the full story. The protagonists prove far more enigmatic. We think we know the story, but we don't. Rather, the story is being presented to us. Certain events are being highlighted and others brushed aside. Truth is, if not 'established by deception',[3] at least dependent upon the perspective of the narrator. Of course, from the perspective of the main players

---

3   Sun Tzu.

in the struggle, there are compelling reasons for presenting the story in particular ways for specific purposes.

None the less, as academics, we are engaged in a different enterprise. Our aim is to produce knowledge of the context from which these tales emerge and to illuminate the function which they serve in practice. We must scrutinise the David and Goliath myth unfolding before our eyes, asking a series of questions such as: Who is David and who is Goliath? Do we see, as Francis Fukuyama suggests in his post-Cold War triumphalist monograph, *The End of History and the Last Man*,[4] David standing with the severed head of Goliath at his feet? Or is this King David, corrupted by power? Regardless of the identity of the protagonists, the battle is underway. And, as is in Bernini's sculptural depiction of the fight, the line between spectator and participant has eroded and Goliath is not yet slain.

SCOPE OF THE COLLECTION

Since the close of the Second World War, interdisciplinary studies of law have pursued the feasibility of theories for understanding how legal narratives are embedded in situations characterised by power disparities capable of application across periods, societies and subject areas. At the close of the 1960s, 1970s and 1980s, the publication of key conference volumes – *Law in Culture and Society*,[5] *The Imposition of Law*[6] and *History and Power in the Study of Law: New Directions in Legal Anthropology*[7] – assessing progress in the field showcased this thematic interest and the broadening of research agendas. Each summed up a decade of socio-legal research exploring the role of power disparities in structuring legal relationships in colonial, post-colonial and industrialised societies. In 1980, Francis G Snyder noted how

> '[m]any scholars have shown that . . . systematic inequalities are inherent in the legal order . . . in studies of: colonial labor law, the transfer of Western legal categories and institutions, patterns of court use; the organization of the legal profession; the role of public enterprise in mediating the domination of foreign capital; the legal regulation of migration and welfare; and the creation of popular justice as survival strategies by dominated classes.'[8]

From the 1980s onward the scope of inquiry has expanded to include studies of the transnational aspects of customary law which was long assumed to be wholly pre-colonial and indigenous,[9] commercial agreements entered into on unequal terms and power disparities in business disputes[10] and also the power dynamics in which the export of human rights, constitutions, judiciaries and democracy are embedded.[11]

---

4 Fukuyama (1992).
5 Nader (1969).
6 Burman and Harrell-Bond (1979).
7 Starr and Collier (1989).
8 Snyder (1980) p 772.
9 See eg Benda-Beckmann (1992); Chanock (1992; 1985); Galanter (1989); Moore (1986); Snyder (1981a; 1981b).
10 See eg Braithwaite and Drahos (2000); Buchanan (2000); Coombe (1995); Hendley (1999); Likosky (forthcomming B) and (in press); Maurer (1997); Piccioto and Mayne (1999).
11 See eg Carothers (1999); Dezalay and Garth (1998); Inoue (1991); Rose (1998); Santos (2000); Twining (1993); Wilson (1997).

This theoretical preoccupation with power disparities and expanding scope of inquiry is demonstrated particularly well by an examination of the progression of the study of liberal legalism. During the law and development movement,[12] which ran roughly from the 1950s to the late 1970s and provided legal assistance to countries in Asia, Africa and South America, the US exported a particular vision of law which David M Trubek and Marc Galanter in a touchstone article, 'Scholars in Self-Estrangement: Some Reflections on the Crisis in Law and Development Studies in America', termed liberal legalism.[13] Under the liberal legalism paradigm:

> 'a legal system is an integrated purposive entity which draws on the power of the state but disciplines that power by its own autonomous and internally derived norms. With some slippage and friction, social behavior is aligned with and guided by legal rules. Moreover, that behavior can be consciously modified by appropriate alternations of these rules.'[14]

In exporting liberal legalism, Trubek and Galanter argued that participants in the movement had exhibited ethnocentrism, over-estimated the power of law and had mistakenly assumed that law was primarily a progressive force. The authors extended this critique of the implementation of liberal legalism to the US, noting that participants in the movement had 'begun to doubt that the model accurately describes legal life even in the United States'.[15] According to Boaventura de Sousa Santos, law and development studies were 'little more than a rhetoric of legitimation which could be appropriated by the more liberal factions of the national bourgeoisies both in the US and in the "Third World"'.[16]

When money dried up for development research, several key players in the law and development movement turned their attention to how liberal legalism functioned within the US. Now as members of the law and society movement, scholars applied their critique of liberal legalism germinated in the development

---

12 Countries such as Belgium, the Federal Republic of Germany, France, the Netherlands, the UK and the US offered advice on constitution drafting and subsequently participated in nation building by drafting legislation and teaching in law faculties: see eg Twining (1997). As transitions were accomplished lawyers continued to provide legal aid in the context of ambitious overseas development efforts funded by international organisations, governments and private foundations. In addition, international law firms played an expansive role drafting concessionary agreements and joint venture contracts. Despite the diversity of forms of legal assistance, our understanding of the role of foreign lawyers in the 1950s through to the 1970s is dominated by the story of the US law and development movement. The literature on the law and development movement is extensive: see eg Carty (1992); Gardner (1980); Ghai, Luckham and Snyder (1987); International Legal Center (1974); Snyder (1982); Trubek and Galanter (1974). A growing body of literature compares these 'development decade' efforts with present day legal assistance, and the 2000 Annual Law and Society Association Meeting, devoted to rule of law exports, made explicit reference to the earlier movement: see eg Chua (1998); Faundez (1997); Ginsburg (2000); Rose (1989); Tamanah (1995); Trubek (1996).
13 Trubek and Galanter (1974).
14 Trubek and Galanter (1974) at 1072.
15 Trubek and Galanter (1974) at 1081. Snyder noted how 'most of the American academic lawyers who had shaped and participated in the movement turned their energies increasingly to domestic legal issues'. Snyder (1982) 374. See also Trubek (1990). Several of these scholars have served as presidents of the Law and Society Association and editors of the Law and Society Review.
16 Santos (1981) p 270.

context to the US system.[17] Marc Galanter made the connection explicit when he recently described the *Law and Society Review* issue in which his now classic 1974 article, '"Why the Haves" Come Out Ahead: Speculations on the Limits of Legal Change',[18] 'as an examination of . . . the U.S. legal system through eyes informed by Indian experience'.[19] Studies of how liberal legalism operates in practice have been a hallmark of the law and society movement ever since.

In the 1996 Presidential Address of the Law and Society Association, Susan S Silbey brought studies of liberal legalism full circle, arguing that in globalisation we see liberal legalism 'recycled for new markets'.[20] Silbey argued that for socio-legal scholars 'globalization is not really a new notion; instead it is a rather familiar, banal story, many of whose elements and narrative structure have been explored and documented in the myriad volumes of law and society research'.[21] Just as the critiques of the law and development movement and the studies of law in the US uncovered power disparities inherent in liberal legalism, Silbey urges that socio-legal scholars in studying liberal legalism within globalisation processes 'must expose and track the power that nonetheless operates below the surface of prices and progress'.[22]

Studies of dispute processing have followed a similar trajectory to liberal legalism.[23] Dispute processing began as a study of disputes in colonised societies and expanded to study alternative dispute resolution in industrialised countries. This work 'illustrates how some people draw an analogy between the situation of colonial people and the poor in industrialized countries'.[24] Recently, alternative dispute resolution studies have turned attention to transnational arenas such as dispute resolution panels of international organisations[25] and international business arbitration.[26] According to Yves Dezalay and Bryant Garth: '[t]he discussions of the role of law and the transformation of alternative dispute resolution do not depend on whether the setting is national or international.'[27]

The purpose of this book is to take the exploration one step further by evaluating the recent shift towards globalisation. Specifically, it evaluates competing conceptual models for understanding transnational legal processes, and also seeks to examine how power disparities inform and are shaped by legal

---

17 The intersection between the law and development movement and the law and society movement is complex. The two movements intersected intellectually and at the level of agency. For instance, Stewart Macaulay wrote his 'Non-Contractual Relations in Business: A Preliminary Study' in 1963 prior to a stint in Chile under the auspices of the Ford Foundation funded International Legal Center. He applied his 'law in action' approach to his work in Chile. Macaulay recalls: 'I was very concerned about the gap between the law in the books and the law in action, and I applied those ideas to the [Ford] foundation and the ILC.' (10.02.02 correspondence).
18 Galanter (1974).
19 Galanter (1999) footnote 3.
20 Silbey (1996) at 210.
21 Silbey (1996) at 210.
22 Silbey (1996) at 232.
23 Similarly, the study of legal pluralism, according to Sally Engle Merry, 'moves from the discovery of indigenous forms of law and law among remote African villagers and New Guinea tribesman to debates concerning the pluralistic qualities of law under advanced capitalism': Merry (1988). For an early study of legal pluralism, see Macauley (1963). Recently, several scholars have argued for a retooling of legal pluralism theories for application to globalisation processes: see eg Moore (2001); Santos (1995); Snyder (present volume); Teubner (1996); Twining (2000; present volume); Wilson (1997; 2000).
24 Moore (2001) at 102.
25 Nader (1999).
26 Dezalay and Garth (1996).
27 Dezalay and Garth (1995) at 29.

relationships in transnational commercial life, within processes of state change and in relation to the unfolding project of public international law. Contributors scrutinise and contextualise conventional legal narratives. In doing so, they recognise that narratives are not merely distortions of reality, but instead are themselves elements of political praxis. Further, just as political narratives are embedded in ongoing struggles for power, so too are academic stories. In fact, as Sally Falk Moore notes, socio-legal scholars increasingly 'treat their own critical commentary as a form of social action';[28] This lends the volume a particular urgency.

PART I: FRAMEWORKS

Since the mid-1990s, several socio-legal scholars have devised frameworks or general approaches to understanding the field of transnational law writ large.[29] Most have attempted to place the present transnational legal processes into an historical context and to explore the significance of power disparities in structuring relationships. While some highlight how elite actors constitute the transnational order, others argue that socio-legal studies should take, to quote Michel Foucault, 'the forms of resistance against different forms of power as their starting point'.[30] However, most acknowledge that any overarching framework must reconcile these two methodological tendencies. These tendencies are both embodied in the approaches put forth in this Part by William Twining, Lawrence M Friedman and David Nelken.

In 'Reviving General Jurisprudence', William Twining explores the role that a revised general jurisprudence might play in underpinning the discipline of law as it becomes more cosmopolitan. Having its origins in the nineteenth century, general jurisprudence traditionally referred to the study of two or more legal systems. Twining distinguishes his own enterprise from the nineteenth century variant in a number of respects, viewing generalisations as inherently problematic, focusing on all levels of legal ordering rather than exclusively on municipal and international law and treating normative and legal pluralism as central. To explore the feasibility of this enterprise, Twining discusses how a revised general jurisprudence might critically engage a number of jurisprudential traditions, including analytical and normative jurisprudence, legal reasoning, historical, social scientific and interpretive inquiries and comparative legal studies. Although sceptical of the feasibility of generalisations, Twining argues that the need to generalise and compare legal phenomena across borders is essential to evaluate the claims and confidences of 'the ideologues of a global economy'.

While Twining enters the field through the concept of general jurisprudence, Lawrence Friedman and David Nelken focus on the concept of culture. However, each has a different thing in mind when talking about culture. In 'One World: Notes on the Emerging Legal Order', Friedman argues that a global culture is driving changes to the legal order. This cultural order, according to Friedman, is undeniably American, emerging from the country's origins as an immigrant society. As the cultural order globalises, changes to the legal order follow. At the same time, borrowing from linguistic studies the term 'diglossia', meaning a 'situation where two very different varieties of language co-occur through a speech

---

28 Moore (2001) at 109.
29 See eg Darian-Smith (1998; 2000); Darian-Smith and Fitzpatrick (1999); Friedman (1996); Jenson and Santos (2000); Santos (1995; 1998). For other approaches, see Shapiro (1993); Tenker (1996); Twining (2000); Trubek, Dezalay, Buchanan and Davis (1994).
30 Foucault (1994) p 329.

community', Friedman argues that an emerging global legal order sits aside and interacts with local legal cultures in most national settings. At the same time, according to Friedman, as cultures converge this global legal order predominates.

In 'Changing Legal Cultures', Nelken draws on a growing body of literature on legal change, making a case for adopting the concept of 'legal culture' as a modality for explaining differences in the ways laws transfer from one social setting to another. The term 'legal culture' is employed to emphasise how law travels in packages. To illuminate how law is transposed from one legal culture to another in an attempt to direct social change, Nelken proposes a number of metaphors. Nelken highlights how these transborder attempts to direct legal change often do not function as intended. This requires particular care in the evaluation of legal efforts, which seek to advance the interests of the disenfranchised. Given that these efforts often are carried out in contexts characterised by extreme power disparities, according to Nelken, they may end up hurting more than helping the targeted group.

PART II: STRATEGISING COMMERCIAL INTEGRATION

In the opening remarks to the Part on strategising commercial integration, Immanuel Wallerstein describes the present transnational commercial order as embodying two conflicting tendencies – the drive to maximise capital accumulation at any cost, on the one hand, and the mobilising of legal and political capital to constrain the deleterious practices associated with global capitalism, on the other. The chapters in this Part elaborate elements of these dual tendencies through an examination of the new international division of labour and the new development regime advanced through the privatisation of infrastructure projects.

The first two chapters examine aspects of the new international division of labour. In what is sometimes referred to as the 'world factory system', transnational corporations disperse segments of their production process among industrial enclaves in various countries around the world. In 'Governing Globalisation', Snyder develops a theory of global legal pluralism to explain the role of law in constituting the new international division of labour. Global legal pluralism refers to 'the totality of strategically determined, situationally specific, and often episodic conjunctions of a multiplicity of institutional, normative, and processual sites throughout the world'. Snyder explains how this global legal pluralism operates with reference to the toy industry. Within this industry, wealthy countries tend to dominate production processes. This dominant position, however, must be maintained against challenges of workers and international organisations.

While Snyder examines macro-level aspects of the global legal order, in 'Transnational Transactions: Legal Work, Crossborder Commerce and Global Regulation', Doreen McBarnet employs a micro-sociological methodology. Like Snyder, McBarnet starts from the assumption that strategic actors construct the transnational legal order by uniting the laws of various sites. In particular, McBarnet looks at how actors draw from the laws of multiple jurisdictions to create transnational legal constructs. By solving problems for specific business clients through this transnational legal work, McBarnet worries that regulations designed to serve the public interest are subverted.

The next two chapters in this Part look at global capital markets providing examples primarily from the infrastructure sector, while the final two chapters in this Part look at the relationship between infrastructure projects and human rights. The findings in these chapters are situated within a shift in the infrastructure sector, initiated in many countries during the 1980s, away from the state-financed approach to the global project finance approach. Under the state-financed approach, the state put up the bulk of the capital to finance infrastructure projects, with the World Bank providing supplementary financing. Also, states established public corporations charged with building and operating infrastructures.[31] In contrast, under the global project finance approach, neither the state nor the World Bank carry out infrastructures. Instead, private companies seek funding for projects through international capital markets and then build and operate projects to recoup sunk costs and to garner a profit. However, as the contributors note, the state does not exit the scene completely under the global project finance approach. Instead the state changes its institutional configuration.

Since the primary targets of non-governmental organisation and community group pressure in the context of state-financed infrastructure projects have been the state and the World Bank, what this shift in the infrastructure field will mean for the advancing of democracy and the protection of human rights is uncertain. We do have some hints, as hundreds of projects have been carried out to date under the global project finance approach. While no study has been undertaken comparing state- and World Bank-financed projects, on the one hand, with global project finance projects, on the other, we do see a subsistence of high-profile abuses from the North-South Expressway in Malaysia to the Three Gorges Dam in China. Also, we are witnessing a shift in the strategies of non-governmental organisations involved in assessing human rights risks of infrastructure projects. New organisations and networks addressing corruption in tendering processes and pursuing litigation to compensate victims of disasters and state violence are popping up and targeting the primary players in the global project finance approach, for example, corporations, investment banks, government export credit agencies and the World Bank's Multilateral Investment Guarantee Agency.[32] The contributors shed light on the elite dimensions of this new development regime and also explore efforts to constrain the regime.

The third and fourth chapters of the Part examine the elite bias of the new transnational development regime as evidenced by the rarefied field of capital markets. In 'Capital Markets, Globalisation and Global Elites', John Flood describes how a small set of elite international law firms, investment banks and government regulators dominate the global capital markets. These markets are tapped by companies seeking to privatise infrastructure projects and to carry them out under the global project finance approach. This monopoly results in decisions with far-reaching implications for how international resources will be allocated being made insulated from democratic processes.

Often these decisions result in externalising the costs of the transnational commercial order on poorer nations. In 'Global Markets, National Law and the Regulation of Business', Eleanor Fox discusses several of the shortcomings of the present regulatory order which is premised on a nation-to-nation regulatory model. Using infrastructure projects which raise regulatory problems, Fox demonstrates the need for a more holistic regulatory order which goes beyond this inter-state logic. For instance, often certain governments lack the institutional capacity to vet proposed deals. To remedy this problem, Fox urges the establishing of a transnational agency to pool the resources of various national securities regulators.

---

31 Ghai (1971; 1981; 1984).
32 Likosky (2002).

As the previous two contributors relate, the transnational infrastructure field is dominated by a small set of actors. International non-governmental agencies and community groups have developed strategies to target these actors. These strategies represent attempts to mitigate the human rights risks posed by infrastructure projects. Here a human rights risk is the possibility that a human rights problem will adversely affect the interests of those persons party to an infrastructure project. As indicated in the Flood and Fox articles, international banks, international law firms, transnational corporations and a segment of elites from industrialised and developing countries are among those persons undertaking infrastructure projects. However, ordinary person are also often party to an infrastructure project.

One particularly successful human rights risk mitigation strategy has been undertaken by Transparency International, an international non-governmental agency addressing corruption in privatisation tendering processes. In 'Corruption and the Global Corporation', Susan Rose-Ackerman demonstrates how anti-corruption strategies have succeeded in establishing that these elite parties to an infrastructure project are under a normative obligation to reduce corruption in the tendering process. This has resulted in the adopting of various legal codes, state and otherwise. Rose-Ackerman argues that not only are these companies are under a normative obligation to refrain from corrupt practices, but also that such practices are economically inefficient. Rose-Ackerman then points to successes in convincing companies that the privileges of doing business in foreign jurisdictions go hand-in-hand with duties to foster public law principles in these countries.

While Rose-Ackerman describes efforts to internalise public interest goals in the infrastructure building processes, Marc Galanter instead examines what happens when something goes severely wrong with an infrastructure project. In 'Law's Elusive Promise: Learning from Bhopal', Galanter examines the efficacy of transnational public law litigation[33] designed to hold companies accountable for human rights problems caused by infrastructure projects, examining the claims process arising out of the massive leak of methyl isocyanate at the Union Carbide plant in Bhopal, India.[34] He argues that tort law proved inadequate to compensate victims of the disaster. In the Bhopal case, the Indian government brought a claim against Union Carbide on behalf of the victims of the disaster in the US federal courts, seeking redress in the high compensation US courts. However, the US judge ruled that the Indian courts were a more appropriate venue for the case (ruling *forum non convenius*). As a result, the case was tried in the low remedy Indian system and the government secured a judgment against the company. According to Galanter, while the Indian legal judgment looked good on its face, in practice, due to inadequate institutions, the tort regime

33 In 1997, Harold Koh noted the emergence of a growing body of 'transnational public law litigation' designed 'to vindicate public rights and values through judicial settings': Koh (1997). One type of transnational public law litigation comprises claims pursued against transnational corporations alleging human rights abuses arising in the context of infrastructure projects. These suits are often brought in the US courts under the Alien Tort Claims Act 1789, targeting US companies for alleged abuses perpetrated abroad: Burley (1989); Herz (2000); Slaughter and Boscoe (2000). Other cases have arisen in the courts of developing countries: Fernandes and Saldanha (2001). Anne-Marie Slaughter and David Boscoe argue that the use of the Alien Tort Claims Act 1789 is a form of 'Plaintiff's Diplomacy' – 'a new trend towards lawsuits that shape foreign policy': Slaughter and Boscoe (2000). See also Compa and Diamond (1996).
34 A case is also being brought under the Alien Tort Claims Act 1789. See *Bano v Union Carbide Corpn* 199 CIV 11329.

failed to deliver on the promises of its judgment. Based on these findings, Galanter advocates transnational tort law reform. According to Galanter, the key to understanding the Bhopal disaster and its legal aftermath lay in approaching it from a transnational vantage. As a possible solution, Galanter argues for the further developing of a transnational private law catering to ordinary persons.

PART III: CHANGING STATES

Although some commentators argue that an extra-state global law is emerging, the chapters in the Part on changing states describe in detail how states maintain and transform themselves in the present transnational order. This is evidenced in the continuing role of the state in privatisation processes, in refusal of states with requisite capacity to deal with immigration flows, in the drafting of new constitutions as elements of nation-building exercises in various countries and the transition of states away from authoritarian government structures and towards human rights-friendly regimes. The chapters take up these topics, describing how, as Saskia Sassen relates in her introductory remarks to the Part, we see the 'denationalisation of certain domains of the state' and 'the re-nationalization of others'.

In 'Dollarising the State and Professional Expertise: Transnational Processes and Questions of Legitimation in State Transformation, 1960–2000', Yves Dezalay and Bryant Garth present a new approach to understanding the change from development states to neo-liberal states. Conventionally, this change is understood as the result of either the imposition of the Washington Consensus or instead as representing an enlightening of local elites. However, little attention is paid to what forces produce these changes. Employing the concepts of international strategy (the way individuals use international capital – degrees, expertise, contacts, resources, prestige and legitimacy acquired abroad – in order to build their positions at home) and palace wars (fights not only over control of the state, but also over the relative value of individuals and expertises that make up and guide the state), Dezalay and Garth tell the story of how internationally well-connected technopols have employed international strategies to rest control over the state from the gentlemen politicians of the law. To do so, Dezalay and Garth elaborate processes of state change in the fields of economics, business law and public interest law.

Richard Abel takes issue with the approach adopted by Dezalay and Garth in 'The Promise and Peril of International Order', a comment on the chapters by Snyder, Flood, Rose-Ackerman, and Dezalay and Garth. To Abel's mind, Dezalay and Garth's focus on palace wars and international strategies obscures how the US has coerced change in Latin America through military means. Further, he thinks Dezalay and Garth overly optimistic about the promise of public interest law to achieve an equitable distribution of transnational power. The argument here is that public interest law has failed to deliver on its promises in the US, so one should expect nothing more in Latin America.

In a short reply to the Abel comment, Dezalay and Garth argue that Abel mistakenly tries to fit their approach into a framework prevalent during the 'law and development movement' in the US which ran from the late 1950s to the early 1980s. This movement, according to Dezalay and Garth, tended to view public interest law as a means of mitigating power disparities caused by inequitable distribution of economic resources. They take explicit distance from this position, arguing that they are not concerned with the emancipatory potential of public interest law. Instead, they address a different set of questions, ie how and why actors in Latin America draw on the division in US law between commercial and human rights orders in specific instances to serve particular purposes.

In 'Cultural Imperialism in the Context of Transnational Commercial Collaboration', Michael Likosky reframes the international cultural wars between Malaysia and the United States. Likosky argues that the 'clash of civilisations', which pits 'asian values' against 'universal human rights', must be understood within the context of extensive transnational commercial collaboration between Malaysia and the United States. This collaboration often creates those 'asian values' assumed to be indigenous and antagonistic to western values. To illustrate his point Likosky examines the Malaysian Multimedia Super Corridor, a high technology national development plan and foreign direct investment scheme designed to leapfrog the country into fully developed nation status by the year 2020. Here he demonstrates how a transnational coalition wields power over the Malaysian state to ensure that the laws of the Corridor are geared towards serving their own interest rather than those of the Malaysian public.

While many studies present globalisation processes as overwhelming the capacity of states, Christian Joppke argues that the limitations of sovereignty in liberal states may be internally imposed rather than externally conditioned. In 'Sovereignty and Citizenship in a World of Migration', Joppke argues that countries in Europe have the capacity to manage immigration. Issue is taken with post-nationalist approaches which, according to Joppke, accentuate the powerlessness of the state to stem the tide of immigration. He asks, assuming state-capacity, whether these post-nationalist theories perhaps unwittingly support political actors who use arguments of diminished state capacity to prevent the flow of immigration into their respective countries.

Ugo Mattei and Kyoko Inoue look at the transnational aspects of state change through an examination of constitution-making in African and Asian countries. Mattei is concerned with how constitutions may curb the power of executive branch-dominated political orders. While typically constitution-making is approached doctrinally, Mattei instead looks at constitution-making as a process. Mattei looks at the relative importance of foreign and local elements in constitution-making exercises in South Africa, the Puntland State of Somalia and Eritrea. He goes on to argue that, in societies suffering from a democratic deficit, the participation of local actors is a more preferable means of ensuring constitutional legitimacy than exclusive use of foreign expertise.

Even when a constitution-making exercise is dominated by foreign forces, as Kyoko Inoue demonstrates with reference to the post-Second World War imposition of a constitution on the Japanese people, local elements may ultimately play a more significant role. Inoue challenges the presumption that the constitutional transfer was a one-way imposition, arguing that the concepts embedded in the constitution are traceable to pre-War Japanese traditions. In particular, Inoue focuses on the concept of individual dignity – *jinkaku* – found in the constitution, arguing that the concept, which was assumed by the US drafters to be exogenous, was indeed present in the Japanese educational institutions before the War.

This Part ends with a chapter on how liberal states transform themselves to increase rather than to lessen their respect for human rights. In 'Transitional Justice as Liberal Narrative', Ruti Teitel addresses the post-Second World War puzzle in which one sees rampant political violence co-existing with unprecedented progress in the field of human rights. Teitel argues that the construction of liberal narratives by transitional trials designed to hold predecessor regimes accountable for abuses holds the key to unravelling this puzzle. The argument is that, through narrative means, the law establishes changed facts – states now respect human rights – which then drives a shift towards the realisation of those facts in practice.

PART IV: PUBLIC INTERNATIONAL LAW AND CONTEXT

At the close of the Second World War, the international order underwent a dramatic transformation as the signing of the UN Charter heralded a new public international legal order, one premised on sovereign absolutism and equality among nation-states. With the subsequent decolonisation movements, nation-states proliferated, enlarging the family of nations exponentially. In their accession to the new international legal order, these new states claimed and were accorded all the rights and duties of long-standing nation-states. However, formal parity understood within the context of inter-state power disparities has meant that formal and substantive equality do not always go hand-in-hand. Also, the state's role as proxy has often been voluntarily legitimised more by the international legal order than it has been by the citizenry of particular states. Further, this dependence on an international community for legitimacy has made states susceptible to international pressures.

A number of chapters focus on this post-War public international legal order and the challenges it faces with the onset of globalisation processes. Studies of international law have been decidedly interdisciplinary since the close of the Second World War, from Myres McDougal and Harold Lasswell's configurative approach to Philip Jessup's transnational law.[35] Several international legal scholars have urged increased collaboration between international lawyers and socio-legal scholars.[36] In the final Part of the volume, these two communities are brought together to examine the relationship between public international law and its context.

In the introductory remarks to this Part, Harold Koh argues that public international law is presently coming to terms with its context – what he terms 'transnational legal process', that is, 'how public and private actors – nation-states, international organizations, multinational enterprises, non-governmental organisations, and private individuals – interact in a variety of public and private, domestic and international fora to make, interpret, enforce, and ultimately internalize the rules of transnational law'. The contributors describe the successes and failures of public international law to internalise these processes, advocate the increased participation of international non-governmental groups in decision-making processes and also propose solutions for filling legal lacunae through legislative drafting, the creation of institutions and compliance mechanisms.

In 'An International Regime in the Context of Conditionality', Sally Falk Moore examines the context from which a piece of UN legislation, 'The Convention to Combat Desertification', emerges and operates in practice. Focusing specifically on implementation efforts in Burkino Faso, Moore demonstrates how the state is encouraged by international donor agencies through conditions placed upon international financial aid to cede decision-making authority to regional and local entities. Due to the political and economic exigencies in the region and pronounced power disparities, refusal of the conditions 'is seldom a choice to be considered'. Accordingly, 'what is in effect a command is conceived as if it were a contract'.

---

35 See eg Henkin (1979); Jessup (1956); Kingsbury (1998); Koh (1994; 1997); McDougal and Lasswell (1960); Slaughter, Tulumello and Wood (1998).
36 See eg Kingsbury (1998); Slaughter, Tulumello and Wood (1998).

While Moore views international law from the perspective of its context, in 'Reframing the Legal Agenda of the World Order in the Course of a Turbulent Century', Richard Falk concerns himself with the converse, that is, how international law should adjust itself to its context. Falk argues that the failure of foreign policy-makers and influential intellectuals to take international law seriously buttresses a power politics which encourages an international politics based on force rather than on the rule of law. None the less, despite this jurisprudential insult which questions the status of international law as law, according to Falk, in practice the record of compliance with international law is quite good. Of course, it can be better, and Falk accordingly focuses on specific areas in which international law may be made more responsive to its context.

The next three chapters examine how international non-governmental organisations and social movements may act as positive agents for ensuring that public interest law responds to justice and equity demands. Like Falk, Stephan Hobe concerns himself with internalising the challenges of globalisation processes into international law approaches. In 'Globalisation: A Challenge to the Nation-State and to International Law', Hobe proposes a recurring solution to transnational power disparities, increasing the participation of non-governmental actors in transnational legal processes. For Hobe, these organisations hold the key for international law to address global problems such as environmental degradation, under-development and terrorism.

Julie Mertus also believes that non-governmental organisations may transform international arenas for the better. For such interventions to be effective, however, Mertus argues that it is necessary to understand the transnational dimensions of civil conflict better. Mertus demonstrates this point by reference to the internal and trans-boundary dimensions of racism in Rwanda and Kosovo. For Mertus, the agents of positive international change are non-governmental organisations and networks of resistance, who in their strategies must address not only the internal dimensions of conflict but also the trans-border aspects.

If Hobe advocates greater participation of non-governmental organisations in public international law decision-making arenas, then Annelise Riles demonstrates how these organisations go about having their influence felt. In 'The Virtual Sociality of Rights: The Case of "Women's Rights as Human Rights"', Riles explores how knowledge professionals orchestrate a movement to have women's rights legitimised as human rights and how the success of this movement paradoxically occurs as the legitimacy of rights themselves were called into question by these same professionals in the academy. Riles details the circulation of persons and ideas between political and academic environments. The ability to hold seemingly self-contradictory stances towards the legitimacy of rights by these professionals could, according to Riles, be explained by a self-reflexivity on the part of actors who, while recognising the inherent limitations of rights in theory, recognised that in practice they possessed social capital in political movements. Riles argues that ultimately the appeal of rights to participants was as a marker of others' commitments. That is, rights were a means of signalling to imagined outsiders the fruits of one's labour.

The final two chapters address attempts to remedy transnational social problems caused by the displacement of people and the failure of states to alleviate hunger. In doing so, they propose specific legislative or institutional solutions to fill legal lacunae. In 'National Legislation and the Role of the Government and UNHCR in the Determination of Refugee Status in Kenya', Koki Muli considers whether the Kenyan government and international organisations provide adequate legal protection to refugees within Kenya's legal borders. Unlike most countries in the region, Kenya has failed to pass refugee-specific legislation. Thus, Muli asks how a legislative lacuna impacts upon the treatment of refugees. Through doctrinal elaboration and fieldwork findings, Muli shows how a piecemeal system has emerged to manage the problem. This system, however, fails to manage the problem adequately, leading Muli to advocate the promulgation of legislation to increase institutional articulation.

Focusing on another pressing transnational social problem, hunger, in 'Geographies of Hunger', Catherine Powell investigates the failure of the US to implement international human rights at home. Powell argues that hunger is typically understood as a problem of developing countries. This framing of the problem ignores pronounced inequalities in wealthy countries. The answer, according to Powell, is to apply a human rights analysis to establish US state responsibility under international law for hunger within its borders. Through doctrinal analysis, normative argumentation and a case study focusing on hunger in New York City, Powell argues that a greater integration between activist networks and international lawyers is necessary to rectify this problem.

CONCLUSION

A frenzy of law-making activity has characterised the latter half of the twentieth century, however, knowledge production has not kept pace with the corresponding changes to the implicated legal orders. At the same time, the sparse extant literature often claims more broadly than is warranted. By approaching the subject matter through the frame of power disparities, the collection begins to take stock of the field writ large, exploring developments in transnational commerce, state change and public international law. Few would dispute that many of the legal relationships and processes occur within a transnational social context marked by power disparities – inequalities among states, international institutions, transnational corporations, non-governmental organisations, peoples, persons, etc. The contributors to the collection are concerned with how these disparities inform and shape the formal legal relationships entered into by states and private actors. To do so, they examine multi-jurisdictional legal techniques and the legal aspects of trans-jurisdictional social phenomena. Relying primarily on field work findings and case studies contributors skeptically engage the grand claims made of and by law while also taking the power and aspirations of law seriously.

Frederick Douglass tells us that 'power concedes nothing without demand'.[37] As a nexus of knowledge and power, law is a site of struggle for control over the transnational social matrix. Still, we know little about the nature of legal demands and the terms of the concessions. Further, as academics of law, we find ourselves not only witnesses of the struggle, but also unavoidably drawn into the fray. Whether we are stratagems of the main players in the struggle is not altogether clear. As transnational legal processes occur in the context of power disparities, do we, as Douglass implores, have a responsibility to 'agitate, agitate, agitate'?[38]

M B Likosky
19 July 2001

37 Quoted in Zinn (1990) p 240.
38 Quoted in Zinn (1990) p 240.

Select bibliography

von Benda-Beckmann, F, (1992) 'Symbiosis of Indigenous and Western Law in Africa and Asia: An Essay in Legal Pluralism' in W J Mommsen and J de Moor (eds) *European Expansion and Law: The Encounter of European and Indigenous Law in 19th- and 20th-Century Africa and Asia*, p 30.

Braithwaite, J, and Drahos, P, (2000) *Global Business Regulation.*

Buchanan, R, (2000) 'I-800 New Brunswick: Economic Development Strategies, Firm Restructuring and the Local Production of "Global" Services' in J Jenson and B de S Santos (eds) *Globalizing Institutions: Case studies in regulation and innovation*, p 53.

Burley, A-M, (1989) 'The Alien Tort Statute and the Judiciary Act of 1789: A Badge of Honor', The American Journal of International Law at 461.

Burman, S, and Harrell-Bond, B, (eds), (1979) *The Imposition of Law.*

Carothers, T, (1999) *Aiding Democracy Abroad: The Learning Curve.*

Carty, A, (ed), (1992) *Law and Development.*

Chanock, M, (1985) *Law, Custom and Social Order: The Colonial Experience in Malawi and Zambia.*

—(1992) 'The Law Market: British East and Central Africa' in W J Mommsen and J de Moor (eds) *European Expansion and Law: The Encounter of European and Indigenous Law in 19th- and 20th-Century Africa and Asia*, p 279.

Chua, A L, (1998) 'Markets, Democracy, and Ethnicity: Towards a New Paradigm for Law and Development' 108 Yale Law Journal 1.

Compa, A, and Diamond, S F, (1996) *Human Rights, Labor Rights, and International Trade.*

Coombe, R J, (1995) 'Interdisciplinary Approaches to International Economic Law: The Cultural Life of Things: Anthropological Approaches to Law and Society in Conditions of Globalization', 10 The American Journal of International Law and Policy 791.

Darian-Smith, E, (1998) 'Review Essay: Power in Paradise: The Political Implications of Santos's Utopia', 23 Law and Social Inquiry 81.

—(2000) 'Review Essay: Structural Inequalities in the Global Legal System', 34 Law and Society Review 809.

Darian-Smith, E, and Fitzpatrick, P, (1999) *Laws of the Post-Colonial.*

Dezalay, Y, and Garth, G, (1995) 'Merchants of Law as Moral Entrepreneurs: Constructing International Justice from the Competition for Transnational Business Disputes', 29(1) Law and Society Review 27 at 29.

—(1996) *Dealing in Virtue: International Commercial Arbitration and the Construction of a Transnational Legal Order.*

—(1998) 'From Notables of the Foreign Policy Establishment to the International Market of Professionals of Philanthropy and Human Rights: Strategies for Power and the Social Construction of a New Field of State Expertise', American Bar Foundation Working Paper Series 9818.

Faundez, J, (ed), (1997) *Good Government and Law: Legal and Institutional Reform in Developing Countries.*

Fernandes, D, and Saldanha, L, (2001) 'Deep Politics, Liberalisation and Corruption: The Mangalore Power Company Controversy', 2001(1) Law, Social Justice and Global Development Journal, available at www.elj.warwick.ac.uk/global/issue/2000-1/fernandes.html.

Foucault, M, (1994) 'The Subject and Power' in J D Faubion (ed) *The Essential Works of Foucault: 1954-1984: Volume Three: Power*, p 329.

Friedman, L M, (1996) 'Borders: On the Emerging Sociology of Transnational Law', 31 Stanford Journal of International Law 65.

Fukuyama, F, (1992) *The End of History and the Last Man*.

Galanter, M, (1974) 'Why the Haves Come Out Ahead: Speculations on the Limits of Legal Change', 9 Law and Society Review 95.

—(1989) *Law and Society in Modern India*.

—(1999) 'COMMENT: Farther Along', 33 Law and Society Review 1113.

Gardner, J A, (1980) *Legal Imperialism: American Lawyers and Foreign Aid in Latin America*.

Ghai, Y, (1971) 'Introduction' in Y Ghai (ed) *Law in the Political Economy of Public Enterprise: African Perspectives*.

—(1981) *The Legislature and Public Enterprises*.

—(1984) 'Law and Public Enterprise in Developing Countries' in V V Ramanadham (ed) *Public Enterprise in the Developing World*.

Ghai, Y, Luckham, R, and Snyder, F, (eds), (1987) *The Political Economy of Law: A Third World Reader*.

Ginsburg, T, (2000) 'Review Essay: Does Law Matter for Economic Development?: Evidence from East Asia', 34 Law and Society Review 829.

Hendley, K, (1999) 'Do Repeat Players Behave Differently in Russia? Contractual and Litigation Behavior of Russian Enterprises', 33 Law and Society Review 833.

Henkin, L, (1979) *How Nations Behave: Law and Foreign Policy* (2nd edn).

Herz, R L, (2000) 'Litigating Environmental Abuses Under the Alien Tort Claims Act: A Practical Assessment', 40 Virg JIL 545.

Inoue, K, (1991) *MacArthur's Japanese Constitution: A Linguistic and Cultural Study of its Making*.

International Legal Center, (1974) *Law and Development: The Future of Law and Development Research: Report of the Research Advisory Committee on Law and Development of the International Legal Center*.

Jenson, J, and Santos, B S, (eds), (2000) *Globalizing Institutions: Case Studies in regulation and innovation*.

Jessup, P C, (1956) *Transnational Law*.

Kidder, R L, (1979) 'Toward an Integrated Theory of Imposed Law' in S Burman and B Harrell-Bond (eds) *The Imposition of Law*, p 289.

Kingsbury, B, (1998) 'The Concept of Compliance as a Function of Competing Conceptions of International Law', 19 Michigan Journal of International Law 345.

Koh, H, (1991) 'Symposium: International Law: Article: Transnational Public Law Litigation', 100 Yale LJ 2347.

—(1994) 'The 1994 Roscoe Pound Lecture: Transnational Legal Process', 75 Nebraska Law Review 181.

—(1997) 'Why Do Nations Obey International Law?', 106 Yale LJ 2599.

Likosky, M, (2002) 'Human Rights Risk, Infrastructure Projects and Developing Countries', 2(1) Global Jurisk Advances Article 2, http://www.bepress.com/gj/advances/vol2/iss1/art2.

—(in press) '"Oligarchising the State": comment on Susan George's Piece' in *Globalizing Rights: The 1999 Oxford Amnesty Lectures* (Oxford University Press).

—(forthcoming) 'Infrastructure for Commerce' 22 Northwestern Journal of International Law and Business.

Macaulay, S, (1963) 'Non-Contractual Relations in Business: A Preliminary Study' 28 American Sociological Review 55.

McDougal, M, and Lasswell, H D, (1960) 'The Identification of Diverse Systems of Public Order' in M McDougal (ed) *Studies in World Public Order*, p 3.

Malcolm X, (1998) *By any means necessary* (4th printing).

Maurer, B, (1997) *Recharting the Caribbean: Land, Law, and Citizenship in the British Virgin Islands.*

Merry, S E, (1988) 'Legal Pluralism', 22(5) Law and Society Review 869.

Moore, S F, (1986) *Social Facts and Fabrications 'Customary' Law on Kilimanjaro 1880-1980.*

—(2001) 'Certainties Undone: Fifty Years of Legal Anthropology, 1949-1999', 7 MAN: Journal of the Royal Anthropological Institute 93.

Nader, L, (ed), (1969) *Law in Culture and Society.*

—(1999) 'The Influence of Dispute Resolution on the Globalization: The Political Economy of Legal Models' in J Feest (ed) *Globalization and Legal Cultures: Onati Summer Course 1997.*

Piccioto, S, and Mayne, R, (1999) *Regulating International Business: Beyond Liberalization.*

Rose, C V, (1998) 'The "New" Law and Development Movement in the Post-Cold War Era: A Vietnam Case Study', 32(1) Law and Society Review 93.

Santos, B S, (1981) 'Science and Politics: Doing Research in Rio's Squatter Settlements' in R Luckham (ed) *Law and Social Enquiry Case Studies of Research*, p 261.

—(1995) *Towards a New Common Sense: Law, Science and Politics in the Paradigmatic Transition.*

—(1998) 'Review Essay: Commentary: Power in Paradise: The Political Implications of Santos Utopia: Oppositional Postmodernism and Globalizations', 23 Law and Social Inquiry 121.

—(2000) 'Law and Democracy: "(Mis)trusting the Global Reform of Courts"' in J Jenson and B S Santos (eds) *Globalizing Institutions: Case studies in regulation and innovation*, p 253.

Shapiro, M, (1993) 'The Globalization of Law', 1(1) Indiana Journal of Global Legal Studies 1.

Silbey, S S, (1997) '"Let Them Eat Cake": Globalization, Postmodern Colonialism, and the Possibilities of Justice', 31(2) Law and Society Review 207.

Slaughter, A-M, and Boscoe, D, (2000) 'Plaintiff's Diplomacy', Foreign Affairs.

Slaughter, A-M, Tulumello, A S, and Wood, S, (1998) 'International Law and International Relations Theory: A New Generation of Interdisciplinary Scholarship', 92 The American Journal of International Law 367.

Snyder, F G, (1980) 'Law and Development in the Light of Dependency Theory', 14(3) Law and Society Review 723 at 772.

—(1981a) 'Colonialism and Legal Form: The Creation of "Customary Law" in Senegal', 19 J Legal Pluralism 49.

—(1981b) *Capitalism and Legal Change.*

—(1982) 'Book Review: The Failure of 'Law and Development', 1982 Wis LR 373.

Starr, J, and Collier, J F, (eds), (1989) *History and Power in the Study of Law: New Directions in Legal Anthropology.*

Tamanah, B Z, (1995) 'Book Review: Law and Development (Vol. 2, Legal Cultures). Edited by Anthony Carty. Dartmouth Publishing Co., Ltd., Gower House (distrib. New York University Press), 1992. Pp. xxiii, 504. Index $150. Law and Crisis in the Third World. Edited by Sammy Adelman and Abdul Paliwala. Hans Zell, 1993. Pp. Xii, 332. Index 40', 89 The American Journal of International Law 470.

Teubner, G, (1992) 'The Two Faces of Janus: Rethinking Legal Pluralism', 13 Cardozo Law Review 1443.

—(1996) '"Global Bukowina": Legal Pluralism in the World Society' in G Teubner (ed) *Global Law Without a State.*

Trubek, D M, (1990) 'Symposium: Back to the Future: The Short, Happy Life of the Law and Society Movement', 18 Florida State University Law Review 4.

—(1996) 'Law and Development: Then and Now', American Society of International Law, Proceedings of the 90th Annual Meeting.

Trubek, D M, and Galanter, M, (1974) 'Scholars in Self-Estrangement: Some Reflections on the Crisis in Law and Development Studies in the United States', 1974 Wis LR 1062.

Trubek, D M, Dezalay, Y, Buchanan, R, and Davis, J R, (1994) 'Symposium: The Future of the Legal Profession: Global Restructuring and the Law: Studies of the Internationalization of Legal Fields and the Creation of Transnational Arenas', 44 Case Western Reserve Law Review 407.

Twining, W, (1993) 'Constitutions, Constitutionalism and Constitution-Mongering' in I P Stotzky (ed) *Transition to Democracy in Latin America: The Role of the Judiciary.*

—(1997) *Law in Context: Enlarging a Discipline.*

—(2000) *Globalisation and Legal Theory.*

Wilson, R, (ed) (1997) *Human Rights: culture and context.*

—(2000) 'Reconciliation and Revenge in Post-Apartheid South Africa', 41 Current Anthropology 75.

Zinn, H, (1990) *Declarations of Independence: Cross-Examining American Ideology.*

Table of statutes

List of cases

Part I

Frameworks

Chapter 1

Reviving general jurisprudence

W TWINING[1]

The literature on globalisation is almost as confusing as the processes it attempts to interpret. There are those who speak in terms of revolutions and paradigmatic change. There are sceptics, like Paul Hirst, who consider most globalising rhetoric to be overblown. There are Marxist, post-modern, free market and religious interpreters. Within each of these groups there are optimists and pessimists. And there are agnostics who claim that the processes are too bewildering in their complexity and too rapid for it to be sensible to make firm judgments, let alone confident predictions. Yet, if one blows away some of the froth from the excited and highly repetitive literature, there seem to be some givens that are widely accepted: that 'globalisation', far from being a new phenomenon, has a history that stretches back for at least two centuries; that the interactions between the local and the global are processes of great fluidity and complexity; that in some areas, such as communications and ecology, we are indeed witnessing important developments; that the significance of national boundaries is changing; that nation-states are not the only significant transnational actors, although it is unlikely that the nation-state will wither away or be superceded by a world government in the foreseeable future.

'Globalisation' in this context refers to those trends and processes which are making the world more interdependent. Whatever one's interpretation of the details of globalisation – strong, weak or agnostic – clearly it has important implications for the discipline of law and for jurisprudence as its theoretical part. In earlier writings, the writer has argued that globalisation presents three specific challenges to traditional legal theory:

1   This chapter builds on and extends themes developed in Twining (1997; 2000). It was written as a prolegomenon to a series of lectures on 'General Jurisprudence' delivered at the Universities of Tilburg and Warwick in 2000–01. The main thesis is that there is a need for a revival of general jurisprudence as a foundation for an increasingly cosmopolitan discipline of law in response to the challenges of 'globalisation'. This chapter was written as a paper while the writer was a Fellow at the Center for Advanced Study in the Behavioral Sciences at Stanford. The writer is grateful for the superb support of the Center and its staff. Thanks for valuable comments and suggestions are also due to the editor, to Terry Anderson, and to participants in seminars at University College London, Wolfson College, Oxford, the Australian National University, and Columbia, Griffith, Stanford, Sydney, Warwick and Tilburg Law Schools.

(1) it challenges 'black box' theories that treat nation-states, societies, legal systems and legal orders as closed, impervious entities that can be studied in isolation;

(2) it challenges the idea that the study of law and legal theory can be restricted to two types of legal ordering: municipal state law and public international law, conceived as dealing with relations between nation states; and

(3) it challenges the adequacy of much of the present conceptual framework and vocabulary of legal discourse (both law talk and talk about law) for discussing legal phenomena across jurisdictions, traditions and cultures.[2]

These challenges all point in the direction of making law as a discipline more cosmopolitan. This in turn requires the revival of the idea of general jurisprudence. The purpose of this chapter is to outline one vision of what might be involved in such an enterprise. It takes as its starting-point a broad conception of the subject-matter of the discipline of law and a particular view of the role of jurisprudence as the general part of that discipline. These assumptions may be controversial, but the case for them has been made elsewhere.

The main assumptions can be summarised as follows: law is concerned with the ordering of relations between agents or persons (human, legal, unincorporated and otherwise) at a variety of levels, not just relations within a single state or society. One way of loosely characterising these levels of relations is geographical. In terms of space they include the global, international, transnational, regional, inter-communal, municipal (nation-state and subsidiary jurisdictions), sub-state local and non-state local.[3] These different levels are not nested simply in a single hierarchy of larger and smaller spaces. Rather, they co-exist, overlap and interact in complex ways. For this reason, normative pluralism, and legal pluralism as part of it, should be among the central concerns of a revived general jurisprudence.[4]

Jurisprudence can be viewed as a heritage, an ideology and as the activity of theorising that is posing, reposing, answering and arguing about general questions relating to the subject-matters of law as a discipline. As an activity within our discipline, theorising has several functions: constructing whole views or total pictures (the synthesizing function); elucidating, constructing and refining concepts; developing normative theories, middle order hypotheses and general working theories for participants; intellectual history; and critically examining the underlying assumptions of different kinds of discourse of and about law.[5]

This chapter is written from the standpoint of an English jurist, who is concerned about the health of the institutionalised discipline of law during the next 10 to 20 years in the face of 'globalisation'. The writer is based in London, has worked in several countries and has travelled widely, mainly in the US, the Commonwealth and, in recent years, the Netherlands. The writer has provenance,

---

2   Twining (2000) chapter 1.

3   For detailed discussion see Twining (2000) chapter 6.

4   Traditional definitional issues concerning what counts as a 'legal order' and how legal and normative pluralism are distinguished have been side-stepped here. In this context, the writer's conception of law is broad enough to include some kinds of non-state and religious law, eg a putative lex mercatoria, Dinka law, Islamic, Hindu or Gypsy law as worthy subject-matters of our discipline, but how one classifies borderline cases is not germane to the argument. Similarly, this characterisation deliberately leaves open questions about the relative importance of different kinds of legal order. On general definitions of law, see Twining (2000) pp 78–80, 224ff.

5   Twining (2000) chapter 1.

experience and outlook which are quite cosmopolitan, but biases and culture which are British, with English as the main language. A jurist from a different intellectual tradition approaching the same issues from another vantage-point would probably present a significantly different picture.

Given a broad conception of law and its study and a functional view of the role of jurisprudence within our discipline, let us look at what may be involved in the idea of general jurisprudence in the context of globalisation.

GENERAL RATHER THAN GLOBAL JURISPRUDENCE

Globalisation has implications for law and its study. It does not follow that what is needed is a global jurisprudence, if that means looking at law solely or mainly from a global perspective. That is too narrow. A good World Atlas does not contain only maps of the world. Rather, it has a combination of large-scale, small-scale and intermediate maps, with a multiplicity of projections and perspectives. The old term 'General Jurisprudence' is broader and more flexible than 'global' just because it refers to discourse about two or more jurisdictions or legal orders from the micro-comparative to the universal. One task of general jurisprudence is to construct overviews of legal phenomena in the world as a whole – global mapping of law – but legal theory needs to be concerned with all levels of legal ordering and their interrelations.[6] Viewing law from a global perspective has its uses, not least in providing context, but understanding law will continue to require detailed focus on particulars at all levels.

In the nineteenth century the term particular jurisprudence referred to the study of the concepts and presuppositions of a single legal system; general jurisprudence referred to the study of two or more legal systems and was quite often confined to advanced or 'civilized' systems; universal jurisprudence was more like global jurisprudence, but was often restricted to the law of sovereign nation-states. Generality and particularity are relative matters. Here the term 'general jurisprudence' will be used to refer to the theoretical study of two or more legal orders (including ones within the same legal tradition or family).[7] This conception has some affinity with nineteenth-century usage, but differs from it in three important respects: (1) it treats generalisation about legal phenomena as problematic; (2) it deals with all levels of legal ordering, not just municipal and public international law; and (3) it treats the phenomena of normative and legal pluralism as central to jurisprudence.

During the nineteenth century English jurists normally assumed that jurisprudence was general. The Natural Law Tradition was universalistic. Bentham developed a universal science of legislation. Austin, more cautiously, developed a general analytical jurisprudence for maturer nations. Holland claimed that jurisprudence was a science and therefore must be general. Leaders of the Historical School, such as Maine, advanced sweeping Darwinian generalisations about law and social change.[8] However, during the early days of academic law in both England and the US the focus became more particular. One reason for this was that the study of the fundamental legal conceptions of one's own legal system was seen to be more practical and relevant to the rest of the curriculum. Austin,

---

6 Problems of mapping law are explored in Twining (2000) chapter 6.
7 On 'comparative common law', see below.
8 For details see Twining (2000) chapter 2.

Pollock, Gray and others explicitly emphasised practicality. There were also signs of a tacit legal relativism, exemplified by W W Buckland.[9]

The story in the US is more complex. Like his English counterparts, John Chipman Gray emphasised that for pedagogical purposes, particular jurisprudence was more practical and relevant to the rest of the first degree curriculum. Hohfeld focused on Anglo-American concepts while emphasising the importance of broad perspectives. Roscoe Pound was a generalist at heart, but normally confined his jurisprudence teaching to postgraduates. During the first decades of the twentieth century Pound, Wigmore, Kocourek and others were cosmopolitan in outlook and pioneered important projects, such as the Continental Legal Philosophy series, which unfortunately did not last long enough to become established as a regular trans-Atlantic conduit for European legal thought. From the 1930s, talented refugees from Nazism provided an important antidote to potential isolationism, but nevertheless for most of the twentieth century the study of foreign and comparative law, international law and other transnational subjects tended to be marginalised in the first degree curriculum and the professional examinations. This had a profound impact on the focus of most US legal scholarship. However, from the perspective of general jurisprudence, there was one crucial difference between the academic cultures of the US and most European countries, including Great Britain. The rise of the national law school in the US led to nearly all US legal education and scholarship being *multi-jurisdictional*. General jurisprudence is concerned with theoretical aspects of law across jurisdictional boundaries; so too is comparative law. In important ways nearly all US academic law has been multi-jurisdictional and comparative, without being transnational. This fact has considerable significance for the theory and practice of comparative law.[10]

For most of the twentieth century the focus of much Anglo-American legal theory has either been quite parochial or else geographically indeterminate.[11]

---

9 Twining (2000) chapter 2.
10 See below.
11 See below. There have, of course, been some notable exceptions. For example, H L A Hart consistently claimed that his book, *The Concept of Law* (1961), was a contribution to general jurisprudence. Some of his writings, eg on causation and on criminal responsibility, were more local, but he did not generally draw a sharp distinction between general and particular jurisprudence. In the Postscript to *The Concept of Law* he tried, unsuccessfully in the writer's view, to revive the distinction in order to suggest that he and Ronald Dworkin were involved in different enterprises: Twining (2000) chapter 2.

 Why does this chapter talk of 'reviving' general jurisprudence, when some prominent contemporary jurists claim to be continuing the tradition of theorising about law across legal cultures and traditions? A brief answer is that the writer's conception of 'general jurisprudence' is much broader than theirs and harks back to a time when jurists as different as Bentham, Austin, Maine, Holland and followers of Natural Law were all conceived as pursuing different aspects of 'jurisprudence'. The label itself is unimportant, although it has sometimes been misused. Furthermore, contemporary jurists who consistently do general jurisprudence are exceptional, for the great bulk of legal theorising in the Anglo-American tradition is confined to modern western legal systems, often very largely to the US and the UK. Second, the concern here is to break away from the strong tendency to confine the concept of law to municipal (state) law and, often reluctantly, public international law narrowly conceived. Religious law, chthonic (traditional) law and other candidates deserving consideration as significant subject matters of the study of law are regularly excluded or marginalised. Finally, this conception of general jurisprudence is intended to challenge tendencies (often latent) to project parochial or ethnocentric preconceptions onto non-Western legal orders, cultures and traditions. See further 'The Province of Jurisprudence Re-examined', Julius Stone Memorial Lecture, Sydney, 2000 (forthcoming).

In his inaugural lecture as Professor of Comparative Law at Oxford, F H Lawson, echoing a wider suspicion of both grand and abstract theory, said: 'Nowadays to be universal is to be superficial.'[12] This was the keynote of most Anglo-American legal theory for much of the twentieth century.[13]

In the last decade of the twentieth century we witnessed two conflicting tendencies: on the one hand, a particularistic tendency that emphasises difference, the uniqueness of history, culture and identity, sometimes even cultural and ethical relativism. On the other hand, awareness of globalisation points to the changing significance of national boundaries and the need for academic law and legal theory to take account of multiple levels of social and legal ordering.

Rather than assume universality, we need to consider difficult issues of the feasibility and desirability of general discourse about law at all these levels. A central question for general jurisprudence is: how far is it possible and desirable to generalise about legal phenomena – conceptually, normatively, empirically, etc – as part of understanding law? So questions of cultural, legal, and ethical relativism become crucial.

Legal theory is concerned with a variety of conceptual, normative, empirical and interpretive issues. Rough distinctions between concepts, values and facts have provided the basis for conventional ways of classifying jurisprudence into different approaches – analytical, philosophical (or normative), historical, sociological and so on. Such taxonomies were convenient and had some use as indicators of differences between lines of inquiry or of emphasis; but they were sometimes misleading in suggesting disagreements among rival 'schools' about a shared agenda of issues. For the purpose of exposition, and in order to indicate some links with tradition, this chapter will consider the idea of a revived general jurisprudence in relation to these conventional categories, but it must be emphasised that it is not intended to present them as designating distinct branches or subdisciplines. Indeed, most particular legal studies involve conceptual, normative, interpretive and empirical dimensions.

ANALYTICAL JURISPRUDENCE[14]

The term 'analytical jurisprudence' is sometimes treated as co-extensive with 'linguistic analysis', or with elucidation of abstract concepts. This is a mistake. For example, Herbert Hart explicitly included as part of analytical jurisprudence the study of the form and structure of legal systems, problems of legal reasoning, problems of definition of law and analysis of legal concepts.[15] He considered that the critical analysis of assumptions and presuppositions of legal discourse was one the main tasks of legal philosophy. He also emphasised that distinctions between different branches of jurisprudence and philosophy of law were matters of convenience, reflecting 'no very firm boundaries'.[16] In this view, the relationship

---

12 Lawson (1950).
13 Twining (2000) p 144. On the differences between 'parochialism' in respect of focus, audience, sources, perspectives, and potential significance, see Twining (2000) chapter 5.
14 This section is a condensed version of the second Tilburg Lecture, entitled 'Have Concepts, Will Travel: Analytical Jurisprudence in a Global Context' (forthcoming).
15 Hart (1967) pp 264–276, reprinted in Hart (1983) chapter 3.
16 Hart (1967). But Hart revived the distinction between general and particular jurisprudence to differentiate his views from those of Dworkin in the posthumously published Postscript to *The Concept of Law*, discussed in Twining (2000) chapters 2–3.

of analytical jurisprudence to jurisprudence is similar to the relationship between analytical philosophy and philosophy in general: it gives an approximate indication of a style and approach that involves the application of a range of techniques of analysis to legal discourse and its concepts. Analytical method here includes not only linguistic and conceptual techniques developed by analytical philosophers, but also tools of analysis such as ideal types, models, metaphors and deconstruction developed in neighbouring disciplines.

The identification of analytical jurisprudence with conceptual analysis has some basis in history. Elucidation of abstract concepts was the main focus of attention of most Anglo-American analytical jurists from Austin through Hart, including Holland, Hohfeld, Kocourek and Salmond. This has been criticised as narrow in two respects. First, in so far as analytical jurists concentrated on such questions rather than on 'substantive' issues of normative, sociological or historical jurisprudence, they could rightly be accused of being over-concerned with conceptual analysis or with mere semantics. At its height the leaders of 'the revolution in philosophy' in Oxford, associated with J L Austin's circle, gave the impression that they believed that most philosophical problems could be solved, or the underlying puzzlements could be dissolved, by careful examination of language, especially ordinary usage. Despite denials that they made any such claim, there is little doubt that in the first flush of enthusiasm some analytical tools were over-used.[17] In both England and the US there was such a strong reaction that 'linguistic analysis' became a by-word for narrow, sterile, over-abstract logomachy.[18]

Some leading mainstream jurists of the next generation, for example Dworkin, Rawls, Raz and MacCormick, quietly assimilated some of the specific techniques of analysis developed by Oxford analytical philosophers, while making clear that they considered themselves to be dealing with issues of substance.[19] However, conceptual analysis as a distinct enterprise largely went out of fashion in political theory and jurisprudence to be replaced by interest in 'substantive philosophical issues', exemplified by the work of Rawls and Dworkin.[20] This was generally a welcome development, but there was, in the writer's view, an over-reaction against sustained conceptual analysis. In taught jurisprudence an almost exclusive focus on analysis of 'fundamental legal conceptions' was indeed narrow; but something was lost when applied analysis of concepts was almost entirely replaced by more abstract discussions on the borders of political philosophy.[21]

A second charge of narrowness bites deeper. Most analytical jurists from Bentham through to Hart have focused on a narrow range of 'legal concepts', that is to say the basic terms for expressing or reconstructing legal doctrine and

17   A good example was T D Weldon's *The Vocabulary of Politics* (1953) which had almost cult status when the present writer was an undergraduate. On the writer's experience of the related disease of 'Korzbyskian paralysis' and Llewellyn's cure, see Twining (1968) pp 5–8. I described my own symptoms as 'an obsession with the definition of terms in seemingly endless regress, a shying away from concrete factual detail in favor of abstract generalizations and an all-or-nothing approach which masquerades as precision': p 6.

18   Gellner (1959).

19   Eg Dworkin (1986) chapter 2 on drawing the semantic sting. Dworkin classifies Hart as a semantic jurist; this seems to the writer to be a caricature.

20   This move is associated with the distinction between 'concept' and 'conceptions' (see eg Dworkin (1986) pp 71–72) and the challenge to the sharp distinction between 'analytic' and 'synthetic'. Rawls (1967) advances his conception of justice in the form of substantive principles and devotes little time to the concept of justice. In the view of some, Hart's book might have been more accurately labelled 'A/My Conception of Law'.

21   Twining (2000) pp 33–34.

their underlying concepts (such as right, duty, legal person, ownership and possession) or the concepts presupposed by such discourse (such as command, rule, sovereignty, sanction and legal system). This focus is associated with a conception of law and of its study that is largely confined to legal doctrine or rules. Analytical jurists hardly ever brought their techniques to bear on concepts such as dispute, process, institution, function and group.[22] One way of expressing this is to distinguish between 'law talk' (the discourse *of* rules and its presuppositions) and 'talk about law' (discourses *about* any legal phenomena).

Jurists in the Anglo-American tradition of analytical jurisprudence largely have confined themselves to analysing law talk, and have tended to neglect the much wider field of talk about law. This partly is attributable to the fact that this kind of work was associated with a rule-oriented picture of law and of its study. Also, the concepts of law talk were considered to be distinctively legal, while many concepts associated with talk about law belonged to, or were at least shared with, other disciplines, such as sociology, economics, ethics and political theory. This chapter adopts a broad conception of the subject-matters of law as a discipline and proceeds on the assumption that the need for conceptual elucidation applies as much to any discourse about law as to the more traditional 'law talk'.

Elucidation and construction of concepts are not a subject apart, but typically are one part of any inquiry. If the methods of conceptual analysis suitable for legal discourse are little more than the principles and techniques of logical analysis and clear thinking, is there any justification for treating analytical jurisprudence as a distinct enterprise? It is suggested here that there are good reasons for keeping it as a focus of attention, but not as a separate subdiscipline.[23] Just as it is useful to consider legal reasoning about questions of law or of fact at a higher level of generality than particular fields of law, so too with conceptual analysis.

Analysis of concepts is only one part of analytical jurisprudence, but it may have a special importance in the coming years. A cosmopolitan discipline of law needs a vocabulary and conceptual apparatus that can be used confidently across jurisdictions and cultures. If jurisprudence is to be general, its vocabulary and concepts need to travel well.[24]

---

22 Twining (1979); cf Twining (2000) pp 34–37. Hart himself often expressed the view that his kind of analysis was applicable to these broader inquiries, but, in practice, very largely he confined his attention to concepts of law talk.

'No very firm boundaries divide the problems confronting these various disciplines from the problems of the philosophy of law. This is especially true of the conceptual schemes of classification, definition, and division introduced by the academic study of law for the purposes of exposition and teaching; but even the historical and sociological statements about law are sufficiently general and abstract to need the attention of the philosophical critic.' (Hart (1983) p 89.)

Cf Hart (1961) Preface ('essay in descriptive sociology').

23 In his important address on 'A Vital School of Jurisprudence and Law' (*Proceedings* of the Association of American Law Schools (1914) p 76ff), Hohfeld acknowledged that students could pick up basic techniques of analysis in the ordinary professional courses through what is now known as 'the pervasive approach', provided that their teachers were reasonably proficient as analytical jurists. But budding teachers needed a separate course on analytical jurisprudence to obtain 'a systematic and extensive grasp of the matters involved' (pp 98–99). The writer's view is that laying the foundation for basic skills is best acquired by direct study, reinforced in other courses, rather than by optimistic 'pick-it-up' approaches: Twining (1997) pp 85–86, 188–189.

24 The metaphor of 'travelling well' is useful in catching the dynamic nature of language and its adaptability to different contexts; but, of course, concepts, like languages, disperse and spread without necessarily leaving their original homes.

At first sight, we seem to be a long way from having an adequate meta-language for this purpose. The literature of analytical jurisprudence and comparative law both send out strong cautionary messages. The early analytical jurists observed that there were only a few 'fundamental legal conceptions' that form part of general jurisprudence.[25] Comparative lawyers from Buckland to the present day regularly have warned of the many pitfalls of translation and comparison because of differences between the conceptual schemes of different legal systems. The dominant movement within mainstream comparative law, represented by Rabel, Kahn-Freund, Zweigert and Kötz, emphasised that convergence between civil and common law systems is normally a convergence of outcomes or solutions to 'shared problems', often reached by different conceptual routes.[26] Within legal anthropology there has been a well-known debate about the extent to which the 'folk concepts' of one culture can be translated or even elucidated in the language of another.[27] The debate ended in a near-consensus that one needs both analytic and folk concepts to give an adequate account of Tiv or Barotse or Cheyenne law-ways and institutions.[28] And, echoing Shaw, Atiyah and Summers have reminded us that 'England and America are two countries separated by the same language'.[29] Not only do we use words like 'trunk', 'boot', 'pint' and 'quite' differently, but we do not even have a shared conception of 'rule'.[30]

Some other considerations can be set against these salutary warnings. Globalisation is not new, nor are transnational legal relations. Trade, diplomacy and commerce have been transnational for centuries and they have developed usable ways of communicating, for example, through the recognition of one or other lingua franca ('the language of diplomacy', 'the language of science') or through the development of specialised vocabularies and conceptual schemes. So have public international law and transnational business. Regional groupings such as the EU, the Council of Europe, and the Organization of African Unity have long experience of struggling with problems of transnational legal communication. Furthermore, the tendency of analytical jurisprudence and mainstream comparative law to concentrate on legal doctrine (law talk) may have obscured the fact that a great deal of talk about law is multi-disciplinary. More or less sophisticated transnational vocabularies have been developed in neighbouring disciplines. Those social sciences that have been particularly

---

25 Bentham, Austin, Hohfeld and other analytical jurists recognised that most legal discourse was specific to a given legal culture and hence belonged to particular jurisprudence. The lists of general legal concepts were quite short.

26 This 'functionalist' approach has attracted growing criticism in recent years. See eg Hill (1989); cf Twining (2000) p 177.

27 For a summary of the debate and references see the Preface to Bohannan (1968). This is sometimes linked to the 'emics/etics debate' in social anthropology.

28 Gluckman's position can be interpreted as a claim that the Barotse had flexible concepts that were functionally equivalent to the English concept of 'the reasonable man'; Bohannan's book on the Tiv (1968) was written mainly in English, using standard concepts from social anthropology in addition to his careful elucidation of Tiv terms. Interestingly, Hoebel acknowledged that he and Karl Llewellyn did not pay sufficient attention to Cheyenne vocabulary and concepts in their classic study, *The Cheyenne Way* (1941): Private communication to the writer.

29 The dictum is often attributed to Bernard Shaw, but *The Oxford Dictionary of Quotations* states that it is not to be found in his published writings.

30 Atiyah and Summers (1987) pp 264–266, 418–420.

influenced by strong conceptions of 'science' have for that reason been concerned to develop general discourses. For example, much of the specialised vocabulary of economics, psychology and geography claims to be transnational. Even anthropology, which has strong particularistic tendencies, has always claimed to be a comparative enterprise.[31] Thus, while the revival of general jurisprudence presents enormous challenges, we are not starting from scratch. But there is a need to take careful stock of the extent to which our existing vocabulary and concepts are adequate for general discourse and how much they are obviously or subtly culture-specific, local, or even ethnocentric.

As a first venture into the exploration of the usability of our stock of concepts in cross-cultural and transnational legal discourses, the writer undertook preliminary case-studies of four groups of concepts: (i) Hohfeld's analytical scheme as one of the highlights of traditional analytical jurisprudence; (ii) transnational discourse about prisons as an example of a body of concepts that seems to travel remarkably well; (iii) corruption as an example of a topic that was thought to be quite culture-specific (but on examination this turned out to be over-simple); and (iv) transnational comparison of lawyers, legal professions, and legal education as an area which is notoriously problematic in respect of usable concepts.[32] The provisional conclusions are as follows:

Hohfeld's analytical scheme for 'rights' travels far and travels well for many purposes. It fits, and can be used in rationally reconstructing almost any normative system. It moves between different levels of legal ordering and, more controversially, can be applied to moral systems[33] and even games, such as chess. It is useful for removing ambiguities and for rational reconstruction of legal rules and many other kinds of norms. However, it is only a starting-point for analysis of discourse about 'rights'. For example, it does not deal with different kinds of 'duty' or 'power' and it does not consider whether there is some underlying connection between the four uses of 'right', nor the relation of rights to other concepts such as interest, benefit or need.

A second case-study examined transnational terminology relating to state prison systems, as illustrated by the Standard Minimum Rules for the Treatment of Prisoners (SMR), Human Rights Watch's national and global reports on prisons and Vivian Stern's *A Sin Against the Future: Imprisonment in the World*.[34] The concepts and terms used in these texts seemed to travel remarkably well, given the great variety in prison conditions, populations, and policies worldwide. For example, the SMR has been widely used in assessing prison conditions and regimes in many countries and has had some influence on standard setting within some state prison systems.[35] The underlying philosophy (essentially based on rehabilitation) is no longer widely accepted, the application of these standards by foreigners is often resented and few prison systems meet these minimum standards in fact; but there appear to be relatively few *conceptual* difficulties about applying these standards worldwide. One interesting feature is that the Standard

31 Eg Bohannan (1963) chapter 1.
32 This is a report on work in progress, which has not yet been completed. This brief summary is included here merely to illustrate the idea of what might be involved in taking stock of the applicability and transferability of existing groups of concepts and vocabularies as part of an expanded conception of general analytical jurisprudence.
33 Eg Gewirth (1983).
34 Stern (1998).
35 Eg it is used in several of Human Rights Watch's recent reports on prison conditions in nearly 20 countries.

Minimum Rules are expressed in non-technical English, which appears to travel better than the terminology of prison laws.

In her powerful survey and polemic about imprisonment as a global phenomenon, Vivien Stern makes a number of sweeping factual generalisations about the state of prisons and shared problems in the world today. As descriptions of conditions these seem at least to represent testable descriptive hypotheses.

The normative generalisations of SMR and Stern's empirical ones refer mainly to prison conditions and prison regimes. They apply less clearly to prison ideology and policies. The main reason for this is probably that 'the modern prison' developed as one of the first institutions of the modern bureaucratic state to be the subject of significant transnational networks of bureaucratising professionals. Prison ideology, rationales and policies are more closely entwined with local politics, history and culture. They may be harder to compare or subject to generalisation.

Corruption, bribery and related concepts used to be considered strongly culture-specific. Since the early 1990s a powerful transnational campaign against 'corruption' has gained ground.[36] It is based largely, but not entirely, on the ideology of the Washington consensus concerning 'democracy, good governance, and human rights' and on free market and related ideologies concerning 'development'. The main target of this campaign is various kinds of deviation from bureaucratic norms of impartiality, efficiency and 'service', especially financial dealings. The focus is primarily on 'public servants' of state bureaucracies. When the campaign is extended to the private sector and 'traditional' contexts it encounters many more grey areas, for instance, in respect of nepotism, patronage, tipping and traditional forms of gift-giving that tend to be more local and culture-specific. Thus corruption and related concepts seem to travel reasonably well in respect of the modern sector of nation-states, especially state bureaucracies, but are more problematic outside this specific context. The strongly emotive language of 'corruption', 'bribes', 'sleaze' and the like seems to fit sensational journalism rather than detached analysis. This sententious discourse tends to direct attention towards individual ethics and personal integrity rather than structural and institutional conditions of large-scale systemic practices.[37] One suspects that here the language often skews both diagnosis and prescription.

Concepts associated with legal education, legal professions and lawyers on the whole do not travel well, even within the same 'legal family' or between contexts in a single jurisdiction. For example, who counts as a 'law student' is problematic within a single jurisdiction, England, and no definition seems to provide a sensible basis for comparison between mass university systems, like Italy, multi-stage processes of professional formation, such as England's, and professional law school programmes in the US. If 'law student' is defined as someone registered for a 'first degree in law', there are serious doubts whether this is a sensible unit of comparison.[38] If the definition is extended to include anyone involved in a professional training programme or in the process ending in initial certification, the problems of comparability are more complex. Any comparative statistics about numbers of law students under any of these

---

36 A good recent assessment by an economist who is a strong supporter of the fight against corruption is Rose-Ackerman (1999); cf Klitgaard (1988).
37 See eg Schofield (1996).
38 Twining (1998).

definitions are almost meaningless, generally misleading and often false. That is only the start of the difficulties. Similar considerations apply to terms like 'lawyer', 'legal profession', 'legal services' and 'legal work', and to a lesser extent to 'judge', 'court' and 'trial'. These conceptual difficulties have been a serious obstacle to the development of comparative studies in this area.[39]

This modest pilot study illustrates the artificiality of trying to maintain sharp distinctions between different branches of jurisprudence. Any transnational study of prison conditions or anti-corruption measures or legal education is likely to involve conceptual, normative, interpretive and empirical dimensions. In the case of prisons and corruption the discourses have travelled as part of a complex process of diffusion. Hohfeld provided some powerful analytical tools for studying normative orders, but how well they fit 'radically different cultures' or all normative systems are questions that still require quite complex empirical and interpretive investigation. The same theme will recur when we look briefly at some implications of globalisation for normative and historical-empirical jurisprudence.

NORMATIVE JURISPRUDENCE

> 'Some think that all justice is of this sort, because that which by nature is unchangeable, and everywhere has the same force (as fire burns both here and in Persia), while they see change in things recognized as just. This, however, is not true in an unqualified way, but is true in a sense.' (Aristotle.)[40]

Normative jurisprudence encompasses general questions about values and law. It deals with the relations between law, politics and morality, including debates between and among positivists and others about the relationship between law and morality; whether law is at its core a moral enterprise; and about political obligation and civil disobedience. It includes questions about the existence, scope and status of natural, moral and non-legal rights; theories of justice; and standards for guiding and evaluating legal institutions, practices and decisions. Whether normative theories of reasoning and rationality and questions of scepticism and relativism about them are subsumed under normative or analytical jurisprudence is largely a matter of convenience.

Issues about universality and generality in respect of values have concerned philosophers throughout history. Western jurisprudence has a long tradition of universalism in ethics. Natural law, classical utilitarianism, Kantianism and modern theories of human rights have all been universalist in tendency. In jurisprudence, most of these ideas have been discussed mainly in relation to the municipal law of nation-states. In recent times liberal democratic political and legal theory have tended either to be geographically indeterminate or to place some limits on their geographical claims. A great deal of recent Anglo-American normative jurisprudence has been relatively local in respect of provenance, audience and even focus. For example, most writings about the new communitarianism, critical race theory and republicanism have been explicitly

---

39 The comparative study of legal professions is one of the most developed fields of transnational legal sociology. The extent to which it is still bedevilled by basic conceptual problems is clearly illustrated in Barcello and Cramton (1999).

40 Aristotle *Nicomachean Ethics* (trans Ross), Book 5, chapter 7 (1134b24–28).

or implicitly or unselfconsciously American.[41] Feminist jurisprudence has only recently begun to be genuinely transnational. John Rawls limits his theory of justice to self-contained liberal societies and in regard to international relations to relations between 'liberal and decent peoples'.[42]

There are some important exceptions to the trend towards greater geographical particularity. The field of international ethics, exemplified by Peter Singer, Onora O'Neill and Amartya Sen, addresses transnational issues from a global perspective.[43] There have been lively debates about human rights and cultural relativism and universalism versus contextualism.[44] In practice, the most politically influential, are probably the ideological assumptions underlying the 'Washington Consensus' which links free market economics to the seductive catch-phrase 'human rights, good governance, and democracy'.[45]

The long tradition of universalism in ethics and the cosmopolitanism of the last three examples suggest that our heritage of normative jurisprudence may have to make fewer adjustments in the face of the challenges of 'globalisation'. This may be partly true. But casting a critical eye on that heritage, especially the work of mainstream or canonical jurists, leads to the conclusion that some rethinking is called for. Let us consider two examples by way of illustration.

First, most juristic discussions of positivism, law and morals, and obedience to law have been almost exclusively concerned with the municipal law of nation-states. For the most part they barely address questions of value in relation to other levels of legal ordering (public international law is a partial exception) nor the phenomena of normative and legal pluralism.[46] A particularly clear example is Rawls' theory of justice, which is explicitly, and, in this writer's view, unconvincingly, limited to nation-states as notionally self-contained communities, and, as a secondary matter, to relations between such states.[47] Just because Rawls' theory is concerned with basic practical principles of institutional design, questions about its extension or adaptability to institutions concerned with ordering at other levels (for example, regional integration or the regulation of exploitation of unappropriated minerals on this or other planets) is of particular significance.

Second, nearly all modern normative jurisprudence is either secular or explicitly Christian. Post-Enlightenment secularism has deep historical roots in the intellectual traditions of Western Christianity. Even those theories which claim universality have proceeded with only tangential reference to, and almost complete ignorance of, the religious and moral beliefs and traditions of the

---

41 Critical legal scholars have quite recently turned their attention to comparative law, international law and Latin America ('Lat-Crits') and issues of globalisation, but it is too early to assess the significance of these developments.

42 Rawls (1999) chapter 1.

43 Eg Singer (1993); O'Neill (1986); Sen and Dre'ze (1999).

44 A convenient introductory anthology is Wilson (1997).

45 A good example of the burgeoning literature challenging the sincerity, coherence and realism of this ideology is Chua (1998).

46 On normative and legal pluralism, see Twining (2000) pp 82–88, 224–233.

47 Rawls (1967) uses such phrases as 'more or less self-sufficient': p 4; 'self-contained national community': p 457; and 'a closed system isolated from other societies': p 8. The fullest critique of this aspect of his theory is Pogge (1992). See Twining (2000) pp 69–75. Rawls gives a partial and, in the writer's view, inadequate response to his critics in *The Law of Peoples* (1999).

majority of humankind.[48] When differing cultural values are discussed, even the agenda of issues tends to have a stereotypically Western bias.[49] A genuinely general jurisprudence will need to do better than that.

LEGAL REASONING

Whether one subsumes 'legal reasoning' under analytical or normative jurisprudence is largely a matter of convenience. However, locating the subject within general jurisprudence brings to the surface some neglected issues.

A 'Cook's Tour' of the heritage of Western literature on 'legal reasoning' might include the following: (1) a remarkably sophisticated, obsessively repetitive body of normative theorising about justification of judicial decisions on questions of law in 'hard cases', and, especially in civil law systems, the rationalisation of systematic exposition of legal doctrine ('legal science'); (2) a largely separate, less developed and rather more diverse literature on reasoning about disputed questions of fact in adjudication, especially contested jury trials in the US; (3) an intermittent and even more diverse body of literature subjecting actual discourse, especially the discourses of argumentation in adjudication, to analysis and criticism from a variety of perspectives;[50] (4) very little sustained work, normative, empirical or interpretive, on the modes of reasoning and argumentation employed in other legal operations (for example, sentencing, negotiation, mediation, rule-making, enforcement); (5) even less about the relationship between reasoning about questions of law, questions of fact and other law-related questions, except occasional indications that all kinds of rational argumentation in legal contexts may possibly be subsumed under a single model of practical reasoning or of problem-solving;[51] (6) very little about the similarities, differences and relations between the various modes of reasoning and argumentation employed in modern municipal legal systems, on the one hand, and other kinds of legal orders (including transnational, religious, and traditional legal orders), on the other; (7) a nascent, but rapidly burgeoning, literature about expert systems and other applications of Artificial Intelligence to law; and (8) a spectrum of sceptical and relativist views of varying degrees of strength challenging one or more of the above.[52]

In contemporary mainstream jurisprudence the enormous literature on legal reasoning tends either to be explicitly particular to a given legal system (for example, American constitutional interpretation), limited to a 'family' or tradition

---

48 It is notoriously difficult to estimate the numbers of adherents of world religions. With the normal caveats, *The Oxford Atlas of the World* (1994) estimates that Christian 'adherents' represent about 40–43% of the world population, Muslims about 25% and other religions the remainder. No figure is given for atheists and agnostics.

49 This tendency is well caught in Ahdaf Salouf's novel *The Map of Love* (1999) p 6. An Egyptian woman, Amal, is expecting an American visitor:
  'Wary and weary in advance: an American woman – a journalist, she had said on the phone. But she said Amal's brother had told her to call and so Amal agreed to see her. And braced herself: the fundamentalists, the veil, the cold peace, polygamy, women's status in Islam, female genital mutilation – which would it be?'

50 'Argumentation' is used here to refer to actual discourses used in advancing arguments, including both 'rational' and 'non-rational' means of persuasion. For a recent survey, dealing mainly with (1) and (3), see Feteris (1999).

51 Twining (2000) pp 194–195, 334–335.

52 This paragraph anticipates the entry on 'Legal reasoning and argument' in the new *International Encyclopedia of the Social and Behavioral Sciences* (forthcoming, 2002).

(for example, common law reasoning) or else geographically indeterminate (is Ronald Dworkin's Hercules a role model for the German judiciary, the ECJ, or an Islamic jurist?). There are a few studies that seek for deep structures underlying Western legal thought in general, but these are exceptional.[53] A largely unexplored question is how far theories of legal reasoning, such as those of Aarnio, Alexy, MacCormick or Dworkin, can be generalised across legal cultures and traditions. Most such theories assert or assume universal principles of logic and/or general principles of practical reasoning, but typically they are set in some more or less local institutional context, such as a country's highest court, or US or common law adjudication. Take the question: 'what constitutes a valid, cogent and appropriate argument on a question of law?' Some criteria of validity may be general, others (such as rules relating to authoritative sources or evidence) may be local; criteria of cogency may be a mixture of general and local, but criteria of appropriateness tend to be context-specific.[54]

The concept of 'questions of law' is also context-dependent. It is a familiar theme in comparative law and legal history that whether an issue is categorised as being a question of law or of fact or of something else (for example, disposition) varies both within and among jurisdictions. In English law 'questions of fact' are classified differently for purposes of allocation of functions of judge and jury, precedent, appeals, statutory interpretation and so on. Dezalay and Garth have shown how, in the context of international commercial arbitration, there are marked differences between common lawyers and civil lawyers as to how they frame the issues in terms of disputed questions of fact or law.[55] If legal theory is to be genuinely transnational and cross-cultural, it must address questions of generalisability not only about legal reasoning in the narrow sense, but also about other reasonings in legal contexts about facts, policy, law-making, sentencing, negotiation and so on.

HISTORICAL, SOCIAL SCIENTIFIC AND INTERPRETIVE INQUIRIES

Analytical jurisprudence has been primarily, but not exclusively, concerned with concepts, and the most stable relations have been with analytical philosophy; normative jurisprudence has been concerned with values, and the most stable relations have been with ethics and political theory. Other theoretical lines of inquiry concerned with interpreting, describing and explaining actual legal phenomena in 'the real world' are sometimes assigned to Historical Jurisprudence and the Sociology of Law.[56]

Such labels are misleading. 'Historical Jurisprudence' came to be associated almost exclusively with the idea of legal evolution, and in the Anglo-American tradition with the rather odd kind of history practised by Sir Henry Maine.[57] This is an important tradition that is due for a revival, but it is only one strand in the

---

53 Eg Samuel (1994) Cover, which 'reflects upon the structural nature of legal reasoning in the perspective of a *ius commune*, focusing on Roman, English and French law ...'.
54 On appropriateness in relation to institutional context, standpoint and style, see Twining and Miers (1999) pp 366–370 passim.
55 Dezalay and Garth (1996).
56 'Sociology of Law' has generally replaced 'Sociological Jurisprudence', which came to be identified quite narrowly with the 'social engineering' perspective of Roscoe Pound and others.
57 Stein (1988) gives an excellent account of the rise and decline of 'the Historical School'.

complex relations between legal theory and historiography. General jurisprudence also needs to take account of intellectual history, comparative or world history, as well as more particularistic kinds of historical enquiry. Similarly, in some contexts terms like 'Sociology of Law', 'Sociological Jurisprudence', 'Law and Society' and 'Socio-legal Studies' may suggest that the main, or even the only, important relationship between law and social science is with sociology. That is, in the writer's opinion, quite obviously wrong.[58]

One function of jurisprudence is to map the relations between law and other disciplines. Professor Julius Stone called Jurisprudence 'the lawyer's extraversion'.[59] This has sometimes been interpreted as encouraging dilettantism and eclecticism. A more positive interpretation is that jurisprudence can have a useful role as a kind of foreign ministry for our discipline in keeping track of relations with other academic tribes and territories. Professor J L Montrose used to bewilder and impress new law students in Belfast by presenting a picture of law in the context of all learning. This may have served a useful purpose by setting particular studies in a broad context, analogous to the Grands Systèmes approach to comparative law.[60] The idea is attractive, provided that is not interpreted in a grandiose or a reductionist fashion. What is needed is not a monolithic synthesis, but rather occasional maps of the main interdisciplinary lines of inquiry that are being, or might be, pursued and the connections between them. Such maps would need to deal not only with the state of relations between law and the subdisciplines and enclaves of every social science, but also with the humanities (including literature and theology) and the physical and applied sciences (including medicine, genetics and engineering).

This chapter cannot attempt to do justice to the details of law's relations with other disciplines. In the run-up to the Millennium there were many overviews, critical stocktakings and programshrifts that can be consulted.[61] The overall picture is diverse, complex, dynamic and uneven. Here we shall limit the discussion to two brief points.

First, every area of interdisciplinary work needs to consider the implications of globalisation and the challenges outlined above. This is a task for specialists. It has already begun in some areas, but not in a very coherent fashion. Second, the chapter has suggested that problems of generalisability should be central to a revived general jurisprudence. Here contrasts between particularistic and

---

58 For example, in the UK the term 'socio-legal studies' was originally coined for bureaucratic purposes to designate those kinds of cross-disciplinary research about law that qualified for financial support from the then Economic and Social Research Council in respect of research that involved perspectives, methods or concepts from any of the social sciences, including anthropology, business studies, criminology, economics, geography, linguistics, penology, politics, psychology, social history and some aspects of statistics. Each of these disciplines has its own complex history, culture, feuds, traditions, external relations and fashions. Their relations to law are correspondingly complex. On the whole, such points have been well understood by those involved in socio-legal research, but this diversity has sometimes been obscured at the level of theory.

59 Stone (1964) p 16.

60 Twining (2000) chapter 6.

61 Useful sources include the introductions to the relevant volumes in the International Library of Essays in Law and Legal Theory, entries in a range of new scholarly encyclopaedias, such as *A Companion to Philosophy of Law and Legal Theory*: Patterson (1996); *Philosophy of Law: An Encyclopedia*: Gray (1999); and the planned new edition of the *International Encyclopedia of the Social and Behavioral Sciences* (forthcoming, 2002). See also, on socio-legal studies, Thomas (1996; 1997); and Gessner, Hoeland and Varga (1996).

scientistic disciplines are quite suggestive. For example, the cultures of anthropology or history tend to be particularistic, emphasising 'thick description', uniqueness, complexity, 'granularity', layers of meaning, multi-factorial causation, and the importance of local knowledge. By contrast, 'harder' social scientists, striving to generalise, invoke Occam's Razor, use simplifying assumptions, stress measurability and look for patterns, trends and correlations. 'How can a historian "explain" an event outside a universe of cases?' ask the scientists. 'How can such thin descriptions, or such unreal assumptions, be the basis for true generalisations?' counter the qualitative scholars? Of course, 'soft' and 'hard', 'qualitative' and 'quantitative' are poles at the ends of a spectrum, with most scholars somewhere in between, looking both ways. The tension can be quite creative, as lawyers well know, because the complexities of relations between the general and the particular – between general rules and concrete cases – are a central part of legal culture.

THE ROLE OF COMPARATIVE LEGAL STUDIES

A cosmopolitan discipline of law will need to be quite general with regard to sources and perspectives, even when the audience is quite local. The appropriate level(s) of focus of a line of inquiry will depend in large part on its purpose and context. To what extent it is feasible and desirable to generalise about a given subject of study will be among the central issues of legal theory.

Here comparative law will have a crucial role. John Stuart Mill treated observation, description, abstraction, comparison, naming, classification and induction as important stages in the process towards generalisation.[62] Without necessarily following Mill's model of scientific inquiry, comparative work in law should play a crucial role in the process of enlarging our understandings of legal phenomena beyond national boundaries en route to exploring problems of generalisability. The idea of general jurisprudence includes study of two or more legal orders; so do comparative legal studies. Comparative law and legal theory should be conceived as interdependent. Only detailed comparative work can provide the essential concrete raw material for constructing and testing general propositions – conceptual/analytical, normative, empirical and prescriptive.

In the Anglo-American tradition 'comparative law' has tended to be treated as a subject apart, peripheral, 'academic' and somewhat given to dilettantism. The mainstream of the institutionalised subdiscipline has in the past tended to be rather narrowly focused on comparing private law doctrine of 'parent' common and civil law systems.[63]

In addition, mainstream comparative law has been criticised for being generally formalistic and atheoretical.[64] However, mainstream comparative law has attracted many outstanding scholars, especially from the extraordinarily influential generation of refugees from Nazism. Taught comparative law may

62 Mill (1843) Book IV Of Operations Subsidiary to Induction.
63 This statement is subject to two caveats: first, it applies to micro-comparative law, which has been the dominant approach especially in the common law tradition. Second, the writer has gently satirised the dominant *conception* of comparative law as 'the Country and Western Tradition'; the practice, especially in respect of research, has been much more diverse in recent years. See 'Comparative Law and Legal Theory: The Country and Western Tradition', in Edge (2000) and Twining (2000) chapter 7.
64 Eg Legrand (1995; 1999); Ewald (1995).

have been narrowly focused for pragmatic reasons, but figures such as Ernst Rabel, Max Rheinstein, Wolfgang Friedman, and Otto Kahn-Freund were the opposite of narrow-minded, intellectually as well as geographically. Indeed several of them played a major role in broadening the discipline of law in the US and the UK.[65]

Comparative law as an institutionalised subdiscipline has diversified and expanded in many ways in recent years. More important, if ever there was a time when a serious legal scholar could concentrate entirely on a single jurisdiction in respect of sources and focus, that time is past. Legal orders are interdependent. Almost all legal scholarship draws on transnational sources, is informed by ideas from other disciplines and legal traditions and, even when the focus is highly local, either implicitly or explicitly makes comparisons with legal phenomena elsewhere. In short, to a significant extent we are all comparatists now.

At this point, let us pause to note two near paradoxes. First, few experienced comparatists compare. By this, the writer means that even within mainstream comparative law sustained explicit molecular comparison is wholly exceptional. Of course, juxtaposition, parallel studies, outsider perspectives and ad hoc contrasts all abound. But systematic analysis and explanation of similarities and differences between legal orders and particular legal phenomena are both rare and fragile. The reasons for this are obvious. The theoretical and practical problems of sustained strict comparison are enormous. Experienced comparatists, usually acutely aware of many of these difficulties, tend to skirt the pitfalls, make disclaimers and lower their sights.[66] Few comparatists compare, for they know the difficulties.

A second near-paradox is that what is frequently perceived to be the most insular tradition in academic law may have the most sophisticated culture involving sustained comparison. American legal scholarship and legal education is frequently accused, by both locals and foreigners, of being 'inward-looking', 'parochial' or 'isolationist'. Yet it is probably the most experienced and adept at handling issues, sources and relations that cross jurisdictional borders. The writer is one of those foreigners who on occasion have chafed at the American tendency to focus 'almost exclusively on American law, American ideas, American institutions (especially courts and law schools) and local American hang-ups',[67] and is not about to recant. But viewed from another perspective, where in the world has there been a scholarly tradition that has had to deal routinely with interpreting, comparing and generalising about relations, problems, sources and 'solutions' that involve over 50 jurisdictions, often simultaneously?[68] The facts behind the images of the US as 'a melting pot' or 'a laboratory' reinforce the thesis that all American legal scholarship, and much of its legal practice, is a sub-branch of comparative law.

65 Eg K Lipstein in Carlebach and Mosse (1991) p 221; Grossfield and Winship (1992).
66 A good example is chapter 1 of David Downes' excellent *Contrasts in Tolerance: Post-war Penal Policy in the Netherlands and England and Wales* (1988) which sets out the main difficulties of comparing criminal justice systems and explicitly disclaims that it is a comparative study of post-war criminal justice policy in the two countries: p 5. The writer has been involved in a number of transnational comparative projects in which at an early stage any pretensions to be doing systematic comparison were abandoned: see eg Dhavan, Kibble and Twining (1989); Malsch and Nijboer (1999).
67 Twining (2000) p 59.
68 The closest approximation might be large empires, but none that the writer is aware of could match the sophistication of American lawyers in dealing with interstate commerce, choice of law issues, federal jurisdiction and the like.

It might be objected that studies of state probate law in Illinois and Michigan,[69] or Federal Jurisdiction, or Native American Law, or the Common Law Movement of the militias (in the prairie states or the US as a whole),[70] do not involve 'real comparison', for this term should be reserved for analysing similarities and differences across legal families or cultures. The basic impulse behind such views is obvious and healthy: law students and lawyers need to be made aware of a wider world. Nevertheless, this conception of 'real comparison' should be treated as a dangerous fallacy. Any comparatist should know that not only is it *easier* to compare and contrast phenomena that are closely related or otherwise similar in important respects, but such comparisons are less likely to be *invalid*. In other words, comparability presupposes some affinity. Psychological research supports this elementary truth.[71]

In this view, comparative legal studies took a wrong turn historically when 'comparative common law' and 'comparative civil law' were excluded from the subdiscipline.[72] For this had the implication that the pioneers of comparative law were not only starting with more difficult kinds of comparison – for which there were some good reasons – but they were excluding from conscious consideration all the accumulated experience, techniques and wisdom that could be found in existing 'best practice' involving more local comparative work. They further increased their own difficulties by trying to exclude the study of 'foreign law' from comparative law.[73] Collectively they purported to run before they had considered what walking involved. The lesson is that comparison begins near home.

This argument is presented here in a deliberately provocative way. If it is broadly correct, it has implications for theory and methodology in comparative law. The mainstream tradition of comparative law has been criticised as being atheoretical[74] and the leading textbook on the subject quotes Gustav Radbruch as saying 'sciences which have to concern themselves with their own methodology are sick sciences'.[75] Max Rheinstein used to suggest that comparative law was more like a way of life than a method.[76] Scepticism about methodology may have been reinforced by a judgment that the theoretical literature about the subject has been rather unhelpful. The writer's preliminary explorations suggest that there have been many reflective practitioners, but almost no outstanding theorists. On the whole comparatists have preferred to get on with the job.

In a participant-oriented discipline such as law, practice very often outstrips theory. But there may be something about the subject matters of law, other than the general impatience with theory of practitioners of an art, that accounts for the reluctance of comparatists to theorise. In so far as many legal phenomena are embedded in specific histories and cultures, one does not have to be a strong

---

69 The writer was taught by Max Rheinstein in a course entitled 'Decedents' Estates' in Chicago. We focused on Illinois probate law; it is left to the reader to imagine the geographical and historical range of his examples.

70 See eg Koniak (1996).

71 Gentner and Markman (1994).

72 Eg Harold Gutteridge, a pioneer of comparative law in England, wrote: 'No special form of technique seems to be called for if the comparison is, for instance, between Australian and Canadian law and the law of the US.': Gutteridge (1946) Preface. Compare Atiyah and Summers (1987). See further Twining (2000) pp 145–148.

73 Discussed in Twining (2000) pp 187–188.

74 Eg Legrand (1999); Ewald (1995).

75 Zweigert and Kötz (1998) p 32.

76 In conversation; cf Rheinstein (1968).

relativist to have doubts about comparing and generalising about them. Some may just not be susceptible to valid comparison at appropriate levels for significant purposes. Yet globalisation and the seeming confidence of the ideologues of a global economy and of free market policies present direct challenges to such doubts. That is one important reason, among many, why we need a revival of general jurisprudence.

References

Atiyah, P S, and Summers, R S, (1987) *Form and Substance in Anglo-American Law.*

Barcello, J J, and Cramton, R C (eds), (1999) *Lawyers' Practice and Ideals: A Comparative View.*

Bohannan, P, (1963) *Social Anthropology.*

—(1968) *Justice and Judgement among the Tiv* (revised edn).

Carlebach, J, and Mosse, W E, (eds), (1991) *Second Chance: Two Centuries of German-speaking Jews in the United Kingdom.*

Chua, A, (1998) 'Markets, Democracy, and Ethnicity: Toward a New Paradigm for Law and Development', 108 Yale LJ 1.

Dezalay, Y, and Garth, B, (1996) *Dealing in Virtue.*

Dhavan, R, Kibble, N, and Twining, W (eds), (1989) *Access to Legal Education and the Legal Profession.*

Downes, D, (1988) *Contrasts in Tolerance: Post-war Penal Policy in the Netherlands and England and Wales.*

Dworkin, R, (1986) *Law's Empire.*

Edge, I, (ed), (2000) *Comparative Law in Global Perspective.*

Ewald, W, (1995) 'What was it Like to Try a Rat?', 143 UPaLR 1889.

Feteris, E, (1999) *Fundamentals of Legal Argumentation.*

Gellner, E, (1959) *Words and Things.*

Gentner, D, and Markman, A B, (1994) 'Structural Alignment in Comparison: No Difference Without Similarity', 5 Psychological Science 152.

Gessner, V, Hoeland, A, and Varga, C (eds), (1996) *European Legal Cultures.*

Gewirth, A, (1983) 'Ethical Universalism and Particularism', 85 J Philosophy 283.

Gray, C, (ed), (1999) *Philosophy of Law: An Encyclopedia.*

Grossfield, B, and Winship, P, (1992) 'The Law Professor Refugee', 18 Syr J Int & Co L 3.

Gutteridge, H, (1946) *Comparative Law.*

Hart, H L A, (1961) *The Concept of Law* (1st edn).

—(1967) 'Problems of Legal Philosophy' in P Edwards (ed) 6 *Encyclopedia of Philosophy.*

—(1983) *Essays in Jurisprudence and Philosophy.*

—(1994) *The Concept of Law* (2nd edn).

Hill, J, (1989) 'Comparative Law, Law Reform, and Legal Theory', 9 OJLS 101.

Hoebel, E A, and Llewellyn, K, (1941) *The Cheyenne Way.*

International Encyclopedia of the Social and Behavioral Sciences, (forthcoming, 2001).

Klitgaard, R, (1988) *Controlling Corruption.*

Koniak, S, (1996) 'When Law Risks Madness', 8 Cardozo SL & Lit 65.

Lawson, F H, (1950) 'The Field of Comparative Law', 61 Juridical Review 16.

Legrand, P, (1995) 'Comparative Legal Studies and Commitment to Theory', 58 MLR 262.

Legrand, P, (1999) *Fragments on Law-as-Culture.*

Malsch, M, and Nijboer, J F (eds), (1999) *Complex Cases: Perspectives on the Netherlands Criminal Justice System.*

Mill, J S, (1973) *A System of Logic Ratiocinative and Inductive* (1st edn, 1843; reprinted 1973).

Patterson, D, (ed), (1996) *A Companion to Philosophy of Law and Legal Theory.*

Pogge, T, (1992) *Realizing Rawls.*

Rawls, J, (1967) *A Theory of Justice.*

—(1999) *The Law of Peoples.*

Rose-Ackerman, S, (1999) *Corruption and Government: Causes, Consequences, and Reform.*

Samuel, G, (1994) *The Foundations of Legal Reasoning.*

Schofield, P, (1996) 'Jeremy Bentham on Political Corruption: A Critique of the First Report of the Nolan Committee', 49 CLP, vol 2 at 395.

Rheinstein, M, (1968) 'Comparative Law – Its Functions, Methods, and Usages', 22 ArkLR 415.

Sen, A, and Dre'ze, J, (1999) *The Amartya Sen and Jean Dre'ze Omnibus.*

Singer, P, (1993) *Practical Ethics* (2nd edn).

Stein, P, (1988) *Legal Evolution: The Story of an Idea.*

Stern, V, (1988) *A Sin Against the Future: Imprisonment in the World.*

Stone, J, (1964) *Legal System and Lawyers' Reasonings.*

Thomas, P A, (ed), (1996) *Legal Frontiers.*

—(1997) *Socio-Legal Studies.*

Twining, W, (1968) *The Karl Llewellyn Papers.*

—(1979) 'Academic Law and Legal Philosophy: The Significance of Herbert Hart', 95 LQR 557.

—(1997) *Law in Context: Enlarging a Discipline.*

—(1998) 'Thinking about Law Schools: Rutland Reviewed', 25 J Law and Society 1.

—(2000) *Globalisation and Legal Theory.*

—(2000) 'Comparative Law and Legal Theory: The Country and Western Tradition' in I Edge (2000).

Twining, W, and Miers, D, (1999) *How to Do Things With Rules* (4th edn).

Weldon, T D, (1953) *The Vocabulary of Politics.*

Wilson, R A, (ed), (1997) *Human Rights, Culture and Context.*

Zweigert, K, and Kotz, H, (1998) *An Introduction to Comparative Law* (3rd edn, trans A Weir).

Chapter 2

One world: notes on the emerging legal order

L M FRIEDMAN*[1]

The globalisation of law is a topic that has entered the consciousness of legal scholars only recently.[2] This is not mere fashion – it is a response to real processes and events. But exactly what do we mean by globalisation? The core meaning of the term refers to a change in *scale* and in *site*. It refers to movement, diffusion and expansion, from a local level and with local implications to levels and implications that are worldwide, or (more usually) that transcend national borders in some way. This expansion and diffusion means that no man, woman or nation is an island, to misquote John Donne. As a result of the process of diffusion, everything seems to be connected with everything else. There are no longer any hermit kingdoms. There are, in fact, hardly any hermits of any sort, on any level, in the world at the threshold of the twenty-first century.[3]

Globalisation, whatever else it may mean, is about movement – of images, goods and ideas – across state borders; and, for that matter, across oceans and mountain barriers as well. Trade relations between tribes, groups and countries are nothing new in human history; quite the contrary. But the sheer scale is new, and also the share of the total world economy that is devoted to transnational trade. Similarly, people have always been on the move, and ideas, images, religions, cultures and diseases have travelled across borders. But the modern diffusion of people and concepts is rather different. For one thing, it is far more *individual*; it is not a migration of peoples but of people.[4] Millions of people in the so-called 'immigration countries', the US or Argentina, migrated by themselves, or in tiny family groups. Today, *all* the rich and developed countries are targets of this kind of movement. We will return to this theme.

Miraculous advances in the technologies of movement and communication make modern diffusion possible. These technologies are the *instruments* or *tools* of globalisation. Without radio, television, satellites, without cars, trains and planes, nobody would be talking about globalisation at all. The Internet is now adding

---

* A previous version of this essay was published in the Stanford Journal of International Law, vol 37 (2001) pp 347–364 (Standford Law School).
1 Marion Rice Kirkwood Professor of Law, Stanford University.
2 The literature is enormous. See eg, Roehl and Magen (1996); Shapiro (1993).
3 In fact, the closest thing to a hermit in our times would be someone alone at home hunched in front of a computer screen, who might well be 'chatting' with other such hermits.
4 Certainly, there are many examples of *mass* migrations still – particularly of the helpless and hapless refugees in places like Kosovo or in central Africa.

another dimension to globalisation. It is possible to send a message around the world in nanoseconds. Even physically to move from one country to another is drastically easier and shorter than it once was. Anyone today can go around the world, if necessary, not in 80 days but in one.

In some ways, the prime carriers of globalisation do not require people to move *anywhere*, or even to get up from their couches and chairs. Globalisation, as we will argue, is basically a cultural phenomenon. But the cultural parts of the process can be beamed directly into the human brain, so to speak. The cultural impact of television, up to now, has been immense. It transports scenes, images, ideas – in short, the grammar and syntax of culture – at great speed across great distances. It insinuates itself into millions or even billions of homes. The Internet promises to make an even greater difference in the future; it has the potential to connect everybody with everybody else in the developed world; and it is already a storehouse of billions and billions of bits of information. It may be too early for us to grasp the significance of the Internet, or to know what this will mean to the global community. The potential impact is immense.

But we must ask exactly *what* is it that the globalising process is globalising – what is its content? The most obvious answer is trade; globalisation is international business, international transactions, international buying and selling and deal-making. It is tankers of oil from Saudi Arabia and container-ships of toys and television sets from Taiwan, shoes and blouses from Indonesia, wheat and walnuts from the US. A second answer is human capital – *people*, to use a less cold and unfriendly term. Human beings have themselves become global; they move rapidly in and out of their countries and all throughout the world – quite ordinary people, travelling as tourists, refugees, in-migrants and out-migrants; not to mention business people, entertainers, academic jetsetters and many others.

Trade and human capital are at the core of globalisation. But both in turn depend on global *culture*. Everything else follows from global culture. Global culture means ideas, images, patterns of behaviour, thought processes which are, to an extent at least, shared all over the world – certainly all over the developed world, and, more and more, elsewhere as well. What is the nature of global culture? In the first place, the developed countries are its main source; it spreads from 'the West' to the east and the south. Bernard defines globalisation ('mondialisation') as 'the invasive influence of cultural, political, and economic models, which are born in the countries of the first world ... and are progressively imposed on a great many other countries'.[5] Some traffic, of course, does flow in the other direction, but the great streams of culture arise in the West.

Television is a powerful carrier of the global culture. The images on television spread all over the world, subtly and invisibly. Every culture that television touches is transformed. Entertainment programmes – comedies, game shows, talk shows, police and detective dramas, sports events – are the most popular programmes on television. Television also devotes attention to 'news', but 'news' must also meet the demand to entertain. Popular programmes are extremely variable, but they carry a definite ideology – a content and a message. In truth, this message is not much different from the message of the commercials, which are another prominent feature of television. The message is one of consumerism, of individualism, of leisure and the ways to enjoy leisure. Television, generally speaking, describes a world of fun, thrill, mystery, adventure; it is a world of celebrities, of the rich and famous; a world primarily of the young and beautiful;

5   Bernard (1999).

a world of people who live exciting lives, sometimes tragic, but rarely humdrum, and rarely reflecting the grinding, daily struggle of most people on earth. These programmes tend to show Western styles, dress and manners. Popular programmes from other parts of the world – for example, soap operas from Latin America – are not very different in kind from the programmes that come from the US. Even the local programmes in India or Egypt share some themes and aspects with Western programmes. In any event, they must compete with Western rivals.

Television is, in general, enormously popular in all but the most underdeveloped places. One very popular programme, all over the world, is *Bay Watch*, one of the US's great gifts to the world. The programme stars some good-looking young people, who are shown mostly on the beach in bathing suits. The programme has an obvious, if rather mild, appeal to lust. Beyond this, it shows a world of fun, leisure and sunshine, interrupted from time-to-time with some more or less serious problem that gets resolved by the end of the programme. The primary image is of slimness, youth, beauty, free time, fun and a healthy dash of sex. Television images like these are tremendously seductive. Foreign television programmes have turned girls in Fiji – where once upon a time fat was beautiful – into bulimics.[6] It is impossible to tell how many people dye their hair, change their style of dress or take up some new habit because of the images they see on television. The programmes arouse, all over the world, a culture of envy and desire.

Movies are another medium of popular culture. Movies are a US success story; in much of the world, it is the US films that bring in the biggest audiences. In country after country, American movies have almost driven the local product to extinction. Americans seem to be world masters of seductive cinematic junk. Germans, Finns, Japanese, Guatemalans, swarm into cinemas to see the latest Clint Eastwood or Bruce Willis movie. The top-grossing film in Argentina in 1991 was *Terminator 2*; in Egypt it was *Dances with Wolves*; in Sweden, it was *Pretty Woman*.[7] In 1993, it was reported that the US 'commands a staggering 85% of the world's film market, and 90% of the European film market'; 88 of the top 100 movies in that year were American.[8] Some countries have been truly alarmed at this threat to their national cultures, as they see it. The French and the Canadians have made serious attempts to protect their culture from the invading Americans. International trade agreements, however, make it difficult to keep out these foreign cultural products. And cultural borders are even harder to protect than physical borders in the age of satellites and receiving dishes.[9] But the underlying problem, of course, is that French audiences *like* American movies, American music, American television. If we ask why this is, the answer has to be that Americans are good at this business. They have a better sense of what sorts of cultural junk-food people enjoy, just as the French seem to have a better grasp of haute cuisine and perfume and the Italians turn out what people consider the world's most wonderful shoes. In short, technology has made it possible to ignore borders, and to diffuse works of popular culture all over the world. The only real barrier is language, which is unimportant in music, and is only a slight obstacle to television and the movies, since they can be dubbed or provided with subtitles. In many

6   Goode (1999).
7   Barber (1995) pp 299–300.
8   Prowda (1996) at 200.
9   Friedman (1999) p 51.

movies, the dialogue is almost irrelevant, anyway, compared with the 'action' and the 'special effects'.

Science and technology have created the industrial world; and have created an immense stock of wealth. The wealth is very badly distributed in many countries, certainly, and even more so between countries; there are millions, even billions, in the world who are condemned to lives of poverty and misery. Their daily lives are a struggle for a piece of bread or a bowl of rice, and a roof to shelter them from rain and wind. The Internet, jet travel and even television may be remote from their world. But in Europe and North America, in Japan, Korea, Hong Kong and Singapore, in Australia, New Zealand and in Israel, there is a huge middle class; in other countries, less well off in general, the middle class grows rapidly in size and influence. The numbers of people who have some affluence or leisure, who no longer live on the razor's-edge of subsistence, run in the hundreds of millions – perhaps billions. These people have money to spend and time to spare to spend that money, after work, on Sunday, on holidays, during vacations. Time and money make them massive consumers; they have, in particular, an insatiable appetite for entertainment; they are avid consumers of fun.

Of course, the economic aspects of globalisation are critically important, especially the development of international trade. The national economies are interlocked; many countries are heavily dependent on international trade. The volume of this trade is simply enormous. Different countries sell different products – oil flows from Saudi Arabia to countries that have no oil of their own; raw materials are extracted where they lie, in the ground, and shipped to countries that process them; some countries specialise in making computers or computer chips; others in shoes and shirts and sealing wax. Peoples have always traded with one another. Today's trade is, however, on the whole, much different from trade in the days when the West had its colonies and bought silk and spices from the East. For one thing, there are now multinational corporations – giant companies that are everywhere and nowhere. Characteristic of these companies is the 'geographic dispersal of firms' factories, offices, service outlets, and markets', and 'the global assembly line in manufacturing'. In the early 1990s, US firms had more than 18,000 'affiliates overseas'; and German firms 'had even more'.[10] An official of Coca-Cola once told a group of students (somewhat grandiosely) that Coca-Cola was not an American company at all, but an international one; certainly, Coca-Cola operates in more than 100 countries. McDonald's cannot be far behind. Sony and Toyota are also ubiquitous.

But the crucial difference in contemporary trade is again a cultural factor: the global nature of both commodities and desires. The hunger for blue jeans, or for Nike shoes, or for cheese pizza is global. If Coca-Cola is sold everywhere, it is because people in Albania and Honduras and Mauritius like the taste. In the 'global marketplace', the Japanese 'eat poultry fattened in Thailand with American corn'; consumers 'on both sides of the Atlantic wear clothes assembled in Saipan with Chinese labour, drink orange juice from concentrate made with Brazilian oranges, and decorate their homes with flowers from Colombia'.[11] The surface point of the quote is about the globalisation of production; but implicit is the globalisation of consumption, the idea that consumers *want* the same things, or much the same things, everywhere. Of course, countries do differ in their

10 Sassen (1996) pp 7, 9–10.
11 McMichael (1996) p 1.

syndromes of consumption, but the similarities are even more striking. The main flow is from West to East, but not exclusively. You can eat sushi in Berlin or Miami as well as in Tokyo. It strikes Americans as weird to see a Pizza Hut in Beijing, but pizza is not American, it is Italian. And it is not really Italian, it is Neapolitan, and probably once as exotic in Milan as it is in Bangkok. Blue jeans, an American gift to the world, were originally designed for miners in California. Their appearance in New York as a fashion statement is as much an example of cultural diffusion as the eruption of blue jeans in Moscow or Jakarta. It is the hunger for the *same* sorts of goods that fuels modern international trade; this hunger creates the converging culture of the global village – indeed it *is* that culture.

No modern phenomenon, perhaps, is as important as this one – that is, the globalisation of patterns of consumption. So many products, ideas, images and patterns are from the US that it is tempting to talk about American imperialism or cultural hegemony. But 'Americanization' is quite selective; some aspects of US culture do not travel well at all. Coca-Cola sweeps the world; but nobody drinks root beer except Americans. The US is, for whatever reason, very good at satisfying tastes of the new middle class. America itself was the first middle class society – the first society in which broad masses of people (with glaring exceptions, of course), owned some property, voted, and *mattered* in society.[12] The talent for understanding, and catering to, mass desires, may come from this tradition of experience.

'America', moreover, has become a kind of symbol of whatever is seductive about modern life; and American products thus become symbols for the US itself. There is, in particular, a peculiarity of American culture which seems unusually attractive to other people. The US is a nation of 'levelers'; it is, of course, full of very rich people who live glamorous lives. But that life-style itself borrows from the life-style of the poor and obscure. Blue jeans, for example, are both chic and classless at the same time; so too are the music and clothes of the urban ghettos. And the American rich do not seem to be aristocrats or intellectuals – they are made out of the same raw material as everybody else.

In any event, the global culture of consumption is the common property of the middle class in almost every country. Is this common culture really as common as it seems? Is it anything more than a veneer? The Japanese have cars, computers, skyscrapers, air conditioners and antibiotics; they dress in a 'Western' style and hordes of young Japanese in Tokyo eat hamburgers at McDonald's. Does this mean that the Japanese are just about the same as the French or the Australians? Many people think not: they feel that the trappings of modernity are deceptive; that there is a Japanese core that remains fundamentally different from the French or Australian core, and has survived over the centuries. Whether this is so is in part an empirical question (and a very tough one), in part a matter of subjective interpretation. The writer's own view is that culture today has become quite fluid and malleable. The engines that produce modern culture are more powerful than the forces of tradition. And if you dress modern, eat modern, use modern tools, then you *become* modern. Your thought processes are, inevitably, altered.[13] It would be foolish to claim that Japanese culture in the late twentieth century had become the twin of French culture. The differences are as obvious as the

12 Friedman (1985) p 230.
13 Inkeles (1983); Inkeles and Smith (1974).

similarities.[14] The question is, is the Japan of today more like the France of today, than it is like the Japan of Lady Murasaki or the Nara court? And is the France of today, in turn, more like Japan, than it is like the France of Charles Martel or Jacques Villon? The answer to both questions, the writer suggests, is yes.

GLOBALISATION OF LAW

If there is a globalised world, and globalised processes, if there is a globalisation of business and trade, and a globalised culture of production and consumption, then it follows that there must also be a globalised sector of law. In the modern world, law is dense, ubiquitous and pervasive.[15] It is logical, then, to expect some kind of legal order or legal culture on the global level, and on a global scale. The question is, what does this global legal order consist of?

We should not exaggerate the scope of the globalised legal sphere. Most lawyers remain firmly rooted in their own legal habits and traditions, even those who work for transnational corporations. They deal mostly with the local management of these corporations – labour issues, tax issues, local contracts. Thousands of lawyers spend their days working on small real-estate deals, drawing up wills, helping couples get a divorce, defending criminals, coping with contract disputes between small and medium-sized companies, arguments over driveways and boundaries, tax audits, land-use planning – all issues firmly rooted in one particular country and even one particular place in that country. The legal world may be, in some ways, one of the more primitive sectors of modern life – less globalised than many other aspects of that life.

Of course, there *is* an international legal sector; there *are* lawyers with international practices; and it seems fairly obvious that this sector of the legal domain is growing rapidly. One symptom is the rise of the transnational law firm. Many large US firms have one, two or even many branches overseas. In 1995, the Wall Street law firm of Sullivan & Cromwell, a famous old firm, had branches in other US cities, plus branches in London, Paris, Hong Kong, Melbourne, Tokyo and Frankfurt. Other large US firms have also broadened their practice in this way; and increasingly it is the case that law firms in other countries similarly have internationalised. A leading firm of solicitors in London has European branches from Brussels to Moscow, as well as offices in Singapore, Bangkok, Hanoi and Beijing. A Hamburg firm has offices in Bratislava, Budapest, New York, Hong Kong and other places; and an Italian firm adds Dubai and Tirana to the list.[16] The leading law firm in Taipei, the writer has been told, does half of its legal business in the English language. 'Transnational law practice' is growing by leaps and bounds.[17]

In a way, then, the legal world has a form of diglossia – a fancy word borrowed from linguistics. It refers to a 'situation where two very different varieties of a language co-occur throughout a speech community', usually divided into a 'high' and a 'low' version. The low version is used at home, on the street and in popular literature and soap operas; the high version in speeches, newspapers and formal

---

14 There is, of course, a huge literature on this issue – and even a large literature on the question of the uniqueness of Japanese *legal* culture. For the latest review of this literature, see Feldman (2000) chapter 7.

15 Friedman (1994).

16 Source: Martindale-Hubbell's *International Law Directory* (vol 1, 1998).

17 Abel (1994).

literature.[18] Diglossia is common in many parts of the world; a mild form of it is almost universal. In the legal world, there is a kind of internationalised law, or globalised law, which exists side-by-side of, or on top of, the national or local sector. It probably represents a minority – even a small minority – of the work of the lawyers. Research on the global sector of the legal order is so far fairly thin, and primarily formalistic. But it is clear that the 'high' culture – the international legal order – has a large and growing impact on legal culture in general. Trubek et al have argued that 'the adaptation of American-style business lawyering methods' is in the process of 'revolutionizing the old European mode of production of law'. Europeans more and more are borrowing the 'tradition of full-service and aggressive "mega-lawyering"'. This is because the 'old European mode of production of law' simply was unsuitable to the new needs of the global markets.[19]

One point is clear: the global sector of the legal world generates (of necessity) a kind of lingua franca. The *formal* lingua franca is (increasingly) English. Estonians may dress internationally, and eat international food, may be eager to join NATO, the EU, the US and any international organisation they can, but they still speak Estonian. None the less, to fulfil their ambitions, they must learn to speak and deal internationally. As they enter the world of international trade, or try to, they cannot expect to find deal-makers from abroad who are fluent in Estonian. Yet business cannot be conducted through grunts or sign language. It is possible to do business through interpreters, but this is a clumsy business at best.[20] A lingua franca must be found; and, as it turns out, for historical reasons, English is the major candidate.[21] Regionally, there are rivals – Estonians probably still need to be fluent in Russian, for example; and they may find German or Swedish useful. But English is winning the battle in transnational lawyering. In a prominent law firm in Warsaw, Poland, for example, 26 of 29 lawyers claimed fluency in English. This was the claim, too, of virtually all of the 150 lawyers in the largest law firm in Korea.[22] The dominance of English is, of course, a terrific boon for those of us who speak it as our native language, and a disadvantage to everybody else; but nobody said life was supposed to be fair.

There is probably another, more subtle, but even more significant, lingua franca – a way of talking and thinking that reflects global culture. Global habits of thought, and global practices, flow almost necessarily from the existence of a global culture. This may mean that American (and English) ways of writing contracts and thinking about law are likely to have more influence than they otherwise would. In some fields of law, indeed, US institutions have been powerful models.[23] These may not really be instances of US power, or US economic and political imperialism; but simply reflect the fact that Americans, for various reasons, were ahead of the game in devising institutions that fit modern legal needs. This is the point that Trubek and his associates make. The others must copy, adapt or

---

18 Crystal (1992a) 104.
19 Trubek et al (1994).
20 For small languages, it is not even practical to use interpreters. An Estonian business that wants to deal with a company from Thailand is not likely to find someone who can shuttle between these two particular languages with ease. Almost certainly both parties will do their business with each other in English.
21 Crystal (1992b).
22 The source of this information is Martindale-Hubbell's *International Law Directory* (vol 1, 1998).
23 See Wiegand (1991).

die. But since it is valuable, in brute money terms, for US law firms and US lawyers to win the race for international business, the use of sheer power and coercion in the process cannot be ruled out.

SUBSTANCE AND STYLE

What makes up the body of transnational or global law? There is, to begin with, a body of hard law; that is, treaties, conventions, GATT and GATT-like arrangements, regional pacts like NAFTA and Mercosur, and the EU. Some of these are truly international; others are regional, but they all, at any rate, aim at cross-national impact. Some of this 'hard law' has also generated the beginnings of what we might call hard institutions – organisations which have the right or the duty to enforce the norms and conventions.

This body of 'hard law' is complex and significant. The key point underlying much of it is the dogma of free trade. At the root of GATT is the economic notion that free trade is good for everybody. Barriers to trade are evil and should be abolished if at all possible, since all nations are certain to gain from the global economy. But the global economy, we have argued, rests on global culture – a culture of global desires and commodities. This too is implicit in the dogma of free trade. If there is no *cultural* barrier to Coca-Cola or Toyota, there should be no *economic* barrier either. If everybody wants the same commodities, then those commodities ought to flow smoothly from where they are made to everywhere else. And they are 'native' to no particular culture or place. Hence the whole tissue of hard trade law presupposes the common global culture we have discussed.

Indeed, this is one reason why international trade law is so unyielding in its faith in the virtues of free trade. It is one reason, too, why this body of transnational law has tended to reject arguments of local tradition or culture. There is basically no 'cultural exception' to GATT and GATS (the corresponding treaty on *services*).[24] The Japanese, for example, argued for the right to limit imports of leather, to protect (they said) the way of life of the 'Dowa', a social caste that specialises in small leather works;[25] they also tried to protect their whaling industry on cultural grounds.[26] These attempts have failed; and Canadian and French attempts to ward off the flood of American films, television shows and magazines have had only limited success, though movies (thanks to French protests) are not covered by GATT, and NAFTA too exempts cultural industries.

Besides this body of 'hard law' there may be what we might call a body of soft law – international customs, practices, behaviours. A large literature deals with what some scholars describe as a new sort of lex mercatoria. The original lex mercatoria was a body of mercantile custom, in the middle ages, associated with the Lombard merchants. These merchants were members of a transnational business class. Some aspects of modern commercial law, relating to banking, negotiable instruments, and the like, grow out of customs and practices that were part of the lex mercatoria. A new kind of law merchant, some say, is now emerging, without benefit of legislation, out of the behaviour patterns of transnational lawyers and business people. Very likely there is less here than meets the eye. Certainly,

24 Cahn and Schimmel (1997).
25 GATT Dispute Panel Report (1985).
26 Boston Globe (2000).

some aspects of international business law have been formalised – standard contract forms, provided by international trade groups, and such devices as the INCOTERMS, which the International Chamber of Commerce publishes. These 'contractual provisions with legal or quasi-legal (customary) character' are supplemented by 'codes of conduct with more or less sanctioning power', and are part of the international 'normative order' – constituting, as Gessner puts it, 'autonomous norm creation within the international economy'.[27] But in the end all such customs and practices have to be validated somehow by national courts, applying what they consider to be national law; or, at any rate, the law that the parties to a contract may have stipulated.

Those who have written about the lex mercatoria associate it, in particular, with the growing field of international arbitration.[28] The world of commercial arbitration is 'global' in the sense that it is not closely tied to any particular system of local law. Parties to international contracts and deals often agree to arbitrate any problems and difficulties that might arise. They avoid the courts, at least initially; they avoid the peculiarities of local legal systems; and they turn their problems over to skilled and prestigious international practitioners. Most of these arbitrators are lawyers. Their decisions, however, are not 'legalistic'. Decisions tend to comply with rules that courts would ultimately apply; but these decisions are also sensitive to norms, customs and understandings of the business world. Arbitration seems much less drastic than litigation. Two firms might well continue doing business while arbitrating a disagreement; it is hard to imagine doing business with someone who has dragged you into court.

The phrase 'lex mercatoria' probably conveys a wrong impression – wrong in suggesting that the norms are hard-edged and precisely known; wrong in suggesting that the norms contradict the legal practices of the great commercial nations; and that international business behaviour is fundamentally or radically different from national business behaviour. Commercial arbitration is common in domestic systems of law as well. Business people everywhere prefer to settle their affairs amicably, if they can, and especially if they are doing business with each other, in a kind of continuing relationship; they also tend to ignore or side-step the 'legalism' of the formal law, and they have their own ideas of the rules of the game, which one can call customary norms if one likes.[29]

It would be interesting to know if there really is a global practice which differs dramatically from local business-law practice, normatively speaking. The original law merchant had this quality. The Lombard merchants were in a way a caste of their own. But the new class of international lawyers and men of business are not a caste in the same sense. Their attitudes and behaviours no doubt reflect the pervasive influence of unplanned convergence – the process that pulls systems of living law in the modern world closer together. Systems of law come to resemble each other, because they share problems and solutions, and because of the spread of global culture; societies which are part of the common global culture of products and desires will tend *legally* to converge.[30] And just as there is a global culture of, say, young people everywhere, who eat hamburgers, wear blue jeans and listen to rock and roll music, so there is a global culture of lawyers and business people

27 Gessner (1994) at 137–138.
28 See the essays in Carbonneau (1998); and the important study of Dezalay and Garth (1996).
29 This is the message of the classic study by Macaulay (1963).
30 Friedman (1994).

who travel on the same jets, who have the same habits, use the same laptops and cell phones, dress the same and speak a common language.

In the age of the Internet, in the age of transnational corporations, in the age of international arbitration, borders come to mean less and less, culturally speaking – for young people and for middle-aged lawyers alike. On the other hand, in other senses, almost paradoxically, *because* borders are weak culturally and economically, national borders come to matter more politically. After all, at one time the majority of people tended to stay where they were; a Spaniard or a Romanian, let alone a Sri Lankan, was born and died at home or near home; moving to Italy was unthinkable. Those days are gone. *Political* control over borders becomes necessary, to prevent the movement of people from places where they do not want to be, to places that glitter with the promise of welfare and jobs.

RISKS AND OPPORTUNITIES

Two more aspects of globalisation should be mentioned, both of which have some importance for the legal order. First is the globalisation of risk and misfortune – the internationalization of problems. These are of all sorts, and this chapter offers little more than a kind of check list. First, there are the problems of what Ulrich Beck has called the 'risk society'.[31] His book, which attracted considerable attention, was stimulated by the Chernobyl disaster. A nuclear reactor in what was then the Soviet Union failed and radioactive winds swept over neighbouring parts of Europe.

The Chernobyl disaster was an example of one kind of global risk. Reckless burning of forests in Indonesia can pollute the air in neighbouring countries. Modern technology makes possible disasters whose sheer magnitude makes a mockery of borders. Some of these – like Chernobyl or the Indonesian forest fires – have a definite source, in one particular country. Another type comes from everywhere at once: global warming, or the depletion of the ozone layer. Still another kind of global risk stems from the increase in travel and trade. In the global age, it is almost impossible to keep various maggots, beetles, weeds and invasive pests from spreading all over the world. They come in cargo ships; they fly on the fastest jets. A plague of tree snakes on one island; mongoose populations on another, killing off local fauna; fruit flies bedevilling California; greedy and invasive plants choking waterways: the list is long and depressing. And the worst may be yet to come. There is always the danger that some exotic virus will make the leap from an animal host to unprotected human beings. And once this happens, the virus might spread from its original focal point, to the rest of the world. This possibly is the history of the AIDS virus; and other diseases, perhaps just as deadly, seem to be lurking in the dark canopies of the jungle.

Global processes are at the root of yet another kind of global problem – one that seems, in a sense, totally local. At first thought, the birth rate in Kenya is nobody's business but the Kenyans; and when we think about globalisation, we do not think about the sex life, marriage patterns, and child-bearing habits of people in Kenya. But, of course, advances in medicine and technology contribute to the soaring populations of African countries. Western medicine has reduced the infant mortality rate, improved the drinking water and provided vaccinations against diseases. The population explosion in Africa or Brazil in turn affects the

31 Beck (1986).

rest of the world. It puts pressure on resources; it creates political instability; it endangers the rain forests. Similarly, the Chinese appetite for turtle-meat or rhinoceros horns is arguably of no concern to anybody else. But these tastes in the first place cannot be satisfied within the borders of China, since China has no rhinoceroses and not enough turtles. The Chinese demand is driving these creatures to the brink of extinction. At one time, this would have been of no particular interest to the rest of the world – nobody protested when Americans slaughtered their buffalo herds – but this is no longer the case. There is a powerful, and international, environmental movement. Indeed, to define the health of rain forests as a problem, and to work to keep giant pandas alive, is one important aspect of the new global culture – or, at least, global *high* culture.

These then are various types of global risk. They each present problems for the international order. Some risks can be, and have to be, dealt with locally: each country must protect itself, as best it can, from roving insect pests. But global warming demands a more universal solution. And voluntary actions, treaties, conventions and the like are unlikely to succeed. For political and economic reasons, countries will always be tempted to break the rules. There has to be some way to control, monitor and discipline them. Even more difficult are such problems as the protection of rain forests. The whole world needs clean air and water, and an ozone layer; but the need for rain forests, steppes, prairies and coral reefs is not quite so obvious, and is often controverted. Moreover, all land and most water habitats are located, legally speaking, within national borders; and a giant, invisible fence, called 'national sovereignty', keeps foreigners, for the most part, out. Yet more and more people recognise that laissez faire is ultimately intolerable. There is a need for hard law, for enforceable law; but where is this going to come from, and how?

REFLECTIONS IN A MIRROR: GLOBAL LAW AT HOME

One can easily describe the world of the international arbitrators and the jetset deal-makers as 'global'. But globalisation also has an enormous impact on strictly local law and the work of strictly local courts. Indeed, global law, in general, depends on the work of local lawyers, courts and judges. The great treaties and conventions would be merely words on paper if this were not the case, if they were not enforceable locally. There is, after all, no real international enforcement mechanism. There are international courts, but they depend on the grace and favour of sovereign nations. Even international arbitration depends, in the last resort, on the national courts for enforcement, if push comes to shove.

In a broader sense, domestic law, even in mundane, local fields, reflects the influence, as it must, of a world which is increasingly interconnected; and responds to the dictates of global culture. Take, for example, the law of child custody. This is a branch of family law, which is conventionally (perhaps wrongly) thought of as intensely local and resistant to change. But this is a world of migration and increasing ethnic diversity – a world in which a Pakistani can move to London and marry an English woman, or an Eritrean woman can form a relationship with an Italian man in Rome. Lo and behold! – children are born who belong to two or three cultural worlds. If the relationship founders, custody issues can take on an international dimension. The problem is especially acute if one parent removes the children to his or her 'motherland'. There are treaties, conventions and legal tools to deal with the issue; but there is no fully satisfying way to resolve problems that come from the clash of cultures, or to prevent bias on the part of local courts.[32]

These sad and difficult cases look like classic examples of culture clash; and in a way they are – African father, American mother; Turkish mother, Norwegian father; Saudi father, Italian mother; insoluble disputes over language, religion, ways of life, gender roles, habits of thought. The culture *clash* is obvious; but what is less obvious is the cultural *convergence* that made the relationship possible in the first place. The global culture created the situation in which these 'clashes' could come about. The cultural divide between the two parents is real enough; but it is incomparably *less* than it would have been a century ago, or even 50 years ago. Only the narrowing of the gap brought two such different people together.

Our times are restless times: thousands of men and women are migrating, legally or otherwise, from one country to another; or trying to. The pressure of this migration spices the population of rich countries with an ethnic and racial diversity they may not particularly want. Some of these countries – Norway, for example – were once fairly monotone, demographically speaking; but no longer. Thousands and thousands bang on the doors of rich countries; this puts pressure on the laws of immigration and citizenship. Immigration, asylum and citizenship rights were not high on the legal agendas of Germany and France in the nineteenth century; now they most definitely are.

The so-called 'immigration' countries (the US or Australia, for example) are not immune to the discontents of global mass movement – far from it. It is often said that the US had no restrictions on immigration in the nineteenth century, until the very end of the century. At that point, laws were passed to keep out the Chinese who were flocking to the West coast, particularly California.[33] Well into the twentieth century, most European countries were not concerned with immigration: they were exporters of bodies, not importers; Swedes and Poles and Greeks and Italians left for the US, Canada, Chile or Australia. The US, like Argentina and Australia, was eager for immigrants; these countries even advertised for immigrants in foreign countries. But the assumption was always that the right sort of people would come. Nobody expected thousands of Chinese peasants or impoverished Tongans or Hindus to knock on the door.[34] In the twentieth century, however, the *cultural* barriers to immigration have broken down. Television and the movies spread the word to remote places; traditional societies are undergoing rapid change; in some places the rapid population growth puts a strain on resources and the land in the villages can no longer feed all the hungry mouths. There is a tremendous pool of surplus labour: high unemployment (in rich countries as well as poor ones); as many as 80,000,000 'expatriate labourers' are working all over the world;[35] and tens of millions more would be only too glad to join their ranks. Moreover, once even small colonies of fellow nationals take root in London, Rome, Sydney or New York, it becomes easier and less alienating to leave your village or your country, and move to the foreign city; after all, there will

32 See Starr (1998); on the bias of local courts (in this case German courts), see (1999) New York Times, 2 August. See also Guibentif (1998).
33 There is of course a very large literature on US immigration history; see, for example, Barkan (1996); on the Chinese immigration issue, see Hing (1993).
34 In the US, Protestant immigrants from northern Europe were the most welcome; and the influx from southern and eastern Europe – Catholic, Jewish, and Orthodox – eventually led to the passage of a restrictive immigration law in 1924.
35 McMichael (1996) p 187.

be people there who speak your language, serve your food and practice your religion. The rich countries build fences around themselves, literally and legally; these fences are a form of protection against movements that reflect the facts of a globalised society, a society in which cultural barriers against immigration have largely, if not entirely, broken down.

Mexico is the largest source of illegal aliens for the US. It might surprise many people to learn that there were no restrictions at all on Mexican immigration before the middle of the twentieth century. The story of legal and social control over Mexican immigrants is, in fact, quite complicated; but in essence it was culture and poverty, not law, that protected the borders of the United States for most of the period in question. There was no border patrol at all before the 1920s. Most Mexicans did not live near the border; they lived on the central plateau. Before a railroad network linked the two countries, most poor peasants and slum-dwellers had no way to reach the glittering world of El Norte. Raging population pressure, and the breakdown of traditional society, removed the other, invisible barriers. Moreover, US agri-businessmen welcomed cheap Mexican stoop labour. Since substantial colonies of Mexicans already lived in the south-west of the US, it was not difficult to find a cousin, neighbour or friend who could lend you a bed and find you a job picking lettuce or washing dishes in Los Angeles.[36] In Europe, the end of colonialism weakened one set of controls over in-migration, and the fall of the iron curtain weakened another set of controls. A politically volatile and controversial immigration 'problem' arose in country after country.

In the palmy days of economic growth after the Second World War, countries like Germany and the Netherlands needed workers; they invited in millions of Italians, Spaniards and Turks. The children and grandchildren of these workers are still around, but the labour shortage is gone, replaced by high unemployment. The 'guest-workers' are at least partially assimilated. In any event, they show no great passion to go 'home'. For most of them, home is where they are right now. Yet some European countries – Germany in particular – are reluctant to admit these 'foreigners' to citizenship.[37]

The foreigners, and their children, and their children's children, are objects of suspicion in part because they seem to threaten national identity and culture (whatever these might mean). But whether they get a passport and citizenship papers or not, they have changed European society simply by *being* there; they have made European countries multicultural in new and dramatic ways.

Immigration is a good example of how the global culture – the culture of wishes, images and desires – sets forces in motion that change the behaviour of masses of people dramatically. The old majority tends to see the new situation as problematic; the public demands barriers against the free flow of goods, people or ideas. Earlier we mentioned attempts to keep out, or control, the 'plague' of US movies and television shows. Self-defence would not be necessary if cultural boundaries were not so weak. Physical boundaries are stronger – but only relatively. The US spends billions of dollars on border control – much of it, apparently, thrown away, since millions of illegal aliens in fact find ways to enter and live in the US. Of course, without border controls there might be millions more. Invisible trade boundaries crumble in an age which is ideologically committed to free trade, and in which economies are interdependent; many countries are afraid to restrict foreign trade for fear of retaliation.

36 On Mexican immigration, see Friedman (1999); Calavita (1992).
37 Friedman (1999) pp 157–159.

Cheap imports and cheap immigrants threaten established values. In Europe and North America, much of the manufacturing base has simply rotted away. The factories have moved to countries where workers are paid less. It is not just jobs that are lost; labour standards also erode. Can countries keep out goods made under conditions that would violate local law? Does 'free trade' mean that a country is helpless against a flood of sweaters and blouses made under revolting conditions, or rugs woven by eight-year-olds? The price of Western goods includes costs of environmental controls and worker safety. Third-world countries pay (on the whole) no attention to these; multinational corporations seem to be beyond anybody's control. Oil companies can pollute the Niger delta in Nigeria – and does – without much fear that the Nigerian government, or *any* government, will do a thing about it. The imperial countries are, in some ways, just as much prisoners of the great multinational corporations as the imperialised countries at the bottom of the heap.

A country, of course, is entitled to keep out products that are harmful or unhealthy; and many do. This right, on the other hand, can easily act as a mask for protectionism. If US farmers pump hormones into cows, does this make the meat unfit to eat, or is this only an excuse for keeping the meat products out? As Martin Shapiro has pointed out, the problem of local standards has plagued the EU too. 'Differing national product standards and rules on advertising and marketing' can become 'very effective barriers to ... trade'. Hence the push, in Europe, toward harmonisation of standards.[38] Hence the push to make 'free trade' an international, and enforceable, norm.

GLOBALISATION OF HUMAN RIGHTS

In the period since the Second World War, there has been an important movement to globalise human rights, that is, to develop, proclaim, publicise and (hopefully) enforce standards of human rights said to be universal. There are all sorts of charters, treaties and pronouncements to this end; and there are organisations (such as Amnesty International) that try to make these rights a reality.

There is an obvious conflict between any concept of universal human rights and national sovereignty, one of the 'sacred cows' of the day. One country is not supposed to meddle in the 'internal affairs' of another. Needless to say, this right is frequently violated. Big powerful countries may get away with a great deal of bullying and interference. We also hear a lot of talk about the erosion of the 'concept of nationality'; supposedly, this has been replaced by 'a concept emphasizing that the state is accountable to all its residents on the basis of international human rights law'.[39] Of course, there is at present no way to force 'international human rights law' down the throat of any satraps, dictators and petty tyrants who may be in power. World opinion counts the least with despots who need it the most. On the other hand, when NATO bombed Serbia over the Kosovo crisis, in 1999, and later sent troops into the area, this was done at least partly in order to uphold standards of human rights. The NATO allies never denied that Kosovo 'belonged' to the Serbs and they never claimed that Kosovo had a right to be independent.

38 Shapiro (1993).
39 Sassen (1996) p 97.

There seems to be general agreement about a common core of human rights and wrongs. Nobody would argue that the state has the right to kill and torture citizens for no good reason. There are plenty of regimes *practising* these black arts; but hardly anybody defends these regimes. Still, beyond a certain basic list, there is controversy over whether any particular right is truly universal. Some scholars and statesmen argue that many so-called universal rights are aspects of Western culture; that these rights are out of place in societies elsewhere in the world – in Asia, very notably.[40]

It is easy to make a case for the cultural relativity of rights. Slavery and torture were in fact once prominent features of western life and law. China and (say) France have very different traditions with regard to human rights (among other things). There is a lively discussion about whether the Western brand of feminism fits other societies; whether female circumcision, for example, is a violation of women's rights, or a precious cultural tradition of African societies.[41] In the modern world, concepts of human rights show real signs of convergence. No doubt, Western concepts of freedom and rights are not neutral, timeless, inherent; and no doubt they found early and eloquent expression in Western ethical and political philosophy, at a time when they were absent in other societies. But these concepts are, in fact, not really Western. Rather, they are *modern*. They developed first in the West, because the West was the first to modernise. Thus they are, as one author put it, 'historically but not culturally relative'.[42] Globalisation is an extension of the process of modernisation; and the spread of the idea of (say) free speech is as much part of the process as the spread of electricity or Coca-Cola. Free speech may be alien to the traditions of (say) Cambodia or Japan; but it was just as alien to Russia or to Germany until quite recently; and how long has it been the norm in Sweden or the Netherlands? The demand for human rights is part of modern legal culture, it is part of global legal culture; it therefore cannot be brushed off with arguments that it is alien to any particular part of the world.

The culture of human rights, if we analyse it carefully, is basically a culture of individualism. It is a culture which locates rights within individuals, not families, clans, tribes or groups. The engines that produced and produce modernity foster this culture. The mass media play an extremely important role. They spread the gospel of a world of individual consumers. They are propaganda engines, consciously or unconsciously, for this gospel. Modern culture, as this chapter has argued, is a culture of leisure and consumption. Such a culture necessarily is focused on the individual. Certainly, modern politics and modern law seem to stress *group* rights in many countries. Racial politics, feminism, the gay rights movement, the various 'liberation' movements of ethnic minorities – all these seem to be flying a banner of group identity, group empowerment, and the like. But, paradoxically, group identity and group empowerment, on closer analysis, turn out to be aspects of individualism. Empowering women means giving women the right, as individuals, to choose their way of life – the right to be whatever they choose to be; and not to be judged in terms of gender stereotypes. If a woman wants to bake cookies and raise children, that is perfectly acceptable; if she wants to be a chief executive officer, mine coal or play football, that should also be her

40 See eg Koh (1995) pp 100–101.
41 Obiora (1997).
42 Bauböck (1994) p 239.

choice. A similar argument can be made for religious minorities, racial minorities, sexual minorities, the handicapped, and so on. This submerged individualism is the base of all 'liberation' movements, racial and otherwise.[43]

Human rights are, of course, meaningless without enforcement; and enforcement means enforcement against those who violate human rights, including the state (a prime offender). Hence the spread of the idea of the 'rule of law', that is, limitations on the power of government to act arbitrarily and unjustly. The phrase is seductive everywhere, even in China, which by and large lacks it, but which seems eager to give it at least lip service. There are many definitions of the 'rule of law', but they have a common core of meaning. In a *Rechtstaat* a body of rules, more or less definite and knowable, governs the state and applies to everybody, including elites and the regime itself. And there must be some institution or structure which can enforce these rules against the violators. This is often taken to mean a strong, honest and independent judiciary; or some functional equivalent.

Some definitions of the 'rule of law' seem to equate the concept with legal formalism – Kermit Hall, for example, speaks of 'a body of rules and procedures ... that have an autonomy and logic of their own'.[44] Law and society scholars, quite properly, are sceptical about the idea of 'autonomy'. The sociology of law has spent much of its energy debunking the idea of strict legal autonomy and neutrality. The logic of the legal order is a cultural logic, not a formal, deductive logic; the legal system is not and cannot be turned into a free-standing machine, one that runs automatically and which is beyond the influence of power, wealth, social elites and prevailing norms. No such system exists or can exist.

None the less, there is a vast gulf between parliamentary democracies, on the one hand, and dictatorships, one-party states and police states on the other. A legal system is not and cannot be 'autonomous', but it can be and often is *independent*, that is, the regime cannot reward, punish or interfere with judges and lower civil servants who follow the rules and apply them honestly. The 'rule of law' ties the hands of the state in important regards. A strong judiciary that is capable of doing this is an institutional feature of many Western countries.

Nowadays, many people would add to the definition of the *Rechtstaat* some degree of commitment to the market system. This would not have figured very prominently in European discussions of the rule of law not so long ago. But today it is quite usual to identify the rule of law with free market economics.[45] Of course, there are many reasons for the triumph of free market capitalism. The collapse of the socialist world is certainly one factor; and there is also a general feeling that the Welfare State has over-extended itself. Still, there is also a cultural factor. Free trade is one of the corner-stones of free market thought (and practice). And free trade is more than an economic ideology; it is necessary for the global *culture*, since that culture is, as we have argued, a culture of consumption and individualism, and a culture of desires and commodities.

That culture also underlies the ideology of the rule of law. Whatever the definition of the rule of law, it implies a strong sense of right and of *rights*. It also depends on rights-consciousness – a willingness, or eagerness, to make use of institutions (like courts) which enforce rights, or which decide when rights have been infringed on or broken. Rights-consciousness is a variable; it is not distributed

43 Friedman (1999).
44 Hall (1989) pp 6–7.
45 See the interesting remarks on this point by Santos (1999).

uniformly over the globe. It comes in different shapes and sizes. Americans are often accused of a kind of addiction to rights and entitlements, and consequently to litigation.[46] At the other extreme is Japan, whose people supposedly work hard to avoid litigation, and where the sense of entitlement is said to be less highly developed than in the US. Whether this is really true of Japan or not remains an open question.[47] The Japanese certainly have a much smaller legal profession than the US, and other Western countries. (They share this trait with Korea and Taiwan.) Undoubtedly there are differences between US and Japanese legal cultures, but this chapter suggests at least some degree of convergence between all modern, industrial nations. Rights-consciousness may vary, but it – and the rule of law – are aspects of legal culture, connected to the decline of traditional, hierarchical societies and the growth of the global culture. This culture permeates and colours all of these societies, though in slightly different flavours and forms.

Select bibliography

Abel, R L, (1994) 'Transnational Law Practice', 44 Case Western Reserve LR 737.

Barber, B R, (1995) *Jihad v. McWorld.*

Barkan, E R, (1996) *And Still They Come: Immigrants and American Society 1920 to the 1990s.*

Bauböck, R, (1994) *Transnational Citizenship: Membership and Rights in International Migration.*

Beck, U, (1986) *Risikogesellschaft.*

Bernard, M-A, (1999) 'Le Droit Comme Instrument de Mondialisation' in J Feest (ed), *Globalization and Legal Cultures* (Oñati Papers, No 7).

Boston Globe (2000) 5 March, at A4.

Cahn, S, and Schimmel, D, (1997) 'The Cultural Exception: Does it Exist in GATT and GATS Frameworks? How Does it Affect or Is It Affected by the Agreement on TRIPS?', 15 Cardozo Arts and Entertainment LJ 281.

Calavita, K, (1992) *Inside the State: The Bracero Program, Immigration, and the I.N.S.*

Carbonneau, T E, (ed), (1998) *Lex Mercatoria and Arbitration* (revised edn).

Crystal, D, (1992a) *An Encyclopedic Dictionary of Language and Languages.*

—(1992b) *English as a Global Language.*

Dezalay, Y, and Garth, B G, (1996) *Dealing in Virtue: International Commercial arbitration and the Construction of a Transnational Legal Order.*

Feldman, E A, (2000) *The Ritual of Rights in Japan.*

Friedman, L M, (1985) *A History of American Law* (2nd edn).

—(1994) 'Is There a Modern Legal Culture?', 7 Ratio Juris 117.

—(1999) *The Horizontal Society.*

GATT Dispute Panel Report (1985) 'Japan, Measures on Imports of Leather', 15–16 May 1984, GATT BISD (31st Supp) 94.

---

46 Kagan (1996).
47 On Japan, see eg Kidder and Miyazawa (1993); Tanase (1990); Feldman (2000).

Gessner, V, (1994) 'Global Legal Interaction and Legal Cultures', 7 Ratio Juris 132.

Goode, E, (1999) 'Study Finds TV Trims Fiji Girls' Body Image and Eating Habits', New York Times (national edn), 20 May, at A13.

Guibentif, P, (1998) 'Cross-border Legal Issues Arising from International Migrations: The Case of Portugal' in V Gessner and A C Budak (eds) *Emerging Legal Certainty: Empirical Studies on the Globalization of Law*, p 241.

Hall, K, (1989) *The Magic Mirror: Law in American History.*

Hing, B O, (1993) *Making and Remaking Asian America through Immigration Policy, 1850–1990.*

Inkeles, A, (1983) *Exploring Individual Modernity.*

Inkeles, A, and Smith, D H, (1974) *Becoming Modern: Individual Change in Six Developing Countries.*

Kagan, R A, (1996) 'American Lawyers, Legal Cultures, and Adversarial Legalism' in L M Friedman and H N Scheiber (eds) *Legal Culture and the Legal Profession*, p 7.

Kidder, R L, and Kidder, M, (1993) 'Long-Term Strategies in Japanese Environmental Litigation', 18 Law and Social Inquiry 605.

Koh, T T B, (1995) 'The United States and East Asia: Conflict and Cooperation' in (1998) *Martindale-Hubbell's International Law Directory*, vol 1.

Macaulay, S, (1963) 'Non-Contractual Relations in Business: A Preliminary Study', 28 American Sociological Rev 55.

McMichael, P, (1996) *Development and Social Change: A Global Perspective.*

Obiora, L A, (1997) 'Bridges and Barricades: Rethinking Polemics and Intransigence in the Campaign against Female Circumcision', 47 Case Western Reserve LR 27.

Prowda, J B, (1996) 'United States Dominance in the 'Marketplace of Culture' and the French 'Cultural Exception'', 29 NYUJIL & Pol 193.

Roehl, K F, and Magen, S, (1996) 'Die Rolle des Rechts im Prozess der Globalisierung', 17 Zeitschrift fuer Rechtssoziologie 1.

Santos, B de S, (1999) 'The GATT of Law and Democracy: (Mis) Trusting the Global Reform of Courts' in J Feest (ed) *Globalization and Legal Cultures* (Oñati Papers, No 7), p 49.

Sassen, S, (1996) *Losing Control? Sovereignty in an Age of Globalization.*

Shapiro, M, (1993) 'The Globalization of Law', 1 Ind J Global LS 37.

Starr, J, (1998) 'The Global Battlefield: Culture and International Child Custody Disputes at Century's End', 15 Ariz JI & C L 791.

Tanase, T, (1990) 'The Management of Disputes: Automobile Accident Compensation in Japan', 24 Law and Society Review 651.

Trubek, D M, Dezalay, Y, Buchanan, R, et al, (1994) 'Global Restructuring and the Law: Studies of the Internationalization of Legal Fields and the Creation of Transnational Arenas', 44 Case Western Reserve LR 407.

Wiegand, W, (1991) 'Reception of American Law in Europe', 39 AJCL 229.

Chapter 3

Changing legal cultures

D NELKEN

Why are legal cultures changing and, in particular, how (far) can they be deliberately changed?[1] These are large questions and this chapter will do no more than summarise some of the rather fragmented relevant literatures and attempt to sort out questions which need to be distinguished if further progress is to be made. The chapter will first suggest some of the issues involved in talking about the relationship between legal change and social change, then go on to discuss what is meant by legal culture, and discuss the problem of describing what is happening to law in the current period.

LEGAL CHANGE AND SOCIAL CHANGE

There are a number of ways of studying changing legal cultures. The most direct of these is to set out to describe and explain the how, when and why of legal change. This raises issues such as the following. Who or what is doing or undergoing the adaptation? What are the typical types and processes of adaptation, and what stages do receptions go through? What is the meaning of 'success' when discussing legal adaptation?[2] How do legal transfers change features of the societies in which they are introduced? What is the part played by institutions, social structure and culture in facilitating or blocking success? Is there a difference between explaining the way law adapts to or produces social change in a given society or context, as compared with what happens when law is transferred from one society to another? Which metaphors can help us theorise different examples of legal transfer and social change, and what is the status of such metaphors?[3] How far can and should we think of legal transfers as exercises in social engineering, how much as efforts to engage in inter-cultural communication?

1   The title of the chapter derives from a series of workshops organised at the Onati Institute of Sociology of Law, 1997–99, which were financed by the Volkswagen Foundation. The workshops were jointly planned and run by Erhard Blankenburg, Johannes Feest (then Director of the Institute), Vollkmar Gessner and the present writer. This chapter is particularly concerned with the issues raised in the third workshop, 'Adapting Legal Cultures', the collected papers of which (edited by Nelken and Feest) are in press.
2   See Nelken (2001a).
3   Lakoff and Johnson (1980).

Alternatively, we may focus on puzzles or anomalies in patterns of legal transfer such as those which are said to upset 'basic tenets of those who believe in the inevitability of the convergence of economic institutions in advanced societies and the functional equivalence of legal constructs'.[4] 'Why', asks Teubner,

> 'has the American tort revolution which led to such a drastic rise of liability that it catalysed an insurance crisis in the United States not occurred in Europe? Why has judicial control over standard contracts not been exercised in the USA as intensively as it has been in Germany? Why do European "general clauses" on consumer protection which are customarily used with little difficulty in France, Italy, Germany, run dry in Great Britain? Why is the legal implementation of Just-in-time distribution networks, a Japanese export, different on the continent than it is in the USA and in Great Britain?'[5]

There are many advantages in starting with the detail of specific cases of change or adaptation of legal culture. But this raises the question how far starting from the particular will allow us to make universal arguments or prescriptions about legal transfers. How far will our arguments apply across different periods or different parts of the world, how far will they encompass the different agencies involved in legal transfers, or other relevant distinctions? Can Roman law expansion be explained in the same terms as that of the Continental European codes in the nineteenth century? Is there anything in common between Japan's method of modernisation and the road currently being taken by the ex-communist countries of Eastern Europe?

Adaptation can take place in a number of ways. It can be imposed, planned, unplanned, a deliberate effort or a result of convergence or divergence.[6] It is a common error to assume that adaptation necessarily must go with attempts at harmonisation, or be a cause or result of convergence between two or more societies, or more general convergence at the level of global society. In practice, legal adaptation can also be a result of planned or unplanned processes of differentiation. Legal adaptation can flow from developments within a society or be a consequence of changes stimulated or imposed by another society. It can take place when a country acts independently to revise its laws in the light of others, or it can come about as part of imperceptible processes, or to deliberate imposition or abrupt revolutionary transformations. Legal change can also be the cause or consequence of action taken by international actors in third cultures and sites. Law can play a variety of roles in the processes through which social, political and economic convergence and divergence come about. It can, for example, be the means by which such convergence or divergence is promoted, can accompany such changes, can be reshaped by such social trends (by law, with law or despite law) or it can be used in attempts to resist (or conceal) such developments.

As this suggests, to overcome the insularity of some debates over legal transfers, there is also a need to relate them to the wider study of social change. Disagreements over the processes of adapting legal culture can and should be related to long-standing debates between 'evolutionists' and 'diffusionists' in

---

4   Teubner (1999).
5   Teubner (1999).
6   The Onati workshops distinguished between adaptations which take place at the pace of day-to-day changes, those which result from interaction between businessmen or the influx of immigration, or those which were the consequence of international communications and exchanges.

the explanation of social and cultural change. We should be asking how far the transfer of law is more or less similar to the transfer of social policies – or to the transfer of technology – or to the spread of fashion or other aspects of culture. We need to examine whether legal changes are really 'inevitable' once certain processes of economic convergence or cultural interchange are under way.[7] We still know little about the relation between the circulation of goods and money and the circulation of law (why, except perhaps in the realm of criminology, is there no drive to import Japanese law?).

Legal change depends on other forces of social change such as social movements, revolutions, evolution or great individuals.[8] But scholars of social change for their part probably underestimate the role of law in its various forms. Sztompka[9] examines normative emergence, evasion and innovation; he distinguishes initiation of change (public or private), filtering (the way change is rejected or adopted) and dissemination and legitimation of change (including negative feedback or amplified-positive feedback). But he assumes that law only comes in at a late stage of social change. Likewise Linz and Stepan[10] in their study of democratic transitions have relatively little to say about law, though when discussing the arrival of democracy in Spain, they too cite it as an example of what they call 'backward legitimation'.

Social scientists try to explain change, but do not have that good a record actually in predicting change; it is enough to consider how the protests of the 1960s caught establishment sociology by surprise or, more recently, of the sudden and unexpected collapse of the Communist bloc. Some legal authors, on the other hand, give a central place to happenstance and the role of contingency in explaining legal adaptation, using such examples as the circumstances which led Ethiopia to accept the French Civil Code, or Turkey to take its codes from Switzerland.[11] Watson seeks to use the vicissitudes of legal borrowing as part of an attack on the very possibility of developing a theory of social and legal change.

Authors differ over whether more importance should be attributed to the 'state' or to 'society' (or culture) as the force behind legal change (or as a drag on such change). Jettinghoff questions the match between law and given social and economic 'needs' in arguing that it was political circumstances which explained why for most of the twentieth century Holland did not have judicial review. Jettinghoff also emphasises the role of the state in preparing for war and dealing with its consequences. He rightly insists that much of the face of law in Europe would now be very different had the Nazis won the Second World War (though there is some controversy over how different private law was under the Third Reich, at least for German citizens). Monateri[12] too gives an important role to war in explaining the changing influence over Italian legal culture exerted by French and German models. In the nineteenth century the elite in Italy, as in so many places, was under the influence of French culture until France's defeat by Germany. But, he adds, after this it was the more academic style of writing of judicial sentences in Germany which played the main part in leading the

7   Friedman (1996); Markensinis (1994); Bradley (1999).
8   Sztompka (1993).
9   Sztompka (1993) p 255.
10 Linz and Stepan (1996).
11 See eg Watson (1974; 1977; 1985); Jettinghoff (forthcoming).
12 Monateri (1998).

university-centred schools of Italian jurisprudence to take their cue from Germany rather than from France.

One of the most fruitful questions in the sociological study of changes in legal culture is to ask who and what is inviting, 'receiving' or enduring such changes. Depending on our theoretical starting points, we can focus on agents, institutions, networks, sub-systems, legal and social 'fields', communities, professions, committees, structures or discourses. It can also be valuable to distinguish the different roles being played, whether they be that of facilitators, educators, guardians of doctrine, planners, regulators, interpreters, activists, mediators or fixers. The bearers of change can include states, national, international and transnational bodies, non-governmental organisations, corporations, banks and other economic actors, politicians, regulators, foundations and philanthropists, bureaucrats, judges, lawyers, accountants and other professionals, and academics. Influential actors are likely to be members of elite groups or other important political and social networks,[13] but legal change can also be brought about through immigration; refugee scholars have been particularly significant in introducing socio-legal approaches to labour law to the US or developing criminological research to Britain. The number of those potentially affected by such change embraces a much wider number of organised or unorganised ordinary citizens.

Some of the groups and individuals who are involved in legal transfers work to a common purpose, as in the earlier US 'law and development' movement of the 1960s or the so called 'Chicago boys' combination of economic realism and legal idealism.[14] But some compete politically, socially and professionally. Comparative lawyers have long devoted considerable attention to the power and prestige of different polities and the competing attractions of different legal systems. In addition, current research on globalisation discusses competition between lawyers and economists, for example in Latin America,[15] between elite international and domestic lawyers, or marginal lawyers or cause lawyers, or between law and accounting firms, in dealing with international bankruptcy.[16] Those who compete at one point may later collaborate as in the way the Chicago neo-liberal economists who first spread the message of deregulation then consolidated their hegemony by rediscovering the merits of legal institutions.[17]

The importance of different groups varies for different periods and different places. In the past much depended on colonial servants, missionaries and settlers.[18] Nowadays, it is more likely to be transnational actors such as NGOs who play the central role in the construction and use of law as regards the environment, human rights, violence against women or indigenous rights. Scholars then and now play a special and often paradoxical role in executing such transfers – they may use their personal connections to construct an ostensibly impersonal legal rationality[19] and the arguments and metaphors they use to explain change easily become part of the phenomenon itself.[20]

---

13 Sklair (1991).
14 It is revealing to compare the account of the competing and yet often symbiotic roles of missionaries and colonists in nineteenth century Africa: Comaroff and Comaroff (1995).
15 See Dezalay and Garth 1997; forthcoming.
16 Flood (forthcoming).
17 Dezalay and Garth (1996; 1997).
18 Comaroff (1995)
19 Dezalay and Garth (1997).
20 See Tanase (forthcoming).

'LEGAL CULTURE' AS TOPIC AND EXPLANATION

Processes of legal change and transfer can involve a wide variety of aspects of law, elements of foreign institutions, procedures or professional organisation and expertise. What evolves, is taken, imitated or imposed can range from single laws of rules, principles and procedures, to codes, constitutions, or entire legal systems. Explicit transfers may involve very different kinds of law, for example, family law, criminal law, human rights law or commercial law – each of which under different circumstances may have greater or lesser difficulty in being accepted. There are likely to be important differences between, on the one hand, transferring technical 'lawyers law' and, on the other, adapting law which is more closely identified with local cultural and national symbols. Some law is more univocal and instrumental, other law is more 'chaotic',[21] aiming at a variety of audiences and addressing and attempting to straddle a multiplicity of (potentially incompatible) values, such as rights and utility or autonomy and community. Some law may be intended to change behaviour in a certain direction, other law only to facilitate choices. Law can be valued as a point of reference, as a bargaining lever, as a form of regulation, or as a threat with sanctions.

The main reason for resorting to the concept of legal culture is the way it reminds us that aspects of law normally come in 'packages' of one sort or another. This means we must go beyond the 'family of law' links identified by comparative lawyers, the discussions of institutional characteristics of different legal traditions,[22] or even valuable insights into the politico-legal frameworks which have an 'elective affinity' with ideal types of 'hierarchical' and 'co-ordinate' types of legal procedure.[23] Instead, the various elements of legal culture are here given the widest definition possible – legal norms, salient features of legal institutions, and of their 'infrastructure',[24] social behaviour in using and not using law, types of legal consciousness in the legal profession and in public – all can and must be shown to be in some way interrelated. Key concepts – such as 'belied'[25] or 'innere sicherheit'[26] both express and offer ways into such interconnections.[27] The idea of legal culture thus points to differences in the way features of law are themselves embedded in larger frameworks of social structure and culture which constitute and reveal the place of law in society.

Any deliberate attempt to change legal culture highlights differences between the legal culture where the adaptation is to take place and that from which the model is taken. These may concern the extent to which law is state-directed or party-led ('bottom up' or 'top down'), the number, role and power of courts and legal professions, the role and importance of the judiciary, or the nature of legal education and legal training. Cultures may have differing idea of what is meant by 'law' (and what law is 'for'), of where and how it is to be found (types of legal reasoning), the role of case law and precedent, of general clauses as compared with detailed drafting, of the place of 'law' and 'fact'. There can be different approaches to regulation, administration and dispute resolution, in what are considered appropriate ways of reaching or of motivating judgment, contrasts

21 Dewar (1998).
22 Merryman (1985).
23 Eg Damaska (1986).
24 Blankenburg (1997).
25 Blankenburg and Bruinsma (1994).
26 Zedner (1995).
27 Nelken (1995; 2000).

in the degree to which given controversies are subject to law, the role of other expertises, the part played by 'alternatives' to law, the role of other religious or ethical norms, and the ambit of the 'informal'.

Accompanying and concretising such differences, explaining and attempting to justify them, there are likely to be competing attitudes to the role of law, formal and substantive ideas of legitimacy, or the need for public participation as compared with legal autonomy. Cultures will also have different ways of combining imported and pre-existing law.[28] Of increasing importance, even the way science is incorporated into law, varies in ways that vary by culture – for example as between the US, Continental European countries, Scandinavia and the UK. Hence what is at stake in adapting legal culture may concern both institutions, models and practices, as well as philosophies, mentalities and ways of conceiving and categorising methods, problems and solutions. Attempting to take over just one part of the larger package can therefore lead to a variety of unexpected difficulties. Indeed, for some scholars the significance of legal culture is such that any effort at faithful borrowing so is doomed to failure – legal transplants are simply impossible.[29]

From its origins, as the German romantic counterpoint to the French term 'civilisation', the term 'culture' often has been invoked (and misused) as a weapon in 'culture wars' between or within cultures.[30] In the context of legal borrowing and resistance, a modern parallel can be found in the call to 'Asian values'. Likewise, some critical discussions of the effects of globalisation conjure up T S Elliot's lament that civilisation must amount to more than banks and insurance companies. Even within a given society, legal culture is a complex, contested and changing phenomenon. The relationship between law and culture varies between one society and another, and one context and another. Of particular relevance for the study of legal transfers, in some times and places law expresses culture whilst in others (or even at the same time) culture can be seen as an obstacle which law has to overcome; if culture can sometimes endow law with legitimacy, at other times law challenges culture. In speaking about legal culture, both at home and abroad, we need to remember the way it is affected by the 'unequal distribution of social and cultural power'.[31] That the question 'whose culture' finds its way into law is unavoidable.

The term legal culture is thus not an easy concept to pin down.[32] It can refer to a variety of types or number of units – from the culture of the local courthouse, of specific types of strong and weak 'community',[33] to that of the nation-state, wider cultural entities such as 'Latin legal culture',[34] or even 'modern legal culture'.[35] It can, with some difficulty, also be applied to so called 'third cultures' of international trade, communication networks or other transnational processes.[36] There are unresolved questions about how to use the concept. Is it really possible to draw a boundary between 'political culture' and 'legal culture' in explaining

28 Galanter (1989); Harding (forthcoming).
29 See Legrand (1996; 1997; forthcoming).
30 Kuper (1999).
31 Legrand (forthcoming).
32 Nelken (1995; 1997a).
33 Cotterrell (forthcoming).
34 Garapon (1995).
35 Friedman (1994).
36 Gessner (1994).

legal developments,[37] or in examining the ways particular regimes of 'governmentality' affect particular ways of seeing and using law?[38] There are basic disagreements on the best way to study legal culture,[39] including the difficult problem of choosing whether or when to use the categories of social structure or of culture in constructing our explanations.[40]

What exactly is embraced by the terms 'French legal culture'[41] or 'Dutch legal culture'?[42] What is being asserted if we characterise Japan as having 'a culture of bureaucratic informalism'?[43] A crucial problem here is deciding whether legal culture should be treated as an explanation or as that which is to be explained. Is legal culture that which is being adapted or that which helps shape the process of adaptation? There are problems with either choice. As something to be explained, it seems to include everything (and therefore have no specificity). Often the term is used as just another way of referring to social structures, formal or informal institutions of dispute processing, or the way social groups make their demands felt and others resist them.[44] Needing explanation, it is of no use as an explanation.

But when legal culture is used as (part of) an explanation it tends to be tautologous, to sum up other findings,[45] and be resorted to only when no other explanation will do. Lawrence Friedman has introduced a useful distinction between 'internal legal culture' (the ideas and practices of legal professionals) and 'external legal culture' (the demands on law brought to bear by those in the wider society).[46] Given the difficulties of the term, however, some authors prefer to talk instead of 'ideology', or law in communities,[47] or of disciplines and expertises, turf wars, or professional markets.[48] But these alternative terms do not cover all that is meant by legal culture, and have their own problems. In order to make progress it will be necessary to address such methodological problems head on, as in the way Prosser recognises both how the idea of legal culture can be used to exaggerate differences and yet does have some real meaning of its own.[49]

Whenever we engage in comparative research (and the study of legal transfers is always that) we also need to ask what shapes our (working) ideas of what is meant by legal culture – given that our idea of what law is and what it is for will itself reflect our culture of origin.[50] The claim that law is inherently more tied to impersonal business behaviour than to the private sphere of family relations[51]

37 Brants and Field (2000).
38 Legrand (1999).
39 See eg Bernstein and Fanning (1996); Blankenburg (1997); Cotterrell (1997); Friedman (1997); Legrand (1999); Nelken (1997b); Nottage (forthcoming).
40 See the debate in Blankenburg (1997) and Nelken (1997b) over the appropriate way to characterise organised 'infrastructural' alternatives to trial. The sense to be given to the idea of 'social capital' is an example of where this choice can be important for current debates over legal transplants and transitions.
41 Garapon (1995).
42 Blankenburg and Bruinsma (1994).
43 Bernstein and Fanning (1996).
44 Friedman (1975).
45 Friedman (1997).
46 Friedman (1975).
47 Cotterrell (1997; forthcoming).
48 Dezalay and Garth (1996; forthcoming).
49 Prosser (forthcoming). But the assumption that we should treat 'culture' as the term to use to describe something blown out of proportion may not always be a safe one.
50 Nelken (1995; 2000).
51 See Cotterrell (forthcoming).

may be less a matter of social science findings than a cultural variable. This is a well known problem regarding non-Western environments where there can be a tendency to think, as Dezalay and Garth put it,[52] that those in Japan and Mexico, for example, have simply got the role of law 'wrong'. But it is just as misleading to assume too much similarity. We should not assume that law works the same way in more centralised societies as compared with more pluralist societies.[53] We need to be open to the possibility that in some societies law is 'doubly removed' from reality.[54]

Finding a neutral standpoint between legal cultures can be a problem. How far does Lawrence Friedman's approach to legal culture presuppose a common law or American background of 'expressive individualism and plural equalities'? From whose perspective can it be said that Latin legal cultures 'have a paradoxical attitude to rule' such that 'they always border on inefficiency'?[55] Or, turning this round, what is the significance of the fact that some legal cultures in Europe aim at 'counterfactual' ideals rather than 'pragmatic reasonableness'?[56] One way of understanding legal cultures involves appreciating the way they (reflexively) constitute themselves by 'difference'.[57] The English common law has long followed this course in relation to the Continent, though this self-understanding has certainly become more complicated after membership of the EU. That such 'identification by difference' is still alive can be seen in recent official reactions to the proposal for a 'corpos juris' aimed at creating a unified prosecution process to deal with Europe-wide crimes.[58]

NAMING THE PRESENT

Whatever meaning we give to the concepts of change and legal culture is likely to be affected by the implicit model we have in mind of the typical processes of legal adaptation and legal transfer we are trying to understand. This applies even more to the use to which we wish to put such concepts when we set out to capture what is new. How far are our theoretical tools adequate for illuminating the range and type of legal transfers currently underway?[59] How should we organise our case studies of present developments so as to help us revise those tools?[60]

Much of the debate about current patterns of changing legal cultures fails to distinguish the question of which description is most appropriate for describing the general trends which affect legal transfers, from that of how best to identify and distinguish the various *different* processes which may be going on in different places at different times. On the one hand, we can ask whether current trends

---

52 Dezalay and Garth (forthcoming).
53 See Harding (forthcoming).
54 Lopez-Ayllon (1995); Rosenne (1971).
55 Garapon (1995).
56 Van Swaaningen (1999).
57 Smandycn (1999).
58 House of Lords (1999).
59 'There is a tension between the more or less static and interpretive comparative project and the dynamic longitudinal project imposed by the resumption of globalisation': Heydebrand (forthcoming).
60 Teubner's attempts to use Luhmann's social systems theory, and in particular to draw out the implications of legal autopoiesis, so as to examine the possibilities of legal regulation under current circumstances, represent a good example of the way new theorising can be linked to new legal and social developments (see Nelken (2001b)).

are best labelled as convergence, as modernisation, as marketisation, as globalisation, as Americanisation, as Europeanisation or all of these (and these trends themselves may sometimes be in a contradictory relationship). On the other hand, we can examine how far these developments affect and are affected by the variety of ways by which law is transferred. Is law driving or being driven by these larger developments? Are there more traditional mechanisms for legal adaptation still at work?

It would be a mistake to assume simply that finding an appropriate label for what is distinctive about current trends automatically will tell us all we need to know about the range of processes of legal transfer under way. If it is important to be open to what is new, we must also avoid the opposite danger of collapsing important differences and putting things together which do not belong under one rubric. The approach to legal transfers which is useful in understanding the efforts at harmonisation presently going on in the EU will probably offer little insight into explaining how new borrowing affects the sedimented patterns of legal pluralism in South East Asia.[61] Dezalay and Garth[62] argue that the role of arbitrators in Paris breaks down the national/international dichotomy. But, in other contexts, the dichotomy may still be alive. In one place the difficulties of transferring Western legal models will be attributable to the weak organisation of 'civil society', in other places it may be a result of civil society being too strong! We should not expect the same considerations to have the same effects in different situations.

In particular, it is doubtful if everything that currently is going on in the way of legal transfer can be captured by the term 'globalisation' without giving this term too expansive a meaning. Is there really any connection between the worldwide spread of human rights talk, the development of 'lex mercatoria', the spread and increased role of constitutional courts and, more generally, the alleged 'globalisation of judicial power'?[63] What really interests us about such developments? The way the world is becoming more alike? (But similar legal trends do not necessarily prove that). Or is the point the fact that these developments all testify to the declining power of the local state? (But does this not depend on which type of state?) Do these trends inevitably mean that businesspeople are more able to bend the law to their purposes (or does it depend which ones)?

Talking of broad trends does not then obviate the need to distinguish the different processes of legal transfer which express, accompany or seek to counteract such developments. Thus we are still far from possessing a theoretical framework for what Friedman calls 'the emerging sociology of transnational Law',[64] Friedman himself suggests that we should distinguish processes of 'borrowing, diffusion or imposition'. Writers who draw on autopoietic theory suggest the value for their purposes of distinguishing 'ad hoc contacts', 'systemic linkages' and 'co-evolution'.[65] In any similar framework we will need to avoid taking the boundaries between our terms so seriously as to fail to see the extent to which processes overlap and interact.

---

61 Harding (forthcoming).
62 Dezalay and Garth (1997).
63 Tate and Vallinder (1995)? Some attempts to put together the rise of constitutional courts with the anti-corruption activities of judges in Continental Europe conflate rather different developments in an attempt to demonstrate that judges now have 'too much' power.
64 Friedman (1996).
65 Paterson and Teubner (1998).

Alternatively, if we proceed inductively, we could choose to bring out what is special about activities linked to national, international and transnational actors – or to the way NGO's such as the IMF or charitable foundations intersect or reconstitute these boundaries. These activities will include not only such central legal activities as those connected to legislation and standard setting, adjudication, regulation, mediation and dispute settlement, but also mutual exchange and networking (as with international meetings of judges, lawyers, academics, police or customs officers) as well as efforts to create new legal, economic, political, social and educational institutions.

Part of this re-thinking must also apply to the metaphors we use as part of (or sometimes in lieu of) attempts to theorise processes of legal transfer. A range of mechanical, organic and discursive metaphors have been applied to the phenomenon of legal transfers. But it has not always been noticed how much these metaphors presuppose and advance different approaches to the relation between law and society.[66] Mechanical metaphors of legal transfer, which make use of terms such as export, diffusion and imposition, tend to accompany talking about law in the language of impact and penetration. They reflect a vision (well illustrated in the work of Lawrence Friedman) of law as a working institution, as an instrument, and as a technique of social engineering. Organic metaphors, on the other hand, speak about grafts, of viruses, and contamination, and, of course, of transplants (whether medical or botanical); legal transfers, when they succeed, blossom, are fertile and set root. They form part of a functionalist vision of law as an interdependent part of a larger whole.[67] Discursive metaphors, finally, speak about transferring law as a matter of engaging in conversation and dialogue – and of translating and reformulating implicit meanings. They approach law as communication, as narrative and as myth.[68] In thinking about changing legal culture, we can easily discover that these approaches have different ideas about what is meant by 'same' and 'different', what it is for a transfer to 'succeed', and how far this depends on the change achieving a given goal, on it helping a given type of social order or system to reproduce itself.

Whatever its value in relation to the past, there is a real risk that continuing to use (and argue about) the significance and possibility of 'legal transplants'[69] may distract us from the need to search for new metaphors and models which may be more appropriate to present day forms of legal adaptation.[70] Should we still be looking for 'advanced' and 'follower' countries?[71] What of the reciprocal effects of transplants in the exporting country?[72] How much does this metaphor prevent us from appreciating processes of imitation and convergence?[73]

Given that we are unlikely to find one metaphor that will serve all purposes, we may want to resort to different metaphors so as to come to terms with different processes. We may, for example, want to distinguish the following (which by no means exhausts all the possible ways of distinguishing different mechanisms and processes of legal transfer):

---

66 Nelken (2001a).
67 See eg Teubner (1998).
68 See eg Legrand (1999b).
69 Watson (1974); Wise (1990); Waelde and Gunderson (1994); Ewald (1995).
70 See Teubner (1997); Nelken (2001a; 2001b; in press).
71 Feldman (1997).
72 Dezalay and Garth (forthcoming).
73 Friedman (1996).

(1) cases where one country borrows or submits to new laws or system from another society,

(2) processes involving the spread of standards, regulations or 'soft law', for example by attempts at harmonisation of private law within the EU,[74] conventions on bio-diversity, genetic engineering or the Internet, labour regulations by the ILO, or international taxation agreements; and

(3) cases where 'third cultures', such as arbitration fora in Paris or Zurich reflect and further processes of the globalisation of law.

The first of these processes could – within limits – be illuminated in terms of the idea of 'legal transplants'; the competing metaphor of 'legal irritation'[75] could be better suited to examining the effects of applying similar laws or regulations in a series of different societies, whereas the idea of 'palace wars'[76] could help to capture the competition between professionals involved in the globalisation of law.[77]

Whilst it is essential not to oversimplify the different reasons for which law changes and the variety of ways it can be transferred, it is understandable that, as far as possible, we also wish to place current developments in a wider framework – and try to trace their interactions.[78] What exactly is new and how is it affecting legal adaptation? In some ways we are probably too close to current events fully to discern their shape. What is summarily referred to as 'globalisation' is a process which has multiple aspects, and its effects are not uniform or predictable. It would also be wrong to attribute to globalisation what are simply parallel but indigenous developments. The global and the local coexist;[79] and if globalisation often marginalises the local sometimes it strengthens it.[80]

But there is broad agreement about a number of major characteristics of the present period. The spread of telecommunications, easier transport, wider markets and political transformation towards neo-liberal models has meant that the world increasingly has become interdependent. There has been a change in the global financial architecture consequent on the move from Fordist, Keynesian forms of capitalist accumulation to strategies of flexible investment and outplacing. Globalisation strengthens an international division of labour in which some societies specialise in high-value goods and services whilst others rely on labour-intensive production or export their raw materials.[81] The same division of labour can be identified within single commodity chains such as toy production.[82]

Globalisation does not mean that the world is necessarily becoming more homogenous or harmonised, since much of the economic and financial integration which characterises globalised markets of production and consumption also presupposes and produces divergence and difference.[83] The national state, it is said, is being 'hollowed out' whereas super-national and federal

74 Joerges (2000) calls this process 'Interactive adjudication' in the Europeanisation Process.
75 Teubner (1998); Nelken (2001b).
76 Dezalay and Garth (1997; forthcoming).
77 It is an open question how far we should be concerned about the problem of mixed metaphors which results from such eclecticism. Much will depend on how far metaphors are seen merely as striking forms of speech and how far they are seen as terms of art within a theory.
78 See eg Santos (1995); Castells (1996; 1998).
79 Santos (1995).
80 Snyder (1999) at 336.
81 Tshuma (1999).
82 See Snyder (1999).
83 Nelken (1997c).

groupings are becoming more important – and the same is often true at the sub-state regional level. But some new nation-states are still being formed, and the lines between citizen and non-citizen status are being drawn with ever-increasing determination. Increasingly, it is obvious that flexible labour processes and footloose capital cannot be regulated at the national level in the old way.[84] In other respects the so called globalisation of law may not be the novelty it appears; rather the identification of law with the nation-states could be considered to have been an exceptional period. Much national commercial law is a result of a period of cross-fertilisation in the nineteenth century, in which domestic law first had to be invented so as to achieve reciprocal agreements with other states.[85]

Globalisation is unlikely to impose any one pattern of legal culture. Heydebrand[86] makes a careful distinction between what he calls the specific consequences of the 'globalisation of law' and the more indirect connections which need to be traced by examining the relations between 'globalisation and law'. It is right to emphasise the connections between neo-liberalism and the increasing adoption of 'bargaining' common law models of law (and at the same time we also witness the spread of the co-ordinate Anglo-American model of the criminal process). But we can also detect processes of political and cultural exchange which mean that that civil law models are also having an influence, as in the increasing importance of judicial review or of rights talk. In some countries, such as the Netherlands, we can see both processes happening together.

Law often does play an important role in seeking to bring about harmonisation or common standards – whether or not the underlying social and economic developments are running in this direction. In part this is pursued through international treaties, court decisions and regulatory action. But in many areas, the main actors are not nation-states but semi-governmental or international agencies and free-riding professionals. In general, we are seeing the increased significance of networks and 'sites' rather than states and the growth of a new 'global legal pluralism' based on episodic connections between 'sites', each with its own history, internal dynamics and distinctive features.[87] A central development in the construction of the neo-liberal post-modern legal order is being played by the so-called new 'lex mercatoria' outside the political structures of national states. A flexible, market-oriented form of contract law based on broad principles accompanies ongoing globalised processes of a highly specialised and technical nature.[88] At the same time we should not ignore the continuing role of old and new political and organisational actors, nor the various other forms of 'soft law' which help shape international trade.[89]

In addition to Heydebrand's categories,[90] however, we might also want to consider others, such as globalisation without law, or even the use of law in the fight against globalisation. The predictability created by the globalised spread of 'Macdonaldisation' or of credit cards[91] in some ways provides an alternative to strengthening the international rule of law or law within a given society. It is remarkable in fact how such forms of:

84 Tshuma (1999).
85 Sherman (1997).
86 Heydebrand (forthcoming).
87 Teubner (1997); Snyder (1999).
88 Teubner (1997) pp 340–343.
89 Picciotto (1997); Snyder (1999).
90 Heydebrand (forthcoming).
91 Ritzer (1995; 1998).

'impersonal trust can spread without the backing of a reliable legal system similar to those in America. Both at home and abroad law may sometimes colonise other norms, but at least as often it is displaced by the rise of actuarial and other expertises, of the so called "normalising disciplines" of social work and psychology, or by new forms of "govermentality".'[92]

The 'local state' may be weakened by some legal developments, but law may also be conditioned by nationalism, even when this is explicitly discouraged.[93] In many states in transition, organised crime groups are used in lieu of courts for the enforcement of civil debts. Mafia and other similar long-established organisations are also taking advantage of globalisation so as to strengthen illegal international networks.

Disagreements over what is special about the present period have direct implications for the legal procedures and ideals it is hoped to transfer. Great efforts are being made to export some version of the 'rule of law' to those countries seeking to make the transition to democracy and the market economy. For many of these societies, the rule of law is seen as valued above all as creating a space for civil rights which were previously denied. Economic advantages are then seen as flowing naturally from greater economic freedoms. But the link between particular types of political and legal structures and economic progress are more complicated than sometimes they are made out to be. How far legal rules actually can guarantee certainty and predictability is hotly debated within the academy; even within developed societies many businessmen simply choose to avoid the courts.

The link between capitalism and market predictability becomes even more moot when we consider variations in time and place. There are at least two competing forms of successful capitalism on offer. On the one hand, Weberian-type rational-capitalism spread by impersonal bureaucracies of production and marketing, as with Benetton or McDonalds, and, on the other, the type of guanxi capitalism more characteristic of Asian economic powers in which networks of family and family-like trust are all important.[94] The difference between these types of capitalism can be exaggerated; US-type capitalism in practice also relies largely on trust built up in continuing relationships more than on contractual entitlements, whilst the personal networks which channel Asian capitalism have their own semi-institutional quality.[95] But observers report important social and cultural differences in the extent to which predictability in everyday life in different societies depends on individual agreements, backed up by law, as compared with bonds between religious, ethnic and other groups. Thus the attempt to introduce greater reliance on legal guarantees may – especially in the short term – lead to *greater* rather than less uncertainty in the market-place.

The technological revolutions and other social developments of late modern forms of capitalism may have very different implications for the rule of law than those of earlier stages of capitalism. We may need to relativise the claim that democracy and the market are inextricably intertwined with the rule of law. According to Scheuerman, in a schematic but provocative analysis of these developments, 'the political and legal infrastructure of globalisation bears little

92 Smandych (1999). According to Murphy (1997) – and against all appearances – 'the legal' as a form of social regulation has had its day.
93 Mertus (1999).
94 Applebaum (1998); Jones (1994).
95 See eg Garth and Dezalay (1998); Friedman (1998).

resemblance to the liberal model of the rule of law'.[96] The rule of law was useful to businesspeople because it helped provide predictability, for example, concerning what would be delivered and when. It met their aspirations to make time and space manageable so as to reduce uncertainty based on distance and duration of commercial exchange. Now, however, with the compression of time and space which characterises globalisation there is less of an elective affinity between capitalism and the rule of law. The risks which the rule of law helped to protect against are now better dealt with by the time/space compression made possible by modern technology, and communication via computer is much quicker than creating and enforcing legal agreements.

Against this background of social change, argues Scheuerman, law loses its autonomy, becomes 'porous' and open-ended. Flexibility is now all important, businesspeople have less need of standard and consistent norms, but thrive rather on opportunities provided by difference between legal regimes, and they see arbitration as the best option in cases of dispute. No less important, the rule of law used to be valued because it protected business transactions from arbitrary interference by the state.[97] But now, at least as far as multinational business is concerned, companies often have the same rights as states themselves (as in the NAFTA agreement). Because poorer states need the investment they bring in, the balance of power is often to their advantage. There follows a competition to reduce legal safeguards and there is by now considerable evidence that economic globalisation flourishes where lower standards in protecting labour, health and the environment is exploited by powerful companies.[98] The need to take account of the needs arising from existing inequalities without sacrificing workers and the environment is a central and not easily resolved issue of legal policy – and leads to conflicting impulses towards greater or reduced regulation within states, and not only as between more and less powerful ones. And the same contradiction dogs the activities of organisations such as the World Trade Organization or the World Bank and the International Monetary Fund.[99]

Select bibliography

Applebaum, R P, (1998) 'The Future of Law in a Global Economy', 7 Social and Legal Studies 171.

Berstein, A, and Fanning, P, (1996) 'Weightier than a mountain: Duty, Hierarchy and the Consumer in Japan', 29 Vanderbilt J Transnational Law 45.

Blankenburg, E, (1997) 'Civil Litigation Rates as Indicators for Legal Culture' in D Nelken (ed), *Comparing Legal Cultures*, pp 41–68.

Blankenburg, E, and Bruinsma, F, (1994) *Dutch Legal Culture*.

---

96   Scheuerman (1999). Concerns similar to Scheuerman's relating to the power of corporate interests were raised by Franz Neumann 50 years ago, well before the current period of globalisation.

97   This part of Scheuerman's analysis seems to underestimate the extent to which capitalist success in Asian countries such as Japan not only did not require an autonomous space for business, but depended on an active state bureaucracy in alliance with big business.

98   Haines (1999).

99   'When all is said and done, the new programmes on law and development have all the hallmarks of the old ones' (Tshuma, 1998).

Bradley, D, (1999) 'Convergence in Family Law: Mirrors, Transplants and Political Economy', 6 Maastricht J European & Comparative Law 127.

Brants, C, and Field, S, (2000) 'Legal Cultures, Political Cultures and Procedural Traditions: Towards a Comparative Interpretation of Covert and Proactive Policing in England and Wales and the Netherlands' in D Nelken (ed) *Contrasting Criminal Justice*, pp 157–182.

Castells, M, (1996) *The Rise of the Network Society.*

—(1998) *The information Society.*

Comaroff, J, and Comaroff, J, (1995) 'The Discourse of Rights in Colonial South Africa: Subjectivity, Sovereignty, Modernity' in A Sarat and T R Kearns (eds) *Identities, Politics and Rights*, pp 193–238.

Cotterrell, R, (1997) 'The Concept of Legal Culture' in D Nelken (ed) *Comparing Legal Cultures*, pp 13–32.

—(forthcoming) 'Is There a Logic of Legal Transplants?' in D Nelken and J Feest (eds), *Adapting Legal Cultures.*

Damaska, M, (1986) *The Faces of Justice and State Authority.*

Dewar, J, (1998) 'The Chaos of Family Law', 61 MLR 1.

Dezalay, Y, and Garth, B, (1996) *Dealing in Virtue.*

—(1997) 'Law, Lawyers and Social Capital: 'Rule of Law' versus Relational Capitalism', 6 Social and Legal Studies 109.

—(forthcoming) 'The Import and Export of Law and Legal Institutions: International Strategies in National Palace Wars' in D Nelken and J Feest (eds), *Adapting Legal Cultures.*

Ewald, W, (1995) 'Comparative Jurisprudence 11: The Logic of Legal Transplants', 43 AJCL 489.

Feldman, E, (1997) 'Patients' Rights, Citizens' Movements and Japanese Legal Culture' in D Nelken (ed) *Comparing Legal Cultures*, pp 215–236.

Flood, J, (forthcoming) 'The Vultures Fly East: The Creation and Globalization of the Distressed Debt Market' in D Nelken and J Feest (eds) *Adapting Legal Cultures.*

Friedman, L, (1975) *The Legal System: a Social Science Perspective.*

—(1994) 'Is there a Modern Legal Culture?', 7 Ratio Juris 117.

—(1996) 'Borders: On the Emerging Sociology of Transnational Law', 32 Stan JIL 65.

—(1997) 'The Concept of Legal Culture: A reply' in D Nelken (ed), *Comparing Legal Cultures*, pp 33–40.

—(1998) 'Comments on Applebaum and Nottage' in J Feest and V Gessner (eds), *Proceedings of the 2nd Onati Workshop on Changing Legal Cultures*, pp 139–149.

Galanter, M, (1989) *Law and Society in Modern India.*

Garapon, A, (1995) 'French Legal Culture and the Shock of 'Globalization" in D Nelken (ed), 4 Social and Legal Studies special issue on Legal Culture, Diversity and Globalization 493.

Gessner, V, (1994) 'Global Legal Interaction and Legal Cultures', 7 Ratio Juris 132.

Haines, F, (1999) 'Towards Understanding Globalization and Corporate Harm: A Preliminary Criminological Analysis', Paper presented at the 1999 American Law and Society Annual Meeting, Chicago, 2 June.

Harding, A, (forthcoming) 'Comparative Law and Legal Transplantation in South East Asia' in D Nelken and J Feest (eds), *Adapting Legal Cultures*.

Heydebrand, W, (forthcoming) 'Globalisation of Law/Globalisation and Law' in D Nelken and J Feest (eds), *Adapting Legal Cultures*.

House of Lords (1999) 'Prosecuting Fraud on the Communities Finances – the Corpus Juris', *Ninth Report of the Select Committee on the European Communities* (HL Paper 62 (1998–99)).

Jettinghoff, A, (forthcoming) 'State Formation and Legal Change: On the Impact of International Politics' in D Nelken and J Feest (eds), *Adapting Legal Cultures*.

Joerges, C, (2000) Special issue on 'Interactive Private law adjudication in the European Multi Level System – Analytical Explorations and Normative Challenges', 8 European Review of Private Law.

Jones, C A G, (1994) 'Capitalism, Globalisation and Rule of Law: An Alternative Trajectory of Legal Change in China', 3 Social and Legal Studies 195.

Kuper, A, (1999) *Culture; the Anthropologist's Account*.

Lakoff, G, and Johnson, M, (1980) *Metaphors We Live By*.

Legrand, P, (1996) 'European Legal Systems are not Converging', 45 ICLQ 52.

—(1997) 'Against a European Civil Code', 60 MLR 44.

—(1999a) 'John Henry Merryman and Comparative Legal Studies: a Dialogue', 47 International Journal of Comparative Law 3.

—(1999b) *Fragments on Law as Culture*.

—(forthcoming) 'What Legal Transplants?' in D Nelken and J Feest (eds), *Adapting Legal Cultures*.

Linz, L, and Stepan, A, (1996) *Problems of Democratic Transition and Consolidation: Southern Europe, South America and Post Communist Europe*.

Lopez-Ayllon, S, (1995) 'Notes on Mexican Legal Culture' in D Nelken (ed), 4 Social and Legal Studies Special issue on Legal Culture, Diversity and Globalization 477.

Markensinis, B, (ed), (1994) *The Gradual Convergence*.

Merryman, J, (1985) *The Civil Law Tradition* (2nd edn).

Mertus, J, (1999) 'The Liberal State vs the National Soul: Mapping Civil Society Transplants', 8 Social and Legal Studies 121.

Monateri, P G, (1998) 'The "weak law": Contaminations and Legal Cultures' in *Italian National Reports to the XVth International Congress of Comparative Law*, pp 83–110.

Nelken, D, (1995) 'Disclosing/Invoking Legal Culture' in D Nelken (ed), 4 Legal Culture, Diversity and Globalisation: special issue of Social and Legal Studies 435.

—(ed), (1997a) *Comparing Legal Cultures*.

—(1997b) 'Puzzling out Legal Culture: A Comment on Blankenburg' in D Nelken (ed), *Comparing Legal Cultures* pp 58–88.

—(1997c) 'The Globalization of Crime and Criminal Justice: Prospects and Problems' in M Freeman (ed), *Current Legal problems: Law and Opinion at the end of the 20th Century,* pp 251–279.

—(ed), (2000) *Contrasting Criminal Justice.*

—(2001a) 'The Meaning of Success in Transnational Legal Transfers' in *Windsor Yearbook of Access to Justice* 19, p 349.

—(2001b) 'Beyond the Metaphor of Legal Transplants? Some Consequences of Autopoiesis Theory for the Study of Cross Cultural Legal Adaptation' in J Priban and D Nelken (eds), *The Consequences of Autopoiesis.*

—(in press) 'Legal Transplants and Beyond' in D Nelken and J Feest (eds), *Adapting Legal Cultures.*

Nelken, D, and Feest, J (eds), (in press) *Adapting Legal Cultures.*

Nottage, L, (forthcoming) 'The Still Birth and Re-Birth of Product Liability in Japan' in D Nelken and J Feest (eds), *Adapting Legal Cultures.*

Paterson, J, and Teubner, G, (1998) 'Changing Maps: Empirical Legal Autopoiesis', 7 Social and Legal Studies 451.

Picciotto, S, (1997) 'Fragmented States and International Rules of Law', 6 Social and Legal Studies 259.

Prosser, T, (forthcoming) 'Marketisation, Public Service and Universal Service' in D Nelken and J Feest (eds), *Adapting Legal Cultures.*

Ritzer, G, (1995) *Expressing America: a critique of the Global Credit Card Society.*

—(1998) *The Macdonalization Thesis.*

Rosenne, K S, (1971) 'The Jeito: Brazil's Institutional Bypass of the Formal Legal System and its Development Implications', 19 AJCL 514.

Santos, B de S (1995) *Towards a New Common Sense.*

Scheuerman, W E, (1999) 'Globalisation and the Rule of Law' in D Dyzenhaus (ed), *Recrafting the Rule of Law.*

Sherman, B, (1997) 'Remembering and Forgetting: The Birth of Modern Copyright' in D Nelken (ed), *Comparing Legal Cultures,* pp 237–266.

Sklair, L, (1991) *The Sociology of the Global System.*

Smandych, R, (1999) *Governable Places: Readings on Governmentality and Crime Control.*

Snyder, F, (1999) 'Governing Economic Globalisation: Global Legal Pluralism and European Law', 5 ELJ 334.

Sztompka, P, (1993) *Sociology of Social Change.*

Tanase, T, (forthcoming) 'The Empty Space of the Modern in Japanese Law Discourse' in D Nelken and J Feest (eds), *Adapting Legal Cultures.*

Tate, C N, and Vallinder, T (eds), (1995) *The Global Expansion of Judicial Power.*

Teubner, G, (1997) 'Global Bukowina: Legal Pluralism in the World Society' in G Teubner (ed), *Global Law without a State.*

—(1998) 'Legal Irritants: Good faith in British Law or How Unifying Law Ends up in New Divergences', 61 MLR 11.

—(1999) 'Idiosyncratic Production Regimes: Co-evolution of Economic and Legal Institutions in the Varieties of Capitalism' in J Ziman (ed), *The Evolution of Cultural Entities: Proceedings of the British Academy.*

Van Swaaningen, R, (1999) 'Reclaiming Critical Criminology: Social Justice and the European Tradition', 3 Theor Crim 5.

Tshuma, L, (1998) 'The Political Economy of the World Bank', 8 Social and Legal Studies 75.

—(1999) 'Hierarchies and Government Versus Networks and Governance: Competing Regulatory Paradigms in Global Economic regulation', Law, Social justice and Global development issue 1999-1. http://elj.warwick.ac.uk/global/issue/1999-1/ hierarchies/.

Watson, A, (1974) *Legal Transplants: An Approach to Comparative Law.*

—(1977) *Society and Legal Change.*

—(1985) *The Evolution of Law.*

Waelde, T W, and Gunderson, J L, (1994) 'Legislative Reform in Transitional Economies: Western Transplants – A Short Cut to Social Market Economy Status?', 43 ICLQ 347.

Wise, E, (1990) 'The Transplant of Legal Patterns', 38 AJCL (Supp) 1.

Zedner, L, (1995) 'In Pursuit of the Vernacular: Comparing Law and Order Discourse in Britain and Germany' in D Nelken (ed), 4 Social and Legal Studies (Special issue on Legal Culture, Diversity and Globalization 517.

Part II

Strategising commercial integration

Opening remarks: legal constraints in the capitalist world-economy

I WALLERSTEIN

For someone who is not a scholar of legal institutions, the primary impression one gets from the chapters in Part II (with one exception) is how weak the authors consider law to be as a constraint on capitalists. These chapters emphasise, thankfully, how the law really works in practice. They seem to share the moral sense that it should work better, that is, be more of a factor of constraint than it is, in terms of the ability of law to provide equity.

Any discussion of the role of law as a constraint in the capitalist world-economy has to start with two basic elements in the situation, not as it has developed in the last 10 to 20 years but as it has existed throughout the entire history of the capitalist world-economy, which means for the last 400 to 500 years. The first fact is that this system is not encased juridically in a world government. Law, both public and private, presumes government. And governments, as we have constructed them in the modern world, mean legislatures that enact laws, executives that enforce them and judiciaries that deal with those who violate them.

Of course, none of this exists to any serious degree at the global level, which is a crucial level, ultimately, for capitalists, especially big capitalists. What we have at the global level, what we have had from the onset, is not merely 'soft law' but 'soft governance'. There exists, certainly, some international law, the product of inter-state treaties, along with a few weak executive institutions (the strongest being the UN Security Council, whose decisions are a function of negotiations between five states), and a toothless international court system. Where rules are really enforced, it is the work, as Flood points out, of two local juridical structures (New York State and England) in the context of a highly monopolistic institutional structure (that of capital markets). Flood says that, in this field, the law 'appears impregnable'. I am more sceptical, since even here the enforcement of the law is subject to political pressures, provided only they be sufficiently organised. Demonstrations in Seattle and quasi-revolutions in Indonesia affect capital markets seriously, and can change IMF policies, for example.

The second basic element in the situation to remember is the *raison d'être* of capitalism. It is the endless accumulation of capital. The major structural element that supports this objective is the fact that the system is so arranged that any individual capitalist/firm that puts any other consideration ahead of maximising capital accumulation is punished sooner or later via the market. This does not mean that capitalists cannot be constrained. They are constrained all the time by laws, as well as by political pressures. Indeed that is the point of a large portion of the laws that are adopted. It is simply that the efficacy of these constraints is limited, and no capitalist/firm can ever be relied upon to constrain themselves, that is, seriously constrain themselves, if they expect to survive economically.

This does not mean that 'society' cannot force capitalists/firms to take into account other considerations than capital accumulation. Of course it can. Two centuries ago, capitalists used slave labour wherever it was profitable. Today the laws, almost everywhere, outlaw this practice. There is considerably less slave labour today than 200 years ago. But it is not down to zero, even in the wealthy countries, despite the fact that it is illegal everywhere. The ability to limit such practices is a function of how much legal and political effort others will put into the effort of constraint.

We see this very clearly when we come to the question of corruption. Corruption is a major concern of scholars and journalists. But is it a major concern of capitalists/ firms? Of course, no capitalist wishes to pay more for services than the minimum they can arrange. Corruption constitutes essentially an increase in the level of taxation from the point of view of the enterprise, which the enterprise may or may not be able to pass on to the buyers of its products. If it cannot pass it on, which is often, it then suffers a cut in the rate of profit.

Who is really interested in creating transnational legal constraints? The strongest states quite clearly have ambivalent attitudes towards creating law-like structures, for fear that they will be applied to themselves as states, or to large enterprises domiciled in their territories. For example, at the moment, the US is hostile to the idea of creating a court structure that can try persons for crimes against humanity for fear that US military might find themselves accused under such a system. The US is also hostile to the proposals of the OECD to curtail money-laundering, again for fear that this will be used against US enterprises.

On the other hand, weak states are often equally hostile to such extension of legal or law-like constraints, for fear that, in the absence of a democratic world government, they have no real guarantee that such laws would be used equitably, that is, not merely against the weak states but equally against all states or all individuals. Those in Serbia who have been resisting extradition demands have argued that Serbians are accused of crimes, but not citizens of the US.

I am not trying here to determine the validity of such fears or assertions. It merely indicates the sense that international legal procedures lack the degree of legitimacy that might be afforded by the existence of a world governmental structure. This is a fortiori true of legal constraints on commercial activities, where equity is far less discernible to the outside observer, and the hand of power far more readily attributed by this same observer the major role in both the creation of the legal constraints and, above all, in their enforcement.

The debate about the Kyoto accords illustrates this well. The Kyoto accords are a typical attempt at international law, a treaty to be ratified by the various sovereign states. They have the ostensible objective of regulating various negative environmental effects resulting from industrial activity. The essential mode of control proposed by the accords is to limit certain kinds of, or elements in, production. And equity is to be achieved by a quota system. The US has rejected the treaty on two major grounds – constraints on less developed states are less than on more developed states; the constraints, even if equitable, would 'hurt' the US economy. The counter-argument is simple. To the first plaint, it is said that more developed states, by definition, have done more environmental damage in the past and should pay the bigger price now; less developed states should not be hindered from 'developing', that is, achieving a status more equal with that of the more developed states. To the second plaint, it is said that, even if true, the benefits to the world environment outweigh any damage that might occur to the US economy.

Once again, it is not a question of the merit of these arguments, but of the fact that in this situation one player, the US, has a de facto veto, and has exercised it. This is not to say that no counter-pressures can be exercised. We have seen in recent years how certain large corporations have been accused of exploiting cheap labour scandalously in some countries in the South. These corporations initially reacted by a refusal to acknowledge the legitimacy of the arguments. These same corporations later made changes in their practices when faced with consumer boycotts in wealthy countries. Such boycotts were the work of militant organisations who, by this method, imposed a constraint on the mode of operation of large corporations.

We live not only amidst soft law and legal pluralism. We are also still subject to a very large degree to the rule of crude power – military, political and economic. The emergence of a web of legal or law-like constraints has been itself, and will continue to be, the outcome of an evolving *rapport de forces* in the world-system. Every increase in a legal structure is not necessarily a move towards greater legal equity. Each such step has to be evaluated in terms of *cui bono?* – not only in the short term, but in the medium term. Law is not supra-political, but a political instrument, a reality aggravated whenever there is a 'democratic deficit' in the state institutions, which is surely true at the world level.

None the less, as these chapters make clear, there has been an increase in the last 20 to 50 years of the amount of international commercial law in all its forms. Why has this occurred? One could argue a thesis of the steady slow evolution of the rule of law, except that it is not true historically, and it certainly has not been steady. What has occurred, of course, since 1945 are two things: an enormous increase in the absolute amount (not necessarily the percentage) of inter-state commercial transactions; an enormous increase in the amount of antisystemic activity, both on the part of governments (although this has in fact receded in the last 20 years) and on the part of movements (which has been surging upward recently).

This pair of conjunctural changes in the world-system has motivated two groups of actors to push for more law-like constraining activities. The first comes from the side of the powerful – powerful states, powerful enterprises. Power is a function of, and reinforced by, monopolistic tendencies. And legal regulations tend to constrain weaker states, weaker enterprises, more than stronger ones. Uniformity regulations, for example, almost always increase costs, with which smaller enterprises find it more difficult to cope than larger ones. The neo-liberal offensive of the last 20 years, far from increasing competition, tends largely to impose concentration of ownership on a world scale. This may be more efficient, but it is not more competitive.

On the other hand, the social movements have realised that, in terms of their objectives, restricting their demands to the national level renders them basically unable to deal with the ability of strong states/strong enterprises to circumvent national constraints. They have therefore moved to obtain transnational guarantees of their social objectives. The Kyoto accords are one such example, but scarcely the only one.

The two sets of law creation go in directly opposite directions. Hence, those who favour the first set tend to oppose the second set, and vice versa. The creation of these legal structures as well as their real enforcement becomes therefore one of the prime political arenas of conflict in the world-system. Since there is no world legislature, one of the key issues is the transparency of the law-making. The strong favour low transparency and the weak high. Transparency thus becomes a meta-issue of the political struggle.

We are a long way from the reign of the reflective, sagacious lawgiver.

Chapter 4

Governing globalisation

F G SNYDER*[1]

INTRODUCTION

How is globalisation governed?[2] This writer suggests that it is governed by the totality of strategically determined, situationally specific and often episodic conjunctions of a multiplicity of sites throughout the world. These sites have institutional, normative and processual characteristics. The totality of these sites represents a new global form of legal pluralism. This chapter, using a case study, aims to explore and, within limits, to substantiate this claim. It invites us to think systematically about how globalisation is governed by global legal pluralism.

The chapter aims to increase our understanding of how globalisation is governed and to improve our capacity to analyse these new forms of governance. It is not intended to promote law reform or advance a specific political or

1   Professor of European Community Law, European University Institute, Florence; Professor of Law, College of Europe, Bruges; Honorary Visiting Professor of Law, University College London; Co-Director, Academy of European Law, Florence; Co-Director, Academy of International Trade Law, Macau, China.
2   Early versions of parts of this chapter were presented at the Institute of International Studies, Stanford University, 2 April 1999, while the writer was Visiting Senior Fellow at the Stanford Law School Program in International Legal Studies; the Conference on 'Transatlantic Regulatory Co-operation', Inaugural Conference of the European Studies Center of New York, held at Columbia Law School, 16–17 April 1999; the Conference on 'The Regional and Global Regulation of International Trade', Institute of European Studies of Macau, 10–11 May 1999; the Guandong International Research Institute for Technology and Economy, 13 May 1999, Guangzhou, China; and the seminar on 'The Juridification of Globalisation' that the writer taught with Christian Joerges and Karl-Heinz Ladeur at the European University Institute, Spring 2000. The writer wishes to thank in particular George Bermann, Coit Blacker, Maria do Ceu Esteves, Jill Cottrell, Chen Yong Quan, Cao Ge Feng, Candido Garcia Molyneux, Tom Heller, David Holloway, Christian Joerges, Karl-Heinz Ladeur, Emir Lawless, Cosimo Monda, Craig Scott, Anne-Lise Strahtmann, Yang Zugong, the Hong Kong Trade Development Council, staff of the European Commission in Brussels and several government and toy industry representatives in the Shenzhen, China, Special Economic Zone, for their contributions to the paper. Jill Cottrell kindly provided helpful material on Hong Kong law. A longer version of the paper has been published as 'Governing Economic Globalisation: European Law and Global Legal Pluralism' (1999) 5 European Law Journal 143 [Special Issue on Law and Economic Globalisation]. A short version of the theoretical argument of the paper will be published as 'Global Economic Networks and Global Legal Pluralism', in Bermann G, Hedeger M, and Lindseth P, (eds), *Transatlantic Regulatory Co-operation* (2000).

institutional agenda. Consequently, its perspective is more sociological than normative. It adopts, as a useful starting point, the standpoint of strategic actors. Relations among strategic actors can be envisaged as involving different types of organisations, whether firms, states, or regional or international organisations. Alternatively, we can see them as implicating different structures of governance, whether market-based structures or polity-based structures. From a third perspective, these relationships put into play global economic networks and various sites of global legal pluralism. This chapter is intended to highlight all of these perspectives.

The argument is divided into two main sections. The first section sketches the main elements of a theory of global legal pluralism. The second section aims to illustrate this theory by reference to the international toy industry. The chapter thus is mainly exploratory, because much theoretical and empirical work remains to be done. A brief conclusion summarises the argument.

TOWARDS A THEORY OF GLOBAL LEGAL PLURALISM

Globalisation

Thinking about how global economic networks are governed requires a concept of globalisation. The term globalisation is used here to refer to an aggregate of multifaceted, uneven, often contradictory economic, political, social, cultural and juridical processes that are characteristic of our time.[3] This chapter concentrates primarily on the economic aspects, but these need to be set within a more general framework.

In economic terms, the most salient features of globalisation, driven by multinational firms, are for the present purposes the development of international production networks (IPNs),[4] dispersion of production facilities among different countries, the technical and functional fragmentation of production, the fragmentation of ownership, the flexibility of the production process, worldwide sourcing, an increase in intra-firm trade, the interpenetration of international financial markets, the possibility of virtually instantaneous worldwide flows of information, changes in the nature of employment and the emergence of new forms of work.

Viewed from a political standpoint, globalisation has witnessed the rise of new political actors such as multinational firms, non-governmental organisations and social movements. It has tended to weaken, fragment and sometimes even restructure the state, but has not by any means destroyed or replaced it. Globalisation has also altered radically the relationship to which we have become accustomed in recent history between governance and territory. It thus has blurred and splintered the boundaries between the domestic and external spheres of nation-states and of regional integration organisations; fostered the articulation of systems of multi-level governance, interlocking politics and policy networks; and helped to render universal the discourse of and claims for human rights. In

---

3   For a recent overview, see Held, McGrew, Goldblatt and Perraton (1999). Unfortunately, as the subtitle indicates, this excellent book pays relatively little attention to law.
4   See in particular the work of the Berkeley Roundtable on the International Economy, for example Borrus and Zysman (1998) pp 27–59.

many political and legal settings, such as the EU, it has raised serious questions about the nature and appropriate form of contemporary governance.

Among the manifold social processes involved in globalisation are the spread of certain models of production and patterns of consumption from specific geographic/political/national contexts to others. Contradictory tendencies have developed towards internationalisation and localisation within as well as among different regions and countries. We have also witnessed the uneven development of new social movements based on different, if not alternative, forms of community.

Seen as a cultural phenomenon, globalisation has implied the emergence of a new global culture, which is shared to some extent by virtually all elite groups. This has enhanced the globalisation of the imagination and of the imaginable.[5] At the same time it has contributed both to the transformation of many local cultures, sometimes strengthening them, sometimes marginalising them, sometimes having both consequences simultaneously. Consequently, it has sometimes increased the range and depth of international and infra-national cultural conflicts, as well as resistance to new forms of cultural imperialism.

Sites

We usually view the legal arrangements that are relevant to such global economic networks in one of two ways. Often we see them essentially in terms of contracts between nominally equal parties, such as individuals, companies or states, whose agreement is consecrated either in bilateral or multilateral form. Alternatively, we conceive of them in hierarchical terms, for example as constituting various regional or international forms of multi-level governance. It was suggested here, however, that both of these conceptions, regardless of their force in normative terms, are descriptively inaccurate and analytically incomplete. There is a fundamental and growing disjunction between our traditional, normative and hierarchical conceptions of the law governing international trade and the shape of the economic networks that are an integral part of economic globalisation. We should not necessarily expect the law and economic relations to be isomorphic. But in order to understand how global economic networks are governed in practice, we need to revise many of our basic ideas about the shape of the global legal order. Global economic networks are the product of and a form of strategic behaviour, and they usually have a particular locus of power and a specific hierarchy. Their dramatic growth has placed in question the credibility of lawyers' claims about the hierarchical nature of global economic governance. At the same time it has provoked demands for the constitutionalisation of global governance and debates about its feasibility and desirability.

The writer suggests that the best way to understand the emerging global legal order is by means of the concept of sites. In order to outline the relationship between economic globalisation and sites, it is useful to engage in a three-step analysis. The first step consists of defining the segments of a global commodity chain or network. The second step then focuses on each segment and asks specific questions about it. The third step takes the answers to these questions as a starting

---

5   For this expression, I am indebted to Prof Pietro Barcellona, oral intervention at the Conference on 'Quelle culture pour l'Europe? Ordres juridiques et cultures dans le processus de globalisation', Réseau Européen de Droit et Société (REDS) and Istituto di Ricerca sui Problemi dello Stato e delle Istitutionzi (IRSI), Rome, 2–3 November 1998.

point to identify the relevant institutions, norms and processes and to analyse their role. Instead of starting with normative systems, this method of analysis thus starts with social and economic relations and then asks how they are organised and governed.

In the first step of the analysis, we can draw on the work of Gereffi and of Hopkins and Wallerstein concerning global commodity chains. The term 'commodity chain' is used to mean 'a network of labor and production processes whose end result is a finished commodity'.[6] Global commodity chains tend to be strongly connected to specific systems of production and to involve particular patterns of co-ordinated trade.[7]

Each global commodity chain, if we follow Gereffi's widely accepted schema, has three main dimensions. The first refers to the structure of inputs and outputs: products and services are linked together in a sequence in which each activity adds value to its predecessor. The second concerns territoriality: networks of enterprises may be spatially dispersed or concentrated. The third dimension is the structure of governance: relationships of power and authority determine the flow and allocation of resources (financial, material, human) within the chain.[8]

Here we are interested especially in the third dimension, the structure of governance which is internal to the chain. Gereffi distinguishes two distinct types of governance structures within global commodity chains. On the one hand are producer-driven commodity chains, in which the system of production is controlled by large integrated industrial enterprises. On the other hand are buyer-driven commodity chains, in which production networks are typically decentralised and power rests with large retailers, brand-name merchandisers and trading companies.[9]

The work of Hopkins and Wallerstein provides another important building block with regard to global commodity chains. They use the term 'boxes' to refer to the separable processes involved in any global commodity chain.[10] I prefer the term 'segment', and I would also stress the importance of keeping in mind the links between the separable boxes or processes. The segments in a global commodity chain may include, for example, invention, production, marketing, distribution, and consumption. The boundaries of each segment are socially defined, and so may be redefined.[11] Technological and social organisational changes play a role in these processes. So too do law and other norms, conceived broadly to encompass the sites of global legal pluralism, with each site comprising its specific institutions, norms and processes, and law. They help to define, to construct and, of equal importance, to link the segments which make up the global commodity chain.

In the second step of the analysis, we can ask a series of questions about the social organisation of the constituent elements of any single box in the chain. They refer, according to Hopkins and Wallerstein,[12] to the following: number of component units; geographical concentration or dispersal; membership in one or more chains; property arrangements; modes of labour control; and links within

---

6   Hopkins and Wallerstein (1986) at 159.
7   Gereffi (1994) at 96. See also Gereffi (1992) at 85–112; Gereffi (1996) at 75–112.
8   Gereffi (1994) pp 96–97.
9   Gereffi (1994) p 97.
10 Hopkins and Wallerstein (1994) p 18.
11 Hopkins and Wallerstein (1994) p 18.
12 Hopkins and Wallerstein (1994) pp 18–19.

a chain. Two further issues have been added here: relations between specific boxes and specific sites, and relations between specific sites and the chain as a whole. Thus, this chapter rephrases, elaborates and adds to Hopkins' and Wallerstein's questions. Special emphasis is given to the institutional, normative and processual components of the sites of global legal pluralism.

The third step of the analysis takes these questions as a starting point. It asks, for example: What institutions, norms and dispute resolution processes are pertinent to these aspects of the social organisation of each segment? What aspects of law or other norms play a role in its governance? This thread will lead us to the institutional, normative and processual sites that together govern the specific global commodity chain. The following paragraphs exemplify this analysis.

Number of component units (monopoly, oligopoly or competition)

To what degree is a box monopolised by a small number of production units? What are the main factors determining this structure? What incentives for a particular structure are provided by legal and other institutions, norms and processes? For example, to what extent and how does the law provide or permit barriers to entry? To what extent does it facilitate or require market access, for instance with regard to production and/or distribution? Do different sites of global legal pluralism provide conflicting incentives, and if so, how are these conflicts managed, if not neutralised? If demonopolisation of any highly profitable box is an important process in the contemporary world economy, as Hopkins and Wallerstein suggest,[13] what role do the sites of global legal pluralism play with regard to this process, for example by encouraging it, by countering it by redefining the boundaries of the box or by other means, or by creating incentives for shifting capital investment to other boxes, or even other chains?

Geographical concentration or dispersal

What is the degree of geographic spread of the units in a specific box? In other words, are the units in a specific box geographically concentrated, or are they dispersed? For example, are the provision of finance, marketing and retailing geographically concentrated, while production is dispersed? Is the prevailing geographic pattern influenced by the sites of global legal pluralism, and if so, how? For example, what incentives do different institutions, norms, and processes provide for either concentration or dispersal of the different sites? Do these institutions, norms, and processes play a role in the extent to which boxes shift from the core to the periphery of the world economy, assuming that, as Hopkins and Wallerstein argue, a box is likely to be relatively geographically concentrated in the core but dispersed on the periphery?

Membership in one or more chains

Is a box located in more than one commodity chain? If so, how many? Do specific sites, including institutions, norms and processes, create a structure of incentives so that a particular box tends to be inserted in more than one commodity chain?

13 Hopkins and Wallerstein (1994) p 18.

To what extent, and how, is this insertion of a particular box in different commodity chains encouraged or facilitated by the law? What role do law and other types of norms play in the management of relations between the different commodity chains in which a particular box is located?

Property arrangements

What property-like arrangements (such as use, ownership, management, control) are associated with the units of a specific box? Which sites of global legal pluralism are the most relevant to these arrangements? Which specific institutions, norms and processes are determinative with regard to the arrangements in a particular site? Why? If different property-like arrangements prevail among the various units in a box, what institutions, norms and processes encourage or tolerate diversity? How is such diversity managed?

Modes of labour control

What modes of labour control are found in each box? Which sites of global legal pluralism are most relevant, and why? Which specific institutions, norms and processes are significant, and why? To what extent are different modes of labour control encouraged or facilitated by legal or other institutions, norms and processes? Are there conflicts among different sites with regard to modes of labour control? If so, how are these conflicts resolved in institutional, normative and processual terms?

Links within a chain

How are the boxes within a particular commodity chain linked to each other? Which specific legal institutions, norms and processes create, sustain or transform these links? What role do different sites of global legal pluralism play in linking different boxes? Is there any overall co-ordination of the boxes, for example, by means of vertical integration, ownership of intellectual property or control of distribution or retail markets? How is the discreteness of a particular commodity chain maintained, and what role does global legal pluralism play in this respect?

Connection between economic relations and specific sites

Do specific sites concern particular aspects of specific boxes? For example, do certain sites deal with labour control, others with financial arrangements, others with marketing, others with dispute resolution, and so on? How, and why? To what extent are particular sites important in governing the social organisation of the constituent units of a box even when the sites are not geographically proximate to the box, in other words when governance, economic processes and territory are not congruent?

Relations between sites and the chain as a whole

What types of relationships, for example, horizontal or vertical, competitive or co-operative, marked-based or state-based or convention-based, exist between the different sites that are relevant to a specific global commodity chain? Does any specific site concern the global commodity chain as a whole? To what extent does the plurality of sites provide an effective way of managing the chain as a whole? Would a single site or a small number of sites be more effective? What does 'effective' mean in this context? In other words, what are our criteria for evaluating the effectiveness of specific sites, and of the totality of sites which we call global legal pluralism, in the organisation and management of the chain as a whole?

Based on this three-step analysis, the concept of sites identifies a series or bundle of institutions, norms and dispute resolution processes. Their empirical unity lies in the activity of strategic actors. Their theoretical unity lies in the concept of global legal pluralism.

Global legal pluralism

Global legal pluralism is an essential concept for understanding the emerging global legal order. We need to take seriously the idea that, as Teubner[14] and Cutler et al[15] for example remind us, there are sources of economically, socially, politically, culturally and juridically significant norms which operate across national borders and to a large extent independently of states. It is important to recall, however, that contract is not the sole legal form. Viewed, for example, from the standpoint of strategic actors in a global commodity chain, such as multinational firms, contract is only one among several legal devices, sources of law and forms of legitimation. Nor should we unduly neglect the state. With regard to international trade, nation-states, regional organisations, such as the EU, and international organisations, such as the World Trade Organisation, as well as other organisations and networks, play a fundamental role. Frequently, the most significant norms are soft law, 'rules of conduct which, in principle, have no legally binding force but which nevertheless may have practical effects'.[16] In the governance of global economic networks, however, both soft law and legally binding norms, or 'hard law', are important. Bundles of norms may be aggregated in the form of a system, and there are a plurality of such systems, including norm-generating processes. The organisation of these norms, and of the systems in which they are embedded, can be envisaged as part of distinct networks rather than in terms of hierarchy.[17]

Global legal pluralism, as I use the term, comprises two different aspects. The first is structural, the second relational.

First, global legal pluralism involves a variety of institutions, norms and dispute resolution processes located, and produced, at different structured sites around the world. Lawyers, political scientists and scholars in other disciplines have described many of them, but no one has tried to unite these different elements. Some basic questions remain therefore to be answered. What is a site? States and regional and international organisations are included, but so are a diversity of other institutional, normative and processual sites such as commercial arbitration,[18] trade associations, and so on. How are sites created, and how do

14 Teubner (1997).
15 Cutler et al (1999).
16 For this definition, see Snyder (1993) at 32.
17 Teubner (1993) pp 41–51.
18 See Dezalay and Garth (1996); Casella (1996).

they grow, survive or die? How are they structured? What does it mean to say that different structured sites are the anchors of contemporary legal pluralism?

Second, the relations among these sites are of many different types, in terms of both structure and process. For example, in terms of structural relationships, sites may be autonomous and even independent, part of the same or different regimes, part of a single system of multi-level governance or otherwise interconnected. In terms of process, they may be distinct and discrete, competing, overlapping, or feed into each other, for example, in the sense of comprising a 'structural set', 'formed through the mutual convertibility of rules and resources in one domain of action into those pertaining to another'.[19] These relations of structure and process constitute the global legal playing field. They determine the basic characteristics of global legal pluralism, such as equality or hierarchy, dominance or submission, creativity or imitation, convergence or divergence, and so on. They influence profoundly the growth, development and survival of the different sites.

Global legal pluralism is not merely an important part of the context in which global economic networks are constructed, in the sense that it is a factor to be taken into account by strategic actors. It is an integral part of these global economic networks. In other words, global economic networks are constructed on a global playing field, which is organised or structured partly by global legal pluralism. Global legal pluralism does more, however, than simply provide the rules of the game. It also constitutes the game itself, including the players.

AN EXAMPLE: THE GLOBAL TOY INDUSTRY

The global commodity chain in toys

Global economic networks take various forms. We focus here on the international toy industry.

The toy industry's global reach and domestic impact can be illustrated clearly by example of the *Barbie* doll. The *Barbie* doll's label states 'made in China'. This suggests, correctly, that, in the production of *Barbie*, China provides the factory space, labour and electricity, as well as cotton cloth for the dress. It conceals, however, the facts that Japan supplies the nylon hair, Saudi Arabia provides oil, Taiwan refines oil into ethylene for plastic pellets for the body; Japan, the US and Europe supply almost all the machinery and tools; most of the molds (the most expensive item) come from the US, Japan or Hong Kong; the US supplies cardboard packaging, paint pigments, and molds; and Hong Kong supplies the banking and insurance and carries out the delivery of the raw materials to factories in Guandong Province in south China, together with the collection of the finished products and shipping. Two *Barbie* dolls are marketed every second in 140 countries around the world by Mattel Inc of El Segundo, California.[20] In Palo Alto, California, there is a *Barbie* doll museum. *Barbie* celebrated her fortieth birthday on 9 March 1999, and in her honour the US Post Office released in June a commemorative US postage stamp.[21] The *Barbie* doll is quintessentially American in origin, style and culture, and of course is the result of a global commodity chain powered by a US buyer. But *Barbie* is a global product, if by 'global' we refer

19 Giddens (1989) p 259.
20 Rone (1996) at 3.
21 Rapoport (1999) at 54–57.

to the fragmentation of the production process, the dispersion of production facilities among different countries and the organisation of production within international production networks.

The international toy industry is a prime example of an international commodity chain dominated by the buyers. It is organised in a hierarchical structure. At the top of the hierarchy are large buyers, as well as large retailers. The buyers include several US manufacturers, two Japanese manufacturers and one European company. The most important buyers are two US companies, Mattel and Hasbro. The key elements in the power of buyers are designs and brands. The large buyers are the node in various networks of inventors and creators of toys. Through contract, they control the access of inventors, intermediaries, and factories to the market. The most important retailers include large specialist stores such as Toys 'R' Us, discount houses such as Wal-Mart in the US, and hypermarkets or catalogue stores in the EU. Taking buyers and retailers together, the power of this group lies in its control of design, brands and marketing.

Buyers and retailers compete, however, with regard to access to retail markets. The powerful buyers are dependent to some degree on large retailers, such as Toys 'R' Us, and discount stores such as Wal-Mart. As economic downturns reveal, however, the two groups have conflicting interests with regard to the retail market. To maintain market share, and to enhance their dominant position in the global commodity chain, buyers have tried recently to lessen their dependence on retailers. Their strategies for doing so include increased direct-to-consumer sales, including catalogue and Internet sales, either from their own website or from on-line retailers.[22]

The US firms have regional headquarters and a significant share of the toy market in Europe. The EU toy market is supplied mainly through importer-wholesalers. In 1995, the EU toy industry comprised about 2,600 firms, producing a great variety of toys and employing just under 100,000 workers, with only 15 firms having more than 500 employees.[23] Each country has its own distinctive retail sector, varying from catalogue stores through hypermarkets to independent retailers.[24] With the exception of Lego, established in Denmark in 1932 and now one of the world's ten largest toy manufacturers, there are no large manufacturers or specialist retailers based in Europe similar to those based in the US. Together with Lego and the Japanese firm Bandai, the US firms dominated the first main peak trade association, Toy Manufacturers of Europe, formed in the early 1990s, and are now the principal players in the current EU peak association, Toy Industries of Europe.

Further down the hierarchy come the Hong Kong companies which act as intermediaries between these multinationals and the toy factories. In East Asia, Hong Kong has been of signal importance in the development of the toy industry. Its role first started in the 1940s as an export platform, then developed in the 1980s as original equipment manufacturers for overseas importers or as intermediaries between local manufacturers and overseas buyers until, starting in the 1990s, Hong Kong became a re-exporter of toys made in China. In 1998, licensing and contract manufacturing for overseas manufacturers, usually to production specifications and product designs provided by the buyers, accounted

22 Anders and Bannon (1999) at B1.
23 Commission of the European Communities (1995).
24 See Hong Kong Trade Development Council (1999) pp 34–58.

for an estimated 70% of total domestic toy exports.[25] US buyers accounted for 51% of Hong Kong's toy exports in the first ten months of 1995.[26] Today, Hong Kong is the location of management, design, research and development, marketing, quality control, finance and usually shipping.[27]

At the bottom of the hierarchy are the factories, most of which are located in China. By 1995, toy production in China involved about 3,000 factories employing more than 1.3 million people.[28] Such factories usually occupy the structural position of original equipment manufacturer, producing to other companies' specifications with machinery provided by the buyer. However, some now operate on the basis of original design manufacturer, producing to designs supplied by the buyer but sharing the cost of machinery and investment as well as markets according to an agreement with the buyer.[29] Today China and Hong Kong account for nearly 60% of world's toy trade.[30]

ECONOMIC GLOBALISATION AND GLOBAL LEGAL PLURALISM

Monopoly or competition

We now turn to the social organisation of the segments and the role of specific sites. For reasons of space, only a few examples can be given to illustrate the roles of particular institutions, norms and processes in organising different segments. Several sites of global legal pluralism shape or determine the number of component units in any given box in the international commodity chain in toys. Leaving aside antitrust law, despite its obvious importance, we focus here on the role played by EU institutions and trade legislation in restructuring the EU toy industry. In fact, through this part of the chapter special emphasis is given to EU law, because so little research has been done so far on the role played by EU law in governing globalisation.

In 1994 the Council of the European Union adopted two major complementary legislative reforms. The first was Council Regulation (EC) 519/94 on common rules for imports from certain third countries, which was the general regulation governing imports from non-market economy countries, except for textile products.[31] EC quotas on seven categories of Chinese products, including toys,

25 'Hong Kong's Toy Industry', *Hong Kong & China Economics*, on the Internet homepage of the Hong Kong Trade Development Council at www.tdc.org.hk/main/industries/t2_2_39.htm, last updated 2 July 1998.
26 (1995) Journal of Commerce January 13.
27 See the statement by Dennis Ting, who as of January 1995 was chairman of Kader Industrial Co Ltd, a leading Hong Kong toy firm, as well as of the Hong Kong trading agency's toy advisory committee and of the Hong Kong Toy Council: (1995) Journal of Commerce January 13.
28 Newton and Tse (1998) at 154.
29 Interviews in Hong Kong, Guangzhou and the Shenzhen Special Economic Zone, China.
30 'Chinese Toy Making: Where the Furbies come from' (1998) The Economist, 19 December, 95–99 at 95.
31 Imports of textiles were governed by one of two other regulations. Council Regulation (EC) 3030/93, on common rules for imports of certain textile products from third countries covered imports of textile products from countries with which the EC has concluded bilateral agreements, protocols or other arrangements. Council Regulation (EC) 517/94 on common rules for imports of textile products from certain third countries not covered by bilateral agreements, protocols or other arrangements, or by other specific Community import rules, covered imports of textile products from non-market economy countries with which the Community had not concluded specific arrangements.

replaced approximately 6,417 national quantitative restrictions, including 4,700 on more than 30 Chinese products.[32] The second was Council Regulation (EC) 520/94, establishing a Community procedure for administrative quantitative quotas.[33] It established a new way of administering quotas, based on a system of licenses issued by the member states according to quantitative criteria established at Community level.[34] Both were part of a package deal, designed to secure acceptance of the Uruguay Round multilateral trade negotiations, to reinforce existing trade policy instruments, and to complete the EC's Common Commercial Policy. Both the new quota regime and provisions for administering it exemplified the Europeanisation of law, the total or partial replacement of the law of the member states by EC law.

The adoption of Council Regulation (EC) 519/94 inaugurated four years of continuous lobbying, negotiation, litigation, law reform, further litigation and further law reform.[35] The UK, which had opposed the measure in the vote in the Council of Ministers, brought an Article 173 action in the ECJ to annul the Chinese toys quota.[36] It argued that the new regulation introduced quotas on imports of Chinese toys into the UK market which previously was free of quotas. Subsequently the Council amended the challenged regulation.[37] However, this compromise itself was challenged in the ECJ by Spain,[38] one of the main initial proponents of quotas on imports of toys from China. Then the European subsidiary of Tyco Toys, Inc[39] brought an action in the CFI to annul the toy quota and to obtain compensation for injury.[40]

The challenge by the UK to the Chinese toys quota[41] has been ascribed to pressure brought on the UK government by the largest umbrella trade association, Toy Manufacturers of Europe (TME). Hong Kong firms accounted for the majority of those affected by the quota, but they could not seek the help of the Hong Kong government, at least directly, because their factories were located in China.[42] Toy

---

32 (1994) Agence Europe, 6272, 13 July, p 9.
33 Council Regulation (EC) 520/94 establishing a Community procedure for administering quantitative quotas.
34 See Snyder, 'International Trade', *op cit* n 2, 190–202.
35 For further details, see F Snyder, 'Chinese Toys', *op cit* n 2, on which the following paragraphs draw.
36 Case C-150/94 *United Kingdom of Great Britain and Northern Ireland v Council of the European Union* [1998] ECR I-7235.
37 Council Regulation (EC) 1921/94, amending Council Regulation (EC) 519/94 on common rules for imports from certain third countries. See also (1994) Agence Europe 6277, 20 July, p 13.
38 Case C-284/94 *Kingdom of Spain v Council of the European Union* [1998] ECR I-7309. The Council was supported by the Commission.
39 Tyco's trade names include *Dr Dreadful, Fashion Magic, Kitchen Littles Cookware, Magna Doodle, Matchbox* and *View-Master*. See its Internet website www.matchboxtoys.com. As of February 1999, Tyco Preschool was a Mattel company. See the Internet website of Toy Manufacturers of America at www.toy-tma.com/MEMBER/.
40 Case T-268/94 *Tyco Toys (UK) Ltd and Others v Commission and Council* OJ 1994, C254/14; see also (1994) Agence Europe 6317, 17 September 1994, p 13. As of 20 April 1999, this case was still pending, but a hearing was expected to be held, according to the services of the ECJ. The writer is grateful to Emir Lawless of the EUI Library for this information. By May 1999, however, the case had been abandoned: interviews in the European Commission.
41 Case C-150/94 *United Kingdom of Great Britain and Northern Ireland v Council of the European Union* [1998] ECR I-7235.
42 Cf Newton and Tse (1999) at 159.

multinationals thus lobbied in Europe through the trade association. TME was formed as a political lobbying group in the early 1990s. It brought together European toy manufacturers, except those in France and Spain and German producers of plastic toys, which were grouped instead in the Fédération européenne des industries du Jouet (FEIJ).[43] The members of TME accounted for approximately 80% of toy manufacturers and distributors operating in Europe and was dominated by American toy multinationals, together with the Danish firm Lego and the Japanese firm Bandai. Its members did not manufacture toys in Europe; their main interest lay in maintaining open markets throughout the world, including the EU, for their main source of production, namely China.[44] They were also concerned to use the EU market and EU law effectively in their strategies for restructuring the international toy sector and ensuring the integration of the EU market into the global commodity chain. TME had opposed the imposition of quotas from the outset.

Lobbying and litigation were two facets of the same political strategy. They paid off in a series of continual legislative reforms, six in total during a brief four-year period. The first occurred when, five weeks after the UK brought its case, the Commission proposed an increase in the quota, largely because of pressure from TME.[45] The member states, however, did not agree.[46] To break the logjam, the Council adopted a compromise solution.[47] It embraced only the toy sector, but it raised the quota for certain toys from China by almost 30% for the period from 15 March to 31 December 1994.[48] This compromise itself, however, provoked further litigation by Spain[49] and the European subsidiary of Tyco Toys, Inc.[50]

The second legislative reform occurred in March 1995 when the Council agreed to raise the toy quota for the year starting 1 January 1995.[51] This was part of a more general revision of quotas on imports from China, in which quotas for some goods were abolished, others increased and others maintained at the then existing level.

The legislative tinkering continued. In April 1996 the Council adopted a third revision, to take effect as of 1 January 1996.[52] This measure was part of a more general revision of imports on goods from China. Like its predecessor, it benefited importers, distributors and processors of Chinese products, met to

---

43 The writer is grateful to Mr Salvador Miro Sanjuan, President of the AEFJ, for this information.

44 Newton and Tse (1999) at 156.

45 (1994) Agence Europe 6272, 13 July, p 9. Newton and Tse (1999) at 159.

46 (1994) Agence Europe, 6275, 16 July, p 14. For the contrasting viewpoint of traders associations, see (1994) Agence Europe, 6289, 6 August, p 8.

47 Council Regulation (EC) 1921/94, amending Council Regulation (EC) 519/94 on common rules for imports from certain third countries. See also (1994) Agence Europe 6277, 20 July 1994, p 13.

48 Council Regulation (EC) 1921/94, art 1. The toys in question were those falling within Code HS/CN 9503 41 (stuffed toys representing animals or non-human creatures), such as *Furbies*.

49 Case C-284/94 *Kingdom of Spain v Council of the European Union* [1998] ECR I-7309. The Council was supported by the Commission.

50 Case T-268/94 *Tyco Toys (UK) Ltd and Others v Commission and Council*, OJ 1994, C254/14 p 14, subsequently withdrawn.

51 Council Regulation (EC) 538/95, art 1, Annex II, amending Council Regulation (EC) 519/94 on common rules for imports from certain third countries.

52 Council Regulation (EC) 752/96 art 1, amending Annexes II and III of Council Regulation (EC) 519/94 on common rules for imports from certain third countries.

some extent the demands of the Chinese government and conferred new advantages on firms by removing quotas in certain markets. While it did not increase the total quota amount for toys, it fused the three existing quotas into one. This introduced greater flexibility in the implementation of the quotas.[53] Hence it empowered certain firms, notably importers, and increased the free play of the market, while maintaining the overall quota. Arguably, it helped industry to meet changes in consumer demand. Fusion of the three quotas into one also created a greater space for restructuring of the toy sector. Small EU firms were faced with international competition from other producers, as well as being squeezed by the dominant international buyers who controlled the major brands and had easy access to large retailers. They were gradually regrouping and restructuring. The Commission's original proposal for fusing the three quotas was intended partly to encourage these economic and social processes, even though the Commission recognised that its legislative proposals were based on very incomplete information.[54] As a result, the large trade associations in the sector supported the Commission's proposals.

The Commission took a further step in May 1996, when it revised the procedures for allocating quota amounts.[55] It reduced the allocations under import licenses for traditional importers by specified percentages, applied to a base equal to average imports for 1992 and 1994.[56] License applications by non-traditional importers were to be met in full within the overall quota limits.[57] In addition, a license issued for a certain category of toys could also be used for the other categories.[58] This revision, as the previous reforms, moved EC law closer to meeting the interests of multinational toy buyers and manufacturers, thus gradually undoing the 1994 compromise. It did so, however, not by increasing or otherwise modifying the quotas themselves, but rather by changing the way they were administered. In particular, it opened more space for new entrants to the import market, while at the same time it increased the flexibility of the administration of licences. In other words, it lowered barriers to entry and the costs of importation, notably for large firms.

In September 1996, litigation in the ECJ bore its first fruit. The Advocate General gave his Opinion jointly in the two cases brought separately by the UK and Spain. He proposed that the ECJ should uphold the policy-making and legislative discretion of the Council, and thus reject the claims by the UK and Spain for the annulment of EC legislation. This Opinion was taken by many in the toy sector as a clear signal that the actions brought by the two governments against the Community legislator would ultimately be rejected. At least some

53 See Council Regulation (EC) 752/96, preamble, sixth recital.
54 Council Regulation (EC) 752/96, at 47. In preparing the report, the Commission solicited information from a wide variety of producers, importers, and traders, either directly or through their trade associations. The response, however, was 'incomplete and rather unsatisfactory': *ibid*, at 3. Nearly all the investigated sectors were composed of numerous small and medium-sized enterprises, 'of which a significant proportion are not even known by the relevant national federations': *ibid*, at 3. Of the importers, the TME, Toys Traders of Europe (TTE), the Hong Kong Toys Council, the Japan Toy Association, and John Lewis Partnership (UK) submitted remarks: see *ibid*, 45-46.
55 Commission Regulation (ECSC) 899/96 establishing the quantities to be allocated to importers from the Community quantitative quotas redistributed by Regulation 612/96.
56 Commission Regulation (ECSC) 899/96, art 1 and Annex I.
57 Commission Regulation (ECSC) 899/96, art 3 and Annex III.
58 Commission Regulation (ECSC) 899/96, Annex I, n 3, and Annex III, n 2.

academic commentators shared this view.[59] Such a perception neglected the fact that the Advocate General's Opinion does not state the law, nor is it legally binding on the court. It captures nicely, however, the real political and symbolic significance of such Opinions, in which, rightly or wrongly, the Advocate General is often seen to be speaking not merely for the public, but also for the court.

Despite its lack of legal force, the Advocate General's Opinion would seem to have had a decisive impact on further reform of the quota legislation. The Council, the Community legislator, enacted a subsequent reform in mid-1997.[60] While maintaining the same overall quota amount for toys, it excluded toy parts and accessories from the quota. It placed these parts and accessories, as well as certain other categories of toys,[61] under Community surveillance, first for the period from publication of the measure on 14 May 1997 until 31 December 1997,[62] and then for the period from 1 January 1998.[63] These changes followed the main conclusions of the Commission's 1996 annual report.[64] The latter, in turn, presented a somewhat simplified version of the recommendations of what were then the two main trade associations, the TME acting on behalf of importers and the Fédération Européenne des Industries du Jouet on behalf of producers. Together these trade associations represented, in the Commission's view, 'almost the entire European toy industry'.[65] The legislative reforms testified to the close co-ordination between firms, both independently and through trade associations, and member states and EC institutions, on the other hand. This co-ordination, in turn, ensured that the adjustments in the law were in step with the changing interests of the EU toy sector, which was then in the process of restructuring within the EU market and of adapting to the new challenges posed by the international market.

The major trade associations had in fact proposed the liberalisation of imports of only 'the components of toys which were meant to be subject to further industrial transformation'.[66] Articulated for political and other reasons in terms of stimulating employment by local assembly and similar processes, this proposal embodied a very clear recognition of the internationalisation of the toy industry and the role of the EU producers in these increasingly global networks. Many EU producers were to occupy a place in these new networks that was very similar to that of producers in China, except that Chinese factories were engaged in original equipment manufacturing, whereas EU producers would be involved merely in the final (though industrial) transformation of the toys, albeit with the possibility in some instances of moving into own brand manufacturing. This proposal

---

59 Newton and Tse (1999) at 161. Doubtless the claimant governments and the large trade associations were more aware of the legal status of such an opinion and its relation to the eventual judgment by the ECJ. Small businesses, however, are often much less aware of these crucial legal and institutional distinctions.

60 Council Regulation (EC) 847/97, amending Annexes II and III to Council Regulation (EC) 519/94 on common rules for imports from certain third countries.

61 Code HS/CN 9503 30 (other construction sets and construction toys of wood, plastic or other materials).

62 Council Regulation (EC) 847/97, art 1, Annexes I and II.

63 Council Regulation (EC) 847/97, art 2, Annexes III and IV.

64 Commission of the European Communities *2nd Report from the Commission to the Council on the surveillance measures and quantitative quotas applicable to certain non-textile products originating in the People's Republic of China* COM(97)11 final, Brussels (29.1.97 p 45).

65 COM(97) 11 final, Brussels (29.1.97 p 38).

66 Quoted in COM(97) 11 final, Brussels (29.1.97 p 38).

signalled the eventual transformation of many small and medium-sized EU firms, and to that extent the nation-states in which they were situated, into flexible, more precarious world-factory sites; dependent, as were Chinese toy factories and their Hong Kong owners, on the multinational firms that occupied the dominant positions and were the key players in the global toy commodity chain. It also implied potentially a shift in legal position. The law governing imports would no longer be the EC quota regulations, but rather EC customs regulations on inward processing and potentially (if China were to accept the relevant annexes) the 1973 Kyoto International Convention on the Simplification and Harmonization of Customs Procedures.[67] To return to our model of the international toy commodity chain, the legal reforms thus fostered a transformation of the number of production units, an increase in their geographic dispersal, and potential changes in the property and other arrangements linking various parts of the chain, as well as a partial transformation of the relevant institutions, norms and processes of governance.

A sixth reform followed soon afterwards. Less than a month after the 1997 reform took effect,[68] the Council once again adopted a further regulation.[69] It abolished entirely, with effect as of 1 January 1998, the quotas of toys falling within Codes HS/CN 9503 41, 9503 49 and 9503 90.[70] It subjected these products (and continued to subject toys of Code HS/CN 9503 30) to prior Community surveillance to ensure adequate monitoring of the volume and prices of imports.[71]

This final step in our saga of legislative reform occurred in the context of – and contributed to – the transformation of the EU toy industry. By definition, therefore, it also affected the gradual restructuring of the global toy commodity chain, including factories in China. By 1996 the EU toy industry had already adapted its production structures and improved production quality to such an extent that, at least from the standpoint of the Commission and most if not all national governments, import quotas were no longer necessary.[72] The EU's restructured toy enterprises imported items that were no longer produced in Europe. As the Commission noted, '[m]ost manufacturers in Europe are also becoming importers of some items which may be necessary for them to keep their market share both in the EU and on export markets'.[73] EU producers were able to compete in foreign markets: exports of European toys outside the EU grew by a record 16.8% in 1996, while imports in the same year rose by only 3%.[74] The European Commission ascribed this successful adaptation to law. In its view,

---

67 Cmnd 5938, OJ L100/2 21.4.75 Cmnd 5938. The most convenient source is the Internet edition: *World Customs Organisation, Handbook: of the International Convention on the Simplification and Harmonization of Customs Procedures* (Kyoto, 18 May 1973) (1st edn, October 1975, Amending Supplement No 13, January 1993). In June 1999 the 1973 Kyoto Convention was revised, but the revised Convention has not yet been ratified by all parties: see www.wcoomd.org/frmpublic.htm.
68 It took effect on the date of publication, 14 May 1997: Cmnd 5398; OJ L100/2, art 3.
69 Council Regulation (EC) 1138/98, amending Annexes II and III of Council Regulation (EC) 519/94 on common rules for imports from certain third countries.
70 Council Regulation (EC) 1138/98, art and Annex I.
71 Council Regulation (EC) 1138/98, art 1 and Annex II.
72 See *Commission of the European Communities 3rd Report from the Commission on the quantitative quotas and surveillance measures applicable to certain non-textile products originating in the People's Republic of China* COM(98)128 final, Brussels (9.3.98 especially pp 26–29, 35).
73 COM(98) 128 final, Brussels (9.3.98 p 28).
74 COM(98) 128 final, Brussels (9.3.98 p 26).

the restructuring of EU industry was due mainly to the temporary protection assured by Community quotas.[75] EC law thus also facilitated the redefinition of the role of EU firms in the global commodity chain.[76]

The abolition of quotas was the culmination of more than a decade of conflict between member states and between competing firms. It represented the temporary conclusion of diverse attempts by EU institutions to manage conflicting interests. Such conflicts were inherent in the process of market building and market management in the EU, partly because of the changes in the way in which the EU market was integrated into the international toy commodity chain. They began with the Chinese opening-up in 1979, the subsequent restructuring of the international toy industry, and the creation of new economic networks and the thin globalisation[77] of this sector of the Chinese economy. Changes occurred in the domestic and international interests in the sector, and the lines between the domestic and the international were not merely blurred but actually reconfigured. These changes were in turn expressed to some extent in legislative form. Just as the 1994 compromise legislation expressed the balance of interests at the time, changes in the structure of interests led to demands for changes in the law. The gradual legal reforms not only represented these new, changing configurations of interests; they also helped to crystallise and perhaps even to create new interests, especially with regard to the number and nature of units of production.[78]

Geographic concentration or dispersal

We have already seen that invention, finance, marketing and retailing in the international toy industry are concentrated: the first in the US, the second and third in the US and Hong Kong, and the last, so far as control is concerned, in the US and, to a lesser extent, Europe and Japan. Production has until recently tended to be concentrated mainly in Asia, though potentially it could be much more dispersed. The geographical separation of production from finance, marketing and retailing is encouraged by international norms concerning the customs operations known in the EU as inward processing and outward processing.[79] It is no exaggeration to describe the existence and increased use of these customs rules as the legal basis for what has been called 'the new international division of labour'.[80]

The overarching international legal framework is provided by the International Convention on the Simplification and Harmonization of Customs Procedures, a

---

75 COM(98) 128 final, Brussels (9.3.98 pp 27–28).

76 Changes in the organisation of political representation in the EU toy sector reflected these changes in the organisation of production and marketing. For a detailed discussion, see Snyder, 'Governing Economic Globalisation: European Law and Global Legal Pluralism' (1999) 5 ELJ 143.

77 The writer is grateful to David Trubek for the expression 'thin globalisation'.

78 Such a transformation is not unique to the EU. Chinese producers of traditional wooden and other toys are being ousted by international toy companies, such as Lego: cf Turner, 'The Fading Tradition of Tang the Toymaker' (1999) International Herald Tribune, January 8, at 8. For an account of the heterogeneity of toy producers in China, see also the short story by Z Xin, 'Where Angels Dare to Tread' [translated by Josephine A Mathews] in *Contemporary Chinese Women Writers VI: Four Novellas by Zhang Xin*, (1998) pp 97–231.

79 On EU law, see F Snyder 83–103.

80 For case studies from an economic standpoint, see Froebel, Heinrichs, and Kreye, 1980.

veritable international customs code. It was first signed at Kyoto on 18 May 1973 and entered in force on 25 September 1974.[81] An updated version was adopted on 25 June 1999 but has not yet been ratified by all parties.[82] The Kyoto Convention is the fruit of the Customs Co-operation Council (CCC), founded in 1952[83] and known since 1994 as the World Customs Organisation (WCO). The WCO now oversees the implementation of the Kyoto Convention.[84] Based in Brussels, the WCO is virtually the sole international body concerned with the harmonisation of technical customs rules and practices.

The Kyoto Convention is an unusual international agreement.[85] The Convention is composed of two Parts. Part I consists of the Convention itself. Part II comprises numerous Annexes, which contain the basic substantive rules. Each Annex usually consists of an introductory summary, definitions of terms, standards, recommended practices, and notes. According to the terms of the Convention,[86] standards are those provisions the general application of which is recognised as necessary for the achievement of harmonisation and simplification of customs procedures. Recommended practices are those provisions which are recognised as constituting progress toward the harmonisation and the simplification of customs procedures, the widest possible application of which is considered to be desirable. Notes indicate some of the possible courses of action to be followed in applying the standard or recommended practice concerned. The number of annexes is not fixed once-and-for-all. Existing annexes may be amended, and new annexes may be added.

The Convention is open to signature by any state Member of the Council and any state Member of the United Nations or its specialised agencies.[87] A state may become a contracting party by signing the Convention without instrument of ratification, by depositing an instrument of ratification after signing it subject to ratification, or by acceding to it.[88] A state which does so must specify which annexes it accepts, and is required to accept at least one annex.[89] A contracting party

---

81 Cmnd 5938.
82 The full text is available on the Internet homepage of the World Customs Organisation at www.wcoomd.org.
83 22 UST 320, TIAS No 7063, 157 UNTS 129. After the Second World War various European governments, drawing on work previously accomplished under the auspices of the League of Nations, formed in Brussels a European Customs Union Study Group, including a Customs Committee. This led in turn to the Convention establishing a Customs Co-operation Council; the Convention was signed in Brussels on 15 December 1950 and entered into force on 4 November 1952.
84 See the WCO Internet homepage www.wcoomd.org. The following three paragraphs are based on the WCO Internet homepage at www.wcoomd.org; McGovern, E, *International Trade Regulation: GATT, the United States and the European Community* (2nd edn, 1986) pp 45–47, 150–151; Jackson, J H, Davey, W J, and Sykes, A O, *Legal Problems of International Economic Relations: Cases, Materials and Text on the National and International Regulation of Transnational Economic Relations* (3rd edn, 1995) p 394; Lasok, D, *The Trade and Customs Law of the European Union* (3rd edn, 1998) pp 237–238, 277–278.
85 Here we are concerned with the 1973 Convention, since the 1999 revised Convention has not yet been ratified by all members. References to the Kyoto Convention in the following paragraphs are therefore made to the 1973 Convention. The 1999 revised Convention is broadly similar in structure, but not identical. The 1999 Convention contains slightly different Annexes and adds a new Specific Annex H on Offences.
86 Kyoto Convention, art 4.
87 Kyoto Convention, art 11 (1).
88 Kyoto Convention, art 11 (2).
89 Kyoto Convention, art 11 (4).

which accepts an annex is deemed to accept all the standards and recommended practices in it unless it enters reservations in respect of particular standards or recommended practices, stating the differences between its national legislative provisions and the provisions of the standards or recommended practices in question.[90] States are not permitted to enter reservations against definitions. The Convention does not preclude the application of prohibitions or restrictions imposed under national legislation.[91] At least once every three years, each contracting party bound by an annex is required to review the standards and recommended practices against which it has entered reservations and notify the Secretary General of the Customs Co-operation Council of the results of the review.[92]

The 1973 Kyoto Convention had approximately 30 contracting parties; the number has increased to 114 for the 1999 revised Convention. For the present purposes, let us focus on the EC, its member states, the US and China in relation to the 1973 Convention, Annex E.6 on inward processing[93] Annex E.8 on outward processing, [94] and Annex F.1 on free zones.[95] As of 1 January 1993, all 15 EC member states had ratified the Convention, but not all have accepted all of these three Annexes.[96] The EC was a contracting party, since a customs union was entitled to be a contracting party if its member states are also parties. The EC had taken advantage of this provision; but it does not have the right to vote.[97] The EC had accepted Annexes E.6, E.8 and F.1, which entered into force for the EC on 26 September 1974. The US had ratified the Convention and had accepted Annex E.8 on outward processing and Annex F.1 on free zones, but not Annex E.6 on inward processing. China had ratified the Convention but had not accepted any of these three Annexes.

These legal provisions have encouraged and facilitated the geographical separation from production of invention, distribution and marketing in the international commodity chain in toys. Since the early 1980s, however, Chinese legislation, both central and local, on Special Economic Zones has also had a

---

90 Kyoto Convention, art 5 (1).
91 Kyoto Convention, art 3. This refers only to provisions of general application enacted either by the legislature or the executive and effective at the national level. However, it includes not only the standard exceptions but also restrictions imposed on economic or any other grounds: see the Commentary on Chapter II, art 3.
92 Kyoto Convention, art 5 (2).
93 Annex E.6 of the Convention concerns temporary admission for inward processing. It was adopted by the Permanent Technical Committee at its 81st/82nd sessions in October 1973. Subsequently, at its 83rd/84th sessions in March 1974, the Committee added a Note to Recommended Practice 43 (compensating products, or setting-off with equivalent goods). This Annex was incorporated into the Kyoto Convention by decision of the Council at its 43rd/44th Sessions held in Brussels on 10 June 1974. It entered into force on 6 December 1977, and, subject to certain reservations, it entered into force for the EEC on the same date.
94 Annex E.8 deals with temporary exportation for outward processing. It entered into force for the EEC, with certain reservations, on 20 April 1978.
95 Annex F.1 concerning free zones.
96 Annex E.6 on inward processing has been accepted by all EC member states except Greece, Luxembourg, Portugal and Sweden. Annex E.8 on outward processing has been accepted by Denmark, France, Germany Ireland, Italy, Netherlands, Spain, and the UK, but not by Austria, Belgium, Finland, Greece, Luxembourg, Portugal and Sweden. Annex F.1 on free zones has been accepted by Austria, Denmark, Finland, France, Ireland, Italy, Luxembourg, Netherlands, Portugal, Spain and the UK, but not by Belgium, Germany, Greece and Sweden.
97 See Kyoto Convention, art 11 (7).

direct influence on the concentration of production facilities.[98] Chinese laws on foreign direct investment (FDI), imports and exports, taxation, and labour are of special importance. Most toy factories in China are located in the Shenzhen SEZ. Shenzhen rules on FDI provide for Chinese-foreign joint ventures, Chinese-foreign contractual joint ventures, wholly foreign-owned enterprises, international leasing, compensation trade and processing and assembling with materials and parts from foreign suppliers.[99] Recently, however, the fact that labour costs in Shenzhen are higher than in the rest of Guandong Province, due partly to law, has encouraged toy companies to establish outside the SEZ, though still in Guandong.[100]

In fact, however, this part of south China belongs to a wider economic area which includes Hong Kong.[101] Toy factories enjoy very close links with entrepreneurs in Hong Kong and often are part of Hong Kong companies. Production, distribution, quasi-political activities such as participation in trade associations, and often personal or family relations, are closely intertwined.[102] Chinese companies, such as Early Light in the Shenzhen Special Economic Zone,[103] produce toys on outsourcing contracts for the world's biggest toy companies, not only Mattel but also Hasbro, Fisher-Price and Ertl from the US and Bandai and Tomy from Japan. These contracts are often arranged and managed by Hong Kong-based entrepreneurs, who, in addition to their role as middlemen, sometimes run their own toy-manufacturing company in China and are also prominent in the main Hong Kong sectoral trade association, Hong Kong Toys Council.[104] More than half of China's toy production is re-exported through Hong Kong.[105] To the extent that power in the toy chain lies in Asia, it is based in

98 See Park (1997).
99 For an introduction, see the Shenzhen SEZ Internet homepage at http://china-window.com/Shenzhen-w/shenzhen.html.
100 Interview, Guangzhou and Shenzhen. It was reported that, as of 1996, the *Barbie* doll factories in China were the Meitei factory in Dongguan and the Zongmei toy factory in Nanhai, both in Guandong Province but outside the Shenzhen SEZ: cf Tempest, 'Barbie and the World Economy' Los Angeles Times World Report [A Special Section Produced in Co-operation with the Korea Times], 13 October, at 3. In 1998, 800 small toy factories closed in Dongguan: 'Chinese Toy Making' (1998) The Economist, December 19, 95–99 at 98. This did not include *Barbie* doll factories.
101 See Willem van Kemenade, *China, Hong Kong, Taiwan, Inc.: The Dynamics of a New Empire* (1997).
102 See, for example, J Smart and A Smart 'Personal Relations and Divergent Economies: A Case Study of Hong Kong Investment in South China' (1991) 15 Int J Urban and Regional Research 216–233.
103 For a brief historical sketch, see 'The tycoon' (1998) The Economist, December 19, at 99. As of 1993, most of the 2,500 registered foreign-funded businesses in the Shenzhen SEZ were small processing and assembly operators from Hong Kong: see G T Crane, 'Reform and Retrenchment in China's Special Economic Zones', in Joint Economic Committee, Congress of the United States (ed), *China's Dilemma's in the 1990s: The Problems of Reforms, Modernization, and Interdependence* (1993) pp 841–857 at 845.
104 As of October 1996, the chairman of the Hong Kong Toys Council was Edmund K S Young, executive vice-president of Perfekta Enterprises Ltd, a leading Hong Kong toy manufacturer: 'Barbie and the World Economy' (1996) Los Angeles Times World Report, October 13, 1996, at 3. In January 1995 Mr Young was described as chairman of Perfekta and vice-chairman of the Hong Kong Toy Council: see (1995) Journal of Commerce, January. As of December 1998, the chairman was T S Wong, head of Jetta, a large toy maker in China: see 'Chinese Toy Making: Where the Furbies come from' (1998) The Economist, December 19, 95–99 at 99. See also Hong Kong Toys Council, Federation of Hong Kong Industries, Members Directory 1999.
105 BBC Monitoring Service: Asia Pacific, 14 June 1995, cited in Newton and Tse (1999) at 154. See also Hong Kong Trade Development Council (1999).

Hong Kong.[106] For this reason, as well as to preserve maximum flexibility in a highly innovative and rapidly changing market, the production of toys for the export market usually takes place in wholly owned subsidiaries rather than joint ventures.[107]

Multiple memberships

A striking contemporary example of multiple memberships is the expansion of major toy companies into other related but distinct sectors, such as television, cinema and the Internet. *Tickle Me Elmo* was heavily marketed during the 1996 Christmas season by Tyco Toys (since acquired by Mattel). It was invented by Ron Dubren of New York and Greg Hyman of Florida. Tyco, according to the inventors, recognised the key ingredient and did the packaging and marketing of their product. For their work, the inventors obtained royalties of somewhat less than 5% of the manufacturer's revenue. The largest share of the royalties went to Children's Television Workshop, which owned the licence.[108]

Property

The highest barriers to entry in buyer-driven commodity chains typically concern product conception, design and marketing. Branding is a key marketing strategy. Consequently, intellectual property law is of crucial significance. Whether under US or EU law, or various national laws or via the WTO TRIPS Agreement, it helps to determine the number of buyers and maintain their market power. In other words, it creates or consolidates barriers to entry.

To give but one example, a number of intellectual property cases have been brought by international buyers in Hong Kong courts. For instance, Mattel, the manufacturer of *Barbie* dolls, sued Tonka Corporation in the Hong Kong High Court in 1991 for infringement of copyright. It alleged that the defendant's *Miss America* dolls copied the *Barbie* doll's head sculpture and that its packaging infringed registered trade marks by stating that the *Miss America* doll's clothes also fit the *Barbie* doll.[109] On the whole, the Hong Kong courts have been favourable to such claims; this is to be expected, since protection of intellectual property is crucial to the legitimacy of Hong Kong from the standpoint of strategic actors and its continued role as a site within the framework of global legal pluralism.[110]

Labour

With respect to labour in the process of production, the labour law of nation-states is not the only relevant law or, in the case of China, even the most important.

---

106 In particular because of the location of branch offices, ownership of local intermediaries and the provision of services.
107 See Newton and Tse (1999) at 149–156; E Tsui 'Marketing Strategies of the Toy Industry in Hong Kong', unpublished MBA dissertation (1988) University of Hong Kong. As of 1995, OEM, including products made in mainland China, accounted for 75–80% of Hong Kong toy sales: see (1995) Journal of Commerce, January 13.
108 Balog 'The untold toy success story: Elmo's evolution is a surprise to those involved' (1996) USA Today, December 11, at 1B.
109 *Mattel Inc v Tonka Corpn* [1991] 2 HKC 411.
110 The writer is grateful to Tom Heller for this point. For other examples regarding the Hong Kong courts, see 'Governing Economic Globalisation: European Law and Global Legal Pluralism' (1999) 5 ELJ 143.

For example, when Mattel acquired Tyco, analysts said that most of the layoffs would come from outside the US, where Tyco had most of its operations.[111] The externalities of the acquisition by one US company of another thus occurred mainly in China, where the applicable labour laws for such factories differed radically from those in the US. In fact, one empirical study of factory regimes in Shenzhen and Hong Kong, albeit in the electronics rather than the toy sector, concluded that the state was much less significant than the social organisation of the labour market as a factor of control of labour and constraint on management.[112]

The codes of conduct elaborated under the aegis of multinational companies and sector-specific trade associations may be much more important in practice than formal national or local legislation. The large toy companies, retailers and trade associations have all adopted sector-specific codes of conduct which are imposed upon or recommended to their factories. Such codes of conduct have been described as 'typically book-sized documents that specify working conditions down to the dimensions of the medical boxes on the wall', and as 'changing China's toy industry more than anything else'.[113]

One example is the Code of Business Practices of the International Council of Toy Industries (ICTI). ICTI was established in 1974 and incorporated under the law of New York. It is an association of toy associations, embracing manufacturers and marketers. Its members, as of February 1999, comprised the toy associations of Hong Kong, China, the US, Japan, Denmark, France, Italy, Spain, Sweden and the UK, as well as Argentina, Australia, Brazil, Canada, Hungary, Korea, Mexico, Philippines, Taiwan and Thailand. The general management functions of ICTI are performed by a president and a secretary, both positions are currently held by the Toy Manufacturers of America. The official language of ICTI is English.

The ICTI Code of Business Practices, which was revised and approved on 1 June 1998, is a voluntary code of conduct containing specific operating conditions which members are expected to meet, for which members are expected to obtain contractor adherence in advance, and to which supply agreements with firms manufacturing on behalf of ICTI members are expected to provide for adherence. The operating conditions refer to labour practices and the workplace. As with other codes, it borrows from core labour rights set out in International Labour Organisation (ILO) conventions, though it omits certain other rights from other ILO conventions, such as the right to organise, collective bargaining and freedom of association.[114] The purpose of the Code is to establish a standard of performance, to educate and to encourage commitment, not to punish. The ICTI Code of Conduct makes elaborate provision for enforcement by the companies through contract. ICTI member companies are expected to evaluate their own facilities, as well as those of their contractors, and request that the latter follow the same with sub-contractors. An annual statement of compliance with the Code must be signed by an officer of each manufacturing company or contractor. According to the Code, contracts for toy

111 Madore 'Mattel confident Tyco deal will pass antitrust scrutiny' (1996) The Buffalo News, November 19.
112 Lee (1997) pp 115–142.
113 (1998) The Economist, December 19, 95–99 at 99.
114 For a comparison of provisions in four major codes of labour practice with the provisions of ILO conventions, see 'A Comparison of Provisions in Base Codes of Labour Practice', available on the website of the Maquiladora Solidarity Network at www.web.net/~msn/3codeslg.htm. The four codes in question are the Code of Labour Practices for the Apparel Industry Including Sportswear (the Netherlands), the Ethical Trading Initiative (UK), SA8000 (US and UK) and the Fair Labor Association Workplace Code of Conduct (US).

manufacture should provide that a material failure to comply with the Code, or to implement a corrective action plan on a timely basis, is a breach of contract for which the contract may be cancelled. Annexes to the Code provide guidelines for determining compliance; their applicability is to be determined by a rule of reason.[115]

These codes have been adopted mainly as a result of pressure from non-governmental organisations (NGOs). For example, the Coalition for the Safe Production of Toys (Toy Coalition) has been instrumental in getting codes of conduct on labour practices adopted by associations of toy manufacturers and companies. The Toy Coalition was started in 1994 by several Thai and Hong Kong groups in response to disastrous fires in several toy factories in Thailand and China.[116] In its campaign, The Toy Coalition campaign was joined by other NGOs, including the World Development Movement (UK), ICFTU, AFL-CIO (US), Trocaire (Ireland), Italian organisations, Workers Party (France), Asia Pacific Workers Solidarity Links, PSPD (Korea), Japan Citizens' Liaison Committee for the Safe Production of Toys (Japan), Indonesian groups, and the Maquila Solidarity Network (Canada).[117] This worldwide network links NGOs in Europe, the US, Asia and other parts of the world. It thus mirrors, to some extent, multinational corporations, and affects conditions and helps to create the norms which are imposed by them.[118]

Despite their political origins, these codes of conduct reflect the organisation of power in the global toy commodity chain in three different respects. First, precisely because the dominant buyers are few in number, they are unusually susceptible to political pressure. Second, the dominant buyers, whose power rests on their control of brands and marketing, are able in effect to determine the content of industry-wide codes of conduct and then to impose them on their suppliers, at least contractually if not always in practice. Third, power struggles within the chain occur latently and sometimes overtly between buyers and original equipment manufacturers. The main US buyers use soft law codes as a way of ensuring their dominance over Hong Kong OEM and Chinese producers; the latter struggle to develop their own ideas and designs, potentially protected by state or WTO intellectual property law, in order to break out of their dependence on foreign buyers and foreign market niches.[119] Conflicts between strategic actors

---

115   This description is based on the ICTI Internet homepage at www.toy-icti.org. The ICTI Code of Business Practices can be found at www.toy-icti.org./mission/bizpractice.htm.

116   The reasons for the establishment of the Coalition and its demands for a Charter on the Safe Production of Toys are described in: Human Rights for Workers: Special Campaigns, 'Our Children Don't Need Blood-Stained Toys', available at www.senser.com/campaign.htm.

117   Asian Labour Update, 19 February 1999, homepage at www.freeway.org.hk/amrc/alu.html. For example, the Maquiladora Solidarity Network, based in Toronto, Canada, promotes solidarity with groups in Mexico, Central America and Asia organising in maquiladora factories and export processing zones to improve working conditions. Its campaigns include The International Toy Campaign. See its website at www.web.net/~msn.

118   For further discussion, see Trubek, Mosher and Rothstein (1999).

119   Cf (1995) Journal of Commerce, January 13. Conflicts are inherent in this relationship: see *Kader Industrial Co Ltd v Galco International Toys NV* [1992] 1 HKC 36; *Galco International Toys NV v Kader Industrial Co Ltd* [1996] HKLY 260. Nor is the relationship free from abuse: in 1996 a senior manager with Mattel Toy Vendor Operations Ltd was convicted in Hong Kong for soliciting and accepting rewards based on the value of turnover between his employer and a Taiwan textile manufacturer: see *A-G v Leung Kin Wai* [1996] HKC 588. Even apparently straightforward international transactions are not free from risk: see *Toymax (HK) Ltd v Redsmith International Ltd* [1994] 1 HKC 714 (holding that signing an order form by adding the words 'as agent for overseas buyer' was sufficient to indicate that no personal liability was assumed by the agent and dismissing plaintiff's claim that defendant was liable for the contractual default by an associated company).

thus involve normative conflicts, not in the sense of conflicting laws potentially applicable to a single, one-off dispute about legally determined facts, but rather in the sense of alternative normative frameworks governing the more long-term relationship between strategic actors.

Based partly on the ICTI example, the Hong Kong Toys Council (HKTC) introduced a Code of Practice for the Toy Industry in July 1997. Although not legally binding, it serves as a reference, educational and promotional device for its members.[120] In fact, however, it is not clear whether it (or another such code) is widely adopted; if adopted, whether it is enforced; or even what enforcement and compliance might mean given that the Code is not legally binding and sanctions for non-compliance are inadequate. It may be hypothesised that such codes have been adopted by and apply more effectively in practice in joint venture between Chinese and western companies or in factories which produce for multinational buyers. It may also be hypothesised that codes of conduct may have little, if any, effect in factories which are wholly locally owned or produce entirely for local markets. But such a simple hypothesis, that the market for norms reflects the market for toys, is given the lie by the fact that even some companies which produce for multinational buyers evaluate the code of conduct recommended by the HKTC and the US buyer as a cost of doing business and decide not to adopt it. They consider to the extent that the items specified in a code of conduct are already dealt with by the US buyer in its specifications to the extent that they are required for marketing the product in the US.[121] But even if a factory has a code of conduct, effective implementation and monitoring thus remain crucial issues.[122]

Links within a chain

In buyer-driven commodity chains, such as that for toys, it is the downstream service activities of marketing and distribution which co-ordinate and drive the chain as a whole.[123] Hence the importance of the Internet, both as a tool for

---

120 'Hong Kong's Toy Industry', *Hong Kong & China Economics*, on the Internet homepage of the Hong Kong Trade Development Council, available at www.tdc.org.hk/main/industries/t2-2-39.htm, last updated 2 July 1998.

121 Interviews, Guangzhou and Shenzhen.

122 A 1996 case study of a Chinese toy manufacturer's code of conduct concluded that the code did not provide for effective implementation, failed to reflect basic international labour standards, in particular concerning freedom of association, and lacked an independent monitoring device: see J Murray, 'Corporate Codes of Conduct and Labour Standards' (International Labour Organisation, Bureau for Workers' Activities [ACTRAV], Working Paper 1996) available on the Internet at www.ilo.org/public/english/230actra/publ/codes.htm. See also J Porges, 'Codes of Conduct', on the homepage of Asian Labour as of 19 February 1999. See also various issues of the *Human Rights for Workers Bulletin* at www.senser.com/b21.htm. As of 1998, the Irish NGO Trocaire concluded that child labour was not a significant issue in China, because of the existence of a large pool of unemployed workers and low wages for women. In its view, the main problem was the working conditions of women. See Trocaire, 'Conditions for Toy Workers', available at www.trocaire.org/toy3.html. On the extent of child labour in Chinese toy factories in the mid-1990s, see 'By the Sweat and Toil of Children: A Report to Congress' (Bureau of International Affairs, US Department of Labor, July 15, 1994) available at www.dol.gov/dol/ilab/public/media/reports/sweat/main.htm; 'Statistics on Child Workers in China', (1996) China Labour Bulletin, n 25, April at www.citinv.it/associazioni/CNMS/archivio/paesi/statistisc.html; and C K Wai, 'Child Labor in China (Change HKCIC-June 1996)' at www.citinv.it/associazioni/CNMS/archivio/lavoro/childlab.html.

123 Rabach and Kim (1994) p 137.

managing and co-ordinating the different sites and also as a form of retailing. Invention, design and marketing tend to be more easily integrated in buyer-driven commodity chains than in producer-driven commodity chains.[124] The conception of toys, intellectual property in brands, and control of marketing and distribution, now particularly via the Internet, are therefore boxes of the chain in which competition is most fierce and attention to law most acute.[125] In other words, the international commodity chain in toys, as with other goods, now depends fundamentally on intellectual property, contract and the provision of services, including legal services.

The major toy companies have spread like a web and onto the Web. The relative lack of regulation of Internet retailing lowers barriers to entry into the retail market. When buyers are squeezed by traditional retailers, they turn without great difficulty to the Internet in order to enter the retail sector themselves, through either their own websites or specialist Internet retailers. Mattel, for instance, has expanded into more high-tech toys and e-commerce.[126] To lesson its dependence on a few powerful traditional retailers, it linked up with the Internet retailer eToys Inc,[127] from Santa Monica, California. Mattel announced a goal of direct-to-consumer sales of $1bn per year, including catalogues and Internet sales, some from Mattel's own website and some from on-line retailers such as eToys. In 1998 total toy retail sales were $23bn, with eToys accounting for only $23.9m.

Connections between economic relations and specific sites

The lack of congruence between governance, economic processes and territory can be illustrated by two examples. The first concerns EC environmental and health legislation. The environmental pressure group Greenpeace put pressure on EU institutions and national governments to ban all toys containing phthalates, an additive used to soften PVC products. As yet, however, no such EU legislation has been enacted. Nevertheless, the risk that such legislation might be enacted in the future has already changed the practices of some toy factories in China. Some factories consider it the major issue confronting Chinese exports of toys to the EU. Their international buyers instructed them to substitute hard plastic for PVC.[128] Some individual EU member states have already banned imports of toys containing PVC or certain other substances, and these measures have affected toy production in Hong Kong and China.[129] In the US, the main buyers stopped using phthalates in certain baby products in early 1999, even though, as in the

---

124 Rabach and Kim.
125 On the growing importance of the Internet for toy distribution, see for example Anders and Bannon (1999) at B1; Davidson 'Net retailer eToys faces big risks as its star rises' (1999) USA Today, 8 April, at B.1; Pollack 'Makeover at Barbie's: Mattel Sheds Jobs and Looks to the Internet', (1999) International Herald Tribune, 17–18 April, at 9; Edgecliffe-Johnson 'Net gains take precedence over bricks and mortar' (1999) Financial Times, 28–29 August, at 25.
126 See the outline history of Mattel in Leibovich and Stoughton 'When keeping us isn't child's play; Mattel to acquire Learning Co. as industry pursues digitally savvy children' (1998) Washington Post, December, at D01.
127 The web page of eToys Inc is available at www.etoys.com.
128 Interviews in Guangzhou and Shenzhen Special Economic Zone, China.
129 See Hong Kong Trade Development Council, Research Department *Practical Guide to Exporting Toys for Hong Kong Traders* (March 1999) p 51.

EU, there is no legislation prohibiting it; these business decisions will inevitably affect toy production in China.[130]

A second example refers to toy safety. It exemplifies the interaction and potential incompatibility of norms, institutions and processes from two geographically discrete sites. The EC 'toys directive'[131] provides that all toys sold in the EU must meet essential safety requirements and bear a 'CE' mark indicating conformity. It was revised in 1996 to be similar to current US requirements,[132] perhaps indicating progress towards mutual recognition and standardisation on toy safety requirements.[133] Such requirements condition Chinese production of toys for export to Europe and the conduct of inspections in Hong Kong. But EU and US safety standards are not the only ones which apply to the marketing of toys produced in Hong Kong and China. In May 1998, the Swedish company Ikea was reported to be facing prosecution in Hong Kong for selling in Hong Kong a toy that caused the death of a boy in Europe; the toy met EU safety requirements but did not meet the more stringent specifications of the Hong Kong Toys and Children's Products Safety Ordinance.[134]

Relations between sites and the chain as a whole

The relations between a specific site and the chain as a whole may take several forms. A simple case, from the theoretical standpoint, is that of a single site that might claim, actually or potentially, to govern the chain as a whole. The GATT/WTO was a crucial conditioning element in the negotiation of the EU quota on toys from China in 1993–94 and the related litigation between 1994–98. The WTO also casts a long shadow with regard to future disputes, notably by holding out, to China and multinational companies 'located' there, the promise of new institutions, norms and processes which would be available on eventual Chinese accession. When China joins the GATT, the firms located there will benefit from Article XI GATT concerning the general elimination of quantitative restrictions. The provision of services and the protection of intellectual property in brand names are likely to be affected by the eventual application of GATS and TRIPS. Companies are already positioning themselves in anticipation of further opening up of China's domestic market to imported toys and foreign toy retailers. One has only to note that in 1997, the same year it purchased a major competitor, Tyco, Mattel launched the *Barbie* doll in China.[135]

130 See Hong Kong Trade Development Council, Research Department 'Review and Outlook of Hong Kong's Toy Exports' (1999) Trade Watch, April, at 6.
131 Council Directive (E 88/378, as amended).
132 EN 71, OJ C190 21.6.97. A complete list of European standards concerning toy safety is available at www2.echo.lu/nasd/dckbl-3.html. See also Hong Kong Industry Department, Quality Services Division 'Health and Safety Standards Circular No. 1/97: International: Toy Safety Standards' (20 January 1997) available at www.info.gov.hk/id/psis/hssc/hssc0197.htm.
133 See Hong Kong Trade Development Council (1998) at 7.
134 Pegg 'Ikea faces threat of illegal toy charges', (1999) South China Morning Post, 12 May, at 3. On the Ordinance, enacted in 1992 as 'a substantial departure from the previous reluctance of government to become involved in this area', see Cottrell 'Product Liability', in Shane Nossal (ed), *Law Lectures for Practitioners 1993* (1993) pp 72–85.
135 See the history of Mattel on the company Internet homepage at www.snc.edu/baad/ba485/spr1998/group8/history.htm.

These examples do not, of course, mean that the WTO is the only site governing international trade. Nor does it necessarily mean that, from a sociological as distinct from a positivist law standpoint, international trade law norms are arranged in a hierarchical fashion, or that the WTO stands at the apex of an institutional and normative hierarchy. The examples do indicate, however, that the WTO affects many aspects of the global commodity chain in toys, perhaps more aspects than any other site. This, in turn, provides a social, economic, political and cultural basis for the WTO's claim *qua* institution to have a dominant position in international trade law, though not necessarily global law generally. It also tends to aliment institutional and often individual support for the argument that international trade law is hierarchical in nature, with the WTO site at the top. Seen sociologically, such developments are processes, not yet acquired positions or states of affairs.

Another case is empirically more frequent, and poses different, and perhaps more complex, issues from the standpoint of a theory of global legal pluralism. This is the case of a single site whose institutions, norms and dispute resolution processes integrate as part of its operation the results – for example the norms – of some/many/all other sites pertinent to the chain. We can describe this as a complex example of a 'structural set', which is 'formed through the mutual convertibility of rules and resources in one domain of action into those pertaining to another'.[136]

For instance, the ECJ in 1998 decided the cases brought by the UK and Spain in 1994 against quotas on imports of toys from China. I focus here on the UK case;[137] the result in the Spanish case was the same in terms of positive law. The ECJ followed its previous case law in concluding that, when assessing complex economic situations, the Council enjoyed substantial discretion, including making findings of fact,[138] and that the exercise of this discretion was subject only to limited judicial review.[139] Similarly, in adopting new Community rules the Council was required to take account only of the general interests of the Community as a whole.[140] In other words, the judiciary will not substitute its evaluation of the facts for that of the legislator, unless the legislator's assessment appears manifestly incorrect in the light of the information available to it at the time of the adoption of the rules.[141] The ECJ therefore dismissed the UK's application for annulment.

These decisions were taken more than four years after the cases were brought, and more than two years after the Advocate General's Opinion.[142] In accordance

---

136   Anthony Giddens (1989) pp 253–259, at 259. For another example, see Francis Snyder, 'Soft Law and Institutional Practice in the European Community', in Stephen Martin (ed), *The Construction of Europe: Essays in Honour of Emile Noël* (1994) pp 197–225.
137   Case C-150/94 *United Kingdom of Great Britain and Northern Ireland v Council of the European Union* [1998] ECR I-7235.
138   Case C-150/94 *United Kingdom of Great Britain and Northern Ireland v Council of the European Union* [1998] ECR I-7235, para 55.
139   See Case C-150/94 *United Kingdom of Great Britain and Northern Ireland v Council of the European Union* [1998] ECR I-7235, para 54.
140   Case C-150/94 *United Kingdom of Great Britain and Northern Ireland v Council of the European Union* [1998] ECR I-7325, para 62.
141   Case C-150/94 *United Kingdom of Great Britain and Northern Ireland v Council of the European Union* [1998] ECR I-7325, para 87.
142   The Opinion of the Advocate General was heard at the sitting of the court on 26 September 1996: see Case C-150/94 *United Kingdom of Great Britain and Northern Ireland v Council of the European Union* [1998] ECR I-7235; Case C-284/94, *Kingdom of Spain v Council of the European Union* [1998] ECR I-7309. The Council was supported by the Commission.

with ECJ practice, the judgment was unanimous, but the length of time taken to reach it suggests that the form of unanimity masked the substance of deep disagreement. I suggest that we can best understand the ECJ judgment as a double-order compromise. First, among the judges themselves: the judgment represented a delicate compromise, articulated in the form of a unanimous judgment, among the judges themselves. Second, among the EU institutions: the judgment, the result of judicial negotiation, protected the integrity of a prior legislative compromise, itself expressed in the form of a complex regulation. This second-order compromise served to ensure the discreteness and integrity of the EC political process and to insulate it to some extent from the judicial process. A member state, or other strategic actor, could not use litigation to upset or revise the results of complex political negotiations regarding external trade.

This double-order compromise was - and is - intimately bound up with the definition of EU rules for the globalisation game. These rules concern relations between strategic actors, relations between strategic actors and governance structures, and relations between different governance structures. But the ECJ did not address these issues directly. Instead, its judgment dealt with them indirectly, by emphasising the importance of judicial restraint in the face of politically sensitive Council legislation. Nevertheless, it had wider consequences. It ensured to some extent the integrity of the EU political process, insulating it from collateral attack by means of judicial review. It maintained a political space, structured to some extent by objective interests, populated by conflicts among subjective interests, and involving member states, firms, trade associations and EU institutions. This space was a political market, in which the EU economic market for toys, structured by the global toy commodity chain, was inter-penetrated with the EU political market, with a supply of and demand for economic regulation and regulatory law. Both of these markets, at least in the UK case, were characterised by what Weber called the factual 'autonomy' of the propertied classes,[143] that is, an asymmetry of property, information, power, and influence upon the member states and thus the EU legislator. The double-order compromise of the ECJ judgment tended to insulate and enhance the integrity of this political space and strengthen its market-oriented normative order. It is important to note, however, that 'market-oriented' does not necessarily mean 'free-market-oriented', but rather that decisions by strategic market actors play an extremely important part.

The ECJ judgment thus occurred in a highly political context, and in fact was highly political. Its main importance did not lie, however, in a short-term economic impact. A judgment either way would probably have had only marginal financial effects on the distribution of resources among EU importers, producers, retailers or others that lost or gained as a result of the existence of quotas between the adoption of the regulation and the date of the judgment. The primary significance of the judgment lay in articulating legal principles for the future and in its broader implications for the relationship between EU law and other institutional, normative and processual sites.

The legal principles concerned the role of the EC legislator in dealing with foreign trade and inter-institutional relations within the EU, in particular between the Council and the ECJ. Their broader implications referred to how much

---

143 *Max Weber on Law in Economy and Society* (Max Rheinstein, ed) [translated by Edward Shils] (1966) p 146.

impact the international commodity chain could have in influencing EC legislation, both by means of its structural position and by direct and indirect pressure on national governments, the Commission and the Council. They also concerned the role played by EU law as part of global legal pluralism. The ECJ judgment sanctioned the integrity of the EU political process and thus the political and law-creating salience of market structure. It thus inserted global legal pluralism into EU law and EU law into global legal pluralism. On the one hand, it imported into EU law the institutions, norms and processes of other global sites, for example, regarding US intellectual property law or the organisation of toy production in the Chinese SEZ of Shenzhen. The latter were incorporated into EU economic, political and legal relations, not just as costs of international or local firms in the EU toy sector, but also as elements which contribute to create, consolidate or structure these relations and thus are an integral part of them. The ECJ judgment incorporated into the realm of EU law the norms produced by institutions and processes in other sites of global legal pluralism, in the manner of invisible legal transplants. On the other hand, the norms produced by the Council and the ECJ in EU legislative and judicial processes became part of the structure of the global commodity chain in toys. They conditioned, shaped and were integral to the decision-making calculus of strategic actors, including governments and firms, in this specific global economic network.

CONCLUSION

It has been argued in this chapter that globalisation is governed by the totality of strategically determined, situationally specific and often episodic conjunctions of a multiplicity of institutional, normative and processual sites throughout the world. The totality of such sites represents a new global form of legal pluralism.

The development of the global economic relations involved in the international toy industry owes much to corporate strategies. Such a view is consistent with the approach taken here, which privileges the perspective of strategic actors. But these strategies themselves have been pursued taking account of the framework of the law and other normative frameworks, and have been elaborated by using them. They take place, are conditioned by and have contributed to the development of global legal pluralism. To put it more accurately, the development of global networks in the toy industry has occurred in conjunction with the development of a variety of structural sites throughout the world, each of which comprises institutions, norms and dispute resolution processes.

One facet of this argument deserves special emphasis. Not only have strategic actors used the law and been shaped by it; they have also been absolutely fundamental in determining which institutional, normative and processual sites have seen the light of day, which have flourished and developed, and which have withered and even died for lack of clients. They have also influenced profoundly the development of sites, so that some have taken on more or less judicial and legal characteristics, while others have not.[144] These strategic actors include governments, businesses, other organisations and sometimes even individuals.

---

144 Though of course these strategic actors are not the only cause of judicialisation and legalisation.

Given their significance for the development of institutions, the production of norms and the functioning of dispute resolution processes, it is surprising that legal scholarship, even in the broadest sense, has given the standpoint of strategic actors relatively little attention.[145] Legal scholarship, except perhaps in the US, usually focuses exclusively on institutions and seeks to reconstruct the system, if any, in which these institutions are embedded. Such a systemic perspective is useful in tracing the elaboration of legal doctrine. This writer would argue, however, that it is not the most fruitful if our aim is to understand how legal institutions and other institutional, normative and processual sites are created, develop, and operate in practice.

Taken together, the different but interwoven sets of institutions, norms and dispute resolution processes that comprise global legal pluralism amount to a novel regime for governing global economic networks. They are, however, less a structure of multi-level governance than a conjunction of distinctive institutional and normative sites for the production, implementation and sanctioning of rules. In the specific case of the toy industry, they testify, in part, to the structure of authority and power within these inter-firm and intra-firm networks, which are characterised by a buyer-driven, rather than a producer-driven, governance structure. These new normative forms for governing global economic networks are among the reasons why the US, EU, and Chinese firms and economies are so intimately linked in the internationalised production and distribution relations which are characteristic of globalisation.

From this discussion we can derive several more specific hypotheses.

First, global legal pluralism is a way of describing the structure of the sites taken as a whole. Seen from the perspective of a specific global commodity chain, global legal pluralism may be described as a network, even if some segments of the network may be occupied alternatively by two or more possible sites.

Second, the sites of global legal pluralism may be classified provisionally into two loose categories. Some sites are market-based, being generated by economic actors as part of economic processes. Some are polity-based, in that they form a part of established political structures; this includes sites which are convention-based, deriving from agreements between governments. This classification scheme distinguishes between different types of sites according to their mode of creation.

Third, the various sites differ in decision-making structure, that is, in their institutions, norms and processes. They vary in the extent to which their institutions, norms and processes are inserted in a hierarchy. They may differ in their reliance on case law, the use of precedent and the binding force of norms and decisions: in other words, in respect of those characteristics which are often associated with law. These factors affect the outcomes of the various sites, including the different ways in which they allocate risk. At the same time, however, it is important not to overlook the extent to which sites are interrelated, for example, in relation to institutional arrangements such as jurisdiction, copying or borrowing of norms, and the interconnection of their dispute-resolution processes.

Fourth, the sites are not all equally vulnerable to economic or political pressures. It is going too far to say that the network of global legal pluralism

---

145 Except perhaps in legal anthropology: see Snyder, (1981) at 141–180; reprinted in revised and slightly different form in Thomas, P A (ed), *Legal Frontiers* (1996) pp 135–179. See also LeRoy (1999).

which is put into play by the economic processes of any specific global commodity chain reflects the structure of authority and power in the global commodity chain in question. Some types of institutions, some types of processes and some types of norms are more permeable to economic processes than others. It should also be noted that in cases of political conflict, for example between NGOs and multinational buyers in the international commodity chain in toys, the struggle between the competing groups is not limited to a single site. Each of the groups may invoke institutions, norms and processes of different sites. This may lead to wider conflicts between different sites, including conflicts of effectiveness and even of legitimacy.

Fifth, different sites may involve different legal cultures and sets of social relations, sometimes in relative isolation from historically different ones, but sometimes in complex hybrid forms.[146]

Sixth, specific sites are affected by conflicts between economic organisations occupying the same box in a global commodity chain. For example, conflicts over markets may pit foreign producers, exporters and importers, on the one hand, against domestic producers, on the other hand. Conflicts over markets also occur between companies occupying similar positions in the chain. The occupants of each of these segments try to enlist the norms, institutions and processes of the various sites of global legal pluralism to improve their position, not only vis-à-vis their direct competitors but also in relation to the occupants of other segments of the global commodity chain. These conflicts involve and have important implications for sites. The most well-known example is the production of case law and the development of legal doctrine. We need to pay more attention to how such conflicts arise, unfold, and are resolved because they are often crucial determinants of the developmental paths of the institutions, norms, and processes of various sites.

Seventh, these sites are not always, or even usually, alternatives in dispute resolution, as might be expected if one presumes that the norms governing global economic networks are ordered in a hierarchical arrangement. Instead, each site deals with, governs, or seeks to govern a discrete part of the global commodity chain. Once a chain is established, its activities are governed by a given set of rules, emanating from a variety of linked sites, except to the extent that normal conflicts of law rules, that is, private international law, allows firms a choice of governing legislation or a choice of dispute resolution.

Eighth, taken as a whole, the various sites are not all necessarily hierarchically ordered in relation to each other. Instead, they demonstrate many other types of interrelationships, sometimes hierarchical, sometimes not, sometimes competing, sometimes collaborative. In other words, even when viewed very broadly, they do not make up a legal system. This contrasts strongly with the usual lawyer's view of the multi-level governance of international economic relations. The latter is a normative view. This chapter has attempted to develop a more sociological perspective.

---

146   Jones (1994) at 195–221. For a useful caveat, see Clarke (1996) at 201–209. Differences in sites are likely to be influenced also by the fact that national structures remain very important for both trade policy and multinational corporate behaviour. On trade policy, see Garcia Molyneux (1999) and his *Domestic Structures and International Trade: The Unfair Trade Instruments of the United States and the European Union* (2000). On corporate behaviour, see Pauly and Reich (1997) at 1–30. Social and cultural differences will also certainly influence the practical implementation of any international competition rules: cf Pape 'Socio-Cultural Differences and International Competition Law' (1999) 5 ELJ 438.

These broad hypotheses need to be tested. In addition, numerous questions remain to be addressed by future research. For example, how are sites created?[147] How are they constituted, developed and legitimated as sites? Which sites have a specific geographical location, and if so, why? What determines the modes and organisation of dispute resolution? What decision processes are involved? Do sites vary in their resemblance to state law (insertion in a hierarchy, reliance on case law, binding decisions, use of precedent, etc), and why? To what extent do the norms of a particular site combine hard law and soft law? To what extent are sites interconnected, and how are they connected? How are groups, hierarchies and networks of sites created, and how if at all are such processes connected to economic and political relations? Do certain sites tend to converge or become more uniform in their institutional characteristics, norms, or dispute settlement processes, and why? How do conflicts between sites arise, what are the consequences of such competition, and how are conflicting institutional, normative, and processual claims handled? The answers to these questions will help us to understand further how globalisation is governed.

Select bibliography

Anders, G, and Bannon, L, (1999) 'Etoys to join web-retailer parade with IPO', Wall Street Journal, 6 April, at B1.

Borrus, M, and Zysman, J, (1998) 'Globalisation with Borders: The Rise of Wintelism as the Future of Industrial Competition' in J Zysman and A Schwartz (eds), *Enlarging Europe: The Industrial Foundations of a New Political Reality*, pp 27–59.

Casella, A, (1996) 'On Market Integration and the Development of Institutions: The Case of International Commercial Arbitration', 40 European Economic Review 155–186.

Clarke, D C, (1996) 'Methodologies for Research in Chinese Law', 30 U Br Col LR 201–209.

Crane, G T, (1993) 'Reform and Retrenchment in China's Special Economic Zones' in Joint Economic Committee, Congress of the United States (ed), *China's Dilemma's in the 1990s: The Problems of Reforms, Modernization, and Interdependence* (M E Sharpe), pp 841–857.

Cutler, A C, Haufler, V, and Porter, T (eds), (1999) *Private Authority and International Affairs.*

Commission of the European Communities, (1995) 'Report from the Commission to the Council on the surveillance measures and quantitative quotas applicable to certain non-textile products originating in the People's Republic of China', COM(95)614 final, Brussels, 6.12.95, p 41.

Dezalay, Y, and Garth, B G, (1996) *Dealing in Virtue: International Commercial Arbitration and the Construction of a Transnational Legal Order.*

---

147 For example, it has been argued that 'the construction of international issue networks and global policy arenas does not constitute a reduction of the scope of interstate politics but rather its pursuit by other means': Picciotto (1996–97) at 1037.

Economist, The, (1998) 'Chinese Toy Making: Where the Furbies come from', 19 December, 95–99 at 95.

Held, D, McGrew, A, Goldblatt, D, et al, (1999) *Global Transformations: Politics, Economics and Culture.*

Froebel, F, Heinrichs, J, and Kreye, O, (1980) *The New International Division of Labour: Structural Unemployment in Industrialised Countries and Industrialisation in Developing Countries* (trans P Burgress).

Gereffi, G, (1992) 'New Realities of Industrial Development in East Asia and Latin America: Global, Regional and National Trends', in R P Appelbaum and J Henderson (eds), *States and Development in the Asian Pacific Rim*, pp 85–112.

—(1994) 'The Organization of Buyer-Driven Global Commodity Chains: How U.S. Retailers Shape Overseas Production Networks' in G Gereffi and M Korzeniewicz (eds), *Commodity Chains and Global Capitalism*, pp 95–122.

—(1996a) 'Global Commodity Chains: New Forms of Coordination and Control among Nations and Firms in International Industries', 4 Competition & Change at 427–439.

—(1996b) 'Commodity Chains and Regional Divisions of Labor in East Asia', 12 J Asian Business 75–112.

Giddens, A, (1989) 'A Reply to My Critics' in D Held and J B Thompson *Social Theory of Modern Societies: Anthony Giddens and His Critics*, pp 253–259.

Hong Kong Trade Development Council, (1998) 'Hong Kong's Toy Industry', Hong Kong & China Economics, www.tdc.org.hk/main/industries/t2_2_39.htm, last updated 2 July 1998.

—(1999) *Practical Guide to Exporting Toys for Hong Kong Traders.*

Hopkins, T K, and Wallerstein, I, (1986) 'Commodity Chains in the World-Economy Prior to 1800', 10 Review 157–170.

—(1994) 'Commodity Chains: Construct and Research' in G Gereffi and M Korzeniewicz (eds), *Commodity Chains and Global Capitalism*, pp 17–20.

Jackson, J H, Davey, W J, and Sykes, A O, (1995) *Legal Problems of International Economic Relations: Cases, Materials and Text on the National and International Regulation of Transnational Economic Relations* (3rd edn).

Jones, C, (1994) 'Capitalism, Globalisation and Rule of Law: An Alternative Trajectory of Legal Change in China', 3 Social and Legal Studies 195–221.

Journal of Commerce, (1995) 13 January.

Lasok, D, (1998) *The Trade and Customs Law of the European Union* (3rd edn).

Lee, C K, (1997) 'Factory Regimes of Chinese Capitalism: Different Cultural Logics in Labor Control' in A Ong and D M Nonini (eds), *Ungrounded Empires: The Cultural Politics of Modern Chinese Transnationalism.*

LeRoy, E, (1999) *Le jeu des lois: Une anthropologie "dynamique" du Droit.*

McGovern, E, (1986) *International Trade Regulation: GATT, the United States and the European Community* (2nd edn).

Molyneux, C G, (1999) 'The Trade Barriers Regulation: The European Union as a Player in the Globalisation Game' 5 European Law Journal 375.

Newton, J, and Tse, L, (1999) "Kids' Stuff: The Organisation and Politics of the China-EU Trade in Toys', in W Pape, 'Socio-Cultural Differences and International Competiton Law', 5 European Law Journal 438.

Park, J D, (1997) *The Special Economic Zones of China and Their Impact on Its Economic Development.*

Pauly, L W, and Reich, S, (1997) 'National Structures and Multinational Corporate Behaviour: Enduring Differences in the Age of Globalisation', 5 International Organization 1–30.

Picciotto, S, (1996–97), 'Networks in International Economic Integration: Fragmented States and the Dilemmas of Neo-Liberalism', 17 Northwestern Journal of International Law and Business 1014.

Rabach, E, and Kim, EM, (1994) 'Where is the Chain in Commodity Chains? The Service Sector Nexus' in G Gereffi and M Korzeniewicz (eds), *Commodity Chains and Global Capitalism*, p 137.

Rapoport, (1999) 'Barbie at 40', *Sky* (Delta Air Lines), March, at 54–57.

Rheinstein, M (ed), (1966) *Max Weber on Law in Economy and Society* (trans E Shils).

Snyder, F, (1981) 'Anthropology, Dispute Processes and Law: A Critical Introduction' 8 British Journal of Law and Society (now Journal of Law and Society) 141–180.

—(1993) 'The Effectiveness of European Community Law: Institutions, Processes, Tools and Techniques', 56 Modern Law Review 1 19–56 at 32.

Strange, R, Slater, J, and Wang, L (eds), (1998) *Trade and Investment in China: The European Experience*, pp 147–165.

Tempest, R, (1996) 'Barbie and the World Economy', Los Angeles Times World Report (special section produced in co-operation with The Korea Times), 13 October, at 3.

Teubner, G (ed), (1993) 'The Many-Headed Hydras: Networks as Higher-Order Collective Actors', in J McCahery, S Picciotto, and C Scott (eds), *Corporate Control and Accountability: Changing Structures and the Dynamics of Regulation*, pp 41–51.

—(1997) *Global Law without a State.*

Trubek, D, Mosher, J, and Rothstein, J S, (1999) 'Transnationalism in the Regulation of Labor Relations: International Regimes and Transnational Advocacy Networks', Labor and the Global Economy Research Circle, The International Institute, University of Wisconsin-Madison.

Chapter 5

Transnational transactions: legal work, cross-border commerce and global regulation[1]

D MᶜBARNET[2]

The topic of law in a global economy is commonly framed as a problem. It is framed as a problem for the *regulation* of transnational business, in the absence of unified norms and global authorities to enforce them. It is also framed as a problem for the *transaction* of transnational business in the face of the conflicting demands of multiple jurisdictions, or in the face of massive 'gaps' in the commercial law of, for example, emergent markets. This chapter focuses on the second of these issues, the legal aspects of *doing business* transnationally, but it has significant implications for transnational *regulation* too.

The research on which this is based was prompted by an apparent paradox. The dominant discourse on global business law is couched in terms of the major problems posed for business by cross-border legal gaps and clashes, and the urgent need to resolve them. Resolution is seen as a matter for international policy and institutional development, in particular by constructing, or constructing further, a global framework of laws or pseudo-laws.[3] In the meantime, however, the global economy appears to be thriving. The empirical reality is that business goes on. Cross-border deals are proceeding, on a massive scale, with or without cross-border law – and they are proceeding as *legal* constructs.

How are these deals legally accomplished in the absence of a fully developed framework of global law? The key to this lies in *legal work*, and the role of legal work in transnational transactions. The term 'legal work' is used here to mean technical work, with and on the law, undertaken usually but not necessarily by

---

1   This chapter draws on a paper presented as 'Legal work in a global economy' at the Law and Society Conference, Miami, May 2000 and written up during a period of sabbatical leave at Edinburgh University Law Faculty, to whom many thanks.
2   Doreen McBarnet is Reader in Socio-Legal Studies at Oxford University and Senior Research Fellow at the Oxford Centre for Socio-Legal Studies. Her main area of interest for some years has been business and the law, in terms of both business practice and its regulation, and, more generally, in the nature of law, legal work and the rule of law. She directs the Centre's research programme on *Business, law and lawyers,* and her own projects have included work on tax avoidance, financial reporting, company law, the Single European Market, and the role of lawyers. Major publications include *Conviction,* and (with Chris Whelan) *Creative Accounting and the cross-eyed javelin thrower.*
3   See eg, Goode (1991); Bonnell (1992).

lawyers, in specific transactions for specific clients. This is a remarkably under-researched aspect of law, whether global or domestic.

To focus research on legal work in a global economy is to adopt a rather different perspective from the main body of transnational research, since it homes in on legal and business practice at the micro level. There is a good deal of debate and research on the need for, or construction of, shared global norms and global institutions to make or enforce them.[4] The focus here is on the macro level and on collective action, whether by states, business associations, legal firms or non-governmental organisations to produce legal, or pseudo-legal, structures.[5]

The writer's research, by contrast, focuses on action at the level of the individual business deal, on the law firm's work for its individual client in specific global transactions. It looks at technical legal work at the micro level.[6] But it also has implications for macro-level analysis. It shows how problems at the macro level are resolved at the micro level. Legal work produces micro-solutions for macro-problems. At the same time, demonstrating how the micro can affect the macro suggests some less benign consequences. If legal work can produce micro-solutions to macro-problems, it also has the potential to undermine the macro-solutions of painstakingly constructed global norms and institutions.

Focusing on legal work means we can not only try to understand the macro through the micro, but to elide analysis of both commercial deals and regulation, and as suggested in the opening paragraph, to draw out the implications of one for the other. Though conventionally commercial law, on the one hand, and regulation, on the other, whether at international or domestic levels, fall into two separate categories – private and public law – and legal academics tend to specialise in one or the other as distinct concerns, the reality is that at the level of legal practice, public and private law are intertwined. Focusing on legal work shows how private law in action affects public law in action and vice versa. Both in terms of solving problems and in terms of creating them, the workings of transnational regulation and the workings of transnational commerce cannot be properly understood in isolation from each other, or from legal work.

This chapter, then, turns the spotlight on the legal construction of global deals, on transnational transaction work. It looks at problems and problem-solving in the context of global business and the law. But it approaches 'problems' not from a policy perspective but from the pragmatic perspective of practising lawyers working for specific clients, and it analyses problem-solving at a micro rather than a macro level. It focuses not on how the problems posed for business by the current state of law in a global economy *should* be resolved in normative or institutional terms in the future, but on how they *are* being resolved in practice now. In this analysis, however, lie some lessons for policy and for the future. For it not only shows how legal work can solve problems; it demonstrates how solving problems for some can create problems for others. It suggests that law in a global society – whether commercial or regulatory – may face more endemic problems than the challenges involved in constructing uniform norms and enforcing them.

4   Eg Gessner and Budak (1998).
5   Teubner (1997).
6   Flood and Skordaki (1997) analyse the role of lawyers and others in a specific case, but with an interest in the collective creation of norms to deal with a cross-border dispute rather than the initial construction of a cross-border transaction.

BUSINESS, LAW AND COMPETITIVE ADVANTAGE

The problems posed for global business by the lack of global law are generally presented, in terms of the substance of law, as:

- clashes between jurisdictions, in terms of basic legal concepts as well as their interpretation and application;
- multiple requirements being imposed. The classic example is the range of different accounting rules to be met if a company wants to be listed on different stock exchanges; and
- gaps, where there are emergent markets, for example, but no legal infrastructure within them appropriate to market dealing.

These are also seen as leading more generally to uncertainty, and uncertainty is underscored by concerns over cross-border enforcement.[7]

Variability in substance has been addressed by numerous strategies of harmonisation. This may be by way of international treaties between states, such as the Vienna Convention on the International Sale of Goods, or by the more ambitious harmonisation of domestic law envisaged by the EU based on the inter-state Treaty of Rome. It may be by way of the work of international organisations such as UNCITRAL or UNIDROIT. It may be addressed by judges, lawyers and accountants working together in specific cases to create special hybrid rules for cross-border contexts.[8] Or it may be initiated by business associations such as International Chambers of Commerce.[9]

The role of business associations themselves has led to the view that global law or pseudo-law is being constructed by business for business as a new lex mercatoria.[10] Business has also been active in setting up its own institutions for international arbitration to deal with disputes.[11] Business can therefore be seen in this sense to be solving its own problems and finding ways to unify the patchwork of varying national laws that obstruct its global deals via collective action at the macro level, the level of shared structures.

This is a macro perspective however. At the micro level, business is also doing it for itself, but by individual rather than collective means, and with a more immediate pragmatic and individual business agenda in mind.

Businesses are responding to the 'global problem' through transactional legal work by their legal advisers. If a desirable cross-border deal is being obstructed by clashing or inadequate laws or enforcement structures, these are no longer policy problems to be solved by negotiating agreed structures for the future but practical problems which management expects its lawyers to solve now. And solving them is exactly what its lawyers do. Indeed solving obstructive legal problems is exactly what legal work – at its most sophisticated level – is all about.

These are, however, individual solutions for individual clients and individual transactions. Often these solutions disseminate to become standard practice. Lex mercatoria is constructed from below, bottom-up from the legal work done to solve problems for individual clients, as well as top-down through standard-setting

---

7 Gessner and Budak (1998).
8 Flood and Skordaki (1997).
9 Goode (1991).
10 See eg, Mertens (1997); Banaker (1998).
11 Dezalay and Garth (1995); Banaker (1998).

bodies. None the less they are solutions that originated in private legal work for private clients, through 'the pragmatic practices of legal entrepreneurs serving their clients' interests', as the writer phrased it many years ago in setting out the concept of law in practice as a 'raw material to be worked upon'.[12]

It should scarcely come as a surprise to find that businesses (and lawyers) operate at the individual as well as the collective level in addressing global problems. Not only do they have to resolve problems in the here and now in order to pursue global business pending future collective developments, but their role in relation to other businesses is not essentially one of collective action. Businesses may have common interests in working together to solve common problems, but they are also in competition. Associates in a sector are also rivals, bent on finding competitive advantage vis-à-vis each other.

Uniformity has the advantages of simplicity and of fostering a sense of certainty and enforceability, and even individual creative solutions can benefit from a wider use that legitimises them.[13] But from a competitive perspective uniformity is a disadvantage. Discussions of global business and the law are often framed in terms of a level playing field. In fact a level playing field is a mixed blessing. From the perspective of any given business, a level playing field is exactly what is wanted – for its competitors. For itself it would prefer to find a nice little molehill of competitive advantage rising above it.[14]

Legal work is one means of securing such competitive advantage. Law is not just an obstacle to business, but a material which can be worked on to its advantage. If creative means can be found to overcome legal obstructions to global deals then those obstructions – still in existence, at least for a time, for others – become not an obstruction but an opportunity, and a route to competitive advantage. There is therefore a constant drive for new legal constructs to solve the global problem, not just at a collective level but at the level of the individual business, the individual deal. That background should be borne in mind as we go on to look in some detail at one example of legal work in a global economy.

GLOBAL LEGAL WORK IN ACTION

The role of legal work in a global economy can best be illustrated through a case study drawn from ongoing research.[15] This particular example concerns the legal construction of cross-border investment in emergent markets, and focuses specifically on a series of deals set up in the late 1990s – and still[16] in play – to

---

12 McBarnet (1984) at 233.
13 See Frankel (1998) for an interesting elaboration of this.
14 For examples in the context of the Single European Market, see McBarnet and Whelan (1994).
15 The project as a whole draws on data on legal transaction work collected in the course of research conducted over several years in the areas of tax, corporate and banking law and practice (all of which inevitably involved transnational deals), along with new work on the specific issue of transnational transactions. The research has involved documentary analysis, including analysis of contracts and transaction structures, participant observation and especially in-depth technical interviews with individuals from major international law firms, international accounting firms, senior in-house legal counsel for multinational corporations, barristers, bankers, regulators and government agencies. Funding sources include the ESRC, the Jacob Burns Foundation and the European Commission.
16 Writing in 2000.

initiate foreign investment via international capital markets in a major company in the Russian Federation. The analysis that follows presupposes no knowledge of Russian law or international finance, but simply an interest on the part of readers in how lawyers work for clients, and work *with* law, in the context of a global economy. The focus, in short, is on the perceptions and legal accomplishments of transnational actors – and particularly international law firms. This chapter looks at some of the problems posed by Russian law for cross-border investment – as perceived by the international firms acting as intermediaries and advisers in these deals – and how they were resolved by legal work, specifically by the legal work of the international law firm acting for the Russian company.

Cross-border legal risk

The Russian Federation example was chosen in particular to explore the issue of jurisdictional variability, as a result of the absence of global law, and especially the resulting issues of 'gaps' in law and legal clashes. Finance now works via global markets, and societies such as the Russian Federation are seen as new openings for financial markets. They are, however, 'emergent' markets, and one of the reasons they are 'emergent' rather than emerged is the fact that they are developing from a different social, political and economic context. Their legal infrastructures are likewise 'emergent'. They are not yet seen by global market players as providing the legal requisites of a market economy. Even where legal provisions have been made there may be concern about their reliability in practice. In short, the economic opportunity for cross-border dealing is there, but there are deemed to be 'gaps' in the legal framework.

At the macro level the question is: How should an appropriate legal infrastructure be created to facilitate investment in emergent markets? How can capitalist legal structures be effectively transplanted? The focus is on development, on changing the legal structures of emergent markets as quickly as possible (though that is fraught with difficulties). At the micro level, however, the question is different. The question here is how *do* transition economies attract investors who are seeking reasonable legal security in a legal infrastructure that does not, in their view, provide it? How *is* global finance, cross-border investment, functioning in such circumstances? The fact is that foreign investment in transition economies does take place on a large scale. Partly this is because investors entering such markets are willing to take more risk – political and economic as well as legal – because of the potential for very high returns. But it is also because legal risk is mitigated through legal gaps and legal clashes being tackled and overcome by technical legal work.

For any Russian company wanting to attract investment from abroad in the late 1990s (and still), and, in this case, for the US/international law firm advising it, there were two general problems posed by the Russian Federation's legal structure. One problem was posed by the lack of legal protections for investors normally available in western capital markets. The other was posed by the existence of special regulatory obstacles in Russian law which meant conventional instruments used for cross-border investment would not work in the Russian legal context. This is then a classic example of both legal gaps and legal clashes, or indeed legal barriers, posing problems for cross-border transactions.

These problems were resolved through legal work: partly through spotting problems and negotiating and drafting contractual solutions; and partly through technical transaction work, some routine, some far more complex, tortuous and creative. We will look first at the more straightforward, at how legal work dealt with regulatory gaps.

Dealing with regulatory gaps: contractual regulation

The first general problem was the lack of standard Western legal protections for investors in the Russian regulatory structure. As the prospectus for one of the share offerings warned:

> 'Russia is still in the process of developing the legal framework required by a market economy.'[17]

Similar problems pervade the 'transition' economies of Eastern Europe in general. In a recent survey conducted in relation to Kazakhstan, 91.6% of respondents saw the legal infrastructure and pace of change in its development as a barrier to trade. Half of those respondents saw this as the major barrier.[18]

In our case study, the strategy adopted was to write in, as contractual obligations, requirements and arrangements normally provided by western regulatory systems, so that what was lacking in Russian regulation was provided for by private agreement. In short, private law substituted for what state law had failed to provide; legal work created private or contractual regulation.[19]

This can be illustrated by two examples, two matters judged particularly important for potential investors: the regulatory structures for share registration and financial reporting. The first was basic. It concerned legal recognition of a shareholder's ownership of the shares he or she had purchased. The second is also seen as fundamental to capital markets. It concerned reliable representation of the company's value and prospects to prospective shareholders, and meaningful accountability to shareholders after purchase.

Establishing ownership: share registration

The first problem for the architects of the securities offerings was evidence, and therefore security, of ownership. Under Russian law, ownership of shares in a company was established solely by reference to the company's shareholder register or the records of a depository. The shareholder's rights were therefore entirely dependent on the accuracy of the company's register or the depository's record. Unless the shareholder was recorded on the register he or she would not have any legal basis for claiming ownership of shares in the company. There is an obvious paradox in being totally dependent for legal rights to the profits and assets of a company on records under the control of the company itself, and one lawyer recounted instances of foreign shareholders simply being struck off the register and so losing the basis of any legal claim to ownership.

---

17 The analysis that follows quotes from some of the documentation studied in detail as part of the research.
18 Kazakhstan Survey, May 1997.
19 Teubner (1997) p xiv also observes relationships between the public and the private in the global context, although in his case in the context of norm creation by non-governmental organisations – 'private governments' with 'a public character'.

At the time of the offerings under analysis, a regulated registration system was just about to come into play. However, there were still concerns over how the system would work in practice. For example, the writer was told that brokers sometimes held shares in their own names, which not only implied continuing risks for the shareholder who was still not registered in person, but which could also produce all kinds of knock-on effects in terms of adverse tax implications.

There were concerns that there was not yet a sufficient infrastructure of independent registrars, especially outside the main urban centres such as Moscow and St Petersburg. There was also concern, expressed in the prospectuses, that even with the new rules –

'many Russian companies are unlikely to be in compliance with the share registrar rules'

by the due date. What is more, a close look at what is legally allowed, even for the 'compliant', raises questions about just how independent of companies the new registrars would be. Under the new laws, companies could quite legitimately own up to 20% of the company registering their shares. Indeed, our case study company (which had hitherto owned and controlled its registrar) intended to comply with the new rules by joining with several other companies to set up (and each partially own) their new registrar.

Such a situation was unlikely to encourage investors. Measures to address this regulatory situation were therefore incorporated into the contractual arrangements for the offerings. The company undertook as a matter of contractual obligation, to –

'take all and any action as may be necessary to assure the accuracy and completeness of all information set forth in the Share Register.'

What is more, the company agreed to provide the intermediary institutions involved in the deal with 'unrestricted access to the Share Register' to check registration 'regularly (and in any event not less than monthly)', along with committing to a whole list of specific duties in specific circumstances.

The company was also to be held liable, under the contract, for any failures on the part of the registrar. This might be seen as converting from disadvantage to advantage the scope under even the incoming Russian law for continuing control of the registrar by the company. The regulatory failings of Russian law, from the perspective of investors, were therefore addressed privately by the introduction of contractual obligations.

Information and accountability: financial reporting

In established markets such as the UK or US, companies are required, as a matter of statutory obligation, to provide public information on their financial status, both in terms of their performance and their assets and liabilities. Lawyers advising the Russian company on foreign capital-raising were faced with a different situation under Russian Federation law. As the prospectuses noted:

'While the Securities law contemplates that any company that issues securities to the public will provide periodic reports to the market, regulations implementing this requirement have yet to be adopted. As a result public information about Russian companies is extremely limited.'

– or, more bluntly, as one lawyer put it –

'company accounts in Russia are absolutely useless.'

This is of course scarcely surprising since the regulations governing them were drawn up for a completely different economy with completely different criteria of accountability. But the net result is that what is seen by capital markets as appropriate information for assessing risk and reward was simply not required in the Russian legal and regulatory structure at the time of the offering.

However, it was required *contractually*. The information given to would-be investors – the offering memorandum – included financial statements drawn up by the company and its subsidiaries not under Russian accounting procedures but under US Generally Accepted Accounting Principles (US GAAP). These were drawn up for the full period of the company's privatisation, resulting in two full annual accounts, and interim half-year accounts for the period prior to the share issue. The annual accounts were audited by a 'Big 5' international accounting firm under US GAAP rules.[20]

The company also undertook –

'in connection with the Global offering, to publish audited consolidated financial statements in respect of its future financial years ... and to publish unaudited consolidated half year financial statements in respect of financial periods ... in each case in accordance with US GAAP.'

It undertook, in short, to comply with the standard legal requirements of western capitalist states, specifically, in this case, US federal law. The company did not even make available to its global shareholders the accounts it prepared under Russian regulations, and the prospectus expressly warned that they –

'should not be relied on by anyone who is unfamiliar with RAR [Regulations on Accounting and Reporting of the Russian Federation] and how they differ from US GAAP.'

So US law is transposed into the Russian deal by private legal agreement. It does not merely supplement Russian legal requirements, but replaces them completely for the purpose of the global deal.

None of this is very complex technically. Rather, it is legal work evidenced in spotting regulatory gaps and filling them by private contractual arrangements, though of course it also involved persuading the Russian company voluntarily to undertake obligations not imposed on it by its own law. This is the more significant when one realises that the state – or at least a vehicle set up to represent it – was itself still the largest shareholder in the company, with a 40% holding of the charter capital, including a 'golden share' with special powers. The state had not yet managed to establish an indigenous regulatory framework satisfactory to foreign investors. None the less, here it was, under another hat, privately contracting to abide by what was in effect a series of imported foreign regulations.

In a sense the state had no choice of course; it wanted foreign investment both in the company and in Russia. The first of this particular set of global offerings was particularly significant. It was to create a marker in the market. There was express reference to this in the prospectus:

20 Not that this alone guarantees reliable reporting. 'Creative accounting' as well as enforcement issues remain a problem even where there are established rules. See Griffiths (1986) and McBarnet and Whelan (1999).

'The Global Offering is being conducted in part in order to establish an active international trading market in [the company]'s shares and thus to facilitate access to the international capital markets in the future.'

What is more, the hope was that this would open the markets to other Russian companies in the future. This company had to succeed to forge a path for others. There was therefore a strong motivation to do what was necessary to make the deal acceptable in the global capital markets. But it also required effort, a point the lawyer in charge was keen to emphasise, to persuade the company to agree.

It is not the lawyer's power of persuasion that is of particular interest here, however. It is the lawyer's technical skills in problem-spotting and problem-solving through contract drafting. In particular, it is the way contract is used to tackle what are perceived, from a cross-border perspective, as regulatory lacunae. The result is legally binding controls constructed through contracts to compensate for regulatory gaps.[21] Legal work creates public law surrogates through private law – it constructs 'private public law'.

Mechanical and functional transplants

In the context of law in a global economy, what we see, in effect, is the problem of regulatory variations across borders being overcome in transnational transactions through legal work, either by transplanting, lock, stock and barrel, ready made protections from established regulatory regimes abroad, as in the financial reporting example – we could think of this as a *mechanical transplant* – or by transplanting an established regulatory function and satisfying it by constructing functionally equivalent rights, duties and liabilities appropriate to the specific situation, as in the share registration example – we could think of this as a *functional transplant.*

Mechanical transplants may be particularly attractive as a means of transplanting *legitimacy*. Teubner[22] suggests that –

'contractual rule-making … is either seen as non-law or as delegated law-making which needs recognition by the official legal order.'

But by using rules already recognised by an 'official legal order' elsewhere, indeed, by the leading market economy, and recognised in practice in the international capital markets this company – and country – were seeking to enter, the issue of legitimacy may be mitigated. The mechanical transplant of established rules may therefore be a less risky strategy, de facto at least, than the invention of new ones.

Transplanting of legal systems, or elements of them, is often discussed at macro level as a policy for global regulation. But cross-border transplants are also the stuff of cross-border deals, accomplished at micro level through private law, and through private legal work by lawyers for private clients. Indeed, what is being accomplished is a kind of private harmonisation. Private treaties may be accomplishing more readily at the micro level what, at the macro level, is still being striven for through public international law or the work of international organisations.

---

21 How legally binding *in practice* these are depends, of course, on the efficacy of cross-border enforcement. This issue is beyond the scope of this chapter but is addressed in McBarnet (2002).
22 Teubner (1997) p xiii.

This is, however, harmonisation with a spin. Indeed it is perhaps more a matter of legal imperialism, with the law of established markets – in this case the US – transplanted privately into the emergent market.[23] There is, after all, a body of international accounting rules, constructed by the International Accounting Standards Committee (IASC). It was not IASC rules that were written into the contract, however, but US GAAP.

From substance to structure: cross-border obstacles and the passport deal

Constructing a cross-border transaction, whether with emergent markets or not, usually involves more than just filling legal gaps. It also means dealing with legal clashes and, indeed, with legal obstacles to what have, in other jurisdictions, become established as standard legal forms in business practice. Such clashes and obstacles are also overcome through legal work – legal work of a different nature to that discussed in the contractual examples given above. This legal work is concerned less with the substance of the deal than with its underlying structure.[24]

Primary and secondary contracts: substance and structure

The contractual work illustrated above, dealt with the *substance* of the deal – the sale of securities. But underpinning this was a body of deeper transactional work, which dealt with its *structure*. Legal work often involves both what we might think of as the *primary* deal, which is the original objective, and a network of *secondary* deals which serve to establish the optimal structure for it.

It is important to distinguish these two levels of legal work. Where socio-legal research refers to commercial law in action it has tended to focus only on what the writer sees as *primary* contracts. But transaction work is about more than primary contracts. The primary contract is, in sophisticated legal work, just the tip of the iceberg, with an often massive, but largely invisible, substructure beneath the surface that needs to be researched too. Researching the primary contract alone would oversimplify the nature of the legal work involved in complex cross-border transactions and understate its subtlety, creativity and technical complexity.

In our case study this deeper structural work was crucial for making the deal work across borders, and in a way deemed commercially, as well as legally viable. Indeed, it was this deeper structural work rather than the surface contractual work that earned the transaction its nickname among those constructing it – the 'passport deal'.

What kind of legal clashes and obstacles were met in the course of constructing these cross-border deals, and how were they resolved? A brief look at one of the underlying structures from our case study may help demonstrate the legal work involved.

The passport deal

An established instrument used these days for cross-border securities (*now* established – but itself a product of creative legal work in the past) is the Eurobond.

---

23 For a more detailed analysis of the nature of legal work at this level, see McBarnet (2002).
24 See Dezalay (1992).

One advantage of the Eurobond form is that it does not attract withholding tax. This maximises yield and makes a security sold in this form an attractive option for investors.

Russian law, however, allowed no exceptions to the payment of withholding tax. This meant that the established advantages of the Eurobond structure would not work for Russian shares. This would reduce their attractiveness vis-à-vis other global offerings. The task for advisers, then, was how to construct a structure that would transfer the advantages of the Eurobond across Russian borders despite the obstacles posed by Russian law.

This was what the construction of the underlying passport deal accomplished. The prospectus for this particular offering could proclaim on its front page:

> 'Payments on the Notes will be made without deduction for or on account of taxes of Ireland or the Russian Federation.'

How does Ireland suddenly come into the picture? In fact, not just Ireland but Luxembourg and Germany – or at least corporate structures and financial institutions in them – became involved in the underlying structure that was finally devised to provide a 'passport' for what in business terms would be seen as a tax-efficient and therefore commercially viable offering.

In the course of construction, other obstacles were met in Russian law. One solution to the withholding tax barrier, involving loans and interest payments between the company and a specially set up foreign subsidiary, which would have worked in other cross-border contexts, would not work in Russia because of its particular rules on VAT, charged (at 25%) on inter-corporate loans. Another barrier concerned Russian rules erected to protect the country from flight of capital abroad. Russian companies wishing to set up an offshore subsidiary company to hold finance abroad could do so only with the permission of the Central Bank.

The solution finally settled on to overcome these barriers involved interpolating a series of legal relationships between the Russian company and its potential investors, involving an Irish subsidiary along with a German bank and its Luxembourg subsidiary.

The role of the Irish company was to issue the securities, Ireland being chosen for its particular tax advantages. The money would not stay in the foreign subsidiary, however, but come back into the Russian company. How would it come back in without attracting tax? Here the foreign bank became important. A German bank would (though only indirectly as we shall see) receive the money paid for the securities and pay it on to the Russian company. This would be paid to the Russian company, however, in the form of a commercial loan. As such it would attract neither withholding tax nor, since it was a bank loan as opposed to a loan between parent company and subsidiary, would it attract VAT.

Finally, as noted above, the securities were issued from Ireland because of tax advantages. However, these particular tax advantages were available only under particular conditions, including the purchase of assets on the secondary markets. Introducing the extra step of the Luxembourg subsidiary between the German bank and the Irish company effectively created a secondary market and so allowed these conditions to be met.

The whole structure involved a network of guarantees, pledges of indebtedness on two levels of priority, certificates of indebtedness and, of course, the aforementioned loan agreement, each of these also transnational, between the Russian company, the Irish company, UK, US, German and Austrian underwriters, the German bank and its Luxembourg subsidiary.

On the face of it then, we have a sale of Russian securities to, primarily, US and UK investors, and this primary deal incorporates a number of contractual safeguards, the product of legal work, to provide safeguards that the law of the transitional society does not yet provide for itself. This contractual legal work fills gaps.

There is also, however, an invisible substructure of secondary deals underlying this primary deal. This too is the product of legal work, highly creative legal work, and itself of a transnational character. The main task of this structural legal work is to overcome barriers posed to a transnational deal by differences in national legal structures. Under the particularities of Russian law the offering, even with the introduction of contractual safeguards, would not have been attractive. Contractual legal work would have helped temper the legal risks, but, to the business world, the impact of Russian-specific tax would have made the deal insufficiently rewarding vis-à-vis other offerings where no tax was involved. The offering would, in short, not have been competing on a level playing field in the global market.

The job of structural legal work was to find a way to make the deal commercially viable through legal means. In this case that meant finding a way to replicate the advantages of a Eurobond-type form across borders despite domestic laws that at first sight made this impossible. From the business perspective, its job was to level the playing field for the Russian offering and allow it to participate in the global market.

That these transnational deals were made both legally and commercially viable in a global market was therefore the product of active legal work at both primary contractual and structural levels, legal work which was often highly technical, complex and creative, and which itself involved a further network of secondary multi-transnational deals in support of the primary cross-border contract.

IMPLICATIONS: LEGAL WORK, CROSS-BORDER COMMERCE AND GLOBAL REGULATION

What does all this mean for the global law enterprise? Does it mean there is no need for global norms and institutions to facilitate cross-border commerce, since legal work can do the job without it? If shared global law is being accomplished, a level playing field established, from the ground up through practice, is there such a pressing need to establish it from the top down through international agreements on policy?

Cross-border commerce and harmonisation

In fact there will still be a drive at institutional level towards uniformity. There is value in standardised mechanisms, and tailor made legal work of the kind described here is expensive – although, of course, what begin as tailor-made mechanisms tend to percolate to become standard practice.[25]

Legal work, as noted earlier, contributes to a growing lex mercatoria.

That said, business has a complex attitude to harmonised law. Although there is a standard rhetoric among businesses complaining about variations between

---

25 McBarnet (1984); Powell (1993); Frankel (1998).

legal regimes, and calling for harmonisation, in practice variation between regimes is routinely exploited by business to its own advantage. This occurs at the level of politics, in negotiations over what kind of legal regime will be acceptable to multinationals operating (in theory)[26] under it, with one regime being played off against another. It occurs too in private legal constructions designed to take full advantage of cross-border variations in a sort of regulatory arbitrage. Complex global legal transactions are often only comprehensible if they are seen as artificial constructs designed specifically to take advantage of gaps and clashes between jurisdictions. In short, far from the lack of a harmonised global law posing a problem for business, it can also provide an opportunity that is routinely exploited. Business, in other words, can find advantage in both uniformity and conflict between regimes.

In the context of legal creativity, advantage can also be found in different ways, with different consequences for harmonisation. In a world in which business is hampered by cross-border gaps and clashes, it may be in the interests of business to use legal creativity to overcome them. Indeed, in a context in which competitors remain hampered by gaps and clashes this can produce competitive advantage. A consequence may be a levelling of the international playing field, both for the transaction in hand and, if the practice disseminates, more generally. But that is not the essence of the practice, nor its purpose. Creative legal practice is not about harmonisation but about innovation, and the purpose is simply to optimise client interests. Any resulting levelling of the playing field for others is purely incidental. Indeed, once such levelling occurs that particular source of competitive advantage through legal creativity is gone. Business needs to find its 'nice little molehill of competitive advantage' some other way.

Legal creativity in pursuit of business interest and competitive advantage is, in fact, much more likely to pose problems for harmonisation than to solve them, because it is continually producing new instruments and practices. As these emerge, so do new challenges for any harmonised law. New forms need decisions on how they are to be treated in law, with the danger of a new patchwork of varying treatments emerging, whether from national legislation, courts or simply the informal decisions of those applying or enforcing the law, until, and unless international consensus on treatment can be accomplished. Creative legal work, in short, can lead to a perpetual dynamic with harmonised law constantly lagging behind. In the Single European Market, many years of labour went into trying to produce a level of harmonisation of corporate financial reporting. But the (much compromised) 'consensus' was no sooner achieved than it was outdated by the development and escalation in use of derivatives and other new financial instruments, on which there was no agreed treatment.[27]

In short, in a business context in which competitive advantage can be gained from legal creativity, legal harmonisation is likely to be constantly chasing legal innovation.

This must make us think carefully about the role of lawyers and legal work in a global economy. Gessner has argued that 'legal certainty cannot be achieved globally at the level of programmes' – my macro level of global norms. Rather, he pins his faith in 'roles' – and so in the shared expectations generated by networks of arbitrators, business communities, and international lawyers.[28] But the role of

---

26 See below: 'creative compliance' is frequently used to escape control.
27 From research by McBarnet and Whelan.
28 Gessner (1998) p 438; see also Banaker (1998) p 382.

lawyers can also be less consensual and collective. Focusing on transnational transactions underlines the more fundamental role of corporate lawyers – working in the interests of clients, often by creative legal engineering. In their role as creative legal engineers, lawyers should be seen as not only having the potential to contribute to harmonisation, but also as having the potential constantly to challenge and undermine it.

Legal work and transnational regulation

Harmonisation is one issue, the effectiveness of transnational regulation, another. And for many the regulation of transnational business is the real concern, with harmonisation merely a potential means to that end. Micro-analysis of cross-border deal-making has implications for this concern too.

The chapter has shown how creative legal work can overcome legal barriers to cross-border deals and create a level playing field, which may seem a benign enough accomplishment. What are 'barriers' from the outside are, however, 'policies' from the inside of the country. They are there for a purpose. They are there to regulate business or to raise tax, and creative legal work undermines those policy purposes.

In the Russian example these policy purposes can be seen as rather more complex than this comment may imply. Indeed, the creative legal work involved could be seen as avoiding Russian law in order to facilitate Russian governmental policy, since it made possible a deal which the Russian government very much wanted to succeed. It was seen as a key step in facilitating the entry of Russian companies into global markets, and in bringing into the country much needed foreign investment. None the less there is a certain irony in the situation. The Federation of Russia was the dominant shareholder in the company in question. Under one hat, then, it stood for the laws of the land, under another it was not only agreeing to US laws overriding its own, but was party to a deal carefully designed to avoid Russian laws.

The point should be considered more generally, however. Creative legal work can undermine or quite simply defeat legal control. This is not a trait confined to cross-border legal work but to legal work more generally. Elsewhere, my own work or work with colleagues has demonstrated how creative legal structuring of deals can facilitate the circumvention and avoidance of regulatory law of all sorts, with knock-on effects for those intended to be protected by it.[29] In short there is a sting in the tail of creative legal work. Legal work involves overcoming legal obstacles, and those obstacles are very often regulations intended to protect others.

This has implications for those concerned not just with the facilitation of global business, but with its control. One long-term concern in globalisation has been the ever-increasing power of multinational corporations and the issue of how to establish effective global regulation of their practices. Since it is recognised that companies currently take advantage of countries with weaker regulations, hope is vested in enhancing and harmonising regulations – and their enforcement – at global level. But this ignores the potential impact of creative legal work.

Creative legal work is not just about playing with the different laws of different jurisdictions, finding tax – or regulatory – havens, set up precisely for that purpose.

---

29 McBarnet (1988); McBarnet and Whelan (1997).

It is about playing with law per se, even within one jurisdiction. It is about constructing 'creative compliance',[30] finding legal forms which fall outside disadvantageous or inside advantageous legal categories. It is about scrutinising legal definitions and thresholds, and repackaging deals to fall within or beyond them – in form though not in substance – as suits. It is about concocting legal forms as yet undreamt of by legislators and regulators. Creative compliance, the product of creative legal work, is likely to remain a problem for regulation even under harmonised and well-enforced global laws. What is more, since creative compliance so often depends on legal work at the 'invisible' substructural level, its occurrence may not be readily detected.

CONCLUSION

So what does a focus on legal work suggest for those concerned with transnational commerce and for those concerned with transnational regulation?

For those concerned with the problems of legal gaps and clashes obstructing cross-border commerce, the immediate message of our case study may be encouraging, since it demonstrates that private legal work by lawyers for business can overcome such problems. It can accomplish a kind of harmonisation in practice from below.

However, that is not the goal of, or driving force behind, legal work. At the macro level, lawyers and law firms, like businesses, may be working for harmonisation in policy, and it is true that the dissemination of their legal work techniques creates a kind of harmonisation in practice – in time and temporarily. But at the micro level of private legal work, the driving force is not collective policy. The goal is merely to serve the interests of the individual private client and to find or innovate legal ways to accomplish that. Though legal creativity can, in the current context, be a force for harmonisation, the driving force of innovation for competitive advantage is more likely overall to frustrate harmonisation than to promote it.

What is more, the driving force of clients' interests means legal work is not concerned to promote effective control but all too often is concerned to undermine it. So for those concerned with the *global regulation* of business through law or law-like structures, the message is far from encouraging. Work at macro level to construct global norms and institutions may face problems – not always readily discerned – at the micro level of practice. Efforts at global control of business may be set up at macro level, only to be destroyed by stealth through routine private legal work.

Select bibliography

Banakar, R, (1998) 'Reflexive Legitimacy in International Arbitration' in V Gessner and A C Budak (eds), *Emerging Legal Certainty: Empirical Studies on the Globalization of Law.*

Bonell, M J, (1992) 'Unification of Law by Non-Legislative Means: the UNIDROIT Draft Principles for International Commercial Contracts', 40 AJCL 617.

Dezalay, Y, (1992) *Marchands de droit.*

---

30 McBarnet and Whelan (1991; 1997; 1999).

Dezalay, Y, and Garth, B, (1996) *Dealing in Virtue: International Commercial Arbitration and the Internationalization of Legal Practice.*

Flood, J, and Skordaki, E, (1997) 'Normative Bricolage: Informal Rule-making by Accountants and Lawyers in Mega-insolvencies' in G Teubner (ed), *Global Law Without a State.*

Frankel, T, (1998) 'Cross-border securitization: without law, but not lawless', 8 Duke Journal of Comparative and International Law 2.

Gessner, V, and Budak, A C (eds), (1998) *Emerging Legal Certainty: Empirical Studies on the Globalization of Law.*

Goode, R, (1991) 'Reflections on the harmonisation of commercial law', Uniform Law Review, vol 1.

Griffiths, I, (1986) *Creative Accounting.*

Kazakhstan Survey, (1997) Kazakhstan, May.

McBarnet, D, (1984) 'Law and Capital', 12 International Journal of the Sociology of Law 3.

—(1988) 'Law, Policy, and Legal Avoidance: Can Law Effectively Implement Egalitarian Policies?', 15 Journal of Law and Society 1.

—(2002) 'Legal work in a global economy: micro-perspectives on macro issues', 1 Socio-Legal Studies: an international journal 1.

McBarnet, D, and Whelan, C, (1991) 'The Elusive Spirit of the Law: Formalism and the Struggle for Legal Control', 54 MLR 6.

—(1994) 'International Corporate Finance and the Challenge of Creative Compliance' in S Wheeler (ed), *The Law of the Business Enterprise.*

—(1997) 'Creative Compliance and the Defeat of Legal Control: The Magic of the Orphan Subsidiary' in K Hawkins (ed), *The Human Face of Law.*

—(1999) *Creative Accounting and the Cross-eyed Javelin Thrower.*

Mertens, H, (1997) '*Lex Mercatoria*: A Self-applying System Beyond National Law?' in G Teubner (ed), *Global Law Without a State.*

Powell, M, (1993) 'Professional innovation: corporate lawyers and private lawmaking', 18 Journal of Law and Social Inquiry 3.

Teubner, G (ed), (1997) *Global Law Without a State.*

Chapter 6

Capital markets, globalisation and global elites

J FLOOD

INTRODUCTION

'Capital Markets are driving the global economy. This is due to the nature of the market in which money moves around the world at the press of a button. Billions of dollars, pounds, deutschmarks and Yen move between financiers every day.'[1]

The e-economy is pushing these billions even faster and harder. No one knows if we are in the midst of a bubble economy or are on the verge of a genuinely 'new' economy, a new economic paradigm for the twenty-first century. Globalisation is being driven by commerce, and Hodgart further comments: 'No legal service is more globally driven than finance and, within this, capital markets work is the purest global service.'[2]

To understand the nature of capital markets, we must explore three elements, namely globalisation, the connection between the creation and the way of death of businesses, and the professionals who service them. Financial services have become increasingly concentrated within the global economy. Banks, international governmental organisations and professional service firms are located in the major financial centres of the world, especially New York and London. Sassen notes: 'Global cities are ... sites for ... the production of financial innovations and the making of markets, both central to the internationalisation and expansion of the financial industry.'[3] The industry seeks homeostasis, that is equilibrium 'amidst the variations of outer shock and change'.[4] Without it risk ascends the register and investors become panicky, the short-sellers proliferate and the 'random walk' persists, as various instances of 'market correction' have amply demonstrated. In partnership with market volatility, bankruptcy is always nearby. And this is the crux of how capital markets work: initial public offerings, mergers and acquisitions, privatisations are all planned with the prospect of their demise in mind and the manner in which the funeral rites should be managed. Although homeostasis is desired, market failure has a way of interjecting disruption. The professionals' roles encapsulate the exigencies and appropriates them into ideally sequenced events that unfold in an orderly fashion – almost.

1 Hodgart (1999) p 6.
2 Hodgart (1999) p 6.
3 Sassen (1991) p 5.
4 McLuhan (1964) p 98.

114

The creation of the documentation captures and represents the essence of homeostasis and attempts to assign chaos to the darkness of randomness, that which lies beyond the logic of the agreement drafted by the lawyers. Agreements and other documentation in capital markets work reach their apotheosis when their normative structures are inscribed in either New York state law or English law, or both. Since the major financial institutions are based in these two jurisdictions, their power usually ensures that there is no deviation from the juridical norm. Thus the global is deeply embedded in the local.

GLOBALISATION

Globalisation is an 'essentially contested concept',[5] in that its meaning is always in dispute. And implanted within the concept of globalisation is an invocation of power as demonstrated by the global financial institutions. McLuhan had the foresight to prognosticate that:

> 'as the new vortices of power are shaped by the instant electric interdependence of all men on this planet, the visual factor in social organization and in personal experience recedes ... [and] there is a steady progression toward commercial exchange as the movement of information itself.'[6]

The power/knowledge ratio becomes a powerful tool in the expansion of the global market economy and through it we can see the manner in which expectations and agendas are shaped by the dominant institutions.[7]

Three models of globalisation currently subsist, according to Held et al: hyperglobalisation, global scepticism and transformationalism.[8] The first is a transmutation of McKinsey (consultants) and McDonalds (hamburgers) as exemplars of world domination. Here globalisation hauls down the barriers between nation states, which become irrelevant: economic activity and cultural identity merge into a multiplex melting-pot and global capitalism emerges triumphant.[9] The process is unilinear, progressive and inexorable. Global scepticism argues against this position, countering the hyperbole of globalisation with statistics demonstrating the failure of economic integration, suggesting at best a process of regionalisation has occurred and that globalisation is a myth.[10] Whereas hyperglobalisation postulates that its progressive movement will lead to radical change for the benefit of all, north and south, scepticism sees internationalisation accentuating the differences between north and south. The transformationalist perspective recognises the contingency of action and the historicity of structure as enabling and constraining globalisation.[11] Whilst transformationalism accepts great change is taking place in the economy, politics and culture, the degree to which it is happening is yet unknown and the redistribution of resources in the world is still unequal, with some getting richer and some areas becoming marginalised.[12] The nation state is able to continue

---

5 Gallie (1955).
6 McLuhan (1964) at 137.
7 Cf Lukes (1974).
8 Held et al (1999).
9 Ohmae (1991; 1995); Ritzer (1996).
10 Hirst and Thompson (1996).
11 Giddens (1990).
12 Held et al (1999) p 8.

claims to power and authority, but they are limited more and more by the emergence of stronger supra-national forms of governance, such as the EU and the World Trade Organization (WTO). Ultimately, the destination of globalisation – if one exists – is unknown. Whichever conception of globalisation is chosen, each represents a threat to homeostasis and each can be shown to function within very loose normative structures.

Globalisation is not entirely anarchic, but nor is it tightly rule-bound. The law of globalisation is almost a new lex mercatoria not dependent on state authority for its legitimacy or its disputing systems.[13] Global law is derived from a number of sources, among the most popular being contract, the drafting of agreements. Contract is able to enmesh states as parties to an agreement without the protection of sovereign immunity. Contract can transcend national boundaries more easily than international law is capable of doing. It is at the level of private ordering that difference is interpreted into a document that resolves the contingencies of jurisdictional conflict. Private ordering emerges away from the centre, as Teubner argues: 'global law will grow mainly from the social peripheries, not from the political centres of nation-states and international institutions'.[14] Global law is *soft law* made by professionals during the construction of legal deals. Without this softness, global law could hardly come into being: it would be brittle and fragile, under constant disputation. Yet soft law has been remarkably successful in constituting the global legal order.[15] Soft law, as a global entity, in this instance has adopted English and New York law as the basis for its palimpsest work.

In the next part, one aspect of private ordering is displayed. Capital markets is one of the fastest growing forms of financial activity in the world, but it can only be understood against the background of its potential and possible failure in bankruptcy and its combined localised and globalised character.[16]

CAPITAL MARKETS

At the end of 1999, the managing directors (the former partners) of Goldman Sachs received remuneration packages to the order of about $10m each.[17] Most was reward for being the top financial adviser and underwriter in the world, being in the biggest deals, such as advising Vodafone in its takeover of

---

13 Dezalay and Garth (1996); Teubner (1997).
14 Teubner (1997) p 7.
15 The rule of law is usually held up as the defining element of civilised society. Under soft law, however, the rule of law often has a harsher, more rugged character, as the following anecdote demonstrates. During the closing of a major deal of an acquisition of a company by another, the documentation was continuously being changed and redrafted. The directors of the selling company came to their lawyers' office in the City of London expecting to sign the documents, close the deal and depart celebrating their new riches. On arrival they were placed in a conference room and told they would have to wait while the last few wrinkles were ironed out. Seventy-two hours later they were released from their confinement when the documents were finally agreed between the lawyers. The lawyers could not let the directors leave the office because they knew they would not return, so they held them until they could sign. There was nothing the directors could do but comply. They were under the force of the rule of law.
16 Santos (1995) p 275 calls this type 'globalized localism' and 'localized globalism'.
17 Garfield (1999) at 13.

Mannesman, and producing a telecommunications company worth £225bn.[18] Capital markets work is high-value service, with enormous premiums for those who do it.

The 50 years following the Second World War constituted a key expansion period for global capital. Foreign direct investment grew, the Eurodollar market increased global capital liquidity, and immense political change issued in a wave of privatisations as states sloughed off their possessions – state industries, utilities and service providers. The market rather than the state was to reign.[19] In the 1980s 'Big Bang' in the UK enabled the global banks, especially those in the US, to establish investment banks free from constricting regulation. For the US banks, the Glass-Steagall Act had corseted their activities by preventing the simultaneous engagement of commercial and investment banking.[20] Stockbroking changed as brokers and jobbers merged and the stock exchange rules outlawing cartels were relaxed. Although the recession of the late 1980s and early 1990s constrained growth for some time, as shown by the rise in insolvency statistics, global investment rose inexorably, as demonstrated by the increases in foreign direct investment flows (FDI).[21] In the last 15 years of the twentieth century, the progress of the economy has subtly altered in that boom and slump can co-exist in different parts of the world. Thus at the end of the century, while the US was economically triumphant, the Asian tigers were limping in a field of thorns. In order to recapture their ferocity, the Asian economies have begun to produce their own big bangs.[22] One other feature of this period ought to be mentioned: the growth in regulatory institutions in the global economy. The most assertive has been the Securities and Exchange Commission (SEC), which now appears to be seeking the role of global regulator. During the 1980s the SEC was dealing with various insider-trading scandals, including the savings and loans industry and the manipulation of the junk bond market (high-yield debt) created by Michael Milken and which subsequently crashed in 1989 causing the downfall of Drexel Burnham Lambert a year later.[23] During the 1990s the junk bond, now high-yield debt, market recovered and was legitimised.[24] The global economy, with the success of the GATT Uruguay Round, has now a transnational watchdog and dispute arbiter in the WTO.

In other ways, the SEC has begun to reduce the barriers to US markets for foreign investors by easing its disclosure requirements.[25] Taking regulatory manoeuvres into account during the economic activity of the last 50 years, capital markets' work has boomed. For example, 'the six largest mergers/acquisitions in 1998 totalled over $300bn and were funded by a combination of equity and debt issues'.[26] Hodgart also notes that 'the six largest auto manufacturers [in 1999] are reported as having a "strategic acquisitions war chest" totalling in excess of $100 billion'.[27]

18 Gow (2000) at 32.
19 Gamble (1994).
20 Finch et al (2000).
21 The bulk of FDI flows among the OECD countries: Held et al (1999) pp 248–249.
22 Kinami (1998); Mannix (2000).
23 Stewart (1991).
24 Drexel Burnham Lambert, and Milken, underwrote 60% of the junk bond market in the second half of the 1980s: Sheldon and Abbondante (1999) p 16.
25 Kamman and Covello (1999).
26 Hodgart (1999) p 6.
27 Hodgart (1999) p 6.

Capital markets work involves gaining access to finance in markets throughout the world. This may be through issues of stock, bonds, securitisation of debt or loans,[28] depositary receipt programmes, initial public offerings (IPOs), or privatisations. The last 20 years have shown bankers' and lawyers' ingenuity in developing new forms of financing and means of packaging them. Demands for creativity have risen as the equities market globalised, and diverse jurisdictions' requirements had to be co-ordinated in strategic ways. If we compare debt markets with equities markets, the difference becomes apparent: trading in debt markets requires less research and availability of information, relies on high quality borrowers with less concern about the underlying credit, and therefore has been able to internationalise more rapidly; whereas information deficits are greater in equities markets, where borrowers are a more diverse group than in debt markets and concepts such as pre-emption rights predominate in some jurisdictions and not others.[29]

The best way to illuminate capital markets work is through case studies of capital markets work in action over the previous two decades. We are fortunate to have records that illustrate the practice. The first is the privatisation of British Gas during the Thatcher premiership.

British Gas[30]

The British Gas privatisation followed that of British Telecom (BT) by two years. BT had been problematic because the value of half of it was £4bn,

> 'some seven times bigger than any previous UK issue and some four times bigger than any issue attempted anywhere in the world. It represented approximately the amount which the big UK investment institutions, the pension funds and insurance companies had put into the equity market over a two-year period.'[31]

The British Gas privatisation was to be bigger than BT's. Three constituencies were identified for the issue: the UK institutions, the UK retail market and the overseas market.[32] The first two required substantial educational investment to create a widespread market: seminars, roadshows and extensive mailshots. This pre-issue publicity was to have deleterious consequences for the US market, since it conflicted with US regulatory norms. The overseas market was further split between the US, Canada, Europe and Japan. Each had a local investment syndicate to nurse the deal to fruition, which would sell only in their territories.[33]

One of the crucial cultural differences between the UK and US practice revolved around the purpose of the prospectus. Within the UK it is seen as a sales document while in the US it is regarded as a liability document. Thus US lawyers influence greatly the content of the prospectus to ensure it is risk averse, even pessimistic.[34] In the UK merchant bankers keen on marketing the offering

---

28 For example, see Lewis' description in *Liar's Poker* of the creation of the mortgage bond market by Salomon Brothers: Lewis (1989: 97 passim).
29 Neate (1987) pp 8–15.
30 Source of case: Neate (1987: 56).
31 Clementi (1987) pp 58–59.
32 The allocations to the three sectors were 40% to UK institutions, 40% to the UK public and 20% to overseas investors: Clementi (1987) p 60.
33 Clementi (1987) p 64.
34 Joyce (1987) p 78. In the US strict liability is imposed on the issuing company for statements in its prospectus.

shaped the prospectus to reflect their interests rather than those of the lawyers. Because the UK was to be the key market for the offering the English lawyers wanted the UK prospectus to be the 'base' prospectus with 'wrap-arounds' for the other jurisdictions. While easy to accomplish throughout Europe, the US, Canada and Japan were difficult to accommodate in this pattern. The statutory requirements of the US system, especially the SEC, threatened to uncouple the US prospectus from the UK base. However, the cardinal rule for the issuers and lawyers was that the *same* message about British Gas should be disseminated everywhere. Thus all drafts of the US, Canadian and Japanese prospectuses had to be checked against the UK base document. Slaughter and May, as UK government lawyers, devoted many associates' hours to the task.[35]

Timing was problematic. The offer and underwriting had to be synchronised, but again the jurisdictions imposed different schedules. Under the UK timetable, 8 December 1986 was the crucial date when the UK underwriting agreement became effective, with all underwriting agreements being signed and the price fixed on 21 November 1986. The overseas' underwriters usually signed agreements only a few days before the effective date; thus, they were being asked to commit to exposure far earlier than normal. Still there were obstacles insofar as the SEC would not have necessarily declared the registration statement effective, nor would the Canadian authorities have sanctioned the statement. Whereas in the US the regulatory material was handled by a single agency, the SEC, in Canada securities regulation was the task of the individual provinces' securities commissions, even though the US lawyers attempted to argue that Canada should not be perceived as an independent market, but merely a subset of the US one, nettling the Canadians. Eventually the US and Canadian lawyers formed a 'North American' group to co-ordinate the offer, but the Americans would often forget to insert the work 'North'.[36] To obviate the need to deal with all ten provinces individually, the commissions agreed to the Ontario Securities Commission being the lead regulator for the issue. Both US and Canadian lawyers had to persuade their regulators to grant various exemptions – for advertising and disclosure[37] – to enable the offer to proceed in synchrony. The SEC insisted that the newspapers the Financial Times and the Economist carry no publicity for the British Gas offer in their US issues, a demand that would be impossible to enforce with the advent of the Internet. As the due date came, all sides had signed various conditions that would manage the failure of the issue if it flopped. The conditions also benefited the North Americans and Japanese financially because of their longer underwriting exposure. The British government's fiscal actions almost damaged the offer when it imposed a tax on American Depositary Receipts (the form the shares would take in the US). Despite the underwriters argument that the government should pay themselves, the tax was passed on to US investors.

Twelve years on, when Deutsche Telekom was being privatised, similar problems came up. In Germany the issue was advertised, which was still against

---

35 Henderson (1987) p 70.
36 Ross (1987) p 84.
37 For example, under US due diligence the lawyers have to examine all legal documents, including oil and gas purchase contracts. The British Gas management were horrified by the request. No one ever looked at their contracts. Ultimately, a Sullivan & Cromwell partner was allowed to read them in a locked room for a day: Henderson (1987) p 81.

SEC rules. The lawyers managed to find a sympathetic hearing at the SEC, who gave them a 'no-action relief'. One of the lawyers concerned noted: 'The SEC was extremely co-operative. They were keen to see the issue happen, as part of their campaign to encourage foreign issuers.'[38] There were also difficulties in co-ordinating the time frames in multiple jurisdictions and for how long the underwriters would have to be exposed. Since this was a major privatisation for Germany, its regulatory structure had to be revised to take account of the new corporate structure. The revisions of the regulatory schemes were coterminous with the preparations for the privatisation, and it was not until the issue was almost due to occur that the rules were finalised. Thus the regulatory framework was a constant moving target for the lawyers.

Following the 'Velvet Revolution' in Eastern Europe in the late 1980s and early 1990s, the pace of privatisations picked up. As the countries of the region, with the assistance of the European Bank for Reconstruction and Development (EBRD), attempted to rejoin the free market system, many state industries were put up for sale, including breweries, automobile manufacturers, utilities and telecoms. The EBRD believed:

> 'a standard view among academics and policy makers in the early days of the transition process was that faster privatisation would automatically lead to faster restructuring of enterprises. Several years into the transition, the relationship between privatisation and restructuring has proved to be more complex.'[39]

Restructuring often meant that private insiders took control of the former state enterprises with little injection of outside capital or expertise. The mere switch from public to private was insufficient; the best results – a 'deeper restructuring' – occurred when there was dominant outside ownership in the form of foreign direct investment (for example the restructuring of Skoda by Volkswagen in the Czech Republic). Capital and corporate governance became crucial determinants of restructuring success.[40] Poland has been in the vanguard of Eastern European countries ready to embrace Western free market capitalism, eagerly helped by economists from Harvard's Kennedy School of Government (for example Jeffrey Sachs). The following privatisation demonstrates Poland's overtures towards the west.

Telekomunikacja Polska SA[41]

TPSA, a Polish telecoms operator, was one of the largest privatisation IPOs undertaken in Central and Eastern Europe at $920m, as the Polish government sold a 15% share in this company. Because of the essentially risky nature of enterprises in Eastern Europe, the EBRD often takes a stake in the enterprise – in this case $75.5m – to shore up confidence. The consortium that won the deal was a partnership of Goldman Sachs and Schroders, advised by Baker & McKenzie as lead counsel. Before the launch of the issue Goldman Sachs

38 International Financial Law Review (1997) at 19.
39 EBRD (1995) p 128.
40 Frydman and Rapacynzski (1994). Another significant requirement is the changeover from a state-planned 'monobank' culture to a more diverse banking sector.
41 Source: IFLR (1999) at 10.

pulled out of the deal, arousing speculation that the deal was dead. It still went ahead and attracted $1.5bn from international investors, that is, two-and-a-half times oversubscribed. Baker & McKenzie prepared the offering and provided opinions for the securities regulators. All was done within a very tight timetable, but the task was anything but simple. For example, the due diligence was vast, with the company spread all over Poland. Lawyers were sent to all parts of the company and country; the final report was over 4,000 pages long. Seventy-five per cent of the offer was in the form of global depositary receipts listed in London.[42] The law firm of White & Case advised the State Treasury of Poland, and TPSA was advised by Hunton & Williams. Even though the bulk of the issue was listed in London, the majority of the legal work was carried out by US law firms. The difference between TPSA and other privatisations in the region was that instead of finding an outside investor partner first, revising the finance and corporate governance, then moving to an IPO, TPSA went for the IPO first, and then sought a partner. Without the due diligence work by the lawyers for the consortium, the deal would have been impossible.

This case does demonstrate the importance of international institutions in enabling emerging markets to participate in global capital markets. Of interest though, is that the World Bank has been criticised for aiding countries that could themselves borrow funds in the capital markets. US Treasury Secretary, Lawrence Summers, said: 'Lending in (emerging market) countries should be confined to the areas where they can increase total financing capacity', adding that sometimes the Bank lending can 'crowd out private sector finance'.[43] However, these institutions are able to help develop legal and regulatory structures in emerging markets that facilitate the growth-free markets, the rule of law and a linkage to capital markets. Indeed, the general counsel for the European Bank of Reconstruction and Development (EBRD) said:

> 'The EBRD's mandate is to foster the transition towards market economies in the countries of the Former Soviet Union and Central and Eastern Europe, and to promote private and entrepreneurial initiative ... Recognising fully the importance to sustainable economic development of stable "rules of the game" and the establishment and continued strengthening of law administration and enforcement institutions, the EBRD has embarked on the provision of legal technical assistance to its countries of operation that will foster the transition process.'[44]

To reinforce its point the EBRD has carried out legal audits on its constituent jurisdictions to determine the receptivity of the legal system to investment. To illustrate its ideas, two examples are given below, one of an immature economy, Turkmenistan, and one more developed, Poland.[45] These examples display the great variability across the EBRD's region.

---

42 Depositary receipts are a means of issuing shares so that investors can purchase publicly traded equity or debt without handling the actual shares. They allow US investors to buy non-US stock, which is forbidden to many. They are also used in 'soft dollar' arrangements. 'Essentially, the depositary receipt has "Americanized" a non-UD share to accommodate the US market' (Bank of New York (1999) p 9).
43 Reuters (2000).
44 Taylor (1996) at 98.
45 EBRD (1995) pp 108–117.

Table 1   Analysis of investment laws in Turkmenistan and Poland

	Turkmenistan	**Poland**
How extensive are legal rules?	Laws exist regulating both foreign and domestic investment. Laws exist regulating the use of indirect investment vehicles, such as securities or investment funds. Foreigners may generally not hold more than 49% of the shares issued by a local company and are prohibited from owning land. Nationals (individuals) may own up to 50 hectares of land. The transfer abroad of fully convertible currencies is subject to central bank approval. Most foreign investment proposals require governmental approval.	Laws exist regulating the use of indirect investment vehicles, such as securities or investment funds. Limited-responsibility partnerships or joint-stock companies may be wholly owned and managed by foreigners. Land ownership is allowed, including by foreigners and foreign-owned local companies, with an appropriate permit. No licence is usually required for the export of fully convertible currencies. Most foreign investment proposals do not require governmental approval.
How clear and accessible is law?	Laws are not always drafted by legally trained personnel and are often based on Soviet Union or Russian models. Legal rules regulating investment are often issued by means of executive decree. The full texts of laws affecting investment are not always published and Ministerial Cabinet decrees are not always available. Important court decisions are not usually published or accessible by practitioners. Legal assistance to private parties in respect of investment matters is very limited and may not be independent from the government. Where available, legal assistance on investment matters is not generally affordable to local investors. Local law firms may not yet have the skills necessary to handle complex investment matters adequately.	Laws are drafted by legally trained personnel. Legal rules regulating investment are prescribed mainly by the legislature. The full texts of laws are published within one month of being passed. Draft laws are not always published. Important court decisions are usually published or accessible to practitioners within 12 months of being issued. Sophisticated legal assistance is available, at least in Warsaw, and is generally affordable to local investors.

	Turkmenistan	**Poland**
How well supported administratively is law?	Although there is a law on pledges, registers of ownership interests and pledges of assets granted by way of security rarely exist. Limited-liability companies and joint-stock companies may take up to two months to be registered. The size and quality of the state civil service in Ashgabad is considered insufficient for the role attributed to it, although the police force is considered adequate.	Legally prescribed registers of interests in respect of land or security exist. No system exists for registration of security interests in respect of movable assets. Records contained in land or share registers are usually current within three months. Limited-liability companies and joint-stock companies may be created; registration may take two to three months. Civil servants are stated to be appointed or promoted principally on the basis of merit rather than declared political allegiance. The size and quality of the state civil service in Warsaw is considered insufficient for the role attributed to it. Criminal laws, particularly those relating to the protection of property and the prohibition of money-laundering and corrupt practices, are viewed as not extensively policed.
How well supported judicially is law?	Judges are appointed by the President for a five-year term. Private parties generally believe that courts would not recognise and enforce their rights against state parties. The annual salary of a judge of a court of first instance is comparable to that of an unskilled factory worker. Courts are often regarded as lacking the financial and human resources, as well as the training, to handle complex investment disputes adequately. Foreign arbitral awards are not required to be recognised and enforced by the courts without a re-examination of their merits.	Private parties generally believe that courts will recognise and enforce their legal rights, including against state parties. Courts are viewed to have the skills to handle investment dispute matters, but still to lack human and administrative resources to ensure a smooth administration of justice. Parties must wait for about one year for their commercial case to be heard on its merits by a court. While the remuneration of a judge of first instance is three times that of an entry-level primary school teacher, it is the reported intention of the state to dedicate further resources to increase the remuneration of the judiciary. The Court of Arbitration attached to the Polish Chamber of Commerce is stated to possess both the human and financial means to handle complex investment disputes approximating to international standards. Foreign arbitral awards are required to be recognised and enforced by the courts without a re-examination of their merits.

The next case concerns a merger and restructuring of a company in western Europe.

ALSTOM[46]

In 1998 the largest non-privatisation IPO was a French company, Alstom, amounting to $3.7bn. Alstom was owned equally by GEC of the UK and Alcatel of France. It had over 400 subsidiaries in over 60 jurisdictions and was registered as a Netherlands NV. Among the advisers, the global co-ordinators were Goldman Sachs and Credit Suisse First Boston, and their advisers were Davis Polk & Wardwell and Stibbe Simont Monahan Duhot & Giroux, a 'large' French law firm.[47] Acting as counsel to the issuer were Shearman & Sterling and Lovell White Durrant. And finally, counsel to the selling stockholders were Freshfields and Gide Loyrette Nouel, another 'large' French law firm. Before the IPO launched, the company's in-house counsel had to take charge of reorganising the company and its various subsidiaries from a Dutch company into a French one. This involved numerous government authorisations, adding to the already complicated and logistically challenging nature of the deal. Preparation for the IPO ran in parallel to the reorganisation and involved French, English, US and international tranches, consisting of a primary offering of shares sold by Alstom and a secondary offering by Alstom's parents. The shares were listed in Paris, London and New York, and were subject to full regulatory review simultaneously by the SEC in the US, the London Stock Exchange in the UK and the COB in France.

The offering involved the issuance of American Depositary Receipts, listed in New York, and the first ever UK Depositary Receipts (UKDRs), listed in London. Lovell White Durrant structured the UKDRs and advised Alstom on its employee share offering, which covered some 35 jurisdictions and ran as part of the public offering. Davis Polk & Wardwell led the due diligence, ensuring that the company's diverse material assets and subsidiaries were intact and included in the deal, or at least making sure that fall-back plans were in place if the reorganisation was not completed by the time of the IPO. The firm also advised on the core disclosure document, the adequacy of the disclosure and the underwriting agreement itself.

Just one month before the closing of the IPO, Alstom acquired Cegelec, an electrical contracting and process control business owned by Alcatel, which was itself a quarter of the size of the combined issuer. All the work which had been to demonstrate what the group would look like after the reorganisation was re-done, taking into account the new business. After five months' work the deal was priced to go.[48] The final case reveals the complexity of legal institutions that can be involved in mergers and acquisitions.

46 Source: IFLR (1999) at 13.
47 In comparison with the large law firms of the US and the UK, the 'large' law firms of mainland Europe are small.
48 In all, in 1998, Davis Polk & Wardwell advised in five major deals: Alstom (France) $3.7bn; Swisscom (Switzerland) $6.43bn; Telefonica (Spain) $2.7bn; Argentaria (Spain) $2.4bn; and Salzgitter (Germany) $483m (IFLR (1999) at 7).

ASAT[49]

Deals have become very complex. ASAT is a large supplier of semiconductor assembly and testing services in the world in Asia. Prior to the transaction QPL International Holdings, a semiconductor manufacturer, was ASAT's parent company. A consortium of buyers used a US-style leveraged buyout (LBO) to acquire a controlling $112m stake in ASAT. This gave them 50% of the parent company holding ASAT's shares. In addition to investors, the consortium included Chase Asia Equity Partners, a $750m fund as lead member. There were three other transactions in the LBO. The second was a $155m high-yield bond offering, including equity warrants, by ASAT. The issue was underwritten by Donaldson, Lufkin & Jenrette and Chase Securities and was sold mainly to US investors. The third transaction was the arrangement of a $65m syndicated loan comprising a $40m term loan due in 2004 and a five-year $25m revolving credit facility. Finally, the first three transactions enabled ASAT to repay its outstanding debt.[50] Because of the number of transactions and complexity of the deal, 15 law firms were involved, based in six countries, giving advice on New York, English and Hong Kong law. Table 2 below shows the distribution of work among the law firms involved.

Table 2   ASAT transaction law firms

Acquisition	**Restructuring of Debt**
Counsel to Buyers	*Counsel to ASAT*
Milbank Tweed Hadley & McCloy (transaction counsel and US law) Lead partner: Hong Kong office	Slaughter and May (English and Hong Kong law) Lead partner: Hong Kong office
Slaughter and May (English and Hong Kong law) Lead partner: Hong Kong office	Milbank Tweed Hadley & McCoy (co-ordinating counsel) Lead partner: Hong Kong office
Counsel to Sellers	*Counsel to QPL*
Richards Butler (transaction counsel; English and Hong Kong law) Lead partner: Hong Kong office	Richards Butler Lead partner: Hong Kong office
Dewey Ballantine (US tax counsel) Lead partner: London office	
	Counsel to Creditors
	Lovell White Durrant (UK creditors) Lead partner: London office

49 Source: IFLR (1999) at 6.
50 IFLR (1999) at 6.

High-Yield Offering

Baker & McKenzie (Hong Kong creditors)
Lead partner: Hong Kong office

Counsel to Issuers
Milbank Tweed Hadley & McCloy
(transaction counsel and US law)
Lead partner: Hong Kong office

Clifford Chance (public note holders)
Lead partner: Hong Kong office

Slaughter and May
(English and Hong Kong law)
Lead partner: Hong Kong office

Counsel to Underwriters
Skadden Arps Slate Meagher & Flom
(transaction counsel and US law)
Lead partner: Hong Kong office

Other Law Firms
Counsel to Co-Investors

O'Melveny & Meyers (Los Angeles)

Denton Hall (English and
Hong Kong law)
Lead partner: Hong Kong office

Paul Weiss Rifkind Wharton &
Garrison (Hong Kong)
Schell Bray Aycock Abel & Livingston
(US)

Other Local Counsel (Re: Formation, etc)

Syndicated Loan

Appleby Spurling & Kempe
(Bermuda)

Counsel to Borrowers
Milbank Tweed Hadley & McCoy

Lead partner: Hong Kong office

Maples & Calder (Cayman Islands)
O'Sullivan Graev & Karabell (New York)
Walkers (Cayman Islands)

Counsel to Banks
Cravath Swaine & Moore
Lead attorney: New York office

Source: International Financial Law Review (1999) 6

CAPITAL MARKETS AND INSOLVENCY

All of this work is done with the knowledge that the possible demise of the business maybe close at hand. This is notably apparent, for example, in the US capital markets, where there is a greater proportion of high-yield debt.[51] During the wild days of Michael Milken, Drexel Burnham Lambert underwrote more than 60% of new junk bond issues in the market.[52] Now no underwriter has any kind of large percentage enabling them to manipulate the market and, moreover, secondary markets have emerged. Underwriters proliferate and many new growth firms are clamouring for funds, especially in telecommunications, Internet and cable television. High-yield debt carries high risk, in the expectation of a big return. In the recession of the early 1990s default rates were over 7%. Market players now have 20 years' of records detailing pricing, default rates and recovery rates. With these data, investors can model their investment strategies. In addition, investors have a better understanding of the insolvency process in the US and the way it can restructure business rather than liquidate it. Thus the expectations of such investors are highly informed, in contrast to Europe, where the high-yield market is very much in its infancy and there are few data to support meaningful predictions.[53]

One of the most interesting aspects of this type of capital markets work is the emergence of secondary debt markets (or distressed debt markets). The writer has analysed in detail elsewhere how the market was created.[54] Briefly, to reprise, during the recession at the end of the twentieth century, lawyers and investors realised that value resided in the distressed debt (paper) of companies in Chapter 11 (the US insolvency regime). The secondary debt market was made creating value out of extremely small margins. As the spreads diminished, traders, often vulture funds, searched elsewhere for markets to exploit. Markets have been made in Europe, especially in the UK, and Asia. The UK situation with respect to distressed debt has disrupted established and settled modes of handling failure.

In the US insolvency regimes are particularly friendly to debtors; not so in the UK. Chapter 11 does not officially exist in the UK. Despite that, from the 1970s onwards the Bank of England has promoted a type of restructuring process called the 'London Approach'.[55] Under the London Approach large companies undergoing financial difficulties can call on their bankers to mount a quasi-Chapter 11 rescue. Unlike Chapter 11 the process is not court or lawyer-driven. It is entirely unofficial, but with the acknowledged blessing of the Bank of England. To those who handle London Approach workouts one of its virtues is that the restructuring is shared equally among bank creditors. No single institution is allowed to hold the others hostage, otherwise it faces the 'threat of the governor's

51 Sheldon and Abbondante (1999) p 16.
52 They were called junk bonds because their risk factor was so high, as were their potential returns, usually because the company desiring the funds was too highly leveraged and could not borrow in the established markets. These corporate bonds were not registered with the SEC. Stewart (1991) even refers to the Wild West atmosphere of the junk bond era.
53 The upshot is that agreements specify English law for the senior debt and New York state law for the high-yield debt: Dignan (1999).
54 Flood (2001).
55 Flood (2001).

eyebrows'.[56] These informal controls have enabled an ad hoc, unofficial workout process to develop and succeed, and it continues as long as participants understand the underlying norms of the London Approach. The secondary debt market has disturbed this genteel process. Outsiders, in the guise of vulture funds, have injected a brash, even rebellious tone into London Approach workouts. Not beholden to the same norms as the regular players, debt traders have generated deep anxiety and nervousness among senior debt holders.[57] As long as these differences in insolvency regimes exist, capital markets players will be able to exploit the fear.

ELITES AND CAPITAL MARKETS

The numbers of active players in capital markets are relatively small. Seven investment banks dominate global capital markets, and of those seven only three comprise the top tier. The bonuses awarded at Goldman Sachs, which is probably the most successful investment bank in the world measured in volume and size of deals' were referred to above. Hodgart noted:

'three investment banks dominated the global adviser market in 1998, handling $2.23 billion of deals, with the next three banks handling $1.18 billion. Within the US the three leading firms (the same as world wide) handled $1.2 billion compared with the next three banks with $690 million.'[58]

By 1999 the big three investment banks, Goldman Sachs, Morgan Stanley Dean Witter and Merrill Lynch, had 'each advised on more than $1 trillion in world-wide mergers and acquisitions …'.[59] The value of the deals also indicates the rewards to the investment banks and others who participate in capital markets work. What is clear about this sector is that the critically decisive players are few in number and their networks are densely structured encouraging repeat-player patterns of activity. Ferguson spells out the connections:

'A small band of major banks call the shots on the big-ticket equities issues. These are the people to impress for law firms looking to develop market share on these deals. Unfortunately for the pretenders, the banks sit comfortably alongside a similarly small band of law firms. On Wall Street, relationships extend beyond even the eldest partners, and banks and forms share a lineage steeped in the history of New York's development as a financial centre. Some of these old-school ties are part of Wall Street folk law [sic]: Goldman Sachs and Sullivan & Cromwell, Morgan Stanley and Davis Polk & Wardwell.'[60]

For example, the relationship between Morgan Stanley and Davis Polk goes back 110 years.[61] If we take some of the key investment banks and match them

---

56 The City of London is a small place where relations are still important in the conduct of commerce. And the Bank of England exerts enormous influence over the City's financial institutions. For example, when Freshfields, the law firm that has traditionally served the Bank, moved premises from close to St Paul's Cathedral to Fleet Street at the western edge of the City, the governor remarked that they could not go any further or they would be in danger of moving to the 'other' side of town.
57 Sheldon and Abbondante (1999) p 18.
58 Hodgart (1999) p 6.
59 Deogun (2000) at 13.
60 Ferguson (1997) at 33.
61 Forster (1997) at 37.

with a sample of their legal advisers, the patterns become evident, as illustrated by Table 3.[62]

Table 3   Major investment banks and legal advisers

INVESTMENT BANK	LAW FIRM
Merrill Lynch	Brown & Wood (NY)
	Cravath Swaine & Moore (NY)
	Davis Polk & Wardwell (NY)
	Freshfields (London)
	Skadden Arps (NY)
Credit Suisse First Boston	Allen & Overy (London)
	Clifford Chance (London)
	Cravath Swaine & Moore (NY)
	Davis Polk & Wardwell (NY)
	Shearman & Sterling (NY)
	Simpson Thacher & Bartlett (NY)
	Skadden Arps (NY)
	Weil Gotshal & Manges (NY)
Goldman Sachs	Allen & Overy (London)
	Cleary Gottlieb (NY)
	Cravath Swaine & Moore (NY)
	Davis Polk & Wardwell (NY)
	Freshfields (London)
	Sullivan & Cromwell (NY)
Morgan Stanley	Brown & Wood (NY)
	Davis Polk & Wardwell (NY)
	Freshfields (London)
	Shearman & Sterling (NY)
	Weil Gotshal & Manges (NY)

In all we are distinguishing around 12 law firms in New York and London that dominate the global capital markets field. They work with each other repeatedly and have adapted to each others' cultural norms. Indeed, they probably do not work with many other firms at all, since they represent the top tier on both sides of the Atlantic. It resembles the Cabots and Lovells of Boston.

Capital markets work requires lawyers who understand the intricacies of both US and UK markets and law. For example, the January 1997 issue of *International Financial Law Review* contained details of the 11 biggest capital markets deals in 1996. The firm with the most deals was Sullivan & Cromwell and it was followed

---

62 These samples were derived from LawMoney.com. Within a given year it is fair to see a preponderance of US law firms involved as legal advisers to the major player investment banks.

by Shearman & Sterling, both blue-chip, Wall Street law firms. On the English side Linklaters and Clifford Chance were the highest ranking firms. In a letter commenting on the new 'aircraft carrier' proposals by the SEC, Sullivan & Cromwell was able to write of itself:

> 'Sullivan & Cromwell has extensive experience in securities transactions. We have represented issuers, underwriters and investors in securities offerings since before the enactment of the Securities Act. In the three-year period of 1996–98, we acted in SEC-registered offerings of corporate securities valued at over $150 billion (based on information maintained by Securities Data Company).'[63]

The situation shows no sign of changing, as the next two Tables on advising in international deals clearly show.

Table 4   International advisers to issuers

International Advisers to Issuers by Total Deal Value

Firm	No. of Deals	Total Value ($m)	Average Value ($m)
Shearman & Sterling	15	18,281.498	1,305.82
Cleary Gottlieb	7	17,146.391	2,449.48
Sullivan & Cromwell	7	11,110.395	1,851.73
Davis Polk & Wardwell	11	7,664.733	696.79
Skadden Arps	2	5,330	2.66
Hengeler Mueller Weitzel Wirtz	3	5,142.341	1,714.11
White & Case	4	4,164.702	1,041.11
Clifford Chance	3	3,495.9	1,165.3
Linklaters & Alliance	16	2,603.832	162.73
Baker & McKenzie	6	1,333.802	222.3

Table 5   International advisers to lead managers

International Advisers to Lead Manager by Total Deal Value

Firm	No. of Deals	Total Value ($m)	Average Value ($m)
Cleary Gottlieb	17	22,889.641	1,430.60
Shearman & Sterling	27	13,471.788	498.955
Sullivan & Cromwell	5	13,038.449	2,607.69
Linklaters & Alliance	11	9,694.325	1,077.147
Allen & Overy	14	7,807.475	557.676
Davis Polk & Wardwell	5	7,321.32	1,830.33
Skadden Arps	5	4,274.921	854.984
Freshfields	15	4,459.304	297.286
Clifford Chance	12	3,018.965	251.58

Source: Mannix (1999)

63 Comments of Sullivan & Cromwell, 10 June 1999.

On all scores the US law firms do best. Between the US firms there is not a great deal of variation. For example, in Table 5 Cleary Gottlieb has the biggest total value, while Shearman & Sterling has the most deals and Sullivan & Cromwell has the highest average value per deal. The profile is not too different in Table 4. The 'magic circle' of firms competes within itself.

The importance of the US capital markets cannot be exaggerated here, which ties in US law firms and investment banks. No other market has such huge resources. This is rendered visible by the high numbers of venture capitalists and hedge funds. Even though London is a major market in its own right, because of obstacles like the Glass-Steagall Act it has been a productive home for many investment banks. But UK capital markets are not as large as the US, hence the hegemony of US institutions in the field.

Cultural differences intrude in styles of working between American and English lawyers. The quest for disclosure in due diligence is quite different. US lawyers think in terms of the litigation potential of disclosure: has the verification process been conducted to the standard expected by a trial judge? This is usually Rule 10b-5 under the Exchange Act 1934, which an investment bank will request of the lawyers. But as one Skadden Arps attorney opined: 'It is negative assurance that nothing has come to our attention that indicates that there are misleading statements or omissions in the disclosure document.'[64] In the British Gas privatisation the Shearman & Sterling lawyer distinguished the difference in disclosure under the American and British regimes:

'One of the conflicts in the Gas offering ... that caused me the most sleepless hours was the contrast between the US system of due diligence ... and the UK system of verification. Now I do not really pretend to understand verification, but it seems to involve taking each sentence of the prospectus and finding someone, either in the government on the company, whose initials can be put next to it. The US system is much more haphazard and less carefully structured but takes a different slant. Under US practice, lawyers for all parties attempt to look at every legal document that can be found to back up the statements in the prospectus.'[65]

These stylistic differences have motivated the English law firms to create US practices that can compete on equal terms with US firms, although the English firms may not be hiring sufficient numbers of US attorneys – one US lawyer commented that just because a big American name joins a UK firm, he still 'needs to go and hire 20 people to convince US underwriters that they can do the due diligence'.[66] Another US lawyer also noted that UK firms:

'have hired some excellent lawyers but the firms as a whole lack some of the resources that we bring to the task and for example some of the sophisticated US tax knowledge for tax disclosure. Also there is the long history and knowledge of how disclosure issues have beenhandled in the past.'[67]

This is where we rejoin Santos' 'globalized localisms' and 'localized globalisms' mentioned above. In order to succeed in the capital markets field, law firms must have multi-jurisdictional skills in sufficient strength that they are accepted as both strong global players and good local players. The investment banks will seek out local expertise as well as global reach.

64 Forster (1996) at 20.
65 Joyce (1987) p 81.
66 Forster (1996) at 21.
67 Forster (1996) at 21.

The key to succeeding in the field is to achieve the capacity to be the global co-ordinator for a deal. This, in effect, means being the adviser to the lead bank in the deal (see Table 5 above). So, even though some UK law firms may involve themselves in a large number of deals, they will not be the global co-ordinator. Instead, they will most likely be a form of local counsel or lead firm for one of the other entities involved in the deal. Only in 1999 did a UK law firm, Linklaters, for the first time advise an underwriter, Merrill Lynch, on an SEC-registered offering.[68] The advantage lies therefore with the US law firms, because of their historical ties with the banks, their long involvement and expertise in capital markets work, and the dominance of US capital markets as sources of funding. In other words, the market is structured through longstanding social and economic ties,[69] which generate high levels of trust.[70] These firms do not have to advertise, they already constitute an index of quality of service.[71] It is therefore feasible for elite, capital markets, US firms such as Cravath Swaine & Moore, Davis Polk & Wardwell and Sullivan & Cromwell to establish London offices that offer only New York law for capital markets work, instead of becoming multinational practices with local capacity; they get ample numbers of UK and European clients eager for access to US capital markets.[72] The corollary being that UK firms cannot depend solely on UK law. As a Chicago lawyer put it: 'Clients are increasingly indifferent to what the governing law of a capital markets transaction is.'[73]

CONCLUSION

Capital markets work is symbolic of the globalisation of finance and professional services. Those endowed with social, cultural and economic capital to carry out the work exist in a rarefied atmosphere inhabited by only a few. The rush to embrace capitalism by the former communist regimes, European and Asian, is matched by the eagerness of the caudillo countries. All want access to the wealthiest market of all, the US. The Securities and Exchange Commission has altered its disclosure rules for registration to enable greater entry to US capital markets by foreigners. Moreover, US lawyers are promoting the US 'way of death' in bankruptcy as more friendly to the debtor, aware that every deal in the capital markets has to be seen in the light of its potential failure. Thus, the two main competitors to service global capital markets – American and English lawyers – have begun to create mutually advantageous legal regimes for deal making and failure. The US has Chapter 11 and the UK has the London Approach. And now UNCITRAL has joined in at their behest.

It is clear that individual jurisdictions remain legitimate sources of state norms, and we have not yet arrived at the hyperglobalisers' utopia nor are we still in the sceptics' dystopia, but these, in many cases are being overridden by soft law created through contract and agreements that usually owes its 'allegiance' to either New York state law or English law. Local law is in the process of becoming subsumed under highly competitive systems of law that market themselves aggressively. The result is that local law declines in importance in spite of whatever changes it may introduce to modernise itself. The Anglo-American axis is too powerful to defeat in the capital markets field. It dominates the transnational institutions such as

68 Mannix (1999) at 9.
69 Granovetter (1985).
70 Cf Baker (1990).
71 Podolny (1993).
72 Lee (1997) at 31.
73 Lee (1997) at 31.

the IMF and WTO; the prime investment banks are based in the US, and the lawyers are either in New York or London. The combination of institutional global reach, normative creativity and pluralism, and professional service flexibility and responsiveness to market changes appears impregnable.

Select bibliography

Baker, W E, (1990) 'Market Networks and Corporate Behavior', 96 AJS 589.

Bank of New York (1999) 'How to Issue and Trade Depositary Receipts', in *US Capital Markets Report.*

Clementi, D, (1987) 'World-Wide Public Offerings of Securities: British Gas', in F Neate (ed), *The Developing Global Securities Market.*

Deogun, N, (2000) 'Top 3 Firms for Deals Set $1 Trillion Mark', Wall Street Journal Europe, 3 January, at 13, 23.

Dezalay, Y, and Garth, B, (1996) *Dealing in Virtue: International Commercial Arbitration and the Construction of a Transnational Legal Order.*

Dignan, C, (1999) 'Are UK Firms Ready for Global Banking?', The Lawyer Online, www.thelawyer.co.uk/TLglobalbank.html.

EBRD, (1995) *Transition Report 1995: Investment and Enterprise Development.*

Ferguson, N, (1997) 'What the Client Demands', IFL Rev 33–35, December.

Finch, S, Macdonald, G, and Walker, J, (2000) 'Replacing the Depression's Final Legacy', IFL Rev 9, February.

Flood, J, (2001) 'The Vultures Fly East: the Creation and Globalisation of the Distressed Debt Market', in D Nelken and J Feest (eds), *Adapting Legal Cultures.*

Forster, R, (1996) 'International Equities Survey: Davis Polk & Wardwell Leads the World's Equity Advisers', IFL Rev 17–25, September.

—(1997) 'New York Firms Seek the World's Business', IFL Rev 36–39, December.

Frydman, R, and Rapacynzski, A, (1994) *Privatisation Eastern Europe: Is the State Withering Away?.*

Gallie, W B, (1955) 'Essentially Contested Concepts', Proceedings of the Aristotelian Society 56, 167–198.

Gamble, A, (1994) *The Free Economy and the Strong State* (2nd edn).

Garfield, A, (1999) 'High-flying Goldman Sees Wage Bill Double to $8.7bn', Independent, 22 December, at 13.

Giddens, A, (1990) *The Consequences of Modernity.*

Gow, D, (2000) 'Now Vodafone Wants Net Alliances', Guardian, 5 February, at 32.

Granovetter, M, (1985) 'Economic Action and Social Structure: The Problem of Embeddedness', 91 AJS 481.

Held, D, McGrew, A, Goldblatt, D, (1999) *Global Transformations: Politics, Economics and Culture.*

Henderson, G, (1987) 'World-Wide Public Offerings of Securities: British Gas', in F Neate (ed), *The Developing Global Securities Market.*

Hirst, P, and Thompson, G, (1996) *Globalisation in Question: The International Economy and the Possibilities of Governance.*

Hodgart, A, (1999) 'Introduction', *IFLR Review of the Year: Capital Markets Forum 1999*, at 6.

IFLR (1999) 'International Equities Team of the Year (Eastern Europe)', *IFLR Review of the Year: Capital Markets Forum 1999.*

IFL Rev, (1997) 'Deals of the Year: Blockbusters Boost Final Months of Record Year', IFL Rev, January, at 18.

—(1999) 'Cutting Edge: Milbank Tweed Leads on First US-Style LBO in Post-Recession Asia', IFL Rev, December, at 6.

Joyce, T, (1987) 'World-Wide Public Offerings of Securities: British Gas', in F Neate (ed), *The Developing Global Securities Market.*

Kamman, E, and Covello, A, (1999) 'New SEC Disclosure Rules for Non-US Companies', in *US Capital Markets Report.*

Kinami, N, (1998) *The Japanese Big Bang.*

Lee, P, (1997) 'Country Survey: US Firms Embrace English Law Capability', IFL Rev, April, at 30–32.

Lewis, M, (1989) *Liar's Poker.*

Lukes, S, (1974) *Power: A Radical View.*

Mannix, R, (1999) 'European Equity Clients Favour One-Stop Shops', IFL Rev, October, at 9–13.

—(2000) 'Foreign Investors Snap Up Korean Bargains', IFL Rev, February, at 28–33.

McLuhan, M, (1964) 'Roads and Paper Routes', in *Understanding Media: The Extensions of Man.*

Neate, F (ed), (1987) 'World-Wide Public Offerings of Securities: British Gas', in F Neate (ed), *The Developing Global Securities Market.*

Ohmae, K, (1991) *The Borderless World.*

—(1995) *The End of the Nation State.*

Podolny, J M, (1993) 'A Status-based Model of Market Competition', 98 AJS 829.

Reuters, (2000) 'US Calls for World Bank Reform', www.altavista.co.uk/content/reu_news_article.jsp?category=business&id=0

Ritzer, G, (1996) 'The McDonaldization Thesis: Is Expansion Inevitable?', 11 International Sociology 291.

Ross, D, (1987) 'World-Wide Public Offerings of Securities: British Gas', in F Neate (ed), *The Developing Global Securities Market.*

Santos, B de S, (1995) *Toward a New Common Sense: Law, Science and Politics in the Paradigmatic Transition.*

Sassen, S, (1991) *The Global City: New York, London, Tokyo.*

Sheldon, C, and Abbondante, T, (1999) 'Great Expectations: High-Yield Debt in European Leveraged Acquisition Finance', in *US Capital Markets Report.* London: Euromoney.

Stewart, J B, (1991) *Den of Thieves.*

Taylor, J, (1996) 'New Laws, New Lawyers and the EBRD', 24 International Business Lawyer 98.

Teubner, G, (1997) '"Global Bukowina": Legal Pluralism in the World Society', in G Teubner (ed), *Global Law Without A State.*

Chapter 7

Global markets, national law, and the regulation of business – a view from the top

EM FOX[1]

INTRODUCTION

Economic liberalisation and technological innovations are changing the dimensions of markets. Both phenomena drive increasing economic integration in the world, making national borders irrelevant to global commerce.

As a result, market problems that were once national are now of international dimension. Many of the problems cannot be solved by a national-only, or nation-to-nation, horizontal view of the world. The global patterns of business and market competition call for a new paradigm for the regulation of business; a paradigm sufficiently copious to view the world as market.

Questions of larger-than-national economic governance have long been treated in the area of trade; particularly in the World Trade Organization (WTO) and its predecessor the GATT. As we enter the new century, similar questions loom with regard to investment, the environment, labour, intellectual property, and the conduct and structure of business. Proposed solutions range from international codes, and thus international economic law, to proactive networking of nations, to continued pursuit of unilateral national policies in the interests of the regulating nation.

This chapter argues that economic reality is diminishing the utility and challenging the wisdom and justice of the supremacy of the nation-to-nation model. Through the window of regulating business conduct and structure, the chapter outlines the problems posed by unbending adherence to the national model, presents case examples that demonstrate the limits of national-based solutions and proposes methodologies for achieving a broader vision.

The questions asked here are questions of world economic federalism: at what level of government or community should regulation be lodged, in view of dual objectives to promote efficiency of regulation for the broader community and to serve the values and choices of the local community? In the EU, the challenge has a name. It is called the problem of subsidiarity. As developed below, the experience of the EU has much to contribute to the world conversation.

---

1   The author thanks Michael Likosky for his stimulating ideas in critiquing this chapter.

The chapter looks in the direction of anchoring liberalisation while assuring as much national or local autonomy as possible consistent with nations' 'pulling together' to achieve an open, productive, unprivileged world-market system.

THE PROBLEMS

As a result of spillovers, nationalism and lack of vision as wide as markets, national law may have a poor fit with transnational problems.[2] There are five particular problems that may call for larger-than-national conceptions. Namely:

(1) National law, because of its bounds, cannot catch all the conduct that harms the nation's citizens.
(2) At the other extreme, national law with a generous reach may regulate other nations' people and transactions and intrude on other nations' prerogatives and order.
(3) National systems of law and regulation tend to clash.
(4) When the problems are bigger than nations, nations lack vision; we need a view from the top.
(5) Nations are increasingly less good representatives of people and firms that reside within their borders but that produce, sell and buy in global markets; and people and firms that reside outside the borders are increasingly regulated without a voice.

The problems are intertwined, as may be seen through the lens of competition law (also called antitrust). In industrialised nations, competition law has largely succeeded in manoeuvring around the first problem – the practical limits of national law. With the US as pioneer in this often controversial enterprise, nations have developed rules of extra-territorial reach of national law. Today, extra-territoriality is largely accepted as a legitimate tool of a nation to catch offshore acts, such as price-fixing cartels, targeted at the regulating nations' commerce or citizens or directly harming them. But extra-territoriality of national law cannot meet the challenge of globalisation.[3] First, it is a tool of mature economies that have power over outsiders sufficient to command obedience. Less developed and developing countries lack the power to reach and discipline offshore actors that harm them. Second, the extra-territorial solution is not complete. Nations may insulate their firms' harmful outbound acts by 'acts of state', putting offenders beyond the legal reach of the harmed jurisdiction. Third, the extra-territorial solution creates other problems that arise from the enforcing nation's intrusion into the domain of another nation; it provokes rather than modulates systems clashes.

While the first problem is that national law may catch too little, the second problem is that national law may catch too much. It may extend so far as to regulate what people do on their home territory by means totally consistent with their home regulation. Aggressively extra-territorial law may intrude on another nation's prerogatives. If the latter nation is likewise industrialised, it is likely to fight back, perhaps by trade war or retaliation. If it is less developed, it may just take what it gets.

---

2   See Christiansen (1994); Trachtman (1992).
3   Fox (2000).

As the third problem postulates, in a world of international transactions and extra-territoriality, systems will clash. In the absence of trade wars on the one hand, or acceptance of protocols on the other, this usually means that the nation with the most prohibitory law 'wins'.

Fourth, as a function of their incentives and powers, national officials in a globalised world can lack vision. When national or local officials see problems through eyes that are blinkered by political borders, vision is parochial. A producing state may want to take what it can get; to use its market power; or to pollute across borders, with no vision of and for the whole.

Fifth, the nation/state is increasingly a flawed agent for international bargains. There has been a shift in the tectonic plates of business.[4] The activity of firms has shifted from national to global environments. Global firms pierce border barriers with the laser speed of e-commerce. The firm looks worldwide for inputs, for production sites and for markets. National agencies, in contrast, look at their bordered domain. In matters of pre-merger notification and clearance, for example, each national antitrust agency sees its own interest in delaying while vetting international mergers (as well as in collecting filing fees). In matters of trade, trade representatives and legislators respond to domestic businesses' 'needs' to protect 'their' markets from low-priced imports. Ideally, the agent for antitrust should be a citizen of the world in the way that European jurists are citizens of Europe. But, typically, national enforcers ask: Why should we look at harms beyond our nation's bounds? Why should we count the costs (for example, of a US export cartel or of a US merger) to the rest of the world?

As a result of this orientation, national enforcers in industrialised countries tend to think of international problems as national, and solutions as horizontal and unilateral or reciprocal. Each nation/community acts in its own interest, usually formulated as a short-term interest. It may call on a neighbour to help it out – in discovery of evidence, in enforcement of law, in non-enforcement of a neighbour's law that hurts 'its' businesses.[5] Perhaps the neighbour will return the favour. There is a failure of will and incentive to see the problems as overarching, to search for solutions in the interests of the common good of the greater community and to appreciate the reality that we are members of the world community.

CASE EXAMPLES

Solutions must be tailored to problems. This chapter presents problem-types exemplified by (1) nation/state regulatory action that imposes costs on outsiders; (2) systems clashes; and (3) failure of vision from the top. Reacting to the particular problems, it suggests avenues for resolution, and each of the avenues suggests unseized opportunities to perfect the world trading system.

Negative spillovers from state regulatory action

Several situations illustrate the problem of negative spillovers from private conduct that has been blessed by government action and that imposes costs on people

---

4   Trachtman (1992).
5   These solutions are called, respectively, positive comity and negative comity.

who have no voice or recourse. First, the problem of the Union Pacific/Southern Pacific merger, approved in the US and harming Mexico, is presented. Second, a problem of standard-setting in one community that has the effect of excluding outsiders with incompatible technology is discussed.

Union Pacific/Southern Pacific

In 1995, the Union Pacific and Southern Pacific Railroads proposed to merge, in a deal that would create the nation's largest railroad. The two railroads ran side-by-side across much of the American West and to and from the Texas Gulf Coast and the Mexican border. The merger would create monopolies or duopolies in numerous markets facing shippers.

In the US, the Surface Transportation Board has the right to approve and exempt railroad mergers and may do so in the 'public interest'. The railroads applied to the Surface Transport Board for approval. They argued that the merger would achieve more than $700m in labour, operational and other savings, and would enable the merged firm to provide better service. The US Departments of Justice, Agriculture and Transportation argued to the contrary and estimated that the merger would cost US shippers and consumers $800m in price rises. The Surface Transportation Board accepted the merging firms' story. It approved the merger subject to modest conditions, exempting it from the US antitrust laws.[6]

Mexican consumers and shippers were clearly in the class of potential victims. Mexican consumers would bear monopoly charges on southbound traffic. Mexican shippers would bear monopoly charges on northbound traffic. But Mexico was not a concern of the Surface Transportation Board.

The merger was consummated. Service deteriorated and prices rose. Mexicans were at the mercy of the new monopolist; and they had had no voice in the process.[7]

Geotek/ETSI

In Europe in the field of wireless communications, including electronic paging technology, the members of the industry belong to a group designed to set the technological standards for Europe and seek their adoption by the private European standards body, ETSI. Only Europeans may belong to ETSI, and all members agree to use its standards. A number of the member states of the EU impose the ETSI standard by law. The European institutions have passed legislation requiring deployment of a mobile telecom services standard by 2002. The ETSI procedures naturally favour EU incumbents. Moreover, because of

---

6   Union Pacific Corpn, Southern Pacific Rail Corpn, et al, Finance Docket No 32760, Decision No 44, 1996 WL 46 7636 (STB Aug. 12, 1996), upheld, *Western Coal Traffic League v Surface Transportation Board* 169 F 3d 775 (DC Cir 1999).
7   The head of the Mexican Competition Commission wrote to the Surface Transportation Board noting the harm to Mexico at the crossing; but the Board was not interested in foreigners. Of course, so too were Americans at the mercy of the monopolist; but they had been heard.

network effects[8] and the fact that other jurisdictions such as the US favour competition among technologies rather than standardisation of them, users around the world gravitate to products complying with the ETSI standard.

The ETSI endorsed a digital standard for electronic paging equipment.

Geotek, a US company that purchased a UK company, was a forerunner in electronic paging that used an analogue technology. It was unable to obtain a license in Europe to use or convert its technology. The single European standard became the gateway to world competition. Geotek now operates under bankruptcy protection.[9]

Analysis

The railroad and the standards cases illustrate an increasingly perplexing problem. Action may be taken by one state that has distinct anticompetitive impacts and the impacts may fall disproportionately outside the regulating jurisdiction. Indeed, as Geotek claims in the ETSI matter, the official action may be strategically designed to benefit nationals (or citizens of a regional community) or may have the clear effect of doing so; thus the benefits may fall disproportionately *within* the regulating state. Moreover, (1) the outsiders have no voice; they lack a right of participation in the making of a decision that will have a major influence on them, and (2) the authority that imposes the regulation or grants an exemption from competition law not only has the power to stack the deck in its favour, but it also has the power to make the political economy choice for the region or the world; and the most regulatory jurisdiction prevails. The most open, competitive economy (for example, with a bias against government-endorsed standards and industry collaboration to set standards) tends to lose.

Solutions

One solution to virtually all of the global-market problems is regulation at a higher level. This solution, however, has all of the shortcomings of 'higher law', including the questions of who will decide what the higher law will be, who will apply it and by what means, how the higher authorities can be held accountable and how the law can be changed as necessary to meet evolving needs. These are daunting problems. They impel us to seek solutions at a lower level.

There are lessons to be drawn from the modes of regulation and due process safeguards of both the EU and the US.

8   The network is useful and valuable in direct proportion to the (increasing) number of people using the network. Network effects are therefore a barrier to entry. While there is no essential difference between a national standard and a regional standard, a regional standard tends to cover a much larger territory; therefore the number of firms required to use the standard will be greater, the open and contestable market will be smaller, and the exclusionary effect will be greater.

9   Waverman (1999).

Lessons from Europe

The EU takes a cosmopolitan approach to member state trade-restraining action in the European internal market. The states have the obligation, under the Treaty of Rome, not to hinder the free flow of commerce from one member state to another, and to carry out the open-market spirit of the Treaty. Any regulation must be non-discriminatory and transparent, and obstacles to internal market trade must be tightly justified. In particular, states must not take measures that advantage their citizens over citizens of other member states.

At European level, the Community often acts by framework directive rather than by uniform substantive rules of law. The framework directive formulates goals and aims of the Community and leaves to the member states the duty and opportunity to implement the directive through legislation of their choice. Thus, in connection with standards for the transmission of television signals, the EU adopted an Open Network framework, obliging the member states' regulatory authorities to provide open architecture and to do so in a transparent and non-discriminatory way.

The EU vision transcends the state. EU law reprehends and punishes excessive, abusive and privilege-granting member state trade-restraining action. The concern is for the citizen of Europe.[10]

Lessons from the US

Lessons from the US also could help to solve the conundrum of anticompetitive regulation that 'binds' (harms) those that have no voice.

The US has strong principles of due process. Its founding tradition condemns taxation without representation. US case law suggests rights of notice, hearing and participation in the event of standard-setting, which by its nature may be both exclusionary and efficient. Thus, the Supreme Court of the US said in a case in which incumbent industry members excluded new entrants by packing a standard-setting meeting with friends:

> 'The hope of procompetitive benefits [from private standard-setting] depends upon the existence of safeguards sufficient to prevent the standard-setting process from being biased by members with economic interests in restraining competition.'[11]

The lessons might be extended to fit the international dilemma. Thus, those who will bear the costs of anticompetitive action adopted by a nation/state, but who are outside the jurisdiction of the state, should have a right to be heard and to participate in hearings. The competition agency of an affected country should be heard. Thus, the Mexican Federal Competition Commission could, in a future *Union Pacific/Southern Pacific* case, have a legal right to participate in proceedings concerning exemption of the merger. It would, in that case, have the opportunity to quantify and present to the agency the costs of the proposed action to Mexico. The US or Geotek might be accorded a similar right, with due process, to participate in hearings by a European standard-setting body that may, as a practical reality, be setting the standard for the world.

---

10 Fox (1994).
11 *Allied Tube & Conduit Corpn v Indian Head, Inc* 486 US 492, 509–510 (1988).

But the right of outsiders to be heard and to explain the harm to themselves and their country is a feeble right if the regulating nation's only incentives and obligations are to act in the interests of its own nation. This dilemma leads to lesson three.

A lesson from economics and practical politics – counting all the costs

We must learn and take seriously the lesson that even the 'harming' nation is better off when it stops imposing economic costs on others, whether by public or private restraints. The externality is a distortion of trade which tends to create inefficiencies throughout the larger community and which also tends to produce retaliation and counter-retaliation, creating further inefficiencies. What seems, in the short term, to advantage a nation comparatively by shifting costs to others directly decreases the welfare of the larger community and indirectly decreases the welfare of the nation.

The phenomenon of the downward spiral is explained in the following passage from an article, co-authored by the present writer, which observes the problem in the context of private as well as public (for example, trade) restraints and which offers as a solution a standard of world welfare (accounting for all costs and benefits in the affected community) instead of the usual standard of national welfare:

'Past the very short run, retaliatory measures and counter-measures taken to offset the first nation's distortion of trade and competition tend to escalate into a downward spiral of increasing impediments to trade. The prospect and reality of the downward spiral have been the impetus to agreements among nations on world trade particularly in the context of the GATT/World Trade Organization. The message that such nationalistic games are harmful was first brought home to nations with regard to government-imposed quotas, tariffs, voluntary export restraints, and similar impediments. It has only recently been recognized with respect to government-imposed non-tariff barriers, including foreign investment limitations, unreasonably exclusionary standards (e.g. in telecommunications) and discriminatory procurement policies.

The lesson has not yet been brought home, however, with respect to private restraints, and (perhaps, peculiarly, because it *is* government action) facilitation by governments of restraints by firms within their territory. Yet governments quite perceptibly and pervasively facilitate private restraints, and the costs to the world possibly amount to billions of dollars a year in lost income. Governments may act in numerous anticompetitive ways. National legislatures may limit the coverage of antitrust laws so as not to reach 'beggar-thy-neighbour' restraints. Executive or administrative decisions may be taken not to enforce antitrust law where the gain from harm to foreigners is judged greater than the loss to the nations' own constituency.

An alternative to the national welfare standard is a world welfare standard. 'World welfare' is used here to mean the aggregate level of consumer benefits and profits realised by consumers and firms in all pertinent countries. The case for a world-welfare standard to guide the two residual areas identified above – private restraints of international dimension, and government facilitation of them – seems rather compelling.'[12, 13]

---

12 Fox and Ordover (1995) at 15–16.
13 See Reinicke (1997) at 131.

The above point is made solely in economic terms. The same phenomenon – disregard of the costs that fall on 'foreigners' – has an important moral and social policy dimension as well. When a nation regulates business structure or conduct that harms outsiders but makes its regulatory decision without taking account of harms to outsiders and the nation stands behind the decision as one entitled to the respect of the world, the decision lacks legitimacy. Thus, the principle of counting all costs has an economic, moral and political policy dimension.

To avoid this problem of narrow or blinkered nationalism, world leaders might adopt a principle such as the following to guide their economic dialogue: when a nation considers regulatory action that may have unwelcome impacts beyond its borders, it should provide rights of process to persons beyond its borders, and it should count the costs and benefits beyond its borders as if all affected areas lay within its borders.[14] Only then, especially if the outside jurisdictions and peoples lack the power to protect themselves, will the regulatory action be both efficient and legitimate.

National law does not reach so far today. Statutory change would be needed. But the more it is the case that national enforcers and regulators resist taking account of the costs 'to foreigners', the sooner will come the day for international regulation; and unnecessary international regulation could straight-jacket the businesses of the world.

Systems clashes

Nations' different and sometimes conflicting laws often apply cumulatively to the same transaction. Sometimes outcomes can be different because local market conditions are different; but sometimes there is only one market and it is the world.

Such was the situation when Boeing, the world's largest producer of commercial jet aircraft, sought to acquire McDonnell Douglas, the third largest. McDonnell Douglas had failed to invest in new generation technology and had a dim future. The only other competitor in the world was Airbus Industrie, the European consortium. In connection with the acquisition, Boeing entered into exclusive supply agreements with the three big US airlines, tying up some 12% of the world market for 20 years.

The US Federal Trade Commission vetted the merger, found no competitive problem because of McDonnell Douglas' probable inability to compete for next generation sales, and closed the investigation. The EU had a different view. Also vetting the merger, the European Commission stressed that Boeing would increase its share of the world market from 64 to 70%. It found serious competitive problems with the merger of the two firms (both US firms, with no assets in Europe), on the theory that Boeing would substantially increase its dominance. The European Commission would have prohibited the merger had Boeing not agreed at the eleventh hour to conditions that included dropping the exclusive contracts and licensing technology that had been subsidised by the US

---

14 Some ask: how can we possibly consider antitrust harm beyond our borders? There are two answers:(1) In cases of world markets, this consideration is a necessary part of the analysis that regulating authorities must undertake. For example, in the merger case of *Boeing/ McDonnell Douglas*, if the merger was price-raising, it was price-raising in the world. Data on the buyers' market would indicate the extent of harm to customers located abroad; and (2) A burden can be put on harmed outsiders to come forward with proof of harm to them.

government. The settlement came only after top-level threats of a trade war, and accusations of nationalistic strategies, on both sides.[15]

Boeing is the tip of an iceberg. Many other conflicts have arisen and will probably arise with increasing frequency. Others that have occurred thus far have usually been less public or less hotly contested than *Boeing*. When Europe's commuter-plane manufacturing consortium sought to acquire its biggest competitor, Canada's de Havilland, Canada cleared and supported the merger but Europe prohibited it. When two platinum mining firms, Gencor and Lonrho sought to merge in South Africa, South Africa cleared and supported the merger but Europe prohibited it. When two Swiss pharmaceutical companies, Ciba-Giegy and Sandoz planned to merge, Europe cleared the merger with no conditions. The US required the spin-off of a line of research activity.[16]

US authorities normally approve a merger if it cannot be proved to raise prices. The European Commission normally disapproves a merger or imposes regulatory conditions if the merger either significantly enhances the market share of a dominant firm, creates joint dominance or seriously unlevels the playing field for competitors. Other countries' laws have yet different nuances. Most outcomes are the same, but there is a not insignificant margin of difference. Mergers affect the basic structure of industry, and the structure of industry within a nation has historically been a subject of national industrial policy. Unarticulated national biases may subtly and invisibly tip the scales in arguable cases. What is to be done?

SOLUTIONS

Possible solutions include a single set of laws for international transactions in global markets; but this would be difficult to accomplish, and harder yet would it be to ensure administration with fairness and legitimacy.

At the other extreme, nations could insist on the right of unilateral enforcement as they deem fit in the interests of their nation, perhaps with bilateral duties of notification consultation, and explanation; as is now the case between the US and the EU and various other jurisdictions.

But the national interest model is likely not to be sufficient in this millennium when one nation's merger affects the world. If nations decide to work towards cosmopolitan principles, an initial set of principles for mergers of international dimension might look like this:

(1) Nations' laws and their mode of analysis should be transparent.
(2) Nations should apply their laws without discrimination based on nationality.
(3) Nations should not allow national champion interests to trump competition interests. They should neither enforce nor withhold enforcement in the interests of a national champion.
(4) If nations apply non-competition objectives, such as national security or environmental concerns, they should do so transparently and by means tailored to achieve their ends.
(5) If a nation's law expressly allows a non-competition policy trump, the trumping value or factor should be applied separately after the competition analysis has been completed.[17]

15 Fox (1998).
16 Fox (1999a).
17 See ICPAC Report (2000).

But even this set of principles may not be enough. What happens when, despite the five principles, systems clash? If there is an interest in countering the state of affairs in which the nation with the most prohibitory law always prevails, we may need either higher law or rules of priority. Assuming that the latter is preferable, if workable, we should consider rules of priority. For example, the right to grant or not grant drastic relief (an injunction or break-up) might be assigned to any nation[18] that is 'home' to both merging firms and/or the one or two nations that are the largest markets for the product or service. But if any nations have rights of priority, there will be no legitimacy unless: (1) the nation with the right of priority counts all costs wherever in the world they fall, and treats all costs and benefits as if they fell within that jurisdiction; and (2) harmed persons or nations outside the regulating jurisdiction have rights of due process before the court or agencies within the regulating jurisdiction.[19]

This proposal is an adaptation to private restraints of the principles suggested above that would constrain state restraints.

LACK OF VISION FROM THE TOP

Lack of vision from the top is a startling missing element in a world in which national law governs global transactions. The blinkered vision problem reasserts itself repeatedly.

One set of problems is exemplified by the state of merger control and pre-merger clearance in the world. This is a problem of excessive unco-ordinated regulation. More than 60 nations now have merger control laws, and more than 40 have laws that require pre-merger notification (usually cumbersome and expensive) and a period of waiting before clearance – which may take five to eight months or more. The thresholds for reporting and waiting are often very low. A small stream of sales into the nation may trigger application of the nation's law; the merging firms may have no assets in the jurisdiction. A small country, like Bulgaria or Romania, can hold up and possibly abort a multinational merger, though the market in that nation is small and the merging firms together have an insignificant market share in the regulating country. A single multinational merger may be required to pass through 20 or 30 national merger systems before consummation, even if the market is global, there is no different impact in any nation and the merger is being seriously vetted by two or more mature agencies in the nations that account for the major purchases.[20]

Despite the large and many nets cast to vet international mergers, few are challenged because few present competition concerns. In the US, approximately 2% of notified mergers become the subject of enforcement actions; in Canada the percentage is 1.5%.

If one were to design an effective merger control system for the world, it would not resemble the ad hoc, unco-ordinated, 'reinvent-the-wheel' merger-control regimes of today.

Second, with a view from the top we would not and could not ignore the less developed world. Demographics and demographic trends, economics, and

---

18 The word 'nation' is used here to include a larger juridic community; thus, the EU.
19 ICPAC Report (2000); Fox, separate statement in ICPAC Report, A-1.
20 ICPAC Report (2000); Ginsburg and Angstreich (2000); Rowley and Campbell (1999).

justice values themselves, require us to move forward on a premise of inclusiveness. Bringing the less developed and developing countries into the core of the world trading system would enhance both world economic welfare and justice. Thomas Friedman has written eloquently about the role of global pressures in squeezing out cronyism and helping to put economies on a base of merit, not privilege.[21] Others have observed how cartels ostensibly targeted at the third world (and thus never challenged) are in fact world cartels that hurt us all.[22] The ripple effects of monopolistic practices that harm nations that lack the institutions or the will to fight back are likely to become large waves on the global ocean. We are, economically (like it or not), one world.

Third, the world trading system is distorted by problems of private restraints that re-close opened markets and undermine the system. Liberal trade law attends to public restraints; competition law is left to deal with private restraints. But competition law is national. National law is not up to the task of opening foreign markets and countering distant restraints; indeed, national law may not apply. To make the world trading system more nearly complete, and to inform the several sectoral instruments of the WTO that already contain competition obligations, we may need to deepen the WTO's competition competences.

Solutions to the vision-deficit problem are elusive. Networking of nations on a horizontal plane is important, but may not be enough. We should work multilaterally towards certain attainable solutions, even while developing deeper, thicker networks of co-operation. For example:

(1) Merger control: pre-merger notification. Nations should establish a common clearing house or a system of mutual recognition of merger filings, available on an opt-in basis to merging parties. Either a clearing-house centre could be established to receive and disperse filings to jurisdictions that file a claim-of-right to receive the notification, or the jurisdiction of the first filing could have a duty to disperse the filings to all possibly interested nations. Recipient countries would be required to accept the first filing in the first instance, with a right to receive codicils for particular, separate markets within their jurisdiction.[23]

Nations would be invited to agree not to assert entitlement to notification unless either the parties have substantial assets in the jurisdiction or there is a credible story of harm to competition in the jurisdiction.

Nations vetting the same merger could be required to co-ordinate their investigations and analysis. Not only would these provisions save millions of dollars in transaction costs for transnational corporations; they would also provide a valuable flow of information to nations that are potential victims but are not capable of assembling the information for themselves, and it would prevent the filing firms from playing off one authority against the others.

---

21 Friedman (1999).
22 Jenny (2000).
23 The merging parties might be obliged to provide a skeleton summary of the planned merger and a list of all possibly interested nations. These nations would receive the skeleton notice, and would either be obliged to come forward, prove their entitlement to notification, and give mutual recognition to the filing, or would waive their right to participate in pre-merger clearance. A similar proposal has been made by Judge Diane Wood: Wood (2000).

(2) Developing countries: First, bilateral co-operation agreements should be multilateralised, to give developing countries protections and opportunities that they themselves would be unable to procure bilaterally. Second, nations should extend their laws to cover outbound cartels; for, of all antitrust restraints, cartel agreements are the most clearly wrong and harmful, and developing countries are usually ill-equipped to successfully challenge offshore cartels that harm them. Third, nations should ratchet back their anti-dumping laws; as a first stage they could be required to give equal weight to their own buyer interests. These laws have particularly harmful effects on developing countries, whose low-priced exports are blocked from sales on the merits. Fourth, developed countries should provide co-ordinated technical assistance to developing countries, with special sensitivity to their context and needs, exploring how competition policy can help the particular developing countries and advising how competition law can be implemented to their advantage. Most importantly, developing countries should have voice and respect in the exploration of multilateral initiatives.
(3) Within the WTO, nations should be obliged not to close their markets, or condone the closing of their markets, by artificial private, as well as public, restraints. For private restraints, the law (for example, competition law) of the excluding nation should apply; as should principles of transparency and non-discrimination and access to courts with due process.[24]

Aspects of each of these proposals meet resistance in the name of sovereignty. This resistance will not, this writer predicts, withstand time.

CONCLUSION

In matters of economics and market conduct, we are on a trend-line toward 'one world'. We can close our eyes and insist on narrow national solutions, or we can be architects of a more nearly open, integrated world.

This chapter is an attempt to stimulate dialogue on liberal solutions to the problem of incoherence between national law and global commerce. It suggests open architecture and the embrace of principles of cosmopolitanism that would link the nations and peoples of the world while giving weighty respect to subsidiarity.

Select bibliography

Christiansen, T, (1994) 'European Integration Between Political Science and International Relations Theory: The End of Sovereignty', European University Institute Working Paper RSC No 94/4.

Fox, E, (1994) 'Vision of Europe: Lessons for the World', 18 Fordham International Law Journal 379.

—(1997) 'Toward World Antitrust and Market Access', 91 AJIL 1.

—(1998) 'Antitrust Regulation Across National Borders: The United States of Boeing versus the European Union of Airbus', 16 Brookings Review 30.

24 Fox (1997; 1999b).

—(1999a) 'Extraterritoriality and the Merger Law: Can All Nations Rule the World?', Antitrust Report, December, p 2.

—(1999b) 'Competition Law and the Millennium Round', 2 Journal of International Economic Law 665.

—(2000) 'National Law, Global Markets, and *Hartford*: Eyes Wide Shut', 68 Antitrust Law Journal 73.

Fox, E, and Ordover, J, (1995) 'The Harmonization of Competition and Trade Law: The Case for Modest Linkages of Law and Limits to Parochial State Action', 19 World Competition Law and Economic Review 5 at 15–16.

Friedman, T, (1999), *Globalution*, Chapter 8: 'The Lexus and the Olive Tree'.

Ginsburg, D, and Angstreich, S, (2000), 'Multinational Merger Review: Lessons from Our Federalism', 68 Antitrust Law Journal 219.

ICPAC Report, (2000) *Report of the International Competition Policy Advisory Committee to the U.S. Attorney General and Assistant Attorney General for Antitrust* (the ICPAC Report), available at www.usdoj.gov/atr/icpac/icpac.htm.

Jenny, F, (2000) 'Globalization, Competition and Trade Policy: Convergence, Divergence and Cooperation', Paper presented at the conference on Competition Policy in the Global Trading System, Washington, DC, 23 June.

Reinicke, W, (1997) 'Global Public Policy', 76 Foreign Affairs 127.

Rowley, J W, and Campbell, A N, (1999) 'Multi-Jurisdictional Merger Review – Is it Time for a Common Form Filing Treaty?' in Policy Directions for Global Merger Review *A Special Report by the Global Forum for Competition and Trade Policy*.

Trachtman, J, (1992) 'L'Etat, C'est Nous: Sovereignty, Economic Integration and Subsidiarity', 33 Harv ILJ 459.

Waverman, L, (1999) '*Standards* WARS: The Use of Standard Setting as a Means of Facilitating Cartels', Presentation to International Competition Policy Advisory Committee to advise the US Attorney-General, 17 May 1999.

Wood, D, (2000) 'International Competition Policy – Convergence/Cooperation?', Outline for Cutting Edge Antitrust Seminar, 18 February.

Chapter 8

Corruption and the global corporation: ethical obligations and workable strategies

S ROSE-ACKERMAN[1]

Do multinational corporations have an obligation to refrain from high-level corruption in the absence of a functioning international legal regime? This chapter argues that they do have such an obligation, but it also accepts the reality that collective action may be the only way to produce widespread changes in behaviour. Interestingly, both norm changes and collective action are occurring in the global business community, aided by international organisations such as the Organization for Economic Cooperation and Development (OECD) and private organisations such as Transparency International and the International Chamber of Commerce. We may be witnessing a change in international commercial norms that, if maintained, could have a noticeable impact on the business environment. This trend is a challenge to the simple normative claim that private firms ought not consider anything other than profit-maximisation. It goes beyond the view that firms have obligations to 'stakeholders' such as employees and local communities and suggests that global firms are beginning to accept a broader set of obligations.[2]

This chapter begins by summarising the international efforts currently under way to involve multinational businesses in the anti-corruption effort. This effort

---

1   This chapter is a revised and shortened version of a paper entitled, '"Grand" Corruption and the Ethics of Global Business', originally presented at a Conference on Measuring and Managing Ethical Risk, Notre Dame Center for Ethics and Religious Values in Business, Notre Dame, IN, 23–24 September 1999.

2   This attitude is expressed by the International Chamber of Commerce in the foreword to its *Rules of Conduct: Extortion and Bribery in International Business Transactions* (1999 revision) [reprinted in Vincke Heimann, and Katz (1999) pp 98–99]: 'In the early 1990s, scandals involving extortion and bribery were a significant factor in toppling government in many parts of the world. This situation, if allowed to continue, could undermine the most promising developments of the post Cold-war era, i.e. the spread of democratic governments and of market economies worldwide. It is all the more unacceptable in view of the liberalization of world trade in goods and services achieved through the Uruguay Round: freer trade must be matched by fair competition, failing which trading relations will be increasingly strained to the common detriment of governments and enterprises. ... The updated [International Chamber of Commerce] report ... confirms ... the need for action by international organizations, governments and by enterprises, nationally and internationally, to meet the challenging goal of greater transparency in international trade. ... [T]he international business community has the ... responsibility to strengthen its own efforts to combat extortion and bribery.'

is then put in context by isolating the costs of high-level corruption in developing and transitional economies. In light of these costs, the ethical obligations of multinational businesses and their managers when they operate in a corrupt environment are considered. Drawing on both political theory and work in corporate ethics, this section argues that businesses have an obligation to avoid payoffs. Finally, the chapter asks whether additional institutional responses are warranted given the difficulty of assuring that business firms will carry out their ethical obligations in the absence of additional collective efforts.

CURRENT INTERNATIONAL EFFORTS[3]

Current attempts to limit corruption in global business focus on reducing the willingness of multinational businesses to pay bribes and on enlisting them to assist the developing world to carry out reforms.[4] This effort appears to be bearing fruit both in changing the rhetoric of the global business community and in producing concrete steps to control corruption.

Multinational initiatives, especially at the OECD and the Organization for American States, have been taken to constrain corruption. Other efforts have been made by the business community to promulgate voluntary codes of conduct.[5] The most important are the OECD's initiatives to criminalise foreign bribery and to induce members to end the tax deductibility of overseas bribes. The OECD Anti-Bribery Convention was signed in December 1997 and has been ratified by enough countries (including the US) so that it entered into force in February 1999.[6] Its basic goal is to extend the principles of the US Foreign Corrupt Practices Act to the international business community.[7] Most countries are required not just to ratify the treaty, but also to pass conforming legislation criminalising overseas bribery. Even the US has made some modest amendments to its own statute.[8] The OECD has begun a process of monitoring country compliance and implementation.

In many countries bribes paid to obtain foreign business are tax-deductible – a legal loophole that obviously encourages payoffs. Thus the OECD Council also recommends that member states 're-examine the tax deductibility of bribes to foreign public officials, with the intention of denying this deductibility in those Member countries which do not already do so'.[9] The US already forbids the tax-deductibility of bribes, and several other countries are in the process of changing their laws to conform with the recommendation.

3   Derived in part from chapter 10 of Rose-Ackerman (1999).
4   De George (1993) pp 54–55.
5   Because of the provisions of the Foreign Corrupt Practices Act 1977, as amended, US firms have a head start in developing corporate codes of conduct, and their experience may be useful to firms elsewhere in the world. The US branch of Transparency International (TI) has sponsored an effort both to compile existing codes and to help companies without such codes to develop them: Transparency International-USA (1996).
6   Convention on Combating Bribery of Foreign Public Officials in International Business Transactions, 11 December 1997. Available at www.oecd.org/daf/cmis/bribery/20novle.htm.
7   The Foreign Corrupt Practices Act, 15 U.S. C.§§ 78m(b), (d)(1), & (g)–(h), 78dd-1, 78dd-2, 78ff(a)(c) (1988 & Supp. IV 1992). See Pendergast (1995).
8   The "International Anti-Bribery and Fair Competition Act of 1998" was enacted into law on 10 November 1998.
9   OECD, Meeting of the Council at the Ministerial Level, Paris, 21–22 May 1996, Communique, SG/COM/NEWS(96)53, section 9(x).

Under the auspices of the Organization for American States, the Inter-American Convention Against Corruption is now open for ratification.[10] The Convention requires a good deal of cross-border co-operation and requires countries to prohibit and punish transnational bribery. The Convention is distinctive in including both developed countries, a number in the middle range and some poor countries.

The development of an international procurement code has proved difficult. The World Trade Organization's (WTO) revised Agreement on Government Procurement entered into force on 1 January 1996, but only 25 countries, mostly industrialised states, have adopted its provisions.[11] Some commentators have urged the WTO to develop a more limited code that focuses only on limiting corruption in the hope that more countries will participate.

Some international professional and business organisations have put anti-corruption initiatives on their agenda. The International Chamber of Commerce asserts that 'as the world business organization, [it] is committed to an efficiently functioning global economy',[12] and considers 'corporate self-regulation an indispensable element of its proposed programme' to fight corruption.[13] It claims that a change in attitude is occurring in the international business community in favour of a more proactive approach to fighting corruption.[14] The International Chamber of Commerce is committed to 'developing a broad international consensus on the need to fight extortion and bribery' as a way of overcoming the reluctance of individual companies to act.[15] It issued a recommendation in March 1996 urging its members to adopt rules of conduct designed to limit bribery in international trade. The rules prohibit bribery for any purpose, not just to obtain or retain business. A 1999 handbook contains more specific guidelines along with the text of the recommendation and the OECD Treaty.[16]

The Council of the International Bar Association adopted a similar resolution in June 1996.[17] The UNDP Aid Accountability Initiative is considering working with the International Organization of Supreme Audit Institutions and the International Federation of Accountants to develop projects to strengthen accountability in developing countries.[18] The American Bar Association has a Task Force on International Standards for Corrupt Practices, and the Business Roundtable has taken up the question of corruption particularly as it affects government procurement processes throughout the world.

These efforts demonstrate how an issue can gain momentum in the international arena in a way that can produce real changes in institutions and in

---

10 OEA/Ser.K/XXXIV.1; CICOR/doc.14/96 rev.2, 29 March 1996.
11 World Trade Organization (2000). Hoekman and Mavroidis (1997) includes the text of the Agreement as an appendix.
12 International Chamber of Commerce (1996).
13 Vincke, Heimann and Katz (1999) p 4.
14 Vincke, Heimann and Katz (1999) pp 15–16, 91–92. The last chapter of this volume includes a section entitled 'Why bribery is no longer tolerable'. The authors claim that a 'significant change' in attitudes has occurred in the last five years and concludes that: '*bribery violates acceptable standards for international competition.* Companies that continue to bribe will do serious damage to their ability to continue as reputable participants in the global economy' (emphasis in original): pp 91–92.
15 Vincke, Heimann and Katz (1999) p 10.
16 Vincke, Heimann and Katz (1999).
17 International Bar Association (1996).
18 United Nations Development Programme (1996) p ii.

behaviour. Many of these efforts are at an early stage, all depend on a co-operative attitude in the business community, even the OECD treaty. The issue has been put on the international agenda by a convergence of several forces, not all of which have moral content. But it appears that the force of the moral argument has helped tip the scales in favour of an anti-corruption effort. Corporate executives and government officials feel that they are doing the right thing as well as promoting the concerns of multinational businesses. The international anti-corruption effort has been spearheaded, on the one hand, by idealistic reformers with experience in the development community, and on the other hand, by business people concerned that they were losing business to corrupt rivals. US firms have been especially active because of the constraint of the Foreign Corrupt Practices Act (1977, as amended) (FCPA). US firms might prefer to see the FCPA repealed but, since that seems an unrealistic hope, they have been active in promoting the extension of similar constraints to firms in other industrialised countries. The global, non-profit-making Transparency International, the leading NGO pushing for reform, is a coalition of these two groups.

The timing can also be explained by the end of the cold war, leading to a situation where wealthy democracies no longer saw the need to support corrupt autocracies, and where the pervasive corruption in many of the countries of the former Soviet bloc led to calls for reform both inside and outside their borders. As a result, even the World Bank and the International Monetary Fund (IMF), long wary of openly addressing the issue, have become leaders in the global anti-corruption effort despite some misgivings among some staff and some member countries. No one can confidently predict the outcome of the various international and nation reform efforts currently in progress, but, at least, a change in the discourse has occurred in a little over five years.

THE COSTS OF 'GRAND CORRUPTION'[19]

The focus in this chapter is on high-level or 'grand' corruption that influences the award of contracts, concessions and privatised firms. Corruption at that level can undermine the functioning of the host state and lower the efficiency of production. The struggle to appropriate the gains of public projects can have a destructive impact on a country's economic and political system. Outside investors and aid organisations can play an active role in maintaining corrupt systems. The impact of corruption in contracting and concessions is discussed below, followed by an analysis of similar problems that can arise in privatisation.

Contracting and concessions

Corruption in contracting and in the award of concessions can introduce inefficiencies that reduce competitiveness. It may limit the number of bidders, favour those with inside connections over the most efficient candidates, limit the information available to participants and introduce added transactions costs. If top officials, including the head of state, are concerned primarily with maximising personal gain, they may favour an inefficient level, composition and time-path of

---

19 This section is derived from chapter 3 of Rose-Ackerman (1999), which includes a richer collection of examples and cases.

investment. Investors' decisions may be affected by the fact that they are dealing with corrupt political leaders.

Consider the officials' decision calculus. The impact of high-level corruption goes beyond the mere scale of public investment and lost revenue for the public budget. Corrupt officials will select projects and make purchases with little or no economic rationale. For example, if kickbacks are easier to obtain on capital investments and input purchases than on labour, rulers will favour capital intensive projects irrespective of their economic justification. One empirical study demonstrates that high levels of corruption are associated with higher levels of public investment as a share of GDP (and lower levels of total investment and foreign direct investment). More corrupt countries spend relatively less on operations and maintenance and have lower quality infrastructure.[20] Corrupt officials will frequently support 'white elephant' projects with little value in promoting economic development.[21]

For large, capital-intensive projects the time-path of net corrupt benefits may be quite different from the pattern of net social benefits. This will affect the choices of rulers. Suppose, as seems likely, that the benefits of bribery are relatively more concentrated in the present than those of the overall project. Then even if the rulers and the populace discount the future at the same rate, the rulers will support projects and policies that have an inefficient time-path of net social benefits. For example, with major construction projects, a country's leaders will extract bribes in the present and may experience few of the future costs of shoddy workmanship or an excessive debt burden. Furthermore, corrupt officials may well have a higher discount rate than the country's citizens. The very venality of corrupt rulers may make them insecure and subject to overthrows. This insecurity induces them to steal more, making them even more insecure, and so forth. As a consequence, they will have a relatively high discount rate for government projects and will support projects with quick short-term payoffs and costs spread far into the future.

Now consider the decision-making calculus of outside investors. To illustrate, consider a logging concession obtained corruptly by a company that out-bribes its competitors. Suppose, to begin, that the corruption market is efficient so that it operates just like an idealised competitive bidding process and that the corrupt ruler's rate of time preference is the same as society's. Suppose that as a result of corruption, the government obtains less than fair market value for the resources under its control.[22] If corruption does not restrict entry and if the official cannot affect the size of the concession, the high briber is the firm that values the benefit the most. It is the most efficient firm that would offer the highest price in a fair bidding procedure. Only the government budget suffers losses, so that the state must either levy extra taxes or cut back public programs.[23] In this simplified

---

20 Tanzi and Davoodi (1997).

21 A study of structural adjustment lending in seven African countries concluded that much investment spending was of dubious worth: Faruqee and Husain (1994) p 6.

22 Evidence that this frequently happens is presented in Environmental Investigation Agency (1996) pp 5, 8. A similar result could occur if suppliers form a cartel. For example, in Indonesia one source estimates that the government had been losing $500m a year in royalty revenues on logging concessions because of the political power of the Indonesian Plywood Association: Schwarz (1994) p 140.

23 A similar situation can arise for government contracts. The most efficient firm will be selected under competitive bribery, but the benefits to the government are reduced. Part of the cost of the bribe is hidden in the value of the contract.

competitive case, the winner is indifferent to whether the concession is won through an honest or a dishonest auction. Bribes paid do not affect the time-path of benefits and costs.

But this extreme case will seldom prevail. In practice, the bribe will be extracted partly from returns that would otherwise flow to government and partly from the profits of the winning firm. If the corrupt official has more leverage than the honest one, he or she will be able to extract a larger share of the profits. In addition, the corrupt official may often be able to structure the deal so that it is more lucrative for firms than an honest contract. The corrupt official may design the concession to maximise the profits available to share between officials and the bidding firm. In so doing, values may be sacrificed that an honestly negotiated contract would include. For example, in a timber contract, environmental damage or harm to indigenous people may be ignored.[24]

Now consider a firm that has obtained a secure long-term timber concession at a bargain price, even if the bribe is added in. If it operates in the international market, its subsequent actions should depend upon the market for timber. The fact that it has underpaid for the concession should not affect its production decisions. It still seeks to maximise profits, and the concession payment is a sunk cost. The cost of corruption is felt by the public fisc, but no inefficiency has been introduced into the international timber market. Even if the total payment is above that expected in an honest system, there should be no impact.

The claim of no impact on a firm's behaviour is, however, too simple to reflect reality. The operative terms are *secure* and *long term*. The corrupt nature of the deal introduces uncertainties that can have additional effects on the way private firms do business. The corrupt nature of the deal may give the firm a short-run orientation.[25] There are two reasons for this. First, the concessionaire (or contractor) may fear that those in power are vulnerable to overthrow because of their corruption. A new regime may not honour the old one's commitments. Second, even if the current regime remains in power, the winner may fear the imposition of arbitrary rules and financial demands once investments are sunk. It may be concerned that the ruler will permit competitors to enter the market or worry that its contract will be voided for reasons of politics or greed.[26] Having paid a bribe in the past, the firm is vulnerable to extortionary demands in the future. For these reasons, the corrupt firm with a timber contract may cut down trees more quickly than it would in more honest countries. Like other investors in risky environments, it may also be reluctant to invest in immovable capital that would be difficult to take out of the country should conditions change. In short, both the timing of production and the input mix may be chosen with an eye to the special risks introduced by the corrupt nature of the system.

Furthermore, corruption will seldom be limited to a one-off payment to top officials. Instead, the winner may be a firm more willing than others to engage in

---

24 On the general issue see Environmental Investigation Agency (1996).

25 For an example of the short-run orientation of corrupt timber concessionaires in Malaysia see Vincent and Binkley (1992). A Malaysian company operating in Guyana was reported to be logging its concession twice as fast as planned: Environmental Investigation Agency (1996) p 28.

26 For example, in Malaysia firms involved in the privatisation of both electricity and telecoms have complained that the government has subsequently admitted numerous additional competitors with strong political links. See Kieran Cooke, 'Malaysian Privatisation Loses Allure' (1995) Financial Times, October 13.

ongoing corrupt relationships up and down the hierarchy to protect its interests. For example, if the timber concession includes a royalty per log that is calibrated by the type of timber, the firm may pay inspectors to misgrade the logs. It may also pay to cut down more trees than the concession permits.[27] The expectation of a long-term, ongoing relationship may be part of the appeal of signing with a corrupt firm in the first place.

Privatisation

Privatisation can reduce corruption by removing certain assets from state control and converting discretionary official actions into private, market-driven choices. However, the process of transferring assets to private ownership is fraught with corrupt opportunities.[28] Many corrupt incentives are comparable to those that arise in the award of contracts and concessions. Instead of bribing a parastatal to obtain contracts and favourable treatment, bidders for a public company can bribe officials in the privatisation authority or at the top of government.[29] Bribes may be solicited for inclusion on the list of prequalified bidders, and firms may pay to restrict the number of other bidders. However, other corrupt incentives are more specific to the privatisation process. Three factors seem particularly important.

First, when large state enterprises are privatised, there may be no reliable way to value their assets, and the tax and regulatory regime that will prevail ex post may be poorly specified. The uncertainties of the process create opportunities for favouring corrupt insiders by giving them information not available to the public, providing information early in return for payoffs or giving corrupt firms special treatment in the bidding process. In extreme cases the firm is simply awarded to those with the best political connections: 'Sales, at unstated prices, have sometimes been made to dubious purchasers, such as ruling party politicians and others lacking in business experience.'[30]

Second, corrupt officials may present information to the public that makes the company look weak, while revealing to favoured insiders that it is actually doing well. The insiders then are the high bidders in what appears to be an open and above-board bidding process. Similarly, corrupt bidders may be assured of lenient regulatory oversight, something an outsider cannot rely upon. Ex post evaluations reveal that the privatisation was a huge success, with the newly private company earning very high rates of return.[31]

---

27 For numerous examples see Environmental Investigation Agency (1996). In Indonesia environmentalists claim that the country's tree-felling rules were violated routinely under President Suharto, in part because of the influence of a close associate who headed the Plywood Association : Schwarz (1994) p 140.
28 Celarier (1996) provides several examples from Latin America, especially Mexico. Manzetti (1999) argues that the privatisation of public enterprises in Peru reduced corruption in the public sector, but then goes on to detail several problems in the privatisation process itself, including lack of transparency. His studies of Argentina and Brazil contain similar examples.
29 Manzetti (1999); Manzetti and Blake (1996).
30 Nellis and Kikeri (1989) at 668. See also Manzetti (1999); Van de Walle (1989); Pasuk and Sungsidh (1994).
31 In Venezuela a major bank was undervalued by the Minister of National Investment amid payoff allegations: Manzetti and Blake (1996).

Third, a privatised firm is worth more if it retains whatever monopoly power was available to the public firm. To an economist, the retention of monopoly rents undermines the justification for privatisation. To an impecunious state and its bidders, assuring monopoly power is in the interest of both. This conflict between revenue maximisation and market competition arises for all privatisation deals. If a state gives lip service to competitive principles, however, it may be unable to endorse monopolisation openly. Corrupt back-channel deals can then accomplish that objective, but with some of the benefits transferred to individuals rather than the government.[32]

Corruption that involves multinational firms can produce serious distortions in the way government and society operate. The state pays too much for large-scale procurements and receives too little from privatisations and the award of concessions. Corrupt officials distort public-sector choices to generate large rents for themselves and to produce inefficient and inequitable public policies. Government produces too many of the wrong kind of projects and overspends even on projects that are fundamentally sound. Corruption reduces the revenue-raising benefits of privatisation and the award of concessions. Firms that retain monopoly power through bribery and favouritism undermine the efficiency benefits of turning over state firms to private owners.

CORRUPTION AND THE OBLIGATIONS OF MULTINATIONAL BUSINESS

Corruption is a two-sided phenomena that can not properly be described as 'imported' by multinational firms into innocent developing countries.[33] It involves both a buyer and a seller, and the co-operation of both is usually needed to make a serious reduction in corruption possible. Nevertheless, multinational firms can contribute to reductions in the incidence and harm of corruption.

The obligations of multinational firms as key actors in the global marketplace and in the societies where they invest are discussed first in this section. The heart of the argument is that an institution's role as a major economic and political actor gives it an obligation in both these spheres. Because firms are legal creations and operate subject to legal constraints, firms' obligations to the legal order are stronger than those of natural persons. However, a firm's political and economic obligations are not always consistent. These tensions are explained and ways to minimise them discussed. Second, even if one accepts the special obligations of legally created entities, one might argue that firms are under no obligation to refrain from bribery because their individual actions will have little or no impact. This argument is challenged on factual and ethical grounds.

The corporation as a moral actor

Corporations have legal personalities. This does not turn them into real human beings, and some commentators insist that this lack of humanity implies that

---

32 Many Latin American privatisations increased, rather than decreased, market concentration and subsequent regulatory oversight often has been weak: Manzetti (1997; 1999).
33 See Rose-Ackerman (1999) for an extensive discussion of the causes of corruption and the policy options available to governments seeking to curtail corruption.

firms cannot have moral obligations. For example, they believe that it is not advisable to hold business firms criminally liable since they cannot have mental states, and since criminal liability would give corporations the same rights as individuals with less justification for these protections.[34] The basic point that organisations should not be anthropomorphized when discussing rights and responsibilities is accepted here. Nevertheless, corporations can still have moral responsibilities, even if we question the application of the criminal law to organisational conduct.[35] These responsibilities cannot always be reduced to individual responsibilities and stem from 'the practices of the organization – the internal and external patterns of relationships – that persist even as the identities of the individuals who participate in them change'.[36]

Another way of thinking about responsibility has to do with volition. Could the person or organisation have acted otherwise? Often this excuse is framed in terms of compulsion – persons claim that circumstances were such that no other action was feasible.[37] In the corruption context, compulsion results from shareholders concerned only with the profitability of the firm and uninterested in moral claims of corporate responsibility. Such owners will sell their shares, and other potential owners will refuse to invest in the scrupulous firm. A community of ethical investors can help here by favouring firms with good ethical principles, but even they face limits. If ethical behaviour drives the firm out of business, the dilemma is at its sharpest. If it just reduces profitability by cutting into monopoly profits, the firm can still be viable. Here the difference between individual and corporate responsibility seems relevant. We might be reluctant to urge a person to face death for his or her beliefs while arguing that a legal person such as a corporation might face situations where bankruptcy is morally preferable to maintaining a corrupt business.[38] In less extreme cases, the firm modifies its business plan to avoid fields subject to corruption.

The modern corporation is a creation of law, and it operates in multiple political jurisdictions only with the permission of governments. Its creation can be justified only insofar as it, on balance, furthers desirable social goals, both economic and political. The basic 'legal personality' of the business firm gives it an obligation at least equal to that of natural persons both to the state that created it and to those jurisdictions that permit it to operate within its borders.

Consider the situation that multinational firms often claim to face. Suppose that the politician insists on a payoff from a firm as a condition for awarding a

---

34 Thompson (1987) pp 76–78; Khanna (1996). In many civil law countries organisations are excluded from criminal liability, although the trend may be changing with the introduction of corporate criminal liability into the French criminal code in 1992. After the French Revolution, France was the source of the prohibition on organisational criminal liability. Its code was adopted widely in Europe and has influenced the criminal law in parts of the world where the civil law tradition has been exported: Orland and Cachera (1995) at 114. A translation of the 1992 French criminal code is in an appendix to Orland and Cachera. The Dutch have permitted corporate criminal liability since the mid-1970s. Italy and Germany have constitutional provisions precluding corporate guilt, and the Belgian courts have refused to find corporations guilty of crimes. In Germany, however, administrative bodies can impose fines on corporations as well as natural persons: Orland and Cachera (1995) at 116; Khanna (1996) at 1488–1491.

35 De George (1993); Donaldson (1989).

36 Thompson (1987) p 76. See also French (1979) and Cooper (1968).

37 Thompson (1987) pp 48–49.

38 As Richard De George (1993, 135) states: "No company has a right to continued existence analogous to a person's right to life."

contract. The firm's management believes that it is the least-cost provider that would win in an honest competition. What are the firm's obligations? Thomas Donaldson's[39] notion of a hypothetical 'social contract' between business and society provides a useful means of framing the issue. In his analysis he asks whether idealised citizens, in setting up a society under similarly idealised conditions, would agree to the creation of private productive organisations (for example, corporations, partnerships). He hypothesises that citizens would accept such organisations if the benefits in increased productivity outweighed the costs. Under this view, it is plausible to ask firms to accept moral obligations as a condition of their right to exist. Donaldson makes clear that it is the hypothetical nature of the contract that gives it moral force.[40] 'Productive organisations and society should act *as if* they had struck a deal. The kind of deal that would be acceptable to free, informed parties acting from positions of equal moral authority (one person, one vote)'.[41] As political philosopher Dennis Thompson writes: 'The legal rights of a corporation (as distinct from the rights of its members) should rest mainly on social utility ...'[42]

Donaldson applies his analysis to multinational businesses by claiming that certain moral conditions are culturally neutral. Thus his argument depends upon widespread agreement with his list of moral commandments.[43] Rather than debate the character of his list, we focus on obligations that are related to the writer's concern with corruption. Two types are important: obligations to enhance the efficiency of the market system and obligations to refrain from undermining legitimate government institutions. Business organisations and individual entrepreneurs have a duty to maintain the systems in which they operate, even when this might be against their narrower goals.[44] These obligations can be viewed as flowing from an implicit 'social contract' that gives legitimacy to legally created productive organisations. Tensions will arise, not only when firm profitability conflicts with these obligations, but also when a country's law and practice facilitates or even requires payoffs and insider dealings.

Furthering market efficiency

Some behaviour may not be individually rational or profitable for the firm, but may nevertheless further the overall efficiency of the market economy. In the purely competitive model no such moral dilemmas exist. That model simply assumes that the rules of the game are fixed and that the assumptions needed

---

39 Donaldson (1989) pp 44–64.
40 Donaldson (1989) p 56.
41 Donaldson (1989) p 61.
42 Donaldson (1989) p 78; see also Dahl (1982) pp 197–202.
43 Donaldson posits three conditions: (1) a productive organisation should enhance the long-term welfare of employees and consumers in any society in which the organisation operates; (2) a productive organisation should minimise the drawbacks associated with moving beyond the state of nature to a state containing productive organisations; and (3) a productive organisation should refrain from violating minimum standards of justice and of human rights in any society in which it operates: Donaldson (1989) p 54.
44 According to the International Chamber of Commerce in introducing their rules of conduct for corporations: 'The highest priority should be directed to ending large-scale extortion and bribery involving politicians and senior officials. These represent the greatest threat to democratic institutions and cause the gravest economic distortions': Vincke, Heimann and Katz (1999) pp 103–104.

for a competitive market are met. The competitive market system operates to produce efficient results even though all the individual actors are only concerned with their own narrow self-interest. None of the actors need have a strong commitment to the preservation of market institutions, and the system is set up so that their amoral views are irrelevant to the market's success. For-profit firms, constrained by the marketplace, cannot survive unless they are single-mindedly devoted to profit-maximisation.

In the real world, of course, this is not true. Firms with nothing more than a commitment to financial gain may engage in actions that destabilise the market or that produce inefficient results. Laws and regulations exist to contain the worst sorts of behaviour such as fraud against customers or intimidation of competitors through threats of violence. Even if the market system operates without fraud and threats, it may still fail to satisfy all the assumptions of the competitive model and so can produce inefficient results. Thus the legal system in most countries seeks to limit monopoly power, requires certain types of information disclosure and controls externalities such as environmental pollution. If these laws created just the right financial incentives for firm compliance, that could be the end of the matter. Even if owners and managers felt no obligation to obey the law, firms would organise their operations to avoid running afoul of these legal constraints.

Obviously, this assumption is also false. Laws express aspirations but are not perfectly enforced. Even when penalties take account of the probability that violations will not be detected, the law in practice seldom provides an incentive for optimal deterrence. This leaves room for firms and their managers to consider their ethical obligations. These considerations will be especially salient in the international arena where there are few realistic legal constraints. As Richard De George states:

'Unless [the market] is perceived as fair, only those who are forced to do so by adverse circumstances or who have no other alternatives will take part. It makes no sense to participate in the market unless one hopes to benefit from it. Lack of fairness undermines the system and works against the norm of efficiency ...'[45]

Firms have an obligation to act in accord with the morality of the marketplace even in countries where that morality is not well entrenched. Firms should not act in ways that undermine contracts or that freeload on benefits of the marketplace without accepting the costs.[46]

Even if an individual corrupt deal is efficient, actions that contribute to the acceptability of corruption in the marketplace undermine efficiency. We saw how this could happen in the discussion of grand corruption. Individual payoffs should not be evaluated only in terms of the proximate deal, but as part of a system that produces inefficiency. The firm is a beneficiary of the market system, and the normative justification of markets rests on their efficiency. Thus the firm has an obligation to act in ways that improve the efficient functioning of the market. Otherwise the entire market system is open to charges of immorality and illegitimacy. Widespread unscrupulous behaviour can erode public confidence in the market and seriously affect the ability of honest entrepreneurs to carry out their activities. If bribery is rampant, those who are honest may refuse to invest.

45 De George (1993) p 421.
46 Bowie (1988) p 528.

Under this view, the firm has a duty not only to refuse the corrupt demand but also to make it public.[47]

Maintaining political legitimacy

Firms are dependent for their success not only on the existence of a functioning market system, but also on a state that facilitates market activity and maintains order and stability. A good deal of recent scholarship points to the close connection between the effectiveness of the state, on the one hand, and economic growth and development, on the other.[48] In particular, foreign direct investment and the success of industrial development policies are linked to the quality of governance and the relative lack of corruption.[49] Thus, just as firms have an obligation to act consistently with the preservation of markets, they also have an obligation to act consistently with the preservation of a 'market friendly' state. One can speak of 'corporate citizenship' in this context. This terminology focuses on the firm as a legal fiction that has been created or permitted to operate by the state itself. One could argue that this only gives the firm an obligation to act in market or efficiency-enhancing ways as outlined above. However, as creatures of the state, firms are also able to affect what the state does. In fact, the firm's capacity to act is likely to be larger than that of unorganised citizens. In response, one might argue that the firm has an obligation *not* to act since it is only a legal fiction. With Thomas Donaldson,[50] the present writer would turn the conclusion around and say that the firm's very dependence on the state for its existence gives it an obligation to consider the consequences of its actions for the state, and sometimes to act affirmatively to preserve political values. Furthermore, as Mark Bovens points out,[51] employees also have obligations as citizens. These obligations may lead them to oppose certain actions supported by the firm, but the firm as an institution in society ought to recognise and accept these obligations, not undermine them. If a firm's top management anticipates such behaviour, it should modify its own policies to fit the citizenship obligations of employees.

Beyond accommodating its employees, the nature of a firm's citizenship obligations are less straightforward than in the case of actions that enhance market performance. The outlines of a competitive market system are fairly broadly accepted, and the nature of market failures well understood. The same cannot be said for the relationship between political and economic systems. The scholarly literature is divided about the relationship between democratic government and economic growth.[52] Furthermore, the causal links between firms' actions and political outcomes are not well understood. Firms that wish to behave responsibly may face difficulties in articulating the values they hope to promote.

In the face of these complex empirical and conceptual problems, firms may simply take the minimalist route and do no more than obey laws that are generally

---

47 Some proposed corporate codes of conduct for transnationals include provisions designed to maintain the integrity of the market by restricting political payments and bribes. Such restrictions are part of the code developed by the OECD and the draft United Nations Code of Conduct on Transnational Corporations. For an overview see Frederick (1991).
48 Keefer and Knack (1995).
49 Ades and Di Tella (1997); Wei (1997).
50 Donaldson (1989).
51 Bovens (1998).
52 Preworski and Limongi (1993).

enforced and refuse to invest in countries where the state is weak or autocratic. Such a position amounts to little more than a refusal to accept any responsibility in the political sphere, although the refusal to invest could generate pro-reform incentives. A slightly more proactive firm would make a good faith effort to comply with the law and to publicise this fact in an effort to induce greater compliance by others. In both cases the firm accepts the legal order and makes no attempt to judge it or modify it.

Under these approaches, the firm merely reacts to the existing legal system without participating in political life directly. Many reformers would like to cabin business firms into such limited roles to leave more room for popular control and, under some conditions, a firm's responsibilities may be stated negatively as an obligation not to interfere with popular control of the state. However, many states are very far from the ideal of democratic control and have legal and regulatory frameworks that restrain market activities without any corresponding benefits for ordinary citizens. Then, firms might actively work for law reform to produce a system that supports a favourable business climate. In other words, their political activity is 'public-spirited', but only with reference to the business community or their own industry, not society as a whole. Finally, firms might actively support purely political reform or, in a well-functioning system, seek to counter reactionary forces. Clearly, as a firm's managers move along this spectrum, they must answer increasingly difficult questions concerning the goals of their actions. Managers who support political reform out of a sense of obligation or responsibility to the state in which their firm operates must have a view of what would constitute 'good government'. At the other extreme, managers just need to know local laws and the nature of the enforcement effort.

Unfortunately, democracy and the 'market-friendly' state are not in all circumstances the same thing. Case studies of foreign direct investment indicate that businesses are not always supporters of democracy, even if they are headquartered in countries where democracy is well-entrenched.[53] Managers may believe that economic success conflicts with the development of democracy in poor and developing countries. Nevertheless, there are some easy cases. Given the firm's dependence on the state for its existence and its ability to operate, it has an obligation not to undermine the constitution of democratic states viewed as legitimate by their citizens. If firms invest in countries trying to establish democratic systems, they should ask if their actions are supporting the development of a viable and legitimate state.[54] New corrupt opportunities are one of the growing pains of economic and political transformation and can undermine otherwise promising reforms by reducing their legitimacy and fairness. As Bowie concludes, firms should support democracy because: 'Otherwise, multinationals would be in the position of benefiting from doing business with the society while at the same time engaging in activity that undermines the society.'[55]

---

53 Armijo (1999).
54 Dennis Thompson writes that 'political ethics provides support for democratic politics in many ways' ((1987) p 3). The present writer would say the same for corporate ethics. The restrictions on bribes and political payments in proposed codes of conduct for transnationals are sometimes justified as attempts to avoid behaviour that interferes with national sovereignty and the internal politics of host countries (Frederick, 1991).
55 Bowie (1988) p 527.

The difficult cases occur when a state's long-term stability is built on an essentially autocratic system that is favourable to business investment and where democracy, if established, could pass through a long unsettled period. If one accepts this writer's argument that firms have an obligation not to undermine a state based on popular sovereignty, then the firm's obligation is clear. It should not engage in corruption to obtain contracts, concessions or privatised firms. Bribery permits a firm to freeload off the framework of rules governing interactions between business and the state. The firm benefits from the rules against corruption without supporting the rules itself.[56] Bribes are illegitimate that 'undermine a democratic system in which publicly elected officials hold a position of public trust'.[57]

Yet, multinational businesses have not generally considered the impact of their behaviour on the long-term prospects of the countries where they invest and trade. One still hears expressions of cynicism and resignation from business leaders. However, in an international environment with no effective means of controlling commercial behaviour, large firms have an obligation to behave responsibly. This obligation is stronger in poor and emerging economies than it is in the developed world, with its network of regulations and its reasonably responsive political systems. A firm that operates within the laws of the US can argue that the constraints imposed by tax, regulatory and criminal laws are sufficient to fulfil its obligations. Such a position is controversial even in developed countries, but it is, at least, a plausible position. This view comes into question when investment and trade occur in overseas environments where legal rules are either poorly specified or overly restrictive, and where the accountability of top government officials to the long-term success of their country's economic and social development is in doubt.

In industrialised countries, firms and their employees cannot choose only to obey laws that they judge to be efficient and just. Firms also have obligations to the state. US and European firms do not generally try to bribe their way out of environmental and health and safety rules or enlist the help of criminals to evade the law. Instead, such firms work to change the laws, make legal campaign contributions, lobby public agencies and bring lawsuits that challenge laws and regulations. One can complain about the importance of wealth and large corporations in the political life of developed countries, but at least well-documented lobbying activities and campaign contributions are preferable to secret bribes in maintaining democratic institutions.

Some of these same firms, however, feel less constraint about violating laws in developing and transitional economies. Survey evidence indicates a wide range of viewpoints among business people. In one US study, 30.3% of the managers surveyed stated that it was never acceptable to pay a 'consulting' fee of $350,000 to a foreign official in return for a contract worth $10m in profits. At the other end of the scale, however, 6.1% found the payment always acceptable.[58]

It seems strange indeed to tolerate business firms' judgments that a well-placed payoff is justified because it increases their profits. Such an attitude can do serious harm in nations struggling to build a viable state. These states need to develop effective mechanisms that translate popular demands into law, that

56 Bowie (1988) p 528.
57 Donaldson (1989) p 88.
58 Longenecker, McKinney and Moore (1988).

provide a credible commitment to the enforcement of these laws and that provide legal recourse to those facing extortionary demands. If investors and ordinary citizens make individualised judgments about which laws are legitimate, the attempt to create state institutions will founder. Bribery will determine not only which laws are enforced, but also which laws are enacted. All states, even those that have most successfully curbed the power of special interests, enact inefficient laws, but no state could operate effectively if individuals could take the law into their own hands and justify doing so by reference to cost-benefit criteria.

The discussion thus suggests that corruption may be more tolerable, not when it increases the efficiency of individual deals, but when it is carried out in clearly illegitimate regimes that can make no claim to popular support. Then, even bribes to avoid taxes seem less harmful than in other contexts because the fewer resources available to the state, the less powerful it is. Still, costs do remain. The beneficiaries of corrupt transactions will be a strong constituency against reform because they will fear the loss of their special advantages. Furthermore, when a reform regime does take power, its efforts will be made more difficult if corruption has become systemic. One of the regime's first tasks must be to change the behaviour of corrupt officials, firms and individuals.

Causation and co-ordination

In 1995 the sales figures for the 20 largest multinational corporations ranged from \$152.5bn to \$61.5bn. The smallest of these companies had sales that exceeded the GDP of 98 of the 138 countries providing data to the World Bank.[59] Such firms have leverage in many of the countries where they invest and trade. Even if foreign direct investment by multinationals and their share of trade are in single figures in a host country, the firms' global reach gives them influence that local firms may lack. Multinational firms may also have superior knowledge based on their global businesses and their access to up-to-date research. A firm may know that a particular factory design will be ineffective in the host country or that a product or input is dangerous. If a country's officials are corrupt, this places additional burdens on the outside investor since the country's officials cannot be assumed to have balanced risk and financial reward in a way that reflects citizen preferences. It will not be sufficient simply to provide officials with information. The firm's managers instead face a starker choice of trading off profits against harm to a nation's citizens in the absence of a strong legal and political framework.

Nevertheless, management may reason that if they do not pay the bribe someone else will, and that the firm has an obligation to its employees and shareholders that supersedes its obligation to act consistently with efficient market principles. Each firm's managers may think that its corruption will not be important in the overall scheme of things. Many moral dilemmas have this form in which individual moral decisions have little impact, but where the situation would be much improved if most people acted morally.[60]

Dennis Thompson proposes an instructive way of framing the issue in his discussion of personal responsibility. In the context of this chapter, this is

---

59 Calculated from data in the World Banks' *World Development Indicators 1997*, Table 4.2, and the United Nations *World Investment Report 1997: Transnational Corporation, Market Structure and Competition Policy*, Table I.7. See also Donaldson (1989) pp 32–33.
60 Regan (1980).

equivalent to the responsibility of managers who must decide whether or not to pay a bribe. He distinguishes between causation and moral responsibility which can apply even if the causal link is weak.[61] However, the duty to act unilaterally is stronger if causation is present along with moral responsibility. Of course, there are very few cases where a multinational firm can single-handedly influence the operation of a state. Some countries are so large that they have market power on their own. However, even in those countries some companies have leverage at the national level, and the regional impact of other deals is large. For example, consumer goods companies with strong international brand recognition may be such a symbol of successful development that they can successfully resist corrupt demands. Other companies with a strong market position in their fields of business can refuse to participate in corrupt arrangements. Even if such firms lose out on corrupt deals, some countries may be induced to operate more cleanly so as not to sacrifice the firms' business. Large, highly diversified firms may have a further advantage if they can credibly threaten to exit a country entirely in the face of corruption in one line of business. Such a firm may also have the bargaining power to protect local subsidiaries from acquiescing to corrupt demands. Firms that successfully use the leverage they have will not only help contribute to a country's long-term growth prospects but also generally will benefit in the short term as well.

Firm managers often assert that they must pay bribes because everyone else does. Bribery persists even though all would prefer an honest environment. Firms are thought to be engaged in a prisoners' dilemma game with their competitors. If so, agreements to refrain from corruption are likely to be unstable since each firm has an incentive to defect. Some claim, however, that the game is actually a co-ordination game, not a prisoners' dilemma, or, at least, that it can be converted into a co-ordination game through dialogue and public relations. The difference is important. In both situations the actors are better off if they all co-operate than if they do not. However, in a pure co-ordination game the co-operative solution is stable. Once everyone behaves morally, there is no incentive for any one to defect. The only problem is inducing firms to move to such a strategy, because being the only honest firm in a sea of corruption is costly. In contrast, under a prisoners' dilemma, the co-operative solution is unstable since each individual has an incentive to cheat when everyone else is co-operating. It seems at least possible to hope that current effort to ratify the OECD anti-bribery convention will prove to be an exercise in co-ordination, not a prisoners' dilemma.

NEXT STEPS

In light of the limitations of moral suasion and of current international efforts, one should ask whether any new international initiatives ought to be developed to deal with the issue. Two are discussed here. The first concerns a stronger effort to control the laundering of corrupt funds. The second involves proposals for international dispute resolution mechanisms that might hear complaints by firms claiming to have lost business to rivals as the result of corruption. In the latter case, the International Financial Institutions might play a role.

---

61 Thompson (1987) pp 47–48.

Controlling money laundering

Anti-corruption efforts should be co-ordinated with another international campaign – the control of money laundering across national borders. Accepting and paying bribes will look more attractive if it is relatively easy to establish secret off-shore bank accounts. However, controls on money laundering should not be the primary focus of anti-corruption efforts. Capital tends to move toward investments with favourable risk-return combinations. So long as poor countries offer an unfavourable investment climate, wealthy residents will try to invest outside their countries' borders. An individual investment project, privatisation deal or concession may be profitably constructed, but the overall set of investment opportunities may be very thin. Thus those in developing countries who accumulate funds – whether from licit or illicit sources – will frequently want to invest abroad. Strict controls on money laundering cannot overcome this basic fact. Controls can make it more costly to accumulate illicit funds and make it riskier for firms to make payoffs, but they can do nothing to change underlying conditions. Deeper reforms in host countries are necessary.

The main international body engaged in ongoing efforts to control money laundering is the Financial Action Task Force set up in 1989 with representatives from the OECD, Hong Kong, Singapore, the Gulf States and the European Commission.[62] It has developed 40 recommendations for appropriate countermeasures, including the prohibition of anonymous accounts. In recent years, more than 50 new laws against money laundering have been passed. In North America, the US passed a broad statute in 1986, followed soon afterwards by Canada and Mexico. Most countries originally focused only on money laundering as it affected drug trafficking. At present, however, many are considering including bribery and corruption as predicate offences.[63] The USA Patriot Act of 2001 includes a section on international money laundering and establishes foreign corruption as a predicate offence for the first time under United States law.[3a]

Money laundering is becoming the specialty of small 'financial paradises' and of some emerging market economies. It is not enough to keep most developed countries pure. A serious international campaign against the worst abusers, including Switzerland, is of increasing importance. At issue is the ease with which corrupt officials in one country can hide their gains in another and structures that permit otherwise legitimate firms to hide their corruption activity.[64]

One role for international organisations and for law enforcement agencies in developed countries is the compilation of information on questionable transactions, combined with the prosecution of individuals and organisations based in developed countries that do business in developing countries. For example, it is possible to compare average product prices in US international trade with the average prices for the same products recorded for US trade with particular countries. The data provide a way to look for over and under-invoicing and have been used by US authorities to direct investigative efforts.[65] Obviously,

---

62 Scott (1995).
63 Paulose (1997) at 263–280.
63a US Congress, 107th Congress, 1st Session, USA Patriot Act, PL 107–56, Title III, section 315, 115 Stat 315.
64 Scott (1995).
65 Paul et al (1994).

price divergences cannot prove anything on their own, but they can provide a starting point for more intensive investigation. These data could point to violations of US tax and customs laws, as well as laws of foreign countries. They can indicate where money laundering may be occurring through mispriced traded goods. This data-gathering effort should be extended to include trade records from other developed countries, and could provide a way for developed countries to help poorer countries control illegal transfers of funds and tax and customs fraud.

Dispute resolution mechanisms and the role of international financial institutions

Limiting money laundering clearly requires international co-operation, but these efforts will not by themselves have much impact on the level of corruption if the underlying incentives arise not from illegal business activity, but from the benefits of controlling the state and of obtaining profitable dispensations from public officials. Obviously, individual states need to consider how to create a less corruption-prone environment, but there may be other steps that can be taken internationally beyond current efforts to ratify and implement international agreements. One proposal is a general forum for resolving disputes involving corruption. Obviously, to make such a suggestion operational one must resolve difficult problems of proof and standards of decision. Nevertheless, some models exist in the international legal arena that can provide ideas about how to proceed.

For example, the World Bank Group's International Center for the Settlement of Investment Disputes (ICSID) resolves disputes under contracts where it is the forum of choice.[66] ICSID panels are not formally courts, and their use is based on the prior consent of the parties, but they do occasionally deal with issues that indirectly are related to corruption. The process has difficulties because the review mechanism lacks finality and sometimes takes an overly technical and formalistic approach. Nevertheless, these problems may have become less severe in recent years.[67] ICSID has not, however, heard disputes arising at the contract awarding stage, and it may not have jurisdiction in such matters. It is also an expensive and time-consuming process that currently is not able to handle a large volume of cases. Serious reforms would be required before it could regularly be invoked as part of a broader anti-corruption effort.

In 1993 the World Bank established an independent Inspection Panel that provides another model for an international dispute resolution mechanism. Unlike the ICSID, which is open only to parties to disputed contracts, the Panel reviews complaints from groups of private persons in borrower countries. Groups must allege that they are suffering or expect to suffer from the World Bank's failure to follow its own policies and procedures.[68] Thus it appears possible for the Panel to hear complaints involving corruption in World Bank projects. For example, the Panel might consider allegations that the Bank did not follow its operational policies and procedures if it overlooked evidence of corruption. In fact, corruption may be behind some recent cases brought on other grounds. Unfortunately, the Panel is a weak instrument and a decision by the Bank's

---

66 Shihata and Parra (1994).
67 Reisman (1992) pp 46–106.
68 Bradlow (1996); Bradlow and Schlemmer-Schulte (1994).

Executive Directors appears to have further limited the institution's power. It cannot proceed with an investigation unless it obtains the approval of the Bank's Board of Directors, and even if the Panel finds against the Bank, it has only advisory powers. Its recommendations are forwarded to the Bank's Board which makes the final decision, and the Panel's own findings are not made public. Of the 12 cases which had come before the Panel by July 1999, the Panel refused to accept two and recommended against an investigation in three. Two cases are pending. In the remaining five, the Board only fully backed the Panel in one case.[69]

The Panel's experience with handling complaints from citizens' groups and non-profit organisations is a useful first step. It is the first international forum in which individuals who do not have a contractual relationship with an international organisation can attempt to hold it accountable.[70] After analysing the Panel's handling of complaints about the Arun III dam project in Nepal, Daniel Bradlow[71] concludes that the Panel can help protect the interests of people affected by World Bank projects, but he raises concerns about ambiguities in the relationship between the Panel, Bank Management and the Board of Executive Directors. A key requirement, and one that will be central to any new institution, is to ensure that the Panel maintains its independence and that its processes are transparent to outside observers.

Alternatively, the international community could establish a forum that could review cases of suspected corruption in privatisation or contracting processes. Cases brought by disappointed bidders or defrauded lenders would require the country involved to make a transparent accounting of its behaviour. Claimants would not necessarily need to document bribes paid. The focus should instead be on the terms of the deal. If it seems to diverge significantly from what an honest process would produce, the court could require that the project be re-bid. One difficulty in making the process operational, however, is that the re-bid will not be simply a more transparent and honest rerun of the old one. All the players have new information as a result of the first round that will affect their behaviour in the second round.

A more serious problem with an international tribunal is to assure obedience to its decisions. One option is to use the leverage of the WTO. The advantage of WTO sanctions is that they are not imposed by the WTO itself but by a country's trading partners. However, the WTO governs relations among nations, not individuals and businesses. Thus, transnational bribery could be controlled *through* the WTO, not *by* the WTO.[72] An international process of this kind would, of course, discourage some investment and privatisation projects from going ahead. First, that might not be such a bad thing. If an inside deal appears inevitable, a country should delay privatisation because a public firm is much easier to monitor than a private one. Similarly, corrupt leaders may design a public works project with bribes in mind, not economic development. Second, the international community might subsidise the cost of any proceeding where the developing country emerges victorious from a challenge. Third, like the WTO procurement pact, participation could be voluntary, with jurisdiction limited to those countries that fulfil WTO conditions or that volunteer to establish

---

69 World Bank (1999).
70 Bissell (1997); Bradlow and Schlemmer-Schulte (1994) at 402.
71 Bradlow (1996).
72 Nichols (1997) at 361–364.

rigorous procurement systems in return for World Bank or UNDP technical advice and other support.

The World Bank and the IMF cannot engage in individualised investigations of corruption. That is for the legal systems of the member countries. However, they can seek to control corruption in their own programs and can help countries design control programs. The World Bank has reformed its procurement guidelines to discipline corrupt firms by restricting their access to future World Bank-financed projects. Both the IMF and World Bank seem more willing than in the past to withhold aid from countries where corruption affects a government's ability to function effectively. For example, under a 1997 policy the IMF required reforms in a country's public sector institutions and in the transparency of its procedures in order to limit corruption and improve the effectiveness of IMF financial assistance.[73]

One method of checking the effectiveness of a country's policies would be to permit firms that are pressured for bribes to report their experience to the IMF. The IMF would not investigate individual complaints, but a pattern of reports could induce the IMF to reopen negotiations. Similarly, top government officials who feel pressured to accept payoffs by businesses seeking favours could also report to the IMF. Such reports, passed on to the World Bank, could be a preliminary step in implementing the World Bank's procurement policy that explicitly contemplates actions to discipline firms by restricting access to projects supported by World Bank loans.

Becoming a clearing house for allegations is a way of revealing to both sides that high-level corruption is a game in which the developing country is the loser and in which neither private nor public actors can absolve themselves of responsibility. If both a top official and a firm complain about corrupt pressures exerted by the other, the stage may be set for meaningful reforms that reduce the underlying incentives for such deals to be made in the first place. Without trying to affix blame, the IMF and World Bank could begin a dialogue with a country's leaders and major investors on ways to improve the situation for the benefit of the country's citizens. If everyone thinks that everyone else is corrupt, then all but the saints will be tempted to engage in malfeasance. If expectations can be changed by clear statements on both sides followed by consistent actions and a credible commitment to report corrupt pressures, progress seems possible.[74] The climate of world opinion may be running strongly enough against corruption to make it worthwhile for major corporations to take a stand against bribery rather than tolerating or encouraging payoffs.

The international business community is beginning to recognise the costs of corruption to the global investment environment. In so far as this is true, it suggests another approach to reform in the developing world and in countries in transition. International businesses themselves could contribute to the effort by providing funds and technical assistance to countries interested in reform. This is already being done through professional associations such as the American Bar Association, but the aid and lending organisations might explore the possibility of collaborative projects. The international organisations might provide a neutral

---

73 International Monetary Fund, 'The Role of the IMF in Governance Issues – Guidance Note,' issued as part of News Brief 95/15, Washington DC: IMF, 4 August 1997.
74 This view is consistent with Regan's (1980) normative position and Sugden's (1984) empirical claim.

forum in which the experience of these companies could be tapped and their suggestions for reform canvassed.

CONCLUSIONS

The important issue for companies operating in a corrupt environment is whether to participate actively, quietly refuse to deal or report corruption to local authorities and to those in the outside world. Keeping quiet is probably the worst option. The firm not only loses the business; it also has done nothing to change the underlying situation for the better. The advantage of the current interest and concern with corruption is that reporting corrupt demands can lead to international embarrassment for the corrupt officials that may, in turn, produce reforms. Companies that claim to abhor corruption while accepting it as a necessary evil are not acting consistently, so long as one assumes that the pressure of international public opinion can have an impact both on corrupt public officials and on bribe-paying business firms. Some writers on business ethics, although accepting the necessity of making payoffs under some limited conditions, nevertheless argue that firms have an obligation to publicise the practice and to work for change at a higher level.[75]

The conclusion of this chapter is a simple one. Corruption in contracting, the award of concessions and privatisation promotes inefficiency and undermines state legitimacy. Business firms, as legally created entities, owe obligations to the political-economic systems in which they operate that go beyond the mere pursuit of profit. Although firms are constrained by the test of market viability, they are obligated both to further overall market efficiency and to uphold democratically legitimate states. Thus they are obligated not to engage in high-level corruption. The obligation goes beyond a mere refusal to deal to an affirmative duty to at least publicise the situation and to build coalitions to work for reform. The experience of recent years suggests that the anti-corruption area is a good case study of how attitudes can change and bandwagon effects can operate to bring in a broader coalition of supporters around an issue of corporate responsibility.

Select bibliography

Ades, A, and Di Tella, R, (1997) 'National Champions and Corruption: Some Unpleasant Interventionist Arithmetic', 107 The Economic Journal 1023.

Armijo, L E, (1999) *Financial Globalization and Democracy in Emerging Markets.*

Bissell, R E, (1997) 'Recent Practice of the Inspection Panel of the World Bank', 91 AJIL 741.

Bovens, M, (1998) *The Quest for Responsibility.*

Bowie, N, (1988) 'The Moral Obligations of Multinational Corporations' in S Luper-Foy (ed), *Problems of International Justice.*

Bradlow, D D, (1996) 'A Test Case for the World Bank', 1 American University Journal of International Law and Policy 247.

---

75 Donaldson (1989) pp 102–106; De George (1993) pp 114, 135.

Bradlow, D D, and Schlemmer-Schulte, S, (1994) 'The World Bank's New Inspection Panel: A Constructive Step in the Transformation of the International Legal Order, 54 Zeitschrift für ausländisches öffentliches Recht und Völkerrecht 392.

Braithwaite, J, (1985) 'Taking Responsibility Seriously: Corporate Compliance Systems', in B Fisse and P A French (eds), *Corrigible Corporations and Unruly Law.*

Campos, J E, and Root, H, (1996) *East Asia's Road to High Growth: An Institutional Perspective.*

Celarier, M, (1996) 'Stealing the Family Silver', Euromoney, February.

Colazingari, S, and Rose-Ackerman, S, (1998) 'Corruption in a Paternalistic Democracy: Lessons from Italy for Latin America', 113 Pol Sc Q 447.

Cooper, D E, (1968) 'Collective Responsibility', 43 Philosophy and Public Affairs 258.

Dahl, R, (1982) *Dilemmas of Pluralist Democracy.*

Deacon, R T, (1994) 'Deforestation and the Rule of Law in a Cross-Section of Countries', 70 Land Economics 414.

De George, R T, (1993) *Competing with Integrity in International Business.*

De Melo, M G O, and Sandler, O, (1995) 'Pioneers for Profit: St. Petersburg Entrepreneurs in Services', 9 World Bank Economic Review 425.

Della Porta, D, and Vannucci, A, (1997) 'The 'Perverse Effects' of Political Corruption', 45 Political Studies 516.

Donagan, A, (1977) *The Theory of Morality.*

Donaldson, T, (1989) *The Ethics of International Business.*

Environmental Investigation Agency, (1996) *Corporate Power, Corruption and the Destruction of the World's Forests: The Case for a New Global Forest Agreement.*

Faruqee, R, and Husain, I, (1994) 'Adjustment in Seven African Countries' in I Husain and R Faruqee (eds), *Adjustment in Africa: Lessons from Country Studies.*

Frederick, W C, (1991) 'The Moral Authority of Transnational Corporate Codes', 10 J Business Ethics 165.

French, P, (1979) 'The Corporation as Moral Person', 16 Am Phil Q 207.

Hamilton, C, (1997) 'The Sustainability of Logging in Indonesia's Tropical Forests: A Dynamic Input/Output Analysis', 21 Ecological Economics 183.

Hoekman, B M, and Mavroidis, P C, (eds), (1997) *Law and Policy in Public Purchasing: The WTO Agreement on Government Procurement.*

International Bar Association (1996) 'Resolution on Deterring Bribery in International Business Transactions', 1 June.

International Chamber of Commerce, (1996) 'Extortion and Bribery in International Business Transactions', Document No 193/15, 26 March.

Kaufmann, D, and Siegelbaum, P, (1997) 'Privatization and Corruption in Transition Economies', 50 J Int Affairs 419.

Keefer, P, and Knack, S, (1995) 'Institutions and Economic Performance: Cross-Country Tests Using Alternative Institutional Measures', 7 Economics and Politics 207.

Khanna, V S, (1996) 'Corporate Criminal Liability: What Purpose Does It Serve?', 109 Harv LR 1477.

Leff, N, (1964), 'Economic Development Through Bureaucratic Corruption', 8 American Behavioral Scientist 8.

Lehman, C K, (1988) 'Moral and Conceptual Issues in Investment and Finance: An Overview', 7 J Business Ethics 3.

Lien, D-H D, (1990a), 'Competition, Regulation and Bribery: A Further Note', 11 Managerial and Decision Economics 127.

—(1990b) 'Corruption and Allocation Efficiency', 33 J Development Economics 153.

Longenecker, J G, McKinney, J A, and Moore, C W, (1988) 'The Ethical Issue of International Bribery: A Study of Attitudes Among U.S. Business Professionals', 7 J Business Ethics 341.

Manzetti, L, (1999) *Privatization South American Style.*

—(1997) 'Regulation in Post-Privatization Environments: Chile and Argentina in Comparative Perspective', *North-South Center Agenda Papers.*

Manzetti, L, and Blake, C, (1996) 'Market Reforms and Corruption in Latin America: New Means for Old Ways', 3 Review of International Political Economy 662.

Nellis, J, and Kikeri, S, (1989) 'Public Enterprise Reform: Privatization and the World Bank', 17 World Development 659.

Nichols, P M, (1997) 'Outlawing Transnational Bribery Through the World Trade Organization', 28 Journal of Law & Policy in International Business 305.

Nickson, R A, (1996) 'Democratisation and Institutional Corruption in Paraguay' in W Little and E Posada-Carbó (eds), *Political Corruption in Europe and Latin America.*

Norcia, V, (1988) 'Mergers, Takeovers, and a Property Ethic', 7 J Business Ethics 109.

Novitzkaya, I, Novitzky, V, and Stone, A, (1995) 'Private Enterprise in Ukraine: Getting Down to Business', World Bank Private Sector Development Division, unprocessed.

Orland, L, and Cachera, C, (1995) 'Essay and Translation: Corporate Crime and Punishment in France: Criminal Responsibility of Legal Entities (Persones Morales) under the New France Criminal Code (Nouveau Code Penal)', 11 Connecticut JIL 111–168.

Pasuk, P, and Sungsidh, P, (1994) *Corruption and Democracy in Thailand.*

Paul, K, Pak, S, Zdanowicz, J et al, (1994) 'The Ethics of International Trade: Use of Deviation from Average World Price to Indicate Possible Wrongdoing', 4 Business Ethics Quarterly 29.

Paulose, M Jr, (1997) '*United States v. McDougald*: The Anathema to 18 U.S.C. § 1956 and National Efforts Against Money Laundering', 21 Fordham International Law Journal 253.

Pendergast, W F, (1995) 'Foreign Corrupt Practices Act: An overview of Almost Twenty Years of Foreign Bribery Prosecutions' 7 International Quarterly 187.

Phongpaicht, P, and Piriyarangsan, S, (1994) *Corruption and Democracy in Thailand.*

Przeworski, A, and Limongi, F, (1993) 'Political Regimes and Economic Growth', 7 J Economic Perspectives 51.

Rashid, S, (1981) 'Public Utilities in Egalitarian LDCs', 34 Kyklos 448.

Regan, D, (1980) *Utilitarianism and Co-operation.*

Reisman, W M, (1992) *Systems of Control in International Adjudication and Arbitration.*

Rose-Ackerman, S, (1978) *Corruption: A Study in Political Economy.*

—(1999), *Corruption and Government:Causes, Consequences, and Reform.*

Rosenberg, R D, (1987) 'Managerial Morality and Behavior: The Questionable Payments Issue', 6 J Business Ethics 23.

Schelling, T, (1960) *The Strategy of Conflict.*

Schwarz, A, (1994) *A Nation in Waiting: Indonesia in the 1990s.*

Scott, D, (1995) 'Money Laundering and International Efforts to Fight It', 48 Viewpoints, Financial Sector Development Department, Vice Presidency for Finance and Private Sector Development, World Bank, Washington, May.

Shihata, I, Parra, F I, and Parra, A R, (1994) 'Applicable Law in Disputes Between States and Private Foreign Parties: The Case of Arbitration under the ICSID Convention', 9 ICSID Review: Foreign Investment Law Journal 9.

Simon, J G, Powers, C W, and Gunnemann, J, (1972) *The Ethical Investor.*

Smiley, M, (1992) *Moral Responsibility and the Boundaries of Community.*

Sugden, R, (1984) 'Reciprocity: The Supply of Public Goods Through Voluntary Contributions', 94 Economic Journal 772.

Tanzi, V, and Davoodi, H, (1997) 'Corruption, Public Investment, and Growth', IMF Working Paper WP/97/139, October.

Thompson, D, (1987) *Political Ethics and Public Office.*

—(1995) *Ethics in Congress.*

Transparency International – USA (1996) 'Corporate Anti-Corruption Programs: A Survey of Best Practices', June.

UN Development Programme (1996) 'Aid Accountability Initiative, Bi-Annual Report, 1 January – June 30, 1996', July.

Van de Walle, N. (1989), 'Privatization in Developing Countries: A Review of the Issues', *World Development* No. 17, 601.

Vincent, J R, and Binkley, C S, (1992) 'Forest-Based Industrialization: A Dynamic Perspective', in N P Sharma (ed), *Managing the World's Forests.*

Vincke, F, Heimann, F, and Katz, R (eds), (1999) *Fighting Bribery: A Corporate Practices Manual.*

Walzer, M, (1973) 'Political Action: The Problem of Dirty Hands', 2 Philosophy and Public Affairs 160.

Webster, L M, and Charap, J, (1993) 'The Emergence of Private Sector Manufacturing in St. Petersburg', World Bank Technical Paper 228.

Wei, S-J, (1997) 'How Taxing Is Corruption on International Investors?', National Bureau of Economic Research Working Paper 6030.

Wiehan, M H, (1997) 'Reform of Government Procurement Procedures: Principles and Objectives', Paper presented at the 8th Conference of the International Public Procurement Association, Kuala Lumpur.

World Bank, (1999) 'The Inspection Panel: Overview September 1997 Update', available at www.worldbank.org/html/ins-panel/overview.html.

World Trade Organization (2000) Government Procurement Code: 2000 Report, November; http://www.wto.org/english/tratop_e/gproc_e/rep_ooe.htm.

Yotopoulos, P A, (1989) 'The (Rip)Tide of Privatization: Lessons from Chile', 17 World Development 683.

Chapter 9

Law's elusive promise: learning from Bhopal

M GALANTER[1]

It is now more than 15 years since the massive leak of methyl isocyanate [MIC] at Union Carbide's plant in Bhopal that killed more than 8,000 people[2] and devastated the lives of tens of thousands. Union Carbide and the government of India reached a settlement in February 1989, bringing an end to the major litigation. As of early 1998, nine years after Union Carbide paid $470m to the government of India, which had appointed itself the victims' exclusive representative, less than half of the sum (including the accumulated interest) had been paid to the victims.[3] The claims process is formalistic, niggardly and corrupt. Some genuine victims have gone without payment for failure to meet the Claims Tribunal's documentation requirements, while less worthy claimants have manipulated the process to secure payment. The majority of victims received minimal payments: more than 90% were paid less than Rs 25,000 (from which nearly Rs 10,000 was deducted for the interim monetary relief paid by the government from 1990).[4] By January 1998, 15,171 death claims were adjudicated. Of these, 3,760 were rejected as inadequately documented and 6,327 were dealt with as injury cases. Of the 5,084 that were found entitled to compensation for death (scheduled to range from Rs 100,000 to Rs 500,000), 98% received the minimum award of Rs 100,000.[5] The payment phase of the Bhopal gas leak affair is a worthy match for the atrocious negligence of the injury phase and the disappointing underperformance of the legal phase.

---

1   John and Rylla Bosshard Professor of Law and Professor of South Asian Studies, University of Wisconsin-Madison. E-mail: MSGalant@facstaff.wisc.edu.
2   Estimates of the death toll vary. Over 2,000 persons died immediately. Estimates of total deaths have climbed over the years. The welfare commissioner in Bhopal listed 8,017 deaths as 'exposure related': Pearce (1998) at 1. A report in the Sunday Times counts at least 12,000: Grey (1998).
3   'Bhopal Gas Tragedy Victims' Woes Continue' (1998) the Statesman, 25 February. Almost all of the payments were made during the latter part of the period since the settlement. In 1994, only 1% of the pending claims had been decided and only 1% of the settlement money distributed. 'Bhopal Survivors' Ailments Go Untreated, Panel Finds' (1994) Cleveland Plain Dealer at 6C. A higher estimate of claims resolved (about 4%) is given by Rettie (1994) at 12.
4   (1998) The Statesman. In the early 1990s, the exchange value of Rs 25,000 was approximately $750.
5   'India NGOs complain about tardy progress in Bhopal gas victims' rehabilitation' (1998) Business Line [available in Nexis News library].

An extensive literature has appeared to unravel the lessons of the disaster.[6] Jamie Cassels' *The Uncertain Promise of Law: Lessons from Bhopal* is the first full-blown work of legal scholarship on Bhopal.[7] It is an achievement of massive scope, bringing together a wealth of hard-won information and a clear exposition of legal theory. It is a wonderfully rich account of the legal aftermath of the Bhopal disaster – or perhaps one should say the legal phase of the Bhopal disaster, a phase which is still unfolding.[8] It is the legal phase, which has attracted far less sustained analysis than the injury phase, that is the subject of Cassels' book. He provides a thorough and imaginative examination of the tangle of legal issues, informed by a sympathetic account of recent developments in the Indian legal system, especially the judicial activism and public interest litigation that flourished spectacularly in the 1980s and have now receded but not withered completely.[9]

Cassels' account joins a new genre of books by scholars of civil justice – the elaborated scholarly account of a large case that uses it as a vehicle to address wider institutional and social problems. It is a genre long familiar in constitutional history[10] and in criminal law.[11] But until recently it has not been prominent in scholarship about private law, where the story may involve an aggregation or congregation of related claims in trial courts rather than a single big case at the Supreme Court.[12] There have been some extended accounts of major civil cases by journalists and lawyer-participants,[13] but these were far outnumbered by the vast 'war story' literature on criminal law. Peter Schuck's *Agent Orange on Trial*,[14] published in 1986, has been joined by a growing collection of analytic scholarly accounts,[15] as well as by outstanding contributions by journalists, most notably Jonathan Harr's *A Civil Action* (1995).[16] Cassels expands this new genre significantly by presenting its first transnational entry.

Being transnational is the key to the Bhopal story. Imagine that this had been a purely US event: suppose the gas had leaked at Union Carbide's MIC operation

6 Eg Morehouse and Subramaniam (1986); Hararika (1987); Srivastava (1987); Jasanoff (1994).
7 Cassels (1993).
8 In addition to the dormant criminal case in India, a new civil case under the Alien Tort Claims Act 1789 was filed in New York in November 1999. 'Bhopal Ghosts (Still) Haunt Union Carbide' (2000) Fortune at 44–46; Appleson (1999) (available at www.bhopal.ord/reuters.html). In November 2001, the US Court of Appeals upheld the District Court's dismissal of the Alien Tort Claims Act claims and remanded plaintiff's common law environmental claims for further action by the District Court: *Bano v Union Carbide Corp* 2001 US App LEXIS 24488.
9 Baar (1990) at 140–150; Baxi (1999); Baxi (1985); Bhagwati (1985) at 561–577; Cassels (1989) at 495; Cunningham (1987) at 494–523; Dhavan (1994) at 302–338; Menon (1985) at 444; Peiris (1991) at 66–91; Sathe (1998) at 399–441, 603–640; Susman (1994) at 58–103.
10 Eg Kutler (1990); Vose (1959); Kluger (1975).
11 Eg Kasserman (1986); Higdon (1975).
12 On the concept of a congregation of cases, see Galanter (1990) at 1201; Sanders (1992) at 301.
13 Brodeur (1985); Charfoos (1981); Stern's (1976) much-taught *The Buffalo Creek Disaster*, a wonderful book and one whose lack of analysis, omissions (much of the Buffalo Creek litigation story is left out) and self-glorification tell us a lot about the limitations of the war stories genre. Shorter critical accounts of well-known cases may be found in Noonan (1976); Danzig (1978).
14 Schuck (1986).
15 Eg Sobol (1991); Bacigal (1990); Bollier (1991); Sanders (1998).
16 See also, Mintz (1985); Werth (1998). During this period we also see the rise of fictional accounts of civil cases in novels (eg John Grisham's *The Runaway Jury* (1997); *The Rainmaker* (1996) and in the movies *Class Action* (Michael Apted, 1991); *Philadelphia* (Jonathan Demme, 1993); *The Rainmaker* (Paramount, 1997); *The Sweet Hereafter* (Atom Egoyan, 1997); and *Erin Bronkovich* (1999).

at Institute, West Virginia, instead of at its undernourished twin in Bhopal. We can readily envision the immense mass tort case, the judicial improvisation of devices to handle it, very likely a settlement for a substantial amount, and possibly even the resulting reorganisation of Union Carbide through bankruptcy. It would have been big and unwieldy and would possibly have strained the capacities of the courts, but it would have delivered significant compensation and broadcast powerful preventive signals to many audiences. In spite of the many imponderables, including problems of causation and the presently unknown extent of injuries, the limited single-event format would have presented a good candidate for more or less satisfactory resolution by the US' high accountability-high remedy-high cost system of private law.

Imagine, now, that it was an entirely Indian event, with a domestic Indian company in the role of Union Carbide. On the basis of all previous experience, notwithstanding the vastly greater scale of this disaster, it is very unlikely that tort law would have been invoked at all. There would have been an ex gratia payment of compensation (quite meagre by Western standards) by the company or the government or both; surely a commission of inquiry, and very likely a criminal prosecution. Buildings collapse, mines cave in, hundreds are killed by poisonous liquor– there is a constant stream of these mini-Bhopals' in India[17] – and the law, courts and lawyers are not involved in establishing accountability or securing compensation.[18] There is no reason to think that an all-Indian Bhopal disaster would have departed from this pattern. (Or, that it would have escaped more than momentarily from the obscurity that surrounded the explosion of a liquefied natural gas storage facility in Mexico City just two weeks earlier in which more than 300 people were killed.[19])

In the case of Bhopal, it was the US identity of the malefactor that coupled the disaster and the legal system as they would not have been connected otherwise. Cassels says expectations 'began to fix upon the promises of law' because of 'the cultural dominance of law' in India.[20] This chapter submits that the origin of these expectations was more specific. The perception of invasive violation and pollution by a foreign intruder generated a sense of shared injury and outrage. At the same time the US connection brought with it the image of a US tort system laden with both sting and largesse. It was this image, given dramatic embodiment by the arrival in India of the US plaintiffs' lawyers just days after the explosion,[21]

---

17 A single, not untypical, example will have to suffice: in December 1995, more than 500 people, mostly children, were killed in a fire that swept through a temporary structure housing a school ceremony. Accounts stressed the inadequacy of safety measures and emergency services. The state government announced that it would provide ex gratia payments of Rs. 100,000 [approximately $2,900] to the families of the dead and half that to those seriously injured. Burns (1995a at 3; 1995b at A9); Bora (1996).
18 For an analysis of the failure to seek legal remedy in an incident in which over 300 were killed after drinking poisonous liquor, see Manor (1993) chapter 7. One notable exception to this pattern is the response to the June 1997 fire at the Uphaar Cinema in New Delhi in which 57 persons, many from affluent families, were killed. Halarnkar and Chakravarty (1997) 30. A group of families launched a co-ordinated campaign of litigation against the cinema owners and negligent regulators.
19 Cassels (1993) p 26. A series of subsequent explosion at the same and other Pemex plants may be found through www.emergency.com.
20 Cassels (1993) p 55.
21 'India may sue Union Carbide in U.S. Courts' (1994) the Hindu. The arrival of US lawyers in Bhopal was first reported on 9 December: 'State to seek damages from Carbide' (1984) The Statesman. According to one account, John Coale arrived on 7 December: Adler (1985) at 128.

that projected the 'uncertain promise of law'. But even before the US lawyers arrived, Indian officials were discussing the possibility of recovery in the US – and at US levels of compensation.[22] It is submitted here that the promise of law was only weakly connected to Indian legal culture but was primarily a reflection of US law as filtered through Indian media and sensibilities. Indeed, the reach for an American remedy was the reverse side of deep pessimism about a remedy in India, coupled with untroubled confidence in the US' legal system and anticipation of enormous recoveries. A few weeks after the gas leak, the Chief Justice of India observed: 'These cases must be pursued in the US. It is the only hope these unfortunate people have.'[23] The export of the legal action to the US provoked hardly a murmur of dissent.

The pessimism about a remedy in India reflected a system of tort law and civil justice that observers of the Indian scene regarded as undeveloped, debilitated or moribund.[24]

India appeared to have tort law modelled on that of England, but this was deceptive. The history of tort in India is quite distinctive. The British brought the common law to India in the eighteenth century; in the quarter-century following the 1857 revolt, the legal system was rationalised and systematised. A unified hierarchy of courts was established in each region. A series of codes, based on English law and applicable throughout British India, were adopted.[25] By 1882 there was virtually complete codification of all fields of criminal, commercial and procedural law; tort was the only major field of law left uncodified.[26]

Few tort cases are brought. There has been little doctrinal development. Tort is little used and has remained largely outside the consciousness of the

---

22 Indian officials were talking about a remedy in the US four days after the leak, before the American lawyers appeared on the scene: 'India may sue Union Carbide in U.S. Courts' (1984) The Hindu, 8 December. The first US lawyers arrived in Bhopal on 9 December: 'State to seek damages from Carbide' (1984) The Statesman, 10 December, or filed suit in the US. A suit against Union Carbide for $15bn was filed in Charleston, West Virginia on 8 December and was reported in the Indian press the following day: Eg '$15 billion suit filed in USA' (1989) The Statesman, 9 December. Three days after the gas leak, V P Sathe, the Central Minister for Petroleum and Chemicals said that he expected Union Carbide to provide the same kind of relief that it would have provided if the accident had taken place in the US: Lewin, (1984). A similar notion was expressed by the Madhya Pradesh Government even earlier: 'Firm Chairman and Experts Denied Entry' (1984) The Statesman.

23 Stewart (1985) (quoting Indian lawyers S Kurshid and V M Tarkunde). Thinking about how Indian legal institutions might be adapted to rise to the occasion surfaced only rarely. See Bakshi (1985). The rudiments of an imaginative scheme by Narasimha Sawmy, an Indian lawyer practicing in the US are discussed in Adler (1985) at 132.

24 The only notable exceptions are the distinguished Indian lawyers who testified on behalf of Union Carbide's effort to remove the case from the US' courts.

25 See Galanter (1968) at 65; Acharyya (1914); Stokes (1887).

26 The need for a tort code was urged by Sir Henry Maine, Sir James Stephen and the Fourth Law Commission, which reported in 1879. An Indian Civil Wrongs Bill, drafted by Sir Frederick Pollock in 1886, at the instance of the Government of India, was never taken up for legislative action: Jain (1966). The failure to enact a code was 'inexplicable' according to Acharyya (1984) p 306. But a decade later the Civil Justice Committee 1924–25, noting that the matter 'had been under consideration for some years', observed that: 'there is no branch of law which is more free from blame of contributing to the law's delays. A large part of this work is done in India, and is better done, by the criminal courts.' Civil Justice Committee 1924–25 (1925).

Indian lawyers and public.[27] Delays of *Bleak House* proportions are routine. The writer conducted a survey of reported tort cases in the ten years before the Bhopal disaster [1975–84] and found some 56 cases in the All-India Reporter, the most widely used series of commercial law reports. Although these cases did not involve matters of great complexity, either logistical or technological, they took an average of 12 years and 9 months from filing to decision.[28]

The sources of the amazing longevity are several. First, there are relatively few courts – about one-tenth as many on a per capita basis as in the US.[29] Lawyers and judges' work habits of dealing with cases piecemeal and lavish provision for multiple interlocutory appeals (originally designed for colonial supervision of unreliable locals) equip the determined adversary with abundant opportunity to prolong litigation almost indefinitely.

Where tort cases are brought, recovery is far from assured and is frequently ungenerous. Of the 56 cases located in this writer's survey, 48 cases seeking money damages had been resolved. Some 23 of these failed to recover anything. The mean recovery of the claimants who won was only Rs 15,159. The median recovery was Rs 7,895.[30]

Neither contingency fees nor legal aid are present to overcome claimants' financial barriers to access. India has a numerous and well-established legal profession. Lawyers in India are courtroom advocates; their role does not include investigation and fact-development; specialisation is rudimentary; barring some recent exceptions, there are few firms or other forms of enduring professional collaboration that would support a division of labour and pooling of resources to support the development of expertise in tort law. The setting in which these lawyers work is devoid of institutional support for specialised knowledge: there are no specialist organisations, no specialised technical publishing, no continuing legal education; nor is there a vigorous scholarly community.

Indian civil procedure does not include effective provisions for wide-ranging discovery that would permit factual investigation of complex problems of technology or corporate management. There are no special procedures for handling complex litigation involving vast amounts of evidence or large numbers of parties. Bar and bench, though they contain many brilliant and talented

27 This absence of tort consciousness is manifested by the invisibility of torts in standard works on the Indian legal system. In Alan Gledhill's authoritative survey, there is not a single mention of tort: Gledhill (1951). M P Jain's widely used *Outlines of Indian Legal History* devotes only two paragraphs in its 700 pages to tort law, that is, to the absence of codified tort law: Jain (1966) pp 649–650, 657–658.

28 In the 22 negligence cases, the most common fact situation was a railroad crossing accident (7); next was a downed electrical line (3). There is not a single product liability case among the 56, nor any case involving any industrial process or chemical mishap. Nor do these cases involve massive amounts of evidence, large numbers of experts or large numbers of parties.

29 Galanter 1984; *Affidavit, Re Union Carbide Corporation Gas Leak Disaster at Bhopal India in December* (1985) Attachment C.

30 The exchange value of the Rupee was approximately 12 to the US dollar in late 1984 and 17 to the US dollar in late 1989. On damages and their determination in India, see Legal Torpor, at 276. A subsequent survey by Mary Versailles (1991) University of Wisconsin Law School) of cases reported in the All-India Reporter analysed recoveries for death of an adult male in motor vehicle accident cases. The mean recovery in cases decided in 1985 was Rs 74,084 and the median was Rs 56,640. Taking inflation into account, the size of recoveries remained constant from 1976 to 1986.

individuals, have a limited fund of experience, skills and organisational capacity to address massive cases involving complex questions of fact.

The cumulative effect of these factors, together with cultural and political predispositions, is that there has been little connection between tort law and disasters in India. Such a negative is hard to document. The writer has never heard of an instance of any industrial explosion, mine cave-in, building collapse, food adulteration or other mass injury leading to tort claims. Surveys of all the tort cases reported by India's leading series of law reports from 1975 to 1984 did not reveal a single case that arose from such an incident.[31] What typically happens in disasters is that the government announces that it is making ex gratia payments of specified amount to the victims.[32] Attributions of responsibility, if pursued at all, would be made by a governmental investigation, or perhaps a criminal prosecution or a commission of inquiry. In each case, the inquiry into responsibility is dissociated from the administration of compensation.

The argument of Cassels' book is that the Bhopal story casts doubt on the reliability/trustworthiness of law's promise. His reading of the appropriate scope of our doubts is framed by his criticism of Judge Keenan's throwing the case out of the US courts and sending it to India on the ground that India offered an adequate alternative forum for the litigation. Cassels concludes that:

> 'Judge Keenan was tragically wrong [in sending the case back to India] – wrong in his optimistic faith in both tort law generally, and the capacities of the Indian legal system, in particular.'[33]

Cassels details with balance and eloquence the problems that beset the Indian response. The book argues that notwithstanding these specifically Indian problems, the performance of the Indian legal system in Bhopal is evidence that Judge Keenan was wrong not only about the Indian system, but about the potential of tort law as such to cope with mass disasters.

For the Bhopal experience to exhibit the outer limits of tort law would require a showing that Indian tort law was sufficiently dynamic and robust to offer a fair test of its capacities. Cassels documents the infirmities of Indian tort law and

---

31 Surveys of cases reported in the All-India Reporter conducted by Gary Wilson (1986) University of Wisconsin Law School and by Mary Versailles (1991) University of Wisconsin.

32 For example, when four people were trampled to death in a March 1989 stampede at the New Delhi railway station, the Railway announced an ex gratia payment of Rs 5,000 [approximately $320 at then current exchange rates] to the kin of the deceased and of Rs 1,000 to the injured. A departmental inquiry was ordered and a criminal case was registered on the basis of the negligent announcement that was thought to have triggered the stampede: 'Toll Rises to Four in Railway Station Stampede' (1989) at 9. On the uneven and capricious character of these payments, see Raghavan (1997).

33 Cassels (1993) p 148. Cassels rightly sees Keenan's judgment as a victory for multi-national corporations (p 205), but it is worth noting that it does contain some seeds of enhanced multinational accountability. The judgment required Union Carbide, the parent corporation, to submit to the jurisdiction of the Indian courts and, in effect to have the parent US corporation and the Indian subsidiary treated as a unit for purposes of liability. It also attempted to make American-style discovery available to the claimants, a possibility never availed of by the government of India. The discovery provision was not eliminated by the Court of Appeals (contra Cassels (1993) p 143), but made reciprocal rather than available only to the claimants. The decision by Judge Keenan and later courts to recognise as binding the Bhopal Act's provision for exclusive representation of victims by the government of India implies that governments, recognised democratic ones at least, can make themselves representatives in US courts of victims of mass disasters: *B v Union Carbide* (1993).

concludes that: 'the law of tort in India is little more than a myth about how people would be cared for in a better world.'[34] How can he then argue that India pushed tort to its usable limits? His argument rests not on India's track record with tort or any other area of private law, but on India's record of public interest litigation. Cassels is convinced that the Indian system is capable of great dynamism because 'under the banner of public interest litigation, courts have sought to enhance access to justice, expedite legal processes, and breath some substantive life into the formal processes of law'.[35] It is the heroic exertions of the judges, lawyers and activists who sustained public interest litigation that is the basis of his argument that the Indian response to Bhopal exhausted the limits of law. At times he suggests that public interest litigation manifests an underlying vitality and dynamism of the Indian legal system. He portrays an idealised Indian legal system that retains the 'flexible and accommodating characteristics of traditional Indian law and society' and that exhibits 'considerable flexibility and diversity when compared to Western models, remaining open to fresh ideas, adopting and absorbing new elements as needed'.[36] In this system judges are activist innovators who 'do not adhere so closely to precedent as do their English or even U.S. counterparts'.[37] They have 'departed considerably from the traditional positivist or legalistic understanding of law...'[38] and 'frequently go beyond the judicial role as it is understood in England and North America, openly pursuing social justice'.[39] It is submitted here that this vastly overstates both the frequency and significance of these judicial excursions and their status as an indicator of the dynamism of the Indian legal system.

At times Cassels shares this scepticism, conceding that such judicial activism does not cut very deep:

'But these developments have been primarily of symbolic value. They address specific rather than structural problems and there is no guarantee that the orders [to enforce industrial safety] will be complied with.'[40]

Indeed one could read his account of the Bhopal litigation in India as a demonstration that heroic interventions were incapable of doing the needful because the problem was an institutional problem. That is, the institutional infra-structure of a high accountability system – the courts, the lawyers, the experts, the procedures – were not in place and could not be constructed at a single bound even by the most adventurous jurist. Good rules were only one missing element – the easiest to supply – but supplying them in a landscape bare of proficient institutional machinery can have paradoxical and even perverse effects. There were several major innovative initiatives in the Indian legal response to Bhopal, but as Cassels documents, each was attended by an ironic reversal in which it became a liability rather than an asset for the claimants:

'•   First, there was the passage of Bhopal Act,[41] establishing the Government of India as the exclusive representative of the victims, intended to banish the private lawyers and to facilitate bringing the case in the United States.

34   Cassels (1993) p 153.
35   Cassels (1993) p 153.
36   Cassels (1993) p 216.
37   Cassels (1993) p 216.
38   Cassels (1993) p 217.
39   Cassels (1993) p 217.
40   Cassels (1993) p 25.
41   Bhopal Gas Disaster (Processing of Claims) Act 1985.

- Second, was the Supreme Court's bold intervention in the Sriram gas leak in New Delhi just a year after Bhopal.'[42]

These interventions became the primary bases for Judge Keenan's estimation of the innovative potential of the Indian system and his dismissal of the case from the US forum.[43] The *Mehta* judgment arising out of the Sriram oleum leak incident,[44] with its doctrine of absolute liability, intended by the Supreme Court to create a major asset in fastening accountability on Union Carbide, never came into play since no Indian court ever reached questions of liability in the Bhopal case. But it raised (probably unfounded, but) troubling doubts about the eventual enforceability of the Indian judgment in the US. Subsequent benches of the Supreme Court minimised the authority of *Mehta*, so that its value as a precedent is marginal at most.[45]

- Third, were the heroic efforts of a public interest intervenor and several judges to fashion interim relief engendered the spectre of additional delays, setting the stage for the settlement.[46]

In spite of the best intentions, none of these innovations helped the victims in Bhopal or left an enduring legacy of improvement. This suggests the limits of rule improvement as a medium of change. Imagine that an Indian court (or legislature for that matter) had in 1984 fashioned an ideal set of substantive rules for dealing with mass disasters, but had left every other feature of the system unchanged. Would the good rules have made a difference? Although Cassels is sensitive to the institutional context, the book is centred on judges and rules rather than institutions and the strategic play of actors in them. This chapter does not claim that doctrine is unimportant, but suggests that many other things are equally essential in producing good legal results, especially on a low-visibility, routine, daily basis. Rules emerge from institutions that have the ability to cope with difficult issues, not vice versa. To focus on doctrine in estimating legal performance is like judging restaurants on the imagination and panache of their recipes. But there are many other elements required for a successful dining experience: pots, pans and stoves, tables, cooks, waiters and buyers and ingredients – all of the elements that translate the recipe into a dish that satisfies actual

42 In December 1985, a gas leak at an oleum plant in Delhi generated panic. At the instance of a public interest advocate, the Supreme Court intervened and set up an investigation of the incident. Although the court's jurisdiction in the matter remained problematic, one year later the court issued a judgment purporting to establish a new standard of 'absolute liability' of large enterprises in industrial disasters: *M C Mehta v Union of India* (1985).
43 Cassels (1993) p 135.
44 *M C Mehta v Union of India* (1985). The case is one of many named after this prominent public interest advocate.
45 In *Charan Lal v Union of India* (1990) Chief Justice Sabyasachi Mukherji observed that the notion that damages would be enhanced in the light of defendant's capacity to pay was 'an uncertain promise of law' and found it 'difficult to foresee any reasonable possibility of acceptance of this yardstick'. In upholding the legitimacy of the Bhopal settlement, the Supreme Court dismissed *Mehta*'s theories of liability as 'essentially obiter': *Union Carbide v Union of India* (1992) at 261.
46 The District Court in Bhopal was persuaded to award interim relief, a remedy almost unknown in tort cases, by Vibhuti Jha of Bhopal, a public interest intervenor. The High Court of Madhya Pradesh upheld the award on different grounds and employing a different formula for payment. The Madhya Pradesh judgment was on appeal before the Supreme Court when the case settled.

diners night after night. Recipes do not create restaurants, but flourishing restaurants rarely suffer from lack of them.

Cassels' assessment of the performance of the Indian legal system curiously parallels Judge Keenan's over-optimistic anticipation of the Indian response. Cassels concludes that 'in many ways the response of the Indian legal system to the plight of the Bhopal victims went well beyond what might have been expected in any other country' and reports himself 'impressed by the dynamism of Indian law'.[47] Thus India displays the full potential of the law as an institution and is eligible to serve as a test case of the 'the limitations of law ...'.[48] This chapter submits instead that Indian law – at least private civil law – is in a pathological or at least a seriously impaired condition.[49] A system so deficient cannot provide a useful test of the inherent limitations of this species of institutions.

The institutional deficiencies of the Indian legal system are not specific to mass torts, but are much more general. The basic problem of low use of the courts and lawyers is that they are able to deliver so little in the way of remedy, protection and vindication. The courts provide a useful facility for those who wish to postpone payment of taxes or debts and those who wish to forestall eviction or other legal action. Generally, they serve those who benefit from delay and non-implementation of legal norms, that is, parties who are in already in possession or satisfied with the status quo. For those who require vindication and prompt implementation of remedies and protections against dominant parties, women from husbands or relatives, labourers from landowners, injured from injurers, the system works only haltingly, partially and occasionally.

Given the long delay (and high interest rates at which future value must be discounted) mounting expenses and meagre damage awards, the present value of most suits for money damages is probably close to zero, if it is not negative. Indeed much litigation in India can be described as a 'sunk cost auction'[50] in which the competitors invest ever-higher amounts in the hope of staving off larger losses. Widespread popular intuition of this produces avoidance of the civil courts and the diversion of potential financial damages cases into criminal cases and claims for injunctive relief.[51]

For large sectors of society and large areas of conduct courts afford no remedies or protections. In spite of a widespread perception that India is a litigious society,[52] the available evidence suggests that rates of use of the courts are low by

47 Cassels (1993) p xi.
48 Cassels (1993) p xi.
49 A long line of external observers have provided different readings of this pathology: Cohn (1959); Kidder (1973); Mendelsohn (1981); Moog (1993). In some respects these critical views echo an earlier literature on the mismatch between British law and Indian conditions: Tucker and Kaye (1853); Moon (1945).
50 A sunk cost auction is a game, often used as a business school exercise, in which some good (say, a lakh of rupees) is awarded to the highest bidder, but the person who bids the second-highest amount also must pay the amount he or she bid. Thus even if the opponent's last bid exceeds one lakh, there is an incentive to bid just a bit more in order to reduce one's loss by the value of the prize, but then the opponent is presented with a similar incentive, ad infinitum. In practice, the game ends when one party runs out of money or grows indifferent to the possibility of reducing the loss by the prize amount.
51 Low (and realistic) public expectations of the courts are described in Rao (1990) p 196.
52 Since so many of the potential meritorious claims are absent from the courts, it is not surprising that the claims that are present there include a significant portion that are 'frivolous' in the sense of being brought for purposes of harassment and delay.

international standards and by comparison with the recent past.[53] When there is sufficient pressure to secure remedies, the solution is typically not to reform the lower courts but to bypass them. In a way, the writ jurisdiction is the prototype for this bypassing strategy, which has been applied to motor vehicle accidents and consumer grievances. The fora created by these measures are court-like: they weigh competing proofs and arguments within a framework of authoritative rules. The notion is that they will do a superior, or at least more efficient, job of adjudication than the regular courts.

BHOPAL AND THE TRANSNATIONAL TRAFFIC IN REMEDIES

Is the lesson of Bhopal that tort is not a promising means of risk control in the third world?[54] On the basis of his dismal conclusion about India's response to Bhopal, Cassels concludes it 'unlikely that private litigation can contribute a great deal to the reduction of international hazardous risk'.[55]

Critical of the partial, uneven and tardy performance of tort in delivering compensation, Cassels' preference is for institutions that are less adversarial and more guided by experts.[56] The ideal would be a comprehensive program of public compensation. But he realises that India could move toward this only in a partial, symbolic way: 'it would be naive to suppose that such a regime is immediately on the cards in a country like India, despite its verbal commitment to democratic socialism and the general welfare.'[57] But he seems to prefer a partial and, admittedly, arbitrarily bounded social compensation system rather than a general upgrading of the tort system on the ground that the arbitrariness of a social compensation system will generate tension that will push the system toward universal coverage.[58]

---

53 Reliable data are scarce and the state of record-keeping makes collecting them a daunting task. But there is sufficient to suggest that India is among the lowest in the world in per capita use of courts. Before his untimely death, the late Professor Christian Wollschlager, the trail-blazer of comparative judicial statistics, presented a comparison of the per capita rate of filing of civil cases in some 35 jurisdictions for the ten-year period 1987–96. Rates of filing in courts of first instance per 1,000 persons ranged from 123 in Germany and 111 in Sweden at the high end to 2.6 in Nepal and 1.7 in Ethiopia at the bottom. Since no national figures are available for India, Professor Wollschlager included in his comparison figures on Maharashtra, which ranked 32nd of the 35 jurisdictions with an annual per capita rate of 3.5 filings per 1,000 persons: Wollschlager (1998) p 582. There is no reason to think that Maharashtra has less litigation than India as a whole, since the data point to a general correlation of court use with economic development.
    An earlier study by Robert Moog, who examined litigation rates in Uttar Pradesh from 1951 to 1976, a stopping point dictated by the fact that the state stopped issuing these statistics then, found that per capita civil filings in all district level courts in Uttar Pradesh had fallen dramatically from the early days of independence, when there were 1.63 per 1,000 persons in 1951, to 1976, when there were only was 0.88 per 1,000: Moog (1993) at 1138. Again, such a fall might reflect the decrease in adults as a portion of the total population and diversion into tribunals, as well as the effect of land reforms. But again we find the data contravene the dominant perception of India as increasingly litigious.
54 Or at home? Cf UPL 102.
55 Cassels (1993) p 51.
56 Cassels (1993) p 258.
57 Cassels (1993) p 267.
58 Cassels (1993) p 268.

His distrust of private law to control risk invites the inevitable question, 'compared to what?' He would prefer a regime of benign, capable, alert governmental regulation. Fully aware that in India enforcement of safety regulation is 'understaffed, underfunded and ill equipped to regulate complex technological processes', he recognises that regulatory reform entails more than formal legal enactments.[59] The problem 'has little to do with applicable standards, but is one of compliance and enforcement'. It requires 'political will backed by sufficient technical and administrative resources'.[60] As the Bhopal story itself reveals, the near-term emergence of such regulation in India is highly improbable.[61]

Cassels sketches a hopeful scenario of an international regime of collaborative control between technology-exporting and importing countries, international organisations, lenders, and non-governmental organisations – to support a regime of enhanced safety requirements. As the writer understands his sketch of this, ultimately the local government would have to enforce these standards. Assuming that such a multi-faceted effort by all these different kinds of organisations would be optimal, would the strengthening of development of tort accountability within the receiving nations impede it or push it along?

Consider a hypothesis that is a plausible alternative both to Cassels' theory that law is an inadequate tool and my notion that India lacked the institutional conditions to test the adequacy of tort law. That is the hypothesis of scale, set out by Durkin and Felstiner,[62] who argue that while tort may usefully address small or mid-size disasters, even the most capable judicial institutions are overwhelmed by outsized occurrences like asbestos or Bhopal, instances in which even the best end up improvising quasi-administrative formulaic outcomes. If we take seriously their 'scale' hypothesis, we might conclude that even if tort is useless for dealing with the elephants, it is indeed useful for dealing with the rabbits, lambs and occasional oxen that populate the world of bad happenings.

We are in the midst of a massive globalisation of law – with multinational corporations and flows of capital has come the development of a transnational network of legal services providers who have assisted corporate actors in translating the mobility of capital into mobility of rights. Union Carbide's operations were serviced by skilled lawyers, articulating their operations to the exigencies of the various regimes that impinged on them and the various forums open to them. But the Bhopal victims were remote from the forum in which they might best pursue a remedy. Both the influx of the US plaintiffs' lawyers and the government of India's attempt to sue in the US can be seen as failed attempts at arbitrage between India's low remedy-low accountability system and the high remedy-high accountability system of the US. Even Judge Keenan attempted to lend to the victims some of the power of the US forum, so long as it could be done without burdening his court. So while the organised corporate side has given rise to a vigorous stream of transnational lawyering, the side of victims, workers, and consumers is left stranded in unappetising puddles. Could there be a second wave of transnationalisation in which these interests can organise to use law where it will serve them best? Do we really have reason to think these interests will be better served by governments and corporations without the goad of private law?

---

59   Cassels (1993) p 38.
60   Cassels (1993) p 282.
61   Cassels (1993) p 280.
62   Durkin and Felstiner (1994).

Select bibliography

Acharyya, B, (1914) *Codification In British India.*

Adler, S, (1985) 'Bhopal Journal: Only the Victims Lack a Strategy', Am Lawyer, April, at 128.

Appleson, G, (1999) 'Bhopal Victims Sue Union Carbide Over '84 Disaster', Reuters dispatch, 16 November.

Baar, C, (1990) 'Social Action Litigation in India: The Operations and Limitations of the World's Most Active Judiciary', 19 Policy Studies J 140.

Bacigal, R J, (1990) *The limits of litigation: the Dalkon Shield controversy.*

Bakshi, (1985) 'Bhopal tragedy and Indian courts', The Statesman, 5 April, at 9.

Baxi, P M, (1999) *Public Interest Litigations.*

Baxi, U, (1985) *Courage, Craft, and Contention: The Supreme Court in the 1980's.*

Bhagwati, P N, (1985) 'Judicial Activism and Public Interest Litigation', 23 ColJ Transnat L 561.

Bora, P, (1996) 'A Man-Made Horror', India Today, 15 January.

Brodeur, P, (1985) *Outrageous Misfortune: the Asbsestos Industry on Trial.*

Burns, J F, (1995a) 'As Fire's Toll Exceeds 400, Indians Seek Bodies of Kin', New York Times, 25 December, at 3.

—(1995b) AP Dispatch, New York Times, 26 December, at A9.

Business Line, (1998) 'India NGOs complain about tardy progress in Bhopal gas victims' rehabilitation', 9 February, available in Nexis News library.

Cassels, J, (1989) 'Judicial Activism and Public Interest Litigation in India: Attempting the Impossible?', 37 AJCL 495.

—(1993) *The Uncertain Promise of Law: Lessons from Bhopal.*

Charfoos, S, (1981) *Daughters at Risk: A Personal D.E.S. History.*

Civil Justice Committee 1924–25, (1925) Report, Government of India.

Cleveland Plain Dealer, (1994) 'Bhopal Survivors' Ailments Go Untreated, Panel Finds', 18 April, at 6C.

Cohn, B S, (1959) 'Some Notes on Law and Change in North India', 8 Economic Development and Cultural Change 90.

Cohn, H, and Bollier, D, (1991) *The Great Hartford Circus Fire.*

Cunningham, C, (1987) 'Public Interest Litigation in Indian Supreme Court: A Study in the Light of American Experience', 29 J Indian Law Institute 494.

Danzig, R, (1978) *The Capability Problem in Contract Law.*

Dhavan, R, (1994) 'Law as Struggle: Public Interest Law in India', 36 J Indian Law Institute 302.

Durkin, T, and Felstiner, W, (1994) 'Bad Arithmetic: Disaster Litigation as Less Than the Sum of Its Parts' in S Jasanoff (ed) *Learning from Disaster: Risk Management After Bhopal.*

Fortune, (2000) 'Bhopal Ghosts (Still) Haunt Union Carbide', 3 April, at 44–46.

Galanter, M, (1968) 'The Displacement of Traditional Law in Modern India', 24 J Soc Issues 65.

—(1990) 'Case Congregations and Their Careers', 24 Law & Society Review 1201.

Gledhill, A, (1951) *The Republic Of India: The Development Of Its Laws And Constitution.*

Grey, S, (1998) 'Cash wait prolongs agony of Bhopal gas victims', Sunday Times, 8 March.

Halarnkar, S, and Chakravarty, S, (1997) 'Tickets to Hell', India Today, June 30, at 30.

Hararika, S, (1987) *Bhopal: The Lessons of a Tragedy.*

Higdon, H, (1975) *The Crime of the Century: The Leopold and Loeb Case.*

Hindu, The, (1989) 'Toll Rises to Four in Railway Station Stampede', 21 March, at 9.

Hindu, The, (1994) 'India may sue Union Carbide in U.S. Courts', 8 December, at 6, col 1.

Jain, M, (1966) *Outlines Of Indian Legal History*, p 658.

Jasanoff, S (ed), (1994) *Learning from Disaster: Risk Management After Bhopal.*

Kasserman, D R, (1986), *Fall River Outrage: Life, Murder and Justice in Early Industrial New England.*

Kidder, R L, (1973) 'Courts and Conflict in an Indian City: a Study in Legal Impact', 11 J Commonwealth Political Studies 121.

Kluger, R, (1975) *Simple Justice; The History of Brown v. Board of Education and Black America's Struggle for Equality.*

Kutler, S, (1990) *Privilege and creative destruction: the Charles River Bridge case.*

Lewin, T, (1984) 'Company Expected to Face Many Claims', New York Times, 7 December, at 8.

Manor, J, (1993) *Power, Poverty and Poison: Disaster and Response in an Indian City.*

Mendelsohn, O, (1981) 'The Pathology of the Indian Legal System', 15 Modern Asian Studies 823.

Menon, M, (1985) 'A Justice Sans Lawyers: Some Indian Experiments', 12 Indian Bar Review 444.

Mintz, M, (1985) *At Any Cost: Corporate Greed, Women and the Dalkon Shield.*

Moog, R, (1993) 'Indian Litigiousness and the Litigation Explosion', 33 Asian Survey 1136, at 1138.

Moon, P, (1945) *Strangers in India.*

Morehouse, W, and Subramaniam, M A, (1986) *The Bhopal Tragedy.*

Rao, V N, (1990) 'Courts and Lawyers in India: Images from Literature and Folklore' in Y K Malik and D K Vajpeyi (eds), *Boeings and Bullock-Carts: Studies in Change and Continuity in Indian Civilization*, vol 3, p 196.

Noonan, J, (1976) *Persons and Masks of the Law.*

Pearce, F, (1998) 'Legacy of a Nightmare', Guardian, 13 August, at 1

Peiris, G L, (1991) 'A Public Interest Litigation in the Indian Subcontinent: Current Dimensions', 40 ICLQ 66.

Raghavan, B S, (1997) 'Ex-gratia whimsy', Business Line, 28 May, at 8.

Rettie, J, (1994) 'Out of Sight, Out of Mind', Guardian, 14 March, at 12.

Sanders, J, (1992) 'The Bendectin Litigation: A Case Study in the Life Cycle of Mass Torts', 43 Hastings LR 301.

—(1998) *Bendectin on Trial: A Study of Mass Tort Litigation.*

Sathe, S P, (1998a) 'Judicial Activism', 10 J Indian School of Political Economy 399.

—(1998b) 'Political Activism (II): Post-Emergency Judicial Activism: Liberty and Good Governance', 10 J Indian School of Political Economy 603.

Schuck, P, (1986) *Agent Orange on Trial: Mass Toxic Disasters in the Courts.*

Sobol, R B, (1991) *Bending the Law: The Story of the Dalkon Shield Bankruptcy.*

Srivastava, P, (1987) *Bhopal: Anatomy of a Crisis.*

Statesman, The, (1984) 'Firm Chairman and Experts Denied Entry', 7 December, at 1, col 1.

—(1984) 'State to seek damages from Carbide', 10 December 1984, at 1, col 6.

—(1998) 'Bhopal Gas Tragedy Victims' Woes Continue', 25 February.

Stern, G, (1976) *The Buffalo Creek Disaster.*

Stewart, J, (1985) 'Why Suits for Damages Such as Bhopal Claims are Very Rare in India', Wall Street Journal, 23 January, at 1, col 1, 16, col 3.

Stokes, W, (1887) *The Anglo-Indian Codes* (2 vols).

Susman, S D, (1994) 'Distant Voices in the Courts of India: Transformation of Standing in Public Interest Litigation', 13 Wisconsin International Law Journal 58.

Tucker, H St G, and Kaye, J W, (eds) (1853) *Memorials of Indian Government.*

Vose, C, (1959) *Caucasians Only: The Supreme Court, the NAACP, and the Restrictive Covenant Cases.*

Werth, B, (1998) *Damages: One Family's Legal Struggles in the World of Medicine.*

Wollschlager, C, (1998) 'Exploring Global Landscapes of Litigation Rates' in J Brand and D Strempel (eds), *Soziologie des Rechts: Festschrift fur Erhard Blankenburg zum 60 Geburtstag* pp 577, 582.

Part III

Changing states

Opening remarks: Producing the transnational inside the national

S SASSEN*

One way of establishing a common thread among these six chapters is to interpret their organising logics as a concern with discontinuities in state form. Five of these chapters examine how states come to incorporate standards, rules and laws associated with foreign states and commercial interests or with international regimes. The sixth chapter does so indirectly, in that it focuses on internal transitions from dictatorship to what are now largely 'universal' standards of liberal democracies. There is enormous specificity in the treatment of these dynamics as each chapter is based on larger projects addressing these issues. Each chapter engages in a detailed examination of how the transition to a new set of standards in a particular institutional order is executed and how their incorporation gets filtered through the distinctive characteristics of the state institutions or larger context involved.

Let me briefly describe how each of these chapters tackles the issues and then proceed to suggest that together they signal the possibility of a more encompassing dynamic that is very much part of the contemporary period but which remains largely unnamed.

Dezalay and Garth explore processes of state change in Latin America by focusing on: (a) the import and export of ideas and institutions and the way individuals use their international capital (degrees, expertise, contacts, prestige and legitimacy acquired abroad) in order to build their positions at home; and (b) 'palace wars',[1] fights not only over the control of the state but also over the relative value of individuals and expertise that make up and guide the state.

Since the 1960s in Latin America these palace wars have increasingly been waged in terms of international strategies. One conclusion for Dezalay and Garth is that states are increasingly embedded in an international marketplace of state expertise centred in the academies and related institutions in the US.

From this perspective, the leading brokers of state expertise beginning in the 1960s were the cosmopolitan gentlemen-lawyers; today, in 2000 that same role is played by technopols, particularly economists in the US tradition. Despite the differences between the US and Latin America, there was a structural similarity

---

* Ralph Lewis Professor of Sociology, University of Chicago and Centennial Visiting Professor, London School of Economics.
1 Cf P Bourdieu (1996) *The state nobility: Elite schools in the field of power.*

in the position of the gentlemen-lawyers regarding political and economic power in their respective states. The similarities in the position and influence of the technopols today are even stronger. They tend to speak the same language, both literally and technically, and they now circulate easily among different countries and multilateral banks, law firms, NGOs, think-tanks.

International strategies deployed in palace wars do not always lead to major institutional or professional transformations; further, 'successful' innovations involving the same technology look very different from place to place. The key to successful transformations is structural parallelism in the importing and exporting countries. It determines whether the imports take hold. Indeed when the structures fit particularly well, the imports are not even recognisable as such. Dominance or dependence becomes invisible, identification of the origins of change as indigenous or imported is impossible. The imports become naturalised. This does not mean that the impact of these ideas and forms of expertise will be the same in all countries involved. What matters is that the exports take root and are eventually assessed by the same universal standards.

A very different type of transfer is at the centre of Inoue's essay: the difficulty of exporting US constitutional notions of individual dignity and equality into the Japanese cultural and legal tradition. Inoue, the author of an impressive book on the Japanese constitution, argues that the concept used in Japanese to capture Western notions of individual dignity does not quite represent what the US framers intended. This is a clear case where the absence of structural homology is an obstacle to the type of outcome described by Dezalay and Garth in their chapter. Inoue shows us how the key term used in the constitution, '*Jinkaku*', underwent changes in meaning over a series of socio-political phases of Japanese history. Yet the term maintained one key feature throughout, including in the post-Second World War new constitution: while concerning individual dignity it always incorporated notions of hierarchy and elitism.

Jinkaku is not about making all equal as a result of the inalienable human attribute of dignity. In earlier versions, there was a strong emphasis on the project of the individual working at making herself a better person, of making herself deserving of human dignity. In later versions there is a democratising in so far as there is a move towards conceiving of individual dignity as a 'man's' attribute rather than an achievement. But hierarchy and differentiation are maintained. According to Inoue, the US delegation never understood this difference. They took the term 'individual dignity' to mean the same as its meaning in the US constitution. Out of this different meaning in the Japanese context also comes the difficulty of appreciating the relation between individual dignity and human rights as inscribed in Western conceptions. The absence of structural homologies made incorporation of a US constitutional transfer far less destabilising of older Japanese notions of rights than the US framers of the post-Second World War Japanese constitution meant it to be. One question I would have, though one not addressed by Inoue in this chapter, is whether the existence of this formal term, along with other such terms that lacked currency in the Japanese culture of the times, might eventually become activated by changes in Japan's society. For instance, when it comes to the case of immigrants, Japanese activists have seized on the notion of human dignity and human rights as ways of securing recognition for immigrants' rights; a similar re-activation under contemporary conditions has taken place with some of the laws oriented towards establishing the difference between economic and government actors, laws which in their origin underwent a shift in meaning when transferred from the US constitutional context to the Japanese one and thereby lost much of their purpose at the time.[2]

Constitution-making experiences are also the subject of Mattei's chapter, but with a focus on three recent African cases: Eritrea, Puntland State in Somalia and South Africa. They represent sharply different African contexts, economic development stages and constitution-making processes. And they elicited varying interest from the international legal community in the constitution-making process, ranging from very high in South Africa to practically non-existent in Eritrea.

Mattei's concern is with the actual constitution-making process rather than the documents themselves. One key feature common to African countries is that the constitutional issues of the state, both in terms of legitimacy and extension, are not solved. The borders of states, largely imposed by colonial powers, and those of nations rarely overlap, making borders the source of much conflict. The existence and extension of the state itself are then problematic in much of Africa, and a process of constitution-making cannot overlook this fact. From whence Mattei's insistence that the process of constitution-making itself and the need for participation to ensure legitimacy are crucial in Africa.

A particular concern is whether participation is necessarily connected to Western-style democratic institutions, such as elections, and what might be the substitutes of such institutions at play today in Africa. In Eritrea, for instance, the lack of elections did not diminish the legitimacy of the leadership that launched the constitution-making process because it had demonstrated its commitment to the country through an extensive armed fight for independence. And in the case of Puntland, the crucial role of elders practising traditional law and enjoying the respect and trust of the people replaced some of the Western-style participatory mechanisms. Even as they lack any resemblance with Western-style democratic institutions, these conditions actually function as structural homologies thereby facilitating the transfer of key Western constitutional elements because they ensured their legitimacy.

Mattei posits that although both the matter of technical transfers and that of the legitimacy of the process are important, it is the latter that is crucial in contemporary Africa where politics rules over law. A focus on the documents alone leads to misunderstandings of how the law works, not only in Africa, where traditional unwritten law is very strong and inflects written law, but also in long-established democracies. The eventual production of a document does not end the process of creation of constitutional law; it might, at most, indicate a new phase. The creation of an African constitutional culture and of an African legal culture are long-term enterprises. This makes evident an important assumption guiding Mattei's analysis: law in general, and constitutional law in particular, are always in flux, from whence his emphasis on process.[3]

---

2   Inoue's analysis helped me understand my experience with activists organising for the rights of immigrants and homeless in Japan. These activists, coming mostly from modest backgrounds and not part of international circuits, invoked human rights as a self-evident truth that once seen would lead to the requisite institutional changes. This is a purist version of the concept of human rights, with a somewhat different sense from what it is in the West.

3   Further, Mattei finds that it is useful to talk about 'Africa' and 'African law' as an object of observation, notwithstanding the internal differences that 'good scholarship cannot overlook'. It is precisely recognition of the multiple differences that allows one to understand the commonalities. And it is the fact of a critical mass of such deep commonalities that allows one to establish that African law is not too broad a category.

Just as Inoue shows us how a transfer of a US legal concept gets reshaped as it enters Japan's political culture, so Mattei shows us how the constitution-making process is filtered through each country's historical, political and legal specificities. One aspect that captures this is the marking condition for which the constitution seeks redress: in South Africa it was apartheid; in Eritrea it was the assertion and international recognition of a new state after a 30-year war for independence against Ethiopia; and in Somalia's Puntland it was the social and political reconstruction of an area of relative peace and prosperity after eight years of civil war that disrupted the whole of Somalia.

A very different instance of state's incorporating 'external' legal transfers is the focus of Joppke's chapter on post-Second World War international migration. He engages the literature that posits that the rise of an international human rights regime reduces the state's capacity to control immigration. He places himself in opposition to what have come to be referred to as post-national interpretations. Joppke argues that far from challenging liberal states, these conditions have led states to internalise the new rights of individuals as these in fact are at the core of the liberal state itself and thereby, if anything, have strengthened liberal states.

While he acknowledges that the growth of transnational and supra-national institutions, and globalisation generally, have weakened certain components of the state, he finds that this is not the case with control over people. Further, he argues that there never was a 'golden age' of state sovereignty assumed in much contemporary writing about the impact of globalisation on state authority. Human rights have long been invoked in one form or another and compromised state sovereignty; hence, for Joppke they do not represent a significant departure in terms of state authority.

Joppke's point that the liberal state incorporates these rights is an important one. Most of the rights gained by immigrants – such as residence, family and social rights – are based in domestic law. Internationally guaranteed asylum and non-discrimination rights cover only a small fraction of immigrants' rights. Empowerment of migrants in the US after 1960 derives largely from rights of personhood, though this began to change again in the 1980s. And even in Europe, which has the highest incidence of inter and supra-national human rights norms and regimes anywhere in the world, most immigrants' rights have domestic roots.

What Joppke does not allow for is that once recognised these facts are subject to interpretation as to their effects on the state even if incorporated by the latter. The key debate for Joppke is between those who argue that sovereignty is becoming globally limited through various international regimes, especially human rights, and those, like the author, who, while not denying the growing weight of these regimes, posit that liberal states have incorporated these rights and in that sense are constitutionally self-limiting their sovereignty. This duality leaves out a third type of interpretation that is emerging and which resonates in many ways with the type of analysis developed in the chapters discussed here. It gives far more weight and transformative potential to internal changes of the state than does Joppke. It is a matter of interpretation to which I return at the end of this commentary.

Likosky examines the continuities and discontinuities between colonial and current transnational legal orders when it comes to the dual goals of universal human rights and sovereign absolutism. He examines this through a particular sphere, that of trans-jurisdictional commercial engagement. Here I want to focus particularly on Likosky's examination of how the recent open political conflicts between Malaysia and the US coexist with extensive transnational commercial transactions between these two countries. Thus even as Gore was criticising and 'exiling' the Malaysian government for human rights abuses, particularly the imprisonment of Anwar, it was encouraging extensive commercial transactions between the two countries and indeed getting praised for doing this. An important feature of these cross-border commercial transactions is that they induce a continuous re-authoring of the Malaysian legal system so as to accommodate their evolving conditionalities. As US criticism of human rights abuses in Malaysia rose, Mahatir succeeded in diluting internal opposition (and weakening the weight of human rights) by invoking US aggression and interference, thereby enhancing the conditions of internal peace and order necessary for US-Malaysia commercial transactions and necessary for domestic law revisions to accommodate this commercial relation.

Likosky shows us the extent to which Malaysia is actually integrated into the global economy and then focuses on a particular instance of transnational commercial engagement and law creation which can be represented as a *localised* event:[4] the 15 by 40km Multimedia Super Corridor, a high-technology foreign direct investment scheme and national development plan. He uses this to illustrate the role of foreign interests in determining the legislative composition of the country and how, in collaboration with local elites, it succeeds in refashioning the domestic legal order. One way of reading the evidence is to posit that Malaysia and the US, together with major commercial actors, have established a transnational 'legal' domain inside Malaysa's political structure. In its most radical formulation, Likosky posits that the legal aspects of 'Asian values' and authoritarian government structures are the product of this transnational commercial partnership.

What is notable about the Malaysian case is that it makes legible a crucial dynamic which is likely to be operative in many different types of countries but perhaps in a more ambiguous fashion, intermediated by market mechanisms[5] rather than embedded in an openly conflictive political relation. And what is notable about Likosky's chapter is not only that it shows us this, but, perhaps most significantly, that it shows how this conflictive political relation actually enables the commercial one in so far as it allows the Malaysian government both to exercise its authoritarianism thereby ensuring 'law and order' and to re-fashion domestic law so as to accommodate the needs of the transnational commercial relation. It is here that I find a strong instantiation of denationalisation: a government's legal and regulatory work that presents itself as oriented to national goals which is in fact doing work for foreign interests. The enabling coincidence is that at least some national elites can share these interests. It is not the fact of foreign investment per se, or setting up a tax-free zone for foreign firms: these are legal

---

4   In this regard it can be seen as a single-variable instance of what I try to capture through the model of the global city, a multiple variable instance.

5   For example, in my research I document the fact that financial services firms entering so-called emergent markets often institute minor regulatory and quasi-legal changes in order to make a country's depository system more congruent with the practices and conditionalities of Western financial systems in the name of transparency, by which is actually meant ensuring (mostly foreign) investors' interests. I conceptualise this as a micro-history of quasi-legislative interventions that is refashioning specific features of a country's legal framework, but doing so through market mechanisms.

and regulatory formats that are designed openly to accommodate these foreign interests. The crucial issue captured by Likosky is of a far more subtle nature.

On a more general level, the chapter posits that Malaysia's authoritarianism and human rights abuses are not the exclusive result of its government but, rather, of this collaboration with US commercial interests. What is constructed from the perspective of the Malaysian government as a conflict between domestic sovereignty and universal human rights is actually centred in a distinct form of collaboration between the two countries. It may well be emblematic of what is happening in other countries as well. In this regard, then, transnational commercial collaboration does not phase out authoritarian rule.

In her chapter, Teitel seeks to explain the coincidence at the end of the twentieth century of both major advances in human rights law along with the growth of grave human rights violations and crimes against humanity. Rwanda and the former Yugoslavia epitomise both of these conditions through the massacres that took place there and the convening of the international tribunals for each of these cases. These and other transitional trials produce, for Teitel, a paradoxical story in this contemporary moment as to the relation international law bears to organised violence. The resolution of the paradox lies in the contribution that transitional justice makes to the construction of a collective liberal narrative, particularly the potential of law in this construction.

Trials have long played a key role in settling historical controversies and thereby constructing collective transition histories. They create public formal shared processes that allow a society and individuals to move on from controversial and divisive conditions. The kinds of truths that are established in such periods are, for Teitel, transitional critical truths that assert the falseness of the predecessor regime and its ideology. Trials make these transitional truths authoritative. And they make possible collective amnesties without neutralising those critical truths.

Out of the interaction of legal and historical constructions of responsibility emerges a complicated understanding of responsibility for wrongdoing under repressive regimes as perpetrated by individuals against a background of systemic policy. 'The question of whether to exercise criminal justice, of whether to punish or to amnesty, is rationalised in overtly political terms, relating to the transition.' Mercy and reconciliation, usually treated as external to criminal justice, become explicitly part of deliberations in transitional justice.

A crucial dynamic that gets constituted here is the normative claim about the relation of a state's past to its prospects for democracy. The narrative structure itself of the transitional justice posits that knowledge of the crimes is relevant to the possibility of personal and social change, from dictatorship to a more liberal future.

Teitel's particular concern and contribution is the distinctive rhetorical form of these transitional narratives, 'beginning in tragedy and ending in a comic or romantic mode'. This form is evident in both fictional and non-fictional accounts of periods of political transformation. Through her examination of various documents issued by various truth commissions, she shows us how in transitional history-making the story has to come out right. Yet typically the processes that led to the transformation preceded the setting up of these commissions, signalling that it is not so much the work of producing the account and establishing the facts about past abuse that are the liberating factor, but the other way around – the demands for change produce the change. This is not without consequences since it subverts one of the crucial truths coming out of such commissions, namely, that had the newly acquired knowledge been known, matters would not have gone the way they did. The process allows persons with particular powers, such as judges, lawyers, experts, to redress evil. In so doing it supports liberal ideology. Liberal rationalist responses to mass suffering and abuses of power have the capacity to rectify the situation. The peacefulness of the proceedings, their grounding in technical rules, all of it strengthens the normative power of liberal political systems, and the 'fact' that the latter produce hope for better futures. Despite major past wrongdoings, the contemporary state can be seen as redemptive and functions as such in transitional justice. The avoidance of tragic repeats becomes associated with the liberal political order.

Summing up, I would like to return to Likosky's introduction to this book where he gives us a glimpse of what we could think of as a 'conceptual architecture' within which he fits the particular and often quite specialised matters covered by the large number of chapters. He does not want the book to be read as a mere collection of authors. At the heart of this conceptual architecture is a crucial dynamic/proposition: that the highly fragmented and partial nature of applicable data limits the value of taxonomies and macro-level frameworks, while at the same time, the existence of multiple literatures and data sets does allow for an encompassing appraisal. As a result, what we need to maximise now is the possibility of producing a larger framework that is strongly grounded in specialised knowledge of a variety of types.

In this spirit then, let me suggest that beyond the multiplicity of subjects and particularities they encompass, the chapters of this section together illuminate some of the key transformations afoot in the world today. In my reading and in my language – not necessarily that of the authors – they contribute to elaborate the distinction between globalisation and what we could think of as 'de-nationalisation'. In making this assertion I must acknowledge that I have followed a rather particular thread through all of these chapters, taking the liberty to produce one of possibly several interpretations as to what they reveal to us. There are many issues discussed by each of the authors that are not present in this brief commentary, though I have sought to produce a precise portrayal of the particular segment of each chapter I chose for discussion.

By 'de-nationalisation' I mean the instituting, often partial and always particular, deep inside national states 'under the rule of law', of standards, norms, laws that respond to a non-national logic.[6] This is not new, but it has sharpened and accelerated over the last decade. Further, de-nationalisation is relative to the preceding period, that of the Keynsian state, one deeply organised along national agendas. Enabling legislation for human rights and neo-liberal economic policy are both emblematic instances. Finally, the denationalisation of certain domains of the state goes along with the re-nationalising of others – two often-connected dynamics.

A key issue distinguishing the novel conditions described by the chapters in this section is that what they describe does not take place necessarily outside, beyond the confines of the national state. Further, these processes need to be distinguished from older notions of extra-territoriality. The chapters by Dezalay

---

6   When I first conceptualised a specific set of dynamics as de-nationalisation in the 1995 Schoff Lectures (Sassen, 1996), I meant to capture processes that take place inside the national state. Particular cases I focused on were a variety of national state agencies and committees which have emerged as the institutional 'home' inside the national for the implementation of various new rules of the game necessary for the development and maintenance of a global economic system and for the implementation of human rights.

and Garth, Mattei, Likosky and Inoue all focus on variants of this dynamic. Joppke, while resisting the interpretation I am projecting onto his analysis, is, in my reading, actually dealing with this as well: his insistence on a polarised debate makes him argue that nothing really has changed, even though his own account suggests that much has but that it cannot be captured necessarily at the global level per se. The argument becomes more difficult in the case of Teitel's chapter, except perhaps for the fact that the aim of transitional narratives is to accommodate a certain type of liberal 'universalism' as part of the structures of the national state that is being rescued.

Chapter 10

Dollarizing state and professional expertise: transnational processes and questions of legitimation in state transformation, 1960–2000

Y DEZALAY and B GARTH

The basic story of transformation of the state in Latin America and the US from 1960 to 2000 can be told by reciting a few conventional terms. In particular, there is a move from 'developmental states' or 'welfare states' to 'neo-liberal states', involving open economics, privatisations and the tenets of the so-called Washington Consensus.[1] The sources of these changes in Latin America and their relationship to the US have been explained in a number of contradictory ways. One explanation is that the International Monetary Fund (IMF) and World Bank imposed the Reagan economic agenda through various 'structural adjustment' programmes. Another view, found especially in the political science literature and in recent journalistic studies, is that 'elite preferences' simply changed from a preference for a 'heavy' state to a preference for a 'neo-liberal' state.[2] The result, according to this view, is that most Latin American states are governed now by 'technopols', who combine sophisticated technical expertise and political sensibilities. The leading examples of these technopols include Pedro Malans and Fernando Henrique Cardoso of Brazil, Domingo Cavallo of Argentina, Alejandro Foxley of Chile and Pedro Aspe of Mexico.[3] Economists are the paradigmatic examples of the technopols.

The scholars who study technopols do not explain how these technocratic politicians came to this particular set of preferences. Most of these scholars assume that the adoption of these preferences simply shows the good judgment of the technopols. The scholars also do not tend to examine those whom the technopols have replaced in the state. They neglect the 'gentlemen-politicians of the law' who occupied the dominant positions and whose generalist knowledge was attacked and discredited by the technopols. As a result, we have very little understanding of what forces produced the change in states captured in the terms with which we began this chapter.

1   A term coined by John Williamson to describe a set of views which, he thought, characterised the position of the US, the Washington financial institutions and a growing number of economists in the south: see Williamson (1990). The term has become a symbol of neo-liberalism and already the World Bank, for example, has published works suggesting that they have moved 'beyond' the Washington consensus toward a more institutional focus: World Bank (1998).
2   Yergin and Stanislaw (1998).
3   Dominguez (1997).

The writers' recent book seeks to explore these processes of state change.[4] It focuses not on the abstract state or labels such as 'developmental' or 'neo-liberal', however, but rather on the people and expertise who produce the state. Since law provides a key language of legitimacy, our point of entry into these transformations is law – more precisely, the position of law in the field of state power. The field includes those who compete on behalf of various forms of capital – familial, religious, economic, legal, international – to gain ascendancy for themselves and what they represent. In addition, two analytical tools are employed:, 'international strategy' and 'palace wars'. The first tool, the concept of 'international strategy', refers to the ways individuals use international capital – degrees, expertise, contacts, resources, prestige and legitimacy acquired abroad – in order to build their positions at home. The importing and exporting of ideas, approaches and institutions is found though these international strategies.

The strategies are often deployed in 'palace wars', the second analytical tool.[5] Palace wars are the fights not only over the control of the state, but also over the relative value of individuals and expertises that make up and guide the state. In the period that can loosely be described as 1960 to the present, we find that palace wars in the south are progressively waged in terms of international strategies. One tentative conclusion of this research, in fact, is that states are increasingly embedded in an international marketplace of state expertise centred in the academies and related institutions in the US.

International strategies deployed in palace wars do not always lead to major institutional or professional transformations, and even 'successful' innovations involving the same technology look very different from place to place. The key to such successful state transformations and institutionalisation of changes is structural parallelism in the importing and exporting countries. The nature of the interaction between these structural settings determines whether the import takes hold. It is possible to make structural comparisons about how different countries relate to the import of northern expertises,[6] but the approach here concentrates on professions and expertises. This chapter therefore will elaborate on the various ways that professions and expertises are imported and exported, and illustrate the processes and role of different structural positions in accounting for those ways. As suggested above, the simultaneous developments that take place in the north and the south are highlighted.

From the perspective of this dual focus, the state of play at the beginning and end of the story of transformation over the period 1960 to 2000 look quite similar. In each case we can point to a seemingly dominant group that matches in the north and in the south. The leading international brokers of state expertise around 1960 were the cosmopolitan gentlemen-lawyers. That same role today is played by the technopols.

As members of a recognisable establishment legitimated through law, the gentlemen-lawyers found common transnational ground. The fields of state power in the different countries were quite different – especially between the US and the other countries of this study. Nevertheless, a structural similarity existed in

---

4   This chapter is based on the writers' forthcoming book – Dezalay and Garth (2002) – which is the product of more than 400 interviews in Argentina, Brazil, Chile, Mexico and the US.

5   Bourdieu (1996).

6   Dezalay and Garth (2002) chapter 3.

the position of the gentlemen-lawyers with respect to political and economic power in their respective states. In the north and the south, the gentlemen-lawyers served as brokers for the major families and enterprises in their countries and also as more statesman-like actors in the government.[7] They helped to facilitate a social consensus and social reform – in very different settings – that promoted stability and protected what could be defined as an establishment. Their similar structural positions promoted interchange and relative successes in the flow of ideas.

Similarly, there are strong – even stronger, in fact – similarities among the technopols who are more influential today. Variations exist, but those who are given or privileged with the name tend to speak the same languages, both literally and technically, and they now circulate relatively easily among different countries – and multilateral banks, NGOs, law firms and think-tanks. Technopols in different countries occupy similar positions with respect to their national fields of power as the gentlemen-lawyers did. Again, national settings vary, and strong differences among the countries exist, but positions of technopols as importers and exporters of ideas and approaches resemble the position previously dominated by gentlemen-lawyers.

Symbolic exports are more likely to be successful when there are structural homologies between the north and the south. When the structural positions of the transacting agents are similar, as they were at the time of the gentlemen-lawyers and now are again with the ascendency of the technopols, the north is able to export its own internal struggles to the south. International strategies that suit the positions of southern actors in their fields of state power connect with the international strategies of northern actors fighting their own fights. Indeed, when the structures fit particularly well, the exports are not even visible as exports. It is not just that all sides believe in the same universals and the same forms, whether the church, human rights, the importance of good credit, sound economics or the environment, although this agreement is important. It is also that their strategies lead the technopols to do the work of their internationalised counterparts.

Accordingly, dominance or dependence in influencing and effecting change becomes invisible, so that identification of the origins of change as indigenous or imported is impossible. The change from the perspective of the importing country becomes internalised and naturalised, making the identity of the source irrelevant. The parallelism is all that matters. As suggested by one of the individuals active in the Summit of the Americas, the idea of an American free trade agreement akin to NAFTA can be traced at least as plausibly to the leaders of Latin America as to the US.[8] This ambiguity does not mean that the impact of these exported (and imported) ideas and technologies will be precisely the same in each country. It certainly will not, but what is important for present purposes is that the exports take root and are subsequently assessed by the same universal standards. The ideas and technologies exported are produced and legitimated through processes inhabited by technopols. Part of the process is determined by developing the menu of acceptable alternatives. Once a model is accepted and legitimated out of a domestic setting, it can be placed on the market for re-export to other places.

7   Eg Bird (1992).
8   Personal interview (1998).

Dollarization – linking the value of currency in the south precisely to buying power in the US – is the key feature of the expertises promoted by the technopols, but it has not operated at the same speed everywhere. The uneven reception stems from the fact that some professional milieux are more global than others. The more established professions, deeply embedded in national histories and the structures of state power, are much more resistant to dollarization than are the newer disciplines such as economics. It is not an accident that the best examples of the technopols come from economics, a relative newcomer in the south.

There is also variation within a single discipline or professional field, as is the case with law. Within the law, corporate lawyering is well ahead of cause lawyering or public interest law. This highly unequal process, which aggravates the current disequilibrium in the market of expertise, is a microcosm of globalisation or dollarization. In order to highlight this unequal process and the structural features that produce it, this chapter will elaborate on the example of economics and two examples from law – corporate lawyering and public interest law. Using these examples, we can examine how a focus on national fields of power and the professions themselves can explain how the national and the transnational connect – or misconnect – at particular moments. Looking beyond the category of technopols, therefore, we see important differences and tensions in the processes of dollarization.

Although we are focusing on internal stories of the development and transformation of national and transnational fields, larger geopolitical processes are crucial in structuring the interactions in particular fields. For instance, looking especially at the period from the 1960s to the present, it is clear that international strategies embedded in national palace wars exacerbated the international competition. The conservative counter-revolution against the reformist foreign policy establishment in the US, for example, battled globally for hegemony against developmental or welfare states. At the same time, international strategies embedded in local palace wars drew on and fuelled that counter-revolution and related international competition – including turf battles between different disciplines, especially economists versus lawyers; and between different 'legal cultures', exemplified by the clash between US legal entrepreneurs and European legal notables. The Cold War and the debt crisis were also key ingredients in shaping the interactions in these fields.

Internal stories relate closely also to the specific structural histories of law and the newer disciplines such as economics. Law was triply embedded in the sense that it played a central role historically in the reproduction and legitimation of the state (even if to a lesser extent in Argentina and Mexico than in Brazil and Chile); it was strongly implicated in the corresponding reproduction (and legitimation) of social hierarchies. Specific national histories also produced relatively rigid internal professional hierarchies, led by the gentlemen-statesmen of the law linked to the faculties of law, the leading families of the oligarchy (especially in Chile and Brazil), and influenced by cosmopolitan learning from Europe.

The story of economics is practically an ideal type for a story of technopols and dollarization. Economics had to conquer its autonomy from law in Latin America, and even to some extent in the US. The first generations of economists after the Second World War were closely linked to the legal establishment in the US and in Latin America (and the governing legal establishment represented by the Partido Revolucionario (PRI) in Mexico). Many of the leading economists in Latin America were, in fact, trained in the faculties of law, and accounting was under the control of the law faculties.

Keynesianism and developmentalism worked very well in the post-Second World War period to sustain relatively strong states that maintained, and modernised, the position of the gentlemen lawyers – especially in Brazil, Chile and the US, but also within the public elite in Mexico. International strategies played an important role relatively early in the evolution of economics in Latin America, since foreign legitimacy could be used to contest the power of the dominant legal elite – which needed relatively less foreign investment because of its more established position.

The Washington consensus in the south and the north developed out of structural similarities in the position of a group of economists standing outside of the establishment. The first key ingredient was scholarly investment as a legitimating basis for what was then an 'unholy alliance'. The University of Chicago economists (the most famous of whom was Milton Friedman) – almost all of whom were first or second-generation immigrants – lacked the social capital and connections of the leading economists of the Eastern establishment and therefore invested more in mathematics, in public choice and in media strategies. They formed early alliances with a then-marginal group of very conservative Republicans and business people hostile to the cosy relationships that made up the establishment. The Chicago economists also developed powerful mathematical arguments to build their position in 'pure' economics against the essayists of Harvard and the powerful Eastern establishment. The fight on the terrain of economics was also a fight against the Keynesian economists among the action intellectuals from the Eastern establishment in the Kennedy administration. The government was denounced as the product of rent-seeking behaviour that led to inflation and economic stagnation.

Chicago economists in the 1950s, at a time when neo-liberal economics was still relatively weak in the US, invested internationally. Led by Arnold Harberger of the University of Chicago, they took advantage of the US Agency for International Development (AID) and the philanthropic foundations to invest in potential counterparts in the south, especially in the Catholic University in Santiago, Chile – the home of the original 'Chicago boys'.[9] The investment in Chile could be directed against the Comisión Económica para América Latina y el Caribe (CEPAL) – the UN organisation in Santiago – and Raul Prebisch – himself the perfect embodiment of the well-bred cosmopolitan economist. The US investment was relatively even-handed between Keynesians and neo-liberals, but the Keynesian or developmentalist economics was the mainstream within the Chilean establishment at the University of Chile. The young economists at the Catholic University came to Chicago in large numbers, and they formed similar political alliances in Chile to those that were being formed among conservatives in the US. They were ready when Pinochet came to power in 1973.

They used their mathematical economics, ties with the media and especially El Mercurio, the Chilean analogue to the Wall Street Journal, and their connection to the Chicago economists, then gaining power within the economics profession in the US, to call for 'shock treatment' – drastic programs to stop the inflationary cycle – and a series of reforms that became the Bible for neo-liberal attacks on the interventionist state elsewhere, including Britain. The almost perfect parallel between Chicago and Catholic made for a remarkable story of export and import, which then helped to build the credibility of the emerging

9   See Valdes (1995).

Washington consensus – and provide the basis for structural adjustment after the debt crisis and the Reagan election in the 1980s.

In Brazil, Delfim Netto, a first generation economist who gained power with the military, used the state and developmentalism against the old establishment that had dominated the state. The second-generation descendants of the establishment, exemplified by Pedro Malans, built their base at the Catholic University in Rio de Janeiro. Since economics was still relatively new in all these countries, the new generation of economists could invest abroad, and upon returning home, essentially take over an economics department and align it with the emerging global market. This generation used US economics and the legitimacy of mathematics against the strong state and relatively high inflation characteristic of the policies of Delfim Netto in the 1970s. The debt crisis further built their position.[10]

Argentina's think tanks – always well-connected internationally – did not need economics to challenge the establishment or the military, but economists, led initially by Domingo Cavallo, relatively easily found their way into the international markets in economic expertise. Mathematics could be used to challenge converted lawyers like Martinez de Hoz, the Finance Minister during much of the military regime in the 1970s. In Mexico, a new generation within the PRI establishment, exemplified by Carlos Salinas, used economics to gain power within the state establishment and to build bridges to economists from the private schools and the private sector, exemplified by Pedro Aspe.

Groups of economists enhanced their domestic positions with the debt crisis of the 1980s. They matched very well with their counterparts negotiating the debt crisis on the other side. Drawing on their proficiency in English, their technical economics, their connections in the economics communities in the US, and the democratic sympathies that they also picked up while swimming in US academic waters,[11] this generation of economists became the core of the technopols celebrated in the US. Indeed, many of the most prominent economists in Latin America met and formed friendships in the US, especially at MIT or Harvard, where much of the post-Chicago generation was educated. They became the southern side of the more democratic version of the Washington consensus.

The market integration of economic expertise has only increased in the succeeding years. It is not just that international degrees are required as a matter of course in order to make any credible claim to economic expertise, but increasingly it is also necessary to have held a position in the US that provides further professional credibility – including visiting professorships, or even tenure track appointments. One result is that there are quite a number of Latin American economists teaching, and even tenured, in US universities, and there are many others who have worked at the World Bank or the IMF. Economists of the state in the south now watch and monitor the careers of their younger compatriots teaching and publishing in the US to determine their suitability for home positions, while those economists working in the US are concerned that returning home will 'ruin their careers'. Some economists will return to their home countries, but many will make their careers mainly in the US, contributing to the brain drain from the south to the north.

10 Dezalay and Garth (1997).
11 Dominguez (1997).

Once in positions of power in the north and the south, in addition, both sides – and the international financial organisations in Washington DC – moved seamlessly toward the new focus on institutions and the state, the so-called move beyond the Washington consensus.[12] The economists were at the same time embedded in the structures of state power – even more so as talented sons and daughters of the elite invested in US economics – and the international market of expertise. The transnational field itself consolidated, moving to legitimate and preserve the basic policies they put into place in the 1970s and 1980s – and also their own positions of power. Some of the interest in court reform in Latin America comes directly from economists in the state and in think-tanks around the state. The economists in power increasingly recognise that, to extend the market, they need strong institutions and international legitimacy. Recent economic attacks on the IMF, from this perspective, which focus on the need for improved governance and better institutions, seek more to consolidate rather than attack the hegemony of economic expertise made in the US.

The situation for law is different in part because of the much longer history of legal institutions in Latin America and their strict embeddedness in historical structures of state power. The positions of the faculties of law and the courts are thus the product of long histories producing patterns of behaviour and hierarchies of power that are very difficult to change. The failure of the law and development movement to have any real impact on legal education in Brazil and Chile shows the way that this mismatch played out in the 1960s and 1970s. Law, the state and legal education in the south completely clashed with what was found in the US, the country seeking to export. The main success of the law and development movement in Brazil was not the transformation of legal education, law, or the state, but rather the building of relationships between people who were in approximately the same positions in their own countries. The elite lawyers of Brazil used their law and development training and connections to follow relatively traditional Brazilian routes to state power. The differences between them and the traditional elite were that their bases of international strength were friendship with leading actors in the US and some familiarity with US business law, which allowed them to advance their positions as the economists came to power.

More generally, we can use this perspective to try to understand the Alliance for Progress.[13] The action intellectuals of the Kennedy era in Washington sought to export what they represented to places with very different structures of state power. They did not find counterparts in the south capable of implementing their technical programmes of anti-communist reform. Even when they were quite successful in making friends, some of the critical technical recipes, such as that favouring land reform, were not accepted by the political establishment in the south. Put another way, individuals in the south who pursued an international strategy of investing in northern reformist expertises, in particular land reform, were not paid dividends proportional to their technical investments. Many ended up being labelled as communists and exiled by the military regimes that came to power. The failure of the 'third way' programs identified with the Alliance for Progress in the 1960s and 1970s foreshadowed and contributed – along with

---

12 Cf World Bank (1998).
13 The Alliance for Progress was established in 1961 as a US technical and financial assistance programme to developing states in Latin America. The immediate catalyst for the programme was the Cuban revolution and the success of Castro in coming to power.

economic decline – to the demise of the reformist establishment in the US a short time later. One of the reasons for Jeanne Kirkpatrick and the Reagan administration to support authoritarian regimes that were identified as anti-communist was that they did not want to see another Allende gain power and confuse the divisions of the Cold War.[14]

Some of the friendships made in the 1960s and 1970s came together again when both sides were removed from power by new groups of conservatives linking the Cold War and neo-liberalism. The international human rights movement is a product of that linkage. To see the legacy of that particular connection, however, and especially what it means for the dollarization of law, it is useful to explore two different aspects of legal intersections. The first is the business law firm, and the second is the public interest law firm in the sense that could be applied to the most famous legally oriented human rights group in Latin America – the Vicariate of Chile. By doing so, we can see the very different ways that these two kinds of law have taken root in Latin America.

The tradition of law firms as family enterprises can be found in varying degrees throughout Latin America. The relatively few law offices with cosmopolitan capital, typically also well-connected to the state and the leading families, served as compradors and double agents for foreign traders and investors. The internationalisation of corporate law firms is thus a joint venture between social capital and legal capital, with the proportions different on each side. The venture could be characterised, as it was in Mexico, as a coming together of local know-who and US know-how – Mexican social connections and US legal technology. In Mexico, in fact, the status associated with this division of labour was made clear with the firm name – Baker, Botts, Miranda and Prieto. The Mexican always came at the end. Those lawyers who made the connections, however, were structurally closer than might at first seem. For Baker and Botts, for example, Henry Holland, the former Assistant Secretary of State for Latin American Affairs, used his connections in Mexico to facilitate the new law firm. Other joint US-Mexico law firms brought US partners who had in effect 'gone native', marrying into Mexican society, gaining law degrees at the National Autonomous University of Mexico (UNAM), and therefore already becoming highly 'Mexicanized'. On the other side, the alliance was facilitated by the fact that those who were willing to be listed with US lawyers in the 1960s and 1970s were descendants of a Mexican elite cut off from careers in the PRI or the Mexican state. They could bear the condemnation that inevitably was heaped on these law firms by Mexican nationalists.

The other model of international joint venture is more frequent and typical of countries where US law firms and US expatriates were not so present. It builds on informal alliances made between local notables of business law who use referrals and apprenticeships to cement relationships and facilitate the exchange of legal technologies. The pioneers of these law firms in Argentina were old family law firms who internationalised very early and obtained degrees and connections abroad; in Brazil, the leading such firm was started by someone outside the faculties of law and the traditional legal hierarchies.[15] The Chilean law firms appear to have developed largely out of the old legal families.[16] The debt crisis and the

---

14 Dezalay and Garth (1999).
15 See Dezalay and Garth (1997).
16 Dezalay and Garth (1998b).

economic activity, especially of the 1980s, put all these law firms in very close contact with US law firms who needed counterparts and local correspondents in the south.

Indeed, legal technologies for the management of the debt crisis were originally worked out in Mexico, and the very same US law firms – mainly Shearman and Sterling for Citicorp and Cleary, Gottlieb for the debtor countries – and often even the same lawyers ensured that the model was put in place in the other debtor countries.[17] The close contact between the various lawyers through seminars and exchanges also facilitated the movement of innovations in one country to another – innovations such as renegotiation according to particular criteria, debt for equity swaps, privatisations and the creation of capital markets in the emerging markets. The law firms on both sides thrived through these innovations that occurred with the restructuring of the Latin American and US states. Law firms in the south that once almost exclusively served a foreign clientele built a much more domestic business clientele by serving a variety of new joint ventures and privatised enterprises.[18]

The contacts also substantially increased the value of US law degrees in all the countries. The family firms grew and divided, making it easy to draw a family tree that explains the community of internationally oriented business law firms. The process led also to a dynamic of family feuds, where *héritiers* and others would fight over the relative values of family capital and legal capital. The growth of these family firms and their spin-offs, their relative prosperity, and the obvious value of the US education, has produced a tremendous increase in the number of lawyers with US law degrees and experience.

A large number of these new hybrid lawyers now face double glass ceilings. The business law firms in their home countries remain for the most part family law firms (with the notable exception of Pinheiro Netto in Brazil), and, while they are much more open than in the past, the opportunities for outsiders remain limited. The hybrid lawyers without family connections typically are still second-class citizens. It is also almost impossible for them to make partner in one of the law firms in the US unless they stay in the US market. The fluidity or dollarization that can be seen increasingly in economics, with relatively few exceptions, does not exist in the field of business law. It appears that this relatively large pool of ambitious and talented people, therefore, is finding opportunities through alliances with non-Wall Street providers of legal services, including Baker and McKenzie, Clifford Chance and the Big Five accounting firms (all of whom are expanding rapidly and have many more foreign partners than do the Wall Street firms).

This growing and somewhat dissatisfied reserve army of talented lawyers may provide a vehicle for change. Potentially they can challenge both the structures of power within the thriving family law firms and the comfortable position of the elite US law firms. They are not, however, so far numerous enough to take on the professional organisations, nor do they as yet express much interest in the courts. But they have helped in a number of countries to mount an offensive against traditional legal academia, which is relatively weak now, by forming new private law schools – many of which are attached to business schools.[19] In a variety of ways,

---

17 Roger Thomas and Mark Walker of Cleary, Gottlieb and Robert Dineen of Shearman and Sterling.
18 Eg Dezalay and Garth (1998b).
19 Especially in Argentina: see Dezalay and Garth, (1998a).

therefore, this reserve army of lawyers may produce a domino effect. Their presence contributes to raise the stakes for the old business elite by enlarging the field and competing with them. At the same time, the activity of the new competitors helps the old business elite demand more recognition and more autonomy within the legal field.

The structural positions of the business law firms from the north and south, in sum, matched pretty well. These brokers between multinational business and the state were able to evolve together to extend and develop the market in corporate legal expertise. The alliance linked especially Latin American social capital with northern legal capital. Results can be seen in legal reforms and practices in such areas as intellectual property, trade, securities and antitrust.

On the 'public interest' side – law for disadvantaged – however, the situation is rather different. There were remarkable successes that came out of the structural conditions that existed in the 1970s and 1980s, but the legacy of that period has not transformed the legal profession to embrace public interest law in the same way that it embraced business law. We can understand these two-stage developments best by recalling first some very substantial historical differences in the position of law and the legal profession in Latin America and the US.

In the US, the legitimacy of law comes in part through the schizophrenic position of those who serve corporate interests. Since the late nineteenth century, corporate lawyers have combined service to business with investment in public service and law reform. An elite career of a US business lawyer, for example, requires investment in the promotion of legal services for disadvantaged persons. This pattern has been reinforced over time and built into elite law schools and careers. Even though the market practically leads most graduates to seek jobs in the corporate sector, the law schools proclaim their commitment to public interest law as well as corporate law; and the profession as a whole recognises and rewards those who act on behalf of the disadvantaged and their legal rights.

The difference in the traditional position in Latin America is quite evident from the reaction of the Argentine corporate bar to the visit to Buenos Aires of corporate lawyers from the New York City Bar in the mid-1970s. As part of their US professionalism, the New York lawyers came to ascertain the human rights situation. The Argentine lawyers, however, simply could not understand why business lawyers would support communists and terrorists. The legitimacy of law and the position of law graduates in Latin America came much less from investment in legal rights for those actors out of power and more in terms of traditional politics. The business lawyers saw relatively little need to invest in the legitimacy of law, and the elite of the profession did not see any place for legal strategies for the disadvantaged or those persecuted by the state. Ambitious law graduates seeking to help or speak for the disadvantaged did not follow professional strategies. Primarily they became active in political parties seeking to gain power in the state.

Law provided some legitimacy for the state, but there was no pattern of professional investment in the development and enforcement of legal rights as a legal career strategy. That would be seen as politics and not a practice that merited professional recognition. Corporate lawyers and faculties of law would not see any reason to invest in this kind of public interest law. Put another way, a lawyer whose career involved high-status public interest law could use that investment in the corporate side in the US. The investment would not be rewarded within law in Latin America.

After Pinochet came to power in 1973 and began to persecute those who had worked with the Allende regime, some lawyer-sympathisers with the Allende group joined with the church – which still strongly reflected the social gospel – and sought to try some legal remedies. They had very few options in politics or the legal profession, and this alternative also provided little in the way of legal success. At that particular moment, however, Amnesty International had worked assiduously to build the idea that human rights were not merely tools for political groups out of power, but reflected universals that proscribed torture and disappearance. A relatively marginal group of legal academics in the US – linked to Amnesty and the International Commission of Jurists – had worked toward the same end by drawing on European principles and post-war developments such as the European Convention on Human Rights. They sought to build the credibility of human rights as international law.

The investment of these groups was recognised and augmented by the split in the foreign policy establishment in the US. The breach in the US side of the Cold War opened up new possibilities. The Democratic doves held hearings in the US following the Pinochet coup and sought to use this human rights expertise to challenge the hawks who had supported and aided the coup.[20] The Cold War split was found also in the Ford Foundation, where young idealists had decided after 1970 to work with Allende despite the pressure of the CIA and the State Department. After the coup, they sought to protect the individuals in whom they had invested earlier. The Ford Foundation did not immediately invest in human rights, but they and the Democratic doves formed an alliance with reformers from the establishment who were now out of power. The alliance was therefore between very close counterparts in the north and the south.

The alliance drew in the first instance on the shared investment in neutral social science, but human rights developed as a legal analogue linked personally and intellectually to the social scientists who had worked with the Allende regime for land reform and other social programs.[21] Both in the north and the south, the opposition actors joined with the media to build the credibility of human rights as a discourse that suited both sides perfectly. Amnesty thrived, winning the Nobel Prize in 1977 and gaining many new members, and Jimmy Carter became President in part on a human rights platform. By 1977, after the Ford Foundation board of trustees had visited the Vicariate in Santiago, the Ford Foundation was willing to create a programme in human rights and use the Vicariate model – which had seemed to be 'curiously legalistic' – to expand to other terrains. During the time of the Reagan administration, which was also the time of the debt crisis and the softening of the authoritarian regimes in Latin America, legally oriented human rights organisations thrived in the north and the south. Responding to the changing field of the state power in the US, in addition, Human Rights Watch challenged Amnesty International and emerged as the leading global human rights organisation.

The model from Chile exerted a great influence around the world, interacting in particular with parallel developments in Brazil and somewhat similar developments in Argentina – where, however, the church offered no support and the Madres of the Plaza de Mayo were the only strong voice at the outset. The growing legitimacy of international human rights discourse in the late 1970s and

20 Dezalay and Garth (1999).
21 See Puryear (1994).

1980s meant also that it came to Mexico to be used by groups who sought to use legal expertise to challenge and to upgrade the PRI. Since, in the words of a Ford Foundation official, 'the model worked everywhere else', the philanthropic foundations also were available to help those who wished to try this international strategy in Mexico.

Human rights organisations were a thriving form of public interest law in the 1980s throughout Latin America and the US. The international market in human rights expertise was a plausible counterpart to the international market in economic expertise. Both were centred in the north, and especially the campuses in the US. Both were closely connected to the media and had become increasingly competitive. The human rights movement helped to make the rules for the transitions to democracy, and lawyers active in the human rights movements became key players in the new regimes.

Once the actors in the human rights movement succeeded in gaining power in Chile, Brazil and elsewhere, however, they abandoned institutions like the Vicariate in order to invest in the new state.[22] The human rights movement hardly exists anymore in Chile in the sense of a movement seeking to hold the state accountable through legal institutions. The same conclusion in general could be reached for Argentina, Brazil and Mexico. For example, Raul Alfonsin in Argentina – the first President after the military dictatorship – came from human rights to elite party politics and the institutions of the state. In all the countries studied by the writers of this chapter, in fact, the investment of the first generation in human rights provided an excellent base for political activity after the transition. What was left behind was not replenished by a new generation eager to mimic the careers of their predecessors. The particular conjuncture that had united moral activism with law through the church and international actors did not continue. The newly created institutional structures that built the human rights NGOs unravelled, revealing the structures that had been in place prior to the 1970s.

Nevertheless, local organisations of human rights, once formed, can continue to exist in the south even if they no longer resemble what they represented earlier. Many, for example, have converted to causes and issues such as the control of crime or the prevention of violence against women. They are much more outposts of international development assistance than activist legal institutions challenging the state. Legal professionals are involved, but it is hard to see these organisations as professional analogues to public interest law.

The patterns may change over time, however, and there may already be some exceptions in the south involving institutions that continue to follow the approach of moral investment in law against the state. In Brazil, for example, Viva Rio is one example of a mix between social movements, religion, politics and law. Its activities, which grew out of the human rights movement, focus on crime, hunger and

---

22 A recent study of NGOs in Chile reaches a parallel conclusion: 'With the end of the military dictatorship in 1990, it soon became difficult for NGOs to justify their existence in the ways that they had previously done so. They were now operating in a democracy in which political resistance per se was not sufficient to justify supporting NGOs ... If this wasn't hard enough, the NGOs now had to compete with the state. This was a democracy whose public institutions became new homes to people who previously worked in the NGO sector ... [T]he state gained the confidence of donors who had previously channelled funds to NGOs. It also slowly became quite critical of NGOs. External funding to NGOs began to fall and has continued to do so': Bebbington and Bebbington (1997) Pt 3.

police violence in Rio de Janeiro, and it draws on elite lawyers as well as social activists. In Chile, activities centred at the University of Diego Portales, a private university originally designed to produce business lawyers, continue to emphasise human rights and public interest law. Argentina seems to offer the most promise for cause lawyering, given the long tradition of professionals investing in institutions and organisations outside the state. Such entities as Poder Ciudadano and a recent and related entity termed the Association for Civil Rights (Associacion por los Derechos Civiles, or 'ADC'), which is dedicated to the protection of civil liberties in Argentina and funded primarily by the Ford Foundation, provide examples.

In contrast to the general pattern in the south, the leading international human rights organisations in the US are thriving in the legal profession. Instead of abandoning their investment in legal expertise to join political parties and movements, human rights organisations continue to invest legal resources and techniques in the cutting edges of US foreign policy. As with power corporate lawyers in Washington, DC, some go into the government on the basis of their experience and expertise, but the legal bases continue to thrive through their symbiotic relationship with the state.

Two further developments relate to the structural asymmetry of the present period. First, those lawyers who have continued to invest professionally in the field of human rights from the south have tended to go abroad, where their expertise and investment in international human rights remains validated and recognised. This legal morality and brain drain from the south to the north helps to legitimate the international human rights organisations based in the north. The northern organisations can use their openness – and make certain modifications that come with that openness – to further legitimate their positions of leadership in the field of international human rights.

The thriving of the human rights organisations in the US, in contrast to the absorption and re-incorporation into the state in the south, is consistent with our structural model. New forms of symbolic capital tend to gravitate toward the more established and dominant symbolic banks where they can be better valued, guaranteed and exchanged. That means in the US that symbolic innovators continue to gravitate around the powerful and relatively autonomous professional milieux – especially given the fairly amorphous and porous US state. In Chile, to make the obvious contrast, the state provides the dominant symbolic bank.

For structural reasons, therefore, the current situation reveals only a partial transplant of the US professional model of legal legitimacy. The partial transplant reinforces US hegemony and helps to sustain the long-term prosperity of the US professional model at home. International activities add a key dimension to a US legal elite that combines hired guns, reformers and public interest lawyers acting on the basis of legal noblesse oblige.[23] In the field of human rights (as well as the environment and the movement to protect women against violence), the local prestige and power of US organisations draws extensively on international activities and expertises. Within national settings outside the US, however, there has been far more lasting success in transplanting US-style business law than US-style public

---

23 Another example is the American Bar Association, which has long relied on a strong institutional commitment to legal services for the poor as part of its professional legitimacy. Now the ABA's activities in exporting the rule of law, especially to Eastern Europe and to Asia, are equally promoted as part of the profession's expression of institutional idealism.

interest law. Within the business law firms, there is a move parallel to that of the economists toward investment in the state and its institutions. The notion of professional strategies of using law against the state and business, however, which is a key ingredient of the legal field in the US, has not been able to thrive beyond a particular time period – when fractions of the establishment united against the authoritarian states that evicted them from power.

The processes of professional dollarization, and the dollarization of state knowledge, captured in the shift from gentlemen lawyers to technopols, are therefore highly uneven. Elite economists can make their professional careers locally through investment in and legitimacy from the international market of expertise centred in the US. They legitimate their superiority to the rank and file economists of their own countries while drawing on the latest economics of the campuses in the north. The US professional ranking of economists outside the US translates directly into professional prestige and recognition at home. There is a brain drain to the north, including to the World Bank and the IMF, but there is enough return traffic to maintain the crucial connections. The development of this international field is traceable through interactions between the north and the south that flourished in the development of the Washington consensus. The relative newness of economics and the need to develop autonomy from law and the legal establishment helped to facilitate these developments.

Business lawyering, falling in line behind the rule of the economists, has also tended to thrive professionally in both the north and the south. A relative abundance of young law graduates now seek graduate degrees abroad and careers as business lawyers. As with respect to economics, the business lawyers are able to build domestic careers by relying on expertise minted abroad. Dollarization is less complete, however, since the relative mixes of social and legal capital are still different in Latin America and the US. The law firms in the south are still largely family law firms, limiting local opportunities.

An overproduction of business lawyers who lack opportunities either with the elite of the US or certain family firms at home may now exist. As a result, these lawyers may be gravitating toward the second-tier transnational law firms and toward the Big Five accounting firms. As a legal professional strategy, however, business lawyering is thriving.

Despite the remarkable professional and legal success that went into the construction of the field of human rights, however, the same enduring pattern of success within the south is not true for public interest law. The institutional prosperity of public interest law in the US draws on the model of schizophrenic corporate lawyers that developed in the nineteenth century. It is closely linked also to the role of courts and to the elite law schools in the US. The professional role of 'public interest lawyer', however, has not taken root in Latin America so far.

The human rights movement fit parallel structural histories in the north and the south, but the south did not have institutions akin to the family law firms that could be used to put public interest law on a more lasting indigenous path. It remains to be seen whether this 'emancipatory side' of US professionalism will take root along side the successful business side – and whether a joint effort might mount a real challenge to the traditional positions of the courts and the law faculties.

In both law and economics, the criteria for legitimate expertise are set according to the international market centred in the US. According to the recently produced hierarchy, elite US professionals are found at the top (regardless of whether they are the product of a brain drain or instead home-grown), and within each country an additional two-tier professional hierarchy exists. The division is between a cosmopolitan elite and an increasingly provincialised mass of professionals in law, economics and other fields who have taken advantage of the expansion of educational opportunity in the post-war period. Each of these hierarchies raises questions about legitimacy that have not yet been confronted.

First, each of these international fields – economics, business law, human rights – is dominated by the US and its mechanisms for legitimating expertise – elite private universities, philanthropic foundations, transnational NGOs, think-tanks, academic journals, the US state and global media. Those who are largely excluded from participating in the making of the governing rules and the operation of these institutions may question the legitimacy of the international expertise as applied to them – and form alliances with those who seek to promote competing expertises (the accountants, for example) and even models of states (the Japanese, for example). Second, at the national level, it is possible to raise similar questions about the cosmopolitan elite. They can be accused by, among others, the professional rank and file of 'selling the state' on the international market in order to promote themselves and their internal power. None of the hierarchies are stable or inevitable, and the legitimacy of states built out of this cosmopolitan expertise is also far from assured.

Select bibliography

Bebbington, D, and Bebbington, A, (1997) *Evaluating the impact of Chilean NGOs: Evaluation and the dilemmas of democracy.*

Bird, K, (1992) *The chairman: John J. McCloy, the making of the American establishment.*

Bourdieu, P, (1996) *The state nobility: Elite schools in the field of power.*

Dezalay, Y, and Garth, B G, (1997) 'Political Crises as Professional Battlegrounds: Technocratic and Philanthropic Challenges to the Dominance of the Cosmopolitan Lawyer-Statesman in Brazil', ABF Working Paper No 9612, Chicago.

—(1998a) 'Argentina: Law at the Periphery and Law in Dependencies. Political and Economic Crisis and the Instrumentalization and Fragmentation of Law', ABF Working Paper No 9708, Chicago.

—(1998b) 'Chile: Law and the Legitimation of Transitions. From the Patrimonial State to the International Neo-Liberal State', ABF Working Paper No 9709, Chicago.

—(1999) 'From Notables of the Foreign Policy Establishment to the International Market of Professionals of Philanthropy and Human Rights. Strategies for Power and the Social Construction of a New Field of State Expertise', ABF Working Paper No 9818, Chicago.

—(2000) *The Internationalization of palace wars: Lawyers, economists and the international reconstruction of the state.*

Dominguez, J, (ed), (1997) *Technopols: Freeing politics and markets in Latin America in the 1990s.*

Puryear, J, (1994) *Thinking politics: Intellectuals and democracy in Chile, 1973-1988.*

Valdes, J G, (1995) *Pinochet's economists: The Chicago School in Chile.*

Williamson, J, (1990) 'What Washington means by policy reform' in J Williamson (ed), *Latin American adjustment: How much has happened?*

World Bank (1998) *Beyond the Washington consensus: Institutions matter.*

Yergin, D, and Stanislaw, J, (1998) *The commanding heights: The battle between government and the marketplace that is remaking the modern world.*

The promise and peril of international order

R ABEL

How is social order possible, and what is its nature? These questions, the starting point of all social science, assume heightened urgency during the present period of accelerating globalisation. The human qualities that make order problematic *within* the nation state are intensified *outside* it: social distance, cultural difference, ignorance, indifference, selfishness, fear and rivalry. This comment focuses on four chapters – by Francis Snyder, Susan Rose-Ackerman, John Flood, and Yves Dezalay and Bryant Garth – which both illuminate the questions and offer fundamentally different responses. They suggest a range of possible sources for international order, radically divergent images and normative evaluations of that order, and reflections on the actual and potential contribution of law and lawyers.

Inevitably, we approach globalisation from the historical perspective of nation states, focusing on the absence of legitimate political power in the international arena. This, of course, exaggerates the importance of the state in creating and maintaining order. Most of the quotidian regularities in our lives, which enable us to plan and to engage in collective action, are very remote from state influence. Social scientists have devoted considerable energy to exploring the bases of co-operative behaviour, pointing to such diverse sources as biology (genetically programmed altruism, developed for its survival value), shared culture (acquired during the lengthy human socialization process), reciprocity (produced by economic incentives) and reputation (investment in human capital). These and other related insights deserve extrapolation to the transnational environment.

The four chapters focus on one vital mode of transnational interaction – global trade (deliberately choosing not to address other equally important manifestations, such as labour migration, cultural dispersion, political influence and warfare). These chapters suggest a variety of institutions and processes that facilitate trade, including lawyers and other professionals (especially economists) whose cultures transcend national boundaries, supra-national bodies whose authority derives from treaties among sovereign states, the mutual benefits conferred by ongoing contractual relations and the value of investments in reputation. The chapters also pose important questions, which call for further empirical investigation. Does competition among jurisdictions inevitably foment a race to the bottom, as states progressively relax regulation to encourage inward investment? Or can jurisdictions engage in a race to the top, endowing compliant economic actors with a reputation for integrity, which enhances the value of their goods and services? Can norms unsupported by the threat of coercion shape

213

behaviour, especially when opposed by strong contrary incentives? It is striking that an economist like Susan Rose-Ackerman feels compelled to argue at length that corruption is morally wrong, even when it may produce efficient outcomes in particular transactions. (That she feels this need exposes the poverty of economic theories exalting efficiency over distribution and wealth over democracy.) But it is far from clear that mere conviction in the wrongfulness of corruption, without more, can significantly reduce it. Dezalay and Garth appear hopeful that lawyers can represent neglected public interests as effectively as they do those of capital. Unfortunately, it is unclear why public interest lawyers should exercise greater influence on the global stage than the lamentably little they do domestically.

One of the most important questions, addressed in several chapters, is the relationship between democracy and economic growth. Supporters of democracy proclaim their hope that it will emerge spontaneously from increases in productivity; market enthusiasts bolster their case for laissez faire and free trade with similarly confident assertions. But there is no convincing or generally accepted theory explaining why democracy and productivity are inextricably linked. And even if there were, much of the evidence tends to disconfirm it. There are far too many poor democracies (most of Africa during the early years of independence) and rapidly expanding economies guided by political autocracies (Hong Kong, Singapore, Taiwan, South Korea, Malaysia, Thailand, Indonesia, even China). Some social scientists have been excessively credulous in swallowing the rationalisations of authoritarian regimes. Samuel Huntington went further and declared that developing countries had governability deficits, making it impossible for them to afford democracy.

We know, of course, that there *is* order outside nation states, just as there was within them before their emergence. The more interesting question, therefore, is the nature of that order, particularly the power relations among crucial actors. Here description quickly shades into – often seems inseparable from – normative judgment. Views rapidly polarise. One extreme embraces an almost Parsonian functionalism in which power is dispersed, influence is invisible, and essential homologies between nations emerge spontaneously. The other sees conflict as pervasive and inevitable and political domination, economic exploitation, environmental degradation and cultural hegemony the inevitable outcome. One talks of globalisation, the other of Americanisation, the triumph of McDo. One sees convergence, at least among elites; the other assails a comprador bourgeoisie in thrall to its metropole masters. One follows Adam Smith in extolling the benefits to *all* of specialisation and trade global trickle down. The other focuses on the plight of workers in both metropole and periphery (exacerbated by the competition fostered by global capitalism), hidden (and sometimes glaring) externalities, and the sacrifice of democracy and human rights. One portrays neo-liberalism as inexorable scientific law, the end of both ideology and history. The other attributes its triumph to a chance political configuration, exposing its idolatry of the market as a rationalisation for the transitory success of particular fractions of capital in making taxes more regressive, robbing labour of its share of productivity gains, demolishing the welfare state and drastically undermining regulation. One trumpets that the fall of the Iron Curtain allows Western democracies to stop propping up puppet dictators as bulwarks against communism. Now we do so for bulwarks against terrorism. The other remembers that the Cold War pressured the West to reform itself (addressing its own racism) and to compete in generosity with its communist rivals in order to woo the Third

World. One sees corruption as an unfortunate but acceptable cost of progress; the other sees it as fatally compromising the fundamental democratic project. One embraces globalisation as the inevitable future; the other resists it as a marginal phenomenon, capable of containment or even reversal.

Although none of the authors approaches either stereotype – global cheerleader or anarchist scourge of WTO and World Bank meetings – Dezalay and Garth certainly offer a rosier view than either Snyder or Flood, while Rose-Ackerman seems to reflect Gramsci's prescription for combining pessimism of the mind with optimism of the will. Certainly Snyder, Flood and Rose-Ackerman locate the primary sources of power in global capital, which explains the dominance of the US, the secondary role of Western Europe and Japan, and the dependence of the rest of the world. Snyder details the linkages among economic actors (creators, financiers, industrialists, workers, intermediaries and consumers) and polities (state and supranational, legislative and judicial). Flood delineates the ways in which both expert services and institutional infrastructure follow capital. And Rose-Ackerman documents the pervasiveness of corruption and the relative impotence of national or international fora to restrain it.

My own biases may already be obvious. I find the account by Dezalay and Garth partial and excessively optimistic. The notion that homology between metropolitan and peripheral elites facilitates interaction between the US and Latin America in which influence is invisible seems to me to omit virtually every important event and trend in the twentieth century. The euphemism of 'palace wars' obscures the dominant role of the US: the brutality of CIA-inspired coups (in Guatemala and Chile); support for anti-democratic guerrillas (in Nicaragua); the 40-year embargo against Cuba; and political, economic and military assistance to repressive regimes throughout the continent guilty of jailing, kidnapping, and murdering thousands of opponents. Land reform did not 'fail'; it was subverted throughout the century by the vested interests of the tiny minority of large landholders. The facade of neo-liberalism cannot conceal the kleptocracy of the new billionaires, who benefited from the corrupt sell-off of state assets (the counterparts of the Russian oligarchs). The unbearable interest burden of Latin American nations was deliberately constructed by Western banks lured by high interest rates and corrupt Latin American officials.

Given these radically inconsistent visions of the world, it is not surprising that the authors also see the role of law and lawyers very differently. The central disagreement turns on conceptualisations of the source of power. Is it wielded by the clients the lawyers serve, for whom they are little more than hired guns? Is it derived from the expert knowledge lawyers possess, which endows them with significant autonomy? Is it still embedded in national legal institutions, which attract foreign actors to their jurisdiction or extend it as domestic actors expand into the global arena? Is it incubating in the emerging supra-national bodies, which attach regulatory powers to the incentives of trade or finance they control? Is it an attribute of the norms themselves, which convince economic actors to choose long-term interests over short-term advantage? Is it exercised by interest groups, which combine ideology, political influence and economic leverage to enact laws, win judgments and enforce compliance? It could, of course, be all of these, in different proportions or varying contexts.

Flood offers extensive evidence that American lawyers have gained their dominant role in global lawyering by riding the coat-tails of their American clients – financial institutions and multinational conglomerates. American procedures (such as bankruptcy and reorganisation) and institutions (like the SEC) have followed in the wake of American economic influence. Dezalay and Garth emphasise changes in the nature of expert knowledge to explain the shift in power from gentlemen-politicians of the law to technocratic economists. In this they seem to be aligning themselves with new-class theorists like Bruce-Biggs, Gouldner, and Konrád and Szelényi. I am sceptical of endowing expertise with such causal significance for the same reason that I am unpersuaded by Andrew Abbott's claim that professional jurisdiction follows knowledge, rather than vice versa. The 'gentlemen-politicians' of Latin American derived their power from the capital – mostly land – which they or their clients owned and the political influence this conferred. As the dominant sources of capital – in the form of foreign investment in the extractive or industrial sectors – have become external, the experts serving global finance (both private and public) have risen to prominence. Since the variables influencing their decision-making are risk and return, the relevant expertise is economic rather than legal. The leading global law firms, based in the US and UK, have pursued new sources of international finance in planning their expansion: first to each other's financial capitals (New York and London), then throughout Europe, Tokyo, Hong Kong, and Singapore, and only now gradually following novel investment opportunities in the former Soviet empire (extractive industries) or Third World (cheap labour for production or assembly).

Snyder documents both the fading national barriers to trade and the rapidly growing influence of supra-national legal institutions, offering a wonderfully detailed account of the global toy industry. Rose-Ackerman looks to both national and international institutions as sources of norms and sanctions against corruption. She also hopes that foreign investors will be swayed by the norms themselves, which accurately express their long-term interests in predictability and institutional integrity.

Dezalay and Garth express bemusement at the failure of Americans to export public interest law in the way they have exported economic technocrats and Wall Street law firms. This strikes me as naive. The reason is not that interest-group politics are inherently less effective in the global arena than in the domestic. Both Snyder and Rose-Ackerman offer telling examples of victories by pressure groups in struggles concerning corruption, labour conditions and environmental dangers. Rather, I disagree with Dezalay and Garth about both the cause and extent of the success of public interest law in the US and the potential relevance of that experience to Latin America. The limited success of public interest law in the US is largely attributable to the (until recently) unique role of judicial review of the constitutionality of legislative and executive action. (This practice recently has been spreading—to Germany, Israel, Canada, South Africa, the EU, and England.) Public interest lawyers have remained outside American political institutions not because those lawyers are powerful but because they are relatively powerless and cannot gain entry or wield influence. On the rare occasions when progressives have flirted with Washington (for instance, during the Clinton Administration), they have been rejected as too ideological (Lani Guinier), co-opted (Donna Shalala), ignored (Robert Reich) or forced to quit in disgust (Peter Edelman). It is no more possible to export US public interest lawyers to Latin America than it was to export American legal education, laws or institutions during the first wave of law and development in the 1960s, or than it has been in the 1990s, for the World Bank to Americanise Third-World judicial systems or the American Bar Association to remake their legal professions in its image.

In the global arena as in the domestic, law and lawyers are largely subordinate to other sources of power, economic and political. At the same time, the ideals of generality, prospectivity and procedural fairness inherent in law and the ideals of service, integrity and disinterest embodied in legal professions offer some potential for curbing global power, protecting vulnerable interests, and reforming corrupt practices.

A response to Richard Abel's reading

Y DEZALAY and B GARTH

Richard Abel has produced many excellent books and articles, shaping the way we and many others think about law and the legal profession. In his comment on four chapters in this volume, he has chosen to single out our chapter for special criticism. We are honoured by the attention, but we would like to respond briefly to his reading of our chapter, since it tries to force our research into a quite specific politico-legal argument. Unfortunately, the process of trying to see where we stand distorts our argument and approach quite radically.

We begin with a few distortions. Abel says the chapters focus on 'one vital mode of transnational interaction – global trade'. That is not our focus. We are also not concerned with the question of whether there is a 'race to the bottom' or a 'race to the top', which he singles out as a common theme. More importantly, we reject the effort to read our chapter to see whether the appropriate stance at this point is 'optimism' or 'pessimism' about current developments. Abel characterises our chapter as offering a 'rosier view' than others and as being 'excessively optimistic'. Finally, we do not feel compelled to take a position as to whether 'global capital' is the 'cause' of the ills that Abel lists.

The basic reason for this lack of relationship between what he attributes and what interests us, we suspect, is that the agenda Abel promotes is relatively narrow. Coming out of the US law and development era, this agenda combines a rather strong materialism – that ultimately it is the power of financial capital and global trade that determines history – with a deeply ingrained legalistic idealism (in spite of doubts there remains a faith in the law through the promotion of progressive lawyering). Abel accordingly wants to take up the issue of 'the actual and potential contribution of law and lawyers' to tame domestic or global corporate power. He then lines up the chapters according to a legalistic explanation of social problems – corruption, races to the bottom, deprivations of human rights, violations of democratic norms – and potential solutions that fit that definition. The question he asks, which is quite familiar in US law schools, especially in the 1960s and 1970s, is whether there are or can be enough progressive lawyers fighting for the public interest to balance the bad lawyers who serve capital or corruption. He is understandably pessimistic that the solution of public interest law will tame global capital.

Since we point to efforts to build public interest law firms in Latin America, he surmises that we are optimistic. Similarly, since we try to understand the way in which ideas and expertises made in the north – including those such as the desirability of public interest law – are exported into the south, he thinks that we are arguing that expertise itself is the 'cause' of change or perhaps even our 'hope' for progressive law. We do not pin any political hopes on the question of whether we should be optimistic or pessimistic about what lawyers will do. The more interesting question is whether Latin Americans will seek to bolster their own positions in palace wars by claiming relevance in their own countries of the US categories of optimism and pessimism about public interest law.

Abel says in passing that our concept of 'palace wars' is a euphemism designed to cover up real power and real capital. On the contrary, we are referring to struggles for control that are often violent. What we try to show is that internationally credible or prestigious expertise and legitimacy – including definitions of problems and solutions that give lawyers a privileged position – can be weapons in national palace wars. Sometimes the mechanisms of influence are invisible or poorly understood. Part of our goal is to make the subtle influences of power relationships, national and transnational hierarchies, better understood. Rather than a euphemism, the image of local palace wars is central to our research. They shape the rules of the game and the winners and losers in the state and the economy.

The image of palace wars allows us to go beyond the contradictions of a whole generation of scholars, especially in the US. It leads to a focus on symbolic capital and symbolic trade, both of which are crucial to the legitimation of hierarchies and privileges. We also can explore the more subtle class hierarchies rarely examined by US academia. Our more complex picture does not correspond to the dichotomies that keep returning under new garb: regulation versus emancipation, races to the bottom or the top, public interest versus private greed. The latest version of these traditional dichotomies can be found in the media portrayals of the virtuous fighters of the NGOs defending civil society against the abuses of the international technocrats. It is not that these fights are pointless or doomed, only that those engaging in them should be better informed – and more reflexive – about the structural history of the battlefields that determines their strategies and resources. The world is not black and white, even if it is continuously presented as such for obvious tactical reasons.

For the same reasons, our research tries to avoid imposing preconceptions about problems and solutions or picking one cause – economic crises, the 'dominant role of the United States', global capital, third world debt, transnational advocacy networks, the opinions of local elites – to explain complex processes that occur simultaneously in the north and the south, even if the power is far from symmetrical. The question whether we should be optimistic or pessimistic about the impact of progressive lawyers against capital and the lawyers who represent it assumes that this framing of the problem has some relevance outside the US. We make no such assumption. Instead, we look at the debates and the sources of the debates and how they relate to national and transnational structures of state power. A 'public interest law firm' found in Argentina is therefore not seen in our research as the hope of the future, but rather as part of an asymmetrical process of transformation or potential transformation in the way law might be used within the Argentine context. We try to see whether and how imported approaches and expertises might gain some form of institutionalisation, but we do not promote the public interest law firm or the elites who staff it as a 'progressive' solution to social problems.

Our sympathies in this respect, therefore, are less with 'new class' theories, as Abel suggests, and more with scholars such as Immanuel Wallerstein, who talk not simply of the 'power' of 'global capitalism', but rather specifically of 'historical capitalism' as the ever-changing product of competition in rules, social hierarchies, efforts to gain wealth, transnational and national alliances, efforts to promote 'universal truths', and struggles over legitimacy in both the north and the south.

Chapter 11

Cultural imperialism in the context of transnational commercial collaboration

M B LIKOSKY*

INTRODUCTION

At the 1998 Asia Pacific Economic Community (APEC) Business Summit dinner held in Kuala Lumpur, Malaysia, then US Vice President Al Gore decried the jailing of former Malaysian Deputy Prime Minister and Finance Minister Anwar Ibrahim on charges of conspiracy and sodomy. APEC is an inter-state forum devoted to promoting commercial integration of its constituent members and to growth of the Southeast Asian region. Members are not limited to East Asian countries and include the US and Canada. The commercial mission of APEC is paramount as member countries are referred to as economies rather than as states. Thus, Gore's discussion of human rights at the Business Summit was a departure from typical diplomatic protocol. Showing solidarity with protestors then outside on the streets of the capital, Gore orated: 'And so, among nations suffering economic crises, we continue to hear calls for democracy and reform in many languages –"people's power", "doi moi", "reformasi". We hear them today – right here, right now – among the brave people of Malaysia.'[1]

The protests and Gore's words were directed at Malaysian Prime Minister Dato' Seri Dr Mahathir bin Mohamad. It was claimed that Mahathir had orchestrated a retaliatory arrest of his protégé Anwar and bore responsibility for the beating he received from guards while in custody. When Anwar held a press conference a number of hours after the jailing, he had a black eye and other visible injuries. While a guard's testimony would legally vindicate Mahathir of responsibility for the physical abuse, Amnesty International placed Anwar on its list of prisoners of conscience[2] where he remains.[3]

Until the jailing, it was assumed that Anwar would succeed Mahathir. However, in 1996 when the currency crisis struck the East Asian region, conflict arose between Mahathir and Anwar. At that time, many countries in the region sought assistance from the International Monetary Fund (IMF). Loans from the IMF were conditioned upon changes to the recipient's domestic political order.

*   mbl@calculus.wolf.ox.ac.uk. I would like to thank Yves Dezalay, Bryant Garth, Jim Harris, Godfrey Hodgson, Sally Falk Moore and Saskia Sassen for their attentive readings.
1   Straits Times Interactive (1998).
2   M2 Presswire (1998).
3   Pereira 2000.

Changes ranged from shifts in state spending for social programmes to curtailment of planned infrastructure projects.[4] Against Anwar's advice, Mahathir refused IMF aid, arguing that conditions attached to the money amounted to attempts to recolonise the country. Also, disagreeing with the presumption that the crisis itself was caused by unsound domestic policies, Mahathir blamed foreigners for the region's economic woes.

Unsurprisingly, Mahathir took offence to Gore's show of political solidarity with the popular opposition at the economic forum. In an interview shortly after the dinner, Mahathir expressed unmitigated disdain, saying '[w]e should fry him' and questioning whether the US had the best interests of the Malaysian people at heart. 'Al Gore does not love Malaysia nor its people', Mahathir declared. 'Al Gore and his government only want to manipulate and control our country.' According to Mahathir a reversion to colonialism was desired: 'They want to make us weak and conquer us again.' Making reference to Anwar he continued, '[t]hey have nurtured a candidate to take over our country. Unfortunately, for America, this candidate failed to be the prime minister because he was ousted. If he succeeds, Al Gore will use this person as his puppet.'[5]

With the end of the Cold War, the tension between the universality of human rights and sovereign absolutism has replaced the battle between free markets and communism. With the preferred economic system apparently well-settled, attention has shifted to whether capitalism, democracy and human rights are fellow travellers.[6] The US takes the position that capitalism necessitates democracy, while Malaysia and Singapore argue that the universality of capitalism does not necessitate the universality of human rights or democracy. Both sides disagree over how to explain the reality of anti-democratic capitalist systems. The US advocates 'peaceful evolution'[7] whereby the development of capitalism will, in time, bring with it democracy. The East Asian counterparts sharply disagree, believing that democracy will never come to East Asia; that is, if democracy means the 'westernising' of Asian political institutions.[8]

Rarely a month goes by without this disagreement manifesting itself in a new conflict or crisis in Malaysian-US bilateral relations reported in the international press. US representatives argue that Malaysia's political system is anti-democratic and that the country does not respect universal human rights. Malaysians retort that their political system and human rights practices reflect culturally specific Asian values and attempts to intervene amount to a violation of domestic sovereignty and an instance of cultural imperialism. From the vitriolic language of the exchanges, one might assume that the countries only talk at each other and rarely with one another.

---

4   Terrill (1999).
5   Agence France Presse (1999).
6   See eg Bartley (1993).
7   The Chinese government initially used the term to express a wariness of the US interest in commercially engaging communist countries. Officials argued that the US sought to erode communism by introducing capitalist culture. US congress people quickly adopted the terminology as a means of promoting commerce in the face of domestic human rights opposition. See eg Congressional Record House (1993).
8   At the same time, many criticise the oppositional character of the debates suggested by phrases such as the 'clash of civilisations'. For instance, Anwar Ibrahim argues for a sincretic model: Ibrahim (1997).

However, this public 'clash of civilisations'[9] occurs in the context of extensive transnational commercial engagement between the countries. The nature of this engagement is such that it engenders a continual transnational re-authoring of the Malaysian legal order so as to ensure the ongoing success of commercial relations. Contrary to the US foreign policy position, transnational commercial collaboration does not phase out authoritarian rule. Instead, commercial engagement itself collaboratively produces cultural practices through a transnational reformulation of the domestic legal order that, in turn, aggravate the tension in public international law between sovereign absolutism and universal human rights.[10] The cultural practices, 'Asian values', at the heart of the public international law controversy are a legal amalgam, a fusion created once the expansion of commerce requires the reformulation of the domestic legal order.

For this reason, the backdrop of commercial engagement forces a reframing of the international culture wars. Malaysia's political system and human rights record are not the sole product of the government, but instead the result of a transnational collaboration. So, US attempts to localise the cause of human rights abuses within the Malaysian government are misconceived. Also, US insistence on the evolutionary relationship between capitalism and respect for human rights is regularly belied by its actions. For similar reasons, the Malaysian retort, which essentialises the domestic characteristics as uniquely and culturally specific 'Asian values', is also mistaken. The debate over the relationship between capitalism and human rights translates into public international law arenas as a conflict between universal human rights and domestic sovereignty.[11]

Colonial legal orders distinguished between the legal aspects of trans-jurisdictional commerce and matters affecting commerce, on the one hand, and the legal aspects of domestic culture, for example, politics, religion, family, on the other. Within the context of dual systems, conflicts often arose when foreign interests sought to impose human rights norms on local cultures. Elements of the local leadership opposed imposition, claiming sovereign inviolability. Further, the practices subject to international scrutiny were at times the product of trans-jurisdictional collaboration. For example, slavery was trans-jurisdictionally conceived and supported by the international slave trade, but was at the same time subject to foreign human rights legal scrutiny. Thus, while the present conflicts bear resemblance to the colonial ones, nominally the term 'colonialism' has undergone a dramatic refashioning as the context in which it is used has shifted with time. Colonialism is a trope.[12] The meaning of the word is context-dependent and thus it may mean different things at different times. Its meaning will also vary depending upon the speaker and audience. At the same time, it is the residual force of history present in the word that gives it linguistic capital.

---

9 Although Samuel Huntington popularised the term, Gerritt W Gong coined the term in 1984. However, Huntington makes no mention of Gong's employment of the term: see Gong (1984); Huntington (1993).
10 On the relationship between universal human rights and sovereign absolutism, see Donnelly (1989); Wilson (1997).
11 For a discussion of the Asian values debate and its relationship to law, philosophy and politics with a focus on China, see Davis (1995). On Asian values, international law and labour, see Woodiwiss (1998). The social science literature on the topic is vast: see eg Laothamatas (1997); Wurfel and Burton (1996).
12 On how various authors define tropes, see Lanham (1991).

Whilst Mahathir is correct in his characterisation of the present order as resembling colonial period orders, at the same time he, along with US governmental and commercial actors, is an active agent rather than an unbiased observer. The colonial elements are in fact the collaborative result of Malaysian elite and foreign commercial and governmental interests rather than a solely Western creation. The argument here is that the use of the term 'colonialism' functionally localises domestic dissatisfaction with the negative externalities of transnational commercial engagement on an entirely foreign actor. Thus, colonialism acts as a powerful rhetorical device to evade domestic scrutiny for one's actions, while transnational commercial relations continue uninterrupted. This point is supported by the fact that, following Gore's comments, not only did transnational commercial relations persist between US and Malaysian actors, but also widespread dissent directed at Mahathir for his handling of Anwar shifted. Mahathir successfully mobilised popular discontent towards the US for its public intervention in Malaysian political life. National solidarity was encouraged by Mahathir through speeches and also an executive order, establishing a day devoted to venting domestic anger towards foreign forces. In addition, a bill was passed in the state of Selangor, officially condemning Gore's intervention into Malaysia's domestic affairs.[13] As animus directed towards the US swelled, opposition to Mahathir dwindled.

At the same time, US attacks on Malaysian political abuses and human rights practices function similarly. Following Gore's speech, many in the US praised his convictions. Commentators argued that the speech had been designed to promote Gore's run for president. The speech would later be published on his campaign website as a representative foreign policy statement. At the time of the speech Gore faced public difficulties for alleged campaign finance improprieties during the Clinton election bid. It was claimed that he had accepted money from the Chinese government, known for its human rights abuses, in exchange for political support for ongoing commercial relations with China. Furthermore, money allegedly had been received illegally, laundered through a religious organisation.[14] Thus, the speech was calculated to make clear Gore's convictions and that he placed human rights above commerce. Yet, while transnational commerce between the US and Malaysia has continued since the jailing of Anwar, resulting in the proliferation of business contracts, Anwar remains in jail and calls for reform to the Malaysian political system continue to be expressed but not acted upon.

Both governments successfully channel domestic discontent with the negative externalities of transnational commerce into international human rights arenas. Since these arenas lack developed enforcement mechanisms, discontent is expressed but not often enacted in policy. For example, the US did not employ the legal tools available to safeguard human rights in Malaysia, such as conditions placed upon TNCs or trade sanctions. Instead, the US took credit for the benefits of transnational commerce, while placing the responsibility for its detrimental effects on the shoulders of Malaysia's government. In fact, in the APEC speech Gore had said: '[a]fter all, we are the nations that, together, created an economic miracle for Asia and the whole Asian-Pacific region.'[15]

---

13 New Straits Times (1999).
14 The Economist (1998).
15 Straits Times Interactive (1998).

While the similarities to the colonial period are plentiful, discontinuities also exist. For example, post-colonial legal orders are comprised of formally equal states enjoying absolute sovereignty over their political territories. In addition, international human rights claims have been secularised and legalised. Also, the economy has shifted away from primary commodities towards high-technology goods. Further complicating cross-period generalisations, colonial legal orders themselves exhibited tremendous intra-categorical variation. Furnivall notes that 'conditions vary from one colonial power to another, from one dependency to another, in different dependencies of the same colonial power, and in the same dependency at different times'.[16]

Historically, Malaysia is the product of the unification of a number of political jurisdictions formerly subject to British overseas intervention. Each jurisdiction has its own history and enjoyed unique legal relations with the British. Also, during the Second World War Japan occupied proto-Malaysia.[17] The nature of relations also varied across time. In addition, the Malaysian state itself was the product of a peaceful constitutional negotiation between the British and Malaysian elites. The internationally composed Reid Commission oversaw the transition.[18] Additionally, British property was often not expropriated by the newly created Malaysian state.[19] Also, English law remained a legitimate legal source after independence and is often cited as precedent in court cases.[20] For these reasons, allusions to colonialism require contextualising in time and place.

This chapter will examine the continuities and discontinuities between colonial and current transnational legal orders with respect to the tension between the dual goals of universal human rights and sovereign absolutism. This tension will be placed within the context of trans-jurisdictional commercial engagement. Before doing so, however, the public international law controversy over 'Asian values' will be elaborated. After presenting the current public international law controversy, the following section will discuss the manifestations of this conflict in the proto-Malaysian legal order.

The trans-jurisdictional commercial context in which the division arose and within which tensions materialised will be elaborated. Within this trans-border engagement, the division between foreign and local rule was highly negotiated and varied according to time and place. In many ways this variation was subsidiary to transnational commercial engagement. That is, the need to maintain an environment conducive to commerce militated towards compromise and continuous renegotiation. Focus here will be on to how commercial exigencies determined the nature and specifics of the division in practice. After illustrating how foreign and local interests collaboratively refashioned the foreign/local divide, human rights demands from the period will be discussed, focusing on their role within this transnational commercial context.

The third section of the chapter will turn to the contemporary era and focus on how transnational commercial interests, including corporations and states, refashion the legal order in Malaysia and, in turn, how the human rights debates occur within this commercial context. To do so, first the degree of Malaysia's integration into the global economy will be elaborated, paying particular attention

---

16 Furnivall (1956) p 9.
17 See Mello (1948).
18 On the Reid Commission, see Harding (1996) pp 28–38.
19 White (1996).
20 Rutter (1989).

to the last several decades. Next, an instance of transnational commercial engagement and law creation supposedly localised within a 15 by 40km strip of land in Malaysia – the Multimedia Super Corridor (MSC) – will be analysed. The MSC is a foreign direct investment (FDI) scheme and national development plan designed to leapfrog the country into fully developed nation status by the year 2020, transforming the country from a manufacturing-based economy to a knowledge-intensive society. This example will be employed to illustrate the role of foreign interests in determining the legislative composition of the country, and how, in collaboration with local elites, the domestic legal order is refashioned. In particular, attention will be paid to how the legal aspects of Asian values and authoritarian government structures are the product of this transnational commercial partnership. After setting this stage of transnational commercial integration and domestic legal reformulation, the public international law debates over Asian values and respect for human rights will be elaborated. To do so, controversy over censoring of the Internet by the Malaysian government in the wake of the East Asian currency crisis and during the aftermath of the jailing of Anwar Ibrahim will receive attention. This government action interacted with the transnational commercial surround in which it occurred. To discuss this interaction, focus will be paid on the relationship between these controversies and the progress of the MSC. In conclusion, the colonial and contemporary transnational manifestations of the tension between foreign expansion and domestic cultural sovereignty will be examined with an eye towards the significance of their continuities and discontinuities.

THE CONTROVERSY

With the close of the Second World War, the Charter of the United Nations (UN Charter) was established in 1945. It set forth the principle of absolute sovereignty and equality among member states.[21] In establishing domestic sovereignty of states over their internal affairs, article 2, number 7 states: 'Nothing contained in the present Charter shall authorize the United Nations to intervene in matters within the domestic jurisdiction of any State.' Three years later, in 1948, the General Assembly of the United Nations adopted the Universal Declaration of Human Rights (UDHR) based on the 'recognition of the inherent dignity and of the equal and inalienable rights of all members of the human family' as 'the foundation of freedom, justice and peace in the world'.[22] These rights, while dependent for protection on co-operative enforcement by nation-states, were to be recognised with 'no distinction' to 'be made to which [nation-state] a person belongs'.[23] The two goals of sovereign absolutism and individually held and universally recognised human rights have often been difficult to reconcile in practice.

The dual goals were given voice in the context of the twentieth-century national independence movements. Prior to these movements, the post-Westphalia international legal order manifest in the UN Charter had also accepted

---

21 Political scientist Stephen Krasner has argued that formal sovereign equality amounts to 'organised hypocrisy': Krasner (1999). For treatment of sovereign equality by international lawyers, see eg Kelsen (1944): Kooijmans (1964).
22 UDHR (1948) preamble.
23 UDHR, art 2, para 2.

colonialism as a legitimate feature of the post-Second World War world. Thus, it was not formally contradictory to say that sovereign equality existed, while political and legal occupation of various sovereign units persisted.[24]

When, in 1960, the UN adopted the Declaration on the Granting of Independence to Colonial Countries and Peoples,[25] new states entered into an international legal order in which sovereign absolutism and respect for human rights co-existed. Article 7 of the Declaration is relevant: 'All States shall observe faithfully and strictly the provisions of the Charter of the United Nations, the Universal Declaration of Human Rights and the present Declaration on the basis of equality, non-interference in the internal affairs of all States, and respect for the sovereign rights of all peoples and their territorial integrity.'[26] This according of full formal citizenship to so many newly formed states was a major innovation on the post-Westphalia order in which a European-determined judgment on a country's level of civilisation was the criterion for determining acceptance in kind and degree into the international legal order.[27] According to the 1960 Declaration, colonialism itself represented a violation of human rights, and remedying the violation was the grounds upon which international state citizenship was accorded.[28]

To ensure that human rights could be effectively exercised by previously colonised peoples, the solution was that newly formed states would act as proxies for the people. So self-determination was expressed as a state-based right.[29] Importantly, newly created states often united previously unco-ordinated political territories. Also, many new states claimed sovereignty over peoples who in turn questioned the legitimacy of this claim. At other times, transitions of power meant the overtaking of colonial legal institutions by an insurgent political community.[30] For these reasons, decolonisation of persons not political territories more aptly characterises the national independence movements.

Through the 1960 Declaration, the dual policies of sovereign absolutism and respect for human rights converged as newly independent states came into being on formal sovereign parity with long-standing European nation-states. However, formal parity understood within the context of inter-state power disparities has meant that formal and substantive equality do not always go hand-in-hand.[31] Also, the state's role as proxy has often been voluntarily legitimised more by the international legal order than it has been by the citizenry of particular states.[32] Further, this dependence on an international community for legitimacy has made states susceptible to international pressures.

As J W Harris elaborates, this cultural sovereignty position operates as follows:

'International protection of human rights is constantly confronted by the challenge that particular formulations of human rights are no more than attempts to foist

---

24 See Asbeck (1976) p 48.
25 United Nations General Resolution 1514, 14 December 1960.
26 United Nations General Resolution 1514 (XV), art 7.
27 See Gong (1984).
28 Art 1.
29 For a discussion of the right to self-determination, see eg Brownlie (1979) pp 552–599; Jennings (1963) pp 78–79; O'Connell (1967); Twining (1991).
30 Specific judges often maintained their colonial period status despite political revolution. The reasonableness of using the theories of Hans Kelsen to justify this continuity was hotly debated in the law reviews at the time: see Brookfield (1969); Eekelaar (1973); Finnis (1973); Harris (1971).
31 See eg Anghie (1999); McDougal and Lasswell (1959); White (1996) pp 19–23.
32 See Chomsky (1991); Falk (present volume).

Western values on other nations in defiance of the facts of cultural pluralism. This can be depicted as bare-faced cultural imperialism.'[33]

Indeed, terms such as 'cultural imperialism', 'economic colonialism' and 'neo-colonialism' are often proffered by opponents of the Western 'imposition' of human rights.

A leading proponent of this position, Mahathir regularly characterises human rights activists as cultural imperialists. In 1994, Mahathir, presenting the opening address at an international conference, 'Rethinking Human Rights', held in Malaysia, argued that, after the close of the Cold War,

> 'neo-colonialism perpetuated the old hegemony ... a new international order was enunciated in which the powerful countries claim a right to impose their system of government, their free market and their concept of human rights on every country. All countries must convert to the multi-party system of government and practice the liberal views on human rights as conceived by the Europeans and North Americans.'[34]

Mahathir cites 'threat[ening] sanctions, withdrawal of aid, stoppage of loans, economic and trade boycotts and actual military strikes' as the tools employed by Western interests 'against those they accuse of violating human rights'. Here, Mahathir takes the position that the sovereign right must be vigilantly defended against attack by human rights advocates who 'have no respect for independence or territorial integrity in their zeal to uphold their human rights principles'.[35] The Chinese, Indian and Serbian governments have taken similar positions.

This anti-imperialist position grew in popularity during the East Asian currency crisis and the subsequent intervention by the IMF in regional economies. Mahathir once again drew an analogy to colonialism, arguing that conditions placed upon IMF bailouts were akin to economic colonialism. Within this context, he characterised the processes of globalisation as creating conditions representing 'a new approach by developed countries to colonize the poor'.[36] This economic colonialism, according to Mahathir, is 'much more insidious' than other forms of colonialism and many developing countries 'have found that we are more dependent than when we were colonies'.[37] Regardless of the veracity of the claims that the present order resembles colonial period orders, the allusions to colonialism have powerful rhetorical purchase.

COLONIAL PERIOD

While these debates assume that colonial legal orders were characterised by the absolute domination of local cultures by foreign forces, in fact, this same tension between the reach of foreign power and local political autonomy was prevalent. For example, British colonial policy similarly internalised these two goals of spreading the recognition and protection of human rights and also the cultural sovereignty of peripheral political units. W C Mommsen, the colonial legal historian, notes:

33 Harris (1997) p 173.
34 Quoted in Xinhau News Agency (1994) at 1.
35 Quoted in Xinhau News Agency (1994) at 1.
36 Quoted in Xinhau News Agency (1994) at 1.
37 Foreign Affairs Malaysia (1997) at 57.

'the pursuit of these two alternative goals, namely the civilzatory mission of the colonial power on the one hand, and the advisability of non-interference with customary law, in order not to arouse the resistance of the local population against the benevolent rule of their colonial masters, could not be easily reconciled with one another.'[38]

Thus claims of 'cultural imperialism' by leaders of developing countries which assume that imperialism or colonialism was equivalent to the absolute and untrammelled imposition of Western legal orders on their peripheral territories are misconceived.

At the same time, critics of these leaders who argue that the absence of absolute domination of domestic legal orders precludes continuities with the colonial period rule are also mistaken. Instead, the central tension between sovereign absolutism and the extent of the legitimate reach of human rights law was also manifest during the colonial period. Similarly, just as this tension during the colonial period occurred within the context of trans-jurisdictional commercial engagement, today many of the most vocal adherents to the 'cultural imperialism' position hail from nations with extensive transnational commercial relations. This commercial engagement involves supporting domestic governments in the East Asian region and also the collaborative refashioning of the local legal orders so as to make them more tailored to commercial needs. As a result of this commercial engagement, foreign interests and local elites collaboratively create customary practices that are subsequently the matter of international scrutiny.

In proto-Malaysia the dual legal system manifested itself in the Resident System. From 1895 until the creation of the Malaysian nation-state, relations between the British and the proto-Malaysian states were solidified through treaties and agreements, establishing the British Resident System.[39] While official policy prohibited intervention in local matters except under specific circumstances, in practice, local laws were regularly refashioned. According to M B Hooker, the conception of sovereignty in nineteenth-century British overseas territories was based upon 'the "amount" of internal regulation assumed or exercised'.[40] So sovereignty was negotiated rather than absolute.[41]

The representations of the British Resident System suggest that customary laws were determined entirely by local political societies. However, since the 1980s scholars have increasingly questioned this assumption.[42] For instance, Sally Falk Moore has termed customary laws 'composite colonial constructions' in which 'current social/cultural systems like souped-up automobiles are constructions made out of new and used parts'.[42a] Francis Snyder explains the making of customary law as follows:

'Though "customary law" implies historical continuity, its origins are actually relatively recent. The notion of customary law in Africa and elsewhere was specific to particular historical circumstances. It belonged to an ideology that generally accompanied and formed part of colonial domination.'[43]

The creation of customary law, according to Snyder, was subsidiary to commercial concerns: 'Both the concrete forms and its conceptualization resulted from changes in social relations associated with the transformation of precapitalist modes

38 Mommsen (1992).
39 Maxwell and Gibson (1924).
40 Hooker (1995) p 312.
41 See eg Johnston (1969) pp 4–6.
42 See eg Merry (1991; 1988); Moore (on file with present author).
42a Moore (1986) pp 5, 10.
43 Snyder (1981) at 49.

of production and the sub-sumption of precapitalist social formation with the capitalist economy.'[44] Thus, negotiations between the Crown's prerogatives and local customary law. What was assumed local was often the product of a collaborative effort between certain foreign and local interests. For example, while the introduction of British law into the Straits Settlements was subject to local customs, when customary law operated 'unjustly or oppressively' it was derogated.[45]

In proto-Malaysia, the movement to abolish slavery is both an instance of the civilising mission of the British and illustrative of the composite nature of customary law. W E Maxwell, a British administrator, was one of the primary compilers of Malay customary law. His two major works, *Laws and Customs* and *Law Relating to Slavery*,[46] were presented as Malay customary law treatises. At the same time, they were designed to effectuate changes in the status quo of customary law in proto-Malaysia. *Laws and Customs* dealt with land law in Perak. The treatise was presented during a time of change as local land laws transformed in response to political and economic changes wrought by British overseas rule. Hooker explains: '*Laws and Customs* is written for the information of serving officers of government and for investors in the area – planters and miners.'[47]

This treatise, like Maxwell's work on slavery, blurred the 'is' and the 'ought'. Maxwell presented Malay custom as static and uniform. As it was neither, Maxwell's articulation of the current state of Malay customary law functionally advocated legal change. By picking and choosing customary practices supporting his position of the current state of the law, Maxwell created a customary law to serve British administrative purposes. Unlike *Laws and Customs*, in *Law Relating to Slavery*, Maxwell explicitly argued for a change in Malay customary law.

During the colonial period the British formed dual legal systems in the proto-Malaysian territories. Generally, the interests of the transnational commercial domain trumped the local political domain's interests. At the same time, British citizens along with local Malays challenged the commercial status quo by asserting 'rights' to civilisation. The following sections move forward to the present era, examining how these same tensions between transnational commerce, domestic politics and human rights manifest themselves in the context of the MSC.

THE CURRENT SCENE

In the last 20 years, globalisation has displaced the Cold War as the dominant geopolitical narrative. While security interests drove foreign policy during the Cold War, globalisation has reoriented agendas towards facilitating national economic competitiveness and effectuating integration into the global economy.[48] In the present era, capitalism and democracy are often expressed as fellow travellers, but the number of international institutions established to promote commerce dwarfs institutions devoted to encouraging democracy. As a result, the growth of transnational commerce has outpaced the development of human rights. In Malaysia, where leaders view commerce and human rights as unnatural partners, democratic and human rights reforms are rarely successfully transnationally effectuated.

44 Snyder (1981) at 49.
45 Buss-Tjen (1958) at 255–256.
46 Maxwell (1890a; 1890b).
47 Hooker (1995) p 365.
48 Falk (present volume).

In its 7th Malaysia Plan: 1996–2000, the government describes how it has shifted its foreign policy orientation away from Cold War mandates and towards the concerns of globalisation. Section 22.02 of the Plan states:

> 'While economic imperatives were a feature of Malaysia's foreign policy, the emphasis has traditionally been on cooperation in the political, cultural and security fields. The consistent purpose of this policy, premised on the principles of respect for the independence, sovereignty, territorial integrity and non-interference in the affairs of other nations, enhanced the country's international standing. In recent years, as national and international considerations became closely interwoven as a consequence of globalization, and given the openness of Malaysia's economy, the economic dimension assumed a more proactive posture in addressing the emerging regional and global issues.'[49]

Malaysian commercial interests and their governmental advocates have found business partners abroad. At the same time, Malaysian democratic and human rights practices have been the subject of intense international scrutiny. However, while criticism has been frequent, the needs and desires of the transnational commercial class generally trump human rights concerns in the priorities of Malaysia's leadership.

Foreign commercial actors have shown keen interest in economic opportunities in Malaysia. In the 7th Malaysia Plan, the government talks of how 'the focus of bilateral cooperation between Malaysia and other countries was on the economic field'. This co-operation had concrete results, facilitating 'an increase in trade and investment between Malaysia and these countries' through bilateral instruments and foreign direct and indirect investment in Malaysia.[50] To accomplish this transnationalisation of its commercial sector, Malaysia reoriented its domestic legal order. Reformulation meant a review of tariff, tax and financial regulations with an eye towards providing foreigners with 'improved market access'.

While the Malaysian government has been willing to reformulate the domestic legal order to serve transnational commercial interests, it has aggressively opposed reformulating the domestic legal order to accommodate foreign demands for democracy and human rights reform. Instead, it has claimed such demands amount to cultural colonialism. Such colonialism, according to Mahathir, is in derogation of internationally derived sovereign rights. When foreign commercial interests make human rights demands, the Malaysian response is publicly less antagonistic. These demands are not frequently made and rarely is compliance vigilantly monitored.

Transnational commercial integration

Post-independence Malaysia has remained highly integrated into the global economy and integration has accelerated since the 1980s. In 1997, Malaysia was one of the five biggest recipients of foreign direct investment in the world.[51] To understand the legal order facilitating this transnational commercial integration, first the economic scene must be briefly recounted.

---

49 7th Malaysia Plan: 1996–2000, s 22.02, para 659.
50 7th Malaysia Plan: 1996–2000, s 22.02, para 661.
51 Islam and Chowdhury (1996).

In the 1980s, a global recession set in and the prices of many commodities were depressed. At the same time, wages increased in the US and Europe in the mid-1980s. These related developments spurred companies to travel away from the US and Europe in search of low-wage labour. Japanese companies also sought out offshore havens in response to the Plaza Accords of 1985, which signalled an elevation of labour costs in Japan.[52] During this period and in response to its own sovereign debt crisis, Malaysia reoriented its domestic economy so as to attract these foreign companies to locate segments of their production processes in the country, passing the Promotion of Investment Act in 1986. This Act provides foreign companies with special privileges and exemptions from domestic tax laws. If a company's investment is in line with Malaysia's development goals, then the government will grant it 'pioneer status'. This status allows the company to benefit from preferential treatment by the government.

Up until the 1980s, Malaysia's foreign trade was dominated by primary commodities such as rubber and tin. Post-independence development was initially geared towards import-substitution.[53] Beginning in the 1970s, Malaysia moved towards a strategy of export-led growth. This strategy involved opening the economy up to foreign TNCs. Opening was not comprehensive and elements of the domestic market remained protected. To facilitate a partial opening, the government established export processing zones (EPZs).[54] Within the EPZs the government lifted legal restrictions on foreign ownership of firms operating within the country. Although the government frequently permitted 100% foreign ownership, it encouraged foreign companies to establish joint venture enterprises with domestic public corporations to promote a transfer of research and development.[55] Foreign companies often found this arrangement agreeable, as a domestic partner provided privileged access to the government's legal processes.

Since 1996, growth in FDI flows into Malaysia have stagnated, leading to a transformation of the country's industrial strategy and the creation of the MSC. Throughout the 1980s and early 1990s, foreign companies have located labour-intensive operations in Malaysia, capitalising on low wages, adequate infrastructure, and a stable political environment. During this period, foreign companies have invested heavily in the electrical and electronics products and food-processing industries. The primary investors by nationality have been Hong Kong, Japan, Singapore, the UK, and the US.[56] Starting in 1996, however, a number of factors have led to slow down in the growth of FDI into the country.

In Malaysia, many of these foreign firms were high-technology TNCs. As Snyder has demonstrated by reference to the toy industry, an understanding of the role of law in transnational commerce requires attention to global production processes.[57] The presence of US high-technology TNCs overseas was the result of 'restructuring' of the high-technology industry.[58] US microchip-makers have progressively moved portions of their production processes overseas as a result of a number of endogenous factors, such as the ability to develop a highly segmented production process. It was thus possible to design microchips in one

52 National Economic Action Council (1998) p 16.
53 Mohamed (1994) p 233.
54 Ariff (1994) p 39.
55 Bende-Nabende (1999) pp 20–21.
56 Eng (1998) p 2.
57 Snyder (present volume).
58 Mazurek (1999) pp 89–112; Siegel and Markoff (1985) pp 179–202.

place and to manufacture them in a distant locale. Exogenous factors such as international competition in microchip-making also forced US companies to seek less expensive labour in developing countries. Additionally, the transfer of production processes overseas allowed the companies to transfer many of the negative externalities of the production process abroad. As environmental groups succeeded in publicising that the supposedly clean high-technology industry polluted heavily, the transfer of the more toxic segments of the production process overseas meant that companies could evade environmental accountability. Malaysia has been a popular overseas manufacturing base for US companies. A large and strictly controlled female population of workers has been provided by the government. The government FDI promotional literature at the time reflected this perceived competitive advantage:

> 'The manual dexterity of the oriental female is famous world over. Her hands are small and she works fast with extreme care. Who, therefore, could be better qualified by nature and inheritance to contribute to the efficiency of a bench-assembly production than the oriental girl?'[59]

Foreign and domestic factors caused a decline in FDI into Malaysia since 1996. The stagnation of the Japanese economy and falling value of the yen have reduced investment flows. Also, as China has opened up to foreign investors and its currency has devalued, companies have shifted production facilities there. At the same time, Malaysia's labour market has become saturated and the government can no longer offer an endless supply of cheap and disciplined labour to foreign companies.[60] As a result, Malaysia has sought to reorient its economy towards multimedia, embarking on strategies to upgrade its domestic labour skills, to attract high-technology foreign transnational corporations, and thus to move up on the international economic value chain.

Malaysia has reformed its domestic legal order to facilitate transnational commerce. For example, the 7th Malaysia Plan states: 'A comprehensive review of IT-related legislation will be undertaken to promote more orderly development of IT and ensure that prevailing laws and regulations do not constrain the nation's efforts of becoming an information rich-society.'[61] This reformulation of the domestic legal order has not been limited to such directly IT-related laws as the Contracts Act 1950, the Telecommunications Act 1950, the Copyright Act 1987 and the Broadcasting Act 1988. In addition, new cyberlaws have been enacted, including the Digital Signature Act 1997, the Computer Crimes Act 1997, the Telemedicine Act 1997 and the Multimedia and Communications Act 1998. Also, amendment of immigration laws, affirmative action laws, and a host of other measures has been undertaken in order to ensure a legislative environment suited to developing the IT sector in the country.

This reformulation of the domestic legal order is largely effectuated by the executive branch. In developing countries, the executive branch often holds more power than the judiciary. In effect, law in these contexts is often what the governing executive determines. Mahathir has the longest tenure of any ruler in East Asia and has used law to maintain his position. For example, Mahathir has

---

59 Quoted in Siegel and Markoff (1985) p 181.
60 National Economic Action Council (1998) p 16.
61 7th Malaysia Plan, s 14.142.

jailed opposition leaders regularly, using the Internal Securities Act 1960 when his position has been threatened. Further, Mahathir's political party, the UMNO, controls Parliament.

The creation of the MSC and also the export-led growth of the country in the last 20 years have depended not only upon the authoritarian executive's domination of the country's legal order, but also upon foreign commercial support. This transnational collaboration is evidenced in the legal process of the MSC.

Creation of culture for commerce

A partnership of foreign commercial and domestic political and business elites produce the legal processes of the MSC. Each party brings with it indispensable capital without which a mega-project like the Corridor would be an impossibility. Together they create the Corridor through a variety of legal mechanisms, including FDI laws, contracts and project finance deals. Roughly put, the Malaysian government provides its public law power, while foreign companies offer financing and expertise. The legal order of the MSC is transnationally conceived and is subject-matter based. It is the global commercial domain of the modern dual legal order. Just as colonial legal orders, the current order includes two domains, the legal aspects of global commerce and matters affecting it, on the one hand, and the legal aspects of local society, on the other.

While the Malaysian government presents the MSC as a national development plan, designed to leapfrog the country into developed nation status by the year 2020, in the first instance, the MSC is geared towards accommodating foreign commercial interests. The government makes clear that it will use its legislative capacity in the service of transnational companies: 'as a cornerstone of its move into the Information Age, Malaysia is transforming its legal and regulatory environment to support companies undertaking multimedia commerce.'[62] As planned, the MSC will be developed in three phases. Temporally, the MSC is geared to serving foreign companies first and the rest of the country later.

According to Malaysia's plan, the end goal of the government's policy is to transform Malaysia into a high-technology-based, knowledge-intensive society by the year 2020. This plan is to be effectuated in three stages. The first phase is devoted to creating 'an ideal multimedia environment to attract world class companies to use the MSC as a hub'.[63] This phase will run until 2003. The second phase will be devoted to linking the MSC to other cybercities in Malaysia and worldwide. This phase will run until 2010. In the third phase, according to the government, Malaysia will be transformed into a knowledge society. Thus, the initial transformation of the Malaysian legal order is tailored to the needs of high-technology TNCs.

The Prime Minister is unambiguous in his enunciation of the government's role. For example, he speaks of the MSC as 'a gift from the Malaysian government'.[64] Further, the Multimedia Development Corporation (MDC), an executive branch publicly backed, privately incorporated company, operationalises the 'business-focused "can do" government' in the service of

---

62 Multimedia Development Corporation (1997) p 6.
63 Othman (1999) p 7.
64 Multimedia Development Corporation (1997) p 2.

transnational commercial interests. The international community has been impressed by Malaysia's 'can do' approach. In its 1993 publication, *East Asia Miracle*, the World Bank praised Malaysia's 'can do' government,[65] speaking favourably about how 'Malaysia shifted from policies that resulted in business-government conflict to highly structured mechanisms to encourage business government cooperation'.[66] The MDC also speaks of the remarkable growth of the Malaysian economy in the past decade in the MDC promotional literature:

> 'Located in the heart of East Asia, Malaysia leads the "tiger nations" that are currently experiencing phenomenal growth. Propelled by massive capital investments, substantial production gains, and business-focused "can do" government, the per-capita GDP of Malaysia's 20 million inhabitants has skyrocked in the last two decades.'[67]

Thus, Malaysia's executive driven growth is promoted and backed by a premier international institution.

This business-friendly attitude is a cornerstone of the government's Malaysia Inc. policy.[68] This policy is an explicit borrowing from the Japanese government's Japan Inc.[69] At the inauguration of the Malaysian Business Council, a government forum designed to strengthen public-private partnerships in commercial matters, the Prime Minister described Malaysia Inc. as 'a concept that is based on a partnership between the government and the private sector, a concept of a nation as a giant corporation in which the public and private together tasked with ensuring its success and are entitled to share the benefits'.[70]

Malaysia, like many developing countries, has a very powerful executive branch. The Malaysian Prime Minister, Dr Mahathir, is a member of the UMNO, which controls Parliament. As a result, Dr Mahathir enjoys broad legislative discretion. The creation of the laws of the MSC evidences this executive discretion. Also, it demonstrates the role played by foreign companies in supporting this governance structure and how the companies benefit from their patronage.

The Malaysian government's business-friendly approach is appealing to foreign high-technology TNCs. John Cage, the Director of Sun Microsystems's Science Office, makes clear that he appreciates the value of a semi-authoritarian state. Speaking of the attributes of Prime Minister Dr Mahathir's impressive political power, Cage says: 'A lot of the business crowd disparages politicians, but you can track Mahathir's performance. He does what he says he's going to do. He'd run any American CEO into the ground.'[71] Frank Sumner Smith III of the Big Five international consulting firm Ernst and Young refers to the Malaysian government as its 'business partner'.[72] Together the Malaysian government and foreign high-technology TNCs recreate the global domain of the dual legal order also manifest in the colonial period.

65 World Bank (1993).
66 World Bank (1993) p 87.
67 Multimedia Development Corporation (1997) p 17.
68 Kuok (1997); Mahathir (1997); Rahman (1997).
69 Mahathir (1999).
70 Mahathir (1997) p 398.
71 Armstrong (1997).
72 Smith (1997).

Two legal orders co-exist within the country, one applying to MSC-status companies and another to the domestic population. The MSC's International Advisory Panel (IAP) members at the Third Annual Meeting spoke favourably of this arrangement, saying: 'A "one country two systems" mode of operation should exist separating the national policies from those of the MSC.'[73] The intra-Corridor policies are founded upon a Bill of Guarantees, granting privileged status to the MSC-status companies. These Guarantees are to:

1. provide a world-class physical and information infrastructure;
2. allow unrestricted employment of local and foreign knowledge workers;
3. ensure freedom of ownership requirements;
4. give the freedom to source capital globally for MSC infrastructure, and the right to borrow globally;
5. provide competitive financial incentives;
6. become a regional leader in intellectual property protection and cyberlaws;
7. ensure no Internet censorship;
8. provide globally competitive telecom tariffs;
9. tender key infrastructure contracts to leading companies to use the MSC as their regional hub; and
10. provide a high-powered implementation agency to act as a one-stop super shop.

The Bill of Guarantees is clearly geared towards facilitating transnational commerce. While the geographic designator 'Corridor' suggests that a legally autonomous corridor exists within the country, just as during the colonial period, the legal order not only manages commerce, but also matters affecting commerce.

Many of the Bill of Guarantees require extra-Corridor legal action. For example, safeguarding the intellectual property rights of TNCs requires extra-Corridor legislative action. Dr Khaw Lake Tee, Senior Manager of the MDC's Legal and Regulation Department, justifies the extra-Corridor enforcement of intellectual property laws: 'with the Bill of Guarantees, Malaysia is set to be a leader in intellectual property protection worldwide. Because of the detrimental effects of piracy on the efforts of the MSC, and on Malaysia's reputation as a whole, we are determined to curb it.' To do so, the MDC brought together a number of government agencies, including the Ministry of Domestic Trade and Consumer Affairs, the Ministry of International Trade, the Attorney-General's Chambers and the MDC, as well as private companies, to develop strategies for ensuring the protection of intellectual property throughout the country.[74] Through these dialogue sessions, the MDC formulated recommendations for enforcement action to the MSC Implementation Committee, the executive branch overseeing the development of the MSC, chaired by the Prime Minister. The upshot of this meeting was that executive action geared towards matters affecting commerce was to occur outside of the legislative confines of the Corridor.

To ensure the MSC-status companies would enjoy their Bill of Guarantee rights, extra-Corridor legislative action was taken. The government established the Special Copyright Task Force, a part of the Enforcement Division of the Ministry of Domestic Trade and Consumer Affairs.[75] This Task Force has the powers 'to

73 Multimedia Super Corridor International Advisory Panel (1997) Annex D, p 5.
74 Cheong and Mirandah (1999).
75 Cheong and Mirandah (1999).

conduct raids on outlets suspected of selling pirated optical discs' and will 'compile data on legal and illegal plants, to enable effective mitigating measures to be instituted'.[76] So rather than a strict geographical delineation of the dual legal order, instead the regulation is subject-matter based. Thus the transnational commercial domain of the dual legal order comprises not only laws regulating transnational commerce, but also matters affecting it. Making Corridor guarantees meaningful requires extra-Corridor regulation. The Malaysian government and transnational companies together drive the extra-Corridor legal reformulation of matters affecting their commercial relations.[77]

The reformulation of the Malaysian legal order by TNCs and the government is accomplished through a number of formal and informal legal mechanisms. One non-traditional forum is the MSC's IAP, a transnational forum comprising international leaders in high-technology. Members include executives of top companies, such as Microsoft, Intel and Sun Microsystems. It also includes leading digital literati, such as Alvin Toffler and Lady McDougall Dougan, and leading writers, consultants and academics, like Kenichi Ohmae and Professor William Miller. The purpose of the IAP is to:

- Provide personal counsel to The Right Honourable Prime Minister of Malaysia on shaping Malaysia's Multimedia Super Corridor (MSC) to the mutual advantage of both Malaysia IAP members.
- Provide direct input to help shape polices and create the perfect environment for realising the full potential of multimedia technologies.[78]

The IAP is both transnational in composition and commercially orientated in focus. The IAP not only provides the legislative capacity to foreign interests, but also a forum designed to attract IAP member companies and other foreign TNCs to locate operations in Malaysia, as well as to attract international project finance money.

The IAP concept was initially proposed by Kenichi Ohmae, an internationally acclaimed high-technology business guru, who worked for years as a principal for the international business consultancy firm, McKinsey & Company. Also the author of hundreds of books and articles on globalisation and business strategy, Ohmae is much in demand as an advisor to businesses and governments as well as a regular visiting professor in US academic institutions. While holding a visiting post at Stanford University's School of Business in 1997, Ohmae conceived the idea of the IAP for the MSC.[79] This meeting was a success and marked the official launching of the MSC.

At the initial IAP meeting, the regulatory groundwork for the Corridor was laid, thousands of miles from Malaysia and remote from the domestic legislative process. According to one Advisory Panel member, at the Stanford meeting, the Prime Minister chaired a brainstorming session with IAP members. Sitting around a boardroom table, Mahathir asked the members to tell him exactly what they desired by way of laws, policies and financial incentives to locate operations within the 40 by 15km strip of land comprising the Corridor.

---

76 Cheong and Mirandah (1999).
77 Microsoft also has used the Malaysian courts to safeguard its copyright protections, suing local companies for copyright infringement and trademark violations: Cheong and Mirandah (1999).
78 Multimedia Super Corridor International Advisory Panel (1997) p 1.
79 Interview with IAP member.

Immediately following the brainstorming session, the Prime Minister proceeded to a news conference at which he announced the Bill of Guarantees. The Guarantees were a distillation of the suggestions proffered by the IAP members. While the Bill of Guarantees was most likely prepared in anticipation of the meeting, the effect was to make clear that not only would the MSC legislative process be driven by foreign commercial needs, but also that the Prime Minister was committed to including foreigners in the domestic legal process. This, according to one IAP member, was how the IAP members perceived the announcement.[80]

The IAP also served an important legitimating function, establishing the international credentials of the MSC project. For a societal project of the MSC's scale to succeed, it needs to establish international legitimacy. By mobilising the backing of so many high-technology luminaries, the MSC ensured it would be taken seriously by international financiers, the media, and high-technology companies. Both the IAP members and the Malaysian government realised the legitimacy function created by their partnership's synergies. At the Third Annual IAP meeting, members made the point that 'positive image is important' and that the 'MSC's image both locally and internationally must be strongly projected'. They suggest 'a general strategy using Internet, press and media blitzes as channels, and targeted markets'.[81] Further, they told the Prime Minister that he could 'make use of MSC companies in making a positive projection'.[82]

The legitimacy conferred on the MSC by the backing of foreign TNCs is not lost on the Prime Minister. The MSC ran into some difficulties in 1998 when a prominent IAP member threatened to leave the Panel in a letter to the International Herald Tribune. At the time, Dr. Mahathir questioned 'if an adviser says "don't invest in Malaysia", what's going to happen?'[83] Culling relationships with key public and private international figures to advance Malaysia's geopolitical and economic position is an explicit function of the Prime Minister's office according to the country's 7th Malaysia Plan. As a planned economy, the government issues regularly plans laying out its approach to development. In line with the statement in the 7th Malaysia Plan, Mahathir 'tends to eschew trips with a primarily symbolic significance and spends more time on "working visits" selling Malaysia to foreign investors and smoothing the way for local companies to break into oversees markets'.[84]

The foreign trips also include legislative action. The Prime Minister uses foreign trips to promote commercial investment in the country. This represents a shift in Malaysia's foreign policy towards commercial concerns. According to the 7th Malaysia Plan:

> 'During the Sixth Plan period, Malaysia cooperated closely with the international community in the interest of national development. Malaysia's international cooperation efforts focused on economic considerations in line with the reorientation of the country's foreign policy. Accordingly, close bilateral relations were forged with both developed and developing countries in order to deepen and accelerate economic interactions.'[85]

---

80 Interview with IAP member.
81 Multimedia Super Corridor International Advisory Panel (1997) Annex D, p 5.
82 Multimedia Super Corridor International Advisory Panel (1997) Annex D, p 5.
83 Porter (1999).
84 Kynge (1997c).
85 7th Malaysia Plan, s 22.03, p 659).

This reorientation marked a general restructuring of Malaysia's foreign policy operation:

> 'During the Plan period, the focus of bilateral cooperation between Malaysia and other countries was on the economic field. Such cooperation facilitated an increase in trade and investment between Malaysia and these countries. In this regard, Malaysia improved market access by streamlining trade-related procedures and reviewing instruments such as tariffs, taxes, and financial regulations. In addition, four new offices were established abroad by the Malaysian External Trade Development Corporation (MATRADE) since its inception in 1993. These efforts partly contributed to an increase in the value of total trade from RM 158.8 billion in 1990 to RM 379.9 billion in 1995. The countries total trade value for 1994 represented 1.4 per cent of the total world trade and Malaysia was then the 19th largest exporter and the 18th largest importing nation in the world.'[86]

An article in the Financial Times describes the Prime Minister as 'the country's chief marketeer'. According to the writer, since 'business and politics are so closely intertwined in Malaysia' this role of the Prime Minister 'seems only natural'.[87]

During Mahathir's trips abroad, he signed bilateral direct investment agreements and also government contracts. From 1991 to 1996, Malaysia entered into 19 bilateral trade agreements, 21 bilateral payment arrangements, 25 investment guarantee agreements, and 19 avoidance of double taxation agreements.[88] These treaties are primarily designed to promote FDI into the country, by providing a legally enforceable guarantee by party states to protect investments of each other's foreign nationals.

While abroad, Mahathir also uses his personal connections with foreign leaders in order to facilitate contracts between his own public and private corporate nationals and foreign states. For example, some suggested that the success of Malaysian power company, YTL Corp, in acquiring a 51% stake in Zimbabwe's state-owned Kwange power plant was made possible by 'Mahathir's close relations with Mr. Robert Mugabe, the Zimbabwe President'. Also, Telekom Malaysia, the state telecommunications company's successful contract with the South African government was, according to some, facilitated by his 'close contacts' with Nelson Mandela.[89] The extensive foreign trips by Mahathir to promote the MSC underscore the place of diplomacy in facilitating commerce.

The MSC is often presented as Mahathir's 'pet project'. In fact, Mahathir took his longest leave of absence from Malaysia, two months, in May 1997 to promote the MSC. The Malaysian government journal, *Foreign Affairs Malaysia*, is replete with speeches given by Mahathir during this period as he travelled to the US, Canada, Europe and Japan, promoting the MSC, signing contracts and entering into inter-state agreements. The importance of these trips extends beyond the tangible contracts; it creates a legitimacy for the MSC which translates into future success.

The IAP itself is an example of the importance of these trips in establishing international credibility. The backing of these companies effectuated during a trip abroad not only encourages other companies to invest directly in the MSC, but also is a means of attracting financing for joint venture partnerships. The IAP

86 7th Malaysia Plan, s 22.07, p 661.
87 Kynge (1997c).
88 7th Malaysia Plan, s 22.06, p 661.
89 Kynge (1997c).

members concurred that for small to medium-sized enterprises, the IAP members endorsement would be instrumental in attracting these companies. In addition, many high-technology TNCs planned to raise international funds to support the MSC.[90] Large scale projects such as the MSC require tremendous outlays of foreign capital, so project finance money is typically provided by a number of sources, including commercial banks, government budgets and inter-governmental agencies. Each of these parties provides a different form of capital with its own conditions and terms. Commercial banks are the most demanding, and often advance short-term loans. Importantly, for our purposes, project financing requires project legitimacy to achieve favourable terms.

One of the key attractions of the MSC is its infrastructure contracts. The creation of the MSC's infrastructure involved a privatisation of several key public utilities, such as telecommunications and transportation, as well as the privatisation of the real estate industry. In the MSC's promotional literature, laws are described as 'soft infrastructure' and telecommunications, property and transportation attributes as 'hard infrastructure'. The creation of this 'hard infrastructure' was the product of a legally effectuated privatisation process in the telecommunications and transportation fields initiated in the 1980s, first with the 1983 privatisation policy, then in 1987 with the creation of Telekom Malaysia, and in 1997 with the building of the Kuala Lumpur International Airport. Both the incorporation of Telekom Malaysia and also the building of the airport was carried forth transnationally through FDI and project finance laws. Following the creation of the MSC's hard infrastructure, a second wave of infrastructure building was internalised in the MSC project itself, with its seven flagship applications.

To facilitate foreign investment in, and to attract international financing for, the MSC, the government privatised the telecommunications industry in the 1980s. While Malaysian law has not legislated a public monopoly, Telekom Malaysia enjoyed a de facto monopoly. Since Telekom Malaysia was a public corporation under the Ministry of Energy, Telecommunications and Posts in the executive branch, the absence of a legislated monopoly provided the Prime Minister with discretion over licensing. Telekom Malaysia has complained that this discretion leaves it vulnerable to the Prime Minister's policy whims.[91]

Telekom Malaysia privatised in 1987. After privatisation, the Ministry of Finance maintained a 76% shareholding, with domestic shareholders holding 16% and foreign investors 8%.[92] At present, it has grown to be one of the most profitable companies in Malaysia, second only to the state-owned oil company, PETRONAS. Telekom Malaysia not only is contracted to complete all MSC telecommunications infrastructure projects, but also owns a portion of Cyberview Holdings and operates the Multimedia University. The land law reforms and telecommunications licensing schemes were undertaken in order to encourage FDI into and project finance for the MSC.

Another major infrastructure project undertaken to facilitate the Corridor in the first place is the Kuala Lumpur International Airport (KLIA). The KLIA was

---

90 Kynge (1997c).

91 Ure (1995) p 57.

92 To give some idea of the relationship between these privatised public companies and project financing, consider a recent deal in which Telekom Malaysia sold equipment to a foreign company and then rented it back for its own use. This deal was conducted under Islamic law and advised on by the UK law firm of Norton Rose. It brought together investors from the Middle East and South-East Asia: Legal Advisors on Telekom Malaysia's $6Million Leasing Facility' (1999).

the largest public project ever undertaken in Malaysia. To accomplish it, both foreign know-how and capital were required. Once again, FDI and project finance went hand-in-hand. The airport-building contracts were awarded by the Malaysian government, which provided much of the project financing. Importantly, it also furnished its executive backing by awarding the contract in the first place. The contract was awarded to an international consortium, comprising Tamen Corporation, a Japanese company, Sapura Holdings, Sdn Bhd, a Malaysian company, and Harris Airport System, a US company. Money for this project came from Malaysian sources, Japanese soft money and Islamic banks.[93] The laws facilitating this financing come from many legal traditions and systems and were co-ordinated for the purpose of a project. Further, the Malaysian government, through guaranteed loans, committed support to the endeavour. This support meant the aid of a friendly state regulator. To ensure close government involvement in the project, the International Airport Berhad was established. This public company was responsible 'for the construction and commissioning of the airport'.[94]

The development of the MSC requires transforming oil and palm estates into the 15 by 40km high-technology Corridor. To do so, the land must be cleared and construction projects undertaken on a wide scale. The transformation of this land was effectuated under the National Land Code and the Prime Minister's Office attained a certificate of urgency to expedite the process. Most of the land was owned by the state government of Selangor, which became a major stakeholder in Cyberview Holdings, along with the largest private sector real estate holder in the region, Golden Hope Plantations.

Much of the real estate investment is handled by Cyberview Holdings. Cyberview Holdings is responsible for developing Cyberjaya, an MSC smart city and the new site for the Malaysian government. This real estate holding company is an international consortium comprised of Setia Haruman Sdn Bhd (55%), Japan's Nippon Telegraph and Telephone (15%), Golden Hope Plantation Bhd (15%), Parmodakan Nasional Bhd (5%), the Selangor State government (5%) and the Multimedia Media Development Corporation (10%).[95] Thus an international consortium comprised of public and private companies is charged with real estate development. The participation of Japan's Nippon Telegraph and Telephone not only provides high profile legitimacy, but also makes the real estate development consortium a more attractive destination for foreign finance money. So FDI and project finance here go hand-in-hand.

The creation of the MSC's legal order has required a major reformulation of the Malaysian domestic legal order. This reformulation has been designed to serve foreign TNCs. As such, sovereignty and domestic law-making capacity have been shared by foreign TNCs and Malaysian political and commercial elites. The recreation of the domestic legal order facilitates global commerce. This reformulation of the domestic legal order by a transnational community has been born from close collaboration. In this partnership, 'Asian democracy' has been an attribute TNCs have been keen not only to benefit from, but also to support. TNCs are quite clear in their interest in benefiting from so-called Asian democracy and also commercialising Asian values.

---

93 Richards (1999).
94 Richards (1999).
95 Ho (1999).

Also a key component is the ongoing infrastructure projects in Malaysia. These projects are termed flagship applications and include telemedicine, smart cards, the development of a paperless government and borderless marketing. The Bill of Guarantees allows MSC-status companies the privilege of bidding on the flagship applications, which are special government-backed projects designed to reformulate the domestic economy. Foreign TNCs, by actively pursuing the flagship applications, which are primarily domestic government and private sector works projects, have buttressed Asian democracy in Malaysia. Through the flagship applications of the MSC, foreign commercial interests are invited to participate in and benefit from Asian values. As noted above, one of the Bill of Guarantee advantages offered to foreign TNCs for basing regional headquarters in Malaysia is to be able to bid on infrastructure projects and the flagship applications – Nippon was rewarded with its place in cyberview holdings because of its early commitment, basing regional operations in the MSC.

A flagship application, the multi-purpose card is a cornerstone of the MSC and will be developed by Malaysia's Bank Negra and Country Syndergy Sdn Bhd in connection with Banksys SA of Belgium. Through this international partnership, the 'Asian way' will be fortified as Malaysia enters into the information age. The multi-purpose card has undergone some changes since its initial conception. Originally the card was to be 'a single and common platform', a credit card with a computer chip, that would 'contain both government and commercial information' to 'radically improve the ease with which ordinary Malaysians conduct routine transactions with government and private companies'. A single card would serve as a national identification, driver's licence, immigration card, health card and electronic purse containing electronic cash and other personal financial information. This merging of consumer and citizenship would, according to the government, 'be symbolically important as a tool of the Information Age'.[96] Subsequently, a decision was made to develop the card initially as two separate cards.

Although two cards would be developed independently, this did not mean that the goal of merging consumer and citizen had been jettisoned, only delayed. Furthermore, foreign TNCs would play a role in facilitating this eventuality. When the contract was awarded to Banksys SA of Belgium, it was based on their developing a common platform for both the bank card and government card. The MDC described the advantages of a common platform: 'Since both cards are to be based on a single technology platform, it will not be too hard to integrate their various applications onto one single card.' Thus, '[u]ltimately there will be just one card that offers all features of the Government and Payment cards'.[97] Of course, this multi-purpose card not only was a symbol of empowerment, but also meant that the business and government communities could share information and offer consumers up as a competitive advantage to foreign TNCs. The interest of TNCs in commercialising Asian values underscores the role the multi-purpose card might play in serving transnational needs, and is fortified by Malaysia's selling of the MSC as a test-bed for multimedia applications. At the Third Annual IAP Meeting, companies made clear to the government that they saw great advantages in Malaysia as not only a growing consumer base, but also for its local knowledge, which would help companies develop Asian values-based, multimedia content for the region.

---

96 Multimedia Development Corporation (1997) at 12.
97 Multimedia Development Corporation (1998).

In order to develop Asian content, local knowledge workers are required. The IAP members suggested a government repatriation policy to supplement the development of multimedia universities in the country, and also relaxing of immigration restrictions by the government to attract regional information technology workers. The IAP advocated 'a mechanism for incentives to encourage the return of Malaysian trained and working abroad as "[k]nowledge workers equipped with multilingual capabilities were required to create software for the region".[98] Asian content was clearly valued, the IAP members in fact suggested 'content creation based on Asian values and cultures' should be a niche area for the MSC.[99] In exuberance the IAP members proposed that 'Asians can create content based on their own culture and propagate that throughout the world'.[100] The desire to capitalise on Asian values was shared by the Prime Minister.

Mahathir had explicitly sold Asian values to high-technology TNCs. By amending the education laws to create the high-technology geared Multimedia University, which would be operated by the transnationalised Telekom Malaysia, the government sought to home-grow Asian knowledge workers for TNCs. Demonstrating the linkages between citizenry and commerce, Malaysia spoke of 'nurturing a whole generation of knowledge workers "custom made" for the needs of MSC firms, through smart schools and the Multimedia University'.[101] Mahathir offered Malaysia up as a site to digitise Hollywood, localising content for the Asian region.[102] Mahathir proposed to Hollywood executives the creation of 'multicultural content creation centres' in Malaysia.[103] Hollywood studios would take advantage of Malaysia's entertainment village in a different way. By filming overseas the studios are able to opt out of the US union-dominated film industry. Malaysian workers, thinking that wages for the same work should be paid the same amount everywhere, demanded higher wages for film work. In response, the government quashed protests to ensure a business-friendly economy. Thus, the Asian values must be viewed as a collaborative product.

These are examples of the reformulation of the domestic cultural sphere for the purposes of facilitating transnational commerce where inter-elite consensus not conflict prevail. The next section will focus on cases in which the spread of human rights standards abuts sovereign absolutism as the jailing of the Deputy Prime Minister and the censorship of the Internet struggled to become matters affecting commerce.

Human rights as a matter affecting commerce

In 1997 at the First Annual IAP Meeting in Stanford, California, Mahathir promised no censorship on the Internet to MSC-status companies. While this policy seemed straightforward enough, it had its ambiguities. For example, what did it mean for a company to hold a right to no censorship on the Internet? Did it mean that a company had a right to a censor-free Internet, or instead that they could freely surf the web themselves? Would this right be enjoyed by both foreign

---

 98 Multimedia Super Corridor International Advisory Panel (1999).
 99 Multimedia Super Corridor International Advisory Panel (1999) p 5.
100 Multimedia Super Corridor International Advisory Panel (1999) Annex D, p 6.
101 Asia Inc. (1999).
102 Petrikin (1999).
103 Goh (1997).

and local knowledge workers of these companies? Would this right apply only to business-related activities? For example, when a foreign executive sat at his computer in his Malaysian home, would he be subject to the laws of the rest of the land regarding censorship on the Internet? By the time the IAP convened for the third time in Cyberjaya, Malaysia in 1999, these questions seemed moot. Malaysian officials represented to the IAP members at their annual meeting that: 'Malaysia does not have censorship on the Internet.' In addition, the recently promulgated legislation designed to overhaul media regulation in the country would boldly assert: 'Nothing in this Act shall be construed as permitting censorship of the Internet.'

This public statement by the government represented a concession. The initial plans for the Corridor as an autonomous legal field, distinct from the rest of the country, did not proceed as envisioned. In fact, as we have seen, the Corridor was not designed as an autonomous legal field, but instead as a semi-autonomous one. The Corridor would draw resources from the rest of the country, but only selectively return the favour. For example, the Employee Provident Fund, a government-controlled retirement scheme with a mandatory contribution by Malaysian workers of 10% of their income, funded much of the Corridor's infrastructure and allowed many projects to proceed during the financial crisis. However, many of these workers would, even if all went as planned, not reap the rewards of the Corridor for another 20 years. The directors of legal change in Malaysia, however, had to reckon with more than simply their legislative imaginations in shaping the contours of the Corridor and its relationship to the rest of the country.

As Sally Falk Moore has noted: 'innovative legislation, or other attempts to direct change often fail to achieve their intended purpose; and even when they succeed wholly or partially, they frequently carry with them unplanned and unexpected consequences.'[104] Not all was predictable, and plans in Malaysia began to unravel, or at least require reconfiguring. A struggle thus ensued over the legislative matrix of the Corridor, as a member of the IAP drew on domestic dissent, international human rights activism, and (he hoped) the commitment to human rights of transnational investors, to make the government deliver on the democratic promise of the Corridor. When the dust settled, however, although plans had been publicly re-articulated, private manoeuvrings as revealed in the legislative record and internal government documents indicated that much remained the same. Demands for democratisation were reframed as public relations challenges, and an external makeover seemed to do the trick.

As Frederick Douglas indicated, 'power concedes nothing without a demand'. And, in the case of Malaysia, a demand certainly existed. This demand was successfully made by a member of the IAP, Alvin Toffler, who threatened to resign from the Panel unless the government released from imprisonment Anwar and a personal friend, Dr Anees. In addition to demanding their release, Toffler indicated that the government's recent crackdown on political speech over the Internet must also cease. While the Prime Minister had met domestic political protest with police crackdowns and raids, when Toffler made these demands the response was less antagonistic. Mahathir was forced to change his position, indicating 'If an adviser says "don't invest in Malaysia", what's going to happen?'[105] While the prisoners were not released, the no-censorship legislation was

104   Moore (1978) p 58.
105   Porter (1999).

promulgated. Thus, a domestic political matter successfully became a matter affecting commerce through the demands made by a member of the IAP. However, although the government boldly proclaimed that no censorship would exist over the Internet, the legislative record indicated otherwise. In fact, the Multimedia and Communications Act 1998, while pronouncing no censorship, was replete with content regulation. This section will explain how this no-censorship guarantee came about and how its meaning changed between 1997 and 1999 as the political and commercial context in which it operated transmogrified.

During this period the transnational commercial sphere extended its reach into the domestic sphere in unexpected ways, forcing a shift in the initial bargain struck in 1997. As the maintenance of transnational commercial relationships became threatened by the inability of the government to maintain a rigid demarcation between the two domains of the dual legal order, Asian values of restricted speech came into conflict with the international human right to the free flow of information.[106] A negotiation ensued over whether free speech on the Internet would be a matter affecting commerce. Before describing the events from 1997–99, it is necessary to clarify the context in which the no-censorship pledge was made and then where, in fact, according to Malaysian law, Internet censorship was in 1999.

When the no-censorship guarantee was announced shortly after the initial IAP meeting to a group in Hollywood by Mahathir, a member of the audience expressed surprise that the same country that banned the film *Schindler's List* as propaganda was now guaranteeing no Internet censorship.[107] Not only was Malaysia not welcoming of certain Hollywood content, but also it forbade foreign advertisements in the mass media. The country also tightly regulated its domestic media under the Printing Presses and Publications Act 1984, including strict provisions curtailing 'the use of printing presses and the printing, importation, production, reproduction, publishing and distribution of publications and for matters connected therewith'.[108] Control over the print industry was localised in the Prime Minister's Department and applied to 'undesirable publications'. The executive power over the media has meant that the press unofficially toes the ruling party line. The close relationship between the press and the government has been characterised by leading East Asian communications scholars as one in which the press operates 'under a guidance concept in their relationship with the government'.[109] Although unreported by the press, this relationship extended to the MSC project. According to the articles of incorporation of the Multimedia Development Corporation, the administrative agency established to carry forth the MSC under the executive branch, the editor of the leading newspaper, the New Straits Times, sat on the board of directors.

This media environment has been presented as one pillar of Asian democracy in which 'respect for authority and hierarchy' mean, according to one commentator, that *apparently* 'most asians consider it unacceptable to criticize publicly a nation's leaders'. According to some, 'criticism of rulers is tantamount to criticism of the state itself'.[110] This domestic context of speech repression was

106   UDHR, art 31.
107   Petrikin (1997).
108   Preface.
109   Glattsbach and Shman (1978).
110   Neher and Marlay (1995) p 15.

clear to foreign investors, who sought for themselves a free speech carve-out within the country. When company executives expressed preference for Malaysia's no-censorship policy as distinct from practices of other East Asian countries, it was then clear that it was their own expression which concerned them and not the rights of the Malaysian public.[111] As such, Toffler's anti-censorship stance was a strategic decision on his part to leverage a promise to TNCs into a more broadly enjoyed right. Importantly, when the dust settled after two controversial years with respect to censorship in Malaysia, the non-Internet-based rules remained. This meant that if an individual printed a forbidden web page, it was subject to censorship by the government. Further, the no-censorship guarantee for the Internet is not so cut and dry.

In April 2000, when pornographic websites were being brought to the attention of government authorities, it presented an opportunity to clarify the government's stance. According to Ohia Kwang Chye, the Parliamentary Secretary to the Energy, Multimedia and Communications Ministry, 'Malaysia is creating [the MSC] because of this, the government can never close down a website'.[112] However, the no-censorship guarantee would 'not stop the police from tracing the sources of such offending materials on the website and taking action against them under existing laws'.[113] In fact, not only was a legal basis for this executive pursuit provided by the Printing and Publications Act 1984, which preceded the Corridor creation, but as well, legislation produced at the impetus of the foreign TNCs, the Communications and Multimedia Act 1998, would lend a hand. In particular, section 211 provides 'no content application service provider or persons using a content applications service, shall provide content which is indecent, improper, obscene, false, menacing and offensive'. While this legislative surround effectively drained the no-censorship guarantee of force, the foreign TNCs could rest assured that these domestic laws created for them would not apply to them, as Mahathir 'reiterated that the licensing provisions under the Communications and Multimedia Act 1998 do not apply to Multimedia Super Corridor (MSC) status companies'.[114]

In 1998, it became clear that MSC-status companies were indeed a privileged class with regard to Internet censorship exemptions. Both other foreigners and domestic nationals were clearly not immune from government oversight of their on-line practices. In August 1998, in the midst of the East Asian currency crisis, three Malaysian citizens were arrested by the police for allegedly spreading rumours of civil disturbances in Kuala Lumpur. In November, Tengku Alaudin Abdul Majid of the Culture, Arts and Tourism Ministry made clear that foreigners could not speak freely over the Internet as 'authorities would begin to monitor the Internet for accurate reports about the country'.[115] In December, the Prime Minister turned his censorial eyes to the country's cybercafes. He required that cybercafes register their users and submit this information to the police.[116] In practice, this meant that cafe owners would keep an official list of Internet users which would then be submitted to the appropriate authorities. In this case, the order was carried out by the Housing and Local Government Ministry.[117] Throughout this period, the

---

111   Armstrong (1997).
112   Deutsche Presse Agentur (2000).
113   Deutsche Presse Agentur (2000).
114   Bando (1999).
115   Index on Censorship (1998) p 92.
116   Computer (1999).
117   Bando (1999).

government reaffirmed its guarantee of no-censorship privileges for MSC-status companies, but matters were soon to get out of control. As a result of several misreports by the foreign press and also a vigilant IAP member, Alvin Toffler, Malaysia would publicly shift its censorship stance.

The arrest of Anwar Ibrahim touched off the alleged Internet 'rumor mongering', and the subsequent police crackdown on the Internet spurred a public stance by IAP member, Alvin Toffler. In addition to Anwar, Dr Anees, a friend of Toffler's, had been arrested. Toffler sent letters to Mahathir through the International Herald Tribune editorial page expressing his disapproval of Anwar and Dr Anee's imprisonment. Both were listed as prisoners of conscience by Amnesty International during this period. The Far Eastern Economic Review published an article claiming that both Toffler and fellow IAP member Kenichi Ohmae had resigned from the IAP in protest. According to the Review, 'they did so through sharp letters to the Premier that professed disappointment'.[118] Given the influential position of the Review, news of the resignations proliferated throughout the international press as established fact.

Ohmae was quick to set the record straight. He announced that he had not resigned. Going further, he said: 'I do not know how the rumours started. I am shocked to receive calls from many people enquiring about the matter ... I see no reason to resign. Therefore it comes as a big surprise.' In fact, Ohmae went so far as to support Mahathir, arguing that Malaysia was the victim of a 'global misunderstanding of the real picture'. He tied the bad reportage to the MSC:

> 'That is why I interviewed the Prime Minister [for a documentary aired in Japan] as things like the progress of the MSC and the economy are not well reported. I told Dr. Mahathir that people in Japan believe the economic crisis has slowed down many projects including the MSC.'

According to Ohmae, public relations was the answer: 'Ohmae felt Malaysia needed to beef up its pubic relations activities in Japan to portray the country in a positive light.'[119]

Ohmae, author of *The Borderless World*, advocating that the end of the nation state was upon us, made clear that he separates politics from commerce. While he expressed his concern about Anwar's jailing to Mahathir, what mattered most was the status of transnational commerce. By pitching in behind Mahathir and reaffirming his support, Ohmae, a very influential international figure, lent credence to Mahathir's legitimacy. Although Toffler had not resigned from the IAP, he was not so accommodating.

In an interview with the New Perspectives Quarterly, Mahathir stated clearly his position when asked to respond to claims by IAP members, Toffler and Bill Gates.

---

118 Mahathir Ordered Expensive Jet, Broke Gag Order: Anwar.
119 New Straits Times (1998). The National Economic Action Council also approached external criticism as a public relations challenge in its *National Recovery Plan*. The Council is part of the Prime Minister's Department. Among its currency crisis recommendations was to 'Improve Public Relations'. According to the Council: 'There is a need to improve the image of the country both domestically and overseas. The government should consider using professional image and public relations consultants to project the country's image both domestically and overseas. Relevant strategic audiences would be targeted with the message that Malaysia should be differentiated from other emerging countries in various ways, including its economic fundamentals, financial sector resilience, and political stability, and its commitment to act on reforms'.

The Quarterly asked Mahathir whether, as claimed by Toffler and Gates, 'the "climate of political fear" in Malaysia today is likely to undermine investor confidence in this kind of Internet Age project, which requires freedom'. Mahathir responded:

> 'Yes, I'm worried because Alvin Toffler is a very influential person. But I'm sorry that he did not first try to find out the truth about our situation. I know he is concerned about Munawar Anees, who is a friend of his, but it is not in my power to release Dr. Anees. I am not that kind of prime minister. Law is the law. He has been sentenced by the courts. What I can do is be sure that Munawar is well treated and I will see to that.
>
> But to link that to the MMSC is unfair. The MMSC is a project which has nothing to do with politics. It is business. Why should that be linked to the internal politics of my party? Do the people live in political fear here? No, they go about their business as usual. Like anywhere else, unless people are throwing stones at the police, they have nothing to fear.
>
> If investors are concerned about stability we have it. This is a multiracial country. How many countries with such different ethnic groups – Chinese, Indians, Malay – are as stable as Malaysia? This is not Indonesia. Malaysians don't go overthrowing governments with street demonstrations. They would rather have their business succeed.'[120]

In his response, Mahathir reaffirmed a tenet of Asian democracy and attempted to determine selectively which 'matters affecting commerce' were to be transnationally created and which were to be off limits.

Mahathir reaffirmed the Asian way, in which commerce and third-wave political freedoms do not necessarily travel together. This position was expressed throughout the Asian values debate as governments challenged the evolutionary relationship between economic growth and political democratisation. The argument runs as follows:

> 'Asian societies are travelling a different path. In their view there is no universal secular culture inherent in the new rich of industrial capitalist societies. Instead national cultures are seen to transcend the processes of social and economic change. Secularism and liberalism are not, in their view, the cultures of industrial societies but the cultures of the west. They have mounted public campaigns exhorting their culture, to look to the Confucian heritage or simply to "look East".'[121]

Thus Mahathir alluded to the different path and its intending mindset. Importantly though the success of the East Asian governments was not achieved alone, and was made possible by transnational commercial collaboration. In addition, the success of the high-technology strategies embarked on with the MSC would also require continued transnational support. Mahathir hoped that companies would see past these domestic political wrangling, recognising them as external to the TNCs and wholly subject to Malaysian sovereign prerogative. Toffler, however, was not easily won over.

Toffler chose a major international media forum to make his stance clear in a letter published in the International Herald Tribune on 15 November 1998. Clarifying that he remained on the IAP, Toffler reaffirmed his support for Anwar and Dr Anees, and made clear that he believed domestic politics are 'matters affecting commerce'. Leaving open the possibility that he would resign from the IAP, Toffler wrote:

---

120 Mahathir (1999) p 14.
121 Robinson and Goodman (1996) p 3.

'Although in my recent correspondences with Prime Minister Mahathir bin Mohamad of Malaysia and in published articles I have sharply criticized the imprisonment in Malaysia of the former Deputy Prime Minister, Anwar Ibrahim, and my friend Munawar Anees, I have not yet formally resigned from the International Advisory Panel of the "Malaysian Multimedia Super Corridor," as reported in the press. I do not believe that this visionary project, which is important for the future of the Malaysian people and serves, in part, as a model and challenge to other countries, can flourish in the present climate of political repression.

I am sure other members of the Panel, including the heads of many giant software computer and telecommunications companies, share this view. And I do not agree, as Mahathir has argued in response to my appeals that the Multimedia Super Corridor is a purely business matter and has nothing to do with politics. The "cyberlaws" that he promised investors – complete freedom of access to information, and other Third Wave freedoms – are, in fact, clearly political. The creation of an Asian Silicon Valley is itself inherently political. That is why I hope that even at this late date a calm and just resolution can be found to the conflict between those calling for reform in Malaysia and a once visionary prime minister, who in the past has prevented ethnic conflict, marginalized religious fanaticism, and helped replace rubber, tin, and timber with semiconductor chips as the country's key export. If Mr. Anwar and Mr Anees are not released from prison as soon as possible, I will resign as, I suspect, will other members of the panel on whose investment the project depends.'[122]

So Toffler took another public stance iterating that Mahathir could not 'expect the world's greatest high-tech companies ... to help the digital future in his country while police throw his former protégé in jail'.[123] Toffler, though, remained on the Panel, perhaps because of the power it continued to afford him with Mahathir. This was in November, before Mahathir ordered the monitoring of the cybercafes. The end of the year also saw riots in Kuala Lumpur on 29 November, with over one thousand people participating. However, with the new year came changes.

In the domestic political sphere on 3 January, the prosecutors dropped sexual misconduct charges in the Anwar case. A week-and-a-half later, Mahathir admitted the importance of international public opinion for the success of the MSC. He tied his shift of position to Toffler's stance, saying, 'If an adviser says "don't invest in Malaysia", what's going to happen?'[124] This capitulation was no small admission. Mahathir's modulated tone and refusal to mount a caustic counter-attack against Toffler was a departure from his usual modus operandi. This was, after all, the same leader who had said that Al Gore should 'be fried', attacked George Soros as a 'moron', and blamed the East Asian currency crisis on 'Jews'. Things had changed publicly. Domestic politics had become acceptable as matters affecting commerce. Mahathir would be rewarded for his public capitulation as the business community would once again rally behind him the following March.

The first five months of 1999 saw a dramatic reshaping of the political discourse in Malaysia. By 23 May, Toffler, in an interview with the Boston Globe, was once again praising Mahathir, although still critical of his handling of domestic politics. Modulated, he said that Mahathir 'has gotten deservedly bad press'. However, he affirmed that he believed Mahathir to be 'the one leader in the Muslim world who had a vision'. Also, by the end of March, several key TNCs had reaffirmed their commitment to Mahathir. In the public sphere, at least, international human rights

122 Toffler (1998b).
123 Toffler (1998a).
124 Porter (1999).

scrutiny, when mounted by the right persons, had an effect, although businesses were not seriously deterred from continuing to invest in Malaysia by these events.

On 22 March, Business Week, a US publication, published a cover story, 'The casualty lying along the Super Corridor', arguing that the progress of the MSC had been meagre. The project had been derailed as foreign TNCs were wary about doing business with Malaysia because of the Prime Minister's authoritarian politics and his virulent attacks on foreigner, George Soros, and claim that 'the Jews' had been responsible for the currency crisis. However, according to the authors of the article, 'Just as damaging to the MSC, however, is Mahathir's reversal of a promise to refrain from censoring the Internet – one of his key pledges outlined in a 'Bill of Guarantees' to investors.'[125] Thus with regard to the Malaysian censorship policy, the authors not only drew a link between extra-Corridor Internet censorship and investor behaviour, but, in doing so, assumed that the original Bill of Guarantees was to apply throughout the nation.

A week before the article went to press in Business Week's Asian edition and two weeks before its was published in the US edition, MDC Chief Executive, Dr Othman Yeop, went on the offensive, rallying the support of key TNCs. On 17 March, Othman held a conference devoted to rebutting the article. The press conference statements would appear in the Letter to the Editors section of Business Week. Throughout the letters, the IAP member companies made clear that they stood behind the Corridor for business reasons, making no mention of the political controversy.

Frank Sumner Smith III, International Director of Ernst and Young's Center for Technology Enablement, spoke of the Malaysian government as its 'business partner'. Ernst and Young would continue not only to invest directly in Malaysia itself, but also would 'continue to seek opportunities for our clients to invest and locate operations in the MSC'.[126] Benedict Lee, Managing Director of Microsoft, likewise reaffirmed its unwavering support: 'Microsoft's commitment to Malaysia's MSC, then and now, has not wavered or has it been altered in any way.'[127] Govinathan Pillai, Managing Director of Sun Microsystems Malaysia, also threw his support behind Malaysia, considering 'Malaysia a key and important market', according to Pillai, Sun was one of 'the first, of a new breed of Internet-savvy companies to step up to support this national initiative by the Malaysian government'.[128] Thus the international business community made clear that it valued Malaysia as a business partner, and that its ability to deliver to them on the promise of individually tailored MSC Guarantees was more important than the domestic political wrangling. So business investment was ongoing, and to ensure its continued success, the IAP members reaffirmed that the Malaysian government could use their legitimacy as international business leaders to ward off the attacks by the international press.

The support demonstrated by the IAP member companies for the MSC underscored the role of the IAP itself as a two-way collaborative enterprise. At the Third IAP Meeting in July 1999, IAP members had made clear to the Prime Minister that they recognised the importance of publicity to ensure the success of the MSC. They represented that in marketing to the world 'positive image is

125 Einhorn and Prasso (1999).
126 Smith (1999).
127 Lee (1999).
128 Pillai (1999).

important', and as such the government '[c]an make use of MSC companies making positive projection'.[129] Thus the compliance with MSC laws depended upon ongoing processes of collaboration negotiated between Malaysian leadership and foreign commercial interests. This collaboration caused Mahathir to make certain public concessions to the IAP members, most notably Toffler, by shifting his position on the applicability of the no-censorship restrictions to the entire country. In fact, this position was used throughout the aftermath of the Business Week article to soften the blow to credibility. However, while statements shifted, and laws were repealed at the impetus of surrounding political goings on, other areas of the Malaysian regulatory matrix were re-emphasised, so as to ensure that the censorship would continue, albeit under a different name. This transmogrifying of the regulatory environment was made possible by the strength of the executive branch in Malaysia.

CONCLUSION

In May 1999, as Toffler reaffirmed his qualified support for the MSC, Malaysia issued a US $1 billion global bond. Legal services were provided by US law firms Cleary, Gottlieb, Steen & Hamilton and Cravath, Swain and Moore[130] as the Malaysian government sought the services of the US investment bank, Salomon Brothers, to bring the bond to international capital markets. This bond was designed to demonstrate international financial support for the Malaysian government, as money would go directly into public coffers. After an intensive tour of financial centres, including Hong Kong, Tokyo, Frankfurt, Milan, London and Boston by the Second Finance Minister, Datuk Mustapa Mohamad, investors were convinced that, despite the reports of Malaysia's human rights problems, the country was economically sound and politically stable.[131] As a result, the bond issue was a tremendous success with 300% over-subscription. Investor confidence in Malaysia was affirmed and the bond issue 'indicated the successful return of Malaysia to the world capital market'.[132]

In this global bond issue, private investors threw their support behind the Malaysian government, literally investing in it. Malaysia's success in pulling out of the East Asian currency crisis, while it did not depend upon assistance from the IMF, was accomplished with the support of transnational commercial interests. The foreign transnational companies stood with the government throughout the aftermath of the currency crisis. Collaboratively, the foreign and domestic interests continually refashioned the Malaysian domestic legal order to ensure that commerce would persist despite currency devaluation and civil unrest. Throughout this process of legal reformulation, foreign human rights organisations attacked the actions of Prime Minister Mahathir and the international press argued that high-technology TNCs would not tolerate his disrespect for basic human rights. However, foreign commercial interests granted the Malaysian government wide latitude in managing its internal human rights affairs. In fact, they both supported and depended upon the government's means of managing its domestic affairs.

128   Multimedia Super Corridor International Advisory Panel (1999) Annex D, p 9.
130   Apparently a ban on foreign lawyers practicing in Malaysia did not apply here.
131   Arifin (1999).
132   Hilfe Country Report (1999).

Despite the reaffirmation of Malaysia's government by foreign commercial interests, the stance taken by Alvin Toffler demonstrates that these TNCs have more power over domestic decision-making than is often assumed. While this power was far from exploited as companies stood by Mahathir, the government was forced to make public concessions in order to maintain its position, which depended upon ongoing transnational support. Thus, just as during the colonial period, the order itself is prone to erosion from the inside. If foreign TNCs had taken a united stance against Malaysia's human rights abuses, then policies would most likely have changed. Despite claims that these companies are inherently independent of nation-states,[133] they are intricately intertwined with them.

In order to manage domestic disruptions, Malaysia embarked on what Yves Dezalay and Bryant Garth have referred to as an 'international strategy'. These strategies comprise 'the ways individuals use international capital – degrees, expertise, contacts, resources, prestige, and legitimacy acquired abroad – in order to build their positions at home'.[134] In Malaysia's case, the government's success in staving off foreign human rights activists and in maintaining Asian values depended upon its success in mobilising the support of foreign commercial actors. Paradoxically, the anti-foreign stance by the Malaysian government was made possible by its openness to, and reciprocal relationship with, foreign nationals.

The success of the national independence movements lay in their ability to identify the role of foreign interests in refashioning peripheral legal orders to suit their own commercial needs. The national independence movements succeeded in uniting a variety of peoples together in common cause against a foreign enemy, the coloniser. The international legal order shifted in response to these demands from the periphery as newly independent states were accorded full sovereignty. However, with time, as the leadership of these new nations consolidated their power with the support of foreign aid, the current transnational order has grown to resemble the colonial legal orders. Transnational commerce has taken precedence in international affairs to the detriment of human rights and democracy throughout the world. As close commercial friends like Malaysia and the US appear publicly as enemies, allusions to human rights and colonialism must be viewed with scepticism. Attention must be given to the speaker and the audience; allusions to colonialism have a function.

Much stands in the way of mobilising TNCs and the Malaysian government to take human rights seriously. An examination of the continuities between colonial and current transnational legal orders highlights important continuities. However, the differences remain crucial. The particular means by which this transnational commercial community has gained its prestige position in the current era must be revealed. This revelation will allow seemingly uncontrollable forces like globalisation to be seen as the product of human agency. Perhaps understanding the roles that a transnational community plays in creating globalisation and also subverting human rights and recreating colonial period relations will permit diagnosing the illnesses of the contemporary transnational legal order. Whether a cure will be forthcoming is far from clear; none the less at least rhetoric will be judged by action rather than by other rhetoric.

---

133 Teubner (1996).
134 Dezalay and Garth (present volume) p 197.

Select bibliography

Agence France Presse, (1999) 'Malaysian PM launches anti-foreign crusade on first leg of national tour', 22 March.

Anghie, A, (1999) 'Finding the Peripheries: Sovereignty and Colonialism in Nineteenth-Century International Law', 40 Harvard International Law Journal 1.

Arifin, Z, (1999) 'Gruelling roadshow that culminated in success', New Straits Times, 28 May.

Armstrong, D, (1997) 'New Asia Inc.: First of Two Parts', The San Francisco Examiner, 15 June.

Ariff, M, (1994) 'External Trade' in Jomo, K S (ed), *Malaysia's Economy in the Nineties.*

von Asbeck, Baron F M, (1976) 'The Relationship between International and Colonial Law' in H M von Panhuys and M van L Boomkam (eds), *Baron F.M. von Asbeck: International Society in Search of a Transnational Legal Order: Selected Writings and Bibliography*, p 48.

Asia Inc, (1999) 'Silicon Island', Asia Inc (Malaysian Edition) 9 and Ministry of International Trade and Industry *Malaysia: Investment in the Manufacturing Sector: Policies, Incentives and Facilities*, MIDA, Kuala Lumpur, Malaysia, p 61.

Asian Development Bank, (1998) *The Role of Law and Legal Institutions in Asian Economic Development 1960-1995.*

Asian Strategy and Leadership Institute (ed), (1997) *Malaysia Today: Towards the New Millennium.*

Bando, S, (1999) 'Guarantee of Non-Censorship of Internet Stays', Business Times (Malaysia), 17 March.

Bartley, R T, (ed), (1993) *Democracy and Capitalism: Asian and American Perspectives.*

Brookfield, F M, (1969) 'The Courts, Kelsen, and the Rhodesian Revolution' (1969) 19 U Toronto LJ 326.

Brownlie, I, (1979) *Principles of Public International Law* (3rd edn).

Buss-Tjen, P P, (1958) 'Malay Law', 7 AJCL 248.

Cardenas, L C, and Buranakanits, A, (1999) 'The Role of APEC in the Achievement of Regional Cooperation in Southeast Asia', 5 Annual Survey of International and Comparative Law 49.

Cheong, E, and Mirandah, G, (1999) 'Companies Pay Price for Piracy', Law Money, 6 July.

Chomsky, N, (1991) *Deterring Democracy.*

Computer, (1999) 'Strategy; High-tech hopes tumble in the jungle', 1 March.

Davis, M C, (ed), (1995) *Human Rights and Chinese Values: Legal, Philosophical, and Political Perspectives.*

Deutsche Presse Agentur, (2000) 'Government won't bar websites of nude Malaysian women', 24 March.

Dezalay, Y, and Garth, B, (present volume), 'Dollarizing State and Professional Expertise: Transnational Processes and Questions of Legitimation in State Transformation, 1960-2000'.

Congressional Record House, (1993) 'Disapproving extension of nondiscriminatory treatment to products of the People's Republic of China', 139 Cong Rec H 4867, 21 July.

Donnelly, J, (1989) *Universal Human Rights in Theory and Practice.*

Dunning, J H, (1993) *Multinational Enterprises and the Global Economy.*

Economist, The, (1998) 'Asia gets too close for comfort', 23 May.

Eekelaar, J M, (1973) 'Principles of Revolutionary Legality' in B Simpson (ed) *Oxford Essays on Jurisprudence* (2nd series).

Einhorn, B, and Prasso, S, (1999) 'Malaysia's grand plan for its Multimedia Super Corridor isn't working and why', Business Week, 29 March.

Eng, P H, (1998) *Foreign Direct Investment: A Study of Malaysia's Balance of Payments Position.*

Falk, R, (present volume) 'Re-Framing the Legal Agenda of World Order in the Course of a Turbulent Century'.

Finnis, J M, (1973) 'Revolutions and Continuity of Law' in B Simpson (ed), *Oxford Essays on Jurisprudence* (2nd series).

Flood, J, (present volume) 'Global Capital Markets, Globalization and Global Elites'.

Foreign Affairs Malaysia, (1997) 'Smart Partnerships: Meeting the Challenges of Globalisation: Speech by Prime Minister Dato' Seri Dr Mahathir bin Mohamad at the First Southern Africa International Dialogue at Kasane, Botswana, on Monday, 5 May 1997', 30(2) Foreign Affairs Malaysia 53, June.

Furnivall, J S, (1956) *Colonial Policy and Practice: A Comparative Study of Burma and Netherlands India.*

Glattsbach, J, and Shman, R B, (1978) 'Malaysia' in J A Lent (ed), *Broadcasting in Asia and the Pacific: A Continental Survey of Radio and Television.*

Goh, C, (1997) 'PM: Hollywood could gain from MSC', New Straits Times, 16 January.

Gong, G W, (1984) *The Standard of Civilization in International Society.*

Gore, A, (1998) Remarks at APEC Business Summit, Kuala Lumpur, Malaysia.

Harding, A, (1996) *Law, Government and the Constitution of Malaysia.*

Harris, J W, (1971) 'When and Why Does the Grundnorm Change?', 29 CU 103.

—(1997) 'Is Self-ownership a Human Right?' in B Galligan and C J G Sampford (eds), *Rethinking Human Rights.*

Hilfe Country Report, (1999) 'Malaysia: Across-The-Board Credit Upgrading', June.

Ho, V, (1999) 'Mahathir Opens Malaysia's Silicon Valley', Japan Economic Newswire, 8 July.

Hooker, M B, (1995a) 'The Law Texts of Muslim South-East Asia' in M B Hooker (ed), *Laws of Southeast Asia: Volume I*, p 358.

—(ed), (1995b) *Laws of South-East Asia: Volume II: European Laws in South-East Asia: Essays on Portuguese and Spanish Laws, the Netherlands, English Law, American Law in the Philippines and the 'Europeanization' of Siam's Law,* p 365.

—(1995c) 'English Law in Sumatra, Java, the Straits Settlements, Malay States, Sarawak, North Borneo and Brunei' in M B Hooker (ed) *Laws of South-East Asia: Volume II: European Laws in South-East Asia: Essays on Portuguese and Spanish Laws, the Netherlands, English Law, American Law in the Philippines and the 'Europeanization' of Siam's Law*, p 299.

Huntington, S P, (1996) *The Clash of Civilizations and the Remaking of World Order.*

Ibrahim, A, (1997) *The Asian Renaissance.*

Index on Censorship (1998) p 92.

Islam, I, and Chowdhury, A, (1996) *Asia-Pacific Economies: A Survey.*

Janow, M E, (1997) 'Symposium – Institutions for International Economic Integration: Assessing APEC's Role in Economic Integration in the Asia-Pacific Region', 17 Journal of International Business 947.

Jennings, R Y, (1963) *The Acquisition of Territory in International Law.*

Johnston, W R, (1969) *Sovereignty and Protection: A Study of British Jurisdictional Imperialism in the Late Nineteenth Century.*

Kelsen, H, (1944) 'The Principle of Sovereign Equality of States as a Basis for International Organization', 53 Yale LJ 207.

Kokkalenios, V, (1992) 'Note: Increasing United States Investment in Foreign Securities: An Evaluation of SEC Rule 144A', 60 Fordham LR 179.

Kooijmans, P H, (1964) *The Doctrine of The Legal Equality of States: An Inquiry into the Foundations of International Law.*

Krasner, S D, (1999) *Sovereignty: Organized Hypocrisy.*

Kuok, R, (1997) 'Malaysia Incorporated: Private Sector-Public Sector Collaboration' in A Sarji (ed), *Malaysia's Vision 2020: Understanding the Concept, Implications & Challenges.*

Kynge, J, (1997a) 'A technological transformation', Financial Times, 19 May.

—(1997b) 'Fatigue on the Road to Growth', Financial Times, 19 May, at 3.

—(1997c) 'Premier is the Chief Marketeer', Financial Times, 19 May, at 3.

Lanham, R A, (1991) *A Handlist of Rhetorical Terms* (2nd edn).

Laothamatas, A, (1997) *Democratization in Southeast and East Asia.*

Law Money, (1999) 'Legal advisers on Telekom Malaysia's $60 million leasing facility', 14 October.

Lee, B, (1999) 'Letter to Business Week by Microsoft Malaysia' reprinted in (1999) 2(1) MSC Comm 23.

M2 Presswire, (1998) 'AMNESTY INTERNATIONAL: Malaysia: Amnesty International Declares Anwar a Prisoner of Conscience', 30 September.

Mahathir, Dr M, (1997) 'Inauguration Speech of the Malaysian Business Council' in A Sarji (ed), *Malaysia's Vision 2020: Understanding the Concept, Implications & Challenges.*

—(1999a) *A New Deal for Asia.*

—(1999b) 'I am not Suharto, or the Shah of Iran', 16(1) New Perspectives Quarterly 14, Winter.

Maxwell, W G, (1890a) *Laws and Customs.*

—(1890b) *Laws Relating to Slavery.*

Maxwell, W G, and Gibson, W S, (eds), (1924) *Treaties and Engagements Affecting the Malay States and Borneo 1924.*

Mazurek, J, (1999) *Making Microchips: Policy, Globalization, and Economic Restructuring in the Semiconductor Industry.*

McDougal, M S, and Lasswell, H D, (1959) 'The Identification of Diverse Systems Public Order', 53 American Journal of International Law 1.

De Mello, A, (1948) 'British Malaya', 30 J Comparative Legislation and Intl L: Rev of Legislation 136.

'Meeting on Rethinking Human Rights Held in Malaysia' Zinhau News Agency (12.6.1994).

Merican, M, (1997) 'Towards a Competitive and Resilient Economy: The External Dimension' in A Sarji (ed), *Malaysia's Vision 2020: Understanding the Concept, Implications & Challenges.*

Merry, S E, (1988) 'Legal Pluralism', 22(5) L and Society Rev 869.

—(1991) 'Law and Colonialism', 25(4) L and Society Rev 889 at 897–906.

Mirandah, G, and Cheong, E, (1999a) 'Malaysia to beef up copyright laws', Law Money, 22 March.

—(1999b) 'Change of pirates' tactics shows success of Malay clamp-down', Law Money, 2 November.

Ministry of Finance, (1999) *Economic Report 1998/1999.*

Mommsen, W J, (1992) 'Introduction' in W J Mommsen and J de Moor (eds), *European Expansion and Law: The Encounter of European and Indigenous Law in 19th- and 20th-Century Africa and Asia,* p 1.

Moore, S F, (1978) *Law as Process: An Anthropological Approach.*

—(1986) *Social Facts and Fabrications "Customary" Law on Kilimanjaro 1880-1980.*

—(forthcoming) 'Certainties Undone: Fifty Turbulent Years of Legal Anthropology, 1949-1999' (on file with author).

—(present volume) 'An International Regime and the Context of Conditionality'

Multimedia Development Corporation, (1997) 7 Flagship Applications 1.

Multimedia Super Corridor, (1998) 'The Smart Way to Tackle Transactions', I(1) MSC comm 9.

Multimedia Super Corridor International Advisory Panel (1999) Report of the Third Multimedia Super Corridor (MSC) International Advisory Panel (IAP), Cyberjaya, Malaysia, meeting, 8–9 July 1999.

Nassar, Dr N, (2000) 'Essay: Project Finance, Public Utilities, and Public Concerns: A Practitioner's Perspective', 23 Fordham LJ 60.

Neher, C P, and Marlay, R, (1995) *Democracy and Development in South-East Asia: The Winds of Change.*

New Straits Times, (1998) 'Japan Consultant: I am still a Member', 20 December.

—(1999) 'Gore, Soros assailed for their interference', 9 December.

O'Connell, D P, (1967) *State Succession in Municipal and International Law.*

Othman, Dr Y A, (1999) 'MSC: Propelling Malaysia into the information era', International Institute of Communications Annual Meeting and Conference, Kuala Lumpur, 7 September (on file with author).

Pereira, B, (2000) 'US Legislators Want New Anwar Trial', The Straits Times (Singapore) 11 January.

Petrikin, C, (1997) 'Malaysian technopolis tries to curry biz favor', Daily Variety, 15 January.

Pillae, G, (1999) 'Letter to the Editor', Business Week, reprinted in (1999) 2(1) MSC Comm 23.

Porter, B, (1999) 'PM admits mistakes over Anwar', South China Post, 14 January.

Rahman, A A, (1997) 'The Malaysia Incorporated Concept' in Asian Strategy and Leadership Institute (ed), *Malaysia Today: Towards the New Millennium*, p 49.

Richards, K, (1999) 'New Airports; New Challenges', Airport Review, 1 January.

Robinson, R, and Goodman, D S G, (1996) 'The New Rich in Asia: Economic Development, Social Status and Political Consciousness' in R Robinson and D S G Goodman (eds), *The New Rich in Asia: Mobile Phones, McDonalds' and Middle-class Revolution*, p 1.

Rutter, M F, (1989) *The Applicable Law in Singapore and Malaysia: A Guide to Reception, Precedent and the Sources of Law in the Republic of Singapore and the Federation of Malaysia.*

Siegel, L, and Markoff, J, (1985) *The Dark Side of the Chip: The High Cost of High Tech.*

Smith, F S III, (1999) 'Letter to Business Week by Ernst and Young', Business Week, reprinted in (1999) 2(1) MSC Comm 23.

Snyder, F, (1981) 'Colonialism and Legal Form: The Creation of "Customary Law" in Senegal', 19 Journal of Legal Pluralism 49.

—(present volume) 'Governing Globalization'.

Straits Times Interactive (1998) 'Malaysians Are Enraged', 18 November.

Teubner, G, (1997) '"Global Bukowina": Legal Pluralism in the World Society' in G Teubner (ed), *Global Law Without a State*, p 3.

Terrill, R, (1999) 'Symposium: Part Three: Private Capital and Development: Challenges Facing International Institutions in a Globalized Economy', 9 Transnational L and Contemporary Problems 303.

Testy, K Y, (1990) 'Note: The Capital Markets in Transition: A Response to New SEC Rule 144A', 66 Ind JL 233.

Toffler, A, (1998a) 'Letter to the Editor; Multimedia Super Corridor', International Herald Tribune, 25 November.

—(1998b) 'Malaysia's high tech dream hit by Anwar trial', The Statesman, 17 November.

Twining, W, (ed), (1991) *Issues of Self-Determination.*

Ure, J, (1997) 'Telecommunications in ASEAN and Indochina' in J Ure (ed), *Telecommunications in Asia: Policy, Planning and Development*, p 49.

White, G, (1988) 'Principles of International Economic Law: An Attempt to Map the Territory' in H Fox (ed), *International Economic Law and Developing States*, p 1.

White, N J, (1996) *Business, Government, and the End of Empire: Malaya, 1942-1957.*

Wilson, R A, (ed), (1997) *Human Rights, Culture and Context: Anthropological Perspectives.*

Wolff, S, (1995) 'Recent Developments in International Securities Regulation', 23 Denver Journal of International Law and Policy 347.

Woodiwiss, A, (1998) *Globalisation, Human Rights and Labour Law in Pacific Asia.*

World Bank, (1993) *The East Asian Miracle: Economic Growth and Public Policy.*

Wurfel, D, and Burton, B, (1996) *Southeast Asia in the New World Order: A Political Economy of a Dynamic Region.*

Zinn, H, (1999) *Declarations of Independence: Cross-Examining American Ideology.*

Zulliger, E, (1997) 'The Malaysia Incorporated Concept: A Key Strategy in Achieving Vision 2020' in A Sarji (ed), *Malaysia's Vision 2020: Understanding the Concept, Implications & Challenges.*

Chapter 12

Sovereignty and citizenship in a world of migration

C JOPPKE

This chapter discusses the relationship between liberal states and international migration after the Second World War.[1] More precisely, it tackles the question of the change or resilience of liberal states in light of this phenomenon. The notion of *liberal* state is not a common one for international lawyers. International law, much like Realism in International Relations Theory, prefers to speak of states in the abstract, independently of their domestic regime form.[2] Insisting on the notion of *liberal state* prefigures the thrust of the following analysis: Though a definitionally inter- or transnational phenomenon, immigration has found a thoroughly national treatment in such states – particularly regarding the legal rules and legitimatory discourses within which immigration has been processed.

However, the domestic perspective that will be presented here is not obvious. In fact, it goes against a dominant trend in sociological and political science writings on states and international migration. For the sake of brevity, and at the risk of simplification, we will call this counter-perspective 'postnational'.[3] It depicts states' treatment of migrants as externally conditioned and constrained by global interdependence (particularly of the economic kind) and by global human-rights norms and principles. Postnationalists have never quite faced up to the paradox why the states in the heartland of liberal stateness – Western Europe and North America – should be reigned by international or global precepts, which after all are only externalisations of their own internal principles and traditions, while the domestically much weaker illiberal or newly liberalising states on the periphery do not seem to be constrained by such precepts.[4]

Before elaborating on both (postnational and domestic) perspectives, and on why this chapter will suggest that the postnational one is wrong, an important distinction must be introduced. States are entangled with international migration

---

1 Liberal states may be defined broadly as 'states with juridical equality, constitutional protections of individual rights, representative republican governments, and market economies based on private property rights': Slaughter (1992) at 1909. Since according to this definition Russia also is a 'liberal' state, the chapter opts for a narrower and geographic definition of liberal states as the states of Western Europe and less-than-a-handful of transoceanic settler countries (the US, Canada, Australia).
2 See the critique by Slaughter (1995).
3 Examples of the postnational perspective are Sassen (1998); Jacobson (1996); Soysal (1994).
4 For the harsh immigration practices of some such states, see Weiner (1995) at 77–83.

both as territorial organisations and as membership associations.[5] As territorial organisations, one can define states – with Max Weber – as entities that monopolise the legitimate use of violence in a given territory. In short, as territorial organisations states are sovereign. As membership associations, modern states are composed of citizens, who possess equality of status and whose collective choices determine who the state is and what it does. One could also say that as membership associations modern states are *nation*-states, because the institution of citizenship is grounded in the modern invention of nationhood.[6] In a (fictional) world without international migration, the scope of sovereignty and citizenship would be identical: sovereignty would be exerted only about the state's citizens. In the real world of cross-border movements, the sovereign jurisdiction of states applies also to non-citizens on their territory, while the citizens who leave their state's jurisdiction do not thereby lose their privileged membership status. International migration thus drives a wedge between sovereignty and citizenship, making them visible as two separate aspects of modern nation-states.

While making them visible as such, international migration may also be seen as a challenge to each of the nation-state's key components, sovereignty and citizenship. Sovereignty is challenged by the phenomenon of unwanted immigration, such as illegal immigration, mass asylum-seeking, or the family unification of labour migrants. Citizenship is challenged by the phenomenon of denizenship (which is permanent resident membership short of citizenship) and – to the extent that citizenship is not only a legal status but also an identity – by ethnic diversification, which undermines the shared identities and homogeneity of the citizenry. Postnationalists suggest a 'declinist' resolution to both migration challenges: states are externally incapacitated in the control of unwanted immigration; and a new form of 'postnational' membership has devalued, perhaps even rendered obsolete, traditional citizenship.

This chapter will argue that on both accounts postnationalists are wrong: liberal states are capable of containing unwanted immigration, and the constraints that they face in this exercise are self-induced rather than externally induced; and postnational membership has not proved to be a viable alternative to citizenship – on the contrary, immigration has reaffirmed citizenship as the dominant form of membership in liberal states. Accordingly, against the declinist picture of postnationalists this writer suggests the resilience of liberal states in the face of international migration.

SOVEREIGNTY

In discussing the relationship between sovereignty and unwanted immigration, one must distinguish between the legal authority and empirical capacity of states. Sovereignty, according to international law and international relations theory means 'legal authority', the formal jurisdiction of states over their territory and people, unimpeded by external intervention from other states or non-state actors. In this view, states are by definition sovereign – otherwise they would not be states. By contrast, 'sovereignty' according to political sociology means 'empirical

---

5   This distinction is eloquently elaborated by Brubaker (1992) chapter 1.
6   See, however, the important observation by Brubaker (1992) chapter 3 that the generalised subjectship of absolutist states amounted to a kind of proto-citizenship that foreshadowed some crucial features of citizenship in democratic, 'national' states.

capacity', the power of states to formulate and implement laws and policies, which is better developed in some (say, 'strong') than in other ('weak') states. In the latter view, sovereign stateness is not a definitional quality, but a 'variable' that can take on a variety of values.[7] Regarding the stipulated decline of sovereignty vis-à-vis immigration, one must therefore ask two separate questions: first, have actors other than the state arrogated unto themselves the formal responsibility for admitting or expelling immigrants; second, have states lost the material power effectively to regulate cross-border movements, even though formally they still may be in charge? On both accounts, the argument of sovereignty-in-decline is on weak empirical grounds:[8] immigration control is no exception to a generally increasing rather than decreasing 'infrastructural power'[9] of the modern state; and where formal authority is delegated to supra- or non-state actors, as most prominently in the EU, the purpose is to increase the empirical capacity of states to keep unwanted migrants out.[10]

Globalisation, which by deterritorialising resource flows and transactions is often seen as weakening the territory-fixed state across its functions, is better seen as an uneven process that weakens the state in some regards, but strengthens it in others. Whereas control over the economy, for example, has indeed been relegated to non-statal, global or regional 'governance' regimes,[11] no such regime is in sight to take control over the movement of people.[12] Whereas money and capital have become denationalised, people continue to be couched in stubbornly national colours. 'Despite the rhetoric of globalization', two British authors observe correctly, 'the bulk of the world's population live in closed worlds, trapped by the lottery of their birth'.[13] Globalisation even upgrades the function of states to be people containers, particularly in the developed parts of the world, where economically disempowered states have found new legitimacy in providing physical 'security' to their domestic populations.[14] The declining number of asylum-seekers across OECD states in the 1990s, which is everywhere the result of restrictive legislation and border enforcement, shows the considerable capacity of migrant-receiving states to live up to their people-containing function.[15]

Having said this, a root image in recent writings on immigration and refugee policies, particularly in those of the postnational persuasion, is this: sovereign states have an interest to keep out migrants; but they meet these migrants protected by universal human rights norms and regimes; and if states accept immigrants, then it is because they give in to externally imposed obligations. Gill Loescher,[16] for example, finds that '(t)he formulation of refugee policy ... illustrates the conflict between international humanitarian norms and the sometimes narrow self-interest calculations of sovereign nation states'. This is a view of the state as externally constrained by global human rights precepts.[17] It is

7 Nettl (1968).
8 See Freeman (1998).
9 Mann (1993) at 59–61.
10 This is reflected in the polemical notion of 'Fortress Europe': see eg Peers (1998).
11 See Reinicke (1998).
12 The one exception of the EU is discussed below.
13 Hirst and Thompson (1995) at 420.
14 See Bigo's (2001) critical analysis of the 'securitization' of migration in Europe.
15 See SOPEMI (1998) at 56–58.
16 Loescher (1989) at 8.
17 See also Jacobson (1996); Soysal (1994).

sometimes combined with a political economy argument, according to which state attempts to control the movement of people in a world of global-factor mobility are futile – if money, goods and ideas flow effortlessly around the globe, people will have to follow eventually.[18]

The juxtaposition of an external human rights regime and sovereign states is entirely appropriate in the case of non-liberal states or fledgling democracies, such as in Africa, Eastern Europe, Latin America or South East Asia.[19] It is misleading in the case of long-established liberal states, in which the protection of human rights is embedded in domestic law and traditions. This changes the root image: sovereignty and human rights are still conflicting principles, but they are located under the roof of liberal states. If liberal states accept unwanted immigrants, then it is because of self-limited, rather than globally limited, sovereignty.[20]

This forces us to disaggregate the domestic state. The typical conflict in immigration control is not a monolithic, sovereign state pitted against, and presumably dodging, external human rights obligations, but a restriction-minded, democratically accountable state executive pitted against independent courts that defend the family or resident rights of immigrants on the basis of domestic law, particularly constitutional law.

The diagnosis of globally limited sovereignty may be countered in two directions. One direction is dismantling its premise of a 'golden age' of state sovereignty, which is said to have come to an end now, in the presumed era of 'globalisation'; a second (and for our purposes more important) direction is tracing the concrete legal sources of crucial migrant rights, such as residence and family unification rights, which leads one to see that they are everywhere domestic, not inter- or transnational.

Regarding the first line of criticism, the Westphalian State – understood as a form of political rule based on territory and immunity from outside interference – has always been compromised: voluntarily by conventions and contracts; and involuntarily by coercion and imposition. As political scientist Stephen Krasner has cleverly argued, 'compromising the Westphalian model is always available as a policy option because there is no authority structure to prevent it'.[21] Human rights considerations, in particular, have been one form of compromising sovereignty since the inception of the modern state system. Examples are the religious minority protections in the Treaty of Westphalia itself; the abolition of the international slave trade under English leadership; or the Wilsonian national minority protections after the First World War, which were forcibly imposed upon the Eastern European successor states to the Ottoman and Habsburg Empires.[22] The universal human rights regime set up after the Second World War is only the latest attempt to discipline states from the outside, and – until recently at least – it has been compromised by a strong norm of non-intervention, which was another lesson to be learnt from the Second World War.

Regarding immigration, the post-war international human rights regime has put two major limits on state discretion: the principle of non-discrimination, which prohibits states, by means of customary international law and conventions, from drawing capricious lines along sex or race in their admission or legal treatment of

---

18 Eg Sassen (1998).
19 These are the regions considered in Risse, Ropp and Sikkink's (1999) comprehensive account of the impact of the international human rights regime on domestic politics.
20 See Joppke (1998).
21 Krasner (1995a) at 117.
22 Krasner (1995b).

aliens on their territory.[23] A second limitation is the right of asylum. The non-refoulement principle in asylum law, according to which asylum-claimants must not be sent back to countries in which they risk torture or death, is perhaps the single strongest external limit on state discretion. This reflects the original impetus of the UN's regime: the protection of individuals qua individuals from criminal states. However, international asylum law still leaves state sovereignty fully intact, because it makes asylum a right of the state to grant asylum, not a right of the individual to enjoy asylum. The first drafts of both the UN Universal Declaration of Human Rights in 1948 and the 1951 Geneva Convention relating to the Status of Refugees contained the subjective right of asylum; in both cases this was eventually erased because of sovereignty concerns.[24] Accordingly, the restrictive asylum laws passed in all Western states in response to mass asylum-seeking in the 1990s are generally not in violation of international asylum law; they rather revoked self-imposed, generous (if convenient in the Cold War confrontation) asylum rules and practices that had exceeded these states' international obligations.

A second objection to the diagnosis of globally limited sovereignty is that internationally guaranteed asylum and non-discrimination rights cover only a small fraction of migrant rights. Crucial migrant rights, such as residence, family and social rights, have domestic, not international, roots. These rights are differently situated, developed and justified in different states. In the US, for example, the post-1960s legal empowerment of legal and illegal immigrants, even of asylum-seekers, draws upon a constitution whose protective due process and equal protection clauses revolve around the category of person rather than citizen. The personhood principle was first applied to aliens in *Yick Wo v Hopkins*,[25] in which the Supreme Court argued that the equal protection clause of the Constitution's 14th Amendment was 'not confined to the protection of citizens', but 'universal in (its) application ... to all persons within the territorial jurisdiction'.[26] However, only the domestic civil rights revolution of the 1960s, as a result of which discrimination on the basis of alienage took on the odour of illegitimate racial discrimination, turned the long-dormant personhood principle into a major source of immigrant rights. In *Graham v Richardson*,[27] the Supreme Court held that states were not entitled to exclude resident aliens from their welfare programmes, also because the latter were a 'discrete and insular minority' that could not be singled out by sub-federal states for discrimination. Following *Graham*, the Supreme Court and lower courts struck down most existing state restrictions against resident aliens regarding professional licenses, civil service employment, welfare programmes, and scholarships. And in the most famous alien rule of all, *Plyler v Doe*,[28] the Supreme Court decided that on equal protection grounds, states were not allowed to exclude the children of illegal immigrants from public schools. The justification underlying these different rules is the same: the Constitution establishes a floor of equality between all persons residing on US territory, and differential treatment on the part of states always requires a special (and, at times, impossible) justification.[29] It is important to add, however,

23 Goodwin-Gill (1978) chapter V.
24 Lavenex (1999) at 51.
25 *Yick Wo v Hopkins* 118 US 356 (1886).
26 Quoted in Bosniak (1994) at 1098.
27 *Graham v Richardson* 403 US 365 (1971).
28 *Plyler v Doe* 457 US 202 (1982).
29 See Rubio-Marin (1998) at 185.

that the Constitution's personhood principle has always been counterbalanced (and in important respects, been trumped) by the judicially constructed principle of 'plenary power', according to which the political branches of the federal government – Congress and the Presidency – have absolute authority over broadly defined 'immigration' matters. Accordingly, constitutional protection for immigrants via 'personhood' is available only at the state, not the federal level. This was affirmed in *Matthews v Diaz*,[30] in which the Supreme Court ruled that it was within the immigration (that is, 'plenary') power of the federal government to exclude long-settled legal immigrants from Medicare benefits if it so wished. An unrepealed plenary power doctrine, which essentially puts the federal government above the (constitutional) law in immigration matters, has been the inroad for the recent exclusion of immigrants from most federal welfare programmes, which is without precedent in the Western world.

In Europe, too, crucial migrant rights have domestic roots. Europe is a particularly interesting case, because it is the region with the highest density of inter- and supra-national human rights norms and regimes anywhere in the world; and still most migrant rights are grounded in the domestic law of European states. Virginie Guiraudon has shown that the very few decisions of the European Court of Human Rights (ECtHR) that dealt with migrant rights[31] postdated the establishment of essential residence and family rights at the national level.[32] To begin with, ECtHR jurisprudence has pronounced itself on only narrow aspects of alien rights, invoking at best article 8 (right to lead a normal family life) and article 3 (protection against inhuman treatment) of the European Convention on Human Rights, but not the more pertinent article 14 (banning discrimination on the grounds of race, national origin, and other ascriptive markers).[33] The ECtHR's favoured recourse to article 8 is not accidental, because strong constitutional provisions for the integrity of family life already existed at that point in most European states. As Virginie Guiraudon characterised the prudent and self-limiting approach taken by the EctHR: 'it tried to coordinate national jurisprudences rather than subjugate national courts and to harmonize preexisting practices rather than impose new ones.'[34] And even when it invoked article 8, as in *Abdulaziz, Cabales and Balkandali v United Kingdom*,[35] the court conceded that:

> '(t)he duty imposed by Article 8 cannot be considered as extending to a general obligation on the part of a Contracting State to respect the choice by married couples of the country of their matrimonial residence and to accept non-national spouses for settlement in that country.'[36]

---

30 *Matthews v Diaz* 426 US 67 (1976).
31 From 1959 to 1993, only about 2.5% of all ECtHR decisions (which is less than a dozen) involved the civil rights of foreigners: Guiraudon (1998) p 15.
32 See also Moravcsik (1995) 173, who found that: '[t]he ECHR is best seen as an instrument to perfect and harmonize preexisting human rights guarantees, rather than to extend basic guarantees.'
33 The ECtHR's famous *Abdulaziz, Cabales and Balkandali* rule (1985), which indicted Britain's exclusion of foreign family members, involved a violation of art 14, but only on the grounds of sex discrimination (at that time foreign husbands were not allowed to join their legal resident or citizen wives in the UK, while foreign wives were allowed to join their UK husbands): see Joppke (1999a) 123ff.
34 Guiraudon (1998) p 20.
35 Judgment of 28 May 1985, Series A no 94, ECtHR.
36 *Abdulaziz, Cabales and Balkandali v United Kingdom* judgment of 28 May 1985, Series A no 94, p 34.

A critical case showing the prevalence of national legal norms over international norms is Germany. This is a country that has ardently incorporated all international human rights treaties and conventions into domestic law, and which has even endowed the primacy of international over domestic law with constitutional dignity.[37] However, the extensive human rights protections in the Basic Law have rendered the resort to international law unnecessary. Crucial protections of guestworkers from deportation, and residence and family rights have all been derived by domestic courts from a constitution that, in response to Germany's own history, has gone further than any other constitution in the world to subject sovereign state powers to universal human rights. As the opening article of the Basic Law stipulates: 'The dignity of the human being is untouchable. To respect and to protect it is the obligation of all statal powers.' Judges, armed by constitutional law, helped make Germany a 'country of immigration', destroying the government's opposite state philosophy 'not' to be a 'country of immigration'.[38]

There are two interesting differences to observe between Germany and the US' constitutional empowerment of immigrants. First, there is no parallel in German constitutional law to the 'plenary power' principle, which had largely exempted the US government from judicial control in immigration matters. This has made the reach of constitutional protection for immigrants even greater in Germany than in the US. Accordingly, a US-style roll-back of social rights for immigrants would not be possible in Germany (nor in any other constitutional state in Europe, for that matter). Secondly, 'freedom' (and not 'equality', as in the US) has been the core value invoked by the Constitutional Court in its immigrant jurisprudence. Here, one must know that the Basic Law's individual rights provisions rest on a distinction between universal human rights and rights reserved to Germans (the so-called *Deutschenrechte*). Among the *Deutschenrechte* are the right of free movement and choice of profession, which are obviously crucial for a secure residence status. However, the Constitutional Court has established in its case law that long-settled aliens are due even the *Deutschenrechte*. Key to this has been article 2(1) of the Basic Law, which guarantees the 'free development of personality'. The court has expansively interpreted this freedom clause as a 'residuary' fundamental right (*Auffanggrundrecht*), which allows long-settled aliens access to the *Deutschenrechte*. The Basic Law's freedom clause has thus been the functional equivalent to the US Constitution's equal protection clause.

In a book that largely (though not exclusively) caters to a British audience, one should not deny that the British case does not quite fit the argument of (constitutionally) self-limited sovereignty. But neither does it fit the opposite argument of globally limited sovereignty. Political scientist Gary Freeman even finds: 'The British experience demonstrates that it is possible to limit unwanted immigration.'[39] One cause of Britain's exceptional efficacy of immigration control is the absence of an autonomous judiciary to keep the executive in check, which is itself due to the absence of a written constitution and of a strong tradition of judicial review of government acts. In Britain, Parliament is sovereign, and it may grant and take away individual rights as it sees fit. It is important to see that this lack

---

37 Art 25 of the Basic Law says: 'The general rules of international law are part of federal state law. The former are superior to the latter and create rights and duties directly for the residents of the Federal Republic (of Germany).'

38 The German Constitutional Court's landmark cases on alien rights are discussed in Joppke (1999a) at 69–75.

39 Freeman (1994) at 297.

of constitutional rights affects citizens and immigrants alike.[40] Accordingly, one can observe that Britain's ferocious fight against immigration via family reunification, which had culminated in an intrusive system of checking the 'primary purpose' of marriages to foreigners, had pushed the family rights of all citizens (not just of immigrants) below EU standard. This was brought to the open in the European Court of Justice's (ECJ) famous decision in *Surinder Singh*,[41] according to which British citizens have more family rights under EC law than under national law.

There are signs, however, that the process of Europeanisation is bringing British exceptionalism to an end.[42] This is visible in an increasing assertiveness of English courts, toward the executive, even in asylum and immigration law. For example, in *'M' v Home Office*[43] – a 1992 case on the refoulement of an asylum-seeker – the Court of Appeal's unwillingness to grant 'Crown immunity' to a high-handed executive that had violated elementary asylum rights ventured on continental-style judicial review. This was in the wake of the ECJ's *Factortame II* decision,[44] which had for the first time instructed British courts to overrule their government in matters of European law.[45] Europe may be the trick to provide Britain with what all other liberal states have long had: effectively divided powers, judicial review, and perhaps even a Bill of Rights.

How does the process of Europeanisation in general fit in with the argument of self-limited state sovereignty and the predominantly domestic sources of immigrant rights? The ECJ, in successfully claiming definitional power over the concept of 'worker' (who according to the founding treaty of the EU are entitled to free movement rights), has incapacitated the so-called 'member states' of the EU to control the entry and residence of EU aliens (provided they are citizens in another member state).[46] This is, by all accounts, a remarkable loss of sovereignty: in the EU, actors other than states control the movement of EU aliens, which in this respect makes these states fail the IR definition of 'formal' state sovereignty. Regarding third-state nationals, for which the Italians have invented the ingenious notion of *extracomunitari*, European nation-states have long resisted being downgraded to impotent 'member states'. But even here a supra-nationalisation of the immigration function is in process, because with the Amsterdam Treaty the control of third-state nationals (that is, immigration control proper) has been moved from the inter-governmental Third Pillar into the supra-national First Pillar. That is, actors other than states will in the future control the movement of non-EU aliens; also, a remarkable loss of sovereignty is likely to occur.

How should one interpret this European development? The answer is as state-building. Certainly, the EU is not a 'state' in the sense of Georg Jellinek's famous triad of territory and people under a sovereign jurisdiction, and it is unlikely to ever become one. But in certain policy domains the EU is taking on state-like features and functions; and control over the movement of people is one of them.

---

40 This distinction is, of course, irrelevant to most post-colonial immigrants, who – as equal 'subjects' of the Empire – arrived with quasi-citizen status.
41 *Surinder Singh* Judgment of 7 July 1992, C-370/90, I-4288.
42 See Levitsky (1994).
43 *'M' v Home Office* [1992] QB 270, CA.
44
45 According to one British lawyer '*M v Home Office* provided a convenient opportunity ... to excise from the law the embarrassing anomaly whereby the procedural protections offered by national law appeared inferior to those afforded by EC law through national courts': Harlow (1994) at 622.
46 See Joppke (1999b).

This development is based on the simple logic that complete market freedoms, as commanded by the Single European Act 1985, are not possible without complete internal freedom of movement of people, which, in turn, requires a common regime of external access, that is, immigration control.

It is important to note that Europeanisation is not, like 'globalisation', a process of eroding boundaries, but instead, one of the redrawing of boundaries. Note that European law by definition excludes third-state nationals from its reach. To the degree that the founding treaty has been 'constitutionalised',[47] through the ECJ's case law, Europe's quasi-constitution is one that applies to member-state nationals only. In this regard, the EU falls behind the practices of liberal states, whose constitutions all contain a space for non-citizen rights, that is, universal human rights, which have been the basis of the legal empowerment of immigrants in liberal states. Being bounded much like nation-states are, Europe is therefore not to be subsumed under a larger 'postnational' trend.

CITIZENSHIP

Closely connected to the argument of globally limited sovereignty is a second 'postnational' argument that a new form of non-citizen membership, legitimised by global human-rights norms, is about to replace traditional citizenship. In one author's words: 'national citizenship is losing ground to a more universal model of membership anchored in deterritorialized notions of persons' rights.'[48] This second argument suffers from the same weaknesses as the first: a hypostasised 'golden age' of citizenship that never was; and a false projection of domestic state functions to the transnational level. In addition, it flies in the face of a recent revaluation of citizenship in Europe and the US alike.

That national citizenship is no longer the predominant mode of incorporating immigrants in Western states has most influentially been argued in Yasemin Soysal's study on guestworkers in Europe, *Limits of Citizenship*.[49] This slim volume is actually two books: one that sorts out the differences of national regimes for incorporating migrants in a fairly standard comparative politics mode; and a second that argues, quite to the opposite, that the rights of settled guestworkers are increasingly standardised across European states and revolving around a new model of 'postnational membership' that has allowed the guestworkers to become integrated into their host societies without becoming their citizens. How both of these quite opposite arguments might go together, the author, curiously, does not say. In any case, the convergence hypothesis only is of interest to us here. Soysal derives her idea from the 'new institutionalism' in organisational sociology, as developed by John Meyer and colleagues. In its earliest and still most succinct version, this new institutionalism argues that the modern model of formal-rational organisation, as first canonised in Max Weber's theory of bureaucracy, is not commanded by the technical nature of the tasks to be accomplished; instead, the model of formal rationality functions as 'myth' and 'ceremony' that organisations adopt from their environment for purposes of legitimation: '(O)rganizations are dramatic enactments of the rationalized myths pervading modern societies.'[50] New institutionalism provides an elegant one-stroke explanation for the

47 See Weiler (1991).
48 Soysal (1994) p 3.
49 Soysal (1994).
50 Meyer and Rowan (1977) 346.

'isomorphism' of formal organisations around the world, from the modern business corporation to the modern nation-state, which are all similarly constituted despite varying local traditions and varying tasks to be accomplished. From this perspective, the contemporary notion of universal human rights appears as one of the environmental precepts (or 'scripts') of the 'global system', which 'provide(s) models for and constraints on actions and policies of the nation-states in regard to international migration and migrants'.[51]

The 'postnational membership' argument invites some generic objections that apply to new institutionalism as such. Most notably, there is a conspicuous absence of agency and process-tracing; new institutionalists do not tell us exactly how global 'scripts' become instantiated in concrete organisations and states.[52]

A more concrete objection to the model of postnational membership is its premise of a colossos of 'national citizenship' that never was. Soysal thinks that in the old nation-states 'rights ... used to belong solely to nationals'.[53] This is a fiction, which builds upon T H Marshall's[54] influential but questionable identification of the whole range of individual rights with citizen rights. Marshall may be excused for conflating 'individual' and 'citizen', because he was writing *before* the great post-war migrations drove a wedge between the two. However, this conflation becomes a serious error if writers in the contemporary age of migrations equate Marshallian citizenship with 'nationality' in the sense of formal state membership, and then derive all sorts of individual rights – civil, political, social – from formal citizen status, at least for the presumed (and now bygone) era of 'national citizenship'. Only against such a peculiar reading of Marshall (that equates 'citizenship' with 'nationality') can the 'postnational' narrative take shape: 'Rights that used to belong solely to nationals are now extended to foreign populations, thereby undermining the very basis of national citizenship.'[55]

The Italian political philosopher Luigi Ferrajoli[56] has powerfully argued against the conflation of individual and citizen that civil and social rights (in contrast to political rights) have never been based on citizenship. Instead, most modern constitutions have conceived of civil and social rights as rights of the person residing in the territory of the state, irrespective of his or her citizenship status. In short, residence, not citizenship, activates most civil and social rights. If one looks at the French Declaration of the Rights of Man and the Citizen, the word 'citizen' (as against 'man' and 'individual') appears first in article 6, which is about the right to political participation; and article 7 of Napoleon's Civil Code states explicitly that 'the exercise of civil rights is independent of citizenship status'.[57] These civil rights, which are invested in personhood rather than citizenship, include the right to freedom (of speech, opinion and the press), the right to private autonomy (that is, to conclude contracts and act in law) and the right of ownership. Later, when states took on welfare functions, civil rights were accompanied by social rights. These were likewise not premised on citizenship, but on residence and labour-market participation. If social rights for long remained the privilege of citizens, this was not because this limitation was

---

51 Soysal (1994) p 6.
52 See Finnemore (1996).
53 Soysal (1994) p 137.
54 Marshall (1950).
55 Soysal (1994) p 137.
56 Ferrajoli (1994).
57 Quoted in Ferrajoli (1994) 266.

notionally inscribed in these rights, but because only citizens enjoyed the right of residence and free access to the labour market, and thus had command over the triggering factors for social rights. The nexus between citizenship and social rights was thus, at best, an indirect one.[58] In any case, since their inception in Bismarckian Germany, social insurance schemes have taken territoriality as their reference point. After all, they had been put into place only in response to industrial-age migrations and the incapability of local poor-relief provisions to cope with them. Accordingly, article 30 of the German Social Statute (*Sozialgesetzbuch*) states: 'The regulations of this statute are binding for all persons who are residents in the realm of its validity.' Since 1789, there has been only one class of rights that has been notionally reserved for citizens: the political right to participate in the formation of the general will and to hold public office.

Ferrajoli notes, rather in passing, that in modern constitutions there are two civil rights that are generally not extended to 'persons' but reserved to 'citizens': residence and free movement in the state's territory. A dramatic moment in the evolution of migrant rights was the decoupling of resident and free-movement rights from citizenship. However, this was not a 'postnational' moment, driven by abstract human rights considerations. Instead, it was a crypto-national moment that equated long-term residence with de facto membership in the national community.

This is especially clear in the notion of *Rechtsschicksal der Unentrinnbarkeit* (legal fate of dependency), which German constitutional lawyers have introduced to justify the extension of constitutional citizen rights to long-settled foreigners.[59] As indicated earlier, the German Basic Law distinguishes between elementary human rights and some rights reserved for German citizens. On the basis of the general freedom clause of the Basic Law (article 2.1), aliens can also get access to the *Deutschenrechte*. However, this leaves open the question *when* the general freedom clause can be invoked – the German state would be a small world-state (or no state at all) if this clause applied to all aliens who happen to set foot on German soil. The 'when' question is answered by the *Unentrinnbarkeit* formula. Its meaning is simple: once the guestworkers have struck deep roots in German society, once a return to the country of origin is no longer realistic, and once these de facto immigrants have become existentially dependent on protection by the German state, the state cannot deny them crucial residence and other rights that are usually reserved for citizens. The underlying motif is communitarian, not universalist: migrants are not perceived as holders of abstract human rights, but as particular members of a community with historically derived entitlements to due consideration and protection.

The German Constitutional Court applied this communitarian logic influentially in the so-called *Indian Case* decision of 1978.[60] This case was about a long-settled Indian migrant worker in Germany, who had been denied a renewal of his annual residence permit by the responsible *Land* (sub-federal state) authority, the latter using the official zero-immigration policy of the federal government as justification. Here the court held that the claimant had a constitutionally protected 'reliance interest' in a renewed residence permit, on the basis of the constitutional principle of *Vertrauensschutz* (protection of legitimate expectations), which the court derived from article 19 of the Basic

---

58 See Eichenhofer (1997).
59 See Isensee (1974); Schwerdtfeger (1980).
60 Decision of 26 September 1978 (2 BvR 525/77).

Law (the so-called *Rechtsstaatsprinzip*).[61] Before this decision, the renewal of annual residence permits was entirely at the discretion of the state, as stipulated by the Foreigner Law 1965, and with each renewal the position of the migrant even became worse, because his or her continued presence could be seen as violation of the government's no-immigration policy. After this decision, past residence created a claim for continued residence in the future, according to the constitutional principle of *Vertrauensschutz*.

The German case adds an important qualification to the communitarian logic of alien rights: the extension of residence rights to non-citizens is not unconditional. It happens only if the state had not clarified beforehand the ultimate termination of residence, and the foreign migrant therefore had reason to plan his or her life in the new society. At least, this is what the German Constitutional Court argued in its *Indian Case* decision: 'If the residence permit had been issued ... with a clear indication of its ... non-renewability, the plaintiff could not have relied on a renewal and derived claims from his integration (in German society).'[62] In short, the German guestworker programme turned into de facto immigration not because of some general logic of postnational membership, but because the state had failed to be firm and explicit about the temporal limitation of its guestworker recruitment – an historical accident turned Germany into an immigration country. And, interestingly, the German state seems to have learned from this experience. Its second-generation guestworker programmes, established in the early 1990s with Poland and other Eastern European countries, include strict termination clauses and legal safeguards to prevent permanent settlement this time round.[63]

The obvious gradation of migrant rights cannot be captured within the postnational membership model, according to which all migrants alike are protected by the same rights of personhood. This model fails to account for one of the most blatant characteristics of contemporary migration: the division of the migrant population into a small group of 'privileged' settled labour migrants or legal immigrants, and the vast, non-privileged remainder of illegal immigrants, asylum-seekers and new labour migrants.

The communitarian logic of investing (some, not all!) labour migrants with permanent-resident and free-movement rights, as revealed in the German case, casts doubt on the postnational hypothesis that 'rights acquire a more universalistic form and are divorced from national belonging'.[64] Wrong is not only the implicit assumption of a comprehensive 'national citizenship' that never was; wrong is also the assumed dualism between rights (that are transposed to the transnational level) and states. This is where the postnational membership argument meets the argument of globally impaired state sovereignty, discussed above. Both invite the same objection: individual rights are not external to, but are an integral part of, liberal states. Otherwise one could not explain why human rights constraints are more urgently felt in the states of the West than, say, the migrant-receiving states in the Middle East – states that do not allow their foreign workers to acquire property

61 Though somewhat weaker, and with some nuances, one can find a similar communitarian justification of expansive alien rights also in the case law of the US Supreme Court. In *Mathews v Diaz* (1976) for example, the court argued: 'Congress may decide that as the alien's tie (with this country) grows stronger, so does the strength of his claim to an equal share of that munificence.' See the discussion of the underlying 'affiliation model' by Motomura (1998).
62 Decision of 26 September 1978 (2 BvR 525/77) p 188.
63 See Groenendijk and Hampsink (1995) chapter 4.
64 Soysal (1997) at 8.

or to be joined by their family, and which routinely practice mass expulsions. Interestingly, recent 'constructivist' International Relations scholarship, which stresses the socialising impact of international human rights precepts on states,[65] has exempted the North Atlantic zone of liberal stateness from the scope of these precepts, obviously assuming that the robust liberal infrastructure and traditions in such states render obsolete the recourse to external norms and regimes.

A final, empirical shortcoming of the postnational approach should be considered: it cannot account for the current revaluation of citizenship in Europe and the US alike. Postnationalists have slighted the role of formal state membership for immigrants, because they deem them enmeshed in a 'transnational' reality, in which the local and the global have pincered the national. In this regard, Soysal starkly delimits her postnational membership model from 'denizenship' models[66] that treat second-tier membership as an anomaly subject to correction and remain 'within the confines of the nation-state model'. She continues:

> 'As I see it, the incorporation of guestworkers is no mere expansion of the scope of national citizenship, nor is it an irregularity. Rather, it reveals a profound transformation in the institution of citizenship, both in its institutional logic and in the way it is legitimated.'[67]

The empirical evidence is against this. Immigrant-receiving Western states have all treated a generation-spanning, non-citizen membership of larger portions of their population as an intolerable anomaly. Throughout the 1990s, most European states reformed their citizenship laws to make it easier for long-settled migrants and their children to acquire the citizenship of the host society. With the exception of Austria, Greece and Luxembourg, all member states of the EU now provide a right to citizenship for second-generation immigrants.[68] Germany, previously the paragon of 'postnational' immigrant integration, had been a member of this club already, *before* its wholesale reform of citizenship law in 1999.[69] In the US, one can observe a similar revaluation of citizenship in response to immigration – even though here the trend is not to make exclusive citizenship more inclusive, as in Europe, but to make initially inclusive citizenship more exclusive, and to tie more substantial privileges than before to the formal status of citizen. The attempt to upgrade citizenship is visible in the recent welfare reforms, as a result of which legal immigrants are now excluded from most federal welfare programmes.[70] The US lesson is this: non-citizens are, inherently, politically vulnerable; political rights, which have always been and continue to be a citizen privilege, matter. By implication, citizenship matters, even in a country where historically it has not mattered much. US immigrants have understood this, as they are now naturalising in record numbers.[71] To be a viable alternative to national citizenship, non-citizen membership would have to be a recurrent, transmittable and positively valued status, with its own institutional infrastructure. It is unlikely to ever meet this test.

While national citizenship continues to be the via regia of immigrant integration, the post-war immigration experience, along with other factors, has started a trend

65 Risse, Ropp and Sikkink (1999).
66 Eg Hammar (1990); Brubaker (1989).
67 Soysal (1994) p 139.
68 Hansen (1998).
69 See Joppke (2000).
70 See Moynihan (1998).
71 New applications for US citizenship rocketed from 543,000 in 1994 to 1,400,000 in 1997: Aleinikoff (1998) at 16. On the problem that instrumentally acquired citizenship is damaging the identity component of citizenship, see Note (1997).

toward the de-ethnicisation of citizenship in Western states. One element of this is the resurgence of territorial *jus soli* citizenship in Europe. Ethnic citizenship, attributed at birth *jure sanguinis*, had once been associated with the modern invention of democracy and nationhood, replacing the feudal principle of *jus soli*, according to which people (like crop and territory) were the property of the lord. Ironically, the smell of modernism is now with *jus soli*, because of its better fit with a world of migration. It is important to see that jus sanguinis remains the predominant mode of attributing citizenship at birth in European states; but – with an eye on integrating later-generation immigrants – it is increasingly complemented with elements of jus soli.[72] To the degree that mere birth on territory confers citizenship, the state-constituting citizenry (ie the nation) can no longer be conceived of in ethnic terms, but transmutes into a politically constituted, territorial body. A second element of de-ethnicised citizenship is the increasing toleration of multiple citizenship, at least in Europe. This is expressed in the Council of Europe's new Nationality Convention of 1997, which allows its signatory states to tolerate dual nationality.[73] A third element of de-ethnicised citizenship is the increasing recognition of minority rights and identities in liberal states.[74] To be a citizen of a liberal state no longer connotes membership in a particular cultural community; the only 'culture' that citizens are asked to share is the 'political culture of liberalism itself'.[75] An expression of this is the 'thinning' of naturalisation requirements in liberal states. Germany, for example, (which until recently had subjected even its Germany-born applicants to an excruciating individual assimilation test) in the early 1990s lowered the threshold in the case of young second-generation immigrants to certain generic residence and language requirements.

Germany is, in fact, still today commonly considered, along with Israel and Japan, as the proverbially ethnic state,[76] is a prime example of de-ethnicisation, introducing conditional jus soli for second-generation immigrants in its new citizenship law of 1999, tacitly tolerating dual citizenship in administrative practice (though as of today in contrast to official political rhetoric) and rejecting the idea of a German *Leitkultur* (dominant culture) that immigrants had to adjust to.[77]

The true galvaniser of de-ethnicised citizenship is the transformation of the North Atlantic region from a Hobbesian zone of war into a Lockean zone of trade. The development of citizenship was historically tied to the development of nations as war-making bodies. With the end of war in the Lockean zone, the 'national' component of national citizenship, rather than disappearing, is undergoing a transformation, from ethnic to civic-territorial. In a word, citizenship everywhere is becoming 'Americanised' – constituted by political values rather than by confrontation with a hypostasised 'Other'. Liberal states are finally living up to the 'liberal' in their name. This is a profoundly different scenario than the one depicted by postnationalists, according to which sovereignty-clenching states are externally kept in check by the 'international-human-rights watchman'. Why the latter scenario has gained so much popularity in recent social science, as well as public discourse, is an interesting question indeed. But it has to be left for another occasion. The

---

72 EU states with jus soli provisions are the UK, France, Portugal, The Netherlands, Ireland and Germany.
73 See Koslowski (1998) at 741–746.
74 Conceptually, see Kymlicka (1995); empirically, see Joppke (1999a) Pt II.
75 Perry (1995) 114.
76 Eg Coleman and Harding (1995) at 51.
77 See the 'Fourth Report on the Situation of Foreigners in Germany', issued by the Federal Commissioner for Foreigner Affairs (Berlin 2000).

chapter concludes by merely hinting at the possibility that globalisation rhetoric helps domestic political elites to evade their responsibilities towards citizen and immigrants alike. Academics should be wary of following them.

Select bibliography

Bigo, D, (2001) 'The Securitization of Migration' in V Guiraudon and C Joppke (eds), Controlling a New Migration World.

Bosniak, L, (1994) 'Membership, Equality, and the Difference that Alienage Makes' 69(6) New York University Law Rev 1047–1149.

Brubaker, R, (1989) 'Introduction' in R Brubaker (ed), Immigration and the Politics of Citizenship in Europe and North America.

—(1992) Citizenship and Nationhood in France and Germany.

Coleman, J A and Harding, S K, (1995) 'Citizenship, the Demands of Justice, and the Moral Relevance of Political Borders' in W F Schwartz (ed), Justice in Immigration.

Eichenhofer, E, (1997) 'Die sozialrechtliche Stellung von Auslaendern aus Nicht-EWR- sowie Nicht-Abkommensstaaten' in K Barwig et al (eds) Sozialer Schutz von Auslaendern in Deutschland.

Ferrajoli, L, (1994) 'Dai diritti del cittadino ai diritti della persona' in D Zolo (ed), La Cittadinanza.

Finnemore, M, (1998) 'Norms, Culture and World Politics' 50(2) International Organization 325–347.

Freeman, G, (1994) 'Britain, the Deviant Case' in Wayne Cornelius et al (eds), Controlling Immigration.

—(1998) 'The Decline of Sovereignty?' in C Joppke (ed) Challenge to the Nation-State.

Goodwin-Gill, G, (1978) International Law and the Movement of Persons Between States.

Groenendijk, K and Hampsink, R, (1995) Temporary Employment of Migrants in Europe.

Guiraudon, V, (1998) Sovereign After All? International Norms, Nation-States, and Aliens (Unpublished manuscript).

Hansen, R, (1998) 'A European Citizenship or a Europe of Citizens?' 24(4) Journal of Ethnic and Migration Studies 751–768.

Hirst, P and Thompson, G, (1995) 'Globalization and the Future of the Nation State' 24(3) Economy and Society 408–442.

Isensee, J, (1974) 'Die statusrechtliche Stellung der Auslaender in der Bundesrepublik Deutschland' Veroeffentlichungen der Vereinigung der Deutschen Staatsrechtslehrer, vol 32.

Hammar, T, (1990) Democracy and the Nation-State.

Harlow, C, (1994) 'Accidental Loss of an Asylum Seeker' 57 Modern Law Rev 620–627.

Jacobson, D, (1996) Rights Across Borders.

Joppke, C, (1998) 'Why Liberal States Accept Unwanted Immigration' 50(2) World Politics 266–293.

—(1999a) Immigration and the Nation-State.

—(1999b) The Domestic-Legal Sources of Immigrant Rights. EUI Working Paper SPS No.99/3. European University Institute, Florence. Published as same title (2001) 34(4) Comparative Political Studies pp 339–366.

—(2000) 'Mobilization of Culture and the Reform of Citizenship Law: Germany and the United States' in R Koopmans and P Statham (eds), Challenging Immigration and Ethnic Relations Politics.

Koslowski, R, (1998) 'European Migration Regimes' 24(4) Journal of Ethnic and Migration Studies 735–749.

Krasner, S, (1995a) 'Compromising Westphalia' 20(3) International Security 115–151.

—(1995b) 'Sovereignty, Regimes, and Human Rights' in V Rittberger (ed), Regime Theory and International Relations.

Kymlicka, W, (1995) Multicultural Citizenship.

Lavenex, S, (1999) The Europeanisation of Refugee Policies. Dissertation, Department of Political and Social Sciences, European University Institute, Florence.

Levitsky, J E, (1994) 'The Europeanization of the British Legal Style' 42 American Journal of Comparative Law 347–380.

Loescher, G, (1989) 'Refugee Issues in International Relations' in G Loescher and L Monahan (eds) Refugees and International Relations.

Mann, M, (1993) The Sources of Social Power, vol 2.

Marshall, T H, (1950) Citizenship and Social Class.

Meyer, J and Rowan, B, (1977) 'Institutionalized Organizations: Formal Structure as Myth and Ceremony' 83(2) American Journal of Sociology 340–363.

Motomura, H, (1998) 'Alienage Classifications in a Nation of Immigrants' in N Pickus (ed) Immigration and Citizenship in the 21st Century.

Moynihan, L, (1998) 'Welfare Reform and the Meaning of Membership' 12 Georgetown Immigration LJ 657–688.

Moravcsik, A, (1995) 'Explaining International Human Rights Regimes' 1(2) European Journal of International Relations 157–189.

Nettl, J P, (1968) 'The State as a Conceptual Variable' 20(4) World Politics 559–592.

Note (anonymous author) (1997) 'The Functionality of Citizenship' 110 Harvard Law Rev 1814–1831.

Peers, S, (1998) 'Building Fortress Europe' 35 Common Market Law Rev 1235–1272.

Perry, S R, (1995) 'Immigration, Justice, and Culture' in W F Schwartz (ed), Justice in Immigration.

Reinicke, W, (1998) Global Public Policy.

Risse, T, Ropp, S and Sikking, K, (eds) (1999) The Power of Human Rights.

Rubio-Marin, R, (1998) Stranger in One's Own Home: The Inclusion of Immigrants as a Democratic Challenge. Published as Immigration as a Democratic Challenge (2000).

Sassen, S, (1998) 'The de facto Transnationalizing of Immigration Policy' in C Joppke (ed), Challenge to the Nation-State.

Schwerdtfeger, G, (1980) Welche rechtlichen Vorkehrungen empfehlen sich, um die Rechtsstellung von Auslaendern in der Bundesrepublik Deutschland angemessen zu gestalten Gutachten A zum 53. Deutschen Juristentag Berlin 1980.

Slaughter, A-M, (1992) 'Law Among Liberal States' 92(8) Columbia Law Rev 1907–1997.

—(1995) 'International Law in a World of Liberal States' 6(4) European Journal of International Law 503–538.

SOPEMI (1998) Trends in International Migration.

Soysal, Y, (1994) Limits of Citizenship.

—(1997) Identity, Rights, and Claims-Making (Manuscript).

Weiler, J, (1991) 'The Transformation of Europe' 100(3) Yale LJ 2403–2483.

Weiner, M, (1995) The Global Migration Crisis.

Chapter 13

Patterns of African constitution in the making

U MATTEI[*]

INTRODUCTION

This chapter focuses on three recent constitutional experiences – South Africa, Eritrea and Puntland State of Somalia – in order to detect new trends in African constitution-making. The focus is not on the constitutional documents, but on the process itself. The latter seems much more important than the former in Africa.

Constitutions are empty boxes until the fundamental question – does the armed man obey the unarmed? – is answered positively.[1] This writer believes, however, that the institution-building exercise necessary for the adoption of a constitutional framework operates as a sort of intellectual and cultural 'gymnastics'[2] that might work in the direction of controlling power within a *rule of political law* system.[3]

The success of an African constitution might therefore be predicted by the extent and the thoroughness of such exercise. The writer detects two important aspects of it: a *technical* one, related to the issue of the transferability and adaptability of foreign legal models in Africa;[4] and a *participatory* one, connected to the degree of involvement of the people in the process. The technical aspect is located in the domain of *professional law*, and plays its role at the semantic level of lawyer's law. Two questions are to be asked here: (a) what are the models used in the process of constitution framing? and (b) does significant local adaptation occur in this process?[5] The participatory aspect is related to the

---

[*] A previous version of this essay was published in the International Conference on African Constitutions. Bologna, 25–27 November 1998 Valeria Piergigli and Irma Taddia (eds) (2000, Giappichelli).
1 Sacco (1997).
2 This expression is owed to Mario Raffaelli, one of the leading international negotiators of the recent success story of Mozambique: see Morozzo della Rocca (1994). Such an idea of law making as an exercise in communication with many spillovers such as, eg, building a sense of belonging to a group is developed also by Habermas (1996).
3 It is argued in this chapter that the separation between law and politics has not occurred in Africa and in other legal systems, and consequently they have been classified here as belonging to a family called *rule of political law*, where politics is not governed by law, but the opposite is true: see Mattei (1997).
4 See Grande (1995); Mattei (2002).
5 See Guadagni (1995).

issue of legitimacy.[6] Two questions should be asked here: (a) is participation necessarily connected with western democratic institutions such as elections?; and (b) what are the substitutes of democratic institutions at play in Africa today?

This writer's conviction is that both the technical and the participatory efforts are important and should be carried on together, although in the present state of African institutional development (*political law* hegemony) legitimacy is more important than professionalism.

Professionalism without participation makes the institution-building gymnastics entirely insufficient, because it does not decentralise the informal institutional constraints that are necessary for the armed man to obey the unarmed. It consequently fails to limit extra-constitutional power. An example of this kind of failure is the Ethiopian Constitution of 1994, a mere top-down introduction of US constitutional rhetoric.[7] Participation without professionalism, however, might affect the quality or the international credibility of the resulting formal institutional setting. The negative impact might be perceived in the long term, but does not seem particularly important at this point.[8]

For the purpose of this chapter, the constitution-making process is viewed as an *informal institutional constraint-building* exercise, usually aimed at the production of some formal document.[9] The formal outcome – principally the production of a written constitutional document – is in itself entirely irrelevant if the fundamental informal institutional constraints are not created and settled.[10] The shortcoming of much scholarship on constitutional law, both within and outside Africa, is its excessive emphasis on the understanding and explanation of the written document. This approach is fruitless in understanding the working of the Western constitutional democracies and is even more senseless in Africa.[11]

Leaving aside such advanced systems as in England, in which the very existence of written constitutional documents is questionable, an approach limited to the explanation of the written constitution would be entirely non-productive in the US, where most of constitutional law is to be found in the working habits of Supreme Courts, both Federal and state. It would certainly be impossible to understand the Italian constitutional system, despite the rather modern and detailed 1948 Constitution, without a serious grasp of the many unwritten dynamics that determine the life of Italian political parties.

Most of the 'real life of the law' dynamics that can be detected in Western law through sophisticated tools (such as the separate analysis of legal formants)[12] are much more transparent in Africa.[13] Africa is a traditional domain of unwritten law, the product of decentralised forces still active and effective at different degrees within a society characterised by a decentralised clan structure. Focusing on final constitutional documents without a secure grasp on how such forces have determined its production is a certain recipe for misunderstanding.

The idea suggested in this chapter is that a close observation of the constitution-making process might show the real-life dynamics of professionalism and legitimacy

---

6 Cf Favali (1998a); Sacco (1995) p 43.
7 See Mattei (1995) p 111.
8 See Lewis (1992).
9 The sense in which the notion of formal and informal institutional constraints is used here is developed and discussed by North (1991).
10 See Van Doren (1994).
11 See Guadagni (1998); Mattei (1998a).
12 See Sacco (1991); Sacco and Monateri (1998).
13 See Grande (1996); Vanderlin (1995).

and is therefore a very promising way to understand the nature of constitutional law in Africa. The constitution-making process is a concentrated institutional drama whose unfolding determines the future constitutional life of a country.

The chapter approaches some preliminary issues, then outlines some historical and political background necessary to understand the constitution-making processes in South Africa, Eritrea and Puntland State of Somalia. The following section tackles the issue of public participation, and the final section approaches the professional dimension from the perspective of import-export of legal patterns, of foreign experts' participation and of international political involvement, and also offers some conclusions.

THE ISSUE OF THE STATE

Two important assumptions of this chapter should be stated at this point. First, the writer suggests that the law in general, and constitutional law in particular, is always in a state of flux. This assumption explains the emphasis on the process,[14] and the process by definition is never over. The eventual production of a document does not end the process of creation of constitutional law. It might, at most, be a convenient way for lawyers to indicate a new phase. In the metaphor of institutional gymnastics, the intensive training might be followed by a less intensive one once the constitution is ready, but this is not necessarily so. The creation of an African constitutional culture and of an African legal culture is, indeed, a long-term enterprise.[15]

Second, the writer believes in the utility and fruitfulness of talking about 'Africa' and 'African Law' as an object of observation.[16] Certainly, within Africa (as everywhere else) there are many different local realities and crucial differences that good scholarship should not forget; one of the objects of this comparative law work is precisely to describe differences between the three countries of my focus. However, knowledge cannot be compartmentalised. By the study of the differences, commonalties – both in terms of problems and of solutions – emerge. The emergence of a sufficient number of such deeply located commonalties justifies a taxonomy that groups the different African countries together. At least for the subject-matter of comparing legal systems, African law is not too broad a category. Many scholars believe that broader categories such as *legal pluralism* or *rule of political law* are needed.[17]

Classification is not an end, but a means for approaching a given observed phenomenon. There is one feature, common around Africa, that connects together and justifies, both from a positive and a normative perspective, the writer's choice of *focusing on the constitutional process*.

In Africa the fundamental constitutional issues of the state, both in terms of legitimacy and of extension, are not solved.[18] Most of the borders of the African states are mere colonial legacies culturally connected with a nineteenth-century European ideal of nation-state that has always been entirely foreign to Africa. Nations and ethnic groups are almost always located across the borders, so that

14 See generally, Cardozo (1921); Hart-Sacks (1994).
15 This point is made in Mattei (1990).
16 See Sacco (1995) p 49ff.
17 See Mattei (1997); Vanderlinden (1982); Reyntjens (1996).
18 See Fortes and Evans-Pritchard (1987).

the boundaries of the nation and those of the state practically never overlap. The consequences of this unprincipled importation of the Western state are extended unrest, war and genocide. Examples are easy to find, and the Rwanda-Burundi-Congo saga between Tutzi and Hutu is just the most recent and bloody. Borders are often the object of armed controversy, such as that presently involving Eritrea and Ethiopia. It would be reductionist to view this conflict, as many other modern African ones, as simply a dispute over a few square kilometres of territory. Within a post-colonial context characterised by what is known as 'internal colonialism', the real issue might be that of the leadership over a great Tigray[19] in the moment in which the Ethiopian leadership, representing only around 10% of the people, simply looks incapable of exerting control over the Oromo in the south.[20]

In this unstable and changing context, a genuine constitutional process might not and should not take for granted the status quo, both in terms of existence and of extension of the state. This is why a peaceful institution-building exercise is more significant than its outcome for the time being. Reaching a constitution perceived as final and emphatically advertised as opening a new era might sometimes even be a step backward from peace and stability. Given the high symbolic value of any constitutional document, if there is no proper participation of all the people concerned (whatever their state of belonging might be at the moment) the whole enterprise might backfire. In other words, as a paradox of modern Africa, flexibility and willingness to experience alternatives to the Western state is strengthened by a negotiated constitution-making process, but might be weakened by the written products of that process.

Even if this paradox were not accurate, it remains true – in Africa as everywhere else – that legal form without informal constraints over the use of armed political force does not solve any of the institutional problems affecting development.

SOME BACKGROUND

This chapter focuses on three of the most recent African experiences that might well be considered still work in progress. South Africa, Eritrea and Puntland (North East Somalia) have recently engaged in thorough constitution-making processes. These are very different African contexts, arguably not representative of the majority of sub-Saharan Africa.[21] Nevertheless, they have been selected for discussion here because the writer has some first-hand knowledge of them and, more importantly, believes that the greater the differences, the more significant are the analogies and general observations. These three countries not only are at very different stages of development (and the patterns of legal transplants among them confirm the well-established theory that more advanced societies affect less developed)[22] but the involvement and willingness of the international community to co-operate has been very uneven. However, their constitutional processes share the crucial characteristic of thoroughly tackling both legitimisation and professionalism. They can, consequently, be interestingly compared.

---

19 The writer owes this view of the present Ethiopia-Eritrea tension to Professor Gianpaolo Calchi Novati.
20 See Battera (1998); Brietzke (1997).
21 See Sacco (1996).
22 See A Watson (1974) arguing that transplants always occur from the more to the less advanced countries.

South Africa[23]

The South African constitution-making process can be considered as beginning in February 1990, when President De Klerk officially announced his intention to release Nelson Mandela, the historic leader of the African National Congress (ANC) who had been detained for 27 years on political charges. The tragedy that the process was aimed to solve was, of course, apartheid. The main target and ambition of the process was an equal society.

Among the reasons, mostly demographic and economic, of the relinquishment of power by the white minority were: high international pressure; internal political resistance, mostly organised by the ANC; and internal division of the whites, not all of whom were racist. It is beyond the scope of this chapter to discuss these issues. Certainly, the South African process has benefited enormously from international participation, both economic and political. It is fair to consider the process the most important success of Boutros Ghali's tenure at the UN.

In September 1991, after some negotiations (and the repeal by the government of the symbol of apartheid, the Population Registration Act), representatives of 27 political organisations signed the National Peace Accord, a 33-page document containing the 'rules of the game' for further negotiations aimed at holding general elections. After more than two years of negotiation in an increasingly violent environment, mitigated by a thorough effort of constitutional education of the population lead by an independent Constitutional Commission, the Provisional Constitution of the Republic of South Africa (Act 200, 1993) was approved in December 1993, and it was agreed that the provisional constitution would enter in force on 27 April 1994, the day after the beginning of elections. This document contained the fundamental principles that the final constitution, to be approved within two years by the newly elected Parliament in a Constitutional Assembly capacity, had to respect.

Within a rudimentary oversimplification of a complex political process, we can say that the main tension that the Provisional Constitution had to solve was between the political parties representing the black majority (notably the ANC) that could easily be predicted to win the elections, and the political forces representing the white minority (and the government) who feared that their rights could be violated by the long-repressed black population. The former political forces were emphasising the lack of legitimisation of the Convention for a Democratic South Africa (Co. De. S.A.), the negotiating body in which formal negotiations were carried on from late 1991, in which only 17 political groups and the government were represented. The government, on the other hand, was emphasising the need to secure the rights of the minorities against the feared tyranny of the majority.[24]

The solution worked out in the Provisional Constitution was thoroughly original: the compatibility of the Final Constitution, with 34 fundamental principles contained in the Provisional Constitution, had to be certified by the newly established, highly independent and respected Constitutional Court. The Provisional Constitution, moreover, institutionalised a power-sharing national unity government to stay in power until the 1999 elections. After the elections (Mandela's ANC 62.6%; De Klerk's National Party 20.4%; the Zulu Inkhata

---

23 For some background see Federal Research Commission of the Library of Congress; S Gloppen (1997).
24 See Du Plessis, Lourens and Corder (1994).

Freedom Party, against the process until the last minute, 10.5%) the new Constitution was approved and voted with the required majority in May 1996. On 6 September of the same year the Constitutional Court, with an impressive review of the whole document, declined certification until some modifications were introduced. After the changes were made by the Constitutional Assembly on 10 December 1996 (Act 108, 1996) the Constitution of the Republic of South Africa was finally promulgated, completing this phase of the constitutional process.

From the perspective of the process, two aspects of the Constitution need to be emphasised. First, that the creation of a Constitutional Court and a detailed Bill of Rights entrusts to the High Court a huge institutional responsibility for the unfolding of South African constitutional life. This institutional solution represents a dramatic break with the previous form of unlimited parliamentary sovereignty inherited from the British Westminster system that has been so much distorted in the racist climate of South Africa. Second, the consciousness of the needs of a difficult transition has lead to the creation of an impressive variety of independent constitutional authorities, which can be seen as sharing the function of thorough constitutional education of the people as well as of continuing an effective constitution-making process in the sense of creating the informal constraints that can make the paper law effective. Among others, we find a Human Rights Commission placed in charge of the effectiveness of the Bill of Rights, a Gender Equality Commission to tackle the difficult issue of the integration of women, a Public Protector, modelled on the Scandinavian Ombudsman, and an Electoral Commission.

Eritrea[25]

Eritrea started the constitution-making process after a 30-year war for independence. This struggle was looked upon with marked indifference, sometimes even hostility, from the international community. Its main purpose can therefore be considered the assertion and international recognition of a new state after decades of oppression from Ethiopia.[26]

The final military victory against Ethiopia came in 1991, ended a war which began in 1961. Asmara was liberated on 24 May, as was the port of Assab the day after.

Menghistu Haile Mariam fled Addis Ababa on 21 May, following defeats by both the Eritrean Front (EPLF) and the tigrean military organisation in Northern Ethiopia (FDRPE). Very short negotiations in London (27 and 28 May) with the assistance of the US were sufficient to persuade the new Ethiopian rulers to recognise the right of the Eritrean people to decide their own future. The deal, ratified by a Conference for Peace and Democracy attended by 25 Ethiopian political groups, held in Addis Ababa in July, was cut in the following way: Eritrea could decide by means of a referendum, to be held by 1993, whether or not to create an independent state. In consideration, Ethiopia was to be granted access to the sea from the port of Assab.

The referendum was held between 23 and 25 April 1993. Ninety-nine point eight per cent of the people cast a 'free and fair' vote for the creation of a new

25 For some updated background, see Guadagni (1998b).
26 See Cliffe and Davidson (1988).

independent and sovereign state. On 24 May 1993 the second anniversary of the liberation of Asmara independence was officially declared. Four days later, Eritrea became an official member of the UN.

More than five years after that emphatic day, the Eritrean people have not been called to the polls. Nevertheless, a fully fledged constitutional process, with a final document approved – but never signed into law by President Issaiah Afeworki – has been ongoing. The legitimating factor has been of an effective and charismatic guerrilla leadership and an almost unanimous vote for independence, interpreted by this leadership as a full endorsement of its power. Interestingly, the legitimating power of military effectiveness has been used as a substitute for elections recently, when the relationship with the new Ethiopian leadership dramatically changed.

The constitution-making process was started very soon by the EPLF, which became both provisional government and the sole political party. In February 1994, in fact, the EPLF was officially transformed into a political party and changed its name to the People's Front for Democracy and Justice (PFDJ). The main formal sources of constitutional law in Eritrea are Proclamations 37/1993 and 52/1994. Such sources set forward the constitutional process aimed at the creation of a Final Constitution (by 1996) as well as to general elections, none of which have so far happend.[27]

According to the Proclamations, the National Assembly (consisting almost entirely of the PFDJ's members)[28] had to create a Constitutional Commission whose duty was to draft a Proposal of Constitution and to develop the instruments necessary to guarantee the participation of the people in the constitution-making process. The product of that process was to be adopted by an 'organ representing the people'.

The Constitutional Commission of Eritrea was established by Proclamation 55/1994. According to Article 4, the Commission had to initiate a national constitutional debate and constitutional educational process by means of public workshops and lectures on constitutional principles and practices. Following this phase, the Commission had to propose a first draft to the Constitutional Assembly. After discussion and more public debate, the final draft was prepared for official approval by a democratically created representative body.

The Constitutional Commission formally took office on 17 April 1994. It was composed of 50 members nominated by the National Assembly in such a way as to represent rural and urban populations, different ethnic and social groups, former guerrilla soldiers and members of the Eritrean people abroad. In total, all individuals capable of contributing to the constitution-making process, in observance of the language of the Proclamation. Ten of the members formed the Executive Committee. Its chair was a prominent Eritrean legal scholar, educated and teaching in the US and for many years active as a supporter of the EPLF from abroad.

A number of subcommittees were created for the different chapters of the Constitution, with the aim to collect information and sources needed for the successful drafting and for a clear perception of the issues and the choices to be made. A Civic Education and Public Debate Committee, possibly framed after the South African experience that lead to the Provisional Constitution, organised

---

27 See Tekle' (1997) at 331ff.
28 According to Proclamation 52/94, of the 150 members, only 75 were to be members of the party, while the other 75 were to be elected by the people. In practice, of course …

hundreds of meetings in the cities, villages and countryside to involve the population and the soldiers in the military facilities. Meetings were also organised abroad within the Eritrean communities. Eventually, even stable offices of the Commission were located in many communities to explain the process and absorb input.

Interestingly, this impressive effort was completed by the creation of two consulting committees. One was composed of 15 foreign experts in constitutional law from the US, Europe, Africa and the Middle East. The other was made up of 45 elders and religious leaders of different groups, who were experts in traditional customary law. While the involvement of the former was technical, or perhaps aimed at international legitimisation of the process, the latter was less technical and more legitimising. Both these committees met, and the different *position papers* created by the Commission were thoroughly discussed in an International Conference held in Asmara in January 1995. The (first) *Draft Constitution* was submitted to the National Assembly in July 1996, and approved with a few amendments. After further discussion involving the whole population, in March 1997 the final draft of the Eritrean Constitution was approved. This was then supposed to be discussed and approved by an ad hoc elected Assembly. In fact, it was approved by a body entirely dominated by the PFDJ and, possibly because of the new international situation, never signed into law by the President. Even after the end of armed conflict with Ethiopia in 2001, the issue of final approval of the constitution, as well as that of elections seems tabled. The present tension in the Horn, following the 11 September events, is likely to encourage and boost the iron fist with opposition as it is presently happening in Asmara.[29]

PUNTLAND STATE OF SOMALIA[30]

Puntland, the territory north-east of Somalia, also known as Mijurtinia, recently started its constitution-making process in an attempt at social and political reconstruction after eight years of a civil war that disrupted all of Somalia. The Puntland constitution-making experience stems from the conditions of relative peace and prosperity of this region, which is mostly populated by Darod people. Midjurtinia (Puntland from the old Egyptian name of this area) was traditionally ruled by a king, the Sultan or Bochor. Traditional leadership, decentralised in many local elders, is still very vital in the region.[31]

When the civil law erupted in Mogadishu and throughout the country after the fall of President Muhamed Siad Barre in January 1991, many white-collar workers in Mogadishu, originally from Puntland, returned home, with a modern political expertise developed during many years in the capital, where many Darod under Siad's rule had been able to occupy important political posts. But Midjurtinia also suffered under Siad, as witnessed by the long incarceration of the first Puntland President Abdullaahi Jussuf, elected in 1998.

A number of the first parties created to resist Siad Barre's dictatorship, most notably the Somali Salvation Democratic Front (SSDF), were created by Puntland people. A number of these anti-Siad politicians came back from abroad. In an effort to regain that law and order indispensable for the thriving trading activity across the sea, this sophisticated leadership, frustrated by the continuous failures

---

29 See Calchi Novati (2002).
30 For some historical background, see Lewis (1988).
31 In the complete absence of scholarly literature, data discussed in this section are based on the writer's direct observation.

of dozens of general Somali peace conferences (in Djibouti, Ethiopia, Yemen, Kenya, Egypt and Somalia, among others) decided to try a different approach.

After total rejection of the agreement among faction leaders signed in Cairo (basically an accord between the Ali Mhadi and Aidid clans), a conference 'to redefine the political destiny' was called in Garowe in March 1998.

At this first conference, a decision was made to start a thorough constitutional process based on three fundamental points.[32] First to abandon the notion of 'creating' Somalia with a top-down approach and replace it with a bottom-up approach. Second, to encourage other Somali groups and territorial entities to create similar administrative systems. Third, after the establishment of regional administrations, to begin negotiations for the reunification of Somalia on a federal basis.

The constitutional process as far as the future federal Puntland State was concerned was scheduled to start on 15 May 1998 with a Constitutional Convention in Garowe, aimed at approving a transitional constitutional charter, and electing all the officials of the new state.

The issue of legitimacy was entirely delegated to the traditional leadership that has been credited with not allowing the north-eastern part of the country to be as badly disrupted as other areas. The traditional leaders were supposed to select, on local bases, the representatives of the regions of Sool, Sanaag, Nugaal, Mudug, Bari and Buuhodle District 'who are descendants of same ancestors' acting as delegates to the Constitutional Convention of Garowe.

A preparatory committee of 25 members, representative of the different areas, as well as of different political groups and religious leaders, was also appointed with the task of drafting a proposal of a Constitutional Charter, to be discussed, changed and approved by the Conference. The process was successfully carried on and resulted in the election and tenure of Abdullaahi Jussuf.

The International community had been approached for help in preparation of the Constitutional Convention, but the request of help received a lukewarm response. Two of the areas involved, Sool and Sanaag, were formally part of the former British Somaliland (North West of Somalia) that had declared itself independent shortly after the beginning of the civil war. Somaliland has never been formally recognised as a state, but, de facto, a large involvement of international NGO's occurred and Somaliland has been both recognised and supported by Ethiopia, the strong player of the region. The fear was that the secession of Sool and Sanaag could create problems. Consequently, the only help provided was a small group of four scholars,[33] under the coverage of the UN Development Office for Somalia. Such experts met with the preparatory Committee in Garowe in April 1998 and a document was produced to serve as a base for the Constitutional Conference.

After hectic consensus-building activity by the preparatory committee, the Constitutional Convention was finally opened in Garowe, under the chairmanship of a senior traditional leader, on 6 June 1998.[34] The Convention was attended by 512 official delegates representing the regions and the Somali Diaspora abroad. The Conference finally concluded on 23 July 1998 with the President and Vice

32 See the Presentation of Puntland State of Somalia's President to the House of Representatives, September 1998, p 3.
33 Two Italian law Professors, including this author, a former US politician, now active as a law professor in Cairo, and an Irish political scientist, partially funded by the Swiss and partially by the Italian governments.
34 See UN Somali Rehabilitation Programme 'Report on the Community Constitutional Conference for the establishment of Puntland State organized by the communities of five regions in Northern Somalia' (prepared by Abdullahi A Ahmed, Observer).

President of Puntland sworn into office with very large majorities. The House of representatives, composed of 69 members duly appointed by the local traditional leaders, was sworn in as well, and many more important decisions taken about the provisional constitutional form of state. When President Jussuf's term expired, in Summer 2001, a new President, Jama Ali Jama was voted into office. Unfortunately, Jussuf's reluctance to relinquish power, and US and Ethiopian intervention in his support due to the fear of Jama Ali Jama's Islamic radicalism, led to much fighting in Garowe, with hundreds of casualties in the aftermath of Enduring Freedom operations. Currently, as through Somalia, with Somaliland being the only exception, two factions struggle for power: a supposedly secular one, supported by the US and Ethiopia (Jussuf in Puntland the Somali Reconciliation and Reconstruction Council in Mogadishu and the South) and a supposedly Islamic one, supported by Saudi Arabia, Yeman and other Islamic countries (President Ysama Ali Jama in Puntland and the Transitional National Government of President Abdiguassim Salad in Mogadishu and the South).[35]

The unfolding of the Conference, a remarkable example of institution-building gymnastics, deserves a study in itself to elaborate. Suffice here to say that unanimous agreement of the elders was always sought on difficult issues before voting, and that a number of significant changes to the document prepared with international assistance were made at the Convention.

The approved provisional Constitution of the State of Puntland does not spell out the next phases of the process in detail. However, a Constitutional Preparatory Commission, inspired by the Eritrean experience, has been provided for in article 28 of the Constitution. The article reads as follows:

'The House of Representatives while consulting with the Executive Council and the High Judicial Council will appoint the Constitutional Preparatory Commission which shall consist of:

Members of the House of Representatives
Members from the Judiciary and Attorney-General's office
Members representing the Executive Council
Valuable members who the Executive Council will appoint – from the public and foreign experts if needed.

28.1   The Constitutional Preparatory Commission will be established as soon as possible considering the magnitude of the task expected from it.
28.3   The Constitutional Preparatory Commission's tasks and responsibilities will be defined by special law.
28.4   The new Constitution of Puntland will be in use on the date in which it is ratified by vote.'

Although Article 28.4 of the Constitution does not spell this out, it is clear that such a vote, consistent with the intention of the Constitutional Convention, should be by popular referendum. Indeed, Article 13 expressly binds the Executive Council to 'organize and support the work of a Constitutional Commission, and prepare a Referendum to endorse the Constitution'. Moreover, President Yussuf, in his first presentation in front of the House of Representatives, expressly pledged that 'after completion of the Puntland Constitution the Government shall establish a committee which carries out the National Referendum and the total

---

35 Updated information was presented at the ISIAO conference cited above. See, in particular, I M Lewis *Muhamad Siyad Barre's Ghost Dance in Somalia*; Ahmed Yussuf Farah *The Process of National Reconciliations*; R Marchal *Mogadiseio dans la guerre civile: rêves d'Etat.*

acceptance and approval of the Constitution by the People of Puntland'.[36] None of this happened.

Finally, it should be mentioned that, realistically, Article 34 of the Constitution provides as follows:

> 'If for any reason after the three transitional years, the Constitution is not ready, the House of Representatives and the Executive Council will automatically be dissolved. The responsibilities of the President should be transferred to the Chief Justice of the Supreme Court, who is required, within thirty days to call for a conference in which all the regions of Puntland will participate to discuss the new circumstances.'

Unfortunately, as mentioned above, only war followed.

Commonalties and differences of background.

The three constitutional experiences that have been briefly described here, although very different from many points of view, share some important aspects. To begin with, these constitutional efforts are responses to genuine revolutionary moments.[37] This is not a process of constitutional reform aimed at improving the existing institutional structure; there is a necessity here for a new start aimed at new basic institutional arrangements. The previous institutional structure (the Apartheid law in South Africa; Ethiopian Law in Eritrea; civil war, tribal legal decentralisation in Puntland) is considered entirely unacceptable; the institutional actors are new, or at least in search of a new formal legitimisation.

These are constitutional processes aimed at genuine change, in the sense of building an institutional structure capable of governing peaceful, wealth-maximising transactions.[38] As all processes of institutional change, these are characterised by important aspects of continuity (not only the undesired kind of institutional continuity, a sort of legal path dependence that might frustrate attempts to change).[39] They are aspects of a desired continuity.

In all the three experiences there was an eagerness to save something of the existing informal institutional structure. South Africa has developed, before and during the apartheid era, a remarkable legal culture that is willing and eager to maintain.[40] Eritrea has organised in the occupied territory an institutional structure based on military hierarchy that was successful in creating a sense of self-sufficiency and of responsibility that the system is willing to keep.[41] Puntland is proud of its traditional leadership and emphasises the role of traditional leadership to an extent that, to the best of the writer's knowledge, is unprecedented.

The various points of departure, however, could not be more different.

South Africa enjoys a modern administrative structure that is the most advanced in Africa. The state has always been strong and well-developed. The constitutional process was aimed at a change in the political leadership, at an enfranchising of the majority of the people. The real issue here was occupation of the positions of power in a well-organised, though traditionally racist, state hierarchy. The equality

---

36 Presentation of Puntland State of Somalia's President to the House of Representatives, September 1998, p 2.
37 See the discussion in Ackerman (1991).
38 See, for a case study of how such institution-building might happen in Africa, Ensminger (1992).
39 See, for a discussion of informal resistance to change, Mattei (1998a).
40 See Zimmermann et al (1996); Mattei (1999).
41 See Tseggai (1998).

of formal possibilities was at stake. Such predominant worry for equality is reflected in the text of the Constitution that, strikingly, never mentions multi-ethnicity in a remarkably multi-ethnic environment.[42]

In Eritrea, the administrative experience of the guerrilla in the territories was more similar to the hierarchical structure of a state or of a Party than to a decentralised model of shared power. Schools, hospitals and other public goods were successfully provided in the guerrilla-occupied territories. Moreover, the Ethiopian state never ceased to claim sovereignty.[43] A state and a hierarchical organisation never really stopped existing in the areas of the country, most notably Asmara, that were still under Ethiopian rule.

Only Somalia completely collapsed as a state. Since the beginning of the civil war, this is *the one spot on earth* in which no state organisation, however tiny and ineffective, claims sovereignty. Puntland was a society that has entirely decentralised its power. Peace and order have been kept by traditional arrangements. There were no hierarchically based police, no army, no schools, no hospitals. All functions usually carried on by the state were de facto privatised. Possibly Islam played an important role from the perspective of organising the society since it was one of the few concentrated depositories of political power. True, the nomadic character of much of the Somali people never allowed the Somali state to develop as a territory-based, centralised organisation as elsewhere.[44] Its absence in Puntland might consequently be interpreted more as a signal of continuity than of change.[45] However, the colonial experience and 30 years of independence had built in Somalia some hierarchy that has now disappeared, and that the constitution-making process of Puntland is trying to rebuild.[46]

Summing up comparatively, we can detect a continuum in the degree of centralisation of power and of development of a state institutional structure from South Africa to Eritrea to Puntland State.

LEGITIMACY AND PARTICIPATION

An important aspect from which to compare constitutional processes is the degree of political pluralism. From this point of view, South Africa and the Puntland State show some analogies; the Eritrean experience stands alone.

Both in Puntland State and in South Africa, the general balance of political power *during the constitutional process* has been very unclear and certainly never clearly in the hands of one group. In a way, both in South Africa and in Puntland, internal political division among different groups (political or ethnic does not matter here) could (and in Puntland did) stop the process at any moment. This apparently negative aspect is nevertheless a signal of genuine competitive constitution-making experience aimed to draft rules of the game with no clearly defined group leading the dance. To return to the armed/unarmed metaphor,

---

42 This point is made by Bernardo Bernardi 'On the Founding Provisions of the Constitution of the Republic of South Africa 1996. Will Multilinguism Subserve or Substitute Multiethnicity?', Paper delivered at the International Bologna Conference on African Constitutionalism, November 1998.
43 See Cliffe and Davidson (1998).
44 See Lewis (1994); Salih (1989).
45 For the situation before the civil war, see Mattei (1990).
46 A complete description of the legal system that was in place before the civil war can be found in Sacco (1988).

the 'armed' were divided and there was substantial competition over arms. Thus constitution-making activity substitutes in a peaceful way armed competition.

In Eritrea, on the other hand, after the success of the armed struggle the power structure and the monopoly of arms has always been clearly in the hands of the EPLF (now PFDJ). There is no ongoing competition for power. The constitution-making activity does not substitute internal armed fighting that would not occur anyway, given the balance of political power.

In other words, the constitutional process has been an 'invisible hand' dynamic in South Africa and Puntland, while in Eritrea it has been the product of a centrally planned decision-making. (This explains the continuing procrastination of the idea of pluralism of political parties.)

This does not mean that important issues were not also at stake in Eritrea.[47] Suffice to think about the issue of gender integration, de facto achieved by women fighters during the war and now creating so many problems in being recognised by the traditional culture. Nevertheless, this issue is possibly less dramatic than the choice between an Islamic and secular system in Puntland, or the degree of effectiveness of minority protection in South Africa. One reason is that the positions achieved by women during the guerrilla period were never threatened at the constitutional level; they were actually fostered by the regime.

In Puntland, the tension between Islamic conservatism and secular leadership is a much closer case. The Constitutional Charter reflects a compromise on a question that is certainly not yet solved.

Something similar can be said for the issue of traditional leadership and monarchy in South Africa – a question that some decentralised aspects of the constitution have been able to push at the local level. More clearly, the issue of effectiveness of minority protection can at any moment strike a blow at the roots of the new constitutional equilibrium.

The idea of involving the masses in the process has been pursued both in South Africa and in Eritrea. This might be a transplant from the former to the latter. In both cases this attitude was not, however, what the writer would regard as a bottom-up experience. It was immediately clear both to the EPLF and to the provisional government stemming from the South African negotiations that the constitutional process could not remain a mere professional business. Public participation in the form of seminars, discussions, conferences, etc had a legitimising function of the power arrangement leading to the Constitution. It possibly also had a fund-raising function (particularly from communities abroad and international institutions).[48]

It is very unlikely that it had much chance of receiving actual observations from the people, if not at a very marginal level. From this perspective, it may be charged with having taken a slightly paternalistic approach. A good example may be the issue of traditional leadership. There is no question that in South African as well as in Eritrean rural society, such kind of leadership still enjoys tremendous influence. Its inclusion in the constitutional process could not be avoided. The political leadership however has been successful in limiting it to a somewhat 'cosmetic' level, rather than allocating genuine powers or considering it thoroughly influential in the making.

To the contrary, in Puntland the real novelty has been the 'bottom up' nature of the effort. The participation at the Garowe Conference and at the preparatory phase was quite spontaneous and the large number of delegates, selected by the

---

47 For a recent in-depth study, see Favali (1998b).
48 This function is clear if one considers the amount of official government publications describing the process targeted at such institutions. For a critical appraisal, see Nelson (1995).

traditional leadership, was possibly evidence of real grass-root involvement of a large number of people other than professional politicians or lawyers. The impact of these people is clear (in the good and the bad) if one compares the document submitted by the preparatory committee with the final Charter produced after the two months of Constitutional Convention in Garowe.[49]

This effective, popular participation in the making of the document was almost absent in Eritrea, where people were more educated about choices taken by others than they were actually involved in making them. The overwhelming vote for independence in 1993 was interpreted as having made up for any other lack of political pluralism. In South Africa, although the election of the Constitutional Conference gives the Charter a much stronger democratic legitimacy – at least for Western eyes – the whole process was framed in order to avoid a majoritarian democracy. The Constitutional Court's decision-making was used to 'certify' that the draft produced by the democratically elected people was not at odds with the deals struck by the political elite. Again, this process was run from the top.[50]

It remains to be seen whether the Puntland experience will actually involve a substantive amount of ordinary people. One only needs to consider the situation in Africa, affected by a high degree of illiteracy, characterising the society to accept that a certain degree of top-down decision-making is completely unavoidable. Nevertheless, the failures of democracy and participation are usually less dangerous than those of authoritarian rule. Certainly, while the former might itself lead to decentralisation of institutional constraints (useful gymnastics), the latter only reinforces present models of African leadership, a leadership that never solved the fundamental problem of the peaceful succession.[51]

PROFESSIONALISM

Generally speaking one can say that the amount of legal professionals involved in a constitution-making process is a variable which depends on a large number of factors. The availability of local professional lawyers and the degree of political openness of the system being the most important. The willingness of the international community to co-operate might be another important factor.

One could detect the optimum level of professionalism in constitution-making somewhere between the two extremes of a purely technical constitution (in which professional expertise dominates the formal document) and a purely political product (in which a document is drafted beyond any technical control). In the first case, the document is likely to have a somewhat cosmopolitan flavour, to be a depository of prestigious international solutions, but at the same time to be poorly adapted to local circumstances. Professional lawyers tend to work outside of contact with the felt needs of the society.[52] A purely political constitution, on the other hand, might be much more original and suited to the local circumstances. The problem is that the lack of professional culture makes it unlikely that the worries of the political forces involved in the process might actually be reflected by the constitutional document in a coherent way. In other words, political desires might be expressed at a semantic level that makes them entirely void of effectiveness once we come down to the real life of the law.[53]

49 See the description under 'Puntland State of Somalia' above.
50 See Du Plessis, Lourens and Corder (1994).
51 See Sacco (1997).
52 See Watson (1974); Sacco (1991).
53 See Vanderlinden (1995).

It is impossible to say *ex ante* what is the optimum mix between professionalism and politics, so that the previous observations have no normative meaning whatsoever. Nevertheless, as an analytical device for comparison, the described trade-off might be quite useful.

Professional law can be either the product of local culture or an import from abroad. Typically, in Africa the latter is the reality.[54] One can generally observe that the more local professionals you have available for constitution-drafting purposes, the less one is in need of foreign experts. One could therefore predict that, given South Africa's well-developed legal culture, it would not import much expertise, whereas Eritrea and Puntland would be much in need of transplants.[55]

The highly developed and educated legal community of South Africa, particularly the academic one, was not, in general, particularly cosy with the apartheid regime. In South Africa, as a consequence, there was plenty of technical legal expertise, although unevenly representing the black majority. Nevertheless, the South African constitution-making process has been significantly assisted by a large number of international experts, mostly from the US and Europe, who have been active particularly in the drafting of detailed technical rules on such things as local administration, taxation, organisation of justice, etc.[56]

Eritrea did not enjoy such a developed community of local professional jurists. A few very well educated lawyers, usually with degrees from the US, France, Italy or the USSR, were available and one of them served as the chair of the Constitutional Commission.[57] This, however, was far from enough, and the reliance on foreign expertise has been more a matter of necessity than of choice.

As to Puntland, the local legal expertise is close to zero.[58] There has not been any significant return from the Diaspora, and even lawyers trained at the Italian University in Mogadishu were not confident. Actually, the desire to co-operate with international scholars was more on their part than on that of the political leadership.

The degree of participation of foreign lawyers is also a function of the openness of the local political and legal culture. The legal culture was traditionally highly open in South Africa, with a large number of internationally recognised legal scholars maintaining contacts in such places as Scotland, Germany and the US.[59] Such academic connections were important in keeping South Africa on the course during the internationally ostracised apartheid regime, and have been even more important in selecting the international experts to be involved in the reconstruction of the rule of law, when experts from all over the world, particularly the US, have been involved.

Eritrea is politically very suspicious, and the relationship between law and politics is realistically considered to be very close by the local authorities. Legal scholarship and research, particularly by foreigners, is not encouraged and the attitude towards customary law seems rather lukewarm at this point.[60] Despite this attitude, some connections have been worked out mostly with US, Dutch and, to a lesser extent, Italian legal scholars. As mentioned above, foreign jurists have been formally involved in the constitution making process, although the degree of effectiveness of their impact is not clear.

54 See Hooker (1975); Grande (1995); Esiemokai (1986).
55 See in general on the state of legal professionalism in Africa, Guadagni (1989).
56 See the special Symposium Issue on 'The Making of the South African Constitution', St. Louis University Law Journal (Winter 1997).
57 See Tekle' (1997).
58 See on the previous state of affairs, Botan, Deghei and Farah (1989).
59 See Zimmermann et al (1996).
60 These remarks stem from the writer's direct observation and discussion with participants in the exchange programme between the Law Schools in Asmara and Trento (Italy).

In Puntland foreign participation has been an issue, particularly because of the very careful attitude of international co-operation and donors after years of failure of Somali peace talks. Foreign experts have been offered for technical help in the preparation of the Garowe Constitutional Conference by the UN Development Office for Somalia. But this was not exactly what the Preparatory Committee, eager and in need of direct financial help, was looking for. As a consequence, part of the more traditionalist components of the Committee had a less open attitude towards foreign participation. Nevertheless, the international contribution to the preparation of the Charter was not trivial, and a foreign participation is contemplated within the Constitutional Commission whose role is described in the Charter approved in Garowe. In a way, both in Puntland and in Somalia, international involvement has been an issue because of the careful attitude of the international community in front of the political process of these countries. To the contrary, in South Africa, where the international participation has been crucial from the very start of the political process, and where a well-developed local academic community was available, international professional involvement came as a matter of course.

In summary, the relationship between law and politics is once again crucial in understanding the process of legal development in Africa. If professional law successfully vindicates its autonomy from the political process, then it becomes entirely natural to take a cosmopolitan approach to the matter and look for foreign technical aid. This has long been the case in South Africa. A high degree of legislative positivism allowed professional lawyers passively to witness the destruction of the rule of law during the apartheid era under cover of legitimacy of whatever was formally law.[61] International institutions such as the World Bank, after the end of the Cold War, gave up the assumption of the connection between law and politics which has long precluded them to invest in the upgrading of legal systems.[62] In South Africa these two conditions have created the ideal environment for a thorough and knowledgeable technical involvement in the constitution-drafting. The outcome is technically admirable and actually sets forth a model for the new generation of African-written constitutions.

In Eritrea and Puntland State, the fiction of the neutral and technical nature of constitutional law has been more difficult to accept. The lack of a local positivistic legal tradition, and the fundamental structural characteristics of legal systems in which political decision-making still imposes its hegemony on law work, in the direction of keeping law and politics strictly connected in the constitution-making process. Consequently, witnessing foreign (technical) involvement in a process that is considered deeply political develops, in some influential quarters, the legitimate fear of neo-colonialism.[63]

Generally speaking, the observation of these three patterns of constitution-making confirms the difficulty of keeping what is technical separate from what is political in constitutional law.

CONCLUSIONS

The beginning of this chapter raised questions; the conclusion sketches some answers.

---

61 See Dugard (1971).
62 See Nelson (1995).
63 Kidder (1979).

In Africa, participation and legitimacy live a life that is entirely independent from elections. Elections have mostly an international legitimating role, with little internal impact. In South Africa most of the constitution-making process was precisely aimed at reducing the foreseen outcome of democratic elections on the Constitution. In Puntland a high level of public participation was reached entirely outside any idea of elections. In Eritrea elections have been promised, but never actually carried out; they have been felt to be useless. Legitimacy of the leadership is grounded elsewhere, typically in the war.[64] Generally speaking, traditional legitimacy and skilful use of force are still leading legitimating factors in Africa. How these notions might become compatible with a formal constitutional framework is the present challenge, which requires creativity and open-mindedness on the part of lawyers and political scientists interested in the phenomenon.

On the professional side, one can observe that the 'shopping around' is quite extensive. Certain aspects of successful Western experiences seem to attract the interest of African constitution-makers. Constitutional adjudication is felt to be important everywhere. The court in which it is vested does not matter so much. It might formally be the Supreme Court or an ad hoc Constitutional Court. What matters is that it is important to limit the authority of the legislative and executive power. Constitutional adjudication is also limited to the highest levels of the judicial hierarchy. Decentralisation, federalism and subsidiarity are also important notions taken from the more advanced constitutional experiences of the West. These are, however, delicate issues, encroaching on the fundamental stake of ethnicity. As a consequence of their being political 'hot button' issues, the choices are wisely kept quite ambiguous. The presidential model borrowed from the US seems the most successful form of government. This scenario offers the impression, seen from the outside, of participation in the Western legal tradition despite differences in details. Among these there is certainly the idea of a strong professional control on the political process through courts and legal culture. While the former are part of the formal institutions and the choices regarding them can be reflected by a formal document such as the Constitution, the latter are part of the informal institution-building that is much more difficult to create.[65]

Even if this chapter was focused on the process and not on the final product, there is one datum that should be considered because it is puzzling and difficult to interpret.

The outcomes of these three processes share an impressive number of fundamental characteristics. This might be interpreted in two ways. Either the connection between constitutional law and the political process is merely

---

64 The war with Ethiopia has removed the process of constitution-making from the stage. The final Constitution produced by the Commission has been 'ratified' by an assembly of mysterious but certainly not elective composition, and transferred to the President for a signature that so far, to the best of the writer's knowledge, has not happened. Apparently the Commission made some final changes before 'ratification' so that the Constitution that is up for signature is different to the official final text published by the Commission itself. This final text is not available. There is no official date for the Constitution to enter in force. According to some statements by the chairman of the Constitutional Commission (known only by hearsay) the decision not to set a date was deliberately taken to allow political choices on the best moment to do so. One theory is that the Constitution will not be signed and enter in force until translations in the official languages are provided. Interestingly, the Constitution itself does not mention what are the official languages. The writer is indebted for these updates to Dr Luca Castellani.

65 Some of these ideas are developed in Mattei (1998).

apparent, and constitutions live a life that is rather independent from the political processes that lead to them, or there are a few fundamental characteristics of African constitutions stemming from a genuine process of local adaptation of the Western formal institutional setting that we call a 'constitution'.

The common basic characteristics are: (a) a strong President who is the chief of the executive; (b) a rather light and weak legislative body; (c) an emphasis on the independence and strengths of the judiciary also empowered to constitutional adjudication; (d) a recognition of traditional law and of a moderate degree of legal pluralism; and (e) a significant number of independent agencies.

On more formal grounds, one can witness a rather detailed language breaking with the Western tradition of short constitutions which are merely depositories of constitutional principles. These constitutions attempt to draft the main lines of the organisation of the state.

While points (a) and (b) seem quite coherent with a strong position of the African chief, the other points are either clear attempts to break with the long tradition of weakness of the judiciary in developing countries ((c) and (e)) or realistic recognition of the fact that the state faces quite substantial competition from alternative decision-making centres. In a sense, points (c) and (e) are the real challenge of modern African constitutional law. The courts, however, have neither the purse nor the sword.[66] Why should the armed man obey them?

Select bibliography

Ackerman, B, (1991) *We the People.*

Battera, F, (1998) 'Ethnicity and State: The Ethiopian Federal Constitution' in L Favali, E Grande and M Guadagni (eds), *New Law for New States. Politica del Diritto in Eritrea.*

Bickel, A, (1986) *The Least Dangerous Branch. The Supreme Court at the Bar of Politics* (2nd edn).

Botan, A, Deghei, H, and Farah, A, (1989) 'Somalia' in M Guadagni (ed), *Legal Scholarship in Africa.*

Calchi Novati, G, (2002) Regional and International Actors. Paper presented at the Giormata di riflessione sulla Somalia, ISIAO, Rome, 15 February 2002.

Cardozo, B N, (1921) *The Nature of the Judicial Process.*

Cliffe, L, and Davidson, B, (eds), (1988) *The Long Struggle of Eritrea for Independence and Constructive Peace.*

Dugard, J, (1971) 'The Judicial Process, Positivism and Civil Liberty', SALJ 181.

Du Plessis, L, and Corder, H, (1994) *Understanding South Africa's Transitional Bill of Rights.*

Ensminger, J, (1992) *Making a Market. The Institutional Transformation of an African Society.*

Esiemokai, E O, (1986) *The Colonial Legal Heritage in Nigeria.*

---

66 See Bickel (1986).

Favali, L, (1998a) 'La Legittimazione e i suoi protagonisti' in L Favali, E Grande and M Guadagni (eds), *New Law for New States. Politica del Diritto in Eritrea*, p 159.

—(1998b) 'Le Risposte del Diritto alle esigenze dello sviluppo. Il caso Eritreo', PhD Dissertation, Universita' di Trieste.

Federal Research Commission of the Library of Congress, (1997) *South Africa. A Country Study.*

Fortes, M, and Evans-Pritchard, E E, (eds), (1987) *African Political Systems.*

Gloppen, S, (1997) *South Africa. The Battle over the Constitution.*

Grande, E, (ed), (1995) *Transplants Innovation and Legal Tradition in the Horn of Africa.*

—(1996) 'L' apporto dell' antropologia alla conoscenza del diritto', Rivista Critica Diritto Privato 467.

Guadagni, M, (ed), (1989) *Legal Scholarship in Africa.*

—(1995) 'Introduction' in E Grande (ed), *Transplants Innovation and Legal Tradition in the Horn of Africa.*

—(1998a) 'Legal Pluralism' in P Newman (ed), *The New Palgrave. A Dictionary of Economics and the Law.*

—(1998b) 'Eritrean Law Between Past and Future', in L Favali, E Grande and M Guadagni (eds), *New Law for New States. Politica del Diritto in Eritrea.*

Habermas, 3, (1996) *Between Facts and Norms: Contributions to a Discourse Theory of Law and Democracy.*

Hart, M B, and Sacks, A M, (1994) *The Legal Process.*

Hooker, M B, (1995) *Legal Pluralism.*

Kidder, R L, (1979) 'Toward an Integrated Theory of imposed law', in S B Burman and B E Harrel-Bond (eds), *The Imposition of Law.*

Lewis, I M, (1988) *A Modern History of Somalia.*

—(1994) *Peoples of the Horn of Africa: Somali, Afar and Saho.*

Lewis, P, (1992) 'Political Transition and the Dilemma of Civil Society in Africa', 46 J Int Affairs 31.

Mattei, U, (1990) 'Socialist and Non Socialist Approaches to Land Law. Continuity and Change in Somalia and Other African States', 16 Rev Socialist Law 17.

—(1995) 'The New Ethiopian Constitution. First Thoughts on Ethnic Federalism and the Reception of Western Institutions' in E Grande (ed) *Transplants Innovation and Legal Tradition in the Horn of Africa.*

—(1997) 'Three Patterns of Law. Taxonomy and Change in the World's Legal Systems', 45 AJCL 5.

—(1998) 'Legal Pluralism, Legal Change and Economic Development' in L Favali, E Grande and M Guadagni (eds), *New Law for New States. Politica del Diritto in Eritrea*, p 23ff.

—(1999) 'Sud Africa', Digesto Discipline Privatistiche IV.

—(2002), Foreign Inspired Courts as Agencies of Peace in Troubled Societies, Global Jurist Topics, vol 2, No 1, art 2; www.bepress.com.

Morozzo della Rocca, R, (1994) *Mozambico. Dalla Guerra alla Pace.*

Nelson, P G, (1995) *The World Bank and Non Governmental Organizations. The Limits of A-political Development.*

North, D, (1991) *Institution, Institutional Change and Economic Performance*, p 40ff.

Reyntjens, F, (1996) 'Note sur l' Utilié d' Introduire un Système juridique pluraliste dans la macro-comparaison des Droits', Re. Droit Int et Droit Comp 659.

Sacco, R, (1988) *Le Grandi Linee del Sistema Giuridico Somalo.*

—(1991) 'Legal Formants. A Dynamic Approach to Comparative Law', 39 AJCL 1.

—(1995) *Il Diritto Africano.*

—(1997) *Perché l' armato ubbidisce all' inerme, Rivista di Diritto Civile*, chapter I.

Sacco, R, and Monateri, P G, (1998) 'Legal Formants' in P Newman (ed), *The New Palgrave. A Dictionary of Economics and the Law.*

Salih, M, (1989) 'Perspectives on Pastoralists and African States', in *Nomadic People.*

Tekle', T, (1997) 'Il Processo Costituente in Eritrea ed il Draft Constitution del 1996', Quaderni Costituzionali 2.

Tseggai, A, (1998) 'The History of Eritrean Struggle', in L Cliffe and B Davidson *The Long Struggle of Eritrea for Independence and Constructive Peace.*

Van Doren, J, (1994) 'Positivism and the Rule of Law, Formal Systems and Concealed values. A Case Study of the Ethiopian Legal System', 3 J Trans Law and Policy 165.

Vanderlinden, J, (1982) 'A Propos des Familles de Droit en Droit Civil Comparé', Hommages Dekkers 363.

—(1995) *Comparer les Droits.*

Watson, A, (1974) *Legal Transplants.*

Zimmermann, R, and Vesser, D, (1996) *Southern Cross, Civil Law and Common Law in South Africa* (1996).

Chapter 14

From individual dignity to respect for *jinkaku* – continuity and change in the concept of the individual in modern Japan[1]

K INOUE

INTRODUCTION

The Americans who occupied Japan in the aftermath of Japan's defeat in the Second World War believed that Japan was a feudalistic country with no experience in democracy, and they were determined to transform Japan into a peaceful and democratic country according to their own image and experience. As part of this project, General Douglas MacArthur's general headquarters prepared a draft for a new Japanese Constitution. In the article that eliminated the legal basis of the Meiji household system, they stated that laws pertaining to marriage and family had to be enacted from the standpoint of 'individual dignity' and the essential equality of the sexes. The Japanese translated individual dignity literally as *kojin-no songen*, but interpreted it figuratively to mean 'respect for *jinkaku*' (moral character).

The word *jinkaku*, consisting of *jin* 'person(s)' and *kaku* 'rank/status', and literally meaning 'the person(s) in some kind of rank', was initially created in the context of law in the late nineteenth century, and only later developed into one of the key concepts in Japanese moral and educational discourse. The moral and educational thinkers who transformed the meaning of the concept, the best known of whom was Inoue Tetsujiro, taught that all people had the responsibility to try to perfect their own *jinkaku* and to respect others' *jinkaku* as well. Initially, the concept had elitist connotations, not only because of the inherent meaning of the characters, but also because it was taught principally to students in boys' middle-school, most of whom were destined to go on to universities and then occupy the leadership positions in government and business. Then, during the so-called Taisho democratic era, political and social activists 'democratised' the concept, stating that ordinary people, because they had *jinkaku*, were not only worthy of respect, but were also entitled to participate in the nation's political process and to receive a greater share of its economic wealth. Yoshino Sakuzo used this newly democratised concept in arguing for universal male suffrage, and Suzuki Bunji used it to justify increased benefits for workers. But, at the same time, these activists also stressed that all people had the responsibility for

---

1 This chapter is largely based on chapter 1 of *Individual Dignity in Modern Japanese Thought: The Evolution of the Concept of Jinkaku in Moral and Educational Discourse*, published by the Center for Japanese Studies, University of Michigan, 2001.

perfecting their *jinkaku*. Thus, Japanese thinkers introduced a tension between the hierarchical and egalitarian senses included in the concept of *jinkaku*, a tension that was never resolved and was ultimately carried over into the post-Second World War Constitution.

This chapter will trace the development of the idea of *jinkaku* in pre-Second World War Japanese intellectual history, focusing on the democratisation of the concept, and will show how the Japanese leaders, by using *jinkaku* to explain the US idea of individual dignity, were able to maintain continuity with pre-war Japanese thought.

The chapter begins with a brief summary of the making of the post-war Constitution and the introduction of the concept of individual dignity by the Americans.

THE MAKING OF THE POST-SECOND WORLD WAR JAPANESE CONSTITUTION

At the beginning of February 1946, a handful of General MacArthur's staff at occupation headquarters prepared the initial draft of the present Japanese Constitution in one week. They handed it to the Japanese government officials and told them to translate it and then present it to the Japanese people as their own creation. After intense negotiations with the Americans, the Japanese prepared a Constitution in Japanese that had only a few changes to the original American draft, and presented it to the 90th Imperial Diet at the end of June 1946. After 100 days of intense deliberation, the two Houses of the Imperial Diet approved the document by an overwhelming majority. Ever since, the Constitution has been regarded as the centrepiece of American effort to democratise Japan; it has survived more than 50 years without a single amendment.

The present writer's book, *MacArthur's Japanese Constitution: A Linguistic and Cultural Study of Its Making*,[2] demonstrated that the story of making the Japanese Constitution is considerably more complex than hitherto believed. This Constitution was created, in large part, in the ambiguities of cross-cultural and cross-linguistic communication. MacArthur approved the document in English, but the National Diet deliberated and ratified the Japanese translation. In translating the US draft, the Japanese made some subtle but significant changes in the text, which neither side appears to have understood. In effect, MacArthur and the Japanese approved two different versions of the Constitution of Japan without reaching complete agreement on its fundamental meaning.

One example of the lack of understanding was the English expression 'individual dignity', which was included in article 24. It reads:

> 'Marriage has to be based only on the mutual consent of both sexes and it has to be maintained through mutual cooperation with the equal rights of husband and wife as a basis.
>
> With regard to choice of spouse, property rights, inheritance, choice of domicile, divorce and other matters pertaining to marriage and the family, laws have to be enacted from the standpoint of *individual dignity and the essential equality of sexes*' (emphasis added).[3]

2   Inoue (1991).
3   This and all other translations of passages cited in this paper are the present writer's, unless otherwise noted.

This article destroyed the legal basis of the Meiji household system, which had given virtually no legal rights to women. The Japanese had no difficulty understanding the legal consequence of the equality of the sexes in matters related to the family and marriage, and they were greatly concerned about it. But they were puzzled about the meaning of the US expression 'individual dignity', and did not understand how it was linked to rights. Government had translated it literally as *kojin-no songen*, but the government officials explained that this meant 'respect for *jinkaku*'.[4]

To Americans in 1946, individual dignity generally meant that each individual was entitled to respect for simply being a human being, and not as a member of some larger group or community. Gunnar Myrdal, the Swedish sociologist, described the US creed as consisting of the 'ideals of the essential dignity of the individual, the basic equality of all men and certain inalienable rights to freedom, justice and opportunity'.[5] For Americans, the idea of equality of the sexes seemed like a natural consequence of the concept of individual dignity, even though they have sometimes been reluctant to draw that conclusion.[6]

The US creed reflected American individualistic values. In contrast, before the Second World War (and even today to a significant degree), the Japanese derived their sense of who they were largely from their membership of the family and other social groups. Membership was a constituent element of their identity, rather than an attribute of each of the individual members. Moreover, most groups were characterised by unequal, hierarchical relationships, and there was no assumption that individuals were equal in the sense of having equal rights.[7] Yet a person could have a measure of self-respect by performing his or her role well. As a result, the US idea of individual dignity, connected as it was to equal rights, was strange to them, and they were not at all certain how it related to the equality of the sexes.

The Japanese understood the notion of respect for *jinkaku*, the moral character of the individual, because this concept had been widely accepted in pre-war moral and educational discourse. But because of its hierarchical connotations, the Japanese believed that persons of high *jinkaku* were entitled to greater respect than those with low *jinkaku*. This idea was far more consistent with their ideas about the place of individuals in social relations. Thus the Japanese choice of 'respect for *jinkaku*' to stand for 'individual dignity' invested the idea of dignity with connotations of hierarchy, and thereby created a significant difference in meaning between the English and Japanese versions of article 24.

---

4   See Inoue (1991) pp 235–265 for a detailed discussion on the constitutional debate over art 24.

5   Myrdal (1944) p 2.

6   While the US has not yet adopted an equal rights amendment to the Constitution, the Americans at MacArthur's headquarters, and the women in particular, believed that Japanese women had been severely deprived of their basic rights, and they were determined to change this in the new Constitution: see *1945-nen-no Kurisumasu: Nihon-koku Kempo-ni 'Danjo Byodo'-o Kaita Josei-no Jiden* ('Christmas 1945: An Autobiography of a Woman Who Added "Equality of Women" in the Japanese Constitution'), narrated in Japanese by Beate Sirota Gordon, and written by Hiraoka Makiko(1995); Inoue (1991) chapter 1.

7   The Japanese have a deeply rooted Buddhist idea of equality (*byodo*), which means that all people are equally endowed with the ability to cope with life.

THE BIRTH OF THE CONCEPT OF *JINKAKU*

It is generally believed in Japan that Inoue Tetsujiro (1855–1944), the first Japanese professor of philosophy at Tokyo University,[8] created the word *jinkaku* as a Japanese translation for the English word 'personality'. This claim is largely based on Inoue's own comment that he suggested this word to Nakajima Rikizo, a colleague at Tokyo University.[9] The present writer's research, however, strongly suggests that Inoue was not the original creator of the word. Moreover, contrary to his suggestion that legal scholars borrowed the word *jinkaku* from ethics, the earliest published uses of the word *jinkaku* appeared in legal writings from the year 1889, or possibly even earlier.[10] Law is where the story of *jinkaku* begins.

Immediately after the Restoration in 1868, the Meiji leaders quickly realised that they needed to establish a modern legal system as the basis for their new governmental and economic system, which required vastly expanding the Japanese legal vocabulary, either by creating new words, or by using old terms in new ways.[11] As in all other areas of modernisation, the Japanese were eclectic, borrowing principally from the French and German legal systems. In 1873, the government invited a French legal scholar, Gustave Emile Boissonade de Fontarabie (1825–1910), to Japan to teach law and create a penal code. In 1879, Boissonade began preparing Japan's first civil code with Japanese colleagues, which is now known as *Kyu-Mimpo* (the Old Civil Code).[12]

It was during the creation of the French-style Civil Code that the Japanese appear to have learned the legal concepts of 'legal person' and 'legal personality', originally derived from Roman law.[13] So far as the writer is aware, the Japanese did not have such a concept during the Tokugawa era, and they initially had a difficult time grasping the idea of a corporate entity having a status similar to that of a human being. For example, when a group of men established the company Maruzen in 1869, Japan's oldest and best-known importer of Western books, they created a fictitious person named Maruya Zenshichi to represent it because they believed that a company had to be represented by a human being.[14] To deal with the unfamiliar legal concept of 'legal person', the Japanese first used the word *mukei-jin*, which literally means 'person(s) without form', to contrast with *yukei-jin* 'person(s) with form', namely human beings. Thus in an 1885 essay explaining the modern banking system, Tomita Tetsunosuke explained that banks that were large enough to have 'company rules, terms of operation, receive the government's approval, and create a *mukei* body – these are the ones that are

---

8   This university was named Tokyo University when it was first established in 1877; its name was changed to Tokyo Imperial University in 1897, and then back to Tokyo University in 1947. Inoue was appointed to assistant professor in 1882 when it was still called Tokyo University. 'Tokyo University' will be used throughout the chapter to avoid confusion.

9   In his reminiscences on Japanese academia, Inoue Tetsujiro states that he and others created many new words in philosophy. Among them is the word *jinkaku*. He says 'I translated "personality" into *jinkaku*. A colleague in ethics named Nakajima Rikizo asked me how he might translate "personality" into Japanese. So I responded that *jinkaku* would be appropriate': Inoue (1973) p 33. But he gives no date.

10 Inoue (1973) p 34.

11 The French-Japanese dictionary of legal terms, *Horitsu Goi Shoko*, published in 1883, has more than 1,000 pages and includes as many as 3,000–4,000 new legal terms (included in *Nihon Rippo Shiryo Zenshu, bekkan* (1989–94) vol 5).

12 Okubo (1977) pp 134–142.

13 Those terms, however, are not included in the 1883 dictionary.

14 Meiji Bunka Kenkyukai (1968) p 42.

publicly called such-and-such bank' (*ginko*).[15] Similarly, in 1887, in a discussion of an article having to do with the right of property, the members of the government's Legal Investigative Committee (*Horitsu Torishirabe Iinkai*) used the word *mukei-jin* to refer to administrative units like 'city' and 'county', as well as hospitals and similar types of institutions.[16]

In 1889, both *ho-jin*, referring to 'legal person', and *ho-jinkaku*, referring to 'legal personality', were used for the first time, both in two documents discussing aspects of the Boissonade draft. The first document, prepared by Yokota Kuniomi and dated 25 April 1889, considered ideas related to inheritance in Roman law. Yokota explained that when the right and property (*kenri zaisan*) of one person was transferred to another person, the new possessor, having *jinkaku*, held rights and duties. He further stated that the estate (*isan*) itself constituted a *ho-jin*.[17]

The second example is found in the Japanese translation of an opinion written by Alessandro Paternostro, an Italian legal scholar, about the state's relationship to individuals. Although this opinion is not dated, it is included in a set of opinions written in the autumn of 1889; it is assumed here that it, too, was written in 1889.[18] In characterising the function of the state, Paternostro said that the state (*kokka*) as a legal person (*hojin*) had two kinds of 'personalite', or *jinkaku*. One was the *jinkaku* of the civil code (*mimpo-teki jinkaku*), and the other was political *jinkaku* (*seiji-teki jinkaku*). The state as a civil person could own property and even profits; the state as a political person performed the duties of the state as a sovereign; as a *jinkaku*, the state could exercise certain rights and duties.[19]

The Boissonade Civil Code was finally completed and made public in October 1890, and the term *jinkaku* began to be used in commentaries on it. For example, the authors of one discussion of property stated that '*hojin*, the product of legal imagination, is recognised legally as a possessor of rights (*kenri-no shukaku*), although physically not a person'. All natural persons (*shizen-jin*), except slaves whose *jinkaku* the law did not recognise, possessed rights.[20]

Three years later, in 1893, the words *hojin* and *hojinkaku* appeared in an essay in *Kokka Gakkai Zasshi* (Journal of the Association for the State Studies). The author, Kishi Kosaburo (1857–1902), who served in the House of Representatives in 1894 and 1898, discussed a maritime accident that occurred in 1892 in which a Japanese battleship collided with a British commercial ship. Faced with the Japanese government's demand for indemnity, the British company that owned the commercial vessel tried to evade its responsibility by arguing that since Japan, as a sovereign nation, was represented by the Emperor, who was above the law, the company had no legal obligation toward Japan. Kishi argued in reply that the state had two kinds of *jinkaku*, public and private. From the viewpoint of the private law, that is, property law, the state was a legal person (*hojin*) that was entitled to compensation. If the British company asked who represented Japan, Japan simply needed to reply that the state of Japan was a legal person that could be represented by an appropriate Minister, in this case, the Minister of Navy.[21]

15 Tomita (1968) p 261.
16 Homu Daijin Kambo Shiho Hosei Chosabu (1984–89) vol 8, pp 1–7.
17 Homu Daijin Kambo Shiho Hosei Chosabu (1984–89) vol 10, pp 161–163.
18 Homu Daijin Kambo Shiho Hosei Chosabu (1984–89) vol 16, pp 2–12.
19 Homu Daijin Kambo Shiho Hosei Chosabu (1984–89) vol 16, p 3.
20 Ishikawa et al (1890) pp 17–18.
21 Kishi (1893) at 1812.

The meaning of *jinkaku* became more explicit in another article by Kuwata Kumazo (1868–1932), a pioneer in the study of social policies in Japan, which was published in the same journal in July 1894.[22] In characterising the relationship between a society and a state, Kuwata said that a society was simply a collection of people without *jinkaku*. A state, on the other hand, had *jinkaku*, that is, it had its own independent will; it had the ability to maintain order and even restrict the activities of its members.[23]

Thus, it appears that the word *jinkaku* initially was used to translate the idea of legal personality. One important aspect of this idea was that *jinkaku* implied that the entity in question had an independent will of its own, a notion that became important when people began to use *jinkaku* in other contexts.

MODERN EDUCATION AND THE TEACHING OF MORALS

The role of education in developing ethical concepts and disseminating them cannot be exaggerated, so the section begins with a short discussion on the early modern Japanese school system in which the term *jinkaku* principally evolved. The leaders of the Meiji Restoration recognised that the success of Japan's modernisation depended heavily on education. Initially, they had considered trying to modernise the country by relying only on the members of the bushi class, but they quickly decided to involve the whole nation. They recognised that this would require educating the populace in Western knowledge and practices in a variety of fields. Therefore, in 1871, the government undertook an ambitious programme of universal education for all Japanese children, adopting systems and practices principally from France, Great Britain and the US. The leaders were initially attracted to Anglo-American utilitarian attitudes toward education and promoted the idea that education, by enhancing knowledge, would help people prosper in life. The government established a separate course on morals called *shushin*, literally translated as 'discipline of one's body', as part of the new elementary school curriculum. But they were not very interested in teaching morals and used translations of various Western books, such as Samuel Smiles' *Self Help* (1860), Francis Wayland's *Elements of Moral Science* (1874), and even Aesop's Fables, as texts.[24]

Around 1880, with the rise of nationalism, strong reactions against Anglo-American utilitarian attitudes toward education began to appear. The government adopted the German idea that it should provide basic education in civic virtues as well as in academic subjects.[25] In 1880, the government prohibited the use of the early *shushin* textbooks, which had been strongly influenced by Christian morality, and began publishing books that incorporated Confucian teachings. With strong support of the Prime Minister, Ito Hirobumi, Mori Arinori, the Minister of Education, introduced various nationalistic programmes and strengthened the central government's control of education.[26]

The Japanese government finally set forth its own philosophy of education in the Imperial Rescript on Education, promulgated in 1890, more than 20 years

22 Kuwata (1894).
23 Kuwata (1894) at 538–539.
24 Tokiomi (1964) pp 507–562.
25 Zaidan Hojin Kaikoku Hyakumem Kinen Bunka Jigyodan (1965) pp 67–116, 187–188.
26 Naka (1967) pp 239–246.

after the Restoration. The Rescript merged two Confucian ideas of loyalty – loyalty to one's lord and to one's parents – into a single idea, loyalty to the emperor as the father of the nation. It encouraged Japanese subjects to be modest, perfect their moral powers (*tokki*), maintain harmonious relationships within their families and communities, and work toward building a harmonious and prosperous nation. Copies of the Rescript were distributed to schools throughout the entire country. It was read to students on important occasions and served as the centrepiece of modern Japanese education until the end of the Second World War. The government asked Inoue Tetsujiro to prepare an official commentary on the Rescript.

Inoue Tetsujiro and the development of *Jinkaku* as a moral concept

In his commentary on the Rescript, published in 1891 and distributed to schools throughout the country, Inoue Tetsujiro used the word *jimpin*, literally translated as 'quality of person(s)', to emphasise the need to strengthen one's ethical and moral character. Thus Inoue introduced the notion that individuals could be ranked according to their strength of the ethical and moral character.[27] Inoue eventually replaced the word *jimpin*[28] with *jinkaku*, which had a clearer hierarchical connotation.

The word *jinkaku* began to be used in boys' middle-school *shushin* textbooks in the latter part of the 1890s. These texts generally consisted of several volumes, used over a period of five years. *Jinkaku* was usually introduced in the final volume of the series, suggesting that developing one's *jinkaku*, which required self-discipline and motivation, was taken to be an advanced concept, appropriate only for students in the fifth and final year of middle-school study.

Inoue was the first person to use the word in a boys' middle-school textbook, *Shimpen Rinri Kyokasho* (A New Textbook on Ethics), published in 1897, which he co-authored with one of his students, Takayama Rinjiro (better known as Chogyu). The book used *jinkaku* twice. One use came in their discussion of the state (*kokka*), in which they gave *jinkaku* the same meaning as legal scholars did. They wrote:

> 'the state (*kokka*) is like an individual in possessing its own will (*ishi*) and purpose. Furthermore, the state is like an individual in possessing *jinkaku* ... Once a state is established, it gives form to a body without form (*mukei–no ittai-o soshiki-shi*)[29] and it performs independent acts using its independent will'.[30]

Inoue and Takayama also used the term *jinkaku* to mean 'character'. They wrote that it was necessary for people to accommodate to one another to facilitate harmonious relationships in society; however, one needed to have great

---

27 Inoue (1891) vol 1, p 66.
28 The word *jimpin* is not commonly used in contemporary Japanese, although the writer was told by her late father that it was commonly used in his youth during the 1920s. The character for *pin*, pronounced as *hin*, used in 'so-and-so has *hin*', refers to the dignified, refined or regal appearance of a person. The Crown Princess, Masako, is a prime example.
29 Although Inoue's language is not very clear, the present writer believes that this translation captures his meaning. It also fits with the Tomita Tetsunosuke's use of the terms *mukei-jin* and *yukei-jin*, discussed above.
30 Inoue and Takayama (1897) vol 4, p 2. Because Inoue and Takayama labeled the first volume *shu-kan* (head volume), vol 4 is the final volume in this series.

determination (*dai-kesshin*) to not yield to others when it came to the principles that derived from one's *hin'i*[31] or *jinkaku*.[32] This is one of the first uses of *jinkaku* to mean 'character' in moral discourse.[33] Inoue may have derived this usage from his knowledge of law.

It is noteworthy that in their discussion about activities necessary for moral discipline, Inoue and Takayama included knowledge (*chishiki*), indicating that learning adorned the spirit of the person (*seishin-no kazari*), which elevated *jimpin*.[34] Moreover, they suggested that students should pursue learning that was not only commensurate with their natural ability (*tensei*) and health, but also their family's finances, and discouraged students from imposing undue financial hardship on their parents and relatives.[35] Obviously, since only a limited number of students could be expected to develop high *jinkaku*, Inoue's idea of *jinkaku* at this time was highly elitist.

Before he began to use the word *jinkaku* regularly in *shushin* texts, however, Inoue had used the word with a moral sense in connection with his criticism of Christianity. When the Imperial Rescript on Education was promulgated, Christian educators and students expressed their opposition to its principal teaching of loyalty toward the emperor, the nation and the family, not only in speeches, but also in what was regarded as 'disrespectful behavior'.[36] They thus instigated a heated debate over whether Christianity was an appropriate religion for Japan. Inoue Tetsujiro was at the centre of this dispute.

In April 1893, Inoue published a small book, entitled *Kyoiku-to Shukyo-no Shototsu* (A Collision Between Education and a Religion), based on an article he had published the previous year. He argued that Christianity was not suited for Japan's body politic (*kokutai*) because Christianity, as a monotheistic religion, resembled a dictatorship which would not allow the Japanese people to worship their own god, *Amaterasu Omikami*, the Sun Goddess. In this discussion, Inoue used the term *jinsei-teki*, literally meaning 'person-like quality' to refer to the Christian God.[37] But in a lecture given in 1899 in which he further criticised Christianity, Inoue replaced *jinsei-teki* with *jinkaku*, and said that the Christian God had *jinkaku*, the essence of which was having a will (*ishi*) of its own, and meddled in human affairs. For this reason, he held that Christianity was not suitable for Japan.[38] Inoue thus seems to have applied this use of *jinkaku* – the idea that God, as a being with *jinkaku*, had an independent will – to people.

---

31 The word *hin'i* consists of *hin*, meaning something like quality, and *i* 'rank'. Thus *hin'i* is another expression that refers to the quality of the person. In modern usage, however, *hin'i* refers more to a regal or dignified appearance than to ethical character.

32 Inoue and Takayama (1897) vol 1, p 55.

33 In 1893, a Buddhist philosopher-educator, Kiyozawa Manshi, used the term *jinkaku* in discussing the conception of the Christian God held by the nineteenth-century German idealist metaphysician, Rudolf Hermann Lotze. Kiyozawa said that the Christian God was a *jinkaku-shin* (*jinkaku* god) and that his *jinkaku* was perfect, unlike the human *jinkaku*, which was imperfect: Kiyozawa (1955) pp 148–151. Kiyozawa's use of *jinkaku* clearly does not come from law, but is linked to morality.

34 Inoue and Takayama (1897) vol 1, p 41.

35 Inoue and Takayama (1897) vol 1, p 37.

36 The most celebrated case involved Uchimura Kanzo, a Christian instructor at the First Higher School, Japan's most prestigious public high school, and prominent intellectual, who did not bow toward the document deeply enough and was eventually forced to resign from the school.

37 Inoue (1893) pp 5–8.

38 Inoue (1902a) p 126. This lecture was published three years later.

Human beings, who were also endowed with a will of their own as well as self-awareness, had the ability to discipline themselves, and improve and eventually perfect their *jinkaku*.

In his next middle-school textbook, published in 1902, Inoue significantly expanded the discussion of *jinkaku*. Furthermore, he no longer used *jinkaku* in characterising the relationship between the state and society – an indication that *jinkaku* had become more exclusively a moral concept.[39] First, in introducing the idea of *jinkaku*, Inoue said that the essence of morality rested in the individual's *jinkaku*. One who did not have *jinkaku* did not have morality (*dotoku*), so to discipline one's *jinkaku* meant to cultivate morality; a person had the responsibility to improve his *jinkaku* regardless of his social position.[40] To quote:

'A person's level of *jinkaku* is determined by the power of his ability to discipline himself … If you have made an error, don't hesitate to correct it, and diligently discipline your *jinkaku* …

Human beings have extensive responsibilities [in life]. Performing them will perfect their *jinkaku*.'[41]

Inoue also discussed the need for individuals to respect others' *jinkaku*, indicating that he was moderating his earlier conservative view. The idea of respecting *jinkaku* applied to all people regardless of their age or position and status within the family and society.[42] In volume 5, Inoue elaborated further, stating that *jinkaku* involved knowledge, emotions and will, and that *jinkaku* distinguished human beings from things and animals. The ultimate goal in life was in developing and perfecting *jinkaku*. But the precise manner in which a person went about perfecting *jinkaku* depended on his role in society, as there was no meaning to *jinkaku* apart from society.[43]

In his 1910 textbook, which he co-authored with Oshima Gishu, Inoue reaffirmed that human beings were superior to animals because human beings had moral responsibility deriving from *jinkaku*, but he emphasised that some people had the ability to reach a higher level of *jinkaku* than others.[44] Finally, in a book aimed at a broader audience, *Jinkaku-to Shuyo*, published in 1915, Inoue emphasised more strongly than before that, because humans were social beings, perfecting *jinkaku* could only be accomplished within the state (*kokka*) and the communal life of society.[45]

The contributions of other moral thinkers

Although Inoue Tetsujiro was the most prolific and influential writer of morals textbooks, a large number of other writers also produced texts, and many of them adopted *jinkaku*.[46] Some of these authors made independent contributions

---

39 Inoue (1902b) vols 3, 4 and 5.
40 Inoue (1902b) vol 3, pp 45–46.
41 Inoue (1902b) vol 3, pp 46–47.
42 Inoue (1902b) vol 4, pp 27–29.
43 Inoue (1902b) vol 5, pp 64–65.
44 Inoue and Oshima (1910) vol 3, pp 41–44.
45 Inoue (1915) pp 532–534.
46 The bibliography of the Tosho Bunko in Tokyo, an education library where the present writer did most of her research, lists 150 *shushin* texts for boys' middle-schools and 216 texts for girls' middle-schools: Tokyo Shoseki (1979) vol 1, pp 3–7, 352–359. Many of these textbooks use *jinkaku*.

to the explication of the concept, adding meanings to the word that appeared only afterwards in Inoue's texts: this section will discuss two of the more prominent writers who gave *jinkaku* a more significantly egalitarian meaning than Inoue.

Takashima Heizaburo was one of the more eminent of the textbook writers. In *Chugaku Shushin Kyokasho* (A Boys' Middle School Textbook on Morals), published in 1903, Takashima introduced the idea that *jinkaku* required an integrated self that was capable of taking responsibility.[47] Then, in 1908 he noted that children had only the potential for *jinkaku* because their sense of integrated self was not developed. Likewise, lunatics and mentally retarded adults did not have *jinkaku*.[48] The same idea appeared in Inoue's book seven years later.[49]

Takashima introduced the idea of equality in his 1908 textbook, stating that husbands and wives were equal in possessing a *jinkaku* worthy of respect. While adhering to the standard idea that the husband's place was outside the home, and the wife's place was inside, he nevertheless wrote that the idea of respect for others' *jinkaku* applied to both men and women, and both the husband and wife had to respect each other's *jinkaku*.[50] This was two years before Inoue and Oshima asserted that it was the essence of ethics for the husband and wife to maintain a monogamous relationship and respect each other's *jinkaku*.[51]

Another scholar was Yoshida Seichi,[52] who presented a more generally egalitarian view of *jinkaku* than Inoue did in 1902. In his *Chugaku Shushin Kyokasho* (A Boys' Middle School Textbook on Morals), published in 1906, Yoshida stated that acquisition of knowledge was irrelevant to developing *jinkaku*: 'because *jinkaku* was the qualification for people being human beings, regardless [of their other qualifications] – the upper and lower classes, with knowledge and without, strong and weak, old and young and men and women – all people were equal (*byodo*) in possessing *jinkaku*'.[53]

Yoshida also had a more active view of the need for respect for *jinkaku*. While Inoue's emphasis was on avoiding tarnishing one's *jinkaku*, by, for instance, accepting bribes,[54] Yoshida emphasised that valuing one's *jinkaku* meant one had to do one's utmost to prevent it from being harmed by others; there might be times when one had to sacrifice one's life and property to adhere to one's ideals, to retain one's *jinkaku*.[55]

Thus, it is clear that by the 1910s, the word *jinkaku* was a key word in Japan's educational and moral discourse. People had the obligation to strengthen and perfect their own *jinkaku* because that was the ultimate purpose of life. *Shushin* textbooks taught that all people were equal in possessing *jinkaku*, and that people

---

47 Takashima (1903) vol 4, pp 28–29. Takashima was a remarkable, self-educated scholar, who grew up in poverty and only completed elementary school. On his own, he pursued his interest in education, wrote many books and articles, and became the principal of an elementary school at the age of 20: Takashima (1983) appendix, pp 2–12.

48 Takashima (1908) vol 3, pp 41–42.

49 Inoue (1915) pp 1–6.

50 Takashima (1908) vol 4, pp 78–79.

51 Inoue and Oshima (1910) vol 4, p 23.

52 Hirai Atsuko claims that Yoshida's importance 'in the educational policy of the Meiji government was second only to that of Inoue': Hirai (1979) in (1979) 5(1) Journal of Japanese Studies 118.

53 Yoshida (1906) vol 3, p 32.

54 Inoue (1915) pp 15–19.

55 Yoshida (1906) vol 3, p 34.

had to respect not only their own *jinkaku*, but also they had to respect others' *jinkaku*. Despite this usage in most textbooks, however, the concept still had an elitist connotation because it assumed that some people would achieve a higher level of perfection than others. Moreover, the concept was being taught mainly to boys in middle-schools who were headed for higher education and were destined to become part of the nation's ruling elite. Only a few graduates of the compulsory elementary schools went on to the middle-schools.[56]

The writers of the boys' middle-school textbooks also wrote texts for girls' middle-schools. But they were not so anxious to teach young women the ideas that all people, irrespective of their social position and gender, had *jinkaku*, although they were just as eager to teach them the importance of morality and virtue. Their discussions of *jinkaku* for girls were not nearly as detailed as those for boys.[57] Moreover, little effort was made to teach *jinkaku* to the lower classes. The Ministry of Education, which published textbooks for *koto shogakko* (higher elementary school) attended by the children from the less privileged classes, did not introduce the concept of *jinkaku* until the early 1930s.[58] None the less, the idea of *jinkaku* became widely known to ordinary Japanese by the 1910s through the movement known as *shuyo undo*, meaning 'movement for self-discipline'.

THE SELF IMPROVEMENT MOVEMENT, *JINKAKU* AND NITOBE INAZO

Japan industrialised rapidly in the first two decades of the twentieth century. Large numbers of young men and women moved from villages to urban centres to work in factories for low wages. Without the support of their families and communities, they needed guidance on how to live their lives in a changing and perplexing society. In response, a broad spiritual movement called *shuyo undo* arose, which encouraged young men and women to discipline and improve themselves so that they might live successfully in their new environment. Through this movement, the word *jinkaku* became familiar to large numbers of ordinary, working young people in villages and growing urban centres.

The most influential figure in this movement was Nitobe Inazo (1862–1933), a distinguished agronomist, educator and highly respected diplomat, who was also a proponent of popular education. During the period between 1911 and 1916, when he was the principal of the First Higher School (*Ichiko*), he published three collections of short, easy-to-read essays on how to live a morally upright and good life in a popular business journal, *Jitsugyo-no Nihon* (Business Japan). These essays, which used the concept *jinkaku*, were published as books shortly thereafter.[59] The first book, titled *Shuyo* (Self Discipline), was so popular that during the first month after its publication in September 1911, *Jitsugyo-no Nihon*

---

56 In 1912, the last year of the Meiji era and the first year of the Taisho era, the number of boys' middle-school (*chugakko*) students totaled 128,973; the same year, there were 7,214,585 children attending elementary schools: Mombusho (Ministry of Education) (1972) *Gakusei Hyaku-nen-shi* (One Hundred Year History of the Educational System), pp 489, 497.

57 Examples are Yoshida (1906a); Inoue (1903).

58 Mombusho (1930–32).

59 The first book, *Shuyo* (1911), focused on individuals and their self-improvement; the second, *Yo-watari* (1912), contained a series of essays on how to live by relating well to other people and society; finally, the third book, *Jikei* (1916), literally meaning 'warnings to oneself', contained somewhat advanced essays on self-discipline and self-improvement.

had to reprint it six times; between then and 1929, it was reprinted 137 more times.[60] During the same period, the second book had gone through 86 editions, and the third, 15 editions.[61]

In the first book, Nitobe wrote that the purpose of *shuyo* was to elevate individuals' *jinkaku*.[62] But what is interesting and important is that while Nitobe emphasised the need for all individuals to strengthen their *jinkaku*, he did not say that all people were equal in possessing *jinkaku*. Although Nitobe had deep respect for young men and women of lesser privilege, he was not a leveller. Like Inoue, he believed both in a hierarchical social order and the need for all people to improve their *jinkaku*, regardless of their social position. In his second book, *Yowatari* (Art of Living), published in 1912, he stated that a society that merely emphasised equality (*byodo*), ignoring hierarchy, could not maintain social order.[63]

Nitobe did, however, differ from Inoue, particular the early Inoue, in that he did not believe that academic learning was essential to developing *jinkaku*. In an anecdote on friendship in the workplace, he noted that there were two types of individuals whom co-workers missed when they left their workplace. The first were those who were useful and competent. The second were people who were honest, diligent, right-minded and who gave pleasure to others. Although those people were often not particularly competent, or skilful, and were seldom appreciated in the workplace, their presence improved the atmosphere, prevented quarrels among people and eliminated unpleasantness from the working environment. They had high *jinkaku*.[64] Lastly, in *Jikei* (Warnings to Oneself), he said that although disciplining and achieving high *jinkaku* was more important than achieving a high level of competence in work, those who were to become successful in their careers – be it politics, business, or scholarly endeavours – had to achieve high *jinkaku*.[65]

Thus, Nitobe, like Inoue and various other leaders in educational and moral discourse, advocated a concept of *jinkaku* that was implicitly elitist, although he contributed to weakening the hierarchical aspects of the idea both by teaching it to ordinary young men and women who were still not learning about it in school, and by clearly indicating that many ordinary people had a *jinkaku* worthy of respect. By softening the hierarchical aspects of the concept of *jinkaku*, Nitobe foreshadowed the so-called Taisho democratic era, when the egalitarian aspect of *jinkaku* became significantly more important.

THE TAISHO DEMOCRATIC MOVEMENT AND THE DEMOCRATISATION OF THE CONCEPT OF *JINKAKU*

Before the beginning of the Taisho period, Japan had been very successful in building a modern, industrial economy. This achievement, however, brought

60 Nitobe (1970) vol 7 [1911], p 691.
61 Nitobe (1970), vol 8 [1912], p 591; vol 7 [1916], p 692. President of *Jitsugyo-no Nihon*, Masuda Giichi, stated that his company published more than 140 editions of *Shuyo*: Nitobe (1970) vol 7, p 691. Although the president does not say how many copies of the journal were sold, Nitobe stated that he had heard that the journal sold 80,000 copies each month; he estimated that each copy was read by three people, expanding its readership to about 240,000: Nitobe (1970) vol 7, p 682.
62 Nitobe (1970) vol 7 [1911], p 31.
63 Nitobe (1970) vol 8 [1912], pp 100–101.
64 Nitobe (1970) vol 8 [1912], pp 227–228.
65 Nitobe (1970) vol 7 [1916], p 439.

new problems to the fore. Rapidly growing industries, with large numbers of young men and women working for low wages and in oppressive working conditions, eventually led to the development of a labour movement that demanded a greater share of economic wealth for the nation's workers. Suzuki Bunji was one of the leaders of Japan's first labour union movement. Another important development was the growth of political parties and a rising interest in politics among the increasingly well-educated and well-informed middle-class citizens, who were demanding a greater share in the nation's political process. In this arena, Yoshino Sakuzo, who led the fight for universal male suffrage, was the most important leader of the democratic political movement. The word *jinkaku* was an important concept in the thinking of both Yoshino and Suzuki. Moreover, these leaders also 'democratised' its meanings by linking it to rights. One other important development was an intellectual movement of self-improvement, called *kyoyo*-movement, a counterpart to Nitobe's *shuyo*-movement, led by Abe Jiro. Abe advocated his own *jinkaku-shugi* (*jinkaku*-ism) that gained a large following among young Japanese. The ideas about *jinkaku* developed by these men informed the concept of *jinkaku* that was later adopted to explain individual dignity.

Yoshino Sakuzo, *jinkaku* and universal male suffrage

Yoshino Sakuzo (1878–1933) was a graduate of Tokyo University and a Christian; he attended a Unitarian church that attracted various other reformers. He is most widely identified with the expression *mimpon-shugi* (government based on the 'people-first' doctrine[66]), which he used to advocate his theory of democracy. One aspect of his theory was a general argument in support of universal male suffrage, in which he used the term *jinkaku* in reference to not only individual moral responsibility to both state and society, but also their political rights.

Between 1919 and 1923, Yoshino wrote three major essays arguing for universal male suffrage. In his 1919 essay, entitled 'Futsu Senkyo-no Riron-teki Konkyo' (A Theoretical Foundation of Universal Suffrage), Yoshino argued that individuals were not free and independent from birth, but had the potential for becoming an independent and free *jinkaku-sha* (a person of *jinkaku*) by self-discipline within society.[67] He did not, however, describe what he meant by *jinkaku-sha*.

In his next essay 'Futatabi Futsu Senkyo-no Riron-teki Konkyo-ni Tsuite' (Once Again, On the Theoretical Underpinnings of Universal Suffrage), published in 1920, the link between voting and *jinkaku* became clearer. In this essay, he used the concept of *jinkaku* in both its hierarchical and egalitarian senses. In what he called the 'passive (*shokyoku-teki*) argument', Yoshino argued against supporters of limited suffrage, who claimed that universal suffrage would increase election crimes committed by voters, and that politics would be controlled by uneducated and ignorant masses. He pointed out that election fraud, or vote buying, was initiated by the candidates and their supporters, and not by voters. Election crimes could thus be controlled by both imposing restrictions on candidates who tried to tempt voters to engage in fraudulent acts and emphasising the selection of candidates. What was most important was that candidates should demonstrate both high *jinkaku* and good judgment

66 Najita (1974) p 119.
67 Yoshino (1948) [1919], pp 177–178.

about politics, and that they educate voters and provide them with opportunities to compare political ideas. He thought that while political office-holders should be carefully selected for their intelligence, special knowledge and skills, it did not require people to have special qualifications to exercise the right to vote.[68] He believed that ordinary people's intellectual and moral abilities were not nearly as low as the opponents of universal suffrage contended, and that they were quite capable of judging the character, the *jinkaku*, of candidates, which was all that was necessary.[69]

In his 'active (*sekkyoku-teki*)' argument for universal suffrage, Yoshino directly presented his ideal of democracy in a modern state, in which he emphasised the need for each individual *jinkaku-sha* to be free to exercise his own will. He believed that voting was an essential right of subjects, who participated in the affairs of the state. To quote:

> 'Focusing on the social nature of the modern state and the fact that modern people are recognized to have politically independent *jinkaku*, we claim that suffrage is a right that properly belongs to the people arising out of their status [as citizens] within the structure of the state. There is no doubt that this is the most important argument for universal suffrage.'[70]

Although it is not entirely clear what Yoshino meant by 'politically independent *jinkaku*', he seems to have thought that all (male) citizens were entitled to the right to vote because they had sufficiently developed *jinkaku* to enable them to participate in the affairs of the country, in part because they were to some extent aware that their activities affected the state. He went on to repeat that democracy as a political ideal would be 'the cooperative management (*kyodo-keiei*) [of the state] based on the free activities of the *jinkaku*'. Co-operative management required a political system that was built on the idea of respect for the freedom of *jinkaku*.[71] His use of the word *jinkaku* in this context is clearly egalitarian.

Finally, in his third essay, 'Senkyo Riron-no Ni-san-ni Tsuite' (A Few Comments on the Theory of Voting), Yoshino reaffirmed his contention that all (male) citizens, who possessed political *jinkaku* (*seiji-teki jinkaku*) as members of a society, had the right to vote. This idea differed fundamentally from the theory of suffrage as a reward for contributions to the state, even if the reward was applied maximally to all citizens in the country, because any such reward would be a grant from the state, rather than an entitlement.[72]

Thus, like Inoue, Yoshino interpreted the word *jinkaku* to mean the moral character of the individual. But, unlike Inoue, he did not emphasise the individual's responsibility to cultivate his *jinkaku*. Rather, he argued that most male citizens had political *jinkaku*, which entitled them the right to vote. In this way, Yoshino 'democratised' *jinkaku*, though he limited it only to males.[73]

---

68 Yoshino (1948) [1920], pp 192–193.
69 Yoshino (1948) [1920], pp 196–197.
70 Yoshino (1948) [1920], p 201.
71 Yoshino (1948) [1920], pp 206–207.
72 Yoshino (1948) [1923], pp 211–214.
73 In his essay on women and suffrage, entitled 'Futsu Senkyo-to Fujin Sansei-ken (Universal Suffrage and Women's Right to Vote)', Yoshino admits that, in theory, there is no justifiable reason for excluding women from the right to vote. He gives the feeble excuse that, for now, women should perhaps be protected from vicious and often unconscionable politics: Yoshino (1948 [1924], pp 244–255).

Jinkaku, the labour movement and Suzuki Bunji

As Japan industrialised, workers formed organisations to promote their interests. Leaders of the nascent labour movement also used the word *jinkaku* in their discourse to refer to individuals who were entitled to economic rights, while retaining its original meaning of moral character. The most prominent of these labour leaders was Suzuki Bunji (1885–1946), who was also a graduate of Tokyo University and who attended the same Unitarian church as Yoshino. He became interested in social welfare activities for industrial workers at an early age. In 1913, he and his associates established a co-operative called *Yuai-kai*, 'friendship association', to help workers educate themselves and strengthen their character so that they could improve their positions in Japan's expanding industrial world. As one might imagine, the association attracted an increasingly large number of members, who found in it a substitute for the village community they had left behind. *Yuai-kai* also became actively involved in labour disputes and attempted to serve as mediator between management and labour and to provide assistance to strikers; it eventually became Japan's first labour union.

Suzuki was very interested in labour relations in Western countries. He initially thought, however, that Western labour relations, which were based on the assumptions of an inevitable conflict of interest between the management and workers, were unsuitable for Japan. He advocated what he called 'family-ism in labour relations', whereby the employers would serve as surrogate parents for their employees, taking care of them with a strong sense of responsibility. Workers, in turn, would devote themselves to contributing their share to building Japanese industry.[74] In his writings, Suzuki told the workers not to be corrupted by the pleasures of life and thereby injure their *jinkaku*.[75] He was obviously referring to the hierarchical sense of *jinkaku* and the need for people to discipline and improve it.

But Suzuki soon realised that employers were exploiting workers, forcing them to work long hours when demand was high, but laying them off when it declined. He decided that his early idea of family-ism did not work. On the one hand, Suzuki continued to tell workers that they had to expand their knowledge about society and strengthen their *jinkaku*, while organising to protect themselves in the labour market. In other words, Suzuki did not simply encourage workers to inform themselves and fight for their rights. He also believed that all workers had to train and discipline themselves as human beings so that they could rightfully demand their equitable share of profits. To employers, on the other hand, he forcefully argued that the nation's economic elite had to respect workers as human beings; they were not simply machines to be used to generate profit. Workers had an independent and self-reliant *jinkaku* that was the same as the *jinkaku* of employers or anyone else in higher social positions. Accordingly, they were entitled to a fair share in the benefits of the economic development, to which they greatly contributed. In a 1918 article entitled '*Mazu Rodosha-no Jinkaku-o Mitome-yo*' (First, Recognize Workers' *Jinkaku*)', Suzuki declared, 'Without recognizing the workers' *jinkaku*, Japanese industry cannot expect to prosper and [the nation] cannot expect to raise its [level of] civilization'.[76]

---

74 Sumiya (1966) pp 187-188.
75 Suzuki (1916).
76 Suzuki (1918).

Thus, as with Yoshino, in Suzuki's economic discourse, the idea of *jinkaku* was clearly linked to rights in society, as well as individual responsibility. Suzuki believed that all industrial workers, even those with lesser education, had the ability to become *jinkaku-sha*, and were therefore entitled to equal economic rights and equal respect. Suzuki, however, did not address the tension between the hierarchical and egalitarian senses of *jinkaku*. Nor did he explain the relationship between respect for *jinkaku* as a right and as a duty.

Abe Jiro's *jinkaku*-ism and the spiritually correct society

While leaders like Yoshino and Suzuki were actively participating in political and labour movements, other intellectuals, who belonged to a group called *kyoyo-ha*, or culture group, believed that social and political action could not solve the political, social and economic problems the nation faced. The *kyoyo*-ism promoted by these intellectuals was the intellectual counterpart of *shuyo* mentioned above; they turned inward in search of moral and aesthetic self-cultivation and liberation. The movement attracted a large number of the better educated new generation of Japanese.[77] They believed in developing the inner strength of individuals and hoped that if the number of morally and ethically upright people became large enough, social ills could be cured.

Abe Jiro (1883–1959), with his theory of *jinkaku-shugi* (*jinkaku*-ism), was at the centre of this movement. Abe's ideas of respect for *jinkaku* and the need to discipline and improve it were very similar to those of Inoue, Yoshino, Suzuki and others. But it differed in that it encompassed, in addition to the moral aspect of character, the inner, or spiritual, self. He also went beyond Yoshino and Suzuki in asserting not only that people had the right to be respected as *jinkaku*, but that they also had the right to expect society to provide an environment in which they could nurture and develop their *jinkaku* maximally, according to their capabilities and talents. A democratic society, as a collective entity, had obligations to the people.

Abe, who taught at *Tohoku* University in Sendai most of his life, began to write about and give lectures on his idealistic theory of *jinkaku* in 1920. Two years later, he published a book entitled *Jinkaku-shugi*, which included the two major essays on his theory of *jinkaku*-ism, Jinkaku Shugi (*Jinkaku*-ism), and Jinkaku-shugi-no Shicho (Thoughts on *Jinkaku*-ism), which was based on a series of public lectures he delivered in Manchuria in the spring of 1920.[78]

Abe emphasised the spiritual side of life. He believed in self-discipline and the pursuit of truth, goodness, beauty and the sacred in life. The goal was a truly liberated *jinkaku*, that is, a person who could free himself or herself of excessive material and physical desires and wants.[79] While Suzuki and other labour leaders argued that workers had the right to share the nation's wealth because they had the same basic *jinkaku* as their employers, Abe believed that the important question was the motivation behind the workers' demands. He would support only a labour movement in which workers sought material goods for the sake of contributing to the growth of their *jinkaku*; he believed that all people, employers and employees alike, were workers and that they should all aim at developing *jinkaku*.[80]

---

77 Kludai Nikon (1959) pp 242–244.
78 Abe (1961) pp 5–459.
79 Abe (1961) p 105.
80 Abe (1961) pp 252–263.

Abe, however, did not believe in complete social equality among people. *Jinkaku-*ism meant that individuals respected each other as possessors of *jinkaku*, even though they performed different roles in society. A husband and wife had distinctly different roles to play, but each had to respect the other equally. Similarly, an employer and employee had different roles to play. Using himself as an example, he explained that he had a calling as a scholar. If he were to neglect his own work and engage in housework, he would be degrading his own calling. His housekeeper had her own calling in housework.[81] Thus, Abe clearly accepted the possibility of social hierarchy.

Finally, Abe linked his notion of improving and perfecting *jinkaku* to democracy. Improving and perfecting *jinkaku* was not simply the individual's responsibility, but it was also a right, to be guaranteed by a democratic society. A truly democratic society was one that allowed all individuals to live according to their own consciences. An ideal democratic society, he said, was 'one that provides equally to all people – not only aristocrats but all common men – the opportunity to develop their *jinkaku* to its highest potential according to their abilities'.[82] He thought that a society of liberated *jinkaku* would not be a complacent society, but a lively one in which people would express their opinions; it would be a contentious society filled with adversaries or rivals (*koteki*), who were nevertheless respected (*keiai-sareru*) as *jinkaku*. It would also be a society in which people with high *jinkaku* would carry the responsibility of leading those with low *jinkaku*.[83] Abe thus combined the notions of hierarchy in *jinkaku* and his own ideas of a democratic society, which respected the individuals' right to develop their *jinkaku*.[84]

While the direct influence of Abe's ideas of *jinkaku* on the development of post-war democratic notions of respect for and perfecting *jinkaku* is not easy to assess, it is noteworthy that parts of Abe's *Jinkaku-shugi* were republished twice by two different publishing houses immediately after the Second World War, when Japan was still suffering from acute shortage of paper – first in September 1947, by Iwanami Shoten, and then in November 1948, by Kadokawa Shoten. The latter published a paperback edition of the same work in 1954, and in 1961, two years after Abe's death, it published his complete works in 17 volumes. This, the present writer believes, is an indication that Abe's ideas about *jinkaku* resonated with the spiritual needs of large numbers of people in post-war Japan. Moreover, the government leaders after the Second World War were not only well acquainted with his *jinkaku*-ism, but many were also Abe's friends and academic colleagues from the pre-war days, who deeply respected both him and his ideas.

THE DIMINISHING ROLE OF *JINKAKU* IN THE ERA OF ULTRA-NATIONALISM

Beginning in the late 1920s, Japan faced a series of domestic and international crises that ultimately led to a catastrophic war against the US and its allies. As the

81 Abe (1961) pp 417–420.
82 Abe (1961) pp 118–119.
83 Abe (1961) pp 119–120.
84 Like Yoshino and Suzuki, Abe was from northern Japan (Yamagata Prefecture). Yoshino noted in one essay that he and Abe were acquainted with each other (*aishiri*) and he had deep respect for Abe's scholarship and *jinkaku*: Yoshino (1995) vol 12 [1922], p 233. In September 1922, he published a short review of Abe's *Jinkaku-shugi* in a journal called *Bunka Seikatsu* (Cultural Life) and praised it not only as an excellent philosophical work, but also an unusually valuable book for moral training (*shuyo-sho*). He said that he had learned much from Abe's book: Yoshino (1995) vol 12 [1922], pp 233–237.

Taisho democrats tried to steer the nation's political, economic and educational life in more liberal directions, the government, fearing the spread of the 'dangerous ideas', moved in the opposite direction. In March 1925, when the Imperial Diet passed the universal male suffrage law, it also passed the Peace Preservation Law that gave the government power to tighten its control over various spheres of citizens' lives.

While the *shoshin* texts continued to discuss *jinkaku*, they also began to include various imperial rescripts to impress upon students the role of the emperor in Japan's body politic. Interests in *jinkaku* diminished and no significant works appeared during the 1930s. In 1944, a year prior to Japan's unconditional surrender, the Ministry of Education published, for the first time, its own *shushin* textbook for boys' middle-schools. Only in this text was there no mention of the need for respecting or developing the *jinkaku* of individuals. The government was entirely preoccupied with teaching militarism and extreme nationalism to the nation's youth.[85] None the less, the concept of *jinkaku* was familiar to any educated Japanese person who survived the war.

CONCLUSION

This chapter has traced the intellectual roots of the word *jinkaku*, which was used in the Japanese translation of the phrase 'individual dignity' included in Article 24 of the post-Second World War Constitution of Japan.

To summarise, the word appears to have been initially created around 1889 in the context of law as a translation for the word '(legal) personality'. Moral and education thinkers, the most prominent of whom was Inoue Tetsujiro, soon adopted the word and began to teach that the goal of life was to discipline and perfect one's *jinkaku*. The Chinese character *kaku* of *jinkaku* had hierarchical implications, and the notion of perfecting it suggested that some would reach higher *jinkaku* than others, and thus would be respected more than others. Initially *jinkaku* was taught only to students in boys' middle-schools, who were destined to be part of the nation's ruling elite. The word gradually acquired a more democratic, egalitarian meaning as textbooks began to teach that all people were worthy of respect for their *jinkaku*.

This trend continued as Nitobe Inazo introduced the concept to ordinary working men and women in villages and urban centres, teaching that all people, irrespective of their social positions and education, had the ability to train and elevate their *jinkaku*. Political and social activists such as Yoshino Sakuzo and Suzuki Bunji further democratised the concept by linking *jinkaku* to rights, claiming that *jinkaku* of all people entitled them equally to participate in the nation's political and economic activities. None the less, all of these thinkers continued to advocate that all people had a duty to perfect their *jinkaku*. The concept thus carried a tension between its hierarchical and egalitarian senses, one that was never resolved.

Thus, when the Japanese government officials adopted 'respect for *jinkaku*' to stand for 'individual dignity', and declared that this was to be one of the principles of post-Second World War democracy in Japan, they were drawing on an important concept from their pre-war democratic experiences. The ideas surrounding

85 Mombusho (1944).

jinkaku came naturally to the members of the post-war leadership because many of them had lived through and, in one way or another, participated in the *Taisho* democratic movement in their younger years. Moreover, many of those leaders, including five out of eight of the Ministers of Education[86] during the occupation, had spent three years at the First Higher School (*Ichiko*) under Nitobe's tutelage.[87] Higher schools in pre-war Japan, the most prestigious of which was *Ichiko*, were the primary, if not the exclusive source of humanistic education for intelligent young men destined for political, economic and social leadership.[88] The core of their education was disciplining *jinkaku*, and one of their favourite authors was Abe Jiro. They thus brought a strong sense of shared values and contiguity to the post-war educational leadership. It is no wonder that they chose respect for and perfecting *jinkaku* as the fundamental concept of post-war democratic education.

In choosing *jinkaku*, however, these leaders also carried its elitist connotations and the unresolved tension between the hierarchical and egalitarian interpretations into the Constitution. Neither the Americans nor the Japanese seem to have realised that the Japanese had significantly altered the meaning of the US ideal of individual dignity. But the use of *jinkaku* enabled them to maintain continuity with pre-war Japanese thought, and thereby bridge the difference between Japanese and American ideas about the individual.

Yet the use of *jinkaku* would cause problems in the long run because the Japanese also had to teach the nation's youth the idea of fundamental human rights, another idea imposed by the US, and one that did not fit well with *jinkaku*. Evidence from post-war textbooks shows that the Japanese initially did not understand the meaning or the sources of human rights and were unable to relate individuals' 'responsibility' to respect their own and others' *jinkaku* to human 'rights'. The hierarchical connotations of *jinkaku* seem to be an important reason for the virtual disappearance of *jinkaku* in recent decades in teaching about democratic ideas about the self.[89]

Select bibliography

Abe, J, (1961) 'Jinkaku-Shugi-no Shicho; Jinkaku Shugi,' in J Abe *Abe Jiro Zenshu* (The Collected Works of Abe Jiro), vol 6 [1921, 1922].

Amano, T, (1970-71) *Amano Teiyu Zenshu* (The Collected Works of Amano Teiyu), 9 vols.

Hirai, A, (1979) 'Self-Realization and Common Good: T H Green in Meiji Ethical Thought 5(1) Journal of Japanese Studies 107–136.

---

86 They were: Maeda Tamon (18 August 1945–13 January 1946); Abe Yoshishige (13 January–22 May 1946); Tanaka Kotaro (22 May 1946–31 January 1947); Morito Tatsuo (1 June 1947–15 October 1948); and Amano Teiyu (6 May 1950–12 August 1952).
87 They acknowledged their indebtedness to Nitobe in various writings: eg Maeda (1963) pp 13–16; Tanaka (1961) pp 18–20; and Amano (1970–71) vol 3, pp 201-210, 326–328. There also are various other acknowledgments: eg Yanaihara (1965) pp 668–674. Yanaihara Tadao (1893–1961), a noted economist and a Christian, who had been forced to resign from Tokyo University during the war, later returned to it; he served as the president from 1951 to 1957. He was an influential figure in post-war educational circles.
88 Roden (1980).
89 This process is discussed in detail in chapter 4 of the present writer's book *Individual Dignity in Modern Japanese Thought: The Evolution of the Concept of Jinkaku in Moral and Educational Discourse*, published by the Center for Japanese Studies, University of Michigan Press, 2001.

Homu Daijin Kambo Shiho Hosei Chosa-bu (1984–89) *Nihon Kindai Rippo Shiryo Sosho* (A Documentary History of Modern Japanese Lawmaking), 32 vols.

Inoue, K, (1991) *MacArthur's Japanese Constitution: A Linguistic and Cultural Study of Its Making.*

Inoue, T, (1993) *Kaichu Nikki*, vol 1 [1884–89]; reproduced by J Fukui (1993) as '*Inoue Tetsujiro Nikki*', vol 1, 11 *Tokyo Daigaku-shi Kiyo* (Journal of the History of Tokyo University), (March, vol II, 25–63).

—(1891) *Chokugo Engi* (A Commentary of the Rescript), 2 vols.

—(1892) '*Shukyo-to Kyoiku-to-no Kankei-ni Tsuki Inoue Tetsujiro-shi no Danwa*' (Mr Tetsujiro Inoue's Comments on the Relationship Between a Religion and Education), 272 *Kyoiku Jiron*, 5 November, at 24–26.

—(1893) *Kyoiku-to Shokyo-to-no Shototsu* (A Collision Between Education and a Religion).

—(1902a) *Sonken Hakushi Rinri Shukyo-ron Hihyo-shu* (A Collection of Critical Essays on Morals and Religion by Dr. Inoue), vol 1.

—(1902b) *Chugaku Shushin Kyokasho* (A Boys' Middle School Textbook on Morals), 5 vols.

—(1915) *Jinkaku-to Shuyo* (On Jinkaku and Self-Discipline).

—(1973) *Inoue Tetsujiro Jiden: Gakkai Kaiko-roku* (An Autobiography of Inoue Tetsujiro: Reminiscences on Academia).

Inoue, T, and Oshima, G, (1910) *Chugaku Shushin Kyokasho* (A Boys' Middle School Textbook on Morals), 5 vols.

Inoue, T, and Takayama, R, (1897) *Shimpen Rinri Kyokasho* (A New Textbook on Ethics), 5 vols.

Ishikawa, K, Osawa S, and Kameyama, N, (1890) *Gakuri Oyo Mimpo Seigi: Zaisan-hen* (A Scientific Commentary on the Civil Code: Property Law).

Kindai Nihon Shisoshi Koza (A Modern Japanese Intellectual History) (1959), vol 1, *Rekishi-teki Gaikan* (A General Survey).

Kishi, K, (1893) '*Kokka-ga Minji Sosho Toji-sha-to Shite-no Shikaku*' (The Status of the State as a Party in a Civil Lawsuit), 6 *Kokka Gakkai Zasshi* 81, 15 November, at 1810–19.

Kiyozawa, M, (1955) *Kiyozawa Manshi Zenshu*, vol 2 [1892–93].

Kuwata, K, (1894) '*Kokka-to Shakai-no Kankei-o Ronzu*' (Discussing the Relationship Between the State and Society), 8 *Kokka Gakkai Zasshi* 89, 15 July, at 533–47.

Maeda, T, (1963) *Maeda Tamon: Sono-bun, Sono-hito* (Maeda Tamon: His Writings and His Activities).

Meiji Bunka Kenkyukai (1968) *Meiji Bunka Zenshu* (A Complete Collection of the Writings of the Meiji Period), vol 12.

Mombusho, (1930–32) *Koto Shogaku Shushin-sho*, 2 vols.

—(1944) *Chuto Shushin* (Middle School Morals), 2 vols.

Myrdal, G, (1944) *An American Dilemma: The Negro Problem and Modern Democracy*. 2 vols.

Naka, A, (1967) *Meiji-no Kyoiku* (Education in the Meiji Era).

Nitobe, I, (1970) *Nitobe Inazo Zenshu* (Complete Works of Nitobe Inazo), vols 7, 8 and 10.

Okubo, Y, (1977) *Nihon Kindai Rippo-no Hito: Boasonodo* (Contributor to Modern Japanese Law-making: Boissonade).

Roden, D, (1980) *School Days in Imperial Japan: A Study in the Culture of a Student Elite.*

Sumiya, M, (1966) '*Rodo Undo-ni Okeru Shinri-to Ronri*' (Truth and Rationale for the Union Movement) in *Kindai Nihon Shiso-shi Koza* (A Modern Japanese Intellectual History), vol 5, *Shidosha-to Taishu* (Leaders and the Masses), pp 187-217.

Suzuki, B, (1916) '*Rodosha Jikaku-ron*' (Thoughts about the Self-awareness of the Workers), 56 *Rodo-oyobi Sangyo* (The Labour and Industry), April, at 266–70.

—(1918) 'Mazu Rodo-sha-no Jinkaku-o Mitome-yo (First, Recognize Workers' Jinkaku)', 85 *Rodo-oyobi Sangyo* (The Labour and Industry), September, at 125–28.

Tanaka, K, (1961) *Watashi-no Rireki-sho* (My Resume).

Takashima, H, (1903) *Chugaku Shushin Kyokasho* (A Boys' Middle School Textbook on Morals), 5 vols.

—(1908), *Shinsen Chuto Shushin-sho* (A New Middle School Textbook on Morals), 5 vols.

—(1983) *Katei, Fujin, Jido. Kindai Fujin Mondai Meicho Senshu: Shakai Mondai-hen (selected works on the Issues Related to Home, Women and Children)*, vol 5 [1936].

Tokiomi, K (ed), (1964) *Nihon Kyoka-sho Taikei, Kindai-hen* (A History of Japanese Textbooks, Modern), vol 3, *Shushin* (Morals Textbooks 3).

Tokyo Shoseki, (1979) *Tosho Bunko Shozo Tosho Kyokasho Mokuroku* (A Bibliography of the Tosho Bunko Textbook Collection).

Tomita, T, (1968) *Ginko Shogen* (A Commentary on Banking), vol 12 [1885], *Meiji Bunka Zenshu*, pp 261-307.

Yanaihara, T, (1965), *Yanaihara Tadao Zenshu* (Collected Works of Yanaihara Tadao), vol 24.

Yoshida, S, (1906a) *Koto Jogakko Shushin Kyokasho* (Girls' Higher School Textbook for Morals), 4 vols, revised edn.

Yoshida, S, (1906b) *Chugaku Shushin Kyokasho* (A Boys' Middle School Textbook on Morals), 5 vols, revised 2nd edition.

Yoshino, S, (1948), *Yoshino Sakuzo Hakushi Minshu-shugi Ronsho* (Collected Lectures on Democracy by Dr Yoshino Sakuzo), vol 2 [1919], *Minshu-shugi Seiji Kowa.*

—(1995) *Yoshino Sakuzo Zenshu* (Selected Works of Yoshino Sakuzo), 15 vols plus supplement.

Zaidan Hojin Kaikoku Hyakunen Kinen Bunka Jigyodan (ed), (1965) *Meiji Bunka-shi* (A History of the Meiji Culture), vol 3, *Kyoiku, Dotoku-hen* (Education and Morals).

Chapter 15

Transitional justice as liberal narrative[1]

R TEITEL[2]

The human rights account at the end of the last century reads as a disjunctive story, a sad litany of grave rights violations and attendant legal responses. So it is that, strangely, Bosnia's massacres, and the Rwandan genocide, go hand-in-hand with the advancement in human rights law, such as the convening of the international criminal proceedings in the Tribunals for Rwanda and for the former Yugoslavia. Attempts to deal with unsettled business relating to the atrocities of the so-called dirty wars of Chile and Argentina under military rule in the early 1980s, such as Spain's extradition request of General Augusto Pinochet, have revolutionised international law, already spurring other similar assumptions of jurisdiction, for example, the case of Habre in Senegal. Globalisation of jurisdiction on behalf of victims in exile will have ramifications for years to come.

Contemporary developments culminate in the call for the establishment of a permanent International Criminal Court. An historic agreement was made in Rome in the summer of 1998 to a permanent body to investigate and prosecute the most heinous war crimes, such as crimes against humanity and genocide. Securing ratification will take time. Yet it is noteworthy that for the first time since the post-war period half a century ago, there appears to be substantial international consensus on international criminal justice. What was *extraordinary* at Nuremberg is now being *normalised*.

Consider this puzzle: how is it that, given the extraordinary political violence of recent decades, there is, nevertheless, the sense of progress in human rights? This puzzle is the subject of this discussion. There is a paradoxical story in this contemporary moment as to the relation international law bears to organised violence. While the violence is not new, the accompanying rhetoric may be. What is the content of international criminal justice in response to the political violence that has characterised this century?

Transitional trials' main contribution, the writer contends, is to advance the construction of a collective liberal narrative. They advance the transformative purpose of moving the international community, as well as individual states in transition towards greater liberalizing political change. This chapter will explore

---

1   This chapter offers a summary of a larger book project: Teitel (2000).
2   Ruti Teitel, Ernst C Stiefel Professor of Comparative Law, Senior Fellow, Yale Law School Orville Schell Center for International Human Rights.

just how this account offers a liberal narrative, in particular, about the potential of law in constructing a story of changed facts, laying a basis for change in political direction. We begin with the trial, but the transformative dimension of the rule of the law can also be seen in other areas.

LAW'S HISTORY: THE USES OF THE HUMAN RIGHTS TRIAL

What is punishment's role in 'historical justice'? Trials long have played the pivotal role in transitional history-making. Criminal justice creates public, formal shared processes that link the relation of past action to the future, and the individual to the collective. Trials are the historic, ceremonial forms of memory-making in the collective, a way to work through community's events in controversy. Even the ordinary criminal trial's purpose is not only to adjudicate individual responsibility, but also to establish the truth about an event in controversy; and the trial's role in settling historical controversies is most significant in periods of transition. Transitions follow regime changes and periods of accentuated political and historical conflict, therefore a primary purpose of successor trials is commonly to advance a measure of historical justice.

But what sort of 'truths' are established in such periods? These are transitional critical truths; truths about the falseness of the predecessor regime and its ideology. Through the trial, the collective historical record produced delegitimises of the predecessor regime, and legitimises that of the successor. While military or political collapse may bring down a repressive leadership, unless the bad regime is also publicly discredited, its political ideology may well endure. An example is the historical trial of King Louis XVI, which served as a forum to deliberate over and to establish the evil of monarchic rule. Other leading historical trials, whether of the major war criminals at Nuremberg or of the public trials of Argentina's military junta (the first in that country's history), are now remembered not merely for their condemnation of individual wrongdoers, but for their roles in creating lasting records of the faces of particular state tyranny.

Transitional criminal processes enable authoritative accounts of past evil legacies and collective history-making. There are many enduring representations: recreation and dramatisation of the repressive past in the trial proceedings, and in the written transcript, trial records and judgment. There are also enhanced representational possibilities in the televising of court proceedings infusing popular culture. Thus, for example, the trial of former Central African Emperor, Jean Bedel Bokassa, offered ex post representation of the past dictatorship. Despite a subsequent amnesty, television and radio broadcasts, offering nationwide reporting of the trial proceeding, gave an oral narrative of the prior dictatorship's brutality, and meant that the offences of the Bokassa regime would not be relegated to oblivion.

Legal and historical judgments regarding persecutory pasts have commonly moved in the same direction, illuminating the role of law in the construction of history in transition. To illustrate, legal understandings of responsibility established at the post-Second World War trials shaped the initial historical understanding of Nazi persecution. Military leaders, and responsibility for wartime persecution established at Nuremberg top-down, Nazi policy, is seen as Hitler-dominated; and responsibility attributed to the top Nazi echelon. Thus, according to the then prevailing historical 'internationalist' school, responsibility for wartime persecution begins with the individual in the top echelons of power.

Over time, a more complicated and nuanced understanding of legal responsibility emerges, which goes together with and shapes changes in the historical understanding of past wrongdoing. Lower-level trials (for example, at the subsequent Control Council No 10 trials) correspond to changes in understandings of responsibility. Historical interpretations shift from the 'intentionalist school', to the 'functionalist school'. A view of responsibility as fragmented, diffused throughout all sectors of German society, and other countries. Thus, the convening of the *Eichmann* trial coincides with Raul Hilberg's *The Destruction of the European Jews*.[3] Most recently, the net of prosecutions expands to include collaborators, even in the lower echelon of power, such as the trials in France of Klaus Barbie in the late 1980s and of Paul Touvier and Maurice Papon in the 1990s. The century ends with the reconstructing of bystander responsibility in legal proceedings convened in the US, England, Scotland and Australia, arising out of these states' granting haven to persecutors at the end of the Second World War. These understandings of third-party responsibility inform human rights law more generally.

The traditional view of punishment does not accord well with its role in periods of political flux. Trials' focus on the individual case are often thought inappropriate to do the political historical work of transition. In such periods, however, contemporary transitional justice mediates the false dualisms of the individual and the collective, through the law, through categories in the law, of policy, membership and motive. Trials play a more significant role as they are well suited to the representation of historical events in controversy, needed in periods of radical flux. Out of the interaction of legal and historical constructions of responsibility emerges a complicated understanding of responsibility for wrongdoing under repressive regimes, as perpetrated by individuals against a background of systemic policy.

While criminal justice ordinarily is justified in dichotomous terms – of backward-looking retributive concerns, juxtaposed to forward-looking, utilitarian concerns – in its transitional form, punishment links up the past and the future. The question of whether to exercise criminal justice, of whether to punish or to amnesty, is rationalised in overtly political terms, relating to the transition. In these periods, the values of mercy and reconciliation, which are commonly treated as external to criminal justice, become an explicit part of transitional deliberations.

The transitional form of punishment, 'the "limited" criminal sanction', is directed less at the individual wrongdoer than at advancing the political transformation's normative shift. This is seen in that the transitional limited sanction is characterised by criminal processes partial in nature, which culminate in little or no penalty. The limited sanction is illustrated historically in post-war policy, but also in the more contemporary transitions – in punishment efforts following regime change – wherever punishment takes the form of select, limited operative acts of formal public inquiry into and clarification of the past, of indictment of past wrongdoing. Even in its arch limited form, criminal processes are a symbol of the rule of law which enables expression of a critical normative message, while advancing the shift that is central to liberalising transition.

Some of the operative effects constructive of transition that are advanced by the limited criminal sanction, such as establishing, recording and condemning

---

3   Hilberg (1961).

past wrongdoing, are also advanced by other legal processes. By its very nature, the massive, systemic wrongdoing that characterises modern repression implies a mix of individual and collective responsibilities. This is seen in the pronounced overlap of criminal and civil institutions and processes in transitions. In these periods of political flux, individualised processes of accountability often give way to administrative investigations and commissions of inquiry; the compilation of public records and official pronouncements about past wrongs. Frequently, these are themselves subsumed in state histories commissioned pursuant to a political mandate for reconciliation, as in South Africa and in much of post-military Latin America. Transitional practices, whether through prosecutions, bureaucratic lustrations or historical inquiries, share operative features to manifest new collectively shared knowledge concerning the past regime in the state's narrative.

What counts as liberalising knowledge? These productions are not original, nor foundational, but contingent on state legacies of repressive rule. The successor truth regimes' critical function is responsive to the repressive practices of the prior regime. Thus, for example, in transitions after military rule, where the truth was a casualty of disappearance policies, the most critical response is the 'official story'. Whereas, after Communism, the search for the 'truth' constituted a matter not of historical production as such – previous uses of official history were deployed as instruments of repressive control – but instead a matter of critical response to repressive state histories and the securing of private access to state archives, to privatise official histories and to introduce competing historical accounts.

NARRATIVES OF TRANSITION

Narratives constructed in transitions, whether through trials, administrative proceedings or historical commissions of inquiry make out a normative claim about the relation of the state's past to its prospects for democracy. The very narrative structure propounds the claim that particular knowledge is relevant to the possibility of personal and social change. Narratives of transition offer an account of the relation of knowledge to the move away from dictatorship and to a more liberal future.

Transitional narratives follow a distinctive rhetorical form; beginning in tragedy, they end on a comic or romantic mode. In the classical understanding, tragedy comprises the elements of catastrophic suffering, injustice or slavery of the plight of individuals, whose fate, due to their status, implicated entire collectives, followed by some discovery or change from ignorance. In tragedy, knowledge seems only to confirm a fate foretold. Contemporary stories of transitional justice similarly involve stories of affliction on a grand scale; but, whereas transitional narratives begin in a tragic mode, they switch over to a non-tragic resolution; there is a turn to what might be characterised as a comic phase. Something happens in these accounts; the persons enmeshed in the story ultimately avert tragic fates somehow to adjust and even thrive in a new reality. In the convention associated with transitional accounts, change involves a critical juncture, where the revelation of knowledge makes a difference. The state's past suffering is somehow reversed, leading to a happy ending of peace and reconciliation.

The structure of transitional narrative is manifest in the form of both fictional and non-fictional accounts of periods of political transformation. The national narratives read as tragic accounts that end on a redemptive note. Suffering somehow is transformed into something good for the state, to a greater self-knowledge, that enhances prospects for an enduring democracy. For example, after 'Night and Fog' disappearance policies throughout much of Latin America, bureaucratic processes were deployed to set up investigatory commissions. Beginning with the report entitled *Never Again*,[4] the truth promises to deter future suffering. Thus, the prologue to the report of the Argentine National Commission on the Disappeared declares the military dictatorship 'brought about the greatest and most savage tragedy' in the country's history; but, catastrophic history provides lessons.

> '[G]reat catastrophes are always instructive. The tragedy which began with the military dictatorship in March 1976, the most terrible our nation has ever suffered, will undoubtedly serve to help us understand that it is only democracy which can save a people from horror on this scale.'[5]

On these accounts, knowledge of past suffering plays a crucial role in the state's ability to make liberating transition.

Other transitional reports follow a similar story line. Confrontation with the past is deemed necessary to democratic transition. The report of the Chilean National Commission on Truth and Reconciliation[6] asserts that the disclosure and knowledge of past suffering is necessary to re-establishing the country's identity. The decree establishing Chile's National Commission declares: 'the truth had to be brought to light, for only on such a foundation ... would it be possible to ... create the necessary conditions for achieving true national reconciliation.'[7] Truth is the necessary precondition for democracy. This is also the organising thesis of the El Salvador Truth Commission. The story line is manifest even in the report's optimistic title: *From Madness to Hope*[8] tells a story of violent civil war, followed by 'truth and reconciliation'. According to the report's Introduction, the truth's 'creative consequences' can 'settle political and social differences by means of agreement instead of violent action'. 'Peace [is] to be built on transparency of ... knowledge.' The truth is characterised as a 'bright light' that 'search[es] for lessons that would contribute to reconciliation and to abolishing such patterns of behavior in the new society'. Even where the reporting is unofficial, the claims are similarly that the revelation of knowledge – in and of itself – constitutes a measure of political transformation and justice. Thus, the preface to the unofficial Uruguayan *Nunca Mas* or *Never Again* report declares that writing in and of itself constitutes a triumph against repression. The claim is that the transitional truth-tellings will deter the possibility of future repression. It is the lack of:

> 'critical understanding which created a risk of having the disaster repeated ... to rescue that history is to learn a lesson ... We should have the courage not to hide that experience in our collective subconscious but to recollect it. So that we do not fall again into the trap.'[9]

---

4   Nunca Mas: Report of the Argentine National Commission on the Disappeared (1986).
5   Nunca Mas: Report of the Argentine National Commission on the Disappeared (1986).
6   Report of the Chilean National Commission on Truth and Reconciliation, Philip E Berryman (trans), 2 vols (Notre Dame: University of Notre Dame).
7   Decree No 365.
8   Report of the Commission on the Truth for El Salvador (1993).
9   Servicio Paz y Justicia, Uruguay, Nunca Mas: Human Rights Violations (1972–1985) trans Elizabeth Hampsten, with an introduction by Lawrence Weschler (1992).

In transitional history-making, the story has to come out right. Yet, the transitional accounts imply a number of poetic leaps. To what extent is it the new truths that bring on liberalising political change; or, is it the political change that enables restoration of democratic government and reconsideration of the past? And, how exactly does the truth deter future catastrophe? The theoretical claim that it is the truth that is liberating – and that the truth enables the move to democracy – seemed wrong as a matter of practical reality almost everywhere. For the transitions out of dictatorship did not await the truth; movement to free elections and a more democratic political processes either preceded or coincided with historical production processes. Nevertheless, despite these ongoing processes of political change, without some form of clarification of the deception and ensuing self-understanding, the truth about the evil past is deemed to be hidden, unavailable, external. So it is, for example, that the post-Communist transitions are characterised by struggling with the accumulated past state archives. The transitional accounts commence with the story of invasion and popular resistance; with the foe represented as foreign outsider, progressing to the ever more troubling discovery of collaboration closer to home and pervasive throughout the society. In the narratives of transition, whether out of a repressive totalitarian rule in the former Soviet bloc, or out of authoritarian military rule, what is most pronounced is the tragic discovery. Whether Latin America's truth reports, or the 'lustration' of the post-Communist bloc, these stories all involve revelation of secreted knowledge.

Knowledge's revelation implies that, through the potential of human action, the possibility of future change is introduced. Knowledge revealed suggests somehow that there was a logic to the madness, and intimates there is now something to be done. What is propounded is the notion that, had the newly acquired knowledge been known, matters would have been different. And, conversely, that now that the truth is known, the course of future events will be different. This hope is the essence of liberalism. Accordingly, processes that illuminate the possibility of future choice distinguish the liberal transition. In the transitional accounts lie the kernels of a liberal future foretold. The revealed truth brings on the switch from the tragic past to the promise of a hopeful future. A catastrophe is somehow turned around, an awful fate averted by the introduction of a magical switch. Transitional justice operates as such a device: legal processes introduce persons vested with particular transformative powers – judges, lawyers, commissioners, experts, witnesses – with special access to privileged knowledge. A reckoning with the past, through mechanisms of revelation, enables the perception of a liberalising shift.

Narratives of transition suggest that, minimally, what is at stake in liberalising transformation is a change in interpretation. Political and truth regimes have a mutually constitutive role. Societies begin to change politically when citizens' understanding of the ambient events change. As Václav Havel has written, the change is from 'living within a lie to living within the truth'.[10] So it is that much of the literature in these periods are stories of precisely this move, from 'living within a lie', to the revelation of newly gained knowledge and self-understanding, affecting and reconstituting personal identity and relationships. These are tales of deceit and betrayal, often stories of long-standing affairs, allegories of the citizen/state relation. But it is the changes in the political and legal regimes that

10 Havel (1992).

shape and structure the historical regime. New truth regimes go hand-in-hand with new political regimes, indeed, they support the change.

The pursuit of historical justice is not simply responsive to or representative of political change, but itself helps to construct the political change, supports the change in political regimes. The transitional historical accounts construct a normative relation, as they connect up the society's past and its future; narratives of transition are stories of progress beginning with the backward-looking reflection on the past, but always in light of the future. The constructive fiction is that had the knowledge now acquired been known then, the national tragedy would have been avertable. New societies will be built on this claim about knowledge. It is this change in political knowledge that allows the move from past evil and suffering to national redemption.

Transitional narratives follow a distinct structured form. Revelation of knowledge of truth occurs through switching mechanisms, critical junctures of individual and societal self-knowledge. There is a ritual disowning of previously secreted knowledge, a purging of the past, as well as an appropriation of a newly revealed truth, enabling corrective return to the society's true course. A new course is charted. The practices in such periods suggest that the new histories are hardly foundational, but explicitly transitional. Certainly, historical narrative is always present in the life of the state, but, in periods of political flux, the narrative's role is to construct perceptible transformation. Transitional histories are not 'meta' narratives, but discrete, 'mini', always situated within the state's pre-existing national narrative. Transitional truth-tellings are not new beginnings, but build upon prior state political legacies. Indeed, the relevant truths are those implicated in a particular state's past political legacies. These are not universal, essential or metatruths, a marginal truth is all that is needed to draw a line on the prior regime. Critical responses negotiated between historical conflict in contested accounts. Transitional histories accordingly offer a displacement of one interpretive account or truth regime for another, as the political regimes change, preserving the state's narrative thread.

Transitional law transcends the 'merely' symbolic to be the leading rite of modern political passage. Law epitomizes the liberal rationalist response to mass suffering and catastrophe, expressing the notion that there is something to be done. Rather than resignation to historical repetition, in the liberal society, hope is put in the air. Ritual acts enable the passage between the two orders, of predecessor and successor regimes. In contemporary transitions, characterised by their peaceful character within the law, legal processes perform the critical undoings of the predicate justifications of the prior regime, through public procedures that produce constitutive collective knowledge, transformative of political identities. The paradigmatic feature of transitional legal response is that visibly it advances the reconstruction of public knowledge, comprehending operative features that enable the separation from the past, as well as integration processes. Establishing a shared collective truth regarding the past repressive legacies has become something of a trope in the literature and discourse of transitions. But, in such periods, the meaning of 'truth' is not a universal, but is fully politically contingent to the transition. The paradigmatic transitional legal processes rely on discrete changes in salient public knowledge for their operative transformative action. Legal processes construct changes in shared public justifications underlying political decision-making and behaviour that simultaneously disavow aspects of the predecessor ideology and justify the ideological changes constituting liberalising transformation. What is politically relevant to transformation is plainly constituted by the transitional context, and by the legacies of displacement and succession of predecessor truth regimes.

Legal processes are ways of changing public reasoning in the political order, for they are often predicated on authoritative representations of public knowledge. Transitional legal processes thus contribute to the interpretive changes that help create the perception of political social transformation. At the same time, transitional legal processes also vividly demonstrate the contingency in what knowledge will advance the construction of the normative shift underpinning regime change. The normative force of transitional constructions in public knowledge depends on critical challenges to the policy predicates and rationalisations of predecessor rule and ideology. What the 'truth' is in transition is discrete and yet of disproportionate significance. For example, simply identifying a victim's status as a 'civilian' rather than as a 'combatant' can topple a regime (at least on the normative level) by undermining a key ideological predicate of the repressive national security policies. These reinterpretations displace the predicates of prior regimes and offer new-found bases for the reinstatement of and adherence to the rule of law.

Law offers a canonical language of symbols and rituals of the contemporary political passage. Legal rituals and processes through trials and public hearings enable transitionally produced histories, social constructions of a democratic nature with a broad reach. Indeed, these rituals of collective history-making construct the transition, dividing political time into a 'before' and an 'after'. Transitional responses perform the critical undoings that respond to the past repression: the letting go of discrete facts justificatory of the prior regime, critical to political change. The practices of historical production associated with transition often publicly affirm only what is already impliedly known in the society, historical inquiry processes bring forward and enable a public letting go of the evil past.

Whether through trials or other practices, transitional narratives highlight the role of knowledge, agency and choice. Though the received wisdom on historical responses to past wrongs is that these are popular in liberalising states emphasising structural causation, transitional histories are complex accounts; dense layered narratives that weave together and mediate individual and collective responsibility. By introducing the potential of individual choice, the accounts perform transitional history's liberalising function. By revealing 'truths' about the past, these accounts are narratives of progress, as they suggest the cause of events might have been different – had this knowledge been previously known – adverting to the potential of individual action. The message is of avertable tragedy. The expression of the hope for prospective individual choice and human action goes to the core of liberalism.

So it is that historical accountings have become a feature of liberalising transition, connected to change in the state's political identity, that transitional narratives advance construction of the contemporary political order. In the transitional narratives, the direction of the story is neither tragically pre-ordained, nor merely a question of brute power. It comports neither to pre-existing world order nor merely to realist politics. Instead, these structured narratives emphasise the possibility of bounded choice, of the reconciliation of the potential for individual agency within a politics situated within parameters of set political circumstances. The notion that, despite past legacies of wrongdoing, there are redemptive possibilities definitional of the contemporary liberal state. Transitional historical narratives emphasising the possibility of societal self-understanding and averting tragic repetition are associated with the liberal political order. The structure of transitional histories is a progressive story of hope.

These responses point to a fragmentary but shared vision of justice that is, above all, corrective. What is paramount is the visible pursuit of return, of wholeness, of political unity. To the extent that transitional justice comprises a turn to the corrective, it offers an alternative successor identity that centres on political unity. Thus, transitional justice offers a way to reconstitute the collective – across potentially divisive racial, ethnic and religious lines – that is based on a contingent political identity grounded in the society's particular legacies of fear and injustice; a juridical discourse of rights and responsibilities offers based on evolving critical processes, a normative vision and a pragmatic course of action.

But, the transitional state's search for political unity can all too easily come to be premised on an inherently unstable formula rendered either of myth or as an unreachable normative vision. The risk is that the state's pursuit of a political identity (based on unity) may even attenuate the possibility of lasting political change. Such static entrenchments of identity are ultimately illiberal. A liberal posture, by contrast, necessitates nurturing the transitional modality as a critical space between the practicable and the redemptive in the political imagination.

Select bibliography

Havel, V, (1992) Open letters: selected writings, 1965–1990 Paul Wilson (ed) (New York: Randam House, Vintage Books, 1992).

Hilberg, R, (1961) *The Destruction of the European Jews.*

Nunca Mas: Report of the Argentine National Commission on the Disappeared (New York: Farrar, Straus, Giroux,1986).

Report of the Commission on the Truth for El Salvador (1993). *From Madness to Hope.*

Teitel, R, (2000) *Transitional Justice.*

Part IV

Public international law and context

Opening remarks: Transnational legal process illuminated*

H H KOH**

In the era of globalisation, a complex new order has supplanted the realist world order dominated by sovereign states. Although still characterised by intense state activity, the new order also embraces proactive international institutions, multinational enterprises, and non-governmental organisations; regional and global markets; a plethora of new decisional fora; transnational networks that link governmental and non-governmental entities; and an exploding information technology that has all but deterritorialised global communication, commerce and finance. Increasingly, individuals owe multiple loyalties, not just to the governments that rule their geographic area, but also to sub-national ethnic groups and broader global religious, ethnic, cultural and issue-based movements.

How has this transformation of the transnational order altered international law's agenda? Some years ago, I argued that in an era of globalisation, international legal scholars should focus their gaze on the study of *transnational legal process:* the theory and practice of how public and private actors – nation-states, international organisations, multinational enterprises, non-governmental organisations, and private individuals – interact in a variety of public and private, domestic and international fora to make, interpret, enforce and, ultimately, internalise rules of transnational law.[1] The concept embraces not just the descriptive workings of that process, but its *normativity* as well: not just how interaction among transnational actors shapes law, but also how law shapes and guides those transactions. A key to understanding whether and when nation-states will comply with international law, I argued, is *norm-internalisation*: the complex process of institutional interaction by which nations come to incorporate international law concepts into their domestic law and practice. In transnational practice, we observe a cycle of interaction-interpretation-internalisation: repeated *interactions* among states and a variety of domestic and transnational actors produce *interpretations* of applicable

* I am grateful to Rebekka Bonner of Yale Law School for her valuable research assistance. This comment shares thoughts with my articles 'The Globalization of Freedom' [2001] 26 Yale J Intl L 305 and 'An Uncommon Lawyer' [2001] 42 Harv Intl LJ 7 (2001).

** Gerard C and Bernice Latrobe Smith Professor of International Law, Yale Law School; US Assistant Secretary of State for Democracy, Human Rights and Labor (1998-2001).

1 H H Koh 'Transnational Legal Process' [1996] 75 Nebraska L R 181. I had previously sketched parts of this argument in H H Koh 'Transnational Public Law Litigation' [1991] 100 Yale LJ 2347 at 2398-2402 and H H Koh 'The "Haiti Paradigm" in United States Human Rights Policy' [1994] 103 Yale LJ 2391 at 2405-09.

global norms which can be and are eventually *internalised* into states' domestic values and processes.[2] Under this theory, various agents of internalisation – which include transnational norm entrepreneurs, governmental norm sponsors, transnational issue networks, issue linkages and interpretive communities – can provoke nations to move from grudging compliance to habitual internalised obedience with international rules.[3] A nation's isolation from transnational legal process thus helps explain its scofflaw status. Conversely, the success of these 'internalisation agents' in spurring a nation's repeated participation in that process can help over time to encourage its obedience with particular norms of international law.

The chapters in this volume – and in this Part in particular – illuminate different facets of this transnational legal process. The conceptual chapters by Falk and Hobe paint in broad strokes the ways in which globalisation has compelled what Falk calls 'reframing the legal agenda of world order'. Setting into historical context the current discussion over globalisation and international law, Falk identifies a set of global logics – including the discipline of global capital, the explosion of cyberspace and the human rights revolution – that have created demand for new global governance structures and created space for more robust global law. While de facto endorsing Louis Henkin's famous maxim that most nations in fact comply with international law most of the time,[4] Falk asks an additional, normative question: '[t]o what extent can international law serve the global public good and provide a vehicle for leadership under American auspices?' Even hegemonic states, he answers, can now lead globally only if they act in ways that affirm the value of human solidarity and are 'bolstered by creative partnerships with other actors, including international institutions, representatives of civil society and the private sectors, as well as with various regional formations'. Hobe similarly argues that the rise of genuinely global problems and the emergence of non-state actors means that international law can no longer simply co-ordinate state interests, but rather, must facilitate state and non-state co-operation in such areas as humanitarian intervention, promotion of democracy and the rule of law, and transnational accountability.

The remaining chapters not only confirm the broad outlines of transnational legal process, they also describe particular agents and mechanisms capable of promoting the internalisation of particular global norms into domestic systems. Muli's chapter, for example, illustrates the extent to which international norms of refugee protection have infiltrated national legislation regarding determination of the legal status of refugees in Kenya. Falk points out how the discipline of global capital has provoked norm-internalisation within numerous domestic orders through imposition of IMF and WTO standards upon domestic

---

2   For elaboration of this argument, see H H Koh 'Why Do Nations Obey International Law?' [1997] 106 Yale LJ 2599; H H Koh 'How is International Human Rights Law Enforced?' [1999] 74 Ind JL 1397.

3   The role of these various 'agents of internalisation' is discussed at length in H H Koh '1998 Frankel Lecture: Bringing International Law Home' [1998] 35 Hous LR 623.

4   Compare Falk, chapter 17 – 'Even with respect to its most problematic areas such as rules governing the use of force or adherence to human rights standards, the degrees of non-compliance are rarely more startling than are those involving upholding problematic areas of domestic law...'– with Louis Henkin *How Nations Behave* (Columbia University Press, 2nd edn, 1979) p 47 – 'almost all nations observe almost all principles of international law and almost all of their obligations almost all of the time'.

public orders. 'Lawmaking treaties', he argues, now 'provide the architecture of a normative order that extends *inwardly* to govern state/society relations and to regulate activities that may have detrimental impacts on the global environment'.

Moore's chapter confirms Falk's assertion by examining the operation of transnational legal process with respect to donor conditions placed upon development funding in West Africa. Moore finds in the political and economic conditionalities attached to development funding under the international Convention on Desertification 'the operational dimension of international relations that is law-like, practiced by the donors on the dependent states' in a manner analogous to domestic legislation. At the core of a new regime of donor-directed international management, however, she finds a disconnect between local realities and grand design. In particular, she wonders whether the donors' quasi-legislative conditions will achieve real compliance by the participating nations, or merely nominal compliance by fulfilling certain of the most visible criteria. For now, she suggests, the donors and recipients have simply agreed to adopt a common vocabulary that may disguise differing conceptions of the future, resulting from differing domestic actions taken in the name of what she calls 'sloganised ideas'.

Significantly, Moore's paper notes the absence of one critical agent for fostering the internalisation of norms of the Desertification Convention into domestic law: a permanent decisional forum in which issues regarding donor conditionalities can be discussed, questioned and contested by the affected countries. In considering how to fill this gap, Moore could profitably look to a panoply of decisional fora that have emerged in other areas of international law: the International Criminal Court, the WTO panel mechanism, the UN Compensation Commission, the Basle Committee of Central Bankers, and the Internet Corporation for Assigned Network Names, just to name a few. Such standing decisional fora can help enforce national obedience with international norms by creating a broader interpretive community which shares knowledge, and fosters mutual compliance with particular legal terms by determining their particular meaning. Such interpretive communities function in what Robert Cover called a 'jurisgenerative' fashion[5] – not simply reducing the kinds of ambiguities that Moore describes, but also giving rise to a transnational network of individuals and organisations that can debate particular legal concepts, share ideas and promote global development of national jurisprudence to support particular international norms.

Riles' chapter uses the 'women's rights as human rights' movement as a case study to explore other ways in which 'knowledge-building' – patterns of cross-fertilisation of ideas within a constellation of academic debates, people, conferences, communities and institutions – can help create interpretive communities and transnational networks to promote articulation of international norms. The 1995 Beijing Women's Conference not only gave the global gender equality movement a new rallying cry – 'women's rights as human rights' – but also energised two constituencies of the movement that had previously been assumed to be antagonistic to one another: human rights academics and human rights activists. Riles concludes that a symbiosis and synergy emerged between

---

5   See R M Cover 'Foreword: Nomos and Narrative' [1983] 97 Harv LR 4 at 40 (describing the 'jurisgenerative,' or law-creating, process as one in which real interpretive 'communities do create law and do give meaning to law through their narratives and precepts').

these two factions that led each to produce projects that the other eventually addressed. The academic critique of the universality of human rights gave activists a new project – networking across national and cultural divides – even while the emergence of women's rights as a human rights law issue finally gave feminist scholars a doctrinal hook for their efforts to bring critical feminist theory to international law. The episode demonstrates, Riles argues, that the ultimate enemy of human rights advancement is categorical, formalistic thinking that maintains rigid compartmentalisation of knowledge. The broad development and advancement of human rights knowledge, she posits, will be best served if many voices and viewpoints, activist and academic alike, are heard.

Riles' analysis is put to the test in Powell's chapter on the geographies of hunger. For if, as Riles argues, the building of transnational networks of activists and academics can put a human rights issue on the map, how should this strategy apply to persuade the US, the most powerful country in the world, to accept international norms of economic, social and cultural rights? Echoing Falk's critique of US exceptionalism, Powell notes that 'the U.S. is the only western democracy that has failed to accept the validity and importance of economic rights, beyond the context of business-related rights'. International human rights rhetoric, enforcement and theory, she argues, have been used largely to target violations of civil and political rights violations in the US, leaving economic rights, such as the right to food, under-analysed, under-articulated and under-enforced. Powell urges us to reconceptualise hunger as a transnational (rather than a geographically isolated or 'Third World') phenomenon, and to apply an international human rights framework to the issue, emphasising the US' role not as a welfare agent or a charitable provider, but as a nation with state responsibilities, duties and obligations. The US' philosophical adherence to a system of federal government and state-supported individualism over communist or socialist values, coupled with long-term resistance to accepting international human rights obligations within its own borders, has led the US to avoid formally ratifying basic international standards to which many other nation-states have bound themselves. As a result, she argues, the US provides limited procedural protections, rather than broad substantive constitutional or statutory protection to economic rights, and fails properly to implement economic rights at a state or local level. To promote broader US embrace of a right to food, Powell endorses a variety of internalisation strategies designed to link the international and the local: for example, federal legislation requiring all levels of the US government to collaborate on a survey of the nutritional status of the American people, convincing state and local governments to adopt resolutions supporting the International Covenant on Economic Social and Cultural Rights, and human rights monitoring to document violations of the right to food in large cities such as New York.

Finally, Mertus' chapter identifies a particular harm against which human rights internalisation strategies should be directed: the internalisation of *racism* as a form of structural violence that engenders and sustains civil conflict. Using Rwanda and Kosovo as case studies, she illustrates how in certain societies, pervasive societal racism combines with other internal factors, such as a state monopoly on speech, and absence of rule of law, independent judiciary, and guaranteed rights for minorities, to create the preconditions for widespread inter-group conflict. When catalysed by such transnational factors as colonial legacies, North-South income disparities, and the availability of modern weapons via the global arms trade, these domestic conditions can enable racism to become a convenient tool for those who would promote widespread violent conflict. Mertus thus sees widespread human rights violation as resulting from a devil's brew that mixes local dysfunctions with global stimulants. Yet by focusing on transnationalism as a cause of racial conflict, she equally suggests how transnationalism can provide a cure. As a policy matter, she concludes, transnational human rights organisations should mobilise transnational legal processes and institutions in an effort to prevent racial conflicts before they occur, by identifying and addressing the conditions that create incentives for national political elites to employ racist ideologies as a method of gaining power and waging war. If patterns of human rights violation are deeply entrenched within a particular society, repeated and persistent invocation of transnational norms and processes by transnational actors can help sympathetic domestic forces to oust those norms of violation and to replace them over time with internalised norms of respect for human rights.

Taken together, these chapters all illuminate different faces of transnational legal process. They also raise a broader question: how, in an age of globalisation, should international legal scholars and lawyers rethink the way they do their work? For international legal academics, I would argue, one lesson is that we should finally start treating *transnational law* as its own category. In time, the domestic and the international will become so integrated that we will no longer know whether to characterise certain concepts as quintessentially local or global in nature. Is the metric system, for example, fundamentally national or international? Is Greenwich Mean Time fundamentally national or international? Is the term 'dot.com' fundamentally national or international? In each case, obviously, the true answer is 'both'. For all have become, over time, genuinely *transnational* concepts in which a global standard has become fully recognised, integrated, and internalised into the domestic system of nearly every nation of the world.

In the era of globalisation, I would argue, the most intriguing legal change has been the emergence and growth of a large body of transnational law that is fundamentally *public* in its character: in such fields as human rights, democracy, and labour law, law and development, environmental law, the law of transnational crime, global cyberlaw, law and public health (for example, the global AIDS crisis) and immigration and refugee law. Around the world, public law concepts are emerging, rooted in shared national norms and emerging international norms, that have similar or identical meaning in every national system: for example, the concept of 'cruel, inhuman or degrading treatment' in human rights law; the concept of 'civil society' in democracy law; the concept of 'the internally displaced' in refugee and immigration law; or the concept of 'transborder trafficking' of drugs and persons in criminal law. For transnational public lawyers, seeking to incorporate these concepts more fully into domestic legal practice have become our equivalent of internalising the global metric system into the domestic practice of weights and measures. To promote better national compliance with international law, we must better understand – and should act aggressively to promote – the agencies and pathways by which these norms are internalised into our domestic legal systems.

In a trenchant comment elsewhere in this volume, Richard Abel argues that 'in the global arena as in the domestic, law and lawyers are largely subordinate to other sources of power, economic and political'. Under his analysis, which bears an odd kinship with that of the political realists, '[p]ublic interest lawyers have remained outside American political institutions because they are relatively powerless and cannot gain entry or wield influence over those institutions. On the rare occasions when they have flirted with Washington', he argues, '(for instance, during the Clinton Administration), they have been rejected as too ideological . . ., co-opted . . ., ignored . . ., or forced to quit in disgust . . .'

As an international human rights lawyer and academic who has only recently returned from Washington, I find Abel's diagnosis overly pessimistic. It is true that for many political actors, including in the Washington political environment, rules of international law are more nuisance than guide. There definitely is a strong and discernible impulse to subordinate law to power and lawyers to their political clients. But if there is one lesson that I have learned, it is that the transnational legal process of norm-internalisation is not self-activating. If international relations are to be more than just power politics, international lawyers must serve as moral actors, who seek self-consciously to promote this process of norm-internalisation. It is the job of international lawyers to promote international norms, to identify legal constraints and to identify ways to channel proposed state actions into normative frameworks. By so doing, public international lawyers help shape policy decisions, which in turn shape legal instruments, which in time become internalised into bureaucratic decision-making processes that promote national compliance with international norms.[6] By so doing, international lawyers who work in the public interest can influence policy, and help influence the development of transnational public law.

Significantly, Abel acknowledges that 'the ideals of generality, prospectivity, and procedural fairness inherent in law and the ideals of service, integrity and disinterest embodied in legal professions offer some potential for curbing global power, protecting vulnerable interests, and reforming corrupt practices'. But these ideals are not self-executing. For if these ideals are genuinely to influence the development of transnational law in the age of globalisation, they must have champions. And those advocates must be international lawyers and legal scholars who see their mission not simply as observing, but as working actively to influence the functioning of transnational legal processes for the good of the global public.

---

6   For a description of Abram Chayes, one public interest lawyer who did this brilliantly, see H H Koh 'An Uncommon Lawyer' [2001] 42 Harv Intl LJ 7.

Chapter 16

An international legal regime and the context of conditionality

S F MOORE

RECONFIGURING THE ORGANISATION WEST AFRICA

Law always emerges in a context. But the surround is often less well known than the formal product. When a new piece of law is supposed to solve an old problem it is important to know how this problem has been conceived by the drafters and others. This chapter explores the context of a piece of international law that emerged from the UN in 1994. The logic of the Convention to Combat Desertification, as it was called, was closely related to the logic of contemporaneous development programmes being played out in West Africa. The Convention was an international agreement about the management of environmental resources in drought-stricken areas, referring particularly to Africa.[1] But the agreement was not just about the environment. That was the functional wedge by means of which a major political change was to be implemented.

Three levels were targeted for change.[2] At the international level, the Convention proposes the establishment of multi-state, intergovernmental regional authorities. That is, it allocates to regional authorities above the level of the state the responsibility of designing and co-ordinating regional action programmes. The African country parties are to 'promote regional co-operation and integration'.[3] The Convention also commits the signatory states to developing their own related national 'action programmes' regarding resource management.[4] And they are to do so while determined to 'sustain and strengthen reforms currently in progress toward greater decentralization and resource tenure as well as reinforce participation of local populations and communities'.[5] The co-operation of rural dwellers obviously is intrinsic to implementation since they

---

1 UN (1994).
2 The 1992 UN Conference on Environment and Development (UNCED) in Rio de Janeiro resulted in the establishment of an intergovernmental committee for the negotiation of a Convention to Combat Desertification. The Comite Permanent Inter-Etats de Lutte contre la Secheresse dans le Sahel (CILSS) participated in five preparatory negotiating sessions between 1992 and 1994. (See CILSS (1994) at 7.)

    The result: UN General Assembly 'Elaboration of an International Convention to Combat Desertification in Countries Experiencing Serious Drought and/or Desertification, particularly in Africa', Draft Final Text of the Convention, A/AC.241/15/Rev.6, Paris, 17 June.
3 Annex 1, art 4, s 1b.
4 Annex 1, art 6, s 1.
5 Annex 1, art 4, s 2b.

are the people who, in fact, live on and use the relevant resources, and constitute by far the majority of the population of the countries involved. It is a package that looks to many different political levels.

The Convention manages to combine a populist rhetoric about rural populations and decentralisation of government within a larger design. The big-scale plan is of new, high-level, centralised, international organisational controls. To be implemented, such a programme would require considerable financing from international donors. They were certainly implicated in the negotiation of the terms of the Convention. Many donor countries signed the Convention.[6] Is

6   A three-level (regional and sub-regional, national and local) track of reasoning is found throughout the 1994 Convention (art 2, 'Purpose'). As conceived in some parts of the Convention, the whole of Africa is one region. The sub-regions foreseen are West, East, Northern and Southern Africa (OECD, CILSS, Club du Sahel, p 10). The Convention establishes a Permanent Secretariat, and clearly contemplates the establishment of sub-regional intergovernmental organisations (Annex 1, art 23; 'Regional Implementation Annex: for Africa', art 10).

The logic of the Convention rests on the fact that most Sahelian countries are small and share many similar problems. Acting in concert on many points they could be much more effective, technically, economically and politically. Any such joining together in an international effort raises questions both about the national level and the small scale, about the role of the African state and about the place of rural people and local communities in helping to develop national schemes of transformation. All levels are mentioned in the Convention as essential to the success of the environmental project.

The political thrust of the Convention clearly is to establish regional organisation, but to give due attention to the participation of local populations, communities, NGOs and national governments in the execution of policy. The Annex for Africa appended to the Convention tries to be all of these things at once, emphasising that 'national action programmes' should do the necessary strategic planning, (arts 4, 5 and 6 of Annex 1). They call for measures encouraging a policy of active decentralisation, and for 'adjusting, as appropriate, the institutional and regulatory framework of natural resource management to provide security of land tenure of local populations' (Annex 1, art 8, s 3c, sub-ss ii and iii.).

The Convention is a lengthy document; its draft was 57 pages long. There is much detail that is of interest, but what is important for present purposes is the political change it postulates. From a donor point of view, regions were conceived as an eventual alternative to negotiating separate agreements with each and every African country, a way of addressing common issues through an authoritative body. It was also thought that if donor funding could be chanelled through multi-state regional entities, these bodies would monitor the member states, and there might be some mutual brake on mismanagement and corruption. What is not clear, of course, is how many West African states shared the same interpretation of this document. The West African ministers with whom I spoke at a subsequent meeting principally were keen to discover whether I had any knowledge when funds for this grand scheme would be forthcoming. Of course, I did not know. And they said that even if it were ratified by most concerned African states, they thought it was not worth the paper it was written on unless vast sums of money were forthcoming from donor countries and agencies.

By 26 December 1996, 124 countries had ratified the Convention. (It had opened for signature on 14–15 October 1994. See n 10, below.) In 1997, at a conference of the parties held in Rome, the decision was made to locate the Permanent Secretariat in Bonn. The Secretariat was to be set up there during 1998.

For present purposes the Convention is most interesting as a reflection of the multiple and contradictory interests it represents, and the clear decision to alter the conditions that constitute the context in which states operate. One can only agree with Vaclav Havel that from the point of view of the Convention, the end of the state as it as previously been conceived is in sight: Havel (1996) pp 4–6.

In this connection see also Schachter (1991) pp 74–81 on 'Law Making Treaties and International Regimes'. On p 75 he says: 'From the standpoint of international law development, the numerous specialized treaty regimes are clearly the "growth sector" of international legal relations.'

the regional and national reorganisation a donor invention to which the receiving countries have signed on in the hope of a new source of funds? That is what I was told privately by some African country Ministers at one of the Club du Sahel meetings. I was a consultant for the Club.

The Club du Sahel was founded in 1976 as a forum where representatives of West African countries and donor agencies could meet to discuss common issues.[7] Funded by AID and the OECD, the idea behind the Paris-based Club was to establish a locale in which an open North-South dialogue could take place about possible projects for the Sahel, and raise funding for these. The initial impetus was to try to address problems of food production and ecological equilibrium.[8]

By 1983, the Club acknowledged that not much had changed through its efforts. In a new initiative, it began hiring experts to generate prescriptions for repairing the Sahel. It then undertook a brokering job, getting both Sahelian governments and funding agencies to agree on the general terms of these prescriptions. But, in fact, most of these plans, though agreed to, were not implemented.

The story is just as Northern-generated as it sounds. The initiative to form this organisation was not African, nor were the guiding policies necessarily African-determined, though the Club included African representatives. The Sahelian end of things already had an organisation, the Permanent Interstate Committee for Drought Control in the Sahel (CILSS), founded in 1973. In 1994 it had nine member states: Burkina Faso, Cape Verde, Chad, Gambia, Guinee Bissau, Mali Mauretania, Niger and Senegal. Its headquarters are now in Ouagadougou.

The relations between the CILSS organisation and the Club have by no means always been smooth. The CILSS began with practically no funds and in the initial years spent its time trying to raise some. Later there were repeated questions about accounting to the donors for monies and other problems of management. By contrast, the Club enjoyed secure funding from the beginning, and the confidence of international donors. The Club came to have a substantial research arm, the Secretariat. By comparison, the CILSS was a kind of poor relative, a Sahelian client of the Club. There were repeated meetings at which the question was raised whether or not to continue to sponsor the CILSS, and at what level. By 1995 the decision to reorganise and revitalise the CILSS had been made and it got moving under a new leadership, and with a new organisation. What matters for present purposes is not the wrangling between agencies, but the picture this gives of the multiple players in this scene. The African countries, the Northern funders, the brokering organisations that lie between them, like the Club and the CILSS. The funding countries and agencies make some of their agreements in concert, and act through the Club. But they also act independently through other outlets. They sponsor particular projects, intervene in the affairs of particular organisations, fund particular NGOs and thus have many separate and independent modes of intervening in African affairs, aside from their collectively agreed upon policies. The situation is unimaginably complex.

Thus in 1991 when I first visited Burkina, there were dozens of NGOs in Burkina, but there was no obtainable master list of them. They did not have any structured system of exchanging information, nor of co-ordinating their activities. This permits gentle European church groups who want to sponsor bee-keeping

7   Giri (1994) at 3.
8   Giri (1994) at 4.

and honey-selling as a development project for peasant women to do so through an NGO, but it also permits the CIA to sponsor a Burkina-organised NGO for the promotion of democracy, without, of course, declaring itself. There are many reasons why it is difficult to assess the overall impact of the many NGOs in existence.

The NGOs and the international donors consider themselves indispensable for the development of West Africa. In 1993, a staff member presented a paper to the Club du Sahel which expressed this view succinctly, and put it in the context of political regionalism:

> 'Aid agencies could be of great assistance in paving the way for regional construction in West Africa. Developed countries have the experience and resources that are lacking in the region where governments are preoccupied with short-term concerns.'[9]

This attitude of technical superiority toward African institutional capacities is not unusual, spelling out as it does the intention of Northern donors to design and finance a reorganisation of interstate relations in Africa; regionalism is not a new idea.[10]

Whatever the underlying attitude, a patronising style of address is treated as politically incorrect in many international communications. In many documents in the mid-1990s, donor countries and agencies came to be referred to as 'partners in development'.[11] This partnership vocabulary commonly used at international meetings is part of the contemporary culture of development. It implies, if not an egalitarian, at least a voluntary relationship, the consent of African countries to the imperatives of outsiders.

This chapter will discuss the development context of the 1994 Convention in parts of West Africa because that is the channel through which I had access to information; reliance is placed on sketchy and intermittent experiences as a consultant to some international development agencies. These experiences, and various documents, are the sources of information about some of the twists and turns in the rhetoric of the planning scene at the time, and for some anecdotal illustrations of what I observed happening on the ground. Undoubtedly, there is a longer and broader history to be searched out in the files of the World Bank and other agencies, but what I saw is telling enough to deserve reflection.

My role as a consultant was modest, but gave an opportunity to see and comment freely on various aspects of the development process. Numbers of meetings in Paris, Washington, Berlin and the like alternated with meetings and field trips in Africa. Development today is a field of action in a 'new regime of unequal international relations'.[12] Directive policies are specified by donors as conditions of funding. The promise of financing generally is accepted by the receiving state as if it had the option of refusing. But under present economic and political circumstances, refusal is seldom a choice to be considered. Interference by donors in the affairs of a state is then justified by the consent of the receiving state. What is in effect a command is conceived as if it were a contract. As Henkin recently wrote:

---

9 Brah, Pradelle and D'Agostino (1993) at 23.
10 See the document available on the Internet at www.odci.gov/cia/publications/factbook/ appd.html indicating which countries had signed the Convention as of 9 August 1999. The full official text of the Convention in English can be obtained on the Internet at www.unccd.ch/ccdeng.htm#parti.
11 See eg Action Collective (1995).
12 Cooper and Packard (1997) p 5.

'elements in state values – the impermeability of state-societies – are dear to all, but there is pressure on many poor to accept scrutiny, advice, even commands, from international financial institutions, from donor states, on matters close to the bone of autonomy.'[13]

This chapter will travel two narrative roads: (1) it will describe glimpses I had of some of those donor conditionalities awkwardly situated in practical West African affairs; and (2) it will describe some of the contacts I had in the course of my African visits, and some of the things I saw and heard. The end of this chapter will raise questions about some conceptual issues imbedded in this material. Are conditionalities attached to development funding in any way analogous to legislation? Should the grand regional reorganisation conceived in the Convention be thought of as an instance of donor-directed internationalism, given that 124 countries have ratified it? At what point in the installation of a new regime of international management is it useful to consider the disconnect between local realities and grand plans? But first we must take account of what I was able to observe.

LAND RIGHTS IN BURKINA FASO: MULTIPLE AND CONFLICTING CLAIMS AND POLICIES

Burkina Faso is one of the poorest countries in the world. The population of the country is somewhere between eight and nine million. Eighty per cent live in rural villages in small, dark huts with dirt floors. Needless to say, the villages usually have no running water or electricity.[14] On average, women in Burkina have six or more children. Since half are girls, in a decade or two they will themselves bear children, and the Burkina population will continue to zoom upwards. The population will at least double in 25 years, and will soon double again even if there is a sharp drop in fertility rates.[15]

I have visited a number of Burkina villages, with and without development projects, and have glimpsed the life of grinding poverty and hard work that the villagers lead. Illiteracy is widespread in the rural areas and health care is hard to come by.

The era of President Thomas Sankara, brought many changes to Bukina Faso. His presidency only lasted four years, from 1984–87. He became head of state through a coup, and his exit took place by means of a coup. He was a young, very popular leader, who talked a populist socialist line. He wore a paratrooper's uniform, a red beret and polished boots, and played an electric guitar. He was a feminist, and appointed three women ministers in his government. Even more impressive, women were prominent members of the motorcycle escort which accompanied him as he travelled around the capital.

But there was a down side to all this great style. He reorganised government by first destroying existing institutions. He abolished the court system, such as it was, alleging that it was a bourgeois institution, and established people's courts, which at the base, in the villages, were not trusted and not used, and at the top, in the capital, Ouagadougou, the higher level people's courts were used to condemn and imprison his political opponents with charges of corruption and

---

13 Henkin (1995) p 167.
14 1990 data from WALTPS Summary Report: Cour (1995) at 31.
15 Cour (1995) at 4.

worse. Sankara replaced many aspects of the pre-existing administrative structure. Thus, for example, he tried to reorganise all the villages. Every village was to be governed by a revolutionary committee, Comite de la defense de la revolution, the CDR. Committee members were to be elected. But, of course, it is unclear how the elections were to be monitored and how much the membership of the new committees really reproduced earlier village organisation with seniors, chiefs and notables running the system while bearing new revolutionary committee titles – another instance of nominal conformity. Since new, equally standardised reorganisations recently have been legislated by the government that overthrew Sankara, there is, as we shall see, real question whether the newly named village committees have really been put in place, any more than their predecessors were.

Sankara also added to the confusion of the landholding system that had previously prevailed. He publicised legislation nationalising all land, and asserted that the land should be assigned to those who had a real social need for it. Decisions regarding allocation were to be made by the revolutionary committees in each village. Sankara had hoped ultimately to revolutionise agricultural production, to make it all communal, reviving the existence of co-operative village groups (Groupement villageois). It was an ambition that was not to be realised in any general form.[16]

The fact is that in addition to their other troubles, rural villages had to deal with major internal migrations within Burkina Faso. Many lands in the central Mossi plateau are severely degraded and their occupants have migrated to other areas. Villages having fallow land or possessing forest or other stretches of land that were not under agricultural production often generously allowed the migrants to cultivate in village territory. Now there are many villages in which migrants outnumber autochthones. In allowing the migrants to cultivate, the villagers now say, quite plausibly, that they had no intention of permanently alienating the land, that it was to have been a loan. However, the Sankara legislation of 1984, the first of several statutes reorganising agricultural land, made the question of permanence very ambiguous.[17] If need was to be the test of rights to land, the autochthones had no special right to reclaim land from the migrants, even if it had once belonged to them. As population increased and land shortage was felt where it had not previously existed, serious tensions arose between populations, and there was no recourse, no one to appeal to who was trusted. Relations between the rural populations and the state were tense.

These legal land problems were the way I became involved in West African affairs. A version of the Burkina situation exists widely in Africa. Many countries have nationalised all land. Complicating the problem of the right to use land, which is all that is left when title has been appropriated by the state, is the fact that the World Bank and other international agencies are pressing all of these countries to permit the individualisation of land titles and to provide for the privatisation of landed property. In Burkina Faso in the 1991 Reorganisation Agraire et Fonciere (the RAF) the proclamation says very clearly that the state may alienate lands from the national domain and individualise them.[18] But it is not at all clear about how one might go about acquiring such property.

16 Tallet (1989) at 47.
17 Tallet (1989) at 43–44.
18 Arts 104, 105, 19.

The proclamation also states that in each village, the attribution of land rights were to be handled by a village committee in charge of land management (Commissions villageoises de gestion des terroirs). This assumes that such committees existed, but in fact they did not yet exist. This legislative statement was a prospective assumption about the way the organisation 'at the base' was to be formed. As appeared in an official summary two years later, in 1993, 'No one knows how these representative organs of the 7000 villages or localities will be constituted ...'.[19]

But problems of attribution of ownership aside, once private property in land was made a condition of international financial assistance, it was immediately seized upon by the government of Burkina Faso. Its representatives rushed to draft and sign new legislation so that funds would be forthcoming. At one point in Burkina when I asked to see a copy of the RAF, the statute reorganising land matters in just that way, I was at first told: 'But madame, we do not even have enough copies for the ministers.' Eventually I obtained a copy, and found, in the mass of print, an allusion to the privatisation of property in land as something the state could do. But the truth was that this clause in the document was given no publicity. Hardly anyone knew that the possibility of a private property regime had been declared, nor were its implications worked out in any detail in the document or anywhere else. No government person whom I met could tell me what its implications were. As far as I could tell it was a pro-forma statement. But it was sufficient for the international funding agencies to come through with the money. Needless to say, the rural villages went on about their affairs as if there had been no change.

No doubt all the informed parties involved understood the situation to be what it was. Surely the World Bank and the other international donors do not believe these mythologies of compliance, nor does the Burkina government. In a rural community where there is no buying and selling of land (and that is the norm in Burkina), and you must be a member of the community to have any land to use, a wave of the legislative wand does not, by itself, change a whole set of established land tenure practices. But conditionalities, once declared publicly as international policy, cannot be easily retracted. So the form, rather than the substance, is accepted, and donor documents extolling the virtues of the individualisation of land tenure continue to be produced.

This legislation about land in Burkina was only one of the country's responses to a set of new plans emanating from the World Bank. The thrust of the World Bank policy was what they called a 'community resource management approach'. (One wonders, parenthetically, who, other than the community, was thought to be managing village resources before this policy was instituted.) The policy had four elements: (1) increased local participation in the identification and implementation of rural development and natural resource management activities; (2) the development of incentives and skills in the local community toward this end; (3) the establishment of clear, openly negotiated agreements between administrative and technical authorities and local communities – a kind of contract approach to development; and (4) the development of multi-sectoral community natural resource management plans (dealing simultaneously with agriculture, livestock and forestry activities) that will result in demand-driven, rather than supply-driven, services.[20] Burkina Faso responded by establishing a

19 Ministere de l'agriculture et des ressources animales, Secretariat general, PGNT, and CILSS (1993).
20 World Bank (1992) at 13.

National Programme for Resource Management (Programme National de Gestion des Terroirs, PNGT). It was the debut of a new set of administrators of this programme that brought me to Burkina for the first time in 1991. I was to go as a consultant for the Club du Sahel, with a specific task to accomplish.

My initial assignment was to talk with the two or three men who were in charge of the PNGT to find out how they envisioned their charge, and then to make a tour of many villages to get some idea of what was happening on the ground. But I was also given more practical directions: in Paris, I had been told that the three men were able and well-trained, yet were bewildered by their new responsibilities and wanted guidance; they had very little idea how to start such a programme and somehow hoped the Club could supply them with advice. One of the three men directing the programme had drawn up a questionnaire to be sent to all villages, all 7,000 of them. Somehow the villages were to muster a literate person to answer appropriately. This questionnaire was to be the initial attempt of the new bureaucracy to take the measure of the domain of their responsibility. I was told in Paris that one of my tasks was to edit and revise this questionnaire. That sounded feasible, but not very exciting.

When I arrived at the PNGT headquarters, the young administrator showed me a painstakingly handwritten 39-page document in French that he had drawn up. It was designed to be sent to every village and to every level of rural administration. It asked such questions as: 'What are the names of all the members of your village committee?' and 'Do you think there should be exchanges of communication among PNGT projects? Yes or No. If yes, in what form? Every month? Every three months? Every year?'. There were pages and pages of questions dealing with the methods to be used to sensitise the various publics involved to the management issues. How should the peasants be informed? How should the authorities be informed? How should the technical services be informed? And under each question there were carefully drawn lines on which the answer was to be written. The questionnaire was interminable and touched on everything from the role of customary chiefs to the frequency with which village committees met.

In view of the widespread illiteracy in the villages, the fact that many Burkinabe do not speak French and the likelihood that if thousands of copies of this document were sent out, very few answers would be likely to be forthcoming, the project seemed daunting. My task seemed clear. How to talk over this maxi-questionnaire with its author, and how to open a face-saving way for him to change course. We talked at length. Among other things, I asked him what he expected to do with the information he collected. Would he count the answers this way and that way. Would he try to make a qualitative evaluation of the answers to some questions? I asked 'What if you found out that half the villages wanted to communicate with others and half did not. What would you do with this information?' He had no reply. He had no plan for the information. Clearly, he wanted to be able to show that his office was aware of what was going on, that it knew about the formal administrative structure of the countryside, no more, no less.

He had been told by a superior that a questionnaire was the way to survey it. I asked him whether really he thought that the questionnaire would produce what he wanted to know. By then we had talked for several days. He understood that I was not finding fault with him, but with the method which I attributed to someone else's mentalite bureaucratique. By then he was laughing and we were ready to get on with an alternative.

We agreed that the amount of diversity in the country would be concealed by a report about the supposedly standard membership of village committees and that it was the diversity of village situations, economic, social and political, that needed to be emphasised in the drawing-up of any national plans. I suggested 10 or 12 quick case-studies, a sample from different parts of the country. The purpose of these would be to show the enormous variation of sociological and ecological situations that I knew existed. A sufficiently persuasive presentation of these *esquisses de cas* would also show that what was needed in the formation of national policy was not a falsely standardised conception of 'the village' as a uniform entity, but a realistic approach to the variety of configurations that actually were out there.

It is no surprise that an anthropologist would recommend field work. I thought that small teams of observers, a person with direct experience in each village, such as an extension agent, in tandem with a scholar, Burkinabe or outsider, would work. This project could produce in sketch form the kind of information that would have an impact on the way the countryside was conceived. It was to be hoped that such materials would deflect administrators of rural programmes from simplistic standardisations of the kind that James Scott recently has illustrated.[21]

Once the young administrator was persuaded, so were the others in his bureau, and the necessary steps were taken to form the field teams, hold a preparatory workshop and make a start. In record time, eight fieldwork sketches were completed, written up and the administrators of the grand national programme to manage rural resources had evidence on which they could base their arguments for local-oriented policy-making. The force of the fiction that for administrative purposes all villages should fit a standard model was undone. Standardisation had once seemed to the administrators the mark of modernity. The Club mission dissuaded them. There was no necessity to maintain such a myth and it might interfere with the very practical tasks they had to face.

For these men, a kind of 'rural realism' became the way to think about the complexity of what they were being asked to do about resource management in the countryside. A national workshop held in Bobo-Dioulasso in 1993 by CILSS and the PNGT used the case-studies to argue that a unified approach was not appropriate where there was such a diversity of contexts as one found in Burkina.[22] The undoing of the questionnaire and its sequel had paid off.

In the course of several visits, I was taken to many villages and got a glimpse of what they were up against. Villages were very varied in ethnic composition, resources, organisation and environmental situation. A village could not be assumed to be a homogeneous social community. The migrants and the transhumant pastoralists did not fit such a model. Even the discrete division and management of geographical space was by no means uniform. In one of the villages that ultimately was contacted, the community depended for part of the year on grazing land in the territory of neighbouring villages. In others, several villages had joined together to exploit and manage common water or forest resources. Thus, even the formulaic idea that for every village community there is one discrete and exclusively utilised territory was acknowledged to be deeply misleading in many cases.

That, however, had not been acceptable to the administrative mentality in the previous decade. One of the most startling things that I was shown on some of these village visits was enormous maps, rolled up like shelf paper. These were extremely detailed aerial photographs. Some administrative mind had concocted

21 Scott (1998).
22 Ministere de l'agriculture et des ressources animales, Secretariat general, PGNT, and CILSS (1993) at 18.

the idea that you could not govern a country unless you knew exactly what the boundaries of the territorial units were at the base, and what use they were making of their land.[23] To achieve this, not only were the aerial photographs taken of the land of pilot project villages, but the villagers were asked to identify the dominant use made of each part of the land so that ecological zones could be delineated on the map. There were four categories used by the questioners: agriculture, fallow, pastoral uses and forest zones. The PNGT report makes it clear that not all local populations were co-operative in informing the bureaucrats about uses. Apart from linguistic difficulties with translating local classifications into French administrative categories, there was also the suspicion held by many populations that the purpose of this surveying of terrain was to organise information about space in order to confiscate the land and redistribute it.[24] But also there were problems with answering because there were many mixed uses of land. Cattle might be pastured in patches of fields in forest areas, or temporarily in the fields of cultivators once the crop was harvested so that the animals might drop manure. The nature of the question about land use also did not take the shifting nature of such uses into account. Neither the identification of zones of use, nor the matching of persons or groups to plots of land was particularly successful in these pilot projects. The villages chosen for the inquiries already had development projects going that were financed variously by such bodies as the Federal Republic of Germany, the World Bank and the Caisse Central de Cooperation Economique.[25] One begins to understand where our young administrator got his ideas. The African reproduction of a donor way of thinking about development occurs very quickly after any message has been put into circulation.

DECENTRALISATION CONCEIVED AS A STRATEGY OF DEMOCRATISATION

One of the best organised and largest resource management projects was funded and planned by various German government agencies and put into effect together with the Ministry of Agriculture of Burkina. It was called Patecore. Started in 1988 in the Central Plateau where desertification had created a complex of ecological problems, it began with seven villages. By the time I visited in 1992, 197 local communities were participating. The project saw itself as the co-ordinator of all the government agencies and NGOs working on resource management in the project region. In short, its mission was heavily administrative. It was at one remove from the villages themselves. Direct contacts with the rural populations were carried out by African extension workers and agents of the NGOs. What Patecore did was get these go-between persons together and provide them with an agenda and training, and it used them as an ongoing mode of communicating with the villages and gathering information about them. The training involved some instruction in teaching with visual aids, one of the principal ones being the aerial photographs of village lands mentioned above.

The first step in village work was to be erosion control, effectuated through the setting up of barriers so that soil would not be as readily carried away by the torrential rains of the rainy season as they had been. These barriers were made of stones placed by the villagers in contour lines. I saw many instances of work

23 PGNT (1989) at 69.
24 PGNT (1989) at 87.
25 PGNT (1989) at 15–16.

parties collecting stones, breaking stones, placing stones and the like. And where large barriers were to be constructed, I saw huge trucks owned by the project carrying the stones to the sites. Many tools were also provided. The second step in village work was to be the launching of the habit of collective planning of village land use, with the aerial photos as maps. Instruction in how to go about this, as well as technical assistance, was filtered down through agents, who, in turn, dealt with village representatives. And after five years of experience, Patecore still described its village land use planning methods as 'still in the "test phase", i.e. as still being experimented with, and improved upon'.[26] In planning village land use, erosion barriers were to be built, compost pits were to be dug and trees were to be planted. Clearing by burning was prohibited, and the like. In a few villages, wells with pumps were provided to help the women. In short, the aim of this huge, many-village effort was to increase agricultural production through simple techniques that could be maintained by the villagers when the project staff left. But neither the trucks, nor the tools, nor the pumps, nor the aerial photographs were simple products of village life, and the paid employment that was provided for the large number of extension workers who were the go-betweens between the local population and the project would not have been sustainable without the project.

One day our PNGT party visited one of the villages unexpectedly. We found no one in their huts. This was their weekly collective work day. They were all together, some distance away in the fields, breaking stones and readying them to be placed in diguettes, the smaller type of erosion barrier. The collective village work party consisted of children, women and old men – there were no young men. I asked where they were. 'Oh, they are all in the Cote d'Ivoire, working' was the answer given (and later confirmed by the extension worker). In short, the young men were pouring into the international migrant labour stream. I later discovered that this was a not unusual feature of rural village life in Burkina. What was astonishing was that at that time none of the development project people had thought it worth mentioning in their characterisation of villages and village dynamics. Very likely almost all of the young men would return, but the very fact of seeking off-farm work, cash and experience, and that this was conceived by their elders to be a regular phase of life, meant that the rural villages were by no means as isolated and out of touch as they were usually depicted. In the development discourse about the Sahel that I heard in Paris and Berlin and in Africa in the early 1990s, I never heard any discussion of training these young people for a more effective role in the labour market into which they were trying to place themselves. This could certainly have been a development strategy, but to acknowledge its importance would have taken some of the steam out of the agricultural improvement side of things, which was a dominant development theme at that time. In the Burkina PNGT the focus of vision was on technical agricultural improvement and ecologically oriented land management.

This exclusive concentration on an agro-oriented policy appeared politically neutral. It did not involve touching the political organisation of the countryside, nor international labour flows, nor even rural-urban economic relations. But there were other agendas in the making. By 1992, one heard some talk of 'decentralization'. The Patecore people put it this way:

---

26 Patecore (1992) at 33.

'There is also a certain political will to practice 'decentralization' in connection with land use, i.e. decisions affecting provinces, districts and villages are no longer to be taken exclusively by the national ministries, but instead at the directly affected levels in each case. So far, however, this is no more than a good intention; the idea of decentralization has yet to be consistently put into practice.'[27]

The decentralisation policy was to be a reallocation of some of the powers and funds of the central government to local collectivities.

What the Patecore project epitomizes is the pre-1990 focus on increased agricultural production as the paramount objective of rural development. The intention of decentralisation was quite different. It was aimed at political reform. Decision-making powers were to be deconcentrated, no longer to be exclusively vested in central governments. While elected village committees were, in theory, to be the bottom level of democratic practice, in 1995 rural villages were not the object of official decentralisation. At that time, in Burkina, decentralised, elected self-government was only put in place in the major towns and cities, called 'communes'.[28]

My first direct experience of decentralisation had been in Mali two years earlier, in 1993, when I was sent to look into how the matter was progressing there. What I came to realise very quickly was that there was a great unease on the part of the central government in transferring political power to rural populations. Since a government had been overthrown in 1991, there was reason for this unease. As was remarked in 1994 in a critical journal published in Bamako:

'The least that one can say is that the technical or even technocratic vision, developed by the Government through the Decentralization Mission hides badly a politics that tries to perpetuate the domination by a minority of urban officials over a community that is 80% composed of rural people.'[29]

I had met the head of the Mali decentralisation mission in the Ministry of Rural Development in 1993. He had made it plain in an interview that at the time there was no intention of changing the place of the villages in the political scheme of things. They were to develop and manage their territories, but, of course, the land still belonged to the state. Most of the population lived in the approximately 11,000 rural villages in Mali, but the government felt too insecure to recognise villages as corporate entities, as 'juridical persons'.

The Chef de Mission Decentralisation said he was occupied with decentralisation at higher levels than the village. There were to be changes in the structure of the three highest levels of rural administration, in the nine regions, the 46 cercles and the approximately 300 communes. Each region had as its head an appointed Governor, each Commune an appointed Commandant. The decentralising changes being contemplated were the installation of elected advisory councils which the Governors and Commandants *could consult*. I was told solemnly that no major decisions would be taken by these executives without consulting the councils.

Both the insecurity of the government and the attitude toward consultation were made dramatically clear to me during my visit of 1993. Among other places to which I went, I spent some days in Mopti. There I paid a courtesy call on the Governor of the region before proceeding. He was cordial, and even jovial. Right

27 Patecore (1992) at 14.
28 Action Collective (1995) at 8.
29 Coulibaly (1994).

next to his desk was what looked like a television set. He saw me glance at it and said 'Do you see what it is?' In fact, what the monitor showed was the corridor in front of the Governor's office and the soldier patrolling up and down the hall. He joked and said 'You see, if there is a demonstration in town and a crowd comes to get me I'll be able to see them before they get into this office. Then I will have time to escape through the back. There.' He pointed to a door at the rear of the office. There were many other remarks in the course of his conversation about popular demonstrations and petitions brought to him by protesting groups. He chuckled bravely! Are such matters, rather casually mentioned, to be taken seriously? Perhaps.

Through the courtesy of the Governor I later met with the Director of Development for the Region. He gave me a little talk on the democratic nature of regional government. He told me that the way things used to be there was a 'gouvernement de commandement'. Now, he said, with evident pride, there is what we call a 'gouvernement de participation', a government of participation. And he provided an immediate illustration. At the time he had just come from presiding over a meeting in another wing of the building. It was a meeting between administrative officials and representatives of the pastoralists. The purpose was to negotiate an agreement regarding the dates of transhumance. Each year official dates are set for the moving of the herds in and out of the area. The dates vary from year to year in keeping with rainfall conditions and other factors. The decision on dates is legally binding on the pastoralists, and is of no small interest to the agricultural communities in the area. They had recently killed a pastoralist whom they found encroaching with his herds. The Director of Development explained that the meeting with the pastoralists was a illustration of the new politics of participation. He said:

> 'It used to be that we administrators decided on the dates without speaking to the pastoralists. Today it is different. Now we have the politics of participation. Now we have a meeting with the pastoralists. We consult them. Then they leave. And *then* we decide.'

He then continued his peroration on democracy, talking about the many structures of participation, the councils at the level of the Cercle, the committees and village councils and the like. But after the structural review he said informatively, 'But of course, at present the councils are not yet functional'. Clearly, in Mali, in 1993, decentralisation was something of which administrators were very much aware, but not too much was being done about it.

A visit to Burkina Faso in 1995 to see how decentralisation was progressing there was not much more encouraging than the earlier visit to Mali. In February 1995, with much democratic rhetoric, the first elections in 30 years had taken place. Mayors had been elected to head the largest towns and cities. They were given no salaries, and new funding for their municipal budgets was not forthcoming.

The mayors of the communes were simply added to the established galaxy of appointed officials.[30] Burkina Faso was divided into 30 provinces, headed by High Commissioners appointed by the President of Burkina. Below them were 300 'departements' administered by Prefets appointed by the Council of Ministers. The communes were 108 in number, comprising the towns and cities,

---

30 Ministere de l'agriculture et des ressources animales, Secretariat general, PGNT, and CILSS (1993).

and of these, the 33 largest ones had mayoral elections in 1995.[31] The larger communes were subdivided into sectors, and each had its own administrative sector head. A multitude of offices and titles existed below that of mayor. There was a plethora of official titles, but since none of these persons was paid, they officiated only occasionally in their official capacities. These very clearly were part-time offices; the officials had other occupations.

The mayoral elections were part of the decentralisation and democratisation effort, a supposed reallocation of powers and responsibilities between the central state and 'local collectivities'.

A National Workshop held in Burkina in 1993 concludes in its summary that 'decentralization is a political decision, issued by the will of the government and of the donors to transfer responsibilities and decisions to the base'.[32] But as they go on to say, the levels of intervention have not yet been clarified, nor the funding of the new levels, nor is it clear what organs will represent the 7,000 villages or localities. The uncertainties were still there in 1995.

I met with three mayors, and heard about others. The finances of the communes were in terrible shape. As a source of income, the mayor of Koupela had resorted to having animals which were found wandering about the streets untethered seized, and requiring their owners to ransom them. This was a pitiful source of monies for the town. And though the mayor had some nominal taxing powers, the possibility of collecting any taxes was zero. She said that only the merchants could afford to pay taxes, but she could not impose them without their consent, which surely they would not give.

Not only were the mayors without necessary funds. They were also overshadowed by the pre-existing structure of administration, which had not been modified in any way to accommodate their election to office. Presidentially appointed High Commissioners continued to head each of the 30 provinces and Prefets appointed by the Commissioner continued to run the 'departements', with no diminution of their authority. There were plans that one day they would be replaced with elected provincial councils, but no move in that direction had taken place when I visited, nor was any date attached to that change. Needless to say, the National Commission on Decentralization, which I visited, was well aware of all of this.[33]

In an effort to strengthen this feeble gesture toward democracy, some meetings of mayors were scheduled, and there was talk of a national association of mayors. The first meeting was organised by an NGO called GERDDES (Groupe d'etude et de recherche pour la democratie and le developpement social). This political-purpose NGO is financed by the US and has branches in a number of other African countries. The American ambassador spoke at the first meeting of mayors. The sponsorship was no secret. The mayors, of course, hoped that funds would come from the US to finance their activities; they had no hope of raising them locally.

This miserable beginning is what decentralisation and the conversion to democracy amounted to in parts of West Africa in 1995. I presume that there have been some further changes in the same direction since. Two things matter for present purposes: the first is that these political moves are a feeble acting out of a much larger strategy of transformation that is not of West African origin. The second is that the Burkina government, for one, continues to imprison anyone

---

31 Action Collective (1995) at 5.
32 Ministere de l'agriculture et des ressources animales, Secretariat general, PGNT, and CILSS (1993) Resume.
33 Commission Nationale de la Decentralisation, Burkina Faso (1995).

who displeases the head of state, and opposition political figures have died mysteriously, even during 1998–99.

IDEOLOGICAL EXPRESSIONS: A REGIONAL CONFERENCE AND AN OFFICAL REPORT ABOUT THE FUTURE

But considerable efforts have been made to give decentralisation and democracy an underpinning of African legitimacy, and to indicate that eventually both would be extended to the countryside. There was, for example, a tremendous groundswell of donor-sponsored interest in the topic manifested at an international Regional Conference on Land Tenure and Decentralization in the Sahel held at Praia, Cape Verde in 1994. The meeting was organised by CILSS and the Club du Sahel. It was extraordinarily large: most of the 200 participants were African, though, of course, also there was a very visible complement of persons from donor countries. A small number of the Africans who attended were leaders of peasant organisations, but most were government officials, journalists, people who worked for NGOs, women, business people and researchers.[34] They came from many countries. Talk was lively. In addition to the plenary sessions, many sub-group discussions were held. It was a great occasion for venting concerns about rural problems; many were raised.

But it was the plenary papers that shaped the record. They focused on three issues. The first, decentralisation, interpreted as allowing for democratic decision-making autonomy and land management at the village level.[35] Left out, of course, was the fact that village organisation as it stood was anything but internally democratic, that villages were run by traditional leaders who wielded unquestioned authority. How this existing hierarchical system would spontaneously convert itself to democratic decision-making was left unanswered. The second and third concerns were with land tenure and resource conservation. The argument was that security of tenure in the hands of the peasantry was essential, whether it was individual tenure or collective tenure.[36] Yet it was also clear that there were many obstacles in the way of legally confirmed tenure, such as conflicting claims, lack of judicial institutions, legal uncertainties involving nationalisation by the state, etc. The contention firmly was made that necessary legal reforms would better fit the needs of the population if they were generated in a process that involved the participation of local populations.

The tone of the plenary papers was overwhelmingly populist and optimist. The presumption was that, left to manage its own affairs, the peasantry would make its decisions in a democratic manner, and that if it were given more information about land law in the local languages, and more of a voice in decisions regarding land legislation and other rural issues, it would have the needed impetus to face its agrarian responsibilities. There were many African administrators, members of the judiciary and other government officials present who agreed that there should be more consultation of rural populations, but who did not concur in the generalised critique that was made of existing government structures. There was general agreement in these papers that the key to the recovery of the Sahelian countries lay in the hands of the rural population.

---

34 Club de Sahel, OCDE and CILSS (1994) at 6.
35 Thomson and Coulibaly (1994).
36 Hesseling and Ba (1994).

Much emphasis was given to the 'principle of subsidiarity', the idea that every problem or decision should be worked out at the lowest level of political organisation at which effectively it could be handled. The implication is that no problem should be referred to a higher level for decision unless it cannot be resolved below. This was appealing to many who wanted to see the West African top-down style of administrative management changed.

Often reiterated was the perception that everything depended on the community at the base. This populist aspect of the Praia meeting aroused a great deal of enthusiasm, focused as it was on African views. What was most obvious to the participants was that it was predominantly an African meeting, composed of delegates of many nationalities, from many walks of life, and not simply a vocalisation of government or donor views.

Almost simultaneously, in June 1994, but unknown to most of the delegates to the Praia meeting was the finalising of the draft of the UN Convention to Combat Desertification and the effects of Drought. A person present at Praia had participated in the negotiation of its terms and I had an opportunity to discuss it with him before I wrote some related papers. The Club du Sahel actively had been involved in setting up the Convention.[37] In contrast to the Praia meeting, with its exclusive focus on the communaute de base, the Convention is oriented to the large-scale, to regional reorganisation. It envisages the drawing together of Sahelian and other states into an immense and complex, long-term international effort to reorganise into multi-state sub-regions, which together would engage in resource conservation and development. While referring very frequently and in some detail to national plans, programmes of decentralisation and local collectivites, these are repeatedly imbedded in the larger background. This primacy of the international dimension is entirely consistent with the provenance of the Convention itself, emanating as it did from the UN.

Aspects of regional integration have been under discussion for decades. A paper presented at an international meeting in Berlin in 1993 reviewed the history of this idea.[38] It also outlined some of the obstacles in the way and indicated that there was disagreement in the donor community about its viability, and some unease about the heavy cost of setting it up. As the introduction to the report said, 'Regional integration is of great importance for West Africa, but it will not arise of its own accord'.[39] It goes on to underline the fact that 'Africa seems to be a continent talking about integration while the process of developing a basic national community of interests in each country has not yet been accomplished'.[40] The report includes a thoughtful paper on the differing attitudes of various donors. What is clear from the report was that all major donors were already involved in regional activities in one form or another, but were not in agreement about the overarching form of regional co-operation and integration that the Convention contemplates. Some of those doubts must have been overcome, since the Convention was filed with the UN a year later.

Meanwhile, at the ranch many related things were happening. A major, very well financed, report on the future of West Africa was published in 1995.[41] It had

37 See Club du Sahel (1995) at 5.
38 Brah, Pradelle and D'Agostino (1993).
39 Brah, Pradelle and D'Agostino (1993) at 18.
40 Brah, Pradelle and D'Agostino (1993) at 20.
41 Cour (1995).

been in preparation over a four-year period.[42] The work was executed by the Secretariat of the Club du Sahel and the Cinergie Project of the OECD and the African Development Bank. The study was a very slick and sophisticated presentation, widely disseminated and discussed at many meetings in Africa, Washington and Europe. This report was known to its sponsors and critics by the acronym WALTPS.[43]

The WALTPS Report largely was a demographic and economic projection from data dealing with changes from 1960 to 1990.[44] But it also gave advice about what should be the investment priorities for donor countries and local states. It is very much a market-oriented study. Its core argument is that the cities provide a market for agricultural products, and the future growth of cities will be the motor of development for the region. It asserts further that population growth will be considerable, that population will tend to migrate to the cities, and principally to the cities of the coast. Many more cities will be established and those in existence will grow.

Its prescription for the countryside is that more persons in rural areas should convert their present modes of production to intensive agriculture. They should become entrepreneurs. The increased production that would result would go to the urban market, to regional markets as well as to more distant export. The authors suggest that regional co-operation should be encouraged, that civil society should be developed, that entrepreneurial activity and financial networks should grow stronger, and so on. They are down on subsistence agriculture and up on agro business. They do not shrink from the fact that the kind of economic activity they recommend, and indeed foresee, would create greater social inequalities and social tensions in the rural areas in which most of the population of West Africa lives.[45]

42 'There are now over 200 African organizations for regional cooperation and integration. West Africa has 45' Cinergie, Club du Sahel, CILSS 'Regional cooperation and integration in West Africa' April 1993: 55. This publication reviews many of these West African efforts and quotes Edem Kodjo, ex-Secretary of the OAU, saying, in 1991: 'Organizations abound, but they remain inert, inactive, ineffective, like corpses in a moonlit graveyard.'

43 In 1991 Canada, France, the US and the Netherlands had suggested that a long-term study of West Africa be undertaken. The idea was to predict what would happen to West Africa in the following 30 years. The study was a substantial investment, $1.5m, financed by The European Commission, the World Bank and the African Development Bank: Dionne (1995) p 1.

44 The report is long and full of charts and maps and is a very sophisticated presentation. It had very little African input, and this has been one of the several objections levelled against it. It also paid limited attention to the political implications of its predictions and recommendations. However, some political attitudes can be deciphered from the text, as when WALTPS talks about the need for interconnected levels of 'development management': Cour (1995) at 46. Its statements about decentralisation are odd because WALTPS uses the occasion to talk about the way the nation-state is politically situated. The state directs land management and decentralisation strategies nationally, yet within the multi-state geographical area of which it is a part, it is itself a decentralised piece of a larger entity, the sub-region. WALTPS maps of settlement patterns, population movements, locations of towns and cities and the like are all sub-regional. When it talks about decentralisation and the local to regional nexus, it makes haste to say: 'Settlement patterns occur at the regional level, markets are sub-regional, river basins and transport corridors cross national borders and the CFA countries have a single currency'. This emphasis on the larger multi-state sub-region is the defining unit of analysis in the WALTPS report (see Schachter (1997) on 'The decline of the nation state' pp 13–28).

45 Cour (1995) at 15, 42.

Their comments on decentralisation are instructive because they indicate that a great deal of state-directed management must not only continue, but also grow to co-ordinate what they call 'development management'.[46] WALTPS notes that efforts to decentralise should promote the development of a local class of entrepreneurs who will be 'eager to become involved in the management of their immediate environment'.[47] They acknowledge that this vision 'is not at all egalitarian'.[48] As for the non-entrepreneurial majority of the rural population:

> 'there will be many farmers ... who will find it hard to make a place for themselves in the changing patterns of agriculture ... this will be the price of progress. It will mean permanent and sometimes acute social tensions. But surely the most important point is that there be progress.'[49]

The WALTPS view of the dynamics of the urban-rural relationship provoked a good deal of disagreement.[50] I cannot review the criticisms here, other than to remark on the reply of the Director of the project to some of them. He argues that the American Africanists around AID and the World Bank are 'ruralistes purs et durs', and that the Americans have a rural bias which interferes with their economic judgment.[51] He reiterates that urban-centred development is the economic lesson of history, that development cannot emerge from this rousseauiste focus on the rural population, on small-holders, on poverty, and on peasant strategies.[52] Like the Convention to Combat Desertification, the organising unit of analysis of the WALTPS Report is the region. But its message is different. WALTPS predicts that the operations of the urban-based market itself will develop and transform the region through associated entrepreneurial activities. The Convention makes a different case. The implication of the Convention is that only with international regulation to co-ordinate the management of regional resources will these be conserved and augmented, and that this regulatory process will only be possible with the active co-operation of the states, and in the presence of decentralised local collectivities.

CONCLUSION

To say the least, this material illustrates the force of a generally convergent rhetoric of development by a particular set of international actors. In this circle donors and receivers have, in general, accepted a similar vocabulary to allude to present problems and the immediate solutions prescribed. The idea of linking grand-scale regional management with democratic participation by small-scale rural settlements seems to have been in prospect for quite a while. It certainly did not begin with the Convention to Combat Desertification. A World Bank paper on population, agriculture and environment, submitted for discussion in 1990 seems to suggest as much. In that connection, it says in its conclusion:

---

46 Cour (1995) at 46.
47 Cour (1995) at 46–47.
48 Cour (1995) at xii.
49 Loc cit.
50 Dionne (1995) for one.
51 Cour (1995) at 1–2.
52 Cour (1995) at 2.

'In each of the above areas, African governments alone cannot manage the monumental tasks identified if the African people, acting individually and in groups, are not brought into the process ... For this a monitoring and research apparatus needs to be created at both the international and the national levels.'[53]

I do not know when or where the associated particulars of decentralisation were formulated, but clearly each West African country did not originate the same formula independently.

At the moment, in the prevalent post-Cold War talk in West Africa, the conditionalities in international discourse involve both economic and political measures. The implied promise, sometimes baldly stated, is that if the receiving states follow the policies laid out for them, they will be able to free themselves of poverty, ignorance, bad health and undemocratic government. They will prosper and have an active civil society. They will enjoy peace, freedom and commerce together.

The paradox is obvious. On the one hand, the receiving country is to become a liberal democracy in order to become free enough to make the choices that will reposition it politically and economically. On the other hand, the liberating trajectory on which it is required to embark to achieve that freedom will be dictated to it by the donors. The donors will lay down the conditions on which funding will depend. These conditionalities are the frameworks for external intervention. There is no permanently established forum where they can be discussed, questioned and contested by the countries to be affected.

What clearly is visible in these conditionalities is that we are in the presence of an operational dimension of international relations that is law-like, practiced by the donors on the dependent states. It is well known that 'Political independence did not bring to new states economic independence'.[54] There are conditions imposed and dependent states must accept the conditions. Does acceptance make it a contract-like arrangement? Or does the fact that the receiving states cannot refuse, the fact that there is a profound asymmetry of power involved – does this circumstance turn the laying down of conditions into a quasi-legislative act? The ordinary legal categories which classify such acts may not be adequate to capture the complexity of the situation.

Besides, one should add that in this domain an acceptance of terms is one thing, compliance is another. Must the receivers really comply to the conditions? And who is to decide whether they have done so? Often the dependent state can achieve nominal compliance by fulfilling certain highly visible but limited criteria signifying conformity. Both the donors and the receivers may know that real and full compliance is a practical impossibility, at least in any short compass of time. But neither party can afford to say that. And even if implementation over the long term is impossible, the donors do not want to hear that bad news at the inception of each new policy initiative. This kind of interaction is one dimension of the international dance between funders and states.

A Club du Sahel publication asserts that there is seldom any sanction attached by the donors to non-compliance with the conditionalities of funding.[55] To my way of thinking, this absence of penalties for non-compliance effectively undoes the contract-like or legislation-like metaphor applied to conditionalities. After

53 World Bank (1990) at 63.
54 Henkin (1995) p 136.
55 Cour and Naudet (1994) p 24.

all, ordinarily both carry sanctions for non-performance. Cour and Naudet also add that there is a big gap between the need for aid and the capacity to use it efficaciously. They argue that this paradox leads to interventionism. Further intervention, then, is the long-term penalty for non-performance.

The logic of the design of conditionalities is supplied by the professional staff of donor organisations and their organisational clients, such as the Club du Sahel, and by consultants. What is ongoing is the virtually industrial mode of production of massive numbers of position papers, conferences, diplomatic overtures, assessments and the like. These are produced in great numbers, both on the African side and on the donor side. Reading this material is a very tedious business, since the same ideas are repeated again and again in the same vocabulary for whatever period they enjoy dominance. The particular actions undertaken in the name of these sloganised ideas, however, are very variable, as we have seen.

This doctrinal reiteration of basic assumptions constitutes a particular, agreed upon, administrative representation of reality, a temporary truth. It subsumes not only the descriptive iterations of social science, demographic tables, maps of desertification, figures on agricultural production and the like. It also includes theories of cause and effect congruent with the designed programmes of change. And most important of all, the programmes encompass conceptions of the future.

This means that international asymmetrical relationships are not only attached to programmes of action. They are imbedded in a pre-defined conception of authoritative knowledge which has a particular content. We might call the mix of action and conceived certainties that surround such agreements as the Convention on Desertification, and that surround the major aid given to West African countries today, 'the cultural nexus of conditionalities'.

But these policies and pronouncements are not the only story going. The official, directed internationalism of development described in the main body of this chapter, however powerful, is not the only field force in the arena. Parallel to the agreed set of conditions imposed in concert by the major donors, there are myriad other conditions imposed by other entities. Some of these are attached to the generosities of individual country donors, of NGOs and other benefactors. Also there are conditions attached to the patronage of politically powerful Africans, and conditions imposed by African traffickers in illegal contraband. In short, there is a parallel world of other pressures beyond the formal conditionalities of unified international development aid. The resulting scene is one of unfathomable complexity, and in many places one of considerable political instability. Authoritative knowledge of this plural totality, and of who controls what, is easier to claim than to have.

Select bibliography

Action Collective, (1995) 'Bulletin bimestrial de liaison de la Commision nationale de la Decentralisation', 01 BP 7027, Ouagadougou 00 January–February, 01 May-June.

Brah, M, Pradelle, J M, and D'Agostino, D, (1993) 'Regional cooperation and integration in West Africa' and 'Donor's Strategic Design and Planning', Cinergie (CILSS, Club du Sahel), two articles presented together at a meeting of the Club du Sahel, Berlin, 19–23 April.

Club du Sahel, (1995) 'The ICD Support Network, A New Club du Sahel Project', Newsletter 14.

Club du Sahel, OCDE, and CILSS, (1994) Conference Proceedings, SAH/ D(94)436, Regional Conference on Land Tenure and Decentralization in the Sahel, Praia, Cape Verde, 20–24 June.

Commission Nationale de la Decentralisation, Burkina Faso, (1995) 'Etat d'avancement de la reflexion sur la decentralisation conduite par la commission nationale de decentralisation', Note de Synthese.

Cooper, F, and Packard, R, (1997) *International Development and the Social Sciences: Essays on the History and Politics of Knowledge.*

Coulibaly, C, (1994) 'Editorial', Cauris (Bamako, Mali), Dossier No 1, December.

Cour, J M, (1995) 'West Africa Long Term Perspective Study, Summary Report', SAH/D(94)439, CILSS, Club du Sahel, CILSS, Cinergie.

Cour, J-M, and Naudet, D, (1994) 'Le financement exterieur du developpement en Afrique de l'ouest: analyse des transferts et reflexion sur l'aide au developpement 1960–1990', Resume of a study by Cour and Naudet, SAH/ D(94)434-juillet 1994, presented at the Annual Meeting of the Club du Sahel, Le Rouret, France, 17–20 October.

Dionne, J, (1995) 'Comments on the WALTPS Results and Implications', FSH Cooperative Agreement, MSU/INSAH-PRISAS, *Food Security Briefing Paper*, No 95-02, January.

Giri, J, (1994) 'What Future for the Club du Sahel', Paper presented at the annual meeting of the Club du Sahel, Le Rouret, France, SAH/D(94)437, Session 10, 17–20 October.

Havel, V, (1999) New York Review of Books, Vol XLVI, No 10, 10 June, p 4.

Henkin, L, (1995) *International Law: Politics and Values.*

Hesseling, G, and Ba, B M, (with the collaboration of P Mathieu, M S Freudenberger and S Soumare), (1994) 'Land Tenure and Natural Resource Management in the Sahel', SAH/D(94)425, CILSS-Club du Sahel, January.

Ministere de l'agriculture et des ressources animales, Secretariat general, PGNT, and CILSS, (1993) 'Atelier national sur la problematique fonciere et la decentralisation, Document de Synthese. Bobo-Dioulasso', Document 1, Synthese.

OECD, CILSS, and Club Du Sahel, (1994) 'A Partnership Mechanism and Enabling Fund for Priority Action in Africa', Proposal submitted to the Club du Sahel Meeting, Paris, 18–19 May, reproduced for the Annual Meeting of the Club du Sahel, Le Rouret, France, 17–20 October.

OECD, and Club du Sahel, (1994) 'Discussion Paper', Annual Meeting of the Club du Sahel, Le Rouret, France, 17–20 October.

Patecore, (1992) *The spark has jumped the gap Case study of a project to improve village land use (PATECORE) in Burkina Faso.*

PGNT, (1989) 'Rapport de synthese et d'analyse des experiences pilotes de gestion des terroir villageois. Programme national de gestion des terroirs villageois', Burkina Faso, May.

Schachter, O, (1991) *International Law in Theory and Practice.*

—(1997) 'The Decline of the Nation-State and its Implications for International Law' in J L Charney, D K Anton and M E O'Connell (eds), *Politics, Values and Functions Essays in Honor of Professor Louis Henkin.*

Scott, J C, (1998) *Seeing Like a State.*

Tallet, B, (1989) 'Le CNR face au mode rural: le discourse a l'epreuve des faits', Politique Africaine.

Thomson, J, and Coulibaly, C, (1994) *Decentralization in the Sahel*, SAH/D (94) 427, CILSS-Club du Sahel.

UNGA, (1994) 'Elaboration of an International Convention to Combat Desertification in Countries Experiencing Serious Drought and/or Desertification, particularly in Africa', Draft Final Text of the Convention, A/AC.241/15/Rev.6, Paris, 17 June.

World Bank, Africa Region, (1990) 'The Population, Agriculture and Environment Nexus in Sub-Saharan Africa', Draft for Discussion, 29 May.

World Bank, (1992) 'Staff Appraisal Report', Report No 10370-MLI, Mali, Natural Resource Management Project, Africa Region, Sahelian Department, Agriculture Department, 1 May.

Reorganisation Agraire et Fonciere au Burkina Faso (1991) ZATU No. AN VIII-0039/FP/PRES, signed by the President 4 June.

Chapter 17

Re-framing the legal agenda of world order in the course of a turbulent century

R FALK

PERSISTING DOUBTS ABOUT INTERNATIONAL LAW

At the end of a century of unprecedented global law-making, two types of debilitating threshold challenges persist. The first involves the jurisprudential insult that arises when influential persons continue to raise the question as to whether international law is really law at all, or in its more moderate form, is a species of primitive law that deserves only qualified respect. The second challenge is the more consequential policy issue about whether leading states should invariably conform their foreign policy to the requirements of international law. This policy question is of particular concern to the US, a powerful country, which currently projects its power globally while enacting a leadership role in world politics. In effect, what is being asked is whether and to what extent a government should constrain its freedom of action by adhering to the constraints of international law.[1] At issue is adherence to international law in settings where its apparent requirements allegedly run counter to the perceived priorities of national interest, or as it sometimes expressed, the tenets of grand strategy.[2]

It is likely that the geopolitical pressures that are responsible for this second challenge also embody some confusion about the nature of law. Without a misleading insistence that a domestic legal order is effective in imposing restraints on the use of unauthorised force, fundamental doubts about the *existence* of international law would not have been taken seriously, and an emphasis would have been placed where it belongs with respect to evaluating international law, namely, on degrees and issue-areas of *effectiveness*. It is Hobbes' insistence that the

---

1   This question posed explicitly by Thomas Franck in his interpretation of the US response to the World Court judgment in the Nicaragua case. See Franck (1986) pp 53–76.
2   As argued below, this assessment seems premised on a realist bias in favour of the efficacy of force in international relations that does not seem accurate in light of recent war/peace experience. There is no careful research on the policy consequences of the question: 'what if international law had been allowed to govern foreign policy?' Would the net policy effects of such a posture be negative or positive? It would continue to be implicit in that legal constraints would be ignored under exceptional circumstances, a doctrine of civil disobedience for states and other political actors.

    There is a separate critique of a legalistic foreign policy that is based on ethical lines of analysis, and became relevant in relation to the NATO campaign against Kosovo that was undertaken in contravention of UN Charter provisions.

absence of a governing authority outside the sovereign state created an anarchy resembling 'the state of nature', which underlies the still-prevalent scepticism about the very possibility of international law. Hobbes influentially postulated a world order consisting of a war of all against all. Ever since, a conceptual scepticism has dominated the political imagination of international statecraft. Such a belief has consistently overwhelmed contrary efforts to insist on the importance and desirability of constructing by stages an effective and humane international legal order.[3] These sceptical attitudes are never far below the surface of political consciousness, especially in the thoughts and actions of powerful countries.[4]

One element that makes dubious such a dismissal of international law is its implicit, and empirically questionable, idealisation of domestic legal order. In fact, very few, if any, domestic public order systems, despite the apparatus of full-fledged government, could survive such a scrutiny. Civil war is far more common over the course of modern history than international war, especially recently, establishing the minimal proposition that the presence of a well-functioning government does not mean that a sovereign state will have the capacity to establish and sustain an assured peace system over time. And yet domestic law is spared the indignity of being asked about whether law exists, at least unless the sort of chaos prevails that leads outsiders to label the reality as an instance of 'a failed state'.[5] Instead, the appropriate inquiry is directed at determining degrees of effectiveness as reflected in crime rates.

If the issue of the existence of an order of legality depends on a general record of compliance, then international law seems rather solid as a legal order. Even with respect to its most problematic areas, such as rules governing the use of force or adherence to human rights standards, the degrees of non-compliance are rarely more startling than are those involving upholding problematic areas of domestic law such as prohibitions on official corruption and criminality of various

---

3   The addition of 'humane' to 'effective' is a relatively recent development, reflecting the emergence of international human rights, humanitarian intervention and self-determination as areas of overlapping legal, political and moral concern over the last half-century, and particularly during the 1990s. For an attempt to delimit this normative foundation of a potential world order, see Falk (1995).

4   See Bolton (1999). In this essay, Bolton, a former US Assistant Secretary of State in the Bush Administration, makes such statements as the following: 'In reality, international law, especially customary international law, meets none of the tests that we normally impose on "law".' And further in the same sequence of argument: '[t]o have real law in a free society, there must be a framework (a constitution) that defines the government's authority, thereby limiting it and preventing the exercise of arbitrary power.': both quotations at 158. Bolton reaches the conclusion that international law meets none of the essential requirements of a genuine legal order, and that the flawed effort to impose criminal accountability on individuals combines arbitrary implementation with utopian expectations in a most unfortunate manner. Of course, such an assessment is self-serving as posited by the world's geopolitical leader, which has frequently engaged in behaviour that is perceived as engaging criminal accountability for its leaders.

5   There is also the opposite question of 'peace at what human cost?' Such a concern exists in relation to highly effective oppressive state structures, as was the case with the former Soviet Union. Such oppressiveness undermines the legitimacy of law from the side of its excessive and unjust effectiveness, as was the case with apartheid in South Africa. Put differently, unless morality and considerations of humane governance are taken into account, the legitimacy of a given legal order cannot adequately be appraised merely by reference to the absence of deviant behaviour.

types or, less consequentially, prohibitions on such social activities as gambling without a license or smoking marijuana. The point here is that the discourse about lawlessness in domestic society takes for granted the background reality of lawfulness, while in international society such a reality is itself routinely called into question. As such, the invidiousness of the comparison implicitly adopts the Hobbesian criterion that law implies government, and the absence of government necessarily entails lawlessness. It is more helpful, in the writer's view, to adopt a flexible view as to the character of law, evaluating its success or failure by measuring the extent of its effectiveness and evaluating humaneness over time and in relation to particular areas of value realisation and substantive concern, such as the reduction of poverty and joblessness.

The writer contends that the persistence of this jurisprudential doubt so damaging to the reputation of international law is a consequence of two main factors. The first is the self-serving acceptance by policymakers of some variant of 'realism' as the proper mode of thought pertaining to international relations. This realist orientation assumes a special importance in the US due to a combination of its allegedly moralistic temptations with its geopolitical stature and role. The US inclination toward moralism is often traced back to Jefferson's suggestion that nations should treat each other with a morality similar to that pertaining to relations among persons, or to early American claims to being an exceptional country, 'a city upon the hill', or even 'a new Jerusalem'.

The modern continuation of such an outlook is, of course, associated with the crusading spirit of Woodrow Wilson, especially his championship of the League of Nations and the idea that the security of states should be increasingly law-based, collective and institutionalised, rather than left to the vagaries of the balance of power, which he and others early in the century condemned as amoral and held responsible for the tragedies of recurrent warfare. With the failure of Wilsonian diplomacy to stem the tide of events that generated the Second World War, the realist perspective gained decisive influence, which was solidified into dogma during the latter stages of the Cold War.[6] Realism flourished in academic circles as well, claiming its share of credit for sustaining the peace during the tense cold war decades despite the periodic intensity of the Soviet/American rivalry.[7] It also served well the academic effort to bring 'science' to the study of international relations, allowing for the emergence of 'rational choice' and other more formal methods of inquiry to flourish.[8] In effect, the discipline was to an extent methodologically driven, with the policy effects seen as derivative.

Realism, in its many varieties, has little or no room for international law in either analysis or prescription. Its policy assessments and prescriptions are primarily based on considerations of power relationships and national interests, devoting its attention mainly to the interpretation of the changing character of 'power', and its effective

6   Of course, this 'failure' so widely attributed to Wilson's approach is misleading in two respects: it was never put into practice; Wilson's own conception was too limited given its goals; see the confusing discussion in Kissinger (1994) pp 218–265; and see pp 804–835 contending that American foreign policy had re-embraced Wilsonianism in the 1990s in the aftermath of the Cold War. For more constructive, less polemical, presentations of Wilson's ideas about world order and their legacies see Knock (1992); Esposito (1996).
7   For two influential realist statements along these lines see Gaddis (1986); (1990).
8   The leading effort here is undoubtedly that of Kenneth Waltz. See particularly Waltz (1993).

use.[9] It focuses on 'national security', with attention given to military and economic capabilities, and alliance relations.[10] International law is treated mainly as a tool of foreign policy, to justify initiatives in international arenas that are diplomatically controversial, to mobilise support for such policies at home, and especially as a legal club with which to strike adversaries.[11] As such, international law is seen by perceptive observers as shaped by a cynical kind of double standards in which one's own side is always legally right and an adversary is always denigrated by being engaged in unacceptable lawlessness.[12] It is not surprising that the more discerning members of the public find such essentially polemical roles for international law as depriving it of the stature of real law. And the less discerning are brainwashed by the media and officialdom, or by militant critics, into believing that in behavioural terms the division of the world into tyrants and outlaws is essentially accurate.

The second reason for the dismissive attitude toward international law has to do with the geopolitical horizons of leading states, again currently conceiving the US as the dominant political actor. To protect widespread interests of the state and exercise the authority of the state is deemed more important than to uphold treaty obligations or other constraining obligations, although some writers on international relations have started to emphasise the instrumental importance of normative reputation to the successful exercise of the hegemonic role.[13] Also confusing is the tendency of the US government to rationalise its *legally* dubious undertakings in a diplomatic language of justification that emphasises selflessness, and *morally* redeeming actions. In the settings of the Gulf War and the NATO campaign over Kosovo this pattern of bypassing law, yet insisting on the moral high ground, was evident.[14] Such a claim to override international law based on a compelling moral imperative can be a plausible and convincing justification for action, suggesting that legality and legitimacy may be in opposition under certain conditions. A good example was the Vietnamese invasion of Cambodia in 1978, which, regardless of its motivation, had the primary effect of ending a genocidal reign of terror by Khmer Rouge.[15]

---

9 Joseph Nye has made an influential argument about reconceptualising power to include what he calls 'soft power', namely the role of information and diplomacy and leadership as instruments of foreign policy. See eg Nye (2000). But for a more geopolitically oriented approach to soft power as the foundation of US predominance in the twenty-first century, see Nye and Owens (1996); Owens was an admiral who had served as the Vice Chairman of Joint Chiefs of Staff in the early years of the Clinton presidency. The basic orientation was set forth in a book outlining a geopolitical strategy designed to perpetuate US global leadership: Nye (1990). See Nye and Owens (1996). But the use of information technology to dominate war-making suggests the interpenetration of soft and hard power.
10 For range of realist views, see Brown, Cote, Lynn-Jones, et al (1998); Keohane (1986).
11 Such realist manipulations of international law draws on the widely shared sense that adherence to law, even international law, is 'moral' and its flagrant violation 'immoral'. Law becomes conflated with and subordinate to morality. Such practices tend to confirm the importance of morality to human identity. They also establish the relevance of law to morality, but do not illuminate the nature and role of law as such.
12 See the strong critique along these lines mounted by Chomsky (1999) especially pp 1–80; Chomsky tends to deploy international law in a manner that is opposite to that of realists, namely as an instrument of critical reaction to official policies emanating from his own government. For more comprehensive reliance on legalist approaches and a principled argument in favor of such reliance, see Boyle (1981); and, more recently Boyle (1999).
13 For an excellent example of such an approach see Knutsen (1999) pp 13, 49–58, 193–203.
14 For a summary expression of the official US position on Kosovo, see Steinberg (1999); a response to a mainstream critique of the Kosovo policies by Mandelbaum (1999).
15 For a scholarly study of the Vietnamese policy that emphasises cultural, strategic and geopolitical considerations, see Morris (1999) especially 229–241.

FROM 1899 TO 1999: POINTS OF COMPARISON

Against such a background, it is possible to trace the achievements and disappointments of international law over the course of the last century. This ebb and flow has been played out mainly in relation to matters of global security, especially the effort of international law to establish a framework governing recourse to, and the conduct of, war. In other sectors of international life, the evolution of international law has marched steadily forward, generally keeping pace with the growing complexity and interdependence of transnational behaviour of all types. This march has been jurisprudentially unproblematic and geopolitically trivial, at least until the advent of the challenge of information technology. These technological innovations, as connected with the growing salience of global economic policy, have raised new doubts about the adequacy of international law. Unlike with regard to the use of force, here questions arise as to the desirability of regulating the operation of market forces and the possibility of protecting intellectual property rights in the age of the Internet.[16]

Despite these new assaults upon the relevance of international law, the traditional concerns about the relations of law and war remain paramount for both practical and theoretical reasons. We turn now to gain some insight into the endeavours of international law in the war/peace area. These endeavours were often less than they seemed, and so the limited results achieved should not be the occasion of surprise.

The Hague Peace Conferences of 1899 and 1907 briefly focused world attention at the start of the twentieth century on the challenge of war prevention. In fact, the agreements that emerged from those gatherings, despite the lofty rhetoric of world peace, related exclusively to the establishment of a legal framework of very generalised and quite vague restraint upon the conduct of war. Such an approach rested on the normative assumption that war was not an unconditional form of conflict in which the only criterion of judgment was its outcome. The overarching goal of the Hague Conventions was to impose some outer legal limits on the tactics of belligerent powers, with the ethical objective of mitigating the suffering associated with war.[17] In practice, such restraints create a minimal challenge to the unrestricted legal discretion associated with battlefield arguments based on 'military necessity'. Perhaps, such restraints do have some marginal impact on the avoidance of large-scale civilian casualties, and on the maintenance of humanitarian values when dealing with matters of no direct belligerent significance, such as the treatment of prisoners of war, wounded enemy personnel and the protection of hospitals, churches and cultural sites.[18] To the extent that the tactics of war seek the demoralisation of the enemy or the stakes of political violence pertain to ethnic identity or religious belief, then the destruction of civilian targets can be regarded as a core objective of the war itself.

16 Both neoliberal orientations toward global economic policy and the libertarian outlook of the Internet elite create a different kind of scepticism about the role of law. With force, the main foundation question is whether regulation can be made effective. With economic activity, the questioning is even more fundamental – whether regulation is needed or desirable.

17 This direction of legal effort has persisted, culminating in the more explicitly humanitarian undertakings of the 1949 Geneva Conventions, as extended by the two 1977 Geneva Protocols. For convenient texts, see Weston, Falk and Charlesworth (1997) pp 154–192, 234–260.

18 See Best (1997).

The enormous carnage of the First World War, combined with its rather inconsequential positive contribution to world order, generated a strong groundswell of support for far more ambitious steps designed to delegitimise war as a discretionary option of sovereign states. War had served as a social institution at the base of international society since the emergence of the modern state system, generally associated with the period of European history following the Peace of Westphalia in 1648. The complex role of war in international life was variously defined, but has been closely associated with providing the only means to register change in the relative power of major states, and to allow international conflicts to be resolved by battlefield results.[19] From this perspective, peace treaties are rightly interpreted as the most important instruments available for restructuring of international relations through the agency of diplomacy, and especially by taking into account shifts in power.[20]

The challenge posed for world order was centred on finding ways to overcome the dependence of states on forcible self-help to uphold their security. International law was invoked to carry forward various approaches to the attainment of a more peaceful world. Each of these approaches exerted some influence in the period after 1918: first, the effort to establish an institutional mechanism for collective security under the auspices of the League of Nations; second, a series of measures embodied in the Versailles Treaty 1919 intended to prevent German remilitarisation and threats to European stability; third, procedures designed to encourage states to settle their disputes by peaceful means before they turned violent; fourth, a variety of disarmament initiatives designed to demilitarise the relations between major states and disrupt the logic of threat and expansionist ambition that induced arms races; and fifth, the establishment of new agreed norms that reflected a consensus that the only permissible use of force by a state was on behalf of a genuine claim of self-defence.[21]

This purported distaste for war after 1918 also induced two kinds of important diplomatic endeavours: the appeasement of fascist expansionism by the European democracies and the reassertion of an isolationist approach to world politics by the US. Such initiatives, designed to prevent the recurrence of major war, were widely interpreted as failures, generating a momentum that was widely viewed as partially responsible for the outbreak and magnitude of the Second World War. It became evident in the 1930s that powerful governments of revisionist states with extremist leadership were prepared to use force, regardless of cost, to satisfy their immense ambitions for greater influence on the global stage. Such expansionist states, particularly Germany and Japan, felt unfairly victimised by

19 For a recent argument along these lines see Luttwak (1999).
20 See Gilpin (1981) and Knutsen (1999); perhaps, even more fundamental changes in international structure arise from non-diplomatic means, shifts brought about by technological innovations, especially those bearing on productive capacities and military capabilities. With the declining relevance of territorial expansion and the unacceptable costs of strategic warfare, the role of international war appears to be diminishing in its role as historical marker.
21 Washington Naval Limitation Agreement of 1922; Pact of Paris of 1928. To the extent that such a view as to the scope of legitimate force was accepted, it did seem to eliminate the relevance of war to change. But such an elimination was not very credible, even on its face, as states retained the discretion to designate a set of facts as giving rise to a valid claim of self-defence. In other words, the subjectivity of self-interpretation was a gaping loophole even if it is granted that the renunciation of non-defensive uses of force was sincerely meant by the governmental representatives who subscribed to The Pact of Paris.

existing economic and security arrangements in international society, and deliberately chose war as the best available instrument by which to achieve their primary goals of enhanced prestige and control, as well as to express their militant nationalist ethos. Without police capabilities, it is obvious that efforts to outlaw recourse to force are vulnerable to any determined violator, but such countervailing capabilities can be generated in a decentralised system of world order only by states. Essentially, and unavoidably, such a structure of 'peace' rests upon the logic of deterrence, and its assumptions of rationality.[22] In essence, norms of peace are not internalised by international actors, but are implemented by an ethos of enforcement and compliance consisting of the willingness of states to avoid recourse to force to the extent possible and to join in collective efforts to oppose violations of the prohibition placed upon aggressive uses of force.

The struggle to prevent strategic war after 1918 was widely thought to have failed because it did not come to terms with the deeply rooted nature of war in a world of sovereign states of changing relative strength and differing goals. Kissinger, among others, popularised the paradoxical view that those who most ardently seek to prevent war set in motion a series of tendencies that make the occurrence of war inevitable, or at least far more likely. Contrariwise, the military approach to foreign policy embodying the Roman maxim 'si vi pacis, vi bellum' (if you want peace, prepare for war), was seen as the best guideline for a peaceful international future, as it ensured attention to deterrent requirements and did not lapse into the complacency of assuming that a legal norm to renounce war could be treated as sufficient unto its goal. In retrospect, this reliance on military capabilities rather than on normative aspirations was seen as far more successful in practice. The acceptance of a realist world picture is widely credited with preserving the peace during the long period of intense East/West rivalry and confronting communism far more successfully than had an earlier generation confronted the menace of fascism.[23] But there is also an ambiguity that is associated with the extension of the function of deterrence, from its defensive role of discouraging recourse to force by adversary states, to the wider undertaking that encompasses a wide range of foreign policy goals, including those involving the projection of power. Thus, the accumulation of deterrent capabilities beyond what is needed to deter others provides some states with a margin of capabilities that enables the pursuit of interventionary and expansionist objectives. It is this circumstance that has converted deterrence in recent decades from its supposed defensive undertaking into an all-purpose underpinning for recourse to force by the US as a hegemonic actor dedicated to the attainment of military *predominance* in conflict situations.[24]

A second influential realist argument was selectively drawn from the deep insight into the nature of international politics attributed to the Athenian historian, Thucydides, especially his supposed espousal of the shaping impact of relative power in the *Melian Dialogue*. This passage has been repeatedly invoked by realists in relation to the reductionist maxim that 'the strong do what they will

22 As compared with centralised enforcement by strong global institutions.
23 See Gaddis (1986); Mearsheimer (1990).
24 Predominance involves more than superiority. It implies victory with minimal losses, and intends to intimidate potential adversaries from mounting challenges. For review of the non-deterrent, non-defensive uses of force in US statecraft during its period of hegemonic status, see Weisburd (1997).

and the weak do what they must', thereby generalising the submission of the Melian generals to Athenian power. Thinkers as liberally inclined as Stanley Hoffmann and Michael Walzer consider the *Melian Dialogue* as a critical pedagogical text that illuminates the whole of international relations, essentially comprehending the decisive role of relative power in shaping the outcomes of international conflicts.[25] The writer would maintain that the relevant passage can be better understood in Thucydides' great historical narrative as an insight into the dynamics of Athenian decline, as expressed by the indication of its abandonment of morality at Melius. This decline manifested itself by reliance on brute strength and ruthless tactics to achieve its will, rather than on the earlier Athenian approach by way of moral example, persuasion and the minimisation of the use of force. If so understood, the *Melian Dialogue* becomes an object lesson, but of an opposite sort – that is, how *not* to conduct statecraft! And as such corresponds with the views of Knutsen, and others, who argue that hegemonic diplomacy depends for its success more on normative leadership and stature than on military prowess.[26] Such an outlook would considerably dilute the current tension between realist thinking and adherence to international law, but it is not likely to gain significant influence in the near future.[27]

Despite the massive impact of realist thinking on the most important foreign policy establishments, the Second World War did not altogether overcome the anti-war sentiments generated by the First World War, although it did give rise to ethical tensions relating to peace and security. The surface response to the Second World War continued to be guided by the conviction that major wars must be prevented in the future, a view apocalyptically reinforced by the use of atomic bombs against Japanese cities in 1945. In essence, the same approach to war prevention was relied upon as after the First World War, but now accompanied by a claim of having learned some lessons from the earlier attempts, including the appreciation that ample authority and power must be made available to global institutions if world-community peacemaking is to be taken seriously. Such an appreciation was translated into a priority effort to involve the US in the work of war prevention, as the leading military, economic and diplomatic force in the world, and to be sure that the norms governing relations between the states were respected and implemented by the major players in the system rather than entrusted to the vagaries of self-enforcement.

This altered view of war prevention resulted in locating the UN in the US and in vesting veto power in the countries victorious (plus China) in the Second World War so as to give the decisions of the Security Council an immediate geopolitical weight. At the same time, endowing powerful states with a right of veto acknowledged that collective security could only hope to succeed if the spirit of co-operation that had been present during the war against European

---

25 For a most thoughtful assessment of Thucydides' approach under the rubric of 'complex realism', see Doyle (1997) pp 49–92; also Walzer (1977) pp 3–13, although discussed in the context of a chapter entitled 'Against Realism'.

26 See Knutsen (1999).

27 Although the rise of human rights and the controversies around humanitarian intervention create some pressure to close the gap between a realist world-view and the normative character of the recent global policy agenda, but not necessarily in a legalist direction. On the contrary, the NATO war over Kosovo encouraged moral and world-order argumentation in support of an abandonment of legal constraints. For two opposed arguments of justification see Glennon (1999); Franck (1999).

fascism and Japanese militarism would be maintained in the post-war world. In the background, also, were tenuous diplomatic commitments to seek disarmament at the earliest possible time and to uphold norms written into the UN Charter 1945 that restricted international uses of force to circumstances of self-defence. The Charter was written in a manner that encouraged a narrow construction of the self-defence exception. The generalised prohibition on force was qualified only by a right of self-defence in situations of response to 'a prior armed attack', and even then, with a further requirement that any claim of self-defence needed to be immediately submitted to the Security Council for review.[28] This textual reining-in of state discretion was never matched by a process of political acceptance and was not effective in limiting behaviour.

As with the earlier efforts, this renewed attempt to rely on international law and institutions to prevent war largely failed, although the failure was not dramatised by a third World War. What ensued instead was a manifest inability to carry out the vision of those that had hoped the UN might be able to keep the peace. As is known, the global atmosphere rapidly degenerated after 1945, leading to the onset of the Cold War that would endure for more than four decades, dooming any hope of co-operation on most matters of global security among the permanent members of the Security Council. Besides this, many influential policy advisors and leaders in the West had interpreted the failures after the First World War from an essentially realist outlook of expecting too much from canons of international law and morality.[29] They underscored 'the lesson of Munich' as teaching that war prevention could be successful only if adversary states were confronted with a prospect of catastrophic consequences in the event of their recourse to aggressive war. And further, the defeat of fascism was seen as itself a momentous contribution to human well-being, giving rise to the prevailing view that reliance on war to achieve the containment and defeat of an evil ideology could be more important than maintaining the peace. Such an insight was central to the opposed ideological positions of the major antagonists in the Cold War, with the West, under the US, committed to liberal democracy and the East, led by the Soviet Union, committed to state socialism. The outcome of wars mattered. The prevailing view believed that it was worth paying the costs of even a highly destructive war to avoid certain undesirable political and ideological results, and further that it was more likely to avoid such wars by conveying to potential aggressors a resolve to fight and win.

Only the deterrent impact of countervailing power was seen as effective in inhibiting a major state with grievances and ambitions. Carrying this deterrent logic to an extreme was converted into foreign policy doctrine due to the impact of nuclear weaponry and the possession of these weapons, along with delivery systems, by both sides in the Cold War, a notion of 'mutual assured destruction', or, more familiarly, 'a balance of terror' was accorded primacy. Norms of international law and institutions designed to provide peace and security for the entire world could not be effective in such an atmosphere, and to rely upon them to attain fundamental goals was generally seen as ridiculous. Such reliance was widely condemned as a dangerous game of wishful thinking. In the course of

---

28 Cf arts 2(4), 51 of the UN Charter.
29 Among the most influential proponents of such views were George F Kennan, Hans Morgenthau and Dean Acheson. See Kennan (1951); Morgenthau (1973); Acheson (1969).

such developments, the self-help nature of world politics was reaffirmed, and the UN and international law were relegated to handmaiden roles.[30]

Nevertheless, the central task of international law continued to be perceived in many quarters as relating to the use of force. Such concerns reflected the sense that peace was precarious in a world bristling with nuclear weaponry and ideological antagonism, as well as the degree to which the primary international law text, the UN Charter, appeared to take such a restrictive view with respect to permissible force. Increasingly, international lawyers themselves realised that law was not in a position to challenge the main practices of world politics, and busied themselves with more technical matters, or at least with concerns that seemed compatible with the self-help structure of world order. A prime law concern became the long negotiating process that produced the UN Convention on the Law of Seas in 1982. Here was a complex negotiation among states with very different ideas about ocean policy that managed in the end to reach an impressively broad-gauged agreement that reconciled divergent interests across a wide spectrum of issues, but, revealingly, by agreeing to leave the regulation of naval activities off the agenda.[31]

Of relevance is the extent to which the normative (as distinct from the functional) side of international law was altered rather than merely disappeared in light of the inability to meet the challenge of war. There was a tacit acknowledgement that steps to curtail dangers of war, especially as related to the problem of avoiding the spread and use of nuclear weaponry, were only politically viable to the extent that such steps could be validated by an appeal to realist logic. The 1999 debate in the US over the ratification of the Comprehensive Test Ban Treaty was dominated by a realist concern with keeping others from acquiring nuclear weaponry rather than with a more idealist interest in initiating a process of denuclearisation of world politics that culminated with total nuclear disarmament. Most mainstream proponents of ratification, including then President Clinton, couched their argumentation in the logic and language of power, and relative gains.[32]

The impact of realist orientation on the role of international law and lawyers is complex, confusing and somewhat contradictory. To the extent that law to be effective needs to comprehend the relevance of power, the realist outlook tends to avoid rather sterile forms of legalism associated with the more extreme versions

---

30 Efforts to rescue the idealistic approach to peace rested on moving the demilitarising logic far beyond what had been agreed upon at the time of establishing the UN. See Clark and Sohn (1966); Millis and Real (1963); Falk (1975). A more recent formulation is Yunker (1993). Such proposals never were viewed seriously, being discounted as 'utopian', or worse, as pathways to global tyranny.

31 See Falk (1997) pp 45–52 in 'Peace in the Oceans'. See also the Report of the Independent World Commission on the Oceans (1998) especially pp 33–52. Even the inflamed ideological atmosphere of the Cold War did not preclude elaborate extensions of international law that could be vindicated by functionalist logic and mutual self-interest.

32 Realism can even adopt an abolitionist view of nuclear weaponry. See argument of the Cold War hawk, Paul Nitze, advocating the elimination of nuclear weaponry on geostrategic grounds: 'To maintain them is costly and adds nothing to our security.' Nitze analyzes threats to security as all capable of being addressed effectively without further reliance on nuclear weapons. But nowhere in this assessment is the further argument even mentioned, namely that these weapons have a dubious legality in light of the 1996 Advisory Opinion of the International Court of Justice and an even more dubious morality in view of their inherently indiscriminate and toxic character: see Nitze (1999); for a normative critique of nuclearism, see Lifton and Falk (1992).

of legal positivism. At the same time, if the interpretations of international law amount to a submission to the will of the powerful, then the regulative function of law is completely lost, and the international lawyer assumes the role, so vividly derided by Kant, of being 'a miserable consoler', in effect, an apologist for the decisions of the geopolitical actor whose nationality he or she shares.

Such a role was virtually formalised in the Soviet Union during its reign, with the legal perspective consistently appropriated to serve the ideological needs of the moment. A subtler version of the same phenomenon occurred in the democratic West during the Cold War, but with more friction due to the possibility of dissent.

The academic realist was more interested in understanding the world, using the history of international relations, to provide a more convincing explanation of past and present, thereby providing insights into policy prescription, and even into a kind of projective assessment that became known as 'future studies'. The adoption of this realist framework by international legal scholars gave their views both a marginal quality (mere elaborations of political patterns) and a greater relevance (no longer detached from the flow of international diplomacy). It is not easy to determine whether this was 'a Faustian bargain' or an advance toward sophistication and modesty.

In the end, the realist domination of intellectual space served well to overcome the legacy of Munich, and given the outcome of the Cold War, seemed to promote peace and stability in a context where the world faced the entirely new challenge of deterring aggression without provoking nuclear war. Whether realism serves the interests of world order since 1989 is more questionable. Here, the opportunities for peace and stability seem to depend on a more normative frame of reference – taking the opportunity to promote nuclear disarmament and a more effective UN.

In such a setting, the ascendancy of realism has not worked well. The efforts to construct a post-Cold War world order have been disappointing and dispiriting. The invocation of human rights and humanitarian intervention by realists has a shrill resonance, especially when such undertakings as Somalia, Bosnia, Rwanda and Kosovo disclose how realist policy-makers (and their academic allies) fail miserably when they undertake normative missions. Their hearts and heads are not truly engaged, or their normative rhetoric offers only a thin disguise for geopolitical motives.

STRUCTURES AND PROCESSES: CONSTRAINING ACTION

Global policy unfolds in response to a series of overlapping, and often contradictory, bases of action, and in a context in which structures of restraint are perceived by decision-makers as restrictive to various degrees. It is the composite global picture established by prominent patterns of initiatives in a given period that provides us with our sense of 'world order'. Such a sense is historically contingent in its superficial aspects, especially as wars come and go, and technological innovations alter the way wars are fought and economic life is organised. There is an evolutionary process that makes comparisons of world order over time relevant, and even illuminating.[33] And yet such comparisons do not help us understand the elements of continuity that have allowed world order

33 See Knutsen (1999); Rosecrance (1963).

as 'a system' to be durable for several centuries. This durability has to do with the persisting pre-eminence of state-centric relations and the extent to which ideas of sovereignty and territoriality dominate the political imagination of those who think seriously about international relations. It is also important to explicate the interplay of several 'logics of action' that together generate the content of global policy.

What is distinctive about the last several decades has been the questioning of these durable underpinnings of world order as understood in Westphalian imagery.[34] It is the cumulative weight of this questioning that makes it plausible to consider conceptual innovations as needed to describe the essential features of contemporary world order. It is here that the various formulations of 'globalisation' assume importance, reflecting a dissatisfaction with the continuing explanatory usefulness of conventional state-centric frameworks of inquiry.[35]

There are various 'litmus tests' that are invoked in the debate as to whether in fact there is a 'new world order'. The phrase gained widespread currency in 1990–91 during the Gulf Crisis. It was repeatedly invoked by George Bush in his presidential efforts to rally political support for a collective forcible response under UN auspices to Iraq's invasion and annexation of Kuwait. The implication of this effort being that if collective security was effectively undertaken by the UN to reverse Iraqi aggression, then it would disclose the emergence of a new world order that contrasted with the former stalemate associated with the Cold War era of East/West confrontation. In such a usage the critical test of a transformative claim is the transition from world order based on 'self-help' to world order based on 'collective security'. Such a transition could be (and was) understood as a revival of Woodrow Wilson's failed crusade at the end of the First World War to institutionalise security in the League of Nations in order to avoid the recurrence of war that seemed to him the result of instabilities in the balance of power approach to international peace and security.[36]

In a more academic vein, this test was relied upon to explore the case for a post-Westphalian world order, and found wanting, by a group of scholars under the leadership of Gene M Lyons and Michael Mastanduno.[37] It is noteworthy that the US government, which initiated this discourse of new world order, quietly abandoned it for undisclosed reasons as soon as the Gulf War was completed. One could surmise that such an abandonment reflected policy considerations

---

34 Stephen Krasner effectively has shown that the strict juridical view of a state-centric world implied by Westphalian imagery never corresponded with actual patterns of statecraft: see Krasner (1999).

35 One of the first comprehensive efforts to capture the newer reality is that of Rosenau (1990) especially pp 21–90; see also Falk (1998; 1995).

36 Part of the explanation for the rise of realist thinking arose as part of a repudiation of such Wilsonian ideas as either ill-adapted to the realities of international political life or as 'utopian'. The Cold War-era was premised on a return to the central idea of relying upon countervailing power and the readiness to use it as the foundation of international stability. Instead of the terminology of 'balance of power', the new language of power referred to 'containment' and 'deterrence'.

37 See Lyons and Mastanduno (1995); compare the more positive assessment in Fisler Damrosch and Scheffer (1991) and Sellers (1996). This latter book, more persuasively, premises the hypothesis of newness on the extent to which Westphalian sovereignty was being undermined from within and without by expanding notions of self-determination that followed the breakup of former Soviet Union and Yugoslavia, and by the increasing salience of international standards of human rights, building support for the legitimacy of circumstances. See Murphy (1996).

in Washington, including a concern about vesting such extensive authority and responsibility in the UN. This concern no doubt partly reflected the view that the US would be expected to provide the lion's share of capabilities for such interventions. It also probably reflected an awareness that widespread 'disorder' being encountered in various parts of the world, including many settings that lacked the strategic importance of Kuwait and whose character did not yield the sort of political consensus that facilitated a unified response to Iraq's aggression. For example, the UN proved incapable of finding a meaningful course of action in response to ethnic cleansing in Bosnia, and has been unable effectively to address most of the problems of recurrent warfare in sub-Saharan Africa.

Another approach to transformation was based on the radical character attributed to the development and use of atomic bombs in the immediate aftermath of the Second World War. Such transformative views regarded the impact as either rendering war obsolete or, more likely, putting the future of human civilisation under a dark shadow of imminent apocalypse.[38] But, in fact, state structures and global diplomacy were resilient, seemingly incorporating the developments of huge nuclear arsenals into the familiar Westphalian framework. Steps toward accommodating these dangerous realities were mainly marginal, consisting of more cautious conflict and crisis management as between nuclear rivals, especially the US and the Soviet Union and the establishment of a non-proliferation regime designed to contain the spread of the weaponry. Recent commentary by a few realists have argued that nuclear weapons are 'useless' or 'superfluous' due to various threats associated with their mere existence, the greater access to the technology of weaponry of mass destruction and taking account of the increasingly devastating character of conventional weaponry as enhanced by information technology.[39] Such anti-nuclear realism remains a fringe position. The dominant view remains that this weaponry, as bolstered by missile defence systems, augments geopolitical influence and performs some deterrent functions.[40]

Undoubtedly the most prominent foundation for proclaiming transformation at the global level is associated with the 'global village' or the 'global neighbourhood' sort of imagery, based on the qualitative significance of integrative tendencies at the regional and global levels and the disintegrative tendencies at the level of the state.[41] The adoption of the language of globalisation is a manner of signalling a fundamental change of conditions in international life, which justifies a new terminology.[42] A somewhat complementary, although quite different, take on transformative developments is to emphasise the defining significance of information technology, the computer and the Internet – developments that radically alter the nature of sovereignty, borders, citizenship, governance and time/space relationships.[43]

---

38 See Schell (1982); also Mandelbaum (1981).
39 See eg Nitze (1999).
40 Gormley and Mahnken (2000). For a more congenial view of the threat, emphasising the danger of retaining possession, see Schell (2000) at 41–56.
41 See the Report of the Commission on Global Governance (1995); for the tension between integrative and disintegrative trends see Clark (1997).
42 For a sceptical perception of this dynamic as an empirical phenomenon, see Hirst and Thompson (1996); for comprehensive overview that includes a comparison of differing assessments of the structural impacts of recent global trends, see Held and others (1999).
43 For a probing and comprehensive argument along these lines see Castels (1995–98).

International law is one factor among several in generating policy outcomes under varying conditions of world order. In 're-framing' the relevance of international law, it is important to take account of how these structures and processes impact upon decisions taken by participants in global policy arenas. The *structures* consist of overlapping frameworks of ideas, norms and limits, and call particular attention to 'world order' and the preceding debate as to whether the impact of change is such as to bring into being a new world order. The *processes* consist of the various logics that exert influence on the perception of appropriate action by decision-makers and their critics. Because perception and interpretation is decisive, and occurs within settings of great unevenness as to capabilities, with respect to civilisational perspective, and as to roles within the world, there are bound to be wide variations in responding to the circumstances of world order at any given historical moment.[44] Nevertheless, by identifying these factors that affect decisions, it is hoped that the normative dimensions of world order at the start of the twenty-first century will be clarified.[45]

The statist logic of sovereign equality

World order for the past several centuries has been formally premised upon the logic of the sovereign rights and equality of all actors that qualify as states, that is, as full members of international society with an accompanying diplomatic status. The defining features of a state include bounded territory, a government and people. States as small as Liechtenstein and Malta or as large as China and Russia are equal from a state-centric perspective, and their diplomatic representatives are accorded a protocol rank in accordance with their seniority. Their territorial domain is exclusively subject to governance by the national government, and overall deference to sovereign rights is acknowledged by non-intervention norms.

Until recently a statist world picture seemed accurate from a juridical perspective, and was generally respected by map-makers. With the growth of international institutions, especially in relation to European regionalism, and as a result of global economic governance (by way of the World Trade Organization, IMF and World Bank) the state-centric image seems less accurate descriptively. Europe often participates in lawmaking conferences as a unified entity, and for many purposes European space has superseded the national space of its constituent states. The international financial institutions exert major influence on the policy options available to governments of sovereign states, especially those in the South. The UN is increasingly subject to criticism as anachronistic because it limits membership to states, excluding not only regional actors, but also representation by transnational market forces and by global civil society.[46]

Nevertheless, for many purposes, statist logic is still the foundation of world order, and in some respects the state has extended its effective reach, as in relation to the oceans and space. Most of human affairs on an operational level

44 Such variation is particularly impressive in this period due to the reassertion of civilisational dimensions of world order. See Jacinta O'Hagan's contribution to this symposium and the extraordinary impact of Samuel Huntington's 'The Clash of Civilizations?' (1993).

45 In important respects this inquiry is kindred to and aligned with the New Haven School of jurisprudence shaped by Myres S McDougal, and his principal collaborators, especially Harold D Lasswell and Michael Reismann. For the most definitive presentation of their framework, see McDougal and Lasswell (1992).

46 On this issue see Falk and Strauss (1999); also Kofi Annan (1999) where 'a global compact' between 'business and the U.N.' is proposed.

continues to be shaped by state/society relations. The state has proved to be a resilient and flexible instrument of governance, and is not likely to lose this prominence, despite the emergence of new actors and the substantial deterritorialisation of economic and financial relationships.[47]

At the same time, it is important to appreciate that the imagery of a state-centric world was always misleading, and at most a kind of political myth disseminated by the powerful, but also expressing an aspiration by subordinated peoples who were stateless. The statist idea does not easily come to terms with the hierarchical character of international relations either in its formal or informal expressions. The colonial order, of course, denied colonial nations statehood, but even within the domain of statism the inequality of states resulted in various modifications of statist logic: spheres of influence, the role of 'great powers', doctrines of 'diplomatic protection' and, more recently, 'structural adjustment programs' (of the IMF), as well as the idea and practice of 'humanitarian intervention'.

The geopolitical logic of hegemonic status: the inequality of states

The shaping role of inequality in modern international history is predominant, as evidenced above all by the role of war as both the purest expression of inequality and the main instrument of ritualised change in boundaries and sovereign rights and duties. Julius Stone usefully called attention to this special function of 'peace treaties' in restructuring international relations even if the war that preceded had itself been illegal and 'a war of aggression'.[48] The UN Charter formally challenges such a role for war, but its impact on the conduct of world politics is controversial, and certainly inconclusive. Surely the strict framework of limitation written into articles 2(4) and 51 of the Charter have not been able to restrict the behaviour of states within such confines except on the rare occasions when geopolitical pressures happen to coincide with these norms. This happened in response to the conquest and annexation of Iraq after the Gulf War, and earlier, in relation to the attack of North Korea on South Korea and in response to the Suez Operation of 1956. But often, force has been used in international relations beyond the Charter limits during the last 50 years. The US and Israel have repeatedly used non-defensive force as alleged instruments of counter-terrorism. Additionally, NATO waged war on behalf of humanitarian claims in Kosovo, despite the absence of any Security Council force authorisation.

The logic of hegemonic authority extends beyond the implications of unequal power and influence to encompass the rather amorphous, yet significant, role of 'global leadership'.[49] Such a hegemonic role in an era of moderated international conflict is premised on military power, but crucially also includes normative reputation as a generally benevolent political actor, a provider of order beneficial for the global public good, and not just action driven by the national interests of the hegemon. Arguably the US fulfilled this role in the period after the Second World War until the fall of the Berlin Wall, but less clearly so in the 1990s.[50]

47 What has occurred recently is the successful evasion of territorial regulatory regimes through offshore banking and by neoliberal pressures to eliminate currency and capital controls.
48 Julius Stone (1954) pp 3–64, 297–413, 635–647.
49 The issue has been persuasively discussed by Hedley Bull in his treatment of the role of 'great powers' in 'upholding the postulates of anarchical society': Bull (1977).
50 See useful discussion in Knutsen (1999).

The discipline of global capital

In this era of globalisation, a series of ideas about the importance of market efficiency have achieved primacy in policy-making circles of governments. These ideas are given practical effect through their institutionalisation in a series of influential arenas of decision: the International Monetary Fund, World Bank, World Trade Organization, Annual Economic Summit (Group of Seven), World Economic Forum (Davos). The coherent presentation of these ideas is often associated with a school of thought developed by economists, known as 'neo-liberalism'. To defy these ideas in any direct way can generate a series of adverse consequences, depending on the situation of a particular state: capital flight, lowering of international credit ratings, refusal of loans, currency fluctuations, legal claims, even nullification of electoral outcomes.[51]

The ascendancy of neo-liberal globalisation has been subject to two sets of challenges in the latter half of the 1990s: first, the largely regional and economic challenge associated with the Asian Financial Crisis that started in mid-1997 and had reverberations elsewhere, including Russia, Japan and Brazil; and second, 'the battle of Seattle' in late 1999, which was global in scope and mainly political in character, raising especially difficult questions about the non-democratic character of global economic governance and the exceedingly inequitable distribution of benefits and burdens of globalisation. The Seattle protests were directed at a ministerial meeting of the WTO being held in the city. In April 2000, a second phase of street protest was aimed at the annual joint meeting of the IMF and World Bank.

At the very least, a widening debate on global economic policy is underway, raising social issues about growing income-wealth disparities, persisting mass poverty and political issues about participation, accountability and transparency, as well as governance issues associated with tensions between territorial policy priorities and global procedures and standards as applicable to labour practices and environmental concerns.

The logic of international law

The acceptance of the binding character of international legal obligations is intended, of course, to condition the behaviour of states, and seems over time, at least for routine, everyday transactions, to be *generally* effective in doing so.[52] The present period exhibits an effort to bring the logic of international law into greater conformity with the discipline of global capital, as through the imposition of IMF standards on domestic public order or more directly through the WTO

---

51 How else to interpret the German social democratic mandate that brought the SPD to power in 1998, but then quickly produced a backlash in the financial community that led to the resignation of Oskar Lafontaine, and the reaffirmation by the German Chancellor, Gerhard Schroeder, of fidelity to neo-liberal principles. 'The third way' represents some effort to soften the impact of the discipline of global capital, but largely it seems to be public relations and rhetoric as enacted by Tony Blair and the British Labour Party. But see the more serious thinking of Giddens (1999).

52 See the much relied upon book by Henkin (1979); also Fisher (1961); as discussed above, the violations of international law receive far greater attention than do patterns of compliance, and overall perceptions are influenced also by governmental propaganda that emphasises the violations of adversaries.

framework, including its compulsory dispute-settlement procedures. Lawmaking treaties provide guidelines for many forms of behaviour, and provide the architecture of a normative order that extends *inwardly* to govern state/society relations and to regulate activities that may have detrimental impacts on the global environment.[53]

The logic of international morality

The spread of a human rights culture has been a notable achievement of the last half-century. This movement has been greatly facilitated by lawmaking initiatives at the UN generating widely respected texts. The recent scrutiny of these texts bears witness to their formidable stature, which might be enhanced by modifications that met criticisms associated with a Western bias. Also important, of course, has been the remarkable growth of human rights NGOs, providing auspices for thousands of activists around the world. The existence of the texts and the emergence of activist pressures are symbiotic, either without the other would not get very far at all.

Finally, the conjuncture of historical forces has created extraordinary opportunities for exercising leverage on unfolding events. Many examples exist, but among the most prominent were the role of human rights in precipitating the collapse of the Soviet Empire in Eastern Europe and then at home, their role in powering the anti-apartheid campaign to the point that it became transformative of the most racist political regime in the world, and their role in awakening the conscience of the world to the diverse and terrible wrongs inflicted for centuries on indigenous peoples throughout the world.

But international morality is more than human rights. It builds on media coverage of human suffering and governmental atrocity. It engenders support (and controversy) relating to 'humanitarian intervention',[54] as in relation to a wide range of abuses and breakdowns of political order. International morality is closing down the exemption from accountability that had been accorded rulers of sovereign states. The International Criminal Court in The Hague relating to former Yugoslavia and Rwanda is a momentous step toward carrying forward the Nuremberg/Tokyo initiatives after the Second World War. The Rome Treaty of 1999 establishing an International Criminal Court is part of the momentum.

Despite these extraordinary moves to implement international morality, abetted by the gaze of a global media in real time and by a mobile corp of transnational activists, there is formidable resistance. This resistance centres in the major power-wielders who refuse to subject themselves to any procedures of accountability. The US is the current leader of this resistance, not surprisingly seconded by China.

There is also evident, in this period of transition from authoritarian rule to constitutional democracy, a morally driven set of compromises between justice and peace. These compromises typically take the form of 'truth and

---

53 In this regard, the whole emergence of international human rights in this period is subversive of the earlier understanding of international law as concerned with the *outward* relations of states. For a creative development of this central metaphor that bears on the understanding of sovereignty see Walker (1993); on the potentially 'subversive' effects of international human rights norms see Falk (1999a) pp 153–178.

54 For useful assessments, see Moore (1998).

reconciliation' commissions that identify past patterns of criminality, but avoid imposing individual criminal responsibility for even the most unforgivable patterns of behaviour.[55]

The logic of cyberspace

Perhaps, the greatest threat to the primacy of the territorial state derives from Information Technology (IT), and its opening of cyberspace. There is an irony present. Most of the innovative momentum underlying the information age derives from the most statist of activities, namely, military research and development, with the fundamental goal of enhancing the intelligence and war-fighting capabilities of the state. The US, otherwise in an internationally hegemonic role, has taken the lead in this transformative undertaking whose implications affect all aspects of human existence, including our sense of collective and personal identity.

Thus understood, IT is an instrument of state power, responsible for a new phase of unequal warfare between those actors that have access to the new technologies and those that do not. At the same time, IT is subversive of state power, greatly facilitating the formation of transnational communities and loyalties, while weakening the hold of territorial communities in the political imagination. The rise of populist resistance to economic globalisation is paradigmatic, exhibiting a strong transnational set of preoccupations relating to global democracy, equity in the world economy and the application of international standards for labour and human rights. Of course, the resistance evident in Seattle and Washington was, in a sense, a backlash against the global influence exerted by market forces as shaped from such non-accountable arenas as those provided by the World Economic Forum at its annual meetings in Davos, Switzerland. In effect, the opening of cyberspace is producing an encounter between market forces aligned with the richer and more developed states (globalisation-from-above) and an array of transnational social forces aligned with governments representing economically disadvantaged states and regions (globalisation-from-below).[56]

The radical element embedded in IT is its boundary-less character, as well as ease of access and communication, and relative anonymity. Governments can forbid or restrict access in various ways, but any comprehensive prohibition imposes serious limitations on the capacity of a society to participate in the world economy, and is likely, in any event, to be ineffective. The economistic priorities that seem to dominate the global arenas since the fall of the Berlin Wall in 1989 alter and erode the political and ideological impulses to regulate territorial space. Such an erosion is reinforced by the Soviet collapse, which is attributed in part to its laggard incorporation of IT into economic activity.[57] The struggle persists, and is revealed in its most significant form in China.

The impact of IT on citizenship and human identity is also unresolved. Along with regionalising, globalising and micro-nationalising trends, the state as the focus of loyalty and as the *sole* vehicle of nationhood is in retreat. As far as cyberspace

---

55 For a sensitive inquiry into this process, see Minow (1998).
56 See Falk (1999).
57 See Castels (1995–98) vol III *End of Millennium* (1998) pp 4–69.

is concerned, the effects are hard to assess at this point, beyond the obvious weakening of national boundaries as a parameter for many dimensions of human existence. Enthusiasts for the Internet have self-consciously articulated a libertarian code that includes a new primary identity, labelled as 'netizen'. More corrosive of state power and authority is the ideological view that market and Internet as self-organising systems are superior problem-solvers to intrusive and inefficient governmental approaches, an outlook that parallels and reinforces the laissez-faire premises of neo-liberalism.

Such orientations have several dramatic effects on the character of world order. First, there is shifted to the private sector a formidable power of initiative to address public issues. Thus, fabulously rich individuals such as Bill Gates, Ted Turner and George Soros commit hundreds of millions of dollars, or even billions, to social and political projects of a transnational character. It cannot be presumed that such private leverage will be always used for philanthropic and benign purposes. Second, the protection of the global public good by international institutions is directly and indirectly under attack. The failure of the UN System to address global challenges partly reflects the unwillingness of states to provide the capabilities and mandates, which in turn expresses a neo-liberal/IT bias against governmental or institutional regulation.

There are important counter-trends present, as well. The growing complexity and interdependence of international life push toward the establishment of regulatory frameworks. Even more relevantly to the logic of cyberspace, transnational social forces promote the adoption and implementation of legal standards, increasingly in coalition with like-minded governments. The Landmines Treaty of 1997 outlawing anti-personnel landmines and the 1999 Rome Treaty establishing an International Criminal Court are notable recent examples of a collaborative state/NGO process that can be identified as 'the new internationalism'.

CONCLUSION

The re-framing agenda for international law derives directly from the changing character of world order. Fundamental shifts in the role and nature of the state reflect both the rise of regional and global market forces and a neo-liberal ideational consensus. This consensus has generated support for minimising the regulatory, entrepreneurial and social roles of the state, while underscoring its role in generating facilitative frameworks for the new geopolitics of economic globalisation. This internationalisation of the state, along with the impacts of information technology on the deterritorialising of commerce and finance, has fundamentally changed the nature and role of the state, but such an impact does not necessarily imply the decline of the state, or even less, an assertion that the state is now obsolete. What has been superseded by the growth of transnational networks and regional and global actors of various sorts is a world order constituted by sovereign territorial states. And as a result, there are shifting identities, with greater attention to both micro-nationalisms and to broader civilisational and religious affinities, and less to the statist command of loyalty over citizens situated within its bounded geographic space.

A related reframing concerns warfare and political violence. The focus of attention has shifted, at least temporarily, from the menace of strategic war to an array of challenges associated with intra-state and transnational violence, ranging from self-determination issues to those involving 'failed states' and humanitarian catastrophes, as well as difficult issues associated with international terrorism and criminal activity. Beyond this, there is a renewed concern with the prospect of further nuclear proliferation and the possible deployment and use of nuclear weapons in such regional settings as South Asia, especially in light of the Indo/Pakistan weapons tests in 1998 and violent confrontation over Kashmir in the following year. Additionally, there have been strong indications that a series of countries in the Middle East and Asia have developed biological and chemical weapons capabilities. Despite the ending of the Cold War and the consequent erosion of deterrence as a rationale for the possession of nuclear weapons, there has been no evident disposition by the five declared nuclear weapons states to pursue nuclear disarmament. The rejection of the Comprehensive Test Ban Treaty of 1996 by the US Senate in 1999 and the pressure to repudiate the ABM Treaty of 1972 so as to pave the way for missile defence deployments seems to be undermining even the modest achievements of an arms control approach to nuclear weaponry. The leadership of Vladimir Putin has at least breathed some signs of life into the start process of bilateral US/Russian nuclear arms limitation.

A further area for reframing, already touched upon in relation to the changing character of the state, is the relevance of cultural difference to the future of world order. There are much-discussed alarmist speculations about inter-civilisational tensions producing wars along the fault lines between Islam and its Western civilisational neighbours, but there are also less consequential problems associated with challenges to the universality of human rights texts, and of international law generally.

A final reframing focal point relates to the emergent salience of normative leadership. To what extent can international law serve the global public good and provide a vehicle for leadership under US auspices? Is political realism of the sort that subordinates respect for law and morality to the calculation of national interests in eclipse? Is the heightening of awareness about human rights and recent calls for humanitarian intervention, or 'principled intervention', suggestive of greater deference to international law?[58] Or might that deference derive from the exponential increase in the complexity and interactive nature of international life? Or the closely related need for greater trust in co-operative method if the trust needed to uphold intellectual property rights is to be forthcoming in a global system in which regulatory effectiveness can no longer be based on territorial authority? Such questions about normative relevance link international law to the practical administration of rights and duties under conditions of growing economic globalisation.

None of these conjectures is meant to encourage a generalised repudiation of realism as a way of assessing relations among international adversaries, especially with respect to security policy within war/peace settings. The mistakes of 'appeasement' remain mistakes under contemporary circumstances. But military and economic prowess more than ever needs to be reinforced by a generally appealing normative project for human betterment. States continue to provide the only source of explicit global leadership, but their capabilities are no longer sufficient unless bolstered by creative partnerships with other actors, including international institutions and representatives of civil society and the private sectors, as well as with various regional formations. In its essence, such a normative

---

58 See Annan (2000).

project to be credible must embody some genuine affirmation of human solidarity. For this reason, the hegemonic leader, to retain its pre-eminence, cannot turn away from humanitarian challenges just because their locus is remote and their impact on strategic concerns seems slight.

Also, the normative horizons of political behaviour need to be given a practical relevance that is precluded by accepting, without essential qualifications, the realist argument about the nature of world order. Among these normative horizons none are more important than the abolition of all weaponry of mass destruction by means of a prudent, adequately verified process and the development of the capabilities and the will to address the outbreak of genocide and severe, prolonged abuse of human rights as a threat to the peace and security of the world. Less substantive, more structural, is the need for a governance structure appropriate to the dangers and opportunities provided by globalisation in all its facets. Humane governance seeks to realise both functional goals of efficient administration and valued ends associated with equitable and sustainable development, as well as the construction of global democracy. To reach such ends, institutional reforms and innovations are needed. These include a stronger, more financially independent UN System, the democratisation of international financial institutions, the creation of a Global Peoples Assembly within the UN, and the creation of a World Environmental Agency.

Even beneath the shadow of a persisting realist climate of political opinion, the possibilities for an enhanced role for international (or global) law are impressive, and perhaps unavoidable given the growing complexity and interdependence of life on the planet.

Select bibliography

Acheson, D, (1969) *Present at the Creation.*

Annan, K, (1999) 'Help the Third World Help Itself', Wall Street Journal, 29 November, at A28.

—(2000) 'The legitimacy to intervene', Financial Times, 10 January, at 13.

Best, G, (1997) *War and Law Since 1945.*

Bolton, J R, (1999) 'The Global Prosecutors: Hunting War Criminals in the Name of Utopia', 78 Foreign Affairs 1 at 157–164.

Boyle, F A, (1981) *The Future of International Law and American Foreign Policy.*

—(1999) *Foundations of World Order: The Legalist Approach to International Relations, 1898-1922.*

Brown, M E, Cote, O R Jr, Lynn-Jones, S M, et al (eds), (1998) *Theories of War and Peace.*

Bull, H, (1977) *The Anarchical Society.*

Castels, M, (1995–98) *The Information Age: Economy, Society, and Culture*, vols I–III.

Chomsky, N, (1999) *The New Military Humanism: Lessons from Kosovo.*

Glark, G, (1997) *Globalization and Fragmentation: International Relations in the Twentieth Century.*

Clark, G, and Sohn, L B, (1996) *World Peace Through World Law* (3rd edn).

Commission on Global Governance, Report of the (1995) *Our Global Neighborhood.*

Doyle, M, (1997) *Ways of War and Peace: Realism, Liberalism, and Socialism.*

Esposito, D M, (1996) *The Legacy of Woodrow Wilson: American War Aims in World War I.*

Falk, R, (1975) *A Study of Future Worlds.*

—(1995) *On Humane Governance: Toward a New Global Politics.*

—(1997) 'A Peaceful Future for the Oceans?' in E Mann Borgese (ed), *Peace in the Oceans: Ocean Governance and the Agenda for Peace.*

—(1998) *Law in an Emerging Global Village: Toward a Post-Westphalian Perspective.*

—(1999a) 'The Quest for Human Rights in an Era of Globalization', in M G Schechter (ed), *Future Multilateralism: The Political and Social Framework.*

—(1999b) *Predatory Globalization: A Critique.*

Falk, R, and Strauss, A, (1999) 'On the Creation of a Global Peoples Assembly: Legitimacy and the Power of Popular Sovereignty', unpublished manuscript.

Fisher, R, (1961) 'Bringing Law to Bear on Government', 74 Harv LR 1130.

Fisler Damrosch, L, and Scheffer, D J (eds), (1991) *Law and Force in the New International Order.*

Franck, T M, (1986) *Judging the World Court.*

—(1999) 'Break It, Don't Fake It', 78 Foreign Affairs 4 at 116–118.

Gaddis, J L, (1986) 'The Long Peace: Elements of Stability in the Postwar International System', 10 I Security 4 at 99–142.

Giddens, A, (1999) *The Third Way: The Renewal of Social Democracy.*

Gilpin, R, (1981) *War and Change in World Politics.*

Glennon, M, (1999) 'The New Interventionism: The Search for a Just International Law', 78 Foreign Affairs 3 at 7–9.

Gormley, D M, and Mahnken, T G, (2000) 'Facing Nuclear and Conventional Reality', 44 Orbis 1 at 109–126.

Held, D, and others (1999) *Global Transformations.*

Henkin, L, (1979) *How Nations Behave.*

Hirst, P, and Thompson, G, (1996) *Globalization in Question: The International Economy and the Possibilities of Governance.*

Huntington, S, (1993) 'The Clash of Civilizations?', 72 Foreign Affairs 22 at 22–49.

Independent World Commission on the Oceans, Report of the (1998) *The Ocean: Our Future.*

Kennan, G F, (1951) *American Diplomacy: 1900–1950.*

Keohane, R O (ed), (1986) *Neo-Realism and Its Critics.*

Kissinger, H, (1994) *Diplomacy.*

Knock, T J, (1992) *To End All Wars: Woodrow Wilson and the Quest for a New World Order.*

Knutsen, T L, (1999) *The Rise and Fall of World Orders.*

Krasner, S D, (1999) *Sovereignty: Organized Hypocrisy.*

Lifton, R J, and Falk, R, (1992) *Indefensible Weapons: The Political and Psychological Case Against Nuclearism* (updated edn).

Luttwak, E N, (1999) 'Give War a Chance', 78 Foreign Affairs 4 at 36–44.

Lyons, G M, and Mastanduno, M (eds), (1995) *Beyond Westphalia? State Sovereignty and International Intervention.*

McDougal, M, and Lasswell, H, (1992) *Jurisprudence for a Free Society.*

Mandelbaum, M, (1981) *The Nuclear Revolution.*

—(1999) 'A Perfect Failure', 78 Foreign Affairs 5 at 2–8.

Mearsheimer, J J, (1990) 'Back to the Future: Instability in Europe after the Cold War', 15 I Security 1 at 5–56.

Millis, M, and Real, J, (1963) *The Abolition of World.*

Minow, M, (1998) *Between Vengeance and Forgiveness.*

Moore, J, (1998) *Hard Choices: Moral Dilemmas in Humanitarian Intervention.*

Morgenthau, H J, (1973) *Politics Among Nations: The Struggle for Power and Peace* (5th edn).

Morris, S J, (1999) *Why Vietnam Invaded Cambodia: Political Culture and the Causes of War.*

Murphy, S D, (1996) *Humanitarian Intervention: The United Nations in an Evolving World Order.*

Nitze, P H, (1999) 'A Threat Mostly to Ourselves', New York Times, 28 October, at A31.

Nye, J S Jr, (1990) *Bound to Lead: The Changing Nature of American Power.*

—(2000) 'The Power We Must Not Squander', New York Times, 3 January, at A19.

Nye, J S Jr, and Owens, W A, (1996) 'America's Information Edge', 75(2) Foreign Affairs 22 at 30–36.

Resenau, J, (1990) *Turbulence in World Politics.*

Rosecrance, R, (1963) *Action and Reaction in World Politics.*

Schell, J, (2000) 'The Unfinished Twentieth Century: What We Have Forgotten About Nuclear Weapons', Harpers, January, at 41–56.

Sellers, M (ed), (1996) *The New World Order: Sovereignty, Human Rights and the Self-Determination of Peoples.*

Steinberg, J B, (1999) 'A Perfect Polemic', 78 Foreign Affairs 6 at 128–133.

Stone, J, (1954) *Legal Controls of International Conflict.*

Walker, R B, (1993) *Inside/outside: international relations as political theory.*

Waltz, K, (1993) 'The Emerging Structure of International Politics', 18 I Security 2 at 44–79.

Walzer, M, (1998) *Just and Unjust Wars: A Moral Argument with Historical Illustrations.*

Weisburd, A M, (1997) *The Use of Force: The Practice of States Since World War II.*

Weston, B H, Falk, R A, and Charlesworth, H (eds), (1997) *Supplement of Basic Documents to International Law and World Order.*

Yunker, J A, (1993) *World Union on the Horizon.*

Chapter 18

Globalisation: a challenge to the nation state and to international law

S HOBE

INTRODUCTION – THE PHENOMENON OF GLOBALISATION

At the threshold of the twenty-first century, we are witnessing a new phenomenon which perhaps in a more profound way than ever before must be understood as a challenge to traditional parameters of statehood and to international law: the phenomenon of globalisation. But although the English journal 'Economist' has declared the notion of globalisation to be the 'economic buzzword of the 1990s',[1] one is left with many unanswered questions if it comes to a more thorough consideration of the legal consequences of this phenomenon. This chapter attempts to shed some light on the legal ramifications and consequences of globalisation. Consequently, it is important to first provide some description of the empirical basis of globalisation before those consequences can be described more accurately.

What is globalisation? It would certainly be to easy to equate globalisation with 'McDonaldisation' or 'Americanisation', an attempt that can be found even in legal literature.[2] Rather, any empirical description of the phenomenon of globalisation has to take into account that we are dealing with a multi-faceted problem, whereby diverse and diverging factors are interconnected with one another.[3]

Without any doubt, the technical pillar of the phenomenon of globalisation is the immense progress of communications technology at the end of the twentieth century. This development, often described as the technological revolution, can easily be compared with the industrial revolution at the beginning of the nineteenth century. Modern means of communication, symbolised by the Internet, enable everybody to worldwide communication at relatively low cost.[4] Obviously, this facilitation of worldwide communication has brought about a slowly evolving change of consciousness in the sense of a global 'belonging together' of the entire world in the 'spaceship Earth'.[5] But this technological revolution is only the basis for important and dynamic changes in the world economy. Here, it is

1 The Economist (1997) at 103.
2 Sur (1997) at 429.
3 See from a legal point of view Delbrück (1993); from a sociological perspective Beck (1997).
4 Malanczuk (1998) p 7.
5 Beck (1997) p 28ff.

not only the factor that, after the end of the Uruguay-Round of the GATT, with the establishment of the WTO and the considerable abandoning of customs for goods and the inclusion of services, the worldwide opening of markets has got its constitutionalised legal framework.[6] Rather the modern means of communication paved the way for an understanding of the world as one single market. As a consequence, enterprises act transnationally more than ever before. Important mergers – one example being the merger of Daimler-Benz and Chrysler in 1998[7] – are but the consequence of this comprehension of the world as one market in which a favourable allocation of – human and capital – resources can best be achieved by so-called 'global players'. Particularly, a global division of labour in the production process by using a most favourable allocation at lowest costs has become reality.[8] The forming of strategic alliances and mergers of enterprises may not even have reached its peak. Those merged enterprises are enabled to transfer capital and resources just within their own realm. It is obvious that under this new setting these transnational enterprises which act beyond boundaries will play an increasingly important role. This is demonstrated by the fact that at the moment approximately one-third of the world trade is just intra-transnational enterprise trade.

Moreover, the progress of technology has stimulated private financial markets to an incredible increase of global financial transactions beyond any state control. Today, the daily volume of such global financial transactions is estimated to be approximately two trillion US dollars.[9]

Besides these technological and economic ramifications of globalisation this phenomenon has still another dimension. What we have been witnessing for the last 20 years or so in an increasing way is the existence of so-called global problems. The destruction of the environment, the depletion of the ozone layer, migration at a worldwide scale as a result of under-development or ethnic problems, a worldwide organised drug traffic, terrorism and the proliferation of nuclear material clearly confront the international community with a new type of problem to which the traditional nation-state alone may not have an appropriate answer.[10]

Finally, the rapid growth of tourism is another facet contributing to an understanding of the world as one global entity.

In summary, therefore, one can observe three elements of globalisation which increasingly challenge the structure of the current international system. First, autonomous transnational actors gain, in a growing way, political negotiation power. Second, global problems demand answers beyond state and inter-governmental regulation. And third, social and political integration is subject to profound change.

Against this empirical background of globalisation, the following sections first, analyse possible challenges to the traditional notion of statehood, then, second, consider possible consequences for international law, which will finally allow for a tentative answer to the question whether globalisation really brings about a change of paradigm to international law, and in which direction the legal regulation of international relations could go in the twenty-first century.

---

6 Stoll (1994); Jackson (1996).
7 Frankfurter Allgemeine Zeitung (1998).
8 Compare Nunnenkamp (1996).
9 Kaiser (1998) p 4.
10 Delbrück (1993); Kaiser (1998) p 705.

CHALLENGES TO STATEHOOD

Based on the introductory description of globalisation, this section is concerned with a more thorough description of possible challenges to statehood. Thereby it should become clear that the new type of problems, as well as new and emerging actors, bring about a tendency to denationalisation.

Policy fields concerning global problems: environment, migration, under-development, terrorism, drug traffic and proliferation of nuclear material

All the problems which we are concerned with here have as their common denominator that they can no longer be solved exclusively by the sovereign nation-state.[11] This becomes very apparent if one looks into environmental degradation.[12] It is already a common saying that pollution can not be limited to national boundaries. Most environmental problems concern the environment per se, so that it makes no sense to preserve the environment in a specific area of a certain state and neglect the surrounding environment of the neighbouring state. Furthermore, difficult problems of transboundary pollution have concerned the international community for the last 20 years. Most importantly, the growing depletion of the ozone layer may threaten the climate of the entire world. The legal answer to these problems increasingly is the establishment of so-called *erga-omnes*-obligations.[13] These are such obligations which do not only exist as obligations vis-à-vis a certain state, but vis-à-vis the entire international community. Examples would be Article 218 of the Law of the Sea Convention of 1982, giving the port state a mandate to sanction a sea-polluting behaviour of others on the high seas on behalf of the international community, the Straddling Stock Convention of 1995, binding third states to a prohibition of fishery of straddling stocks, and those rules in the Convention for the Protection of the Ozone Layer of 1985 which for the protection of the ozone layer put serious restrictions on the sovereignty of states and of third parties.

With regard to the other global problems under consideration, international legislation has not yet achieved that standard. As regards migration and under-development, the international community has only very slowly started to develop concepts of more global character. In particular, in the field of environmental protection since the Rio Conference on Environment and Development of 1992, there is a growing tendency to link those fields, in the sense that an effective combat against environmental degradation can be achieved by developing countries only with the help of the developed world. But as regards migration, we are witnessing a very slow process of recognising that elements of under-development contribute a great deal to worldwide migration. The very slow process of establishing minority rights at the international level can furthermore be regarded as a first attempt to combat another factor contributing to the problem of migration.

In the areas of terrorism, drug traffic and the proliferation of nuclear material also we have some attempts to international legislation. It thus becomes apparent

---

11 Delbrück (1993).
12 For the environmental aspects of globalisation see Dolzer (1998) p 39.
13 Ragazzi 1997; Delbrück (1998).

that, particularly in Europe, the opening up of boundaries, coinciding with the abandoning of border controls, may call for deeper international co-operation to combat these problems. Finally, with regard to the proliferation of nuclear materials we are confronted with the fact that under the umbrella of the Non-Proliferation Treaty,[14] the obligations derived from this Treaty concern states and become ineffective if a state as implementing force does not have effective control of proliferation any longer, as seems to be the case in the former Soviet Union.

In summary all these problems show a global character. They fall short of solutions made by and within the nation-states themselves, and require an intensified international co-operation. In some cases, as, for example, with regard to the depletion of the ozone layer, it is even questionable whether a state-based solution, ie a solution by way of interstate co-operation, may still suffice. At least the establishment of already existing *erga-omnes*-obligations indicates very clearly a tendency of modern international law to transcend the traditional pattern of interstate co-operative rules and establish objective legal regimes.[15]

TRANSACTIONS OF PRIVATE ACTORS BEYOND STATE CONTROL

The second type of problem we are confronted with demonstrates even more clearly the new character of global problems. As we have seen in the introductory section, international financial markets have emancipated themselves to a certain extent from any state control. Private actors like individuals, banks or other private investors are capable of transferring enormous amounts of money or stocks around the entire globe at any given time. This may affect the economic performance of states considerably. As in the case of the recent Malaysian financial crisis, markets simply react with higher interest rates for those states, which try to cut themselves off from the global financial market. But the rather crucial point is that states may try only to a certain extent to set a legal framework for those economic transactions, but that they can neither fully regulate, nor effectively control them any longer.

And the same (ie a diminished control function of states) can be observed with regard to the Internet. The Internet provides global, decentralised, timeless, cheap, easy, digital, individual, secure, secret and anonymous communication. Because of its extra-jurisdictional and extra-territorial character, any international regulation for the Internet based on state jurisdiction is enormously complicated.[16] Yet the use of the Internet can bring about obvious dangers for providers and users as well as for states. Therefore, the regulatory and control function for this new medium must be considered a crucial question for the future. Should states still try to regulate a medium which, however, is characterised by its extra-territorial and extra-jurisdictional reach? This is a first and very important question; as a second problem, the question must be asked whether the traditional patterns of international legislation by states are still an accurate description of international law-making. With regard to this problem, due to this decreasing influence of states on the legal regulation of the use of the Internet, it seems to be most likely that regulatory regimes have to more intensively include the interests of the users, which may not necessarily be represented by states any

---

14 Of 1 July 1968, 729 UNTS 149.
15 Delbrück (1998).
16 See Mefford (1997) at 221.

longer. An example for the establishment of a code of conduct for the use of this new medium is the establishment of a 'netiquette', even though it does not have a very strong legally binding force.[17] At least, the use of the Internet indicates very clearly a need for transnational rules. Internet providers and Internet users need an effective representation of their interests as interests of international legal society as opposed to states.

New and emerging actors: transnational corporations and non-governmental organisations

As becomes clear from the preceeding section, the core structures of the international system are subject to profound changes. Transnational corporations as well as representatives of the international society become more and more active in international affairs and marginalise to a certain extent the formerly exclusive control function of states.[18] Thereby, on the one hand, the importance of the role of transnational corporations has been subject to discussion for some time. Their role has grown in more recent times; in an unprecedented way, they may influence the performance of the international economic and monetary system.

On the other hand, we can observe the growing importance of NGOs.[19] Those organisations generally do not involve any public or state element in them. Rather, they formulate interests which may even be directed against state interests. This becomes apparent if one looks into the role which is played, for example, by such important NGOs as Amnesty International or Greenpeace. Amnesty, on the one hand, organises campaigns for the protection of human rights. Their campaigns for 'prisoners of conscience' directly challenge states on human rights matters. On the other hand, their activities are even institutionalised within the human rights monitoring system due to their close involvement with the supervisory organs of international organisations for the protection of human rights. Not so clear is the current function of Greenpeace. Greenpeace is not *officially* involved with matters protecting the environment. Rather, its actions, again directed against states, are very often based on a self-given mandate.[20] Obviously, this causes problems.[21]

Nevertheless, both non-state actors and transnational corporations, as well as NGOs, are important representatives of the international civil society and cannot therefore be disregarded any longer by international law. As an answer to their increasingly important function, international law even recognises their status in specific areas.

Summary: the state is losing control and its uniqueness as actor in the international system – the tendency to denationalisation

In summary, the era of globalisation brings about serious challenges to statehood. The state has been the exclusive controlling actor of the international system

---

17 Mefford (1997) at 228.
18 For transnational corporations generally, see Muchlinski (1995).
19 See Hobe (1997).
20 Hobe (1997) at 198.
21 Hobe (1999) p 27.

since the modern international system came into existence after the Peace of Westphalia in 1648, which ended the Thirty Years War. Characterised by the notion of sovereignty, the state was the only manager of international relations. But, as we have observed, the current global problems involve as a common denominator a tendency towards denationalisation. Current financial transactions, as well as the use of the Internet, can no longer be regulated solely by interstate co-operation. Rather, the new and emerging actors demand for a fair share in the process of formulating rules of behaviour for activities in the international system. It may therefore be crucial to observe how international law can react to these challenges to statehood which, as discussed below, is itself subject to profound challenges in the era of globalisation.

CHALLENGES TO INTERNATIONAL LAW

Traditional international law as a law of co-ordinating state interests

The establishment of the modern sovereign state as an entity imposing government not only on people but also on a territory demarcated by boundaries is considered to have taken place at the end of the Thirty Years War with the Peace of Westphalia in 1648.[22] Both the peace instruments of Münster and Osnabrück laid down the right to warfare and to conclude peace as a privilege of the sovereign emperor. This brought about the capacity of emperors to act internally as sovereigns, in the sense of Jean Bodin, and externally to determine the course of international affairs.[23] Sovereignty at that time was understood in an absolute sense, and involved the natural right of the emperor to go to war. Until the middle of the nineteenth century these basic structures of the international system and of international law as a set of rules regulating the behaviour between independent actors changed relatively little. The peace system of the Vienna Congress of 1815 was a typical example for this co-ordinating character of international law. Preservation of peace was based on the co-ordination of interests of the sovereign powers of the Holy Alliance, as a 'Steering Committee' of the international society of states in the nineteenth century. The famous American international lawyer of German descent, Wolfgang Friedman, has characterised this international law as a 'law of coordination' in order to distinguish it from a 'law of cooperation' which started to develop in the middle of the nineteenth century and grew rapidly after 1945.[24] The Permanent Court of International Justice had described the law of co-ordination in the famous *Lotus* case of 1927 as follows:

> 'International law governs relations between independent States. The rules of law binding upon States therefore emanate from their own free will as expressed in conventions or by usages generally accepted as expressing principles of law and established in order to regulate the relations between these co-existing independent communities all with a view to the achievement of common aims. Restrictions upon the independence of States cannot therefore be presumed.'[25]

22 See de Zayas (1984) p 534.
23 Bodin (1583).
24 Friedman (1964).
25 Permanent Court of International Justice (1927), series a, No 9 p 18.

The crucial new development of the nineteenth century was the beginning of international institutionalised co-operation of states. This began in non-political fields, for example with the foundation of international River Commissions, for the administration of international watercourses and the International Telecommunication Union, for the regulation of telephone and telegraph traffic. These 'unions' for the first time in history established international bureaus and thus established a new era of institutionalised, ie permanent, state-to-state co-operation,[26] and were an expression of the states' growing perception of their own incapability to regulate independently areas of international concern.

The Hague Peace Conferences of 1899 and 1907 brought about the second line of development of international institutionalised co-operation: an establishment of rules of warfare with the final aim to eliminate the right to warfare.[27]

This institutionalised peace-keeping machinery was combined with the idea of a permanent establishment of state-to-state co-operation for the first time in the League of Nations of 1919. Here we can find an, albeit rather ineffective, peace-keeping machinery for the establishment of a system of collective security.[28]

The incapability of the League of Nations effectively to preserve international peace – as was clearly demonstrated with regard to the League's inactivity concerning Germany's aggressions at the outbreak of the Second World War – led to the establishment of a second international organisation of universal character, the Organisation of the United Nations, in 1945.

The first change of paradigm: from a law of co-existence to a law of co-operation

The Charter of the United Nations was the founding document of the United Nations Organisation and a basic document of international law which is often referred to as a 'Magna Carta' of international law, indicates the first change of paradigm of international law.[29] This becomes very apparent if one looks at the broadened notion of international peace as contained in the UN Charter, which gave the notion of peace a much broader scope. Not only did it involve the absence of war but the overall aim of the United Nations Organisation was to preserve peace by establishing conditions for the co-existence of states which would not give rise to further warfare. It is important to note that the Charter included the observance of human rights and a satisfactory standard of living for all states, to name but two of the most important contributing factors to international peace.[30] Most importantly, in article 2(4), the Charter completely abandoned the use of force. This was even more than the abandoning of the right to warfare in the Briand-Kellogg Pact which had characterised classical international law since 1928, and a revolution for classical international law since its inception 300 years ago. Today the non-use of force principle may be designated not only as being contained in the UN Charter, but also as a principle

---

26 Wolfrum (1983).
27 Duelffer (1998).
28 Delbrück (1992).
29 See for the normative impact of this change of paradigm in the preambula of the UN Charter: Hobe (1997).
30 See eg Delbrück (1996) p 14; Ermacora (1974) p 69.

of customary international law of ius cogens[31] character. It is therefore important to note that within these three centuries the notion of sovereignty had changed. It no longer involved any right to warfare. Moreover, the way was paved for a more intensive co-operation of states. Many problems of international character could no longer be resolved by the sovereign states themselves. The growing number of states – the number of UN member states has more than tripled from 51 founding members to the current 188 members – brought about a further need for intensified interstate co-operation. Co-operation in this sense means to compromise. And this again involved a changed notion of sovereignty. It is therefore fully justified to characterise the post-Second World War international law as a *law of co-operation*.

But at the threshold of the twenty-first century, the crucial question is whether this law of co-operation will be followed by a change of paradigm and replaced by a 'law of *globalisation*'. This involves two more detailed questions which will be addressed in the following and summarising section. First the question must be answered whether the new global problems will eventually lead to the complete replacing of the law of co-operation. Second, the characteristics of international law in the era of globalisation must be laid down.

THE ANSWER: A NEW CHANGE OF PARADIGM AT THE THRESHOLD OF THE TWENTY-FIRST CENTURY? TOWARD A TRANSNATIONAL LAW?

The concluding remarks will try to give some answers to the questions asked in the preceeding section; and it may be concluded that the denationalising effect of globalisation may indeed constitute a new change of paradigm of international law.

But this by no means includes a complete replacement of the law of co-operation of the second phase of the development of international law. Rather, based on the achievements of the international co-operative legal order some further development of international law may indicate some new directions as well.

The achievements of the international legal order based on a law of co-operation may be characterised by three major developments.

First, notwithstanding all the current problems of disregard of the UN and its Security Council in the case of regional attempts to secure international peace, the current trend since the end of the Cold War to UN 'humanitarian interventions'[32] must fully be supported.[33] It is a logical consequence of the broadening of the notion of peace that states can no longer treat their citizens as they like. One might even go so far as to understand international law in the new globalised environment as to imply an obligation for states to intervene in the affairs of other sovereign states, even by military means, in cases of severe humanitarian tragedies. The most recent example of such an understanding of human rights as being the necessary precondition for peace could arguably be NATO's military intervention in Kosovo, notwithstanding the problems of a lack of authorisation by the UN's Security Council.[34] Severe humanitarian tragedies of a certain intensity are therefore subject to public intervention. As has been

31 For the notion of ius cogens, see generally Hannikainen (1988).
32 Beyerlin (1995) p 926.
33 See generally to humanitarian interventions Gading (1996).
34 For a discussion of these problems in terms of a reincarnation of the theory of just war, see Hobe (2001).

indicated by the Security Council in the cases of the Kurds in Iraq,[35] and the humanitarian tragedies in Rwanda and Somalia, as well as in the case of restoring democracy in Haiti,[36] the severe infringement of basic human rights gives rise to international intervention. This is fully in line with the shrinking notion of state sovereignty in terms of the preservation of human rights.[37] Human rights are not *granted* by states, but have to be recognised by them as the basic characteristic of human dignity. If states cannot guarantee their responsibility for the preservation of human rights it is for the international community to intervene if, and under the condition that, it can better preserve the observance of human rights.

The second important development is the growing recognition of principles of the observance of the rule of law and of democracy. The Summit of the Security Council in January 1992 gave an impressive example for the strengthening of the rule of law within fora of international institutionalised co-operation; and the intervention of the UN in Haiti in order to restore democracy is a strong indication of the commitment of the international community to secure democratic government.[38] As indicated by Thomas Frank, the 'emerging right to democratic governance' is an expression of a widespread development all over the world.[39]

Moreover, and third, the establishment of the International Criminal Tribunals for the Former Yugoslavia and for Rwanda,[40] as well as the adoption of the Statute of the International Criminal Court in 1998[41] are important and encouraging signs for the securing of an international legal minimum order. Thereby the still existing difficulties, mostly in the area of enforcing the jurisdiction of the ICTY as well as of the upcoming International Criminal Court may not be overlooked. This 'enforcement' is still very much based on consensus and co-operation of states. But the visible influence of the new international criminal law even on national courts might encourage a new form of co-operation between national courts and international criminal tribunals. We must also not overlook the fact that the principle of individual criminal responsibility is an important step not only of the recognition of the individual as a growing subject of international law, but also of the fact that international law may directly impose rights, and in this case obligations, upon individuals.[42]

All these developments centre around the core achievement of the post-Second World War legal order, the prohibition of the use of force in international relations. And these developments indicate that the formerly completely independent and sovereign nation-state has fundamentally changed its character since 1648, and even since 1945.[43] Independence as the core characteristic of the international system, as demonstrated by the Permanent Court of International

---

35 Malanczuk (1991).
36 Glennon (1995).
37 See Hobe (1997) p 136 and (1998) p 216.
38 Schachter (1984).
39 Franck (1992).
40 UN SC Resolutions 808 (1993) of 22 February 1993 and 827 (1993) of 25 May 1993 establishing the Tribunal of the Former Yugoslavia, in (1993) ILM p 1203; and UN Resolution (1994) 955 of 8 November 1994 (Rwanda), in (1994) ILM p 1602. For a review of the general development see M Cherif Bassiouni *The Ad Hoc Tribunal of the Former Yugoslavia: Commentaries on Statutes and Rules* (1995) passim; and P Manikas *The Law of the International Tribunal for the Former Yugoslavia* (1996) pp 1ff, 199ff.
41 Ambos (1998) p 3743.
42 Hobe (1999) p 115.
43 See for this and the following Hobe (1997) p 136 and (1998) p 216.

Justice in 1927, has now been replaced by interdependence of all states. And it has brought about an interstate co-operative order which has not abandoned sovereignty, but rather altered its notion. The modern 'open' sovereign state is not allowed to use force in international relations any more; it is not allowed to treat its citizens below a minimum standard of human rights; it shows a tendency to observe the principles of the rules of law and democracy; and it accepts rules of criminal law, even for individual 'acts of state'. These are all important indications of the fact that the need for international institutionalised co-operation has become a core ingredient of modern statehood. This modern statehood recognises the need for international institutionalised co-operation by opening up its own legal order toward the international legal order and by giving inputs to the international legal order by way of an expansion of its own legal achievements, for example, the observance of the rules of law and democracy.

Any effective regulation of the current global problems must therefore be based on the existing legal co-operative order. This, first of all, means that the UN, as the universal international organisation, has still to build the organisational framework for efforts to come to terms with global problems. But the crucial new element of the international legal order in the era of globalisation is the new dimension of global problems, as well as the emergence of the new actors.[44] Therefore, a logical consequence of the enlargement of actors must be their involvement in international law-making. Partly, this involvement already can be observed today. If one looks, for example, into the role which is played by NGOs, one can give some examples of their at least indirect involvement in international law-making: Landmine Convention of 1997; Convention on the Right of the Child of 1989; Desertification Convention of 1994. On the other hand, the involvement of, for example, NGOs and transnational corporations in the international legal order is of course the bearing of a legal responsibility of these entities. Here the international legal order is still at a very early stage of formulating rules. These are still rather unbinding, for example, in the form of so called 'codes of conduct'. But international criminal law indicates a direction in which it is possible to bind even non-state actors to international legal rules. And those legal rules must be elaborated not only by states, but also by these non-state actors.

We are, therefore, obviously also confronted with the necessity of rethinking the sources of international law. Traditionally all of the main sources as listed in article 38, paragraph 1 of the Statute of the International Court of Justice – international conventions, custom and the general principles of law as recognised by peace-loving states – very much centre around the law-making function of states. It is the state which, besides inter-governmental organisations – ie organisations composed of states – enters into agreements and thus creates conventional international law. It is mostly states (and inter-governmental organisations) which form, through their practice and opinio iuris, customary international law. And the general principles of law themselves refer to the legal order of states all over the world. But it is quite questionable whether this description still holds true if new actors enter the international scene, as is the case in the era of globalisation. Questions of liability for Internet providers or for multinational enterprises or, as in the case of the oil-platform 'Brent Spar', for NGOs such as Greenpeace, seem to be a logical consequence for their future activities. But can these rules solely be drafted by states, as has been done

---

44 See for this and the following Hobe (1997) p 191 and (1999) p 28.

traditionally? The growing activities of NGOs in the legislative sector seem clearly to indicate that interests of the international society, as apart from states, somehow must be represented and included in the new type of international law. Consequently, the practice of NGOs and multinational enterprises will undoubtedly have greater significance in the future if they come to formulate rules of customary international law.[45]

It seems therefore to be justifiable to speak of a new character of international law in the era of globalisation. If one looks, for example, for a legal regime for the use of the Internet or some ground rules of behaviour for transnational corporations with regard to the observance of human rights (for example, children at work) and if one furthermore takes into account that most probably those rules have to be negotiated as a co-operative effort of states and non-state actors one may be inclined not to speak of international law as state-made law any longer but of a *transnational* law,[46] thus indicating the substantial further development of this law. This new law is, on the one hand, based on the law of co-operation, but transcends it by the new formation of law-creating entities. On the other hand, it is characterised by the recognition of an objective legal régime of certain ground rules of just cogens and erga omnes character which binds even the new actors. As a bottom line, the new transnational law also will recognise state sovereignty as one core pillar of the international legal order. But this state sovereignty will again be subject to important changes and, if you will, important restrictions. Because in view of the global problems, for example of environmental degradation, and in view of the state's incapability exclusively to shape regulations for the use of the Internet or for international financial transactions of transnational corporations, the new approach to sovereignty should be designated as '*enlightened sovereignty*'.[47] Enlightened sovereignty pays tribute to the fact that living on 'spaceship Earth' involves the living in a community of responsible states and the taking into account of non-state interests.

Also, enlightened sovereignty pays tribute to the fact that those tasks which can only be fulfilled by international regulation must be performed at the adequate level of government, be it at universal, at regional or at state level. The maxim of subsidiarity thus requires to fulfil tasks always at the adequate level of government whereby the presumption in favour of national solutions is in principle a rebuttable one.

Only if the international community perceives itself in this enlightened way as acting for present and future generations may it fulfil its responsibility in a satisfactory manner. It may therefore be hoped that the international community can live up to this responsibility in the twenty-first century. If this is the case, the writer is convinced that the new transnational law will help to guarantee the survival of mankind.

---

45 Charney (1993).
46 Others, like J Delbrück 'Von der Staatenordnung über die internationale institutionelle Kooperation zur "supraterritorial or global governance": Wandel des zwischenstaatlichen Völkerrechts zur Rechtsordnung der Menschen und Völker?' in *Liber Amicorum for Carl Friedrich v Weizsäcker* (forthcoming) (quoted from manuscript, p 13) speak of a 'third legal order' like the lex mercatoria; see to lex mercatoria Lord Mustill 'The New Lex Mercatoria: The first Twenty-Five Years' in *Liber Amicorum Lord Wilberforce* (1987) p 149. Very critically with regard to transnational law, O Kimminich *Einführung in das Völkerrecht* (6th edn, 1997) p 32; more moderate, the 7th edn, by O Kimminich and S Hobe *Einführung in das Völkerrecht* (2000) pp 14, 15.
47 Hobe (1999) p 31.

Select bibliography

Ambos, K, (1998) Der neue Internationale Strafgerichtshof – ein Überblick, 51 Neue Juristische Wochenschrift, p 3743.

Bassiouni, M C, (1995) *The Ad Hoc Tribunal of the Former Yugoslavia: Commentaries on Statutes and Rules.*

Beck, U, (1997) *Was ist Globalisierung?*

Beyerlin, U, (1995) *Humanitarian Intervention, Encyclopedia of Public International Law,* vol II, p 926.

Bodin, J, (1583) *Les six Livres de la République, Paris.*

Charney, J, (1993) 'Universal International Law', 87 AJIL 529.

Delbrück, J, (1992) 'Collective Security', in *Encyclopedia of Public International Law,* vol I, p 646.

—(1993a), 'Globalization of Law, Politics and Markets – Implications for Domestic Law. A European Perspective', 1 Ind J Global Legal Studies 9.

—(1993b) 'A More Effective International Law or a New "World Law"', 68 Ind JL 705.

—(1996) 'Menschenrechte – Grundlage des Friedens' in K Dicke, S Hobe, et al (eds), *Die Konstitution des Friedens als Rechtsordnung,* 241.

—(1998) 'Laws in the Public Interest – Some Observations on the Foundations and Identification of erga omnes Norms in International Law' in V Götz, P Selmer and R Wolfrum (eds), *Liber Amicorum G. Jaenicke,* p 17.

—(forthcoming) 'Wandel des zwischenstaatlichen Völkerrechts zur Rechtsordnung der Menschen und Völker?' in *Liber Amicorum for Carl Friedrich v Weizsäcker.*

De Zayas, A-M, (1984) 'Westphalia, Peace of (1648)' in R Bernhardt (ed), *Encyclopedia of Public International Law,* Instalment 7.

Dolzer, R, (1998) 'Konzeption, Finanzierung und Durchführung des globalen Umweltschutzes', in V Götz, P Selmer and R Wolfrun (eds), *Liber Amicorum Gúnther Jaenicke,* p 37.

Duelffer, J, (1998) 'Regeln gegen den Krieg? Die Haager Friedenskonferenzen von 1899 und 1907 in der internationalen Politik' Berlin.

Economist, The (1997) 'On Globalisation', 18 October, at 103.

Ermacora, F, (1974) *Menschenrechte in der sich wandelnden Welt,* vol 1.

Franck, T M, (1992) 'The Emerging Right to Democratic Governance', 86 AJIL 46.

Frankfurter Allgemeine Zeitung (1998) Nr 109 , 12. 5, p 3.

Friedmann, W, (1964) *The Changing Structure of International Law.*

Gading, H, (1996) *Der Schutz grundlegender Menschenrechte durch militärische Maßnahmen des Sicherheitsrates – das Ende staatlicher Souveränität?, Berlin.*

Glennon, M, (1995) 'Sovereignty and Community after Haiti: Rethinking the Collective Use of Force', 89 AJIL 70.

Hannikainen, L, (1988) *Peremptory Norms (ius cogens) in International Law, Helsinki.*

Hobe, S, (1997a) 'Global Challenges to Statehood: The Increasingly Important Role of Nongovernmental Organizations', 5 Ind J Global Legal Studies 191.

—(1997b) 'Statehood at the End of the 20th Century – The Model of the "Open State": A German Perspective', 72 Austrian Review of International and European Law 127.

—(ed), (1997c) *Die Präambel der UN-Charta im Lichte der aktuellen Völkerrechtsentwicklung*, Berlin.

—(1997d) 'Global Challenges to Statehood: The Increasingly Important Role of Nongovernmental Organizations', 5 Ind J Global Legal Studies 191.

—(1998) *Der offene Verfassungsstaat zwischen Souveränität und Interdependenz*, Berlin.

—(1999a) *Völkerrecht im Zeitalter der Globalisierung – Perspektiven der Völkerrechtsentwicklung im 21. Jahrhundert*, Köln.

—(1999b) 'Individuals and Groups as Global Actors: The Denationalization of International Transactions', in R Hofmann (ed), *Non-State Actors as new Subjects of International Law. International Law – From the Traditional State Order Towards the Law of the Global Community*, p 115.

—(2001) 'NATO Intervention im Kosovo – Eine Rückkehr zur Lehre vom gerechten Krieg?', in D Dörr, U Fink, Chr Hillgruber, B Kempen and D Murswick (eds), *Die Macht des Geistes Liber Amicorum Hartmut Schiedermair*, p 819.

Jackson, J H, (1996) 'Appraising the Launch and Functioning of the WTO', 39 German Yearbook of International Law 20.

Kaiser, K, (1998) *Globalisierung als Problem der Demokratie, Internationale Politik*, p 3.

Kinninich, O, and Hobe, S, (2000) *Einführung in das Völkerrecht* (7th edn).

Malanczuk, P, (1991) 'The Kurdish Crisis and Allied Intervention in the Aftermath of the Second Gulf War', 2 EJIL114.

—(1998) 'Globalization and the Future of Sovereign States', in F Weiss, K Ginther and P de Waart (eds), *International Economic Law with a Human Face*.

Manikas, P, (1996) *The Law of the International Tribunal for the Former Yugoslavia*.

Mefford, A, (1997) 'Lex Informatica: Foundations of Law on the Internet', 5 Ind J Global Legal Studies 211.

Muchlinski, P, (1995) *Multinational Enterprises and the Law*.

Mustill, Lord, (1987) 'The New Lex Mercatoria: The first Twenty-Five Years' in G Slynn (ed), *Liber Amicorum Lord Wilberforce*, p 149.

Nunnenkamp, P, (1996) 'Winners and Losers in the Global Economy: Recent Trends in the International Division of Labor, Major Implications and Critical Policy Challenges', 39 German Yearbook of International Law 42.

Permanent Court of International Justice (1927) Series A, No 9, p 18.

Ragazzi, M, (1997) *The Concept of International Obligations Erga Omnes*.

Schachter, O, (1984) 'The Legality of Pro-Democratic Interventions', 78 AJIL 645.

Stoll, P-T, (1994) 'Die World Trade Organization, neue Welthandelsorganisation neue Welthandelsordnung. Ergebnisse der Uruguay-Runde des GATT', 54 Zeitschrift für ausländisches öffentliches Recht und Völkerrecht 214.

Sur, S, (1997) 'The State between Fragmentation and Globalisation', 3 EJIL 421.

UN Charter (1945) 557 UNIS.

UN SC Res. 808 (1993) of 22 February 1993, resp. res. 827 (1993) of 25 May 1993, I.L.M. 1993, p. 1203, and UN res. 955 of 8 November 1994 (Rwanda), in: I.L.M. 1994, p. 1602

Wolfrum, R, (1983) 'International Administrative Unions', 5 Encyclopedia of Public International Law 42.

—(ed), (1998) *Liber Amicorum G. Jaenicke.*

Chapter 19

Racism in civil conflict: domestic and global dimensions

J MERTUS[1]

This chapter examines the role of racism in civil conflicts and identifies the internal and global dimensions of conflict that transnational lawyers must appreciate if their efforts for conflict prevention are to be effective. 'Racism' as understood here is a programme of political action whereby one group finds justification for domination of the other. Political mobilisation for domination can take many forms, but the ideology of racism relies upon perceived notions of genetic superiority and acts and processes of de-humanisation of the 'naturally' inferior 'other'. Through racial ideology, both an aggressive and defensive consciousness can be articulated. 'Racial thinking is not merely an expression of the need to dominate and oppress', Frank Füerdi explains, '[a]t times, it expresses a *defensive* response; a manifestation of the fear of losing power'.[2]

The state of racism is a state of violence. Racism constitutes *structural violence* to the extent that it produces and institutionalises a pervasive pattern of discrimination and disadvantage for specific ethnic and racial groups. The lived reality of structural violence is a continual negotiation of conflict. None the less, racism does not always lead to concerted, co-ordinated violence between two or more groups. While racism may be a tool for proponents of violent conflict, it alone does not result in widespread violence, absent the added input of certain conditions and catalysts. The concept of race or ethnicity is socially constructed within the context of power struggles.[3] As such, it is possible to identify and address the conditions that create incentives for political elites to employ racist ideology as a method of gaining power and waging war. This chapter finds that the societies in which racism plays a role in violent conflict share identifiable internal characteristics and, in particular, historical systems for differentiation

1   Julie Mertus is an associate professor in the Department of International Peace and Conflict Resolution at American University, School of International Service. She gratefully acknowledges the research assistance of Katherine Guernsey and the critical input of Pita Ogaba Agbese, Mohammad-Mahmoud Mohamedou, Sakile Camara, Kevin Hill, Janet Lord and the participants in the International Council on Human Rights Policy's Consultation on Racism and Human Rights, Geneva, 3–4 December 1999.
2   Füredi (1998) p 25.
3   See Agbese (1999). Agbese explains: 'Contestation over material resources frames the context under which social identities of race and ethnicity are constructed. Once racial or ethnic classifications have been made, social relations are then conditioned on those categorisations.' (At 8.)

and extreme social polarisation, structural violence, racist propaganda and a culture of victimisation. Still, these internal dimensions of conflict are unlikely to lead to violent conflict without the influence of additional catalysts of a global/ trans-boundary nature, such as increased marginalisation of economies of the South, the expanding power of diaspora communities, a burgeoning arms trade and the increased willingness of international bodies to intervene in civil conflicts.

Legal scholars have remarked on the increasing relevance of transnational law for civil conflict, including humanitarian and human rights law as well as customary and treaty law pertaining to the recognition of states, state secession and the use of force.[4] As David Wippman observes: 'virtually all of the central issues arising out of ethnic conflict implicate key aspects of international law and, from a lawyer's standpoint, should be regulated by international law.'[5] This chapter does not pretend to catalogue all of the transnational legal issues pertaining to conflict. Instead, it takes a step backwards and identifies underlying domestic and global/trans-boundary dimensions of conflict. Such a discussion is considered a necessary component of understanding the relevance of transnational law as applied to cases of civil conflict. An underlying theme considers that the process of globalisation, marked both by increased interconnectedness and accelerated fragmentation,[6] acts as a stimulant for conflict, but that in some instances this is unavoidable, and even desirable. It is in this context that transnational legal processes and transnational human rights non-governmental organisations (NGOs) are considered for their potential to help manage conflict before it escalates into violent conflict.

The conflicts in Rwanda and Kosovo serve as case studies where racist ideology served as the impetus for brutal racist acts, as hate manifested itself in attempts to destroy the 'other'. The mass killings in Rwanda and massive deportation of the population in Kosovo were, at their core, stridently racist acts. In each case, violent conflict was made possible because of the dehumanisation of a conceptual 'other.' The 'other' symbolised all those outside the realm of moral obligation; severe and systematic violent acts were said to be necessary to 'preserve' the superior groups, that is the Serbs or Hutus. And yet racism did not *cause* the outbreak of war in Rwanda and Kosovo. The mainstream media portrayed both conflicts as inevitable in its characterisation of the unleashing of primordial ethnic hatred and the eruption of primitive tribalism. It is clear, however, that violent results were not pre-ordained by ancient hatreds in either case. Rather, violence in Rwanda and Kosovo emanated from systematic public structures of differentiation that contributed to the development of a nationalist/racist ideology ripe for manipulation by elites. The violence was fostered by the structural and institutional shortcomings of societies, while global/trans-boundary factors tipped the scale to all-out war.

The purpose of this chapter is to explore the interaction of internal and global/trans-boundary conditions that give rise to identity conflict. The discussion is divided into three parts. First, the chapter provides historical context to the case studies in briefly outlining the use of group classification schemes in Kosovo and Rwanda, describing their role in the conflicts and analysing the responses of

---

4   See generally Wippman (1998).
5   Wippman (1998) p 2.
6   See Picciotto (1996–97); Falk (1997).

the international community in each case. Second, building on the Kosovo and Rwanda illustrations, the chapter identifies the internal characteristics of societies where conflicts have a discernible racial dimension. Finally, the chapter suggests global/trans-boundary factors which aggravate conflict on the one hand, and those which hold the potential for ameliorating conflict, on the other.

CLASSIFICATION SYSTEMS IN RWANDA AND KOSOVO: POTENT FOR CONFLICT

In fundamentally different ways, political elites in Rwanda and Kosovo used group classification schemes to gain power and maintain control. While Rwandan history is marked by colonialism and Yugoslavia's history was shaped by a Tito-style, decentralised federal government, the impact of extreme social polarisation in both cases was strikingly similar. In Rwanda and Kosovo politicians had the incentive and ability for political mobilisation to ground itself in a racist ideology. Each society was transformed from one in which group difference was 'one among many political dimensions of conflict, to one in which it [became] the sole dimension of conflict'.[7] Further, in each case, the international community issued empty promises to uphold transnational legal norms.

Rwanda

The strategy of racial classification: from colonialism to modern times

Traditionally, there had been 'no age-old animosity' between the Hutus and Tutsis of Rwanda. The tensions between the groups were of relatively recent origin, largely spurred on by European pseudo-science and perpetuated by African politicians as a tool for gaining and maintaining power.

Prior to European colonisation, Hutus and Tutsis lived in a somewhat divided society, but not one based upon racism. Hutus farmed and Tutsis raised cattle, but otherwise they intermarried, fought together, shared a national god ('Imana'), a national language (Kinyarwanda), lived in villages together and were loyal to their Mwami (king), regardless of his tribal background.[8] The mixing of the groups was so extensive that 'ethnographers and historians have lately come to agree that Hutus and Tutsis cannot properly be called distinct ethnic groups'.[9] Prior to the 1950s, there were no reported incidents of racism or violence between the two groups.

Germany was the first to colonise Rwanda, and Germans colonisers subscribed to the 'Victorian race theory' according to which Hutus were the descendants of Ham and, therefore, were destined to be slaves.[10] This gave rise to the colonial tendency to favour Tutsis over Hutus, a practice that was continued in more elaborate fashion by the Belgians, who assumed administering authority over Rwanda after the First World War under the League of Nations system. Belgian 'scientists' undertook physical studies of Hutus and Tutsis in order to establish

---

7 De Figueiredo and Weingast (1999) p 293.
8 Corry (1998).
9 Gourevitch (1998) p 48. See also Parker (1994); Kagame (1999) pp 71–72; Lemarchand (1970); African Rights (1995) pp 2–10; Prunier (1995).
10 Corry (1998).

the physical differences between the two groups. The Belgians believed that because the Tutsi nose was narrower and longer (and closer in resemblance to the Belgian nose), the Tutsis were somehow more noble and innately cognitively superior to the Hutus and other Africans.[11] As a result, the Belgian officials reserved the best jobs in the administrative system for Tutsis. Thus, Tutsis dominated local rule in Rwanda during the colonial period, at which time they constituted 17% of the population.

The post-colonial government of Rwanda continued the practice of political mobilisation along ethnic lines. In 1959, Rwanda's first president, Gregoire Kayibanda, rode a wave of anti-Tutsi violence to come to power.[12] The 1959 revolution in Rwanda gave an ostensible democratic respectability to Hutu rule, but it failed to give institutional expression to the rights of the Tutsi minority.[13] Instead, it perpetrated systematic racial classification and discrimination based upon group lines. This reversal of the country's original colonial policy in which power was concentrated in the Hutu majority was accomplished with the blessing – and even at the instigation – of the Belgian colonialists. As Philip Gourevitch explains, in 1960 a Belgian colonel named Guy Logiest staged a coup d'etat by executive fiat, replacing Tutsi chiefs with Hutu chiefs and giving tacit approval when Hutus began organising violence against Tutsis.[14] The ensuing violence led to the flight of about half of the Tutsi population to neighbouring states.[15]

In late 1960, Colonel Logiest proudly proclaimed that 'the revolution is over'. On taking office, Gregoire Kayibanda declared, 'democracy has triumphed over feudalism.'[16]

The 'democratic turn' pleased some Western observers but, as Gourevitch observes, it was a democratic charade. 'So Hutu dictatorship masqueraded as popular democracy, and Rwanda's power struggles became an internal affair of the Hutu elite, very much as the feuds among royal Tutsi clans had been in the past.'[17]

From their posts in Uganda and Burundi, exiled Tutsi leaders repeatedly launched attacks on Rwandan territory to regain power. Rwanda's Hutu leaders repelled those attacks and perpetrated reprisals against local Tutsis. The worst violence occurred shortly before Christmas in 1963 when several hundred Tutsis crossed into Rwandan territory from their camps in Burundi and advanced to a position within 12 miles of Kigali. Rwandan forces under Belgian command wiped out the insurgents, and President Kayibanda unleashed a reign of terror over Tutsis by announcing a state of national emergency to combat 'counter-revolutionaries'.[18]

The fighting had subsided by the time a 1973 coup brought to power Juvenal Habyarimana, a Hutu from a clan in the north. Habyarimana's clan-based oligarchy, known as the *akazu* ('little house'), practised discrimination against both Hutus from southern Rwanda and Tutsis.[19] 'Habyarimana and the *akazu* had learned the lessons of the Hutu-Tutsi opposition in the Kayibanda regime and used

11 Chege (1996–97).
12 Jones (1999) p 123.
13 See Lemarchand (1993).
14 Gourevitch (1998) p 60.
15 Watson (1991).
16 Watson (1991).
17 Watson (1991) p 61.
18 Corry (1998).
19 Newbury (1992).

ethnic tension to strengthen their own rule', Bruce Jones observes.[20] While the ethnic tension manifested itself as discrimination and abuse, it did not erupt into communal violence for 16 years.

In the late 1980s, the international community introduced structural adjustment programme conditionalities and exerted diplomatic pressure to push for democratic and human rights reforms in Rwanda. As a result of the structural adjustment initiatives, the government's budget was slashed in half, taxes rose and famine grew widespread. Habyarimana announced democratic reforms in early 1990, only to shelve them months later when a group of Ugandan Tutsi invaded Rwanda in October 1990, under the banner of the 'Rwanda Patriotic Front' (RPF). Hutu leaders battled the invaders and attacked domestic Tutsis thought to be RPF sympathisers. In contrast to the conflicts of the 1960s, however, the Tutsi invaders made significant advances. Not only did the RPF gain a small parcel of territory in northern Rwanda, they also garnered the support of opposition Hutu and the sympathy of much of the international community. The akazu intensified their rhetorical and violent attacks against Tutsis, thereby attempting to unify all Hutu against a common enemy. The Rwandan government, however, was dependent upon foreign aid and vulnerable to international pressure for political negotiations.

In April 1992, international pressure led to the creation of a coalition government in Rwanda, whereby power was shared with opposition parties and political negotiations were undertaken with the RPF. Culminating in 1994, the Arusha Peace Accords represented a radical transfer of power, from the akazu to a coalition government that would include the regime, opposition parties and the RPF. The Arusha settlement 'produced violent reactions among power holders in Kigali'.[21] In particular, the ruling regime was insulted by being assigned a weak position in the transitional government and felt threatened by the powerful role the RPF was to have in the integrated army.

Supporters of the regime would not relinquish power so easily; instead they launched an intensified racist propaganda campaign against the Tutsis and 'created widespread fear among the Rwandan population – not out of nothing, but through the skilful manipulation of an existing social cleavage, ethnicity'.[22] These fears were not allayed by the international community's promise at Arusha to deploy a multinational force in Rwanda to guarantee peace and security. This force, the UN Mission in Rwanda (UNAMIR),[23] was slow to be deployed and was generally regarded by locals as a paper tiger.

The outbreak of genocidal conflict

On 6 April 1994, a plane carrying President Juvenal Habyarimana of Rwanda and the president of Burundi was shot down while attempting to land at Kigali.[24] The Hutu government blamed the attack on Tutsi rebels of the RPF. The violence, however, represented instead an effort by the akazu and its supporters to consolidate Hutu power by wiping out the Tutsis. As Human Rights Watch observed in their 1999 report:

20 Jones (1999) p 123.
21 Jones (1999) p 124. See also Adelman, Suhrke and Jones (1996).
22 Jones (1999) p 126.
23 Established under Security Council Resolution 872, 5 October 1993.
24 Anonymous (1994c).

'This genocide resulted from the deliberate choice of a modern elite to foster hatred and fear to keep itself in power. This small, privileged group first set the majority against the minority to counter a growing political opposition within Rwanda. Then, faced with RPF success on the battlefield and at the negotiating table, these few power holders transformed the strategy of ethnic division into genocide. They believed that the extermination campaign would restore the solidarity of the Hutu under their leadership and help them win the war, or at least improve their chances of negotiating a favourable peace. They seized control of the state and used its machinery and its authority to carry out the slaughter.'[25]

Supporting evidence for the strategic nature of the conflict includes the speed with which the killings began and the methodical nature of the violence. Rwandan authorities had been distributing weapons as early as 1992, with more extensive distributions occurring in 1993 and 1994.[26] Within one hour of the president's plane crash, Kigali, the capital of Rwanda, had been surrounded by roadblocks and the killings had begun.[27] Within a week of the plane crash, approximately 20,000 people had been killed in Kigali and the immediately surrounding areas. The total killed ran into the hundreds of thousands.

Further support for the premise that the conflict was strategically manipulated comes from the evidence of killings of non-Tutsis. Some of the earliest victims included Prime Minister Agathe Uwilingiyimana and President of the Supreme Court Joseph Kavaruganda, both Hutus.[28] In addition, those who formed part of the opposition politicians were killed along with independent journalists, human rights activists and senior civil servants.[29] Other groups targeted at an early stage included members of the international community, and, in particular, ten Belgium peacekeepers who were first taken hostage and later killed.

The existence of other victims does not detract from the fact that the violence in Rwanda was, at its core, a planned genocide.[30] The attack was an attempt to destroy the whole Tutsi population. The international community had knowledge of the planned atrocities[31] and yet it failed to take effective action, either to prevent the violence or to take action to stop it once it had already begun. On the contrary, the killing of the Belgian peacekeepers led to a withdrawal of all but a handful of UN troops. While the UN eventually sent fresh troops into Rwanda, they did not arrive until the genocidal killings were over.

Kosovo

Manipulation of group classifications: from Tito's Yugoslavia to Milosevic

In Tito's Yugoslavia, officially everyone enjoyed Yugoslav nationality and stood united for 'brotherhood and unity'. In constitutional terms, however, the Yugoslavia people were divided into two categories – in Zoran Paijic's terms, the 'hosts and the historical guests'.[32] Under this system, the hosts, or 'nations' (*narod*)

---

25 Human Rights Watch (1999b) p 1–2.
26 Human Rights Watch (1999b) p 2.
27 Human Rights Watch/Africa (1994) pp 1, 3.
28 Human Rights Watch/Africa (1994) p 3. See also Parker (1994).
29 African Rights (1995) p xxi. See also Anonymous (1994a).
30 Human Rights Watch (1999b) pp 1–2.
31 Scheffer (1998) p 163.
32 Paijic (1995) p 162.

included: Serbs, Croats, Slovenes, Macedonians, Montenegrins and Muslims. The guests, or 'nationalities' (*narodnosti*), included groups with a national homeland elsewhere: Albanians, Hungarians, Italians, Bulgarians, Turks, Slovaks, Czechs and Russians. Those without a homeland elsewhere, such as the Romany and Vlachs, were ignored. These divisions according to three classifications were significant, as national status was an indicator of belonging and privilege.

Under the 1974 Constitution, power was decentralised from the federal to the republic level. Thus, each of Yugoslavia's six republics and two provinces had a central bank and separate police, educational and judicial systems. These units, with the exception of Bosnia-Herzegovina, were de facto organised largely around national identity, based on the majority nation of the region. Thus, rewards were based on national status. Through such arrangements, national status, 'which had seemingly been buried by the 1971 intervention [Tito's crushing of nationalist movements in Croatia], returned by the back door'.[33]

The 'nationality key' system was another institutional arrangement which pushed national identity to the fore. A proportional representation scheme – the 'key' system – became a means for many incompetent and/or corrupt party members to achieve positions of importance on the basis of the national status. Within each republic or province, members of the majority nation complained of the incompetence of the members of the minority nation who were promoted to high positions of power; widespread backlash against the 'key' system led to a widening of national divides.[34]

During the years after Tito's death, the population of Yugoslavia was increasingly forced into alignments based upon national identity. Many politicians used the notion of 'sovereignty' as a rhetorical device, claiming that their own group's 'sovereignty' was being violated by another group.[35] Similarly, national status was used as a rhetorical device, with each side, beginning with the Serbs, pitting themselves against the 'evil other'. As Mary Kaldor has observed, the discrediting of Marxist-Leninist discourse left a void.[36] No alternative discourse emerged that proved capable of reconstructing legitimacy, apart from ethnic nationalism.

In the first democratic elections, nationalism became the mechanism for political differentiation.[37] Few alternative categories existed to distinguish candidates; the previous authoritarian regime had not encouraged the development of a civil society in which sophisticated differences might have emerged. Political and economic structures swayed under the weight of internal bickering as new leaders struggled for power and international financial institutions pressed Yugoslavia to restructure its economy.[38] This situation fostered intense nationalist bureaucratic

---

33 Schopflin (1993) p 190.
34 Other key attributes of the Yugoslav constitutional system pertaining to national minorities included poly-ethnic rights, such as the right to use one's own language in public and to primary education in one's own language, counterbalanced by constitutional prohibitions *against* propagating or practising national inequality and incitement of national, racial or religious hatred and intolerance.
35 A prime example of this tactic is the Memorandum of the Serbian Academy of Sciences and Arts which warned of attacks on 'the status of Serbia and the Serb nation'. An English version of the Memorandum can be found in Mihajlovic and Krestic (1995).
36 Kaldor (1994) p 89.
37 For a summary of election results, see Bugajski (1995) pp 3–192.
38 For one review of the economic situation, see Cohen (1995) p 45.

competition and corruption, often along national lines.[39] Certainly, nationalism was not the only force pushing Yugoslavia towards collapse, but as manipulated by politicians, it became a crucial ingredient.

Kosovo helped foster the path to war in Croatia and Bosnia-Herzegovina. Developments in Kosovo 'led to a fundamental realignment of politics in Serbia and the growth of dangerous, defensive, populist, and officially sanctioned nationalism'.[40] An anti-democratic coalition within Serbia of nationalists and communists manipulated the myth of Kosovo to formulate its nationalist ideology and to produce racially inspired propaganda. Serbs were said to be the victims of Albanians in Kosovo in dire need of the protection of a strong leader like Slobodan Milosevic. Incrementally, Milosevic and his supporters applied this strategy of victimisation to the rest of Yugoslavia, and the list of victimisers grew. In this way:

> 'Kosovo provided the time-fuse, and Slobodan Milosevic provided the detonators for a chain reaction of explosions in which first Serbs and then Albanians, Slovenes, Croats, and others came to believe, often to the point of obsession, that part or all of their nation was already or could be faced with extinction.'[41]

The Kosovo Wars

While the onset of hostilities in Kosovo is open to debate, few would disagree that tensions were exacerbated after Serbian politicians aligned with Slobodan Milosevic stripped Kosovo of its status as an autonomous province in 1989. This move subjected Kosovo to Belgrade's direct control and ushered in an era of draconian marshal law and other 'emergency provisions'. Kosovars resisted the Milosevic regime with non-violent tactics under the leadership of Ibrahim Rugova, the leader of the 'League for Democratic Kosova' (LDK). In protest at the Serbian takeover of government institutions, Kosovars established their own parallel civil administration, schools, healthcare facilities and welfare programmes. During this period, international human rights groups issued successive reports of gross and systemic human rights abuses in the troubled region, nearly all detailing crimes committed by Serb civilians and Serb police against Albanian civilians.[42] They warned of escalating violence and impending forced deportations, and implored inter-governmental organisations and individual countries to take preventative action.[43]

A defining moment for many Kosovars occurred during the negotiations over the Dayton Peace Accord in 1995, when Kosovars were excluded from the negotiation process and from the resulting document itself. After the signing of the peace plan for Bosnia, Serb violence in Kosovo continued. Many Albanians grew impatient with their campaign of 'passive resistance' to Serb aggression and instead supported a new tactic of aggressive, armed resistance, with the Kosova Liberation Army (KLA) emerging as the leader of this resistance by the end of 1997. In the spring of 1998, 51 members of a single Albanian family were killed by Serb forces in retaliation for KLA provocation. The US Secretary of

---

39 See Woodward (1995) pp 47–81.
40 Denitch (1994) p 116.
41 Rusinow (1995) pp 19–20.
42 See eg, Helsinki Watch (Mertus and Mihelic) (1994); Anonymous (1998b); Human Rights Watch (1998b).
43 Amnesty International (1998a;1998b); Anonymous (1998a).

State, Madeline Albright, immediately condemned the attacks, warning: 'We are not going to stand by and watch Serbian authorities do in Kosovo what they can no longer get away with in Bosnia.'[44] In June 1998, NATO staged practice bombing raids in Albania and Macedonia in an attempt to force Milosevic to back down. Milosevic called NATO's bluff. In the summer of 1998 Serb forces began a scorched-earth policy of destroying whole villages throughout Kosovo.[45] Up to 300,000 people were displaced from their homes at this stage of the conflict.[46]

In October 1998, US special envoy Richard Holbrooke negotiated an agreement with Serbian President Slobodan Milosevic to reduce Serb forces in Kosovo and to allow 2,000 unarmed 'verifiers' into the territory under the control of the Organisation for Security and Cooperation in Europe (OSCE). The UN Security Council issued a resolution 'welcoming' the October agreement and 'demand[ing] immediate action from the authorities of the Federal Republic of Yugoslavia and the Kosovo Albanian leadership to cooperate with international efforts to improve the humanitarian situation and to avert the impending humanitarian catastrophe'.[47] The verifiers were deployed, but Milosevic reneged on his agreement to reduce his forces in Kosovo. Despite the presence of the international verifiers, sporadic fighting continued.[48]

In January 1999, Serb forces killed 41 civilians in the Kosovo village of Racak.[49] Despite the attempts of Serb authorities to block international war crimes investigators from entering Serbia, international forensic efforts managed to investigate the incident. They found that the dead were indeed civilians, and not KLA troops as Serbian officials claimed. The KLA retaliated and the fighting in Kosovo escalated.

In March 1999 a group of six nations – 'the Contact group' (the US, the UK, France, Germany, Italy and Russia) – brought Kosovar and Serbian negotiators together in Rambouillet, France. The agreement on the table required autonomy to be restored to Kosovo, a NATO peacekeeping force to be installed, the KLA to disarm and Milosevic to reduce his troops in Kosovo. Neither side liked the arrangement. The agreement was unacceptable to Kosovars because it failed to require the complete withdrawal of Serbian troops and the guarantee of independence. At the same time, it was unacceptable to Serbs, who refused to give up Kosovo and to permit the presence of an armed international military force. NATO threatened both sides: Kosovars would be cut off from any international support if they failed to sign; Serbia would be bombed if they failed to sign. Kosovars eventually signed the agreement, but Serbia refused.

All international verifiers were pulled out of Kosovo in preparation for the threatened bombing. Meanwhile, Serb forces and heavy weapons flooded into Kosovo. US Special Envoy Richard Holbrooke continued to meet with Milosevic, but the Serbian leader refused to sign the Rambouillet agreement. On 23 March 1999, NATO war-planes commenced military air operations and missile strikes against targets in Serbia proper, Montenegro and Kosovo. Milosevic responded not by capitulating, but by digging in and unleashing a violent programme of

44 Smith (1998).
45 See Human Rights Watch (1998c). See also Physicians for Human Rights (1998a; 1998b).
46 This is the estimate of the UN Office for the Coordination of Humanitarian Affairs (OCHA). See Relief Web (1999).
47 Resolution 1203 (1998).
48 Human Rights Watch (1998a).
49 Human Rights Watch (1999a; 1999c).

deportation against Kosovar Albanians. The international community was left wholly unprepared for the sea of humanity that rushed across Kosovo's borders.

The NATO bombing campaign lasted for 78 days. During that time, Serbian forces (regular and paramilitary troops) swept through Kosovo, pushing over one-and-a-half million people from their homes, many in the first weeks of the campaign.[50] Refugees gave eye-witness accounts of summary executions of civilians and the pillaging and burning of entire villages by Serbian forces.[51] The bombing ended abruptly during the first week of June 1999, with Serbia agreeing to a somewhat less demanding peace accord than that offered at Rambouillet. The agreement reaffirmed Yugoslavia's sovereignty over the province, confined NATO troops to Kosovo and required UN authorisation for the peacekeeping force.[52] Kosovars flooded back into Kosovo and took revenge on the few Serb civilians who remained.[53] Today, the international community insists on maintaining a multi-ethnic Kosovo, despite the fact that Kosovo is virtually completely ethnic Albanian.

INTERNAL DIMENSIONS

A core characteristic of societies where conflicts have an important racial dimension is the existence of an historical system of group differentiation and extreme social polarisation. In both Rwanda and Kosovo, schemes for group differentiation were created and sustained through the dominant institutions of the state. Even as the state system of classification was viewed by many citizens as illegitimate (particularly by those in the 'out' group), the notion that difference could and should be institutionalised was none the less accepted as legitimate. Those who stood outside the ruling power structures sought not to do away with group differentiation schemes altogether, but merely to install their own chosen scheme. State institutions established the co-operative and competitive incentives in society by virtue of their rules, norms and procedures. In Rwanda and Kosovo, these institutions served to legitimise and normalise identity conflict.

Structural violence is another characteristic of societies marked by racialised conflict. In both Rwanda and Kosovo, over a period of many years, racism ensured a permanent state of violence, where there were severe deprivations and human rights abuses. While the stories of these abuses are complex, at their core was an attempt to deny groups their legitimate identity and individuals their human dignity. Other categories of structural violence contributed to the unstable situation, such as poverty, gender violence, unmet human development needs and the absence of human rights. Identity plays an important role in conflict where one group feels the impact of the deprivations in a disproportionate and unfair manner. Comparative deprivations based on race are particularly suspect. While such differences are passed off as 'natural' and even as evidence that one group is 'inherently' inferior, they are the result of structural violence and historical discrimination.

---

50 UNHCR estimated that by May 1999 at least 800,000 people had fled Kosovo for Macedonia, Albania or further abroad: UNHCR (1999).
51 The writer took testimony from refugees in Albania in May–June 1999.
52 Resolution 1244 (1999).
53 Surroi (1999).

The existence of structural violence fosters fear and instability. Wherever an identity group perceives a threat to its interests and values, rising counter-elites find playing the racist/nationalist/chauvinist card a particularly useful tool for gaining power. Political mobilisation based on identity is made possible where the state's administrative structures and legal institutions distribute scarce resources based on ethnic or national differences.[54] Such was the case in Rwanda and Kosovo. The problem is particularly acute where, as in Rwanda and Yugoslavia, lead positions in military and police forces are distributed based upon group identity.[55]

Yugoslavia and Rwanda are textbook examples of cases in which the controlling entity – the state, the party, the coloniser – 'for its own administrative convenience and in order to improve control over local elites, may select certain ethnic elites and organisations as collaborators or channels for the transmission of government patronage'.[56] This favouritism based on group identity serves to further polarise societies and, additionally, to institutionalise and make acceptable intra-group suspicion and hatred. Over time, identity conflict changes from being *a means* for political mobilisation to *the only means* for political mobilisation.

Political mobilisation based on racism is aided by a history of real and imagined oppression and a culture of victimisation. Where one is made to feel the victim, it becomes far easier to become the perpetrator. Individuals driven by fear of victimisation are willing to support violence for, as Rui de Figueiredo and Barry Weingast have observed: '[p]otential victimisation implies that citizens do not view the choice as between peace and violence but between fighting and being a victim.'[57] Many varieties of propaganda are useful in creating a culture of victimisation, but racist discourse wields particularly potent power. Once a person can be deemed genetically inferior, or not human at all – the pinnacle of racism – killing becomes justified, easy, noble. In both Rwanda and Kosovo, hate propaganda was used in this manner to play upon memories of real and imagined past domination by the minority.

The enemy in Rwanda[58] and Kosovo[59] was often portrayed in racialised terms by the media and in public addresses of elites. Racist ideology in Rwanda and Kosovo was expressed in the following terms:

- *Debates about physical fitness.* The 'other' was regarded as coming from polluted and inferior stock. In Rwanda, the newspaper Kangura published the 'Hutu ten commandments', which referred to the Tutsis as 'evil', and characterised intermarriage among Tutsi and Hutu as a pollution of 'pure Hutu'. Similarly, in the former Yugoslavia, Albanians were depicted as genetically inferior and polluted by Turkish influence. In Rwanda, those married members of the opposing group were said to produce children who were 'hybrids'. In the former Yugoslavia, intermarriage between Albanians and Serbs was extremely rare.
- *Sub-human imagery.* In Rwanda, Tutsi were called *Inyenzi* ('cockroaches') in political speeches and depicted as such in political cartoons – that is, they

54 See generally Horwitz (1985) p 151; Lipshutz and Crawford (1998).
55 Enloe (1977).
56 Lipset et al (1997) p 91.
57 De Figueiredo and Weingast (1999) p 292.
58 The examples in this section are drawn from: Human Rights Watch; Chalk (1999) pp 93–107; Human Rights Watch (1996) p 18; Article 19 (1996) p 64; Africa Watch (Omaar and de Waal) (1994); Thompson (1994).
59 All of these have been drawn from Mertus (1999c).

were less than human. Those Tutsis who had reached positions of importance in government were said to have slipped 'like snakes' into their positions. In the former Yugoslavia, Albanians were called parasites and devils.

- *Attacks on reproduction and competitive fertility.* In Rwanda, propaganda especially encouraged the killing of Tutsi children, so that Tutsi genes would not re-emerge. In Rwanda and Kosovo, Hutu and Serb militias subjected Tutsi and Albanian women to acts of sexual violence. In the former Yugoslavia, Albanian women were said to be 'baby factories' and Serbs were said to be threatened by their overproduction.
- *Portrayal of the enemy as savage.* Radio-Télévision Libre des Mille Collines (RTLM) in Rwanda broadcast propaganda about the RPF, claiming that they not only killed people, but also dissected and ate them, thereby contributing to their dehumanisation of the other. Media throughout the former Yugoslavia portrayed Albanians as 'less civilised' and less cultured. Images of Albanians in the press rarely depicted educated, urban Albanians. Albanian men were branded as rapists, although they were statistically less likely to be accused of rape than members of other national groups. Whenever the public needed to be reminded about the victimisation of Serbs and the barbaric nature of Albanians, the image of Djordje Martinovic was conveniently invoked. Martinovic was the ethnic Serb who claimed to have been raped with a bottle by two Albanians. As a violent crime of the most 'unspeakable nature', the act itself was 'written on the body'. The power of the Martinovic case lay in its ability to invoke the primary and potent image of Serb oppression: the Ottoman Turk's practice of impaling their victims with a stick.
- *Portrayal of the 'other' as foreigner.* In Rwanda, propagandists played upon the theme that Tutsis were not originally from the area and, therefore, they were outsiders who could not be trusted. Similarly, in Kosovo, Albanians were regarded as the new arrivals. With respect to the Martinovic case and other cases, the media tapped relentlessly into historic racism against Turks and Muslims. Albanians were equated with Turkish and Muslim peoples (while in reality Albanians do not identify as such; they are not 'Turks' and some Albanians are Catholic or Orthodox).
- *Portrayal of the 'other' as enemy from within.* In the former Yugoslavia, Albanians were also portrayed as fanatical, sly and evil – enemies from within. When a young Yugoslav army recruit named Aziz Keljmendi shot dead four men in his barracks, Albanians as a group were accused of aiding the crime. In Rwanda, Tutsis were portrayed as the internal enemy who was trying to destroy Rwanda from the inside, with the help of the international community.

In Kosovo, state-sponsored and state-condoned hate propaganda offered support for a virulent chauvinist agenda that included military and paramilitary abuses. In Rwanda, the connection between militias and racist media was even closer: the media was used to disseminate instructions as to when and how to kill.[60] Although some of those participating in the killings were government army and militia members, many of those who joined in the killings were 'peasants',[61] and the young and young adults formed a large part of the audience for such stations as RTLM. Although they would not normally have engaged in the torture and killing of their fellow citizens, many claimed that the propaganda broadcast by the government

---

60 See Human Rights Watch (1999b) pp 89–90.
61 Anonymous (1994b).

radio convinced them that they had no alternative. One man reported: 'I did not believe the Tutsis were coming to kill us, but when the government radio continued to broadcast that they were coming to take our land, were coming to kill the Hutus – when this was repeated over and over – I began to feel some kind of fear.'[62]

The problem in the former Yugoslavia was not the complete absence of free speech. While the government restricted the activities of some nationalist journalists and others critical of Tito's legacy, the most virulent hate speech in Yugoslavia was made possible due to an *increase* in free speech.[63] By contrast, in Rwanda, information was suppressed through direct government harassment of and control over journalists and through tight controls on the right to freedom of movement, which made it easier for authorities to cover up human rights abuses and to present their own version of state-sponsored and state-condoned violence.[64] Despite the differences in relative degrees of free speech, the core problem in Rwanda and Kosovo was the same. In both places, speech went unchallenged due to the absence of institutions to break up governmental and non-governmental informational monopolies, the lack of common public forums for the free and safe exchange of diverse ideas, and the absence of a prerequisite for a 'well developed' civil society: 'the set of institutions and social norms that make pluralism a civil process of persuasion and reconciling of differences.'[65] The electronic media proved to be the most powerful force in both Kosovo and Rwanda due to its ability to reach rural populations (Rwanda relied largely on radio, the former Yugoslavia, on radio and television), and in both cases an ethic of biased journalism prevailed.

The remaining defining features of societies in which racism plays a role in violent conflict include the absence of: (1) the rule of law; (2) an independent judiciary; and (3) minority rights guarantees. The historical failure of the court systems in both Rwanda and Kosovo to address fairly and adequately inter-group violence gave perpetrators the sense that violence for political ends was legitimate and that such actions could be undertaken with impunity. 'The effects of genocide', as Helen Fein notes, 'may persist after its perpetrator is overthrown by undermining any notion of law and justice, creating pervasive motives for retribution'.[66] The absence of the rule of law, coupled with economic deprivations and a lack of democratic institutions, made Rwanda and Kosovo structurally violent societies susceptible to a culture of hate. The outbursts of murderous violence, then, were 'not something new, but primarily part of a continuum of ever-present violence in which violence is the answer to violence, and in which victims temporarily become perpetrators and then victims again'.[67]

GLOBAL/TRANS-BOUNDARY DIMENSIONS

The above discussion identified the following core domestic characteristics of conflicts with a racial dimension:

(1) an historical system of group differentiation and extreme social polarisation; structural violence;

(2) political mobilisation linked to real and imagined group differences;

---

62 Anonymous (1994b).
63 See Mertus (1999c).
64 Article 19 (1996) p 44.
65 Snyder and Ballentine (1997) p 65.
66 Fein (1990).
67 Uvin (1996).

(3) a history of real and imagined oppression and a culture of victimisation;
(4) a portrayal of the enemy in racialised terms;
(5) a state or counter-elite monopoly over speech; and
(6) the absence of the rule of law, an independent judiciary and minority rights guarantees.

The identification of these characteristics, however, does not explain in full why and when conflicts with a racial dimension will erupt into violence. Some countries exhibit all of these characteristics and yet they are devoid of communal violence. Why is this? The explanation lies in global/trans-boundary factors, factors which are themselves shaped by racism.

Global factors profoundly affect issues, cleavages and potential rivalries between ethnic groups and the willingness and ability of the international community to respond to ethnic conflict. The central global factors influencing the emergence of and response to conflict are:

(1) the end of the Cold War and the emergence of an ethnically fragmented multi-polar world;
(2) the legacy of colonialism[68] and the proliferation of transitionary regimes;
(3) enhanced tension between state and non-state actors, with non-state actors increasingly vying for power;
(4) the globalisation of production, growing power of international financial institutions and increased disparities in wealth between North and South; and
(5) the emergence of international and regional bodies willing to respond to intra-state conflict.[69]

All of the foregoing factors are racialised. After all, it is at the level of global power that racial fears are most systematically articulated. Anxieties about the changing balance of international power are often articulated through the concept of a race war, a 'clash of civilisations', primitive, tribal conflict. Transitional struggles of post-colonial and formerly Soviet satellite-states are painted solely as racist/tribal/primitive atavistic struggles, when, as pointed out above, racist ideology is a tool but not a cause of the conflicts. Racist reporting by the media can act to confirm stereotypes held by outsiders – the inevitability of violent conflict – and thus dissuade outsiders from intervening before the conflict starts.[70] In situations like Rwanda, as Jose Alvarez observes, an 'emphasis on race, ethnicity, or religion can become a comfortable rationale for passivity for those outside the affected region'.[71] When journalists and analysts depict conflicts as primitive and irrational, they convey to their readers that 'it might be best simply to leave the parties to fend for themselves, or even kill themselves off'.[72]

Racist thinking structures the way the international community approaches conflict. 'Increasingly', Frank Furedi writes, 'the vocabulary applied to the South is morally different than that which is used in the North'.[73] Societies of the

---

68 As explained above, colonialism introduced racist ideology into societies and this thinking was then perpetuated by post-colonial regimes. Ndayambaje and Mutabaruka (1999) pp 30-51.
69 Klinke et al (1997) p 9.
70 Alvarez (1999) at 381.
71 Alvarez (1999) at 381.
72 Alvarez (1999) at 381.
73 Füredi (1998) p 240.

South, especially those of Africa, but also those of the Balkans, are treated in pathological terms. Rwandans, Serbs and Albanians, for example, are routinely represented as 'naturally' devoid of morality; they do not know right from wrong. People of the South are regarded as subject to easy co-option by terrorists and fundamentalists and are characterised as breeding at too rapid a rate. Such expressions are racism in its grossest form. It is no wonder, then, that Western states have intervened to protect Christians and white 'Westerners', and that they have declined to intervene in wars between non-white/non-Western combatants.[74]

The new moral equation between a morally superior North and an inferior South helps legitimate a two-tiered international system.[75] The neo-colonial relationship between benefactor and beneficiary allows the benefactor to judge the beneficiary's capacity for 'civilisation' and prescribe what it deems the appropriate plan of action.

When Western states have intervened in the South and on behalf of non-white/non-Western people, they tend to run in with a club, and not with the soft sale of 'rebuilding civil society'. Civil society programmes are reserved for societies deemed more capable of rational and moral thought.[76] The amount of effort spent on rebuilding civil society in Africa and Asia pales when compared with reconstruction efforts flooding into Europe. While the international community arrived en masse with the civil society banner waving in the seemingly more Western parts of the former Yugoslavia, a relative trickle of funding went to Albanian (read predominately Muslim) Kosovo. In Rwanda, the international community used the country's dependence on foreign aid to demand 'democratisation', but, reminiscent of old-time colonialism, the project constituted democratisation on command of outsiders, not democratisation valuing the will and experience of locals. Some commentators have argued persuasively that the denial of the agency of local actors led to the akazu's decision to plan the 'final solution' that was ultimately manifested as genocide.[77]

Some commentators have contended that the failure of the international community to act promptly and effectively has contributed to the outbreak, intensity and persistence of violent conflict.[78] As this writer has argued in detail elsewhere,[79] Yugoslavia in the 1980s could have benefited from civil intervention aimed at eliminating or mitigating the factors outlined above. The same reasoning applies to Rwanda. In the 1980s, Rwanda was forced to agree to a structural adjustment programme with the World Bank. Domestic tensions rose when salaries eroded, the expansion of public services jobs halted and the increased shares of the remaining government budget were taken up by debt reimbursement.[80] In both Yugoslavia and Rwanda, international intermeddling only increased deprivation (in both cases with real and/or perceived disparate impact along identity lines) and permitted elite-instigated racism/nationalism to continue unabated. Instead of calling in bank loans and ordering fiscal austerity measures in Yugoslavia and Rwanda, the international community could have supported the development of civil society and an independent media, addressed poverty

74 See Finnemore (1996) p 169.
75 Füredi (1998) p 240.
76 The writer has developed this thesis elsewhere: see Mertus (1999e).
77 Jones (1999) p 125.
78 See Carnegie Commission on Preventing Deadly Conflict (1998).
79 See Mertus (1999c) pp 227–268.
80 Uvin (1996) p 29.

and other forms of structural violence, and fostered the development of the rule of law and an independent judiciary. Serious questions arise as to whether the failure of the international community to undertake an extensive, early civil society approach in Rwanda and the former Yugoslavia was based on a reading of the people of Africa and the Balkans as primitively predisposed to conflict, thereby rendering outside preventative efforts futile.[81]

Only a crystal ball could tell us whether effective and early civil intervention could have prevented violent conflict in Rwanda and the former Yugoslavia. At some point, the time for civil intervention passed and only military intervention and strong-armed diplomacy could have changed the progress of events. Ultimately, the untimely and ineffective interventions in Kosovo and Rwanda failed to prevent mass deportations and genocide.[82] In Rwanda, the UN was given repeated warnings of a planned genocide, but, as African Rights observes: 'when the storm broke [the UN] appeared to be caught unawares.'[83] Three-quarters of the Tutsi population had been killed before a UN-authorised intervention began in earnest and, even then, the response was confused and largely ineffectual. Human Rights Watch suggests that, while the Rwandans who organised and executed the genocide must bear full responsibility for the genocide, the US staff as well as the three governments principally involved in Rwanda also bear great responsibility:

> 'the UN staff for having failed to provide adequate information to the Security Council; Belgium, for having withdrawn its troops precipitately and for having championed total withdrawal of the U.S. force; the U.S. for having put saving money ahead of saving lives and for slowing the sending of a relief force; and France, for having continued to support a government engaged in genocide.'[84]

Similarly, the tell-tale signs of explosive conflict in Kosovo were well known to the international community long before the killing and forced displacement of Albanians had begun. Yet half of the Albanian population was forcibly deported, and most of the remaining population was internally displaced before NATO's air campaign compelled a withdrawal of Serb forces.[85]

Some commentators have theorised that a more useful explanatory variable for the eruption of conflict is not international omission, but international commission, especially the application of transnational legal norms to civil conflict. Alan Kuperman hypothesises that 'the substantial level of attention already paid to nascent conflicts by the international community is actually a causal variable in exacerbating their violence'.[86] The identification of human rights violations worldwide and the increasing application of human rights norms

---

81 For example, Robert Kaplan's book (Kaplan (1993)) was used by many politicians to support the thesis that conflict in the Balkans was inevitable. For an analysis of the impact of racist thinking in the media and the decision to not intervene in Rwanda, see Alvarez (1999) at 380–381.

82 With respect to Rwanda in particular, the international community could have intervened militarily once the plan of genocide was leaked and it became clear that a massacre was imminent, but it failed to do so. The watery intervention in Rwanda backfired as it served only to demonstrate the lack of will on behalf of the international community. Similarly, the withdrawal of civilian monitors and President Clinton's announcement that he would not send ground troops to Kosovo gave a green light to ethnic cleansing within Kosovo.

83 African Rights (1995).

84 Human Rights Watch (1999b) p 17.

85 Kuperman (1999).

86 Kuperman (1999) at 1. See also Klinke et al (1997) p 8.

across borders, Kuperman argues, inspires subordinate groups to believe that they will be supported in their pursuit of equal rights, political autonomy, secession and/or the revolutionary overthrow of the existing regime. 'Genocides and ethnic cleansing may occur when a weak and vulnerable subordinate group rises up because it miscalculates optimistically that it will receive assistance from an outside source.'[87] Kuperman claims that false expectations can be attributed to two sources: the willingness of politicians to critique foreign leaders for oppression of subordinate groups within their own borders, and the use of humanitarian military interventions on behalf of victimised groups. Where violence has not yet broken out: 'weak subordinate groups have a perverse incentive to initiate violent challenges against much stronger opponents in order to provoke a violent crackdown against their own people, in hopes of compelling sympathetic media attention, Western threats, and ultimately military intervention.'[88]

Certainly the facts of the Kosovo case appear to support this thesis. Kosovo Albanians have always optimistically defined their struggle in terms of transnational human rights norms.[89] They optimistically believed that the US and NATO[90] would support their claims to human rights, including some degree of political self-determination short of outright secession. After the international community failed to offer effective support, Albanians took up arms. By failing to act early in support of human rights, the international community did indeed send a message to future subordinated peoples who decide to stand up for their rights: we will not help you unless you provoke all-out war. There is a problem here, but it is the failure of the international community to stand by its professed commitment to human rights, not the Albanian insistence on adherence to respect for transnational legal norms.

The transnational human rights demands of Albanians in Kosovo did indeed cause conflict, but this in itself is unproblematic. The US and its NATO allies claim to support democracy. In a democracy, in contrast to a totalitarian state, subordinate groups advance not only transsocial objectives – such as guarantees for basic rights for all citizens – but more particularistic interests.[91] The demand of any minority group for rights is bound to inspire conflict of some type. The problem with the Kosovars' demands was not that they caused conflict, but that institutional mechanisms and structures for the management of conflict did not exist in Kosovo and Serbia proper, and transnational legal mechanisms proved inadequate to stem the tide of violence. Conflict turns violent when the international community insists on the application of transnational legal norms and yet does nothing to help the community manage the conflict that inevitably arises when subordinate groups demand implementation of these norms.

The situation in Rwanda was quite different. In that case, the numerical and political majority struck out against the minority group. While the Hutu majority, first under the Kayibanda and then the Habyarimana regime, cloaked itself in a façade of democracy, no one spoke of human rights. It was a 'democracy' of majority rule, authoritarian leadership, the absence of minority rights and limited

---

87 Klinke et al (1997) p 3.
88 Klinke et al (1997) p 4.
89 This is discussed in Mertus (1999f) p 171.
90 Since the early 1990s, Kosovar Albanians have looked to the skies for US and NATO planes. Observation drawn from the writer's work in Kosovo, 1993 – present.
91 Woodward (1999) p 233.

personal freedoms (for example, there was no freedom of movement with respect to residence and labour could be forced). In this 'democracy', Habyarimana and his family grew rich while the general population grew increasingly impoverished and ethnic tensions mounted. International actors could have pierced the veil of the sham democracy and demanded the institution of human rights for all citizens of Rwanda. Instead, international donors were pleased that the regime had brought a sense of order to troubled Rwanda, and they rewarded the government with large amounts of foreign aid.[92] In this respect, then, the ultimate problem was similar to Kosovo in the notable lack of international support for human rights' principles. When the international community finally did act, it was too late.

International action supportive of human rights may in many cases ameliorate conflict, but additional trans-boundary factors explain why unaddressed conflicts eventually erupt. The main explanatory global/trans-boundary factors for the emergence of violent conflict are economic in origin. Globalisation has led to the increased uniformity of 'production possibilities across national borders' (largely due to technological advances) and the integration of markets, meaning that decisions regarding jobs and investment are now made on an international rather than purely domestic level. As a result, those with the resources to take advantage of these conditions are able to make great profits, and those without the necessary resources find themselves pressured to 'sell their labour, family life or environment cheaply in order to make a living'.[93] These conditions lead to inequalities in the distribution of wealth. An already massive gap in income and wealth among the richest 10% and the poorest 10% of people worldwide has increased almost tenfold during the 1980s.[94] In 1998, the combined income of three billion people in the South was less than the collective assets of 358 multibillionaires.[95] While transnational law facilitates trade and investment, it does little to address growing poverty, and even contributes to the growing North/South divide.

This divide means different things for different people within societies, as at a local level people are divided into winners and losers in the new globalised economy. Whenever international financial institutions order austerity measures, a disproportionate burden of the adjustment to harsh circumstances falls on the shoulders of the women, children, the elderly, disabled and the already poor, as social and educational provisions serving these populations are reduced.[96] Those who do manage to take advantage of the global restructuring are more likely to be the elite, but the winners may also be those of the politically powerless group. In either case, the globalisation of the economy can result in exacerbated racial/ethnic tensions at a local level. For example, Kosovar Albanians may actually be regarded as the winners in the global economy over Kosovar Serbs. Pushed out of their government jobs in mines, factories and schools, Kosovar Albanians benefited from the global economy by becoming members of the large migratory work force of Western Europe, and by becoming small traders of (often smuggled and sometimes illegal) goods from Turkey

---

92 Philip Gourevitch writes that aid arrived from Belgium, France ('ever eager to expand its neocolonial empire'), Switzerland ('which sent more development aid to Rwanda than to any other country on earth'), Washington, Bonn, Tokyo and the Vatican: see Gourevitch (1998).

93 Edwards et al (1999) at 118.

94 Gill (1996) p 215.

95 Edwards et al (1999) at 117.

96 Gill (1996) p 215.

and further east. As a result, despite the intense oppression against Kosovar Albanians in the early 1990s, rural Albanians in Kosovo tended to have more material goods than their neighbouring rural Serbs (with fewer freedoms). The success of Albanians in the global economy only contributed to the rise in tension between the two groups, resulting in further crackdowns by Serb authorities and cases of Serb police burning and destroying Albanian jewellery shops and other small businesses.[97]

The local impact of globalisation plays out differently in more industrialised areas. In the globalised economy, many jobs have disappeared from industrial centres, as transnational corporations transfer labour-intensive manufacturing to low-wage countries, creating a new class of unemployed, and often unemployable, people. A systematic economic crisis has emerged in the marginal areas of the economy, spurring poverty and famine. This crisis has enhanced antagonism between ethnic groups as a shrinking resource base has reinforced the value of subsistence assets, thus shifting conflict down to the most local level.[98] Ethnically structured competition between dominant and subordinate groups over the shrinking resource base only worsens the economic situation and increases the vulnerability of subordinate groups.[99] At its most extreme, ethnic competition contributes to the failure of states and the collapse of formal economies.

The collapse of formal economies has enabled the emergence of autonomous, ethnically defined war economies. Mark Duffield explains:

'These structures are based upon control and development of parallel economic activities, internal taxing, asset appropriation and manipulation of relief aid. They enable political movements to function beyond the bounds of conventional relations. To a large extent the dominant groups within these economies are sanction proof ... Lacking legal means of survival, extralegal structures have emerged.'[100]

International actors cannot use traditional means of influencing these war economies as they operate separate from and, at times in defiance of, the operation of law and the threats and promises of international financial institutions. In both Rwanda and Kosovo, active underground economies existed, immune to international control.

Another factor in the global economy with importance for racialised conflict is the ghost of colonialisation. Entrenched in much of the colonialist ideology was the view of 'the North as rightly and naturally dominant over the South'.[101] During colonisation, the North dominated the South by turning 'Southern economies into satellites of the Northern economies'.[102] Thereafter followed a large-scale transfer of resources from the South to the North. The extraction of these indigenous resources resulted in the under-development of the Southern economies and the shift from a self-reliant economy to one dependent on both imports from and exports to Northern markets. Such inequalities between economies of the North and South have persisted in the post-colonialist era,

97 This is discussed in Mertus (1999c).
98 Duffield (1997) p 206.
99 Keen (1994).
100 Duffield (1997) p 205.
101 Thomas (1999) at 6. Some of the other traditional views of concepts associated with the North and South respectively are also discussed.
102 Thomas (1989) at 4.

perpetuated in part by the Northern perception that the disparity is caused by inherent differences in culture.[103] These inequalities lead, in turn, to economic conditions ripe for conflict. In addition to economic inequality, many Southern post-colonial states are viewed as having 'a shortage of the institutional features that characterise fully sovereign Western states'.[104] Thus, in the post-colonial era these states have not had their sovereignty and self-determination fully restored and they are not equipped to deal with the diverse ethnic and cultural subgroups that continue to maintain tenuous relationships with central authorities. As noted in the case of Rwanda, colonialism introduced a crippling racist ideology into the society that was perpetuated by the willingness of subsequent international benefactors to overlook racist and authoritarian practices in favour of 'order'. At no point did the international community sincerely support the sovereignty of the people of Rwanda. Rather, through the support of authoritarian regimes, the international community contributed to their denial of self-determination.

The policies behind distribution of aid have also been identified in a variety of instances as an additional factor in the inducement of conflict in aid-receiving societies.[105] During the 1980s, the focus on 'promoting stabilisation and growth, marketisation, privatisation, and minimal government' often led inadvertently to ethnic conflict.[106] For example, aid intended to facilitate rapid modernisation frequently resulted in confusion among indigenous peoples with regard to unfamiliar market economics.[107] In addition, aid in some instances has resulted in the migration of workers, where already present populations have 'charged settlers with encroachment on their lands and livelihoods'.[108] Many aid agencies have been unwilling or unable to respond adequately to the misuse of foreign aid by receiving governments, who sometimes use the aid to bolster corruption.[109] Thus, aid which could have positively affected conditions in which ethnic conflict is fostered, is instead diverted by the very parties who are often responsible for stirring up conflict. Rwanda is a primary illustration of a pattern of development support (to regimes that failed to respect human rights) and emergency aid (largely to the instigators of genocidal conflict) which served to fortify structural violence and contribute to the outbreak of violent conflict.[110]

Globalisation has also inspired massive migrations. Migration of peoples can often place ethnic groups in locations and situations where they are unwelcome by the indigenous peoples and, where the two groups compete for resources and control, conflict may ensue. Increasing levels of migration worldwide make growing numbers of refugees and migrant workers vulnerable to various forms of abuse by sending and receiving states. 'The rise in xenophobia and overtly racist practices' writes Joe Oloka-Onyango, a member of the UN Sub-Commission on the Protection and Promotion of Human Rights, 'has led to serious diminution in the legal protection of refugees, migrant workers and asylum seekers in many countries'.[111] In an environment of

103 Thomas (1999) at 7–9.
104 Grovogui (1996) p 179.
105 Esman (1997).
106 Esman (1997).
107 Esman (1997) at 3.
108 Esman (1997).
109 Esman (1997).
110 Uvin (1988).
111 Stavenhagen (1999).

restrictive immigration laws, it becomes easy for judicial authorities to 'criminalise' certain ethnic and racial minorities.[112] These practices can lead to racial/ethnic conflict outside the host country. In the case of Rwanda, the difficulties experienced by Tutsi refugees in neighbouring Uganda influenced their decision to join the Rwandese Patriotic Army (RPA), the military arm of the Rwandese Patriotic Front[113] and, similarly, substandard treatment of Albanians in Western Europe was one factor influencing young Kosovar Albanians to join the Kosovar Liberation Army.[114]

The new patterns of migration have created new and powerful diaspora communities. The existence of a diaspora helps to explain both when conflicts begin and when states intervene. Diaspora support their kin by exerting pressure on political leaders in their newly adopted states and by bankrolling the purchase of weaponry. For example, the Albanian diaspora in the US and Western Europe at first economically supported Kosovar's 'passive resistance' movement and then, having grown impatient, the arming of a Kosova Liberation Army; the Tutsi diaspora in Burundi and Uganda provided manpower and military support for the Rwandan Patriotic Front. While the Tutsi had the support of the Burundi government, Kosovar Albanians lobbied hard in the US for the support of the Bush and then Clinton administrations.

As Kamila Valkova Valenta has demonstrated, whether states intervene on behalf of their own ethnic minority in another country is largely related to what type of nationalism exists there.[115] Civil nationalism denotes membership in a nation that is determined by birth, and residence and political participation which can be acquired. Ethnic nationalism, by contrast, is perceived as inborn and inherited through a common ancestry and is difficult or impossible to acquire. Countries where ethnic nationalism prevails are more likely to intervene on behalf of their minorities abroad than countries where civic nationalism prevails. Valenta has found that:

> 'countries where nationalism is based on blood and ethnic ties will perceive their ethnic minorities abroad as being an integral part of their nation, and on the basis of this perception, they will be more inclined to protect them. On the other hand, countries that perceive their nation as being defined on the basis of the territory of their state will not feel such a strong tie with their ethnic minorities living outside the state boundaries and will therefore be more reluctant to initiate military disputes for their protection.'[116]

The outbreak of violent conflict can be explained not only by the existence of a powerful diaspora, but also in terms of the understanding of the concept of nation in potentially supportive countries.[117]

Another global/trans-boundary catalyst for violent conflict on racialised lines is the availability of modern weaponry through the global arms trade. Examples of this phenomenon abound. Fighting between Burundi Hutus and Tutsis was fuelled by sales of arms by French gun-runners to both sides (with the alleged

---

112 Stevenhagen (1999).
113 See Watson (1991).
114 This insight is drawn from the writer's interviews with participants.
115 Valenta (1999).
116 Valenta (1999) at 15.
117 Certainly the decision to intervene is also based on other factors, such as the self-interest of the intervening state, public support for intervention and the likelihood of victory. See Klinke et al (1997) p 8.

acquiescence of the French government) and money from South American drug dealers, who were attempting to launder their money through the sales.[118] Trade in Soviet-made arms was linked to conflict between the Konkomba and Dagomba tribes in Ghana. There, arms were allegedly purchased by youth groups, who used money donated by tribe members across the country to so-called 'war funds'.[119] In the name of 'francophonie' France played the role of 'external patron' in Rwanda, providing the akazu with substantial military, logistical and economic aid against the 'anglophone' Tutsi refugee-warriors.[120] A report of a French parliamentary committee concedes that from 1990 to April 1994, France sold 137 million francs worth of arms to Rwanda, and provided more than 10,000 mortar rounds, one million bullets and six Gazelle helicopters.[121] While the 1994 Rwandan genocide was carried out mainly by people wielding machetes and knives, the steady supply of arms by France to the akazu gave them the strength to repel an earlier Tutsi insurgency and contributed to the knowledge that, in an all-out campaign against the Tutsi, they would have the military advantage. In this sense, the international arms market was a crucial, enabling ingredient in the akazu's 'final solution'.

A related global/trans-boundary factor influencing the emergence of conflict is the transformation of social relations. Enhanced poverty and economic insecurity encourages banditry and trade in arms. The hallmarks of the global economy – increased interconnectedness and ease of communication and transportation – makes drug and arm smuggling ever more possible and profitable. The emergence of armed militias and income available through banditry erodes the position of elders and community leaders opposed to violent and illegal means.[122] Intensified labour migration further undermines the position of elders as power shifts to the young migrants, who now have the wealth and influence to support an armed insurrection back home.[123] Finally, the global economic shifts and migration patterns have a profound influence on family and gender relations. Where families are split by migration and war, new burdens are placed on the women and children left behind. Shorn of the sanctions of kinship, children are susceptible to being recruited as soldiers, and rape and the sexual exploitation of women become a common adjunct to ethnic violence.[124] A common impact of post-war and transitional rebuilding is a rise in prostitution and trafficking of women and children.[125] Human rights researchers in Kosovo, for example, have documented post-war incidents of forced prostitution and the trafficking of Ukrainian and other Eastern European women.[126] Transnational legal institutions and mechanisms have yet to address these social problems, which only contribute to the structural violence spurring racial/ethnic conflict.

---

118 Anonymous (1995).
119 Ephson (1994).
120 Lemarchand (undated). See also Prunier (1995) p 243.
121 See Whitney (1998).
122 Duffield (1997) p 206.
123 The KLA, for example, was funded almost entirely by younger Albanian migrants living in the US and Europe.
124 Duffield (1997) p 206.
125 Byrsk (1999) p 3.
126 Telephone conversation between writer and Martina Vandenberg, Human Rights Watch, May 2000.

CONCLUSION

Unelected global institutions such as the World Bank, UNHCR and international peacekeepers increasingly control the lives of the most powerless citizens. The bright side of globalisation is the growth of power among the powerless. The losers in global restructuring and in civil conflicts have attempted to redefine their roles at home and in the emerging global order. These groups, James Mittelman explains, 'aim to augment popular participation and assert local control over the seemingly remote forces of globalisation'.[127] The new space created by globalisation makes possible cross-boundary linkages among citizens of different states, and encourages the growth and development of social movements demanding human rights and transformative social justice.[128] Stephen Gill optimistically declares: 'Even the poorest members of world society are combining politically to oppose their oppression.'[129]

The 1980s and 1990s have indeed witnessed a flourishing of NGOs and a growth of 'informal, quasi-spontaneous networks of resistance'.[130] All actors involved in this movement for 'democratisation from below' face an incredible challenge in their struggle for peace and justice. They must address not only internal dimensions of conflict, but global/trans-boundary dimensions as well, addressing in particular the ramifications of globalisation of the economy.[131] Transnational law is increasingly relevant to this endeavour, but any efforts for conflict prevention will fail to prevent violence without a multi-dimensional approach that appreciates the root causes of conflict. This chapter has demonstrated that race and ethnic-based conflicts must be understood not only by reference to a history of internal structural inequities, but also in terms of trans-boundary factors. It is a combination of these domestic and trans-boundary factors which lead to violent inter-group conflict.

Select bibliography

Adelman, H, Suhrke, A, and Jones, B, (1996) *Early Warning and Conflict Management, Study 2 of the Joint Evaluation of Emergency Assistance in Rwanda.*

African Rights, (1995) *Rwanda – Death Despair and Defiance.*

Africa Watch (Omaar, R, and de Waal, A,), (1994) *Rwanda: Death, Despair and Defiance.*

Agbese, P O, (1999) 'Racism and Ethnic Conflicts as Root Cause of Refugee Flows', Background Paper presented at the Seminar of Experts on Racism, Refugees and Multiethnic States, 6–8 December, UN High Commissioner on Human Rights, Geneva, HR/GVA/DR/SEM/1999/BP.1.

Alvarez, J E, (1999) 'Crimes of States/Crimes of Hate: Lessons from Rwanda', 24 Yale JIL 365.

---

127 Mittelman (1994) p 325.
128 See generally Mertus (1999d).
129 Gill (1996) p 217.
130 Gill (1996) p 217.
131 The potential for transnational NGOs to take up this task is explored in Mertus (1999a;1999b; 1999g).

Amnesty International, (1998a) 'Violence sweeps through Kosovo province: International effort needed to prevent further killings and beatings', Press Release, 5 March, available at www.amnesty.org.uk/news/press/releases/5_march_1998-1.html.

Amnesty International, (1998b) 'Federal Republic of Yugoslavia: Time the authorities listened and acted!', Press Release, 29 April, available at www.amnesty.org.uk/news/press/releases/29_april_1998-5.html.

Anonymous, (1994a) 'Rwanda: No end in sight', The Economist, 23 April, at 331.

—(1994b) 'Sounds of violence', The New Republic, 22 August, at 211.

—(1994c) 'The bleeding of Rwanda', The Economist, 16 April, at 331.

—(1995) 'Drug cartels and French arms dealers linked to Burundi bloodshed', Deutsche Presse-Agentur, 10 July .

—(1998a) 'Kosovo: Time is running out', Budva, Montenegro, 30 August, available at www.ihf-hr.org/appeals/980830.htm.

—(1998b) 'Systematic rights abuses reported in Kosovo', New Europe On-Line, 28 August, 1998 WL 24015766.

Article 19 (The International Centre Against Censorship, Broadcasting Genocide), (1996) *Censorship, Propaganda & State-Sponsored Violence in Rwanda 1990-1994.*

Bugajski, J, (1995) *Ethnic Politics in Eastern Europe: A Guide to Nationality Policies, Organisations and Parties.*

Byrsk, A, (1999) 'Globalisation and Human Rights: Transnational Threats and Opportunities', Paper prepared for the American Political Science Association Annual Convention, 2–5 September.

Carnegie Commission on Preventing Deadly Conflict, (1998) *Preventing Deadly Conflict: Final Report.*

Chalk, F, (1999) 'Hate Radio in Rwanda' in H Adelman and A Suhrke (eds), *The Path of a Genocide: The Rwanda Crisis From Uganda to Zaire.*

Chege, M, (1996–97) 'Africa's murderous professors', 46 The National Interest 3.

Cohen, L, (1995) *Broken Bonds: Yugoslavia's Disintegration and Balkan Politics in Transition.*

Corry, J, (1998) 'A formula for genocide', 31 The American Spectator 9, 2 September.

Denitch, B, (1994) *Ethnic Nationalism: the Tragic Death of Yugoslavia.*

Duffield, M, (1997) 'Ethnic War and International Humanitarian Intervention: A Broad Perspective' in D Turton (ed), *War and Ethnicity: Global Connections and Local Violence.*

Edwards, M, Hulme, D, and Wallace, T, (1999) 'NGOs in a global future: marrying local delivery to worldwide leverage', 19(2) Public Administrative Development: A Journal of the Royal Institute of Public Administration 117.

Enloe, C H, (1977) 'Police and Military in the Resolution of Ethnic Conflict', 433 Annals of the American Academy of Political and Social Science 137–149.

Ephson, B, (1994) 'Ethnic tension threatens northern Ghana', Agence France Presse, October 26.

Esman, M J, (1997) 'Can Foreign Aid Moderate Ethnic Conflict?', 2 United States Institute of Peace "Peaceworks" 13.

Falk, R, (1997) 'The Right to Self-Determination Under International Law: The Coherence of Doctrine Versus the Incoherence of Experience' in W Danspeckgurber (ed), *Self-Determination and Self-Administration: A Sourcebook.*

Fein, H, (1990) 'Genocide: A Sociological Perspective', 38 Current Sociology 1 (Special Issue).

de Figueiredo, R J P, and Weingast, B R, (1999) 'The Rationality of Fear: Political Opportunism and Ethnic Conflict' in B F Walter and J Snyder (eds) *Civil Wars, Insecurity and Intervention.*

Finnemore, M, (1996) 'Constructing Norms of Humanitarian Intervention' in P J Katzenstein (ed), *The Culture of National Security: Norms and Identity in World Politics.*

Füredi, F, (1998) *The Silent War: Imperialism and the Changing Perception of Race.*

Gill, S, (1996) 'Globalization, Democratization and the Politics of Indifference' in J H Mittelman (ed), *Globalization: Critical Reflections.*

Gourevitch, P, (1998) *We Wish to Inform You That Tomorrow We Will be Killed With Our Families.*

Grovogui, S N, (1996) *Sovereigns, Quasi Sovereigns, and Africans.*

Helsinki Watch (Mertus, J, and Mihelic), (1994) *Open Wounds: Human Rights Abuses in Kosovo.*

Horwitz, D, (1985) *Ethnic Groups in Conflict.*

Human Rights Watch, (1996) *Shattered Lives: Sexual Violence during the Genocide.*

—(1998a) *Detention and Abuse in Kosovo,* December, available at www.hrw.org/hrw/reports98/kosovo2/.

—(1998b) *Report, Federal Republic of Yugoslavia: Humanitarian Law Violations in Kosovo,* vol 10, No 9(D), October, available at www.hrw.org/reports98/kosovo/.

—(1998c) *Humanitarian Law Violations in Kosovo,* October, available at www.hrw.org/hrw/reports98/kosovo/.

—(1999a) *Human Rights Watch investigation finds: Yugoslav Forces Guilty of War Crimes in Racak, Kosovo,* 29 January, available at www.hrw.org/hrw/press/1999/apr/kosovo402.htm.

—(1999b) *Leave None to Tell the Story – Genocide in Rwanda.*

—(1999c) *Yugoslav Government War Crimes in Racak,* January, available at www.hrw.org/hrw/campaigns/kosovo98/racak.htm.

Human Rights Watch/Africa, (1994) *Genocide in Rwanda April-May 1994,* 6(4), 1 and 3 (May).

Jalali, R and Lipset, S M, (1997) 'Racial and Ethnic Conflicts: A Global Perspective' in D J Caralay and B B Hartman (eds), *American Leadership, Ethnic Conflict, and the New World Politics.*

Jones, B, (1999) 'Military Intervention in Rwanda's Two Wars: Partisanship and Indifference' in B F Walter and J Snyder (eds), *Civil Wars, Insecurity and Intervention.*

Kagame, F, (1999) 'The Artificial Racialization at the Root of the Rwandan Genocide' in J A Berry and C Pott Berry (eds), *Genocide in Rwanda: A Collective Memory.*

Kaldor, M, (1994) 'The New Nationalism in Europe' in R Elias and J Turpin (eds), *Rethinking Peace.*

Kaplan, R, (1993) *Balkan Ghosts: A Journey Through History.*

Keen, D, (1994) *The Benefits of Famine: A Political Economy of Famine and Relief in Southwestern Sudan, 1983-1989.*

Klinke, A, Renn, O and Lehners, J-P, (1997) 'Ethnic Conflicts and Cooperation Among and Within States' in A Klinke, O Renn and J Lehners (eds), *Ethnic Conflicts and Civil Society: Proposals for a New Era in Eastern Europe.*

Kuperman, A, (1999) 'Transnational Causes of Genocide: Or How the West Inadvertently Exacerbates Ethnic Conflict in the Post-Cold War Era', Paper presented at the Annual Meeting of the American Political Science Association, Atlanta, Georgia, 2 September.

Lemarchand, R, (1970) *Rwanda and Burundi.*

—(1993) 'Burundi in Comparative Perspective: Dimensions of Ethnic Strife' in B O'Leary and J McGarry (eds), *The Politics of Ethnic Conflict Regulation.*

—(undated) 'Genocide in Comparative Perspective: Rwanda, Cambodia and Bosnia' (manuscript on file with writer).

Lipshutz, R D, and Crawford, B (eds), (1998) *The Myth of 'Ethnic Conflict': politics, economics, and 'cultural' violence.*

Mertus, J, (forthcoming 1999) 'Doing Democracy "Differently": The Transformative Potential of Human Rights NGOs in Transnational Civil Society', Third World Legal Studies 1998–99, 205–234.

—(1999a) 'From Legal Transplants to Transformative Justice: Human Rights and the Promise of Transnational Civil Society', 14(5) American University International Law Review at 1335.

—(1999b) 'Human Rights and the Promise of Transnational Civil Society' in B Weston and P Marks (eds), *The Future of International Human Rights.*

—(1999c) *Kosovo: How Myths and Truths Started a War.*

—(1999d) 'The Liberal State vs. the National Soul: Mapping Civil Society Transplants', 8 Social & Legal Studies 1.

—(1999e) 'Mapping Civil Society Transplants: A Preliminary Comparison of Eastern Europe and Latin America', 53 U Miami LR 4 at 921.

—(1999f) 'Women in Kosovo: Contested Terrains' in S P Ramet (ed), *Gender Politics in the Western Balkans Women and Society in Yugoslavia and the Yugoslav Successor States.*

Mihajlovic, K, and Krestic, V, (1995) *Memorandum of the Serbian Academy of Sciences and Arts: Answers to Criticisms.*

Mittelman, J, (1994) 'The Globalization of Social Conflict' in V Bornschier and P Lengyel (eds), *Conflicts and Departures in World Society: Volume 3.*

Ndayambaje, J D, and Mutabaruka, J, (1999) 'Colonialism and the Churches as Agents of Ethnic Division' in J A Berry and C Pott Berry (eds), *Genocide in Rwanda: A Collective Memory.*

Newbury, C, (1992) 'Rwanda – Recent Debates Over Governance and Rural Development' in G Hyden and M Bratton (eds), *Governance and Politics in Africa.*

Oloka-Onyango, J, (1999) 'Globalization in the Context of Increased Incidents of Racism, Racial Discrimination and Xenophobia' (unpublished manuscript).

Paijic, Z, (1995) 'Bosnia-Herzegovina: From Multiethnic Coexistence to 'Apartheid' and Back' in P Akhavan (ed), *Yugoslavia: The Former and the Future: Reflections by Scholars from the Region.*

Parker, F J, (1994) 'The Why's in Rwanda', 171 America 5.

Physicians for Human Rights, (1998a) 'Action Alert: Kosovo Crisis', August, available at www.phrusa.org/campaigns/kosovo.html#INVESTI.

—(1998b) 'Medical Group Recounts Individual Testimonies Of Human Rights Abuses in Kosovo', 24 June, available at www.phrusa.org/research/kosovo2.html.

Picciotto, S, (1996–97) 'Networks in International Economic Integration: Fragmented States and the Dilemmas of Neo-Liberalism', 17 Northwestern Journal of International Law and Business 1014.

Prunier, G, (1995) *The Rwanda Crisis: History of a Genocide.*

Relief Web, (1999) 'Revision of the 1999 United Nations Consolidated Inter-Agency Appeal for the Southeastern Europe Humanitarian Operation', (the 'OCHA Report'), 26 July, available at www.reliefweb.int.

Rusinow, D, (1995) 'The Avoidable Catastrophe' in S P Ramet and L S Adamovich (eds), *Beyond Yugoslavia: Politics, Economics and Culture in a Shattered Community.*

Scheffer, D J, (1998) 'U.N. Engagement in Ethnic Conflicts' in D Wippman (ed), *International law and Ethnic Conflict.*

Schopflin, G, (1993) 'The Rise and Fall of Yugoslavia' in J McGarry and B O'Leary (eds), *The Politics of Ethnic Conflict Regulation: Case Studies of Protracted Ethnic Conflicts.*

Smith, R J, (1998) 'Yugoslavia Will Pay a Price, Albright Warns', Washington Post, 8 March.

Snyder, J, and Ballentine, K, (1997) 'Nationalism and the marketplace of ideas' in M E Brown, O R Cote, S M Lynn-Jones and S E Miller (eds), *Nationalism and Ethnic Conflict.*

Stavenhagen, R, (1999) 'Structural Racism and Trends in the Global Economy', Paper presented at the International Council on Human Rights Policy, Consultation on Racism and Human Rights, Geneva, 3–4 December.

Surroi, V, (1999) 'Victims of Victims', New York Review of Books, 7 October, p 21.

Thomas, C, (1999) 'Causes of Inequality in the International Economic Order: Critical Race Theory and Postcolonial Development', 9 Transnational Legal and Contemporary Problems 1.

Thompson, M, (1994) *Article 19, Forging War: The Media in Serbia, Croatia and Bosnia-Herzegovina.*

UN, (1998) 'Resolution 1203', adopted by the Security Council at its 3937th meeting, 24 October, available at www.nato.int/kosovo/docu/u981024a.htm.

UN, (1999) 'Resolution 1244', adopted by the Security Council at its 4011th meeting, 10 June. The full text of the UN Resolution on Kosovo can be found at www.nato.int/kosovo/docu/u990610a.htm.

UNHCR, (1999) 'Concept Paper on a Proposed Framework for Return of Refugees and Internally Displaced Persons to Kosovo', 12 May.

Uvin, P, (1996) *Development, Aid and Conflict: Reflections from the Case of Rwanda.*

—(1988) *Aiding Violence: The Development Enterprise in Rwanda.*

Valenta, K V, (1999) 'Protecting Minorities: Domestic Causes of Foreign Military Intervention on Behalf of Ethnic Minorities', Paper prepared for the American Political Science Association Annual Convention, 2–5 September.

Watson, C, (1991) *Exile from Rwanda: Background to an Invasion.*

Whitney, C R, (1998) 'Panel Finds French Errors in Judgment on Rwanda', New York Times, 20 December, at A17.

Wippman, D, (1998), 'Introduction: Ethnic Claims and International Law' in David Wippman, (ed), *International Law and Ethnic Conflict.*

Woodward, B, (1999) 'Civil Society in Transition' in R Elias and J Turpin (eds) *Rethinking Peace.*

Woodward, S, (1995) *Balkan Tragedy: Chaos and Dissolution After the Cold War.*

Chapter 20

The virtual sociality of rights: the case of 'women's rights are human rights'

A RILES[1]

It is 5 September 1995, mid-way through the staid and laborious proceedings of the UN Fourth World Conference on Women in Beijing. The delegates' seats, usually filled only with a handful of bureaucrats who nap or doodle through the ministerial speeches, are suddenly brimming with anticipation as Hillary Rodham Clinton takes the podium to thunderous applause. In marked contrast to the speeches delivered to that point, Clinton's is a political speech in the American style, and it hits its target with the delegates assembled in this room, as with the activists at the non-governmental organisations (NGOs) meeting watching by closed-circuit television, as each paragraph elicits cheers and applause:

> 'I believe that, on the eve of a new millennium, it is time to break our silence. It is time for us to say here in Beijing, and the world to hear, that it is no longer acceptable to discuss women's rights as separate from human rights ... It is a violation of *human rights* when babies are denied food, or drowned, or suffocated, or their spines broken, simply because they are girls.
>
> It is a violation of *human rights* when women and girls are sold into the slavery of prostitution.
>
> It is a violation of *human rights* when women are doused with gasoline, set on fire and burned to death because their marriage dowries are deemed too small.
>
> It is a violation of *human rights* when individual women are raped in their own communities and when thousands of women are subjected to rape as a tactic or prize of war.
>
> It is a violation of *human rights* when a leading cause of death worldwide among women ages 14 to 44 is the violence they are subjected to in their own homes.
>
> It is a violation of *human rights* when young girls are brutalized by the painful and degrading practice of genital mutilation.
>
> It is a violation of *human rights* when women are denied the right to plan their own families, and that includes being forced to have abortions or being sterilized against their will.

1   I am grateful to Bryant Garth, Hirokazu Miyazaki, Kunal Parker, Lisa Pruitt, Doug Cassel, Karen Knopf, Ed Morgan, Eve Darian-Smith and the participants in the faculty workshop, University of California at Davis School of Law, and the Human Rights Workshop, Yale Law School where this paper was presented, for their comments on this chapter, and to Beth Olds for research assistance. Funding for ethnographic research and writing was generously provided by the American Bar Foundation, the Howard Foundation, the American Couil of Learned Societies, the National Endowment for the Humanities, the Social Science Research Council, the Cambridge Commonwealth, Livingstone and Overseas Trusts and Trinity College, University of Cambridge.

If there is one message that echoes forth from this conference, it is that human rights are women's rights ... And *women's rights are human rights.*'[2]

From the point of view of the delegates assembled in the audience, the speech was courageous and path-breaking in its demand for action; indeed it *was* action.[3] (That afternoon, the young programme officer for the Fiji Women's Rights Movement, with whom the writer come to Beijing, and who had always displayed a good deal of cynicism about US interests in the Pacific, exclaimed 'you must be so proud to be an American today!') Yet the audience for Clinton's speech, of course, was as much her political enemies in Washington who had denounced her attendance at this meeting[4] as the delegates assembled in Beijing, and she addresses these quite explicitly. Indeed, one can read her speech as much as a defence of UN conferences as a defence of women's human rights.[5] The human rights message seemed to strike just the right note, in the context of Washington politics, to put her critics on the defensive. At the same time, the slogan included nothing to generate a controversial sound-bite on that evening's news broadcast.

The speech also anticipated another audience. As Clinton's speechwriters would have understood, for several years prior to the Beijing Conference a coalition of organisations had spearheaded a campaign around these precise words.[6] At issue were several related goals. The first was to gain new purchase for feminist concerns by associating these with the powerful language of human rights. The second was to gain acceptance for so-called 'second and third generation' human rights – rights that extend beyond the political and civil rights of the Cold War era[7] which proponents imagined only governments to owe to their citizens – from the right to development to the recognition of violence between private parties, as a human rights violation by associating these with the popular cause of women's rights.[8] The strategy, then, was to understand these two goals and these two domains – human rights and feminism – as versions of one another so that each might take hold through an engagement with the other.[9]

The 'women's rights are human rights' strategy has a long and distinguished pedigree, and one of great importance to its practitioners, from the inception of the UN Commission on the Status of Women in 1946 to the establishment of

2   Clinton (1995).
3   Cf Riles (2000).
4   Bogert (1995); BBC (1995).
5   'There are some who question the reason for this conference. Let them listen to the voices of women in their homes, neighborhoods, and workplaces. There are some who wonder whether the lives of women and girls matter to economic and political progress around the globe ... Let them look at the women gathered here and at Huairou ... the homemakers, nurses, teachers, lawyers, policymakers, and women who run their own businesses.
    It is conferences like this that compel governments and peoples everywhere to listen, look and face the world's most pressing problems.
    Wasn't it after the women's conference in Nairobi ten years ago that the world focused for the first time on the crisis of domestic violence?': Clinton (1995).
6   Bunch (1993).
7   Dezalay and Garth (forthcoming).
8   Bunch and Frost (1997); Cook (1994a).
9   Of course, 'first generation' human rights only appear as a stable, settled category from the point of view of the campaign to expand the category. As described in the final section of this chapter, the category becomes real only through an engagement with the 'outside'. For a discussion of the conflicts over the status of first generation human rights at the UN, the terms of which structurally mirror the material presented in this chapter, see Gaer (1996).

women's rights groups that followed its proceedings as official observers lobbied for women's political rights and the legal rights of married women.[10] However, the 'second generation' of women's rights NGOs which became active at the UN during the UN Decade for Women (1975–85) self-consciously emphasised a new and broader slate of 'issues', from peace to domestic violence to nutrition.[11] What is new, then, about the latest turn to 'rights' is the attempt to recast some of these second-generation 'issues' (most notably violence against women) as a matter of 'rights'.[12]

What is also new about the recent return to rights is the lack of contention over this agenda. While the project met with some initial scepticism from activists in the developing world, that scepticism has not taken the form of any concerted organisation against it. This is in marked contrast to the bruising conflicts among 'first' and 'third world' feminists in the 1970s and 1980s over the direction of the global women's movement.[13] Indeed, this chapter must be read as an account of a campaign that by 1995 had largely succeeded.[14] Human Rights Watch, for example, notes that governments, donors and NGOs now at least must nominally recognise that women's rights issues fall within the purview of human rights.[15] The campaign's organisers illustrate this success most often with reference to the language of the documents negotiated at recent UN world conferences, including especially the World Conference on Human Rights held in Vienna in 1993 and the UN Fourth World Conference on Women.[16] This newfound unity around rights may strike academic readers as surprising given the vigorous critique of rights and of universalism more broadly that permeated legal scholarship during exactly the same period. During the period described in this chapter, then, rights emerged as the focal point of both an intensive, self-reflexive, feminist critique and a flurry of activist 'networking'.

As an anthropologist, as well as a very minor participant in the events described here, my aim is not to contribute to the arguments for or against women's rights as human rights per se, nor is it to offer a defence or critique of the movement

---

10 Connors (1996) p 154. For a discussion of the history of the Commission on the Status of Women and of the NGOs that participated in its activities, see Galey (1995).

11 Connors (1996).

12 Reichert (1998).

13 Fraser (1987). Keck and Sikkink (1998) p 177 quote activist Charlotte Bunch as explaining that violence as a human rights issue was selected largely to overcome North-South divisions in the global women's movement.

14 As described in more detail below, the campaign defined its goal as to insure that women's rights became an accepted part of the mainstream human rights agenda.

15 Cf Boyle and Preves (1998); Keck and Sikkink (1998); Human Rights Watch (1999). Human Rights Watch notes that 'one concrete example of this rhetorical success is the inclusion of rape, sexual slavery, enforced prostitution, forced pregnancy, and enforced sterilization as war crimes and crimes against humanity' in the 1998 Treaty of Rome for the creation of an International Criminal Court new world criminal court: see Human Rights Watch (1999).

16 Eg Bunch and Frost (1997). The Beijing Declaration explicitly refers to women's human rights several times, eg paras 8 and 9, and also directly asserts that 'Women's rights are human rights': United Nations Fourth World Conference on Women (1995) para 14.

In a more recent critique of the limitations of the 'women's rights as human rights' strategy, Dianne Otto ((1997) at 128) points out there is no discussion of 'rights' at all in the sections of the Beijing Platform for Action devoted to poverty and economic structures, and that this suggests that the campaign has succeeded more in including women in the existing human rights framework than in transforming or expanding the category of human rights itself.

– all of these projects have already been performed better than I could hope to do. Rather, my interest in the constellation of academic debates, people, ideas, conferences and institutions associated with 'women's human rights' circa 1995 is in understanding how causes like 'women's rights as human rights' are made, and what kinds of institutions, professionals and further causes they make in turn. In recent years, anthropologists have begun to address the special problems of research into the character of late modern institutions and the knowledge they produce. Science Studies scholars have learned much about the micro-sociology of institutions within which the givens of scientific knowledge are constructed,[17] and others have pursued parallel insights into the character of bureaucracies,[18] of professionalism,[19] and even of the academy.[20] One theme emerging from this work concerns the articulation, appropriation and circulation of academic or artistic knowledge in commercial, bureaucratic and professional contexts.[21] The chapter aims to extend this project to an understanding of the work of what I call legal knowledge professionals – academics, bureaucrats, activists, self-consciously acting in a transnational and legal domain.[22] I take the 'women's rights are human rights' campaign and the activities of so-called 'women's NGOs' more generally as one sphere for such an inquiry. The objective, in other words, is a better understanding of how knowledge practices are shared and not shared between different classes of professionals self-consciously acting in a transnational legal domain.

To academics, it is largely self-evident that academic and activist knowledge practices are worlds apart. In fact, the distance between academic and bureaucratic or activist knowledge has often served as a useful grounding for analysis – a means of reflecting, for example, on the character of academic thought through the lens of comparison.[23] The divide seems equally real for the activist community in a different sense: academics and their insights hardly figure explicitly in activist networks at all. Offhand comments by activists about the privileged access of academics to UN bureaucrats[24] or about mutual misunderstandings,[25] offer some evidence of overt tensions.[26] Perhaps, then, academics and practitioners are as distant from one another as anthropologists once took 'Western' and 'non-Western' knowledge practices to be. Perhaps we should be wary of assuming that what motivates 'them' is transparent to 'our' analysis.

---

17 Eg Haraway (1992).
18 Eg Herzfeld (1992).
19 Eg Mol (1998a).
20 Eg Kuhn (1996); Bourdieu (1988); Strathern (1991); Reading (1996).
21 EG Brenneis (1999); Born (1995); Marcus and Myers (1995); Latour (1990); Rabinow (1989); Dezalay and Garth (1996); Radway (1997); Riles (2000).
22 Riles (manuscript).
23 Eg Kennedy (1985).
24 Eg Adams (1993) p 117.
25 Eg Cook (1994b) p 31.
26 Rebecca Cook (1994b) p 31 concludes her summary of the proceedings of a 'consultation of lawyers' on women's human rights with the comment that:
    'The consultation showed that among lawyers there must be better interaction in the work of theoreticians and practitioners. Academic lawyers working on the integration of women's human rights into the universal human rights movement must be aware of how theoretical concepts depend for effectiveness on applicability according to the rules of practice and needs of documentation of human rights committees, courts, and commissions. Legal practitioners must recognize that their work will be enriched by awareness of feminist analysis, and the relation of practical goals to the transcending evolution of the human rights movement.'

Yet the critiques of the West/non-West divide in anthropology[27] as in human rights might lead us to conclude that perhaps this concern is misplaced. How do we come to terms with the 'overlap' between 'communities' (a wholly unsatisfactory metaphor) as when sociologists serve as 'consultants' to human rights organisations or law professors become bureaucrats? Or how do we theorise alternating motivations – the feminist legal scholar's self-understanding as both theorist and activist, for example? Indeed, in practice there is such continual contact between the two camps that it is impossible to define either with any clarity: an academic pitched recent theory to activists by telling them why they should care about the dominance of the state in human rights law, for example;[28] or a key organisational player in the women's human rights campaign co-sponsored panel discussions at the World Summit on Social Development with a network of academic women from the South. One might also note activists' frequent use of academics' statistical studies in their campaigns and publications. There were even post-structuralist arguments by young employees of NGOs produced to dispute claims about the cultural specificity of human rights.[29] Some of the most interesting evidence of cross-fertilisation was a genre of advocacy that took the form of historical[30] or sociological[31] studies of the women's human rights movement itself.

This leads us to the question of reflexivity. Simply put, how can the present writer make human rights accessible, in sociological terms, given that the issues are as much 'mine' (the academic's) as 'theirs' (the activist's, the bureaucrat's)? No longer is it possible to debunk one discourse in terms of another – to apply one set of tools (academic, for example) to uncover the truth about the other knowledge practices (activist, for example). The relationship between academics and activists also presents a problem of ethnographic description. Some scholars and activists know one another personally, while many do not. There are periodic conferences at which an always slightly different list of participants assembles. Volumes of articles are produced; speeches are made and circulated – read or filed away. It is difficult, in other words, to describe any singular 'community' that might be the subject of ethnographic inquiry here. In a previous work on international institutions, I handled this dilemma by creating a certain synthetic distance between my own knowledge practices and those of her subjects, by turning away from the 'message' or 'issues' ('women's rights are human rights', for example) to focus instead on matters of 'form' in institutional practices.[32] However, in the hands of the social scientist, this synthetic distance can easily be taken for a 'real' one. I raise this issue in response to a debate concerning whether socio-legal studies might have something to contribute in return to the disciplines from which it has borrowed so heavily over past decades.

As we will see, the 'problem' of reflexivity was a question with profound effects circa 1995 on both scholarship and activism. 'Reflexivity' is not just a matter of methodology, however: it also has a sociology. How 'issues' become rights – real and independent of the analysis – and then how these rights in turn become the

27 Eg Thomas (1991).
28 Knopf (1994).
29 Eg Rao (1995).
30 Eg Bunch and Frost (1997).
31 Friedman (1995).
32 Eg Riles (1998; 2000).

subject of self-reflexive analysis – is one means of bringing that sociology into view. The challenge, then, is to understand the 'reflexive turn' as both a methodological question and something to be observed.

The puzzle that animates this chapter is the following: how was it that at the very moment at which a *critique* of 'rights'[33] and a re-imagination of rights as 'rights talk'[34] had proved to be such a fertile ground for academic scholarship did the same 'rights' prove to be an equally fertile ground for activist *networking* and lobbying activities? We will begin with the following hypothesis about this activity: Human rights 'action' among both academics and activists circa 1995 occurred in two genres. The first we will call 'human rights as representation' and the second, 'human rights as project'.

HUMAN RIGHTS AS PROJECT

'Those of us with the opportunity to be here have the responsibility to speak for those who could not.'[35]

In 1995, the women's human rights campaign was one of the most important activities of the handful of NGOs whose niche is advocacy for women on the 'international level'. The Center for Global Women's Leadership (CGWL) at the University of Rutgers, founded in 1989 with the goal of relating women, human rights and violence issues, is often credited for organising the campaign.[36] Other organisations at the centre of the campaign included the International Women's Tribune Center (IWTC), an organisation founded after the first UN conference on women held in Mexico City in 1975 and located across the street from UN headquarters in New York, and the Women's Environment and Development Organization (WEDO) also based within a stone's throw of the UN in New York. Although these organisations were based in the US[37] their target was the UN version of the global. Activities centred on UN processes, conferences and documents, and in this the human rights campaign was no exception.

Each of these organisations was associated with the personality of one figure at its helm. The director of CGWL was a lawyer and professor of women's studies, Charlotte Bunch. Anne Walker, a former YWCA employee who holds a PhD in communications, was the founder and director of IWTC. Former New York congresswoman Bella Abzug was the co-founder and President of WEDO. These leaders were senior, seasoned women's rights activists with the management-level contacts at UN agencies and at the major funding agencies necessary to survive in the highly competitive world of human rights activism. They had worked closely with one another for many years. Most were veterans of the 'second wave' feminist movement of the 1960s and 1970s in the US and overseas, and had been involved in UN activities since the UN First World Conference on Women held in 1975. Periodic criticisms of Euro-American bias were also addressed by assembling a geographically and racially diverse staff and board of directors or by involving equally seasoned women's rights activists from different regions of the world in periodic strategy meetings. In sum, the

---

33 Eg Unger (1983).
34 Eg Glendon (1991).
35 Clinton (1995).
36 Eg Keck and Sikkink (1998) p 184.
37 One exception is the International YWCA, which is based in Geneva.

leadership of the 'movement' consisted of a small and tight circle. I will refer to these organisations as 'global women's organisations' in order to capture their own understanding of the character of their mission.

Of course, in order for the global women's organisations to garner funding for their campaigns, 'women's rights as human rights' had to have already crystallised as an 'issue' – something that might be funded – in the minds of donors.[38] It is at this point that the conversation among activists, bureaucrats and academics was relevant from activists' point of view. Contemporaneous with the activities described above, a growing academic literature, curriculum and conference agenda began to appear on the question of 'women's human rights'.

The central agents of these other academic kinds of projects were international lawyers who served as experts on consultants bodies and national governments, made speeches at the UN, served as experts in the media and gave lectures at activist conferences. These academic practitioners shared with the global women's organisations an interest in influencing UN processes to gain acceptance and enforcement of 'women's rights as human rights' and a detailed knowledge of UN procedures and actors – the implications of different theories of government accountability in human rights law, the possible uses of reporting systems under the various relevant treaties, the institutional politics of UN bodies.[39] This work was not the limited province of law professors, however: there were research 'projects' as well as bureaucratic and legal projects. Political scientists served as 'gender' consultants to UN bodies,[40] anthropologists 'documented' instances of bride-burning, and some academics even took as their own activist project the task of sparring with their less project-oriented colleagues over their failure to engage with rights as a project.[41]

Activities for the 'women's rights are human rights' campaign included a global petition drive calling on the inclusion of women's rights in the agenda for the UN World Conference on Human Rights held in Vienna in 1993, panels and seminars at UN conferences in 1993, 1994 and 1995, much lobbying within the UN bureaucracy and among national bureaucracies, and the publication of newspaper and academic articles.[42] The concrete goal of the campaign was simply to have the phrase 'women's

---

38 Cf Riles (2000).

39 Cook (1994a; 1994b); cf Rishmawi (1994); Fitzpatrick (1994).

40 For example, a key UN document for the Beijing Conference – the Secretary General's mandated report on 'existing technical and financial programmes in favor of women' – was prepared by an academic 'consultant' described in the report as an 'expert in gender and organizational behaviour'. The report is peppered with political science terminology and citations: see United Nations Economic and Social Council (1995).

41 Consider, for example, the way the following conclusion to a recent review article on anthropology and human rights takes academics to task for their 'relativism' on human rights questions:
    'Over the last 45 years, the world, the discipline of anthropology, and the human rights framework have changed ... Anthropologists since 1947 have moved from criticizing universal human rights ... and are now expanding the scope filling in the content, and participating in organizations for the enforcement of these rights. The mid-century anthropologists struggled with questions of cultural relativism mostly as a debate over cultural values ..., but changing world conditions, the clear violations of human decency and dignity on the part of non-Western political leadership under the banner of cultural relativism, as well as the expansion of the human rights concept – to incorporate people's rights, a range of socioeconomic rights, the rights of indigenous peoples, and the rights to development (as defined by Third and Fourth World peoples) – have all changed the human rights problematique and correspondingly anthropologists' responses to it.' See Messer (1993) at 240.

42 The most celebrated of these is Bunch (1990).

rights are human rights' appear as prominently as possible in as many UN documents as possible. The women's human rights campaign focused primarily on the example of violence against women, as Bunch and colleagues explained:

> 'Prior to the Vienna conference, the Global Campaign made a strategic decision to emphasize issues of gender-based violence since they illustrate best how traditional human rights concepts and practice are gender-based and exclude a large spectrum of women's experience of abuse.'[43]

In interviews, however, Bunch has suggested that her interest in violence predated her interest in human rights by several years[44] – that the turn to human rights was a strategic means of foregrounding the issue of violence among the many possible feminist causes rather than a means of promoting the concept of women's rights as human rights. As we will see, this ambivalence over whether human rights was a tool to a greater end, or a final end in itself, pervaded the campaign's agenda and self image.

It is important to note that even among the group of insiders assembled by the Center for Women's Global Leadership for the purpose of developing the campaign's strategy there were doubts at the outset about this campaign.[45] The cosmopolitan leaders' appreciation of others' confusion and even disagreement over the campaign figured prominently in their actions.

The high point of the campaign for 'women's rights as human rights' is said to be the UN World Conference on Human Rights held in Vienna in 1993.[46] At that conference, the global women's organisations successfully lobbied delegates to adopt the slogan as one of the conference's central themes.[47] The UN conferences that followed – the World Summit on Development held in Copenhagen in 1994 and the UN Fourth World Conference on Women held in Beijing in 1995 – were something of a disappointment in contrast, as it proved impossible to secure statements that rights to development are human rights at the former, and the 'opposition' was far more organised opposition at the latter.[48] Indeed, one of the

---

43 Bunch, Frost and Reilly (1999) p 95.
44 Keck and Sikkink (1998).
45 Bunch, Frost and Reilly (1999) p 97 write: 'Some women were concerned that the focus on gender-based violence in Vienna detracted attention from other types of human rights issues, especially abuses associated with the actions of non-state actors like international financial institutions and transnational corporations.'
46 Eg Bunch, Frost and Reilly (1999).
47 Vienna Declaration and Programme of Action (1993). Statements about women's rights as human rights appear repeatedly in that document. The Declaration states that the UN is '*Deeply concerned* by various forms of discrimination and violence, to which women continue to be exposed all over the world': p 3:
    'The human rights of women and of the girl-child are an inalienable, integral and indivisible part of universal human rights. The full and equal participation of women in political, civil, economic, social and cultural life, at the national, regional and international levels, and the eradication of all forms of discrimination on grounds of sex are priority objectives of the international community. The human rights of women should form an integral part of the United Nations human rights activities, including the promotion of all human rights instruments relating to women.' See Vienna Declaration and Programme of Action (1993) p 10, para 18.
48 Leo (1995); Buss (1998). In a press release entitled 'Women's Human Rights: A Neglected Part of the Agenda for the United Nations Fourth World Conference on Women', the Human Rights Caucus (1995), which lists as its contact members Charlotte Bunch, Alice Miller of the International Human Rights Law Group and Regan Ralph of Human Rights Watch's Women's Rights Project, laments that: 'Governments seem to have forgotten that less than two years ago they declared that "women's rights are human rights".'

most interesting twists in the blockage of the global women's organisations at the Beijing Conference was the Vatican's own adoption of 'universal human rights' as its rallying cry against the inclusion of language supporting reproductive rights. For the campaign, therefore, a high point of the Beijing Conference was Hillary Clinton's metered, purposeful repetition of the slogan. This was the project: the repetition of a phrase in the documents as in the conference hall. What defined the project mode of thinking about human rights in contrast to the alternative discussed below, then, is what motivated its proponents: the documents, the language, the compaigns and the research programmes 'human rights' as a project generated.

HUMAN RIGHTS AS REPRESENTATION

'[H]ow can the notion that there are rights applicable to women everywhere incorporate the fact of diversity among women? Is it useful to develop international or universal understandings of the position of women? Is human rights law simply the product of the eighteenth century European "Enlightenment" and inappropriately extended to non-European societies?'[49]

Consider another position that crystallised in the academy around 1995. Once Hillary Clinton's speech, an anecdote tailor-made for CNN, is recast as the opening anecdote for a chapter on the anthropology of human rights, it demands something like the following commentary:

'Human rights is a powerful term. It is the media through which a politics, a particular politics of our time, occurs. It is imperative, therefore, to understand how the deployment of this term shapes the parameters of debate in a variety of contexts, what can and cannot be recast as a fight for human rights, what effects this recasting has on the causes and constituencies at issue.'

This statement is one I would have uttered at conferences circa 1995 and also would have recognised as a position in a debate, as the parameters of a politics of its own.[50] Circa 1995, scholars made this claim forcefully and eloquently,[51] if not without a certain degree of anguish at the concern that in 'exposing the reality' of human rights discourse they might rob causes in which they believed of their most effective weapon,[52] nor without a good dose of self-reflexivity about the situated 'politics' of such a claim itself. This mode of thinking about women's human rights was more readily associated with self-consciously academic feminist law professors who participated only rarely in UN activities and whose community of peers was feminist scholars in law and other disciplines.[53]

---

49 Charlesworth (1999). Citing feminist theorist Rosi Braidotti's claim that feminists must 'relinquish the dream of a common language': p xxi.
50 Cf Riles (1993); Engle (1992).
51 Eg Romany (1994).
52 Eg Charlesworth (1994).
53 Given anthropologists' claims on the reflexive turn to discourse and representation in lawyer's imaginations (eg Clifford and Marcus (1986)), it is interesting that this highly ambivalent focus on human rights as discourse and representation proliferates in the legal literature far more than in the anthropological one. Anthropologists traditionally have served more as foot soldiers for human rights than as its ethnographic observers: see eg American Anthropological Association Executive Board (1947); American Anthropological Association (1999).

In the classic academic statement on the question, Charlesworth, Chinkin and Wright borrow the insights of feminist theory to critique the 'abstract rationalism' of international law, but also to insist that there is 'no single school of feminism' from which to critique the work of international lawyers in the first place.[54] For this reason, the authors are highly critical of the rights-based framework of human rights.[55] Referencing a wider feminist and critical legal studies critique,[56] they note that to focus on human rights is to reduce the complexity of power inequalities to a model in which possessive individualism becomes the goal, in which it is difficult to see rights as in tension with one another or as operating to the benefit of some only to the detriment of others.[57] In the introduction to a prominent volume on women's human rights, Charlesworth further challenges the very project the volume's contributors espouse. Noting that 'It is interesting that there are few doubts expressed about the value of the whole enterprise, unlike, for example, the well-known postmodern skepticism about the use of rights discourse to remedy structural disadvantage',[58] Charlesworth concludes that 'The euphoria sometimes prompted by the vocabulary of human rights may occasionally distract us from the deeply entrenched nature of injustice and the many obstacles to change'.[59] Lest their analysis be read to support those who would derail the progress of women's human rights, however, Charlesworth, Chinkin and Wright hasten to add that rights can exude symbolic force and hence become a source of empowerment.[60]

An interest in human rights as representation, then, was an interest in the *meaning* of human rights, the expression of that meaning in documents and other genres, the limits of such representations, and hence the politics of expression more broadly. Its style of self-presentation was explicitly self-reflexive: drawing on the uses of narrative and autobiographical insight in feminist theory, scholars sought to make their own questions and concerns about rights explicit, and to use these as an engine of theory. In the final section of an article that perhaps epitomizes the discursive critique of women's human rights,[61] Karen Engle abandons her careful analysis of 'human rights discourse' and recounts, in first person form, her own experience working one summer as a human rights activist and her commitment to feminist and human rights causes. This exercise in self-reflexivity (a revelation of personal experience and the commitments, as

---

54 Charlesworth, Chinkin and Wright (1991).
55 Charlesworth, Chinkin and Wright (1991) at 634.
56 Charlesworth, Chinkin and Wright (1991) at 634, fnn 133 and 134.
57 Charlesworth, Chinkin and Wright (1991) at 634–37.
58 Charlesworth (1999) p xxii.
59 Charlesworth (1999) p xxiii. As mentioned above, this account takes 1995 as its ethnographic present. Writings since that time seem to devote more energy to the rehabilitation of women's human rights rather than its critique. For example, Dianne Otto (1997) borrows 'post-structuralist' methods to demonstrate that both positions in the debate over the universality or cultural specificity of human rights are mutually dependent. She is blunt, however, in her criticism of the activities described in this chapter:
   'the global women's human rights strategy has had the unintended effect of endorsing the post-Cold War dominance of civil and political rights. Further, although the campaign against gendered violence was designed with careful attention to women's diverse experience of violence, more public effort has been directed towards condemning certain non-Western practices.' Otto (1997) at 124.
60 Charlesworth, Chinkin and Wright (1991) at 638.
61 Engle (1992).

well as the anxieties it produced) is more than a crude assertion of activist credentials in anticipation of the (mis)reading of one's work by activists as an attack on their enterprise; it is a recounting of the ambivalence that served as the impetus for discursive analysis in the first place.[62]

One of the interesting features of the two genres of rights talk and action described above is that one could not take both positions – representation and project – at once. Like poles of a magnetic field, they could not be brought together. It may even seem that these two modes are opposites, and their proponents, adversaries. It is as if each genre of rights talk and action was unravelling what the other was weaving. As a case for a new right emerged it was deconstructed; as a new theory emerged, its relevance to the 'real action' was questioned.

Yet in order to disagree, one must first share a register of contention that renders the conflict explicit to oneself and others. Indeed, if the *genres* of rights talk could not be brought together, in participants' own imagination, the *people* who took these positions moved very much in the same circles. Almost everyone involved in the campaigns had university affiliations, higher degrees, academic publications. Likewise, almost everyone involved in the circle of scholars with interests in women's human rights was a veteran of feminist and human rights activism of some kind. Both 'sides' were intimately aware of, and concerned about, the response their work was likely to generate with the other. Scholars and activists met at conferences, over e-mail list-servs, and where each crossed over into the other's terrain (the activist took on a visiting lectureship; the law professor held a consultancy at the UN) and they addressed one another's views cautiously, amicably, directly or indirectly. In practice, there was no explicit conflict, or even contention.

Indeed, whenever a person more accustomed to one register of human rights talk and action crossed over into another, her work became virtually indistinguishable from other work of the same genre. Academics who participated in UN programmes lobbied for rights, drafted documents, or just kept quiet, but they did not give voice to the critiques they would have mounted of such activities in another setting. A most powerful example of this was the absence of debate about the 'meaning' of terms like 'woman' and 'gender' among government and NGO delegates alike at the Beijing Conference, despite the heavy representation of academics at the conference and parallel NGO Forum.[63]

In her published articles addressed to a more academic audience, for example, Charlotte Bunch makes it clear that she is well-versed in the discursive critiques of her project and that, moreover, she *agrees* entirely with her critics. She herself is staunchly against 'trying to twist women into existing human rights categories',[64] she points out, and she expounds a far more self-reflexive notion of human rights than some critiques allow: the women's human rights campaign is simply a discursive strategy, a marker for a set of practices, she argues.[65] She accepts 'the challenge to universality' with the claim that she and other proponents of women's human rights are working hard to overcome first-world bias, and she demonstrates this fact with citations to poststructuralist feminist theorists of colour and from the developing world.[66] Indeed, despite self-positioning to the contrary, it is

---

62 Engle (1992) at 599–606.
63 Riles (forthcoming).
64 Bunch (1993) p 141.
65 This article was written together with an academic who served as a 'consultant' to the Center: Bunch and Frost (1997).
66 Bunch, Frost and Reilly (1999) p 103.

impossible to find any explicit point of disagreement between the activists and academics working for and around women's human rights during this period. The difference was rather a matter of emphasis, of self-presentation, of where one chose to put one's energies. As mentioned at the outset, what must be explained sociologically, then, is this surprising amount of consensus around the notion that 'women's rights are human rights' at the very moment at which rights emerged as a subject of critique in the academy.

At the outset, we can acknowledge the symbiotic relationship between academics and activists working and writing about women's rights as human rights circa 1995. Each side produced problems or projects the other addressed: the academic critique of the 'universality' of human rights gave activists a new project – networking across national and cultural divides. Likewise, the emergence of women's rights as an issue in human rights law gave feminist scholars a doctrinal hook for their effort to bring feminist and critical race theory to bear on international law. The end points of one kind of analysis served as the beginning points of the other. This was possible because each side was intimately familiar with the aspirations and activities of the other. One simple conclusion one can draw from this material at this juncture, then, is that the anxious choice scholars and activists were making circa 1995 between promoting and critiquing human rights discourse was always a false one. The one was never tearing down what the other was building.[67] Yet there is more to it than that.

RIGHTS INSIDE OUT

What interests me most about projects and representations as genres of human rights work circa 1995 is the shared ambivalence that both modes of engagement produced: at times, those who looked at human rights in the genre of representation stepped back from the abyss and asserted that they too supported projects. Likewise, at times, those who worked with human rights as projects emphasised their own appreciation for the critique of rights and their misgivings about rights as a strategy. One characteristic of the sociality of the women's rights as human rights campaign, in other words, was the way each side momentarily switched positions and looked at the issue from the other point of view.

For both genres, this ambivalence had productive effects. It was as though the foreclosure of one kind of possibility enabled another. Ambivalence about rights was the very impetus for analyses of rights as representation. Likewise, arguably, the greatest outcome of the women's human rights campaign – the creation of several major regional networks'[68] was the result of the campaign's cosmopolitan leaders' desire to do something about their own ambivalence concerning criticisms of liberal, first world feminist bias:

'Just as [Chandra] Mohanty argues that a coherent third world feminism can be located despite the multiplicity of locations and identities of third world women, the experience of the women's human rights movement suggests that a global feminism driven by international feminist networking is also possible. Such networking does not require homogeneity of experience or perspective, or even ongoing consensus across a range of issues.'[69]

67 Cf Mol (1998).
68 Bunch, Frost and Reilly (1999) p 104.
69 Bunch, Frost and Reilly (1999) pp 103–106.

What work does this ambivalence do? Here we must return to some features of projects and representations. In the campaign, as epitomized by Hillary Clinton's speech, human rights work was talk and writing about itself. This 'talk' was not just *about* (political) action – it *was* the action: the goal of the campaign, as we saw, was the repetition of a slogan. The words Clinton so forcefully uttered did not 'stand for' an 'issue' rather, they were a set of words to be repeated in diverse contexts, from document to document. Activists took the adoption of human rights statements as the fulfilment of a goal, an accomplishment, a step forward. At the same time, academics had a theory known as 'discourse' and a method, the study of 'representation', which sought to analyse human rights action as talk and human rights talk as action. Representation and project were two versions of the same representation.

Projects and representations also shared a common ancestor and enemy – the boxed in, formalistic reasoning that dominated both academic thinking about legal rights on the one hand, and the institutional structures that had defined human rights on the other. For both, the antidote to this categorical thinking was relationality[70] – an emphasis on loose, complex, multi-layered connections (networking in the mode of projects or deconstruction in the mode of representation), and a sense that this relationship was the source of their (intellectual or political) power. For an example of this shared fascination with their own relational capacities, consider the statement of the Asia Pacific Forum of Women, Land and Development at the Beijing Conference:

> 'Issues of women's rights are human rights which are universal, indivisible, inter-dependent and inter-related. They therefore encompass the whole sphere of rights, economic, social and political. No issue of women's rights can be viewed outside of the human rights framework. The Women's Conference in Beijing would, in that context, be a follow-up of women's achievement in Vienna at the World Conference on Human Rights. Let us, therefore, remember that the road for women goes from Nairobi to Beijing, but only through Vienna.'[71]

In this statement, women's rights are related to human rights; human rights are related to one another; each UN conference is related to the next. Relationality has emerged in this statement as a fact, an achievement and a political cause of its own.

What projects and representations shared, in other words, was a particularly late twentieth-century way of analysing problems, of which a 'gender perspective' is perhaps the pinnacle achievement.[72] They shared, for example, a notion of the multiplicity of perspectives on the meaning of human rights. Indeed, it was this perspectivism that had enabled the critical gendered analysis of the old Cold War human rights paradigm in the first place: the activist's campaign to expand and transform the category of human rights was the outcome of a particular kind of academic analysis – a critique of what is taken as self-evident, a demonstration that surfaces are different from underlying realities.

Ambivalence, then, was the engine of common progress, the rejection of opposites in favour of a third indeterminate, even indefinable way. From this perspective, I believe we can read the 'women's rights are human rights' campaign *and* its critique – the deployment and the deconstruction of 'rights' as 'rights

---

70 Cf Strathern (1995).
71 Asia Pacific Forum on Women, Law and Development (1995).
72 The innovation of the term 'Gender' over 'sex' was precisely to draw attention to the socially constructed *relations* between men and women rather than to innate qualities of men or women. Cf Strathern (1991).

talk' – as a chapter in the twentieth-century excess of representation. Here is what I mean by an excess of representation: unlike political activism around torture, for example, where the problem is the indescribable, unspeakable nature of the harm,[73] the harms to women that activists sought to associate with human rights were already too easily represented – they were the mundane, casually talked-about harms: the daily incidents of food shortages, domestic violence or being passed over for a promotion. The problem for activism was that this very *over-representation* seemed to numb the activist's audience to the harm itself. Yet to solve this problem of over-representation by turning to further 'rights talk' and critiques was to add more layers, more of the same.

What was unique about this particular academic-activist relationship, then, was that both groups shared a common problem. Of course, they shared a sense of being on a common periphery from the human rights and UN establishment.[74] Yet there was something more: once unleashed, representations and perspectives proliferate beyond their framers' control. As we saw, the singular stumbling block for the women's human rights campaign was not so much the intransigence of the international community as the divisions within the global feminist community. As the leaders of the campaign repeatedly insisted, women's human rights was selected as the ultimate goal precisely because, in the aftermath of the bitter conflicts over the dominance of first-world agendas of the 1970s and 1980s, human rights was believed to be less contentious than other agendas. Likewise, the reflexive turn in the study of rights, and the critique of rights as representation was a response to similar divisions within the academy – in particular to the emergence of a 'third world perspective' critique of academic international law.

Yet, as we saw, the ambivalence and self-reflexivity that dominated discussions of women's human rights during this period – the outcome, I have suggested, of a particular epistemological moment and set of political conclusions, an awareness of the indeterminacy of things, the multiplicity of possible perspectives – engendered a need to see things from *others*' point of view. In a recent study of the emergence of a medical specialty in pain therapy in France, Isabelle Baszanger[75] argues that the division of the community of specialists into two camps who follow different theories and practices and seemingly have little to do with one another at the very moment at which the new specialty emerges and fights for respectability with the medical profession must be understood as an act of self-constitution centred in the:

> 'dual manner in which all actors involved treat a vital resource [the scientific theory of pain] even though this group is structured around internal differences gradually fashioned into practice, this theory, acting as a 'boundary object' between different groups, is the source of its stability.'[76]

Her point is that it is the internal division which allows pain, as a theory and a set of professional practices, to take form.

In a similar way, the emergence of a virtual sociality of 'groups' of activists then responded to a concrete political problem. The turn to rights, and in particular

---

73 Scarry (1985).
74 'Women's rights discourse is generally positioned at the periphery of human rights discourse, both challenging and defending the dominant human rights model as it attempts to fit causes into that model.' Engle (1992) at 519.
75 Baszanger (1998).
76 Baszanger (1998) p 120.

to rights talk (projects, representations) momentarily, anxiously, ambivalently resolved what was acknowledged as ultimately unresolvable only by drawing that conflict into a debate among virtual groups and their virtually opposed projects and representations. Rights served as a marker, an empty box around which a more contentious conversation could be cautiously continued.

The claim here is that the shared ambivalence generated the *effect* of two *groups*, activists and academics, where what was really at stake was two *modes* of engagement – representation and project. To imagine another register for doing what one does (talking about rights) is to imagine an outside vis-à-vis oneself. For participants in rights talk, then, project and representation worked as inside out views of the same device – each an 'inside speak' versus an 'outside speak' to the other. A preliminary conclusion one can draw from this short ethnographic sketch, then, concerns the sociology of 'groups' such as academics and activists: what these two 'groups' might have to do with each other is an impossible question, it is contended here – for participants as much as for outside analysts – because the groups are not 'real' entities but rather simulations produced by the discursive phenomenon of rights. The sociology cannot be described, in other words, other than in the language of rights.

This leads to a final question: why rights? Why do rights emerge as the source of a flurry of deconstructive, self-reflexive endeavours, on the one hand, and of networking projects, on the other, circa 1995? Drawing on the previous analysis, I can only offer my own conjecture: What is interesting about 'human rights' is that they can alternatively be conceived as tools – means to other ends such as women's empowerment – and as real entities, ontologically distinct from and prior to any political claims or strategies one might have or analyses one might make. They encourage the kind of double view that, in the case of projects and representations, fuelled the virtual sociality described here. Academics have tended to fixate on one possibility entailed in this dual perspective or the other – either to show how the 'real' issues serve as the focal point for a new transnational sociality,[77] or to demonstrate that human rights are in fact nothing more than a set of rhetorical strategies.[78] I find knowledge professionals' movement between these alternatives more interesting and challenging to apprehend.

Here we should look to what activists and academics alike explicitly say about the pull of rights. They are drawn to rights not because of their inherent significance, they insist, but because *others* value them. Consider, for example, the confusion about the meaning of 'women's rights are human rights' routinely heard among the women's organisations among whom I conducted ethnographic research in Fiji. For Fiji's women's rights professionals, 'human rights' were part of the global agenda, and hence to be included in their list of stated commitments if they wished to signal their status as transnational actors.[79] Women's rights as human rights evoked UN processes and documents, as when a newsletter simply reprinted under the topic of women's human rights, the portions of the Vienna document that referred to women's rights.[80] Yet rarely did activists describe events in Fiji as 'human rights violations'. Rather, human rights conjured up images of violations *elsewhere* – female infanticide in China or female genital mutilation in Africa being two common examples.

77 Eg Keck and Sikkink (1998).
78 Eg Engle (1992).
79 Cf Boyle and Meyer (forthcoming).
80 Eg Ganilau (1995).

Rights, in other words, index the outside, the other – others' interest in rights, violations of rights elsewhere. One dimension of the outside is the law. Rights of course are 'legal' entities – they generally are acknowledged to be among the subjects that lawyers and legal scholars should be concerned about. For both feminist legal scholars and activists circa 1995, lawyers were proximate outsiders to their own circle. For human rights activists, the legality of rights located their projects beyond their own activities, in the realm of the established, the settled, the mainstream.[81] The same could be said for feminist and deconstructivist legal scholars. The cartoon-like simplicity of rights, in both projects and representations, then, might be understood as evoking this otherness of law is the simplicity of something viewed from afar, something imagined to be *others'* commitment.

In this sense, for both the producers of representations and of projects, making 'rights' the focal point takes the project outside, beyond their own inner circle. We might say that it helps to turn their commitments and activities inside out,[82] and hence to make those projects and representations real to themselves. The 'beyond' quality of rights generates a sense of an outside, an *audience* of lawyers, of UN Diplomats, for example, for whom rights – and hence one's representations of them – might 'mean something'. The deployment of 'rights', whether as a matter of projects or representation, then is the virtual experience of 'our group' as apart from 'theirs', of one's own community and the 'mainstream', or the 'third world', or the 'first world', or the 'academy'. I want to suggest that this is the inherent appeal of legality and hence of rights: as a marker of *others'* commitments, rights signal to imagined outsiders the fruits of one's labour, and hence virtually establish one's social existence as apart from those imagined as beyond.

Select bibliography

Adams, B, (1993) 'The UN, World Conferences and Women's Rights' in J Kerr (ed) *Ours by Right: Women's Rights as Human Rights.*

American Anthropological Association, (1999) 'Proposed Declaration on Anthropology and Human Rights. As presented in William E. Davis', American Anthropological Association Memorandum, 23 April.

American Anthropological Association Executive Board, (1947) 'Statement on Human Rights Submitted to the Commission on Human Rights, United Nations', 49(4) American Anthropologist 1.

Asia Pacific Forum on Women, Law and Development, (1995) 'Statement for the 39th Session of the Commission on the Status of Women', 15 March–4 April (on file with present writer).

Baszanger, I, (1998) 'Pain Physicians: All Alike, All Different' in M Berg and A Mol (eds) *Differences in Medicine: Unraveling Practices, Techniques, and Bodies.*

---

81 Interestingly, the phrase of 'legal rights' had far more appeal with activists in Fiji than 'human rights'(eg Jalal (1998)) and was often used in the very contexts the global women's organisations hoped to deploy the notion of human rights such as violence against women and married women's citizenship rights. Women's groups also sought to associate these issues with the more gender-neutral theme of 'development'. Cf Fiji Women's Rights Movement (1995a; 1995b); Prakash (1994).

82 Riles (2002)

BBC Summary of World Broadcasts, (1995) 'Hillary Clinton's "improper" speech contained "nonsensical and preposterous arguments"', 18 September, Part 3, Asia-Pacific, UN Fourth World Conference on Women; EE/D2411/S2. Source: Zhongguo Tongxun She news agency, Hong Kong, in Chinese, 16 September.

Bogert, C, (1995) 'Women In China: We Turned This Around', Newsweek, 18 September, at 50.

Born, G, (1995) *Rationalizing Culture: IRCAM, Boulez, and the Institutionalization of the Musical Avant-Garde.*

Bourdieu, P, (1988) *Homo Academicus.*

Boyle, E H, and Meyer, J, (2002) 'Modern Law as a Secularized and Global Model: Implications for the Sociology of Law' in Y Dezalay and B Garth (eds), *The Production, Exportation and Importation of a New Legal Orthodoxy.*

Boyle, E H, and Preves, S E, (1998) 'Sovereign Autonomy Versus Universal Human Rights: The Bases for National Anti-Female-Genital Excision Laws', (manuscript).

Brenneis, D, (1999) 'New Lexicon, Old Language: Negotiating the "Global" at the National Science Foundation' in G E Marcus (ed) *Cultural anthropology now: Unexpected contexts, shifting constituencies, changing agendas.*

Bunch, C, (1990) 'Women's Rights as Human Rights: Toward a Revision of Human Rights' 12 Human Rights Quarterly 486–489.

—(1993) 'Organizing for Women's Human Rights Globally' in J Kerr (ed) *Ours by Right: Women's Rights as Human Rights.*

Bunch, C, and Frost, S, (1997) 'Women's Human Rights: An Introduction' in C Bunch and S Frost (eds) *The Encyclopedia of Women's Studies.*

Bunch, C, Frost, S, and Reilly, N, (1999) 'Making the Global Local: International Networking for Women's Human Rights' in K D Askin and D M Koenig (eds) *Women and International Human Rights Law.*

Buss, D E, (1998) 'Robes, Relics and Rights: The Vatican and the Beijing Conference on Women', 7(3) Social and Legal Studies 339.

Charlesworth, H, (1994) 'What are "Women's International Human Rights?"' in R Cook (ed) *Human Rights of Women: National and International Perspective.*

—(1999) 'General Introduction' in K D Askin and D M Koenig (eds) *Women and International Human Rights Law.*

Charlesworth, H, Chinkin, C, and Wright, S, (1991) 'Feminist Approaches to International Law', 85 AJIL 613.

Clifford, J, and Marcus, G (eds), (1986) *Writing Culture.*

Clinton, H R, (1995) 'Statement at the United Nations Fourth World Conference on Women', Beijing, China, 5 September. United Nations Development Program (UNDP), available at gopher://gopher.undp.org/00/unconfs/women/conf/gov/950905175653.

Connors, J, (1996) 'NGOs and the Human Rights of Women at the United Nations' in P Willetts (ed) *'The Conscience of the World': The Influence of Non-Governmental Organisations in the UN System.*

Cook, R, (1994a) 'State Accountability Under the Convention on the Elimination of All Forms of Discrimination Against Women' in R Cook (ed) *Human Rights of Women: National and International Perspectives.*

—(1994b) 'Women's International Human Rights Law: The Way Forward' in R Cook (ed) *Human Rights of Women: National and International Perspectives.*

Dezalay, Y, and Garth, B, (1996) *Dealing in Virtue: International Commercial Arbitration and The Construction of a Transnational Legal Order.*

—(2002) *The Internationalization of Palace Wars: Lawyers, Economists and the Contest to Transform Latin American States.*

Engle, K, (1992) 'International Human Rights and Feminism: When Discourses Meet', 13 Mich JIL 517.

Fiji Women's Rights Movement, (1995a) 'Putting an End to the Crisis', Balance, November–December, at 1.

—(1995b) 'Drafting Bill on Domestic Violence', *Balance.* May–June, at 14.

Fitzpatrick, J, (1994) 'The Use of International Human Rights Norms to Combat Violence Against Women' in R Cook (ed) *Human Rights of Women: National and International Perspectives.*

Fraser, A S, (1987) *The U.N. Decade for Women: Documents and Dialogue.*

Friedman, E, (1995) 'Women's Human Rights: The Emergence of a Movement' in J Peters and A Wolper (eds) *Women's Rights Human Rights: International Feminist Perspectives.*

Gaer, F D, (1996) 'Reality Check: Human Rights NGOs Confront Governments at the UN' in T G Weiss and L Gordenker (eds) *NGOs, the UN, and Global Governance.*

Galey, M E, (1995) 'Women Find a Place' in A Winslow (ed) *Women, Politics and the United Nations.*

Ganilau, B R, (1995) 'The Road to Beijing', 1(3) S'Pacifically Speaking: Newsletter of the PNGOCG, May, at 8.

Glendon, M A, (1991) *Rights Talk: The Impoverishment of Political Discourse.*

Haraway, D, (1992) *Primate Visions: Gender, Race, and Nature in the World of Modern Science.*

Herzfeld, M, (1992) *The Social Production of Indifference: Exploring the Symbolic Roots of Western Bureaucracy.*

Human Rights Caucus, (1995) '*Women's Human Rights: A Neglected Part of the Agenda for the United Nations Fourth World Conference on Women*', Press Release, (on file with present writer).

Human Rights Watch, (1999) *Human Rights Watch World Report 1999: Women's Human Rights*, available at www.hrw.org/hrw/worldreport99/women.

Jalal, I P, (1998) *Law for Pacific Women: A Legal Rights Handbook.*

Keck, M E, and Sikkink, K, (1998) *Activists Beyond Borders: Advocacy Networks in International Politics.*

Kennedy, D, (1985) 'Spring Break', 63 Texas LR 1377.

Knopf, K, (1994) 'Why Rethinking the Sovereign State is Important for Women's International Human Rights Law' in R Cook (ed) *Human Rights of Women: National and International Perspectives.*

Kuhn, T S, (1996) *The Structure of Scientific Revolutions* (3rd edn).

Latour, B, (1990) 'Drawing Things Together' in M Lynch and S Woolgar (eds) *Representation in Scientific Practice.*

Leo, J, (1995) 'A Near Hijacking at the U.N.', 119(12) U.S. News & World Report 32, 25 September.

Marcus, G E, and Meyers, F R, (1995) 'The Traffic in Art and Culture: an Introduction' in G E Marcus and F R Meyers (eds) *The Traffic in Culture: Refiguring Art and Anthropology*.

Messer, E, (1993) 'Anthropology and Human Rights', 22 Annual Review of Anthropology 221.

Mol, A, (1998) 'Missing Links, Making Links: The Performance of Some Atheroscleroses' in M Berg and A Mol (eds) *Differences in Medicine: Unraveling Practices, Techniques and Bodies*.

Otto, D, (1997) 'Rethinking the "Universality" of Human Rights Law', 29 Columbia Human Rights Law Review 1.

Prakash, L, (1994) 'Crime Against Women', Balance, December, at 9.

Rabinow, P, (1989) *French Modern: Norms and Forms of the Social Environment*.

Radway, J, (1997) *A Feeling for Books: The Book-of-the-Month Club, Literary Taste, and Middle-Class Desire*.

Rao, A, (1995) 'The Politics of Gender and Culture in International Human Rights Discourse' in J Peters and A Wolper (eds) *Women's Rights Human Rights: International Feminist Perspectives*.

Reading, B, (1996) '*The University in Ruins*'.

Reichert, E, (1998) 'Women's Rights are Human Rights: Platform for Action', 41(3) International Social Work 371.

Riles, A, (1993) 'Note: Aspiration and Control: International Legal Rhetoric and the Essentialization of Culture', 106(3) Harv LR 723.

—(1998) 'Infinity Within the Brackets', 25(3) American Ethnologist 378.

—(2000) *The Network Inside Out*.

—(forthcoming) '[Deadlines]' in A Riles (ed) *Documents: Artifacts of Modern Knowledge*.

—(manuscript) The Transnational Appeal of Formalism: The Case of Japan's Netting Law, available at www.SSRN.com.

Rishmawi, M, (1994) 'The Developing Approaches of the International Commission of Jurists to Women's Human Rights' in R Cook (ed) *Human Rights of Women: National and International Perspectives*.

Romany, C, (1994) 'State Responsibility Goes Private: A Feminist Critique of the Public/Private Distinction in International Human Rights Law' in R Cook (ed) *Human Rights of Women: National and International Perspectives*.

Scarry, E, (1985) *The Body in Pain: The Making and Unmaking of the World*.

Strathern, M, (1991) *Partial Connections*.

—(1995) 'The Relation: Issues in Complexity and Scale', 6 Prickly Pear Pamphlet.

Thomas, N, (1991) *Entangled Objects: Exchange, Material Culture, and Colonialism in the Pacific*.

Unger, R M, (1983) *The Critical Legal Studies Movement*.

United Nations Economic and Social Council, Commission on the Status of Women (1995). 'Preparations for the Fourth World Conference on Women: Actions for Equality, Development and Peace: Technical Assistance and Women: From Mainstreaming Towards Institutional Accountability', E/CN.6/1995/6, 19 December.

United Nations Fourth World Conference on Women (1995) Beijing Declaration in *Report of the Fourth World Conference on Women*. A/Conf. 177/20.

Vienna Declaration and Programme of Action, (1993) UN World Conference on Human Rights, A/Conf.157/23, 25 June.

Chapter 21

National legislation and the role of the government and the UNHCR in the determination of legal status of refugees in Kenya

KOKI MULI

INTRODUCTION

One interesting aspect of Kenya is that, while being a host to many refugees, it does not have a refugee-specific law or an official policy on refugees, other than that Kenya is a temporary[1] country of host. One would ask then what procedures does it follow in determining their legal status and how does it manage its refugee population? Kenya relies on immigration and restriction of aliens laws to deal with matters regarding and relating to refugees, citizenship laws are applied on refugees as and when they become necessary. The Constitution of Kenya is also an important law when it comes to guaranteeing the human rights of everyone within the territory of Kenya. Whether or not refugees enjoy these rights is a moot question. An ad hoc committee was established after independence to deal with the issue of determining the legal status of asylum-seekers and refugees. The United Nations High Commissioner for Refugees (UNHCR) has been assisting the government in providing for the welfare of the refugees and in protection activities.

A refugee is a person whose definition and identity is contained and provided for under international conventions. Likewise, their protection is governed under international instruments and overseen by an international organisation, the UNHCR. A refugee becomes thus by virtue of crossing international borders. National systems define and bestow legal status to refugees pursuant to the international definition of a refugee, whether or not they have ratified these international refugee conventions. Therefore, a person must satisfy the criteria and the definition of a refugee in order to deserve international protection. Thus the process of determining the legal status of a refugee is crucial to his or her protection. Countries pursue different procedures of determining the legal status of refugees. The common procedure being that set down by the UNHCR Handbook for the determination of refugee status.[2] Although contracting states are not obliged to admit refugees in their countries, they cannot return a refugee to a country where he or she is at risk of torture, persecution or death without examining their claims in detail.

---

1   Although there is a question on how temporary is 'temporary' in this regard because refugees from Somalia, The Sudan, Ethiopia, etc have been in Kenya from the late 1980s and early 1990s to the present day, yet they are still considered to be in Kenya on a temporary basis: refer to Hyndman and Nylund (1998) at 21.
2   UNHCR (1992).

440

This chapter is divided into three parts. The first part discusses the existing legal framework, which directly or indirectly regards or relates to refugees. The main argument here being that the existing legal framework does not adequately deal with refugees and address their protection needs. The upshot of this is that the lacunae in the refugee-specific legislation undermines Kenya's efforts in protecting refugees' rights and it cannot be filled by the existing legislation. Part two discusses the role played by the government in determining the legal status of refugees, specifically focusing on some concerns regarding the current practice. The argument is that lack of a procedure for the determination of legal status undermines the process itself, which as a result is seriously flawed and therefore ineffective. Part three examines the role of the UNHCR in processes of determining the legal status of refugees. The main argument here is that although UNHCR is clearly overwhelmed by the task of determining the legal status of most of the refugees coming into Kenya since 1991, its activities do not conform to its mandate and to international human rights standards regarding due process of law and fairness.

THE CURRENT LEGAL FRAMEWORK

Laws dealing with immigration

The main argument in this section is that the laws described here which are relied on in dealing with refugee issues are inadequate and cannot fill the gap created by lack of a refugee-specific legislation. Further, the process of determination of refugee status requires legally sanctioned procedures and their lack thereof undermines the process of refugee status determination.

Some people[3] argue that adoption of a legislation, which would establish in Kenya a procedure for refugee status determination, would not make much difference especially to prima facie refugees. The writer disagrees with this argument for the following reasons. First, legal procedures bestow legal status without which protection cannot be provided. Second, legal procedures ensure that refugees are protected by law and as a right and do not depend on the magnanimity and the discretion of the officials they encounter when they enter the country. Third, legal procedures guarantee some form of uniformity and universality in the manner with which refugees are dealt throughout different entry points in the country. Fourth, legal procedures provide an official sequence of the process of application for refugee status, determination of legal status, due process including appeals, etc – processes which could be undermined when not set out in some official procedures. This also reduces instances of abuse of office and corruption, conditions, which are unfortunately rampant in Kenya. Finally, legal procedures will help those concerned determine durable solutions faster, including local integration if provided for. It is precisely because there are no legal procedures that the prima facie refugees continue to languish in camps without any durable solution in sight, as the government continues to argue that they must remain in camps while it is enacting a refugee-specific legislation which will determine what should be done with them.[4]

---

3   Hyndman and Nylund (1998).
4   This does not mean that a refugee-specific legislation is a panacea of all the problems regarding and relating to refugees in Kenya, but it certainly will not make the situation any worse.

The main Immigration Restriction Ordinance[5] was first enacted in 1906. This Ordinance mainly dealt with the restriction of immigration to the Kenya colony. It did not deal with the issue of citizenship and persons lawfully in Kenya. Prohibited immigrants[6] included those who were convicted of serious offences and who might have threatened the peace and security of the colony. It also prohibited persons likely to immigrate to the colony and become a liability or a public charge.

An important feature of this Ordinance was that it allowed immigration into the colony of persons who had been convicted of offences of a political nature 'not involving moral turpitude' and were fleeing to the colony to seek some kind of peace or refuge,[7] thus denoting for the first time the concept of providing asylum for those suffering political persecution. The Ordinance established the foundation for the protection of these kinds of people.

In 1956, The Legislative Council enacted a new Immigration Ordinance, the Immigration Ordinance, Number 35 of 1956, which was adopted almost wholly, with only minor modifications and amendments, at independence in 1963.

The Miscellaneous Amendments Act 1964[8] facilitated a number of amendments to existing legislation to enable the new government to consolidate its authority and power with regard to security issues. Its aim was 'to amend certain Acts in the interests of security and to make other minor, consequential or incidental amendments' to the already existing Ordinances. It amended the Immigration Ordinance[9] to provide that the Ordinance should not apply to citizens of Kenya and other Africans, with certain exceptions. The Amendment Act also gave the power to prohibit immigration to Kenya on the ground of security by allowing the minister to declare a person a 'prohibited immigrant' whose presence in Kenya was contrary to the interests of national security.

The current Immigration Act[10] repealed the provision that an aggrieved person could appeal to the Supreme Court by making the appeal to the minister concerned with immigration final. This provision makes it difficult for any one aggrieved by the decision of the minister to appeal to the courts.

This Act, among other things, makes it a crime to harbour, aid or employ a prohibited immigrant and for a prohibited immigrant to remain in Kenya, thus making it very difficult for people to assist refugees, who in many cases could be classified under the category of prohibited immigrants for the purposes of this Act.

Immigration laws deal only with matters of immigration and do not expressly deal with refugees except in so far as crimes related to unlawful presence in Kenya are concerned. The Immigration Act is used in this regard as a basis upon which refugees who do not remain in the camps, as is required by the government policy, are charged in courts for being in Kenya illegally. The prosecution argues that the government of Kenya does not recognise any refugees outside the camps unless they have permission from the government to be outside the camps. This situation is unfair and curtails the refugees' right of movement and of association.

---

5 Ch 62 of Colonial Ordinance, Kenya; Ch 172 of the Laws of Kenya.
6 S 5(a)–(h).
7 S 5(d).
8 The Immigration and Deportation (Miscellaneous Amendments) Act, No 1 of 3 March 1964.
9 S 1(2) of the Immigration Ordinance 1956 (Cap 172).
10 Immigration Act, No 25 of 1967, commenced on 1 December as 'an Act of Parliament to amend and consolidate the law relating to immigration into Kenya, and for matters incidental thereto and matters connected therewith'.

Colonial laws were adopted by the independent government and have not been repealed to accommodate the changing circumstances of the free movement of persons, instead only some provisions have been amended and added into the existing legislation to address in part some contemporary issues.

The Immigration Act was amended in 1972[11] to incorporate a definition of a refugee in accordance with the 1951 UN Geneva Convention relating to the Status of Refugees (hereafter the 1951 UN Convention).[12] However, while this definition only related to work permits and was aimed at providing that a person recognised as a refugee might be granted an M type[13] of entry permit enabling him to engage in gainful occupation, it nevertheless defined a refugee within Kenyan law for the first time. This classification presupposed that there were procedures for determining and identifying persons fitting the definition and criteria of a refugee.

This amendment might well be considered the most important amendment in relation to recognition of refugees. Although it did little more than provide for a category of persons known as refugees, its effects were quite marked. In practice, the amendment did more than just provide for this category of permits, and it had some positive as well as negative effects.

Some of the positive effects include the following:

(1) It amended the Immigration Act 1967 to include the M category of permits.[14] The effect of this amendment was that as regards applications for permits, refugees were recognised for the first time as legal persons requiring their own category of permits. The net outcome was that refugees became a category of persons recognised under the laws of Kenya, thus bestowing them with some kind of legal status, albeit with regard to issuance of permits only.

(2) Permit M[15] does not apply to the child of the refugee under the age of 13. What this means is that any child of the refugee over the stated age can engage or make use of the permit granted to his or her father to carry on their independent business, profession, trade, etc. The same case applies to the wife[16] of the refugee granted a permit, thus enabling the adult family members to engage in income-generating activities on the same permit.

(3) Under the added subsection,[17] all persons issued with this permit are also issued with identity cards, the effect of which bestows the same rights to refugees that are enjoyed by ordinary Kenyans, with the exception of voting

11 The Immigration (Amendment) Act, No 6 of 1972, Ch 176 of the Laws of Kenya, s 5 provides for Class M entry permit applicable to persons recognised as refugees.
12 Entered into force on 22 April 1954. Kenya acceded to this Convention on 16 May 1966 without any reservations and to the 1967 Protocol to this Convention on 13 November 1981, also without any reservations.
13 The Schedule to the Immigration Act providing for classes of entry permits, in accordance to s 5 of the Act was amended to include class M: 'A person who is a refugee, that is to say, is, owing to well-founded fear of being persecuted for reasons of race, religion, nationality, membership of a particular social group or political opinion, unwilling to avail himself of the protection of the country of his nationality or who, not having a nationality and being outside the country of his former habitual residence for any particular reason, is unable or, owing to such fear, is unwilling to return to such a country; and any wife or child over the age of thirteen years of such a refugee.'
14 S 5(3) of the Immigration Act 1967 (Ch 172 of the Laws of Kenya).
15 Under the added s 6(3) of the Act.
16 Amendment to the Schedule to the Immigration Act to include category M: '... (b) and any wife (c) Any child over the age of 13 years of such a refugee.'
17 S 17(da), which requires that registers be kept for permits issued under M category.

rights and the right to join the armed forces. These identity cards are recognised as having the same effect as identity cards issued to Kenyans.[18] In essence, the sum effect of this subsection is that people issued with an M-type permit enjoy asylum rights in Kenya as soon as they engage in the activities allowed under the permit. After the requisite residence period they have an option of applying for registration as citizens of Kenya.

There are also some difficulties arising from the 1972 Amendment because the wording is unclear, somewhat ambiguous and confusing – allowing for different interpretations that might be used against a prospective applicant. Although there is no doubt that the definition of a 'refugee' is consistent with article 1A(2) of the 1951 UN Convention, the 1972 amendment leaves out the words '*is outside the country of his nationality and is unable or, owing to such fear*' immediately after enumerating the grounds for well-founded fear of persecution. This can be assumed to be a drafting omission, but it raises the question: does it affect the definition of a refugee in this sense as a result? In practice, perhaps not, since little attention is paid to this definition largely because there are no legal procedures for determining refugee status anyway and it is often assumed that applicants for a Class M permit have in one way or another been confirmed as refugees. There remain serious concerns about this definition however. For example, the definition is gender-specific and does not include women[19] refugees, prima facie refugees and some refugees sur place, and it is not clear whether or not such refugees are entitled to this class of permit.

Some of the negative effects of the 1972 Amendment are noted as follows:

(1) The amendment to the Schedule defining a refugee is very restrictive and is based only on the 1951 UN Convention definition. This means that most of the refugees in Kenya are not eligible for Class M permits because they fall under the added category of persons fitting the description of a refugee under the Organization of African Unity: 1969 Convention on the Specific Aspects of Refugee Problems in Africa (the OAU Convention[20]). Also, the fact that only the wife and children of a refugee are covered under the M permit definition excludes the many refugees in Kenya who seek refuge as part of an extended family. Furthermore, the fact that the amendment defines the refugee as a man whose wife and children can enjoy the benefits of the permit omits single mothers and widows altogether, and in essence discriminates against them. Therefore, since the majority of refugees are widows, single mothers and children,[21] they are disqualified, under the law, from making the application for an M permit. As a consequence they are condemned to the harsh and deplorable living conditions of the camps.

(2) The decision of the minister,[22] on appeal, to grant or deny a permit under Class M is final and cannot be challenged in any court. Although this section

18 S 9 of the Registration of Persons Act (Cap 107).
19 This is not just about the use of 'he' word in the definition only, but because of the use of the word 'wife' instead of 'spouse' or both 'wife' and 'husband'. Some women refugees have argued that they have been denied permits because it is difficult to prove that they do not have a male guardian and it took a lot of time and convincing to change this perception by Immigration Officers to allow the women applicants to apply for the permit.
20 Organization of African Unity (1969)
21 UNHCR Nairobi branch Office statistics, April 1999, as well as from the writer's personal observations.
22 The amended s 5(3) of the Act.

does not discriminate against refugees as a class of persons, since it applies to all classes from E to M, it gives the minister wide discretionary powers that present opportunities for abuse, and, since no reasons need be provided for denial of a permit, it is possible for permits to be denied arbitrarily.

(3) A person granted a Class M permit must engage, within 14 days of issue of the permit, in the activity for which the permit was issued, failure to do which invalidates the permit.[23] For whatever reason, if the grantee is unable to engage in the activity for which the permit was granted within the required time limit, he has to repeat the application procedure. The writer suggests that 14 days is an unfairly short and rather arbitrary time allowance before a licence is invalidated, when it takes so long to acquire in the first place.

Therefore, although this amendment bestows certain benefits to refugees, it cannot be substituted for a comprehensive and appropriate refugee-specific legislation, since it does not assist the government in ensuring the legal protection of refugees in Kenya. Consequently, the necessity of an appropriate refugee-specific legislation cannot be over-emphasised. Furthermore, the enforcement of refugee rights and responsibilities through the courts in Kenya is an alien concept because international refugee conventions are unenforceable since they have not yet been incorporated into Kenyan law through Parliament, as is the tradition. Thus, the amendment discussed above remains an ornament in the Immigration Act 1967 with regard to the protection of refugees, even though it recognises them as legal persons for the purposes of the Act.

LAWS DEALING WITH RESTRICTION OF ALIENS

Laws dealing with restriction of movement of aliens into Kenya are also used to govern matters concerning refugees. This is mainly with regard to denying entry into Kenya of refugees, as was the case with Somali refugees in 1990, when security officers arrested and turned away boats arriving in the coastal region from Somalia, leading to many of the boats capsizing. Security officers also detained refugees in boats for days in the Kenyan harbour of Mombasa under conditions unfit for human habitation.[24] Matters regarding refugees are also classified as affecting national security, thus the justification to categorise them under these laws.

The Aliens Restriction Ordinance 1918[25] was aimed at restricting entry of aliens into the Protectorate, and specifically gave powers to the Governor needed to prohibit aliens from entering or leaving Kenya at any time during a state of war or during a situation of imminent danger or a great emergency. The meaning of 'alien' was any person who was not a British subject or who was not a native of the Protectorate.[26] At the time, because of the hostilities in Europe, it was perhaps understandable that an Ordinance of this nature would be enacted to enable Protectorate officials to take measures necessary or expedient to guarantee the safety of the Colony.[27] This is one example of legislation enacted to safeguard national security.

---

23 The amended s 6(1) and 6(1)(a) of the Act.
24 Refer to Africa Watch Report (1991) chapter 119, p 342.
25 The Aliens Restriction Ordinance (Ch 189, Colonial Ordinances, Kenya), No12 of 11 May 1918, enacted towards the end of the First World War.
26 Aliens Restriction Ordinance 1918, s 2.
27 Aliens Restriction Ordinance 1918, s 3(1).

The 1918 Ordinance was not subject to any review or amendments throughout the colonial period, and was adopted 55 years later by the independent government of Kenya as the Aliens Restriction Act 1973,[28] with very minor alterations, and indeed the substance and the essence of the 1918 Ordinance was retained.[29]

The Aliens Restriction Act 1973 has, in the writer's opinion, outlived its usefulness and should be repealed as it is only used to oppress aliens, and especially refugees since other 'aliens' are adequately provided for under the Immigration Act 1967. One interesting factor is that the 1973 Act has not been subject to any interpretation by the courts and it remains ambiguous as to what 'a situation of imminent danger or a great emergency' is. As a result, this section has been subject to abuse, in the writer's opinion, by immigration and security officers when they arrest refugees claiming that they are in urban centres without the permission of the government and that by their sheer numbers and presence in urban areas they pose a security threat to Kenya.[30]

The Aliens Restriction Act 1973 is one of the very brief Kenyan laws. It contains three substantive sections, the first providing for the short title, the second providing for the interpretation of the meanings of 'alien', 'alien order' and 'the minister' and the third outlining the powers to be exercised with respect to aliens, specifically what the minister may do 'at any time during a state of war', during an 'occasion of eminent danger' or when a 'great emergency' has arisen. Section 3 provides that the minister may by order impose from time to time restrictions on aliens:

'(a) For prohibiting aliens from landing in or otherwise entering Kenya either generally or at certain places and for imposing restrictions or conditions on aliens landing or arriving at any port in Kenya.
   ...
(c) For requiring aliens to reside and remain within certain places or districts.
(d) For prohibiting aliens from residing or remaining in any areas specified in the order.'

As mentioned above, these provisions have not been subject to any interpretations by courts and are therefore applied at the discretion of the officers in charge and often are not uniformly interpreted by the officers who, in the writer's experience, often overstep their jurisdiction in the zealous manner in which they apply the provisions to harass refugees. On the basis of these provisions the Aliens Restriction Act 1973 appears to have been enacted

28 Ch 173 of the Laws of Kenya, Legal Notice No 5 of 1973. This Act commenced on 18 May 1973. It was first revised in 1974 by Legal Notice No 65 of 1974 and again in 1977. This Act was enacted at the beginning of mass exodus of people from Uganda, and it can be deduced that one of its aims was to restrict entry into Kenya by, among others, persons expelled from Uganda in 1972 who were pursuant to that expulsion stateless.

29 Modest changes were made to the 1918 Ordinance by making it an Act of Parliament instead of an Ordinance, expounding s 2 by including 'aliens order', replacing the words 'Governor' or 'Governor in Council' with 'Minister' and replacing 'His Majesty' with 'Kenya' (s 3). However, the substantive sections and their effects remained the same.

30 Although it is a government policy that refugees remain in camps unless with express permission from the government to be outside the perimeters of the camps, there is no law that echoes this policy and therefore courts cannot base decisions against refugees on the policy. It is the writer's experience that the police and immigration officers arrest refugees on the basis of this policy and charge them under offences created by the Immigration Act 1967, for example for being in Kenya unlawfully (s 8) or falling under the category of prohibited immigrants (s 3).

more for administrative purposes than for the *protection* of the aliens and it is used for this purpose. It is also incompatible with refugee and human rights provisions, which permit reasonable freedom of movement,[31] the right to seek and enjoy asylum[32] and the right of non-refoulement.[33]

Does the fact that this Act remains in effect in Kenya in the absence of any refugee-specific legislation mean that the government is unwilling to deal in any other way with refugees? Furthermore, with a law like this it matters little whether Kenya has ratified any international refugee Conventions, which protect refugees, especially when such are not part of Kenya's domestic legislation, because national legislation overrides international law in Kenya. Incorporation of treaties and conventions through an Act of Parliament in Kenya is a prerequisite for their implementation at national level. As a consequence, signature, accession and/or ratification alone is not sufficient to guarantee their effective implementation and enforcement in Kenya. The cases of *Okunda and anr v R*[34] and *The East Africa Community v R*[35] establish in Kenya the principle as argued above. In the latter decision, the Court of Appeal held that treaties do not become part of the law of Kenya, until made so by law of Kenya and having been made the law of Kenya, any such treaty which is in conflict with the Constitution is void. Therefore, the Aliens Restriction Act 1973 by its very existence undermines any efforts to bestow legal status and protection to refugees.

The Aliens Restriction Act 1973 defines 'alien' as any person who is not a citizen of Kenya. Therefore, although the Act does not especially deal with refugees *per se*, as mentioned above, it does in so far as the definition of an alien includes all non-Kenyans. It is important, however, to draw the distinction between an 'alien' in this regard and a 'refugee' because the distinction matters a great deal to the protection of the refugee. There is a big difference between refugees and aliens. Aliens can still enjoy the protection of the countries of their nationality, while refugees cannot because they may be fleeing their governments and have lost the protection of their governments. Aliens can also call on their governments to protect them against violation of their rights, and can seek remedies at national and international level, unlike refugees. Refugees are thus a special category of vulnerable persons requiring international protection. The generally accepted definition of a refugee is that of the 1951 UN Convention[36] in which a refugee is defined as a person who:

> 'Owing to a well founded fear of being persecuted for reasons of race, religion, nationality, membership of a particular social group or political opinion, is outside the country of his nationality and is unable or, owing to such fear, is unwilling to avail himself of the protection of that country; or who, not having a nationality and being outside the country of his former habitual residence ... is unable or, owing to such fear, is unwilling to return to it.'[37]

---

31 Art 26 of the 1951 UN Convention, which provides that contracting states shall accord to refugees lawfully in their territories the right to choose their residence and to move freely therein. Also, see art 13 of the UN Universal Declaration of Human Rights 1948 (UDHR) and art 12 of the International Covenant of Civil and Political Rights 1966.
32 Art 14(1) of the UDHR. Also art II of the 1969 OAU Convention.
33 Art 33(1) of the 1951 UN Convention and art II(3) of the 1969 OAU Convention.
34 [1970] EA 453 (HC of Kenya at Nairobi), per Mwendwa CJ, Chanan Singh and Simson JJ, 21 October and 3 November 1969.
35 Criminal Appeal 156 of 1969 [1970] EA 457 (CA, Nairobi), per Sir Charles Newbold, Duffus V-P and Spry JA, 22 January and 22 February 1970.
36 Also contained in the 1969 OAU Convention: Organization of African Unity (1960).
37 Art 1(2) of the 1951 UN Convention.

The 1969 OAU Convention is more liberal in that its definition protects a wider category of people, encompassing the above definition and adding other categories of people whom:

'Owing to external aggression, occupation, foreign domination or events seriously disturbing public order in either part or the whole of his country of origin or nationality, is compelled to leave his place of habitual residence in order to seek refuge in another place outside his or her country of origin or nationality.'[38]

It is this latter definition that actually covers the majority of refugees hosted in Kenya,[39] who are mainly recognised under the UNHCR mandate as prima facie refugees. Unfortunately, these refugees, who are required to remain confined in camps and whose legal status is not clear, are treated as aliens for the purposes of the Aliens Restriction Act 1973. They are not allowed to move freely to other parts of Kenya, nor are they allowed to seek gainful employment.

The Aliens Restriction Act 1973 prescribes the manner in which aliens may be dealt with in relation to registration but it does not provide for a procedure for the determination of status of the different types of aliens entering Kenya. This factor which puts refugees in a precarious situation, since the very status of a refugee is the basis upon his or her protection but any person claiming protection as a refugee must first be determined as a refugee.

The Aliens Restriction Act 1973 does not provide any particular rights and privileges for aliens. As the name suggests, and from its contents, its main purpose is to regulate for the restriction of aliens entering Kenya.

From this discussion we can conclude that the Aliens Restriction Act 1973 is inappropriate and should not be applied to refugees. It was enacted to restrict movement into and within Kenya, and to guarantee the security of the state by empowering the minister concerned to remove aliens from Kenya. It does not provide any rights for refugees or any other aliens; thus its punitive character. It goes against the spirit and the grain of international refugee conventions and the Constitution of Kenya, and the writer suggests that in the absence of any other refugee-specific law, it should not be relied on to fill the gap since it does not even begin to address the refugee problem in Kenya.

The Constitution of Kenya

Although Kenya is a signatory to international human rights treaties,[40] it has not enacted any legislation specifically to make provision for human rights,[41] but instead enacted fundamental rights and freedoms in Chapter V of the Constitution of

---

38 Art 1(2) of the 1969 OAU Convention.
39 According to UNHCR monthly statistics on the categories of refugees hosted in Kenya released in May 1999, the majority of the refugees present in Kenya come from Somalia and the Sudan having fled these countries following civil war and inter-clan fighting, 'events seriously disturbing public order' in those countries.
40 The International Covenant of Civil and Political Rights and the International Covenant on Economic, Social and Cultural Rights, both in 1976, etc.
41 When interviewed regarding this, the head of the Legal Department of the Ministry of Foreign Affairs and International Cooperation recalled that sometimes in the late 1980s and after the re-introduction of multi-party politics in Kenya in 1992, there was a debate aimed at pressurising the government to enact human rights-specific legislation. However, the government argued that there was no need for such a legislation as human rights were adequately covered by the Constitution.

Kenya. However, Chapter V has been amended incrementally, resulting in the rights and freedoms being so qualified as to render their enjoyment untenable. Section 70 of the Constitution, which falls under Chapter V providing for the protection of fundamental rights and freedoms of the individual, states as follows:

> 'Whereas *every person in Kenya* is entitled to the fundamental rights and freedoms of the individual, that is to say, the right, whatever his race, tribe, place of origin or residence or other local connexion, political opinions, colour, creed or sex, but subject to respect for the rights and freedoms of others and for the public interest, to each and all of the following, namely – (a) life, liberty, security of the person and the protection of the law; (b) freedom of conscience, of expression and of assembly and association; and (c) protection for the privacy of his home and other property and from deprivation of property without compensation.
>
> The provisions of this Chapter (V) shall have effect for the purpose of affording protection for those rights and freedoms subject to such limitations of that protection as are contained in those provisions, being limitations designed to ensure that the enjoyment of those rights and freedoms by any individual does not prejudice the rights and freedoms of others or the public interest.' (Emphasis added.)

The importance of this provision lies in the fact that it does not discriminate against foreigners or aliens, but affords protection of the rights and freedoms of 'every person in Kenya' without exception. Therefore, aliens and refugees in Kenya are protected by the Constitution in the same way as Kenyan citizens are.[42] The principle of non-discrimination against everyone in Kenya was reaffirmed in the case of *Madhwa and ors v City Council of Nairobi*[43] where the court held that the Constitution provided for the rights of the individual as a human being without reference to any matter of nationality, citizenship or domicile. Further, the Constitution entitles any such human being to seek redress from Kenyan courts without restrictions, as any other Kenyan would.

However, there are serious limitations to what rights refugees can enjoy in Kenya, especially limitations created by lacunae in law. Refugees have found it very difficult to enforce the enjoyment of their rights in the courts for a number of reasons, including the fact that the Constitution denies them some rights, for example, the protection of the freedom of movement, a right that is reserved exclusively for the citizens of Kenya.[44] Furthermore, since refugees in Kenya cannot boast legal status in the sense of the law, they have almost no legal capacity to bring actions in the courts of law and, in the few cases where they do, they cannot afford to do so because legal aid is not available, even to Kenyans, as a right.

In conclusion, the Constitution exists in this sense to provide some hope for refugees in the future, while at present the situation remains gloomy.

THE ROLE OF THE GOVERNMENT IN THE PROCESS OF DETERMINATION OF REFUGEE RIGHTS

Structures and procedures

There are no specific structures or institutions established for the purpose of determining refugee status. However, in the 1970s and 1980s there existed an

42 S 81 of the Constitution.
43 [1968] EA 406.
44 S 81 of the Constitution.

ad hoc committee charged with this responsibility, known as the Eligibility Committee. It was based within the Ministry of Home Affairs, National Heritage, Culture, and Social Services (Home Affairs) which traditionally deals with refugee affairs. The Eligibility Committee comprised of representatives from different government departments, vide the Immigration Department, Provincial Administration and Internal Security, all under the Office of the President, and the UNHCR.[45]

The Eligibility Committee operated on an ad hoc basis, as it did not have legally sanctioned procedures. It received applications and interviewed applicants, after which the successful applicants were passed on to a Security Committee convened specifically to vet applicants who successfully had passed through the Eligibility Committee. The Security Committee comprised of security officers from the Office of the President. Appeals were allowed to the same Eligibility Committee, this time comprising of representatives of a senior level from the same departments. If applicants failed at the appeals level, the minister's decision was final. No reasons for the decisions of the Eligibility Committee, the Security Committee, the Appeals Committee and the minister were given.

After this detailed verification process, the successful applicants were then issued with Convention documents, including an identity card which was co-signed by the government and the UNHCR and allowed the refugees to settle and work as they pleased anywhere in Kenya. If the applicants constituted a threat to national security,[46] they were asked to leave the country within 72 hours or were declared persona non grata in Kenya. There were very few of this kind of person. The majority who fell under this category did not remain in Kenya long enough to make a further application to the UNHCR; they were more likely to flee to another secure country of asylum as soon as they suspected that this was likely to be the case.[47] Applicants who were denied asylum for political reasons were also passed on to the UNHCR for resettlement, repatriation or for search for protection in a third country[48] if the UNHCR considered them as mandate refugees. If it did not, they were expected to leave the country immediately.

The National Council of Churches of Kenya (NCCK), one of whose other functions was the provision of social services to both the applicants and those whose refugee status was determined, carried out the registration of the applicants. After registration, the lists of the applicants and their application forms[49] were forwarded to the Eligibility Committee. Determination of refugee status was conducted on an individual basis, although in some cases groups or clans from

---

45 UNHCR then maintained a small office constituting the representative, his or her deputy, programme division, protection and social services, and shared an office block with the other UN agencies based in Nairobi.

46 There have been very few refugees who for political reasons have met with hostility from the government. According to sources from the Immigration Department, all of these refugees, without exception, immediately left the country and sought refuge from third countries, away from Kenya. The majority of refugees, according to the same sources, who sought asylum in Kenya between the 1960s and late 1980s were granted it. Those the government found it could not protect for political reasons were passed to the UNHCR, which dealt with only a handful of cases then.

47 Home Affairs files, February 1999.

48 Home Affairs files, February 1999.

49 These forms were printed by the UNHCR, which also provides administration expenses to both the NCCK and the Home Affairs, including cars, faxes, etc.

the same country were recognised but vetted or screened individually[50] by the Security Committee. The activities of these committees were suspended in 1991 because of the influx of Somali refugees and the Sudanese arriving from Ethiopian refugee camps.

The determination of refugee status is a quasi-judicial function in which the applicant should be afforded a fair hearing within a reasonable time by an independent and impartial body established by law. The Constitution[51] makes provisions to secure protection of law to every person in Kenya. This section requires that an authority determining the existence of a civil right or obligation be established by the law and be independent and impartial.[52]

'A court or other adjudicating authority prescribed by law for the determination of a civil right or obligation shall be established by law and shall be independent and impartial; and ... the case shall be given a fair hearing within a reasonable time.'

Such a process requires that a person be afforded adequate time and facilities to prepare his or her case,[53] a free interpreter[54] if he or she does not understand the language in use, legal representation and, after the final decision, be availed a copy of the proceedings of the matter for his or her appeal or other use.[55] This section echoes other international human rights treaty provisions regarding fair trial and protection by law.[56] As is shown here, the Eligibility Committee is an ad hoc committee, not established by law, and the process of determination of refugee status by the Eligibility Committee can hardly be termed as fair and just while the independence and impartiality of these government officials, all of who have an interest in the process,[57] is questionable.

Between 1979 and 1981 the government, in co-operation with the UNHCR, had established a refugee reception camp in Thika town, near Nairobi. The UNHCR financed the running of the camp and provided resources to the government to manage the camp. The camp was mainly used as a reception camp, where the interviewing and screening of refugees took place. After 1991 the camp was mainly used for security purposes, where refugees whose security was at risk were hosted. The camp was closed in 1995 as a result of logistical difficulties.

The post-1989 period was different. After the collapse of Somalia in 1990, a large number of Somali refugees fled into Kenya. Meanwhile, a large number of Sudanese refugees were fleeing from Ethiopian camps after the government was overthrown there. Kenya was suddenly faced with almost a quarter of a million

---

50 According to the Home Affairs archives, the total number of people granted refugee status up to 1991 did not exceed 15,000.
51 S 77.
52 S 77(9) of the Constitution.
53 S 77(2)(c) of the Constitution.
54 S 77(2)(f) of the Constitution.
55 S 77(3) of the Constitution.
56 The right to an effective remedy by a competent national tribunal (art 8 of the UDHR and art 14 of the International Covenant on Civil and Political Rights (ICCPR), Resolution 2200 A (XXI) of 16 December 1966), the right to a fair hearing (art 10 of the UDHR and art 14(1) of the ICCPR), the right to a free interpreter (art 14(3)(f) of the ICCPR) and the right to appeal (art 14(5) of the ICCPR).
57 All government representatives on the Eligibility Committee are there to safeguard their departments' interests; indeed, that is the rationale for their being there at all. Even the UNHCR is represented to protect its interests primarily, and those of the refugee as a secondary concern.

refugees.[58] As a result, it was impossible for the government and the UNHCR to continue granting legal status to refugees on an individual basis.

The National Secretariat of Refugees (NSR)[59] was established within the Home Affairs Department in September 1993 to co-ordinate relief activities and carry out other administrative duties. After the re-establishment of the Eligibility Committee, it also became its base and chair. In September 1998 a new Eligibility Committee was established to deal with the growing urban refugee problem.[60] The Eligibility Committee comprised the representatives from departments of the earlier Eligibility Committee, plus an additional two from the office of the Attorney-General and the Ministry of Foreign Affairs and International Cooperation. Just like the earlier Eligibility Committee, it did not have legally sanctioned procedures or a clearly defined institutional framework, and it operated on an ad hoc basis. Unlike the pre-1991 committee, it had a bigger urban refugee problem to deal with.[61]

The government has always maintained an individual determination of refugee status and refused to recognise refugees otherwise; even prima facie refugees who have been consigned to the camps continue to suffer a malignant government neglect.[62]

The first meeting of the Eligibility Committee was to be held on 4 November 1998 to determine the status of some Eritrean refugees whose application was under review. This meeting did not take place because although there were enough members present to constitute a quorum, it was explained that the two members who had not attended or sent representatives were crucial to the Eligibility Committee.[63] The second meeting, a postponement of the first one, was to take place on 11 November 1998, but before it could, the President publicly, through the media,[64] called on the UNHCR to repatriate all the refugees hosted in Kenya! This created some confusion within the relevant Ministries and the meeting did not take place. Although the Ministry of Home Affairs denies the announcement by the President had anything to do with it, no reasons were given as to why the meeting did not take place. The meeting was rescheduled for 2 December 1998 after UNHCR's high-profile interventions with the President, but was not held because the UNHCR representative was away on a mission, and

58 Interview with a Home Affairs official in charge of the refugee affairs in the Ministry, Nairobi, 3 May 1999.
59 Unlike other countries, for example, Malawi and Tanzania, where there are established refugee councils, in Kenya issues relating to refugees are dealt with by a small division in the Home Affairs Department comprising one officer and two assistants, who are often overwhelmed by the work they have to do and only manage some administrative aspects of the problem of refugees.
60 Sources: Home Affairs archives, institutional files and interviews with the officials in NSR, Nairobi, May 1999.
61 The estimated number of refugees and people of concern to the UNHCR by September 1998 in Nairobi alone was 150,000 according to an unofficial UNHCR count (about 50,000 official count); according to the government, 100,000; and about 150,000 according to UNHCR's implementing partners.
62 Home Affairs archives, February 1999. There are two categories of refugees in Kenya: (1) Those that are interviewed on an individual basis - mainly urban refugees, political refugees and refugees sur place, and (2) those who fall in the general category of prima facie refugees, de facto refugees and rural refugees who get absolved amongst friends, relatives and other benefactors. Usually the first category of refugees is known or their presence in Kenya documented. However, in many cases, only the first class of refugees in the second category is documented, but only those who are resident in refugee camps.
63 Home Affairs officer 2, interviewed in Nairobi, 16 April 1999.
64 Kenya Television Network, 21.00 News Bulletin, 9 November 1998.

the meeting was again postponed to 9 December 1998. Eventually the meeting took place early 1999.

The 1998 Eligibility Committee initially insisted on having all UNHCR mandate refugees appear before it individually. It could, however, not cope. It lacked resources, its members were busy, as they had other jobs, and many of them were untrained in determination of refugee status processes. There were also other political events taking place which took priority over refugees. Eventually the Committee, after meeting only a handful of times, suspended its activities towards the end of the first quarter of 1999. Now no official refugee status determination is carried out, except under the UNHCR mandate. The government does not, however, recognise such refugees, who are required to remain in the camps until some durable solution is found for them.

Some problems with the structures and the processes

There is a problem of a lack of defined institutional framework to deal with refugee affairs. There has always been a conflict between the Immigration and Home Affairs Departments in relation to refugee issues. The Immigration Department has often argued that they should have a strong say in matters relating to refugees. They contend that since Kenya does not have refugee legislation and refugees are dealt with under the Aliens Restriction Act 1973 and the Immigration Act 1967, the responsibility of refugees falls within the ambit of the Immigration Department.[65]

Second, when refugees enter the country, the first government officers they encounter are immigration officers, who have the responsibility of vetting them and allowing or denying them entry into the country.

Third, the immigration officers are responsible for issuing entry permits and travel documents to refugees whenever necessary. The Immigration Department has often insisted that the Home Affairs Department had no business dealing with refugees, and as a result of the Home Affairs Department's involvement there has been confusion and bad blood between the two.[66] Indeed, they claim that because of the confusion as to which department is responsible for refugees and what particular duties each should perform, neither department is doing much about the large numbers of refugees in urban areas, not to mention those hosted in far-away camps. This has led to illegal aliens hiding amongst genuine refugees and the general harassment of genuine refugees by the police and immigration officers. The Immigration Department argues that the Home Affairs Department should take over responsibility for the refugees only after the Immigration Department has granted them status. That is to say, the responsibility of the Home Affairs Department should not include the determination of refugee status, as is the case now, but only the management and the running of the refugee camps, should the government find camps necessary.

The writer suggests that these arguments make a lot of sense as there is no central register for all the refugees in Kenya, thus making the authorities

---

65 Immigration officer 2, interviewed on 27 April 1999 in Nairobi. The immigration officer also argues that in the absence of a refugee-specific legislation, refugees as foreigners are under the control of the Immigration Department.

66 Immigration officer 1, interviewed on 27 April 1999 in Nairobi Immigration Department. Also immigration officer 2 interview, conducted on 17 November 1998 at Lokichoggio next to the Kenyan border with the Sudan.

vulnerable to fraud. The Immigration Department handles all applications for travel documents and must encounter serious difficulties when attempting to distinguish between genuine refugees and fraudulent claimants since they do not keep the records of all refugees.[67] The problem is compounded by the fact that the UNHCR also maintains a separate list of its mandate refugees with whom the government wants nothing to do. The Home Affairs Department maintains a list of Convention refugees and those granted asylum by the government, while the Immigration Department maintains a record of those to whom it has issued documents and of all prohibited immigrants.

The Home Affairs Department on the other hand, argues that the fact that they are in charge of refugees is an historical one, because they have a great deal of experience on the subject, and claim they are justified to conduct the determination of refugee status. Indeed, before 1978 the Immigration and Internal Security Departments came under the Home Affairs Department, which was the Ministry held by the Vice-President. However, after he became the President in 1978, these departments were relocated to the Office of the President, thus the confusion. According to the Home Affairs Department, when these departments were all within Home Affairs there was closer co-ordination of duties and no confusion. Now, the duties for each have not changed but they fall under two different Ministries, thus the confusion.

Therefore, according to both the Immigration and Home Affairs Departments, only a refugee-specific legislation, establishing an independent organ to deal with refugees, with legally sanctioned responsibilities, functions and procedures will clarify the situation and end the confusion. This, they argue, is the reason why the government has suspended the Eligibility Committee and given the drafting of a refugee-specific legislation new impetus.[68]

The Departments of Internal Security and Provincial Administration have also added to the general confusion. They maintain that, because of the nature of their flight and the easy access to weapons in their countries of origin, refugees pose a security threat to the host country, especially when they flee into the country without giving security personnel the opportunity to disarm them. These departments argue that refugees are a concern for them for this reason and also because they come into contact first with provincial administration upon their entry into Kenya.[69] The departments wish to play a critical role in the process of refugee status determination in order to ensure that when granted refugee status, refugees do not pose a security threat to the nation.[70] The writer suggests that claims by politicians and government officials that refugees are a threat to national security should not be taken seriously, because more than three-quarters of the refugees in Kenya are old men, women and children, who are hungry, emaciated and unarmed. Furthermore, this threat has never been proved; it is only the perception of those making the claims. Fortunately, no refugee has been subjected to refoulement from Kenya.[71]

The government disagreed with the UNHCR over recognition of refugees on a prima facie basis because, if it allowed this kind of recognition, refugees would be

---

67 Unless an independent body like a refugee council with branches at all entry points into Kenya is established.
68 Interviews with Immigration and Home Affairs Department officials on why the 1998 Eligibility Committee is not functioning, Nairobi, January 2000; also interviewed on 27 April 1999 in Nairobi.
69 District Officer, Kakuma, 1 February 1999.
70 Officer Commanding Station, Kakuma Police Station, 4 February 1999.
71 UNHCR (1998–99).

allowed to compete for the country's resources and opportunities with other Kenyans, as full status refugees enjoy same rights as Kenyans. This would have posed a great challenge to its capacity to provide for its citizens. The government was also afraid of the response by Kenyans against the influx if refugees were allowed to mix with locals, arguing that this was likely to result in clashes over resources and would greatly undermine the government's efforts to maintain public order and security.[72] So, since the government could not expel the refugees, it allowed the establishment of refugee camps, which were to be organised and managed by the UNHCR until some other mechanisms were put in place.[73]

Between 1991 and August 1998 no serious and firm mechanisms and institutions were put in place by the government. During this period, refugees were expected to remain in the camps with no solutions in sight, which led to a lot of frustration among refugees. The government argues that it will deal with the problem once a refugee-specific legislation is enacted, but in the meantime nothing is happening. So the UNHCR continues to admit more and more Sudanese and Somali refugees under its mandate and the government remains silent over the issue of the legislation and does not recognise these refugees. It does appear that the government would like to maintain the status quo, as currently it does not have to put itself out for the refugees. Naturally, this is an unacceptable situation, which cannot be allowed to go on, because Kenya has agreed to secure the effective implementation of its refugee treaty obligations in good faith.

Some concerns about the Eligibility Committee

There were many shortcomings associated with the Eligibility Committee. First, there are established procedures and guidelines to deal with the process of determination of refugee status, but important decisions are taken on discretionary basis[74] and the criteria relied upon for consideration by the Committee are unclear. Lack of consistency and uniformity in decision-making bedevilled the whole process of determination of refugee status, resulting in some refugees from the same country, fleeing similar events under similar circumstances, receiving different treatment from the Eligibility Committee.[75]

Second, there is a great deal of confusion about the role played by the security officers. Indeed, the interference from the Office of the President and internal security with the work of the Eligibility Committee on the basis of national security saw many applicants refused asylum on security grounds without any justification. No reasons for grant or denial of asylum were given. This was done arbitrarily, and it was difficult for the Home Affairs Department to object because there is no basis for such objections.[76]

---

72 The influx of refugees and the deteriorating economic conditions resulted in Kenyans competing for dwindling resources, resulting in hostility directed towards refugees.
73 Interview at offices of the President – Internal Security Nairobi, 1 February 1999.
74 This is a concern which was expressed by all the persons interviewed during this study, including staff of the UNHCR, the Home Affairs and Immigration Departments, the Office of the President, Provincial Administration, the Directorate of National Intelligence, the Attorney-General's Chambers, Foreign Affairs, the Judiciary, and even some refugees.
75 Home Affairs Department archives and files from the NSR in which some Ethiopian and Somali refugees were granted refugee status while others from their home areas were denied status.
76 Interviews with Office of the President official 2 and Home Affairs Department official 2, Nairobi, 18 February 1999.

Third, there seems to be a great turnover of the officials sitting on the Eligibility Committee: for example, between September 1998 and February 1999 more than two-thirds of the members of the Committee were replaced through inter-ministerial transfers. This resulted in a lack of consistency and continuity. Also, individual experience is lost, meaning that most of the time the people in the Committee are not particularly well-versed in the work they are supposed to perform.[77]

Fourth, in the writer's opinion, and from the views expressed by Home Affairs and immigration officials, the government does not consider refugees a priority concern and therefore does not allocate adequate resources to deal with them.[78] The NSR also does not have the institutional capacity to deal with refugee affairs, as there are only three officers dealing directly with refugee concerns. Lack of resources also results in the Eligibility Committee being unable to provide the services of interpreters, a very necessary service to the refugees. In addition, it is unable to conduct investigations and gather information about the situations of human rights in the countries of the origin of refugees, and often bases its decisions primarily on the cases presented by the applicants.[79]

Fifth, the fact that there is no recourse to a court of law for an aggrieved refugee is tragic. Many refugees' lives are jeopardised because they are required to return to countries which may still be unsafe.[80] Even when they are protected by the UNHCR, they are still not allowed to remain in Kenya. If the UNHCR is therefore unable to relocate or find them resettlement, they are in Kenya illegally, a situation which is criminal.[81]

Finally, the Eligibility Committee is partial and lacks independence. All the representatives to the committee except the UNHCR are from the government and when the refugee appears before it, he or she has no representative and no recourse to facilities to enable him or her present their case. The applicant is required to show cause why they should be granted refugee status and is reduced

---

77 All members of the Eligibility Committee are experts in the field in which they specialise; however, not in the area of refugee protection.

78 UNHCR and Home Affairs Department files, February 1999. According to Home Affairs officials, lack of legislation and resources has placed them in such a precarious situation that they feel they simply 'rubber stamp' what the UNHCR asks of them and in practice it is the UNHCR running the programme of refugees in Kenya. These officials are angry with the government and bitter against the UNHCR, who they accuse of arrogance and disrespect.

79 Some Ethiopian Oromo refugees were denied recognition on the basis of an argument that they had no reason to flee their country because the members of the interviewing panel did not have information about what was happening in Ethiopia at that time. Fortunately, these refugees were later granted mandate status by the UNHCR and later resettled: interviews conducted in Nairobi in May 1999.

80 Although refugees are not 'forcibly returned to any country where their lives may be at risk', interviews with protection officers and implementing partners of the UNHCR based in the Kakuma refugee camp show that there is a continuous flow of Sudanese refugees back to the South of Sudan, even though the civil war there still rages on. Of course, the UNHCR cannot hold refugees in camps by force, but it is clearly a situation complicated by the fact that refugees claim it is better for them to die in the Sudan than to die as refugees in Kenya because of violent clashes in the camps, or to be depressed because of the situation in Kakuma: interviews conducted in Kakuma refugee camp, 17–19 November 1998.

81 An example can be drawn from a case of four Eritreans whose case was pleaded before the 1998 Eligibility Committee in early 1999 by the UNHCR and were denied refugee status, after which they were required to leave the country. Even after the UNHCR granted them mandate status, the requirement that they leave the country remained.

to a beggar before the Committee. Furthermore, the 1998 Committee did not even entertain personal appearances by the applicants, as it only insisted on hearing presentations on behalf of refugees from the UNHCR.[82]

THE ROLE OF THE UNHCR

International protection and the UNHCR

The 1951 UN Convention recognises the international nature of refugee protection and calls upon member states to promote international co-operation and the principle of burden-sharing in dealing with the problems occasioned by forced migration. It also urges states to co-operate with and assist the UNHCR to fulfil its mandate under article 35, which provides that:

'(1) The Contracting States undertake to cooperate with the office of the United Nations High Commissioner for Refugees, or any other agency of the United Nations which may succeed it, in the exercise of its functions, and shall in particular facilitate its duty of supervising the application of the provisions of the Convention.

(2) In order to enable the office of the High Commissioner or any other agency of the United Nations which may succeed it, to make reports to the competent organs of the United Nations, the Contracting States undertake to provide them in the appropriate form with information and statistical data requested concerning: (a) The condition of refugees, (b) the implementation of this Convention, and (c) laws, regulations and decrees which are, or may hereafter be, in force relating to refugees.'

This co-operation is reiterated in the Statute of the Office of the UNHCR and article II of the 1967 Protocol to the 1951 Convention. The call for co-operation is also echoed by article VIII of the 1969 OAU Convention.

What is the UNHCR and what does it do?

The 1950 Statute of the Office of the United Nations High Commissioner for Refugees (the Statute)[83] created the office of the UNHCR, gave it a mandate to oversee the implementation of 1951 UN Convention and called upon governments to co-operate with the UNHCR in its work and in the protection of refugees and those falling within its competence. The UNHCR is a subsidiary organ of the UN under the authority of the UN General Assembly (UNGA), which essentially requires it to follow policy directions given by UNGA or by the Economic and Social Council (ECOSOC).[84] In its general provisions, the Statute states that:

'The UNHCR, acting under the authority of the General Assembly, shall assume the function of providing international protection, under the auspices of the United Nations, to refugees who fall within the scope of the present Statute and of seeking

---

82 The refugees had mandate status already and the representations resulted in endorsing their status thus enabling them to enjoy full Convention status. This process was aimed at dealing with the large number of refugees in Nairobi, who the government argued were there illegally.

83 UN General Assembly Resolution 428(V) of 14 December 1950.

84 Goodwin-Gill (1996) p 214.

permanent solutions for the problem of refugees by assisting Governments and, subject to the approval of the Governments concerned, and private organisations to facilitate the voluntary repatriation of such refugees, or their assimilation within new national communities.'[85]

The Statute, in its definition of who falls within its mandate, lays down categories of persons falling under the definition of a refugee, thus accepting a 'group approach' to the determination of refugee status in cases involving mass influxes of asylum-seekers, as well as the movement away from the strict definition of a refugee to one more accommodating to displaced persons.[86] This requirement does not limit the determination of refugee status by the UNHCR to groups and categories only, and it has been involved in determination of refugee status on individual basis.[87]

'The work of the High Commissioner shall be of an entirely non-political character; it shall be humanitarian and social and shall relate, as a rule, to groups and categories of refugees.'[88]

The subsystem of solution entails voluntary repatriation, integration into the local community in the country of first asylum and resettlement in third countries.

'These solutions are implied in the Statute of the UNHCR under which the principal responsibility of the UNHCR is to provide international protection to refugees and to seek permanent solutions for the problem of refugees by assisting governments and, subject to approval of the governments concerned, private organisations to facilitate the voluntary repatriation of refugees, or their assimilation within new national communities.'[89]

This subsystem is also pointed out in the UNHCR *Handbook on Voluntary Repatriation: International Protection*:

'The purpose of international protection is not ... that a refugee remain a refugee forever, but to ensure the individual's renewed membership of a community and the restoration of national protection, either in the homeland or through integration elsewhere.'[90]

How does the UNHCR function?

The UNHCR has offices in many countries where refugees are hosted and deals directly with them in the host country. The Executive Committee (EXCOM) of the UNHCR was established in 1958[91] and its terms of reference include advising the High Commissioner, on request, in the exercise of the statutory functions

---

85 Ch 1, para 1 of the Statute of the Office of the UNHCR.
86 Rwelamira (1989).
87 'The individual dimension to the protection function is a natural corollary to the declared task of supervising the application of international conventions': Goodwin-Gill (1996) p 213.
88 Ch 1, para 2 of the Statute of the Office of the UNHCR.
89 Bonaventure Rutinwa, 'forced displacement and refugee rights in the Great Lakes region', paper presented at the Conference on Peace and Human Rights in the Great Lakes Region of Africa: Prospects for the New Millennium, Makerere University, Kampala, Uganda, 11–12 December 1997, also quoting the Statute, para 1 and UNGA Resolution 428(V).
90 As quoted by Rutinwa, fn 88 above, from UNHCR (1996) p 3.
91 Pursuant to Ch 1, para 4 of the Statute, which provides for the establishment of an advisory committee on refugees consisting of representatives of both member and non-member states of the UN.

and advising on the appropriateness of providing international assistance through UNHCR in order to solve specific refugee problems as may arise.[92] At the request of UNHCR, EXCOM has made pertinent conclusions on international protection and issues relating to the functions of UNHCR. Rule 32 of the EXCOM Rules of Procedure[93] requires the reports of EXCOM in its executive capacity to be attached to the UNHCR's Annual Report to the United Nations General Assembly (UNGA). Subsequently, UNGA makes a resolution based on these reports, which are directed to all members of the UN but not necessarily to the members of the EXCOM. UNGA has in this manner managed to extend the mandate of UNHCR to other persons not necessarily covered under the UNHCR Statute or the 1951 UN Convention and its 1967 Protocol.

Thus, EXCOM decisions have had far-reaching effects on the protection of refugees and other people of concern to UNHCR and in providing guidelines to states with regard to how they are expected to treat refugees and other persons in need of international protection. EXCOM decisions have been made on practically all issues concerning refugees, internally displaced persons and other persons of concern to UNHCR and the UN in general, and have had far-reaching influence on the practice of states. Some examples include: in establishing procedures for the determination of refugee status;[94] calling on states to grant temporary refuge in relation to large-scale influxes of refugees[95] and for protection of asylum seekers in situations of large-scale influx;[96] on the problem of manifestly unfounded or abusive applications for refugee status or asylum;[97] on voluntary repatriation;[98] urging states to accede to international instruments on refugees and ensure their implementation;[99] on refugee children;[100] urging international solidarity and refugee protection;[101] on cessation of refugee status;[102] on safeguarding asylum;[103] on the safety of the UNHCR staff and other humanitarian personnel;[104] and on refugee children and adolescents.[105]

92 Goodwin-Gill (1996) pp 9, 215.
93 United Nations General Assembly, 47th Session, 'Rules of Procedure', A/AC.96187/ Rev 5, 10 April 1997.
94 EXCOM Conclusions, No 8(XXVIII) of 1977, available at www.unhcr.ch/refworld/unhcr/ excom/xconc/excom8.htm.
95 EXCOM Conclusions, No 19(XXXI) of 1980, available at www.unhcr.ch/refworld/unhcr/ excom/xconc/excom19.htm.
96 EXCOM Conclusions, No 22(XXXII) of 1981, available at www.unhcr.ch/refworld/unhcr/ excom/xconc/excom22.htm.
97 EXCOM Conclusions, No 30(XXXIV) of 1983, available at www.unhcr.ch/refworld/unhcr/ excom/xconc/excom30.htm.
98 EXCOM Conclusions, No 40(XXXVI) of 1985, available at www.unhcr.ch/refworld/unhcr/ excom/xconc/excom40.htm.
99 EXCOM Conclusions, No 42(XXXVII) of 1986, available at ww.unhcr.ch/refworld/unhcr/ excom/xconc/excom42.htm.
100 EXCOM Conclusions, No 47(XXXVIII) of 1987, available at www.unhcr.ch/refworld/ unhcr/excom/xconc/excom47.htm.
101 EXCOM Conclusions, No 52(XXXIX) of 1988, available at www.unhcr.ch/refworld/unhcr/ excom/xconc/excom52.htm.
102 EXCOM Conclusions, No 52(XXXIX) of 1988, available at www.unhcr.ch/refworld/unhcr/ excom/xconc/excom52.htm.
103 EXCOM Conclusions, No 82(XLVIII) of 1997, available at www.unhcr.ch/refworld/unhcr/ excom/xconc/excom82.htm.
104 EXCOM Conclusions, No 83(XLVIII) of 1997, available at www.unhcr.ch/refworld/unhcr/ excom/xconc/excom83.htm.
105 EXCOM Conclusions, No 84(XLVIII) of 1997, available at www.unhcr.ch/refworld/unhcr/ excom/xconc/excom84.htm.

EXCOM uses subcommittees to facilitate its work and increase its effectiveness. One of the main subcommittees is the Sub-committee of the Whole on International Protection, established in 1975, which has made great contribution in the area of international protection.[106] This subcommittee prepares periodic notes on international protection which are incorporated in the general conclusions on international protection of EXCOM or are submitted to the UNGA by the UNHCR as part of the EXCOM Report.[107] These Notes deal with protection issues including security, asylum, determination of refugee status, non-refoulement, issues relating to the functions of the UNHCR and the effective implementation of international refugee conventions.[108]

What are the functions of the UNHCR?

The functions of the UNHCR discussed above are detailed specifically as being concerned with non-refoulement, access to the procedures of determination of refugee status, the grant of asylum, prevention against expulsion unless compelling grounds of national security and public order prevail, and only after due process of law has been observed, physical security of the refugee, personal liberty, the right to identity and travel documents, ensuring certain rights are secured for the refugee within reasonable limits; and seeking durable solutions for refugees. The UNHCR is also expected to urge the implementation of the 1951 UN Convention and its 1967 Protocol by states parties and to urge those who have not done so to ratify these instruments. Most importantly, UNHCR works in close co-operation and co-ordination with states party to the Convention, who facilitate the functions of UNHCR and use it as a forum to exchange and channel their views. The member states voluntarily bind themselves to assisting and co-operating with UNHCR in its work.

> 'The Contracting states undertake to cooperate with the Office of the United Nations High Commissioner for Refugees, or any other agency of the United Nations which may succeed it, in the exercise of its functions, and shall in particular facilitate its duty of supervising the application of the provisions of this Convention.'[109]

The UNHCR does not have a monitoring role or capacity to ensure that the contracting states comply with the provisions of the 1951 UN Convention. Indeed, one of the main weaknesses of the Convention and the Statute of the UNHCR is their failure to grant UNHCR this function. The UNHCR also does not have express mandate to interpret the provisions of the Convention although the

---

106 Report of the 26th Session (1975) UN doc.A/AC.96/521, para 69(h).
107 A good example is the Note on International Protection submitted to the UNGA by the UNHCR on 27 August 1990, available at www.unhcr.ch/refworld/unhcr//notes/750.htm. The Note addresses the protection function of the UNHCR and current protection problems – operational problems, the asylum crisis, financial crisis and protection – and proposes longer-term approaches to these problems, etc. Protection notes have been appearing under this title since the subcommittee was formed and under this website since Refworld was established by UNHCR on the Internet in 1995.
108 An example of general conclusions on international protection is contained in EXCOM Conclusions, No 41(XXXVII) of 1986, available at www.unhcr.ch/refworld/unhcr/excom/xconc/excom41.htm, which deals with a variety of protection issues, including voluntary repatriation, security of refugee camps, states' compliance with international refugee conventions, national legislation on refugees, etc.
109 Art 35(1) of the 1951 UN Convention. Also art II of the 1967 Protocol to the Convention.

EXCOM Committee has in the past played this role even though its decisions and recommendations are not binding on contracting states. The nearest the UNHCR comes to the role of monitoring the activities of contracting states is through its reporting requirements to the UNGA, which reports also include those provided by contracting states pursuant to the Convention.

> 'In order to enable the Office of the High Commissioner or any other agency of the United Nations which may succeed it, to make reports to the competent organs of the United Nations, the Contracting States undertake to provide them in the appropriate form with information and statistical data requested concerning:
>
> (a) The condition of refugees,
> (b) The implementation of this Convention, and
> (c) Laws, regulations and decrees which are, or may hereafter be, in force relating to refugees.'[110]

This reporting requirement, however, is not sufficient to guarantee enforcement and implementation of the provisions of the Convention. Furthermore, the UNHCR, as discussed above, depends on the goodwill and co-operation of contracting states to carry out its duties. Indeed, UNHCR, as an organ of the UN, is principally a forum for member states to work together, as well as to pursue their interests and to ensure that the goals of the UN are achieved. Although the UNHCR in its humanitarian work tries very hard to protect the interests of refugees, collectively and as individuals, its manoeuvring space is restricted and has first and foremost to serve the interests of the UN and its member states. However, in practice the UNHCR has managed through its protection work to achieve much more than its statute and the Convention envisaged.

> 'UNHCR with its principal function of providing international protection to refugees, can be seen to occupy the central role in an analogous legal system of supervision. Indeed, though discretions continue to favour States in certain of their dealings with the refugees, the peremptory character of the principle of *non-refoulement* puts it in a higher class than the intangible and almost nominal obligation to consider in good faith a recommendation of a supervisory body, such as Judge Lauterpacht discerned in the *Voting Procedure* case ... There, the court read into the rights and duties of the United Nations Organization, as a necessity intendment, the capacity to exercise a measure of functional protection on behalf of its agents.'[111]

When the UNHCR was established it was not directly mandated to intervene publicly on behalf of refugees and persons of concern to it; instead it accomplished this through quiet diplomacy. However, as the numbers of refugees and asylum-seekers increased and the problem of forced migration became more complicated, the UNHCR continually finds itself at loggerheads with governments who are unwilling to provide protection to refugees and to admit them into their territories. Yet the UNHCR must maintain its non-political objectivity in order to gain the confidence and the co-operation of asylum states, as well as countries of origin, in order to secure protection for the refugees and to find durable solutions to their plight.

110 1951 UN Convention, art 35(2).
111 Goodwin-Gill (1996) p 217.

The role of the UNHCR in the process of refugee status determination

The UNHCR has always played an active role in the process of refugee status determination since it established its presence in Kenya in the early 1970s. As discussed above, in the 1970s and 1980s it worked in joint co-operation with the government and participated in the interviewing of applicants and decision-making. However, since 1991 the UNHCR went its separate way and has been conducting refugee status determination under its mandate and screening prima facie refugees. This section concentrates on the role of the UNHCR since 1991.

Prima facie refugee status

After the collapse of Somalia in 1990, Somalian refugees were recognised on a prima facie basis because of the events taking place in their country. Ethiopian and Sudanese refugees were also recognised on this basis after the collapse of Mengistu regime in Ethiopia.[112] When these refugees arrived in Kenya they were only required to assemble in reception camps where they were screened, registered and provided with food and non-food items. Later on they were required to go to camps where they were (still are) hosted. In 1994, following the genocide in Rwanda, refugees from that country were also recognised on a prima facie basis. However, for unknown reasons, many refugees from Rwanda and Burundi managed to remain in urban areas, and the majority of them are in Nairobi.

The UNHCR insisted on recognising refugees on a prima facie basis against the wishes of and without the assistance of the government, which claims to find the regime untenable, resulting in alienation of these refugees, who were required to remain in the camps indefinitely. The government wants nothing to do with them. Therefore, the UNHCR must not only guarantee protection for the refugees but must also find them durable solutions, mainly on its own. There are more than 200,000 of these refugees.[113] The government policy that these refugees remain in the camps indefinitely and only leave with its permission, returning after the purpose for which they were permitted to leave has been served, curtails their freedom of movement, their freedom of association, their right to choice of residence, their right to pursue a better livelihood outside the camps and to participate in the normal life of the host community.

Due to the nature of this kind of recognition, refugees, especially from the Sudan, by 1997 began to pose as new arrivals (known as 'recyclers') so that they could receive more benefits. Many of the recyclers claimed that they did this because this was the only way of achieving a (necessary) increase in their food rations. The problem of 'recycling' by refugees also artificially inflates the numbers of refugees actually hosted in the camps.

Also because of the nature of the recognition, many Sudanese refugees 'return' to the South of Sudan, to their livestock and farms and to visit relatives in the

---

112   Many of the Sudanese refugees coming into Kenya were arriving from refugee camps in Ethiopia. Refugees from Ethiopia stopped being recognised on a prima facie basis after 1991 and those who fled after the fall of Mengistu have since ceased to be refugees. However, Oromo refugees from South of Ethiopia are still recognised as refugees.

113   The UNHCR has come under a lot of criticism over its handling of these refugees in the camps and for failing to offer them protection: interviews with refugees, UNHCR staff, NGOs working as partners of the UNHCR, November 1998 (Kakuma), February and March 1999 (Nairobi). Also interviews with a Human Rights Watch delegation, May 1999.

rainy seasons, only to return to the refugee camps for the dry seasons or to bring their children to school or their relatives to hospital. As a result, there is a lot of traffic between the South of Sudan and the Kakuma refugee camp.[114]

Prima facie recognition has the benefit of recognising groups of people as refugees, thus dispensing with the expensive process of individual recognition. However, it bestows nothing on the refugees in terms of rights and the legal capacity to them, and in Kenya it is a status on which a refugee cannot rely for protection by the government. Indeed, even with the UNHCR, such a refugee must go through an individual interview to qualify for resettlement in Europe, Australia or North America. '*Prima facie* regime as it has developed over the past few decades for the purpose of protecting refugees in countries, like Kenya, is legally insufficient and sorely lacking in terms of humanitarian standards of practice.'[115]

Another problem associated with prima facie recognition is that it is supposed to be temporary in nature. In Kenya, this has resulted in a malignant neglect of refugees by the government, which insists that it need do nothing since they are in Kenya only temporarily as the reasons for their flight are expected to be resolved, at which point they will be repatriated. Refugees have, as a result, been waiting in camps since 1993, some even longer.

UNHCR mandate refugee status

Persons coming from countries and the North of Sudan and Khartoum also have to go through an individual status determination process under the UNHCR mandate. These people must fall within the definitions and criteria of a refugee set out in the 1951 UN Convention, its 1967 Protocol and the UNHCR Statute. Persons recognised by the UNHCR alone under this regime are said to have mandate refugee status.

In 1992 UNHCR set up procedures for determining refugee status under its mandate and commissioned one of its partners to manage the process outside the UNHCR offices.[116] Some applicants were, however, interviewed in the Branch Office of UNHCR because 'they may require speedy assessment and speedy solutions, for example those subjected to torture, sexual violence and special medical cases'.[117] This joint project was discontinued at the recommendation of the implementing partner, Jesuit Refugee Service (JRS), which decided that determination of refugee status was logistically untenable and because the

114 The writer was surprised when told this by refugees from the Sudan, but interviews with the UNHCR staff and their implementing partners confirmed this fact. In fact, one of the implementing partners of the UNHCR said that refugees, in their requisition forms, often request mud-boots even though Turkana District, where Kakuma is located, is a semi-desert and mud-boots are not necessary. The boots, they found out, were for use in the South of Sudan!
115 Hyndman and Nylund (1998).
116 The Jesuit Refugee Service established a joint project funded by the UNHCR in which refugees were registered and interviewed by local lawyers and protection officers. This project also provided other services to refugees, eg community, social and counselling services. The local lawyers received training on interviewing skills, international refugee law and procedures of determination of refugee status, communication and recording skills for two weeks, after which they were expected to learn 'on the job' and through observing colleagues at the UNHCR Office.
117 Interview with protection officer 2, Nairobi, 6 May 1999.

co-ordination of its activities with the UNHCR became difficult.[118] As a result, all determination of status and eligibility processes were transferred to the UNHCR's Protection House (PH) in January 1999. Some three lawyers working under the JRS/UNHCR joint project were transferred to PH, joining two other lawyers who had been working there already. From the date of appointment for an interview to the decision, a case took an average of four months, during which period most of the applicants received assistance from the UNHCR.

The lawyers interviewed applicants and made a recommendation to the protection officer regarding what decision should be made for the applicant. If the protection officer agreed with the recommendation, he or she endorsed the decision. When the decisions were in the negative, the applicant was given an opportunity to appeal. Appeals went to one of the other lawyers, who had not conducted the interview, and the final appeal was made to the senior protection officer, who then may or may not interview the appellant.[119] This procedure is seriously flawed and does not conform to standards of justice and fairness. In many of the interviews observed by the writer, the applicant behaved as though he or she was intimidated and defensive.[120] Although applicants were afforded a free interpreter, many refugees claimed that the interpreter did not translate what they were told, but instead said what they thought the UNHCR should know.[121] The fact that the appeal is heard by a colleague of the lawyer who conducted the first interview is questionable itself. This is because, even if a negative decision on appeal is justified, the applicant and other observers will not be satisfied that the appellate lawyer would be prepared to decide against his or her colleague. In addition, the colleague may find it uncomfortable to overturn the decision of his or her colleague. Justice must not only be done, but also be seen to be done.

In 1997 the UNHCR also came under serious criticism regarding their handling of refugees from Rwanda who were suspected of having taken part in the 1994 genocide. As a response to the criticisms, UNHCR instituted a screening process for both Rwandese and Burundi refugees to determine those refugees who, although qualifying as such, are excluded from international protection as a result of their participation in the genocide. UNHCR took this opportunity to interview refugees who had arrived in 1994–95 and were recognised on a prima facie basis individually. The process of exclusion began in June 1998, and required

118 Interviews with protection officer 2 and the Jesuit Priest in charge of the Programme, Nairobi, 6 May 1999.
119 These were very rare cases and dependent on the senior protection officer's prerogative and discretion. Often, the applicant was allowed the two interviews with the two lawyers, after which a protection officer would go through both files and confirm or reject the decision on appeal. According to the lawyers and the protection officer, most rejections were confirmed on appeal. The applicant was then told the grounds of the rejection and advised that the appeal was final.
120 The writer was not quite sure why in the interviews observed the applicants appeared intimidated and were literally begging for recognition. To the credit of the lawyers at the interviews, they conducted them in a professional manner, at least the ones observed by the writer.
121 Some refugees claim that their applications were rejected because the interpreters did not like them or they came from a different tribe. The UNHCR officers interviewed on this question said that there were some cases in which the interpreters may have failed to communicate the cases of some applicants, but that, in cases where such claims were made, the applicant was afforded another interview. Some applicants contest the UNHCR' assurances.

Rwandese and Burundi refugees in Kenya to submit themselves to UNHCR protection officers for individual interviews. Many of the refugees refused to submit to the interviews. The process of exclusion followed the same pattern as discussed above, although in the cases of exclusion the lawyers were trained and appraised of the situation of human rights in the country of origin.

All refugees who were granted mandate status were required to travel to the camps.

CONCLUSIONS

This chapter has argued that although there is no refugee-specific legislation, the government and UNHCR have survived in just managing to deal with some aspects of the refugee problems in Kenya as best as they could under the circumstances. However, the issue here is not about survival or just managing, it is about ensuring that, first, the government has a legal framework to guide it in adhering to its international obligations over refugees. Second, that refugees are accorded legal protection as is required under international refugee law, that their rights and responsibilities are legally sanctioned and their legal status be recognised. Third, that there should be mechanisms to ensure that the government and the UNHCR do not function in a discriminatory manner and to enable refugees and interested parties to hold the government and UNHCR accountable. The processes of determination of refugee status by both the government and UNHCR do not fully conform to international human rights standards. Finally, it is suggested that there must be mechanisms to enable refugees and interested parties to enforce refugee rights through the judiciary.

Select bibliography

Africa Watch Report, (1991) 'Kenya Taking Liberties', July.

Goodwin-Gill, (1996) The Refugee in International Law (2nd edn).

Hyndman, J, and Nylund, B V, (1998) 'UNHCR and the Status of Prima Facie Refugees in Kenya', 10 IJRL 1/2.

Organization of African Unity (1969) Convention on the Specific Aspects of Refugee Problems in Africa, Adopted in Addis Ababa, Ethiopia in September 1969 and came into force on 20 June 1974, 1000 UNTS 46.

Rutinwa, B, (1997) 'Forced Displacement and Refugee Rights in the Great Lakes Region', Paper presented at the Conference on 'Peace and Human Rights in the Great Lakes Region of Africa: Prospects for the New Millennium', Makerere University, Kampala, Uganda, 11–12 December.

Rwelamira, M R, (1989) 'Editorial 1989 – An Anniversary Year', 1 IJRL 4.

UNHCR, (1992) *Handbook on Procedures and Criteria for Determining Refugee Status under the 1951 Convention and the 1967 Protocol Relating to the Status of Refugees.*

—(1998–99) Annual Protection Report.

Chapter 22

Geographies of hunger[1]

C POWELL[2]

Hunger is a global problem requiring transnational[3] responses that address human rights and State responsibility.[4] However, US policy and scholarship focused on world hunger often 'distance hunger',[5] by viewing the subject as a remote phenomenon occurring primarily in poor countries. Others have argued that by distancing hunger, such treatment of the subject masks responsibility of Western industrialised States for policies that create or maintain hunger in poor countries.[6] The assumption that the West bears no responsibility for such a distant phenomenon justifies viewing the subject through a development aid or charity paradigm, rather than through a rights framework.[7] This chapter begins closer to home by focusing on the ways in which the practice of distancing hunger obscures the fact that it is a serious and widespread problem in one of the world's more affluent countries. Despite its affluence and status as the world's only superpower, the US is the only industrialised country with widespread hunger,[8] due in part to its failure to address economic insecurity. Moreover, the US is the only Western

1 This chapter is based on a paper delivered by the writer at the 1999 Annual Meeting of the American Society of International Law. The writer would like to thank Catherine Albisa, Jose E Alvarez, Lori Damrosch, Radhika Balakrishnan, Heidi Dorow, Louis Henkin, Henry P Monaghan, Gerald Neuman, Mark Quarterman and Susan Sturm for their generous advice, support and encouragement. She would also like to acknowledge Llezlie Green, Carrie Gustophsen, Christine Strumpen-Darrie and Tamika Thomas for their invaluable research assistance, as well as Michael Likosky of Oxford University for his editorial assistance.
2 Associate Clinical Professor of Law, Columbia Law School, Faculty Director, Human Rights Institute; BA, Yale University (1987); MPA, Princeton University, Woodrow Wilson School of International and Public Affairs (1991); JD, Yale Law School (1992).
3 The term 'transnational' is used here to reflect the '*transnational* legal process' approach, which describes 'the theory and practice of how public *and* private actors – nation-states, international organizations, multinational enterprises, non-governmental organizations, and private individuals – interact in a variety of public and private, domestic and international fora to make, interpret, enforce, and ultimately, internalize rules of transnational law' (in contrast to '*international* legal process' which refers to state-to-state interaction): see Koh (1996). See also H Koh's opening remarks to this part of the present work.
4 In this chapter, capitalised 'States' refers to States in the international law sense, and de-capitalised 'states' refers to the 50 states of the US.
5 Balakrishnan and Narayan (1996) pp 231–233.
6 Balakrishman and Narayan (1996).
7 Balakrishman and Narayan (1996) pp 239–242.
8 Urban Justice Center (2000) p 13 (citing Bread for the World (2000)).

democracy that has failed to accept the validity and importance of economic rights,[9] beyond the context of business-related rights.[10]

This chapter evaluates State responsibility for hunger in the US by applying a human rights analysis that benefits from a transnational legal process approach. Although the US has not ratified the relevant international and regional instruments containing the right to food, as a signatory to these instruments, the US must 'refrain from acts which would defeat the object and purpose of a treaty[.]'[11] US failure to take meaningful steps toward incorporating the right to food as binding law – while also holding itself out to be a human rights leader in the world – provides an interesting point of departure from which to consider the universality of human rights.

In fact, the human rights paradigm is relatively under-utilised as a framework of analysis for evaluating any social justice concerns in the US. To the extent human rights discourse is invoked to address domestic policies in the US, it is mainly in the context of civil and political rights,[12] to which the US is unquestionably bound. While rights rhetoric, enforcement and theory have been used to mobilise shame against civil and political rights violations, economic rights, such as the right to food, remain under-analysed, under-articulated and under-enforced, both inside and outside the US.

Viewing hunger in the US through an international human rights lens spotlights ways in which hunger is a transnational (rather than a geographically isolated or solely 'Third World' problem) phenomenon. A human rights framework also places the US within the context of a community of States that have agreed to a set of international standards concerning the right to food, reflected in human rights law.[13] Finally, rather than characterise the State's role as a welfare agent or a charitable provider, the rights paradigm insists on state responsibilities, duties and obligations.

According to the human rights idea, all humans have certain rights simply by virtue of their humanity. We live in an Age of Rights – an era in which the idea of human rights is pervasive; it is internationally accepted and universally shared.[14] Yet, because of differences in cultures, histories, political structures and economic systems, the particular local incorporation, articulation and implementation of human rights vary across borders. Generally speaking, this particularity is not a threat to the idea that human rights are universal; rather, it allows states to best

9 Alston (1990) at 375.
10 US law recognises property rights and freedom to contract.
11 The 1969 Vienna Convention on the Law of Treaties (hereinafter the Vienna Convention) (entered into force 27 January 1980, 1155 UNTS 331, reprinted in (1969) 8 ILM 679), art 18: 'A State is obliged to refrain from acts which would defeat the object and purpose of a treaty when: (a) it has signed the treaty or has exchanged instruments constituting the treaty subject to ratification, acceptance or approval, until it shall have made its intention clear not to become a party to the treaty; or (b) it has expressed its consent to be bound by the treaty, pending the entry into force of the treaty and provided that such entry into force is not unduly delayed.'
12 But see Edelman (1998).
13 See eg Universal Declaration of Human Rights 1948 (UDHR), art 25 ('Everyone has the right to a standard of living adequate for the health and well-being of himself and of his family, including food, clothing, housing and medical care and necessary social services ...'). The argument here is not that the *entire* UDHR is binding law. Rather, the point is that the standards in the UDHR represent universal and international standards, accepted by virtually all of today's states.
14 Henkin (1990).

protect human rights in light of local realities. In certain instances, however, the particular is so at odds with the universal that it undermines the claim that human rights are in fact universal. While Islamic and Asian cultural practices are often singled out as being at odds with universality, failure by the US to recognise and implement the substantive right to food (and other substantive economic rights) also provides a stark example of the tension between particularity and universality.[15]

This chapter investigates the failure by the US to implement the right to food and proposes strategies to remedy the situation. The first section examines the right to food under international law. The second section defines the scope of US obligations under international law. The third section reviews the US approach to economic rights under its domestic legal framework. Fourth, the chapter turns to a discussion of the cyclical nature of US recognition of economic rights. The fifth section of the chapter analyses the dialectic between universality and particularity in the context of the US commitment to the right to food. The sixth section examines opportunities to rethink rights and responsibilities using a transnational legal process approach, and suggests that the US evades its responsibilities for its role by 'distancing hunger'. The seventh section examines how the structure of federalism fails to support substantive commitments to the right to food that could be cultivated at the subfederal level. Finally, the eighth section concludes by examining possible strategies for analysing, articulating and enforcing the right to food in the United States.

THE RIGHT TO FOOD UNDER INTERNATIONAL LAW

The right to food is a universal human right, expressed in various international human rights instruments,[16] as well as in regional

---

15 For a discussion of the selective ways in which human rights non-compliance is described as 'cultural' and therefore relativist in non-Western sites, while in Western sites non-compliance is characterised as non-cultural and therefore rational and normalised, see Powell (1999). Both that article and this chapter are part of a broader research agenda designed to explore this dichotomy in contemporary human rights scholarship and policy.

16 The right to food is contained in the following international instruments:
   Universal Declaration of Human Rights (UDHR), art 25: 'Everyone has the right to a standard of living adequate for the health and well-being of himself and of his family, including food, clothing, housing and medical care and necessary social services, and the right to security in the event of unemployment, sickness, disability, widowhood, old age or lack of livelihood in circumstances beyond his control.'
   International Covenant on Economic, Social and Cultural Rights (ICESCR), art 11: 'The States Parties to the present Covenant recognize the right of everyone to an adequate standard of living for himself and his family, including adequate food, clothing and housing, and to the continuous improvement of living conditions.' Art 11 goes on to require State Parties to take the measures needed to fulfil the right, 'recognising the fundamental right of everyone to be free from hunger.'
   Convention on the Rights of the Child (CRC), art 24: 'States parties shall pursue full implementation of [the child's right to the highest attainable standard of health] and ... shall take appropriate measures ... to combat disease and malnutrition ... through the provision of adequate nutritious foods.' Art 27: 'States Parties recognize the right of every child to a standard of living adequate for the child's physical, mental, spiritual, moral and social development ... States Parties ... shall in case of need provide material assistance and support ..., particularly with regard to nutrition, clothing and housing.'
   For a more exhaustive listing, see Tomasevski (1987).

instruments.[17] In addition to being a freestanding right, the right to food is also inherent in and central to realising human dignity and the right to life.[18] Moreover, because nutrition is central to child health and development,[19] the Convention of the Rights of the Child recognises that states parties 'shall in case of need provide material assistance and support programs, particularly with regard to nutrition' as 'childhood is entitled to special care and assistance'.[20]

The most elaborate expression of economic rights, including the right to food, is the International Covenant on Economic, Social and Cultural Rights (ICESCR). Two concepts serve to define the scope of obligations regarding the rights contained therein: (1) the minimum core content of a right, and (2) progressive realisation of the right.[21] The first concept envisions an obligation on States to observe, at a minimum, the core content of the right. In the case of the right to food, the minimum core content is freedom from hunger. The ICESCR draws a distinction between the right to 'adequate food' and the 'fundamental right of everyone to be free from hunger', which implies that the minimum core content of the right to food is freedom from hunger.[22] The second notion envisions an obligation on states to take steps to progressively realise rights. Article 2(1) of the ICESCR requires governments to 'take steps ... to the maximum of its available resources, with a view to achieving progressively the full realization of the rights recognized' in the ICESCR. This requirement, which is evaluated in light of 'available resources', offers States more flexibility than does the International Covenant for Civil and Political Rights (ICCPR). The ICCPR requires immediate (rather than progressive) realisation of rights, and the state's obligation to realise rights is not

17 The relevant regional instruments for the US include the following.
    American Declaration of the Rights and Duties of Man, art 11: 'Every person has the right to the preservation of his health through sanitary and social measures relating to food, clothing, housing and medical care, to the extent permitted by public and community resources.'
    Charter of the Organization of American States, art 34: '[t]he Member States agree that equality of opportunity, the elimination of extreme poverty, equitable distribution of wealth and income and the full participation of their peoples in decisions relating to their own development are, among others, basic objectives of integral development.'
    To achieve these basic objectives, the member states 'likewise agree to devote their utmost efforts to accomplishing the following basic goals [including] ... j) proper nutrition, especially through the acceleration of national efforts to increase the production and availability of food ...'
    American Convention on Human Rights, art 26: 'The States Parties undertake to adopt measures, both internally and through international co-operation ... with a view to achieving progressively ... the full realization of the rights implicit in the economic ... standards set forth in the Charter of the Organization of American States.'
18 Obviously, food is required to live. The right to life is located in the UDHR, art 3 and in the International Covenant on Civil and Political Rights (ICCPR), art 6. The right to food is also necessary for the preservation of human dignity. The ICESCR states that the rights contained therein 'derive from the inherent dignity of the human person': ICESCR, preamble.
19 For discussion of the health impact of hunger and malnutrition on children as well as on pregnant women, see Urban Justice Center (2000) p 38 (citing Food Research and Action Center *Hunger in the U.S.: Health Consequences of Hunger*).
20 CRC, art 27 and preamble.
21 Committee on Economic, Social, Cultural Rights, General Comment No 12 (on the right to adequate food), para 6, UN doc no E/C.12/1999/5. Note that while the notion of minimum core content of a right is an interpretation of the Covenant, progressive realisation is express in the Covenant itself. In referring to 'the right to food', this chapter refers to both dimensions of the right unless otherwise indicated.
22 Compare ICESCR, art 11(1) with ICESCR, art 11(2).

expressly conditioned by availability of resources.[23] While the right to adequate food is to be realised progressively, states parties to the ICESCR must not delay in taking steps toward realising the right.[24] Also, the concept of progressive realization prohibits retrogressive measures.[25]

As with any other human right, the right to adequate food imposes three levels or types of obligations: to respect, protect and fulfil rights.[26] First, the government has a duty to *respect* the rights of individuals through restraint of power, by not actively depriving people of a guaranteed right. For example, the government cannot impede an individual's ability to feed him or herself by imposing a food blockade. Second, the government has a duty to *protect* by preventing third parties from depriving individuals of their access to adequate food. For example, the federal government has a duty to enact and enforce laws that prevent state and local welfare officials from withholding federal food aid from needy individuals.[27] Third, the government has a duty to *fulfil* rights through establishment of political, economic, and social systems and infrastructure that create conditions whereby individuals can exercise and enforce their rights. While a government need not necessarily feed everyone within its borders (since many people living there may already have resources to feed themselves), it must create conditions for individuals to feed themselves and provide subsidies to those who are unable (ie children, the elderly, individuals with disabilities, and those who are economically marginalised).[28]

23 Compare ICESCR, art 2(1) ('Each State Party to the present Covenant undertakes to take steps ... to the maximum of its available resources, with a view to achieving progressively the full realization of the rights recognized in the present Covenant') with ICCPR, art 2(1) ('Each State Party to the present Covenant undertakes to respect and to ensure to all individuals within its territory and subject to its jurisdiction the rights recognized in the present Covenant').
24 Alston (1990) at 379 (citing the travaux preparatoires – or negotiating history – for the Covenant). See also, the Limburg Principles on the Implementation of the International Covenant on Economic, Social and Cultural Rights, Annex to UN doc no E/CN.4/1987/17, reprinted in (1987) 9 Hum Rts Q 122 ('to begin immediately to take steps toward full realization of the rights contained in the Covenant').
25 The UN Committee on Economic, Social and Cultural Rights notes that 'any deliberately retrogressive measures ... would require the most careful consideration and would need to be fully justified by reference to the totality of the rights provided for in the Covenant and in the context of the full use of the maximum available resources'. UN Committee on Economic, Social and Cultural Rights, Annex III, General Comment No 3 of the Committee on Economic, Social and Cultural Rights, The Nature of State Party Obligations (art 2, para 1 of the Covenant), UN doc no E/1991/23 (E./C.12/1990/3).
26 Committee on Economic, Social, Cultural Rights, General Comment No 12 (on the right to adequate food), para 15, UN doc no E/C.12/1999/5. See also, The Maastricht Guidelines on Violations of Economic, Social and Cultural Rights, para 6 ('Like civil and political rights, economic, social and cultural rights impose three different types of obligations on States: the obligations to respect, protect and fulfil').
27 The federal regulation requiring state and local welfare officials to notify households of their statutory right to file a Food Stamp application the same day they contact the Food Stamp office could be seen as a way of facilitating this type of obligation: see 7 CFR 273.2(c)(2). The federal government can generally regulate or place conditions on the conduct of state governments where federal funding or regulation of interstate commerce are involved. Consider, for example, the fact that the federal government conditions receipt of federal highway funds on states' raising the drinking age to 21. Also, in the civil rights context, the federal government has enacted statutes that regulate the conduct of state and local officials: see eg 42 USC, s 1983.
28 Eide (1998). See also 'Implementation of the Right to Food in National Legislation' in The Food and Agricultural Organization of the United Nations (ed) (1998) *The Right to Food: In Theory and Practice*, available at www.fao.org/docrep/w9990e/w9990e03.htm.

THE SCOPE OF US OBLIGATIONS UNDER INTERNATIONAL LAW

The ICESCR and the CRC were signed and sent to the US Congress by Presidents Carter and Clinton respectively. Although the US has not ratified either of these instruments, its signature obligates the US to 'refrain from acts which would defeat the object and purpose of a treaty[.]'[29] Interestingly, 180 states – including every other major industrialised nation – have ratified the ICESCR, and 191 states have ratified the CRC.[30] In fact, the US is the only nation in the world, except for Somalia (a country without a functioning government throughout much of the 1990s) that has yet to ratify the CRC.[31]

The US has also accepted the UDHR. Parts of the UDHR may have attained the status of customary international law norms, which are binding on all states, including the US. However, it is not clear that the right to food in article 25 of the UDHR has attained the status of customary international law.

At the regional level, article 26 of the American Convention on Human Rights requires state parties to adopt measures with a view to achieving progressively full realisation of the rights implicit in the economic standards set forth in the Charter of the Organization of American States (OAS), which includes proper nutrition as a basic goal in article 34. The American Convention (which effectuates the goals of the OAS Charter) was signed by the US on 1 June 1977. While the US has not yet ratified the American Convention, again, its signature obligates the US to 'refrain from acts which would defeat [its] object and purpose[.]'[32]

Additionally, the American Declaration of the Rights and Duties of Man, which, provides the right to food,[33] was approved with the vote of US.[34] The Inter-American Court notes: 'The General Assembly of the [OAS] has also repeatedly recognized that the American Declaration is a source of international obligation for the member states of the OAS.'[35]

THE US APPROACH TO ECONOMIC RIGHTS UNDER DOMESTIC LAW

Both as a matter of constitutional and statutory law, the particular approach to hunger in the US largely involves providing procedural protections in its national food assistance program, the Food Stamps Program, rather than guaranteeing the underlying substantive right. Such procedural guarantees are under-enforced and will remain inadequate[36] so long as the federal government gives state and local governments enormous incentives to reduce the number of people enrolled in poverty relief programs. This chapter challenges the complacency with which the US relies on a process-oriented solution in an area where substantive

29 Vienna Convention, art 18.
30 Office of the United Nations High Commissioner for Human Rights (2000).
31 Urban Justice Center (2000) at 16.
32 Vienna Convention, art 18.
33 'Every person has the right to the preservation of his health through sanitary and social measures relating to food, clothing, housing and medical care, to the extent permitted by public and community resources.' American Declaration, art 11.
34 Case 2141, para 16.
35 'Interpretation of the American Declaration of the Rights and Duties of Man within the Framework of Article 64 of the American Convention on Human Rights', Advisory Opinion OC-1089, para 45, Inter-Am C.H.R. (Ser A) no 10 (1989).
36 In his critique of contemporary liberal theory, David Kennedy points out that liberalism has been 'Thatcherized or Reaganized' – cleansed of its earlier substantive commitments and narrowed to focus on proceduralist democracy: Kennedy (1999).

benchmarks may be necessary, because economic and political incentives for states to diminish assistance to poor families are embedded in current federal law.[37]

Despite the aspiration expressed in the preamble of the US Constitution to 'promote the general Welfare',[38] the US Supreme Court interprets the Constitution and relevant federal statutes as providing procedural protections for social welfare programs to prevent arbitrary termination from these programs,[39] but has repeatedly refused to recognise the existence of the underlying substantive economic rights at stake.[40] Moreover, the Court has rejected claims that the federal government has affirmative obligations to guarantee rights.[41] Instead, federal law provides minimal procedural guarantees that, for example, require state and local welfare officials to notify households of their statutory right to file a Food Stamp application the same day the household contacts the Food Stamp office.[42]

While the approach to economic rights is a proceduralist one under US domestic law, at least two approaches to the right to food link it to substantive civil and political rights approaches. This linkage not only underscores the interdependence of rights, but also places the right to food within the mainstream of American legal culture. One such approach – sometimes characterised as the 'full belly approach' – advances the idea that political rights can be exercised and enjoyed only by people who are maintained by basic subsistence. Frank Michelman, for example, contends that the Equal Protection clause of the Fourteenth Amendment to the US Constitution should be interpreted as requiring government to satisfy certain minimal economic requirements.[43] How, after all, is the homeless citizen able to exercise the right to vote if lack of housing (and therefore lack of an address) prevent him from registering to vote? Akhil Amar makes a similar argument with regard to basic entitlements as prerequisites to exercising the rights of citizens, such as the right to vote.[44] Amar supports his theory by observing that the Reconstruction Amendments to the US Constitution (which extended the

---

37 Cashin (1999) (describing how the new federal welfare reform law uses both financial rewards and penalties to incentivise states to reduce their public assistance rolls).

38 US Constitution, preamble.

39 See eg *Goldberg v Kelly* 397 US 254 (1970) (finding that a statutory entitlement to public assistance is a 'liberty' or 'property' interest protected by Due Process and requires a pre-termination evidentiary hearing). But see *Mathews v Eldridge* 424 US 319 (1976) (finding that administrative procedures that failed to provide pre-termination hearing for disability benefits comports with Due Process).

40 See eg *United States Department of Agriculture v Moreno* 413 US 528 (1973) (applying 'mere rationality' test to determine constitutionality of federal statute denying Food Stamps to households containing unrelated people). See also *San Antonio Independent School District v Rodriguez* 411 US 1 (1973) (failing to recognise a constitutional right to education); *Dandridge v Williams* 397 US 471 (1970) (no right to welfare); *Lindsey v Normet* 405 US 56 (1972) (no right to housing); *Massachusetts Board of Retirement v Murgia* 427 US 307 (1976) (no right to work).

41 The Court has found that the federal government has no affirmative constitutional obligations or duties to create the conditions necessary to protect rights. See eg *DeShaney v Winnebago Co Department of Social Services* 489 US 189 (1989) (finding no government duty to remove a child from a severely abusive home). Not only is the government under no affirmative obligation to provide protection, it also has full discretion to eliminate or limit social programs. *Harris v Mcrae* 448 US 297 (1980) (finding no government duty to provide funds for medically necessary abortions).

42 7 CFR 273.2 (c)(2).

43 Michelman (1969).

44 Amar (1990).

franchise to former slaves following the US Civil War) were enacted by the same radical Republican Congress that supported the idea of 'forty acres and a mule' for the newly freed slaves. Congress thereby acknowledged that these new citizens could not truly be citizens (making the Reconstruction Amendments meaningless), without being provided a basic level of subsistence. As far as US constitutional law is concerned, the Supreme Court has rejected similar arguments made in the context of the right to education.[45]

A second approach linking the right to food to civil and political rights is based on Amartya Sen's theory about the role of civil and political rights in preventing famine. According to Sen, famines are typically caused by political failures (that is, the failure of governments to deliver food), rather than by crop failures.[46] By creating vehicles of accountability that expose corrupt and inefficient government policies, the existence of a free press, regular elections, free speech and democracy assist in preventing famines. Arguably, hunger in the US results from political failure, as the US government has the resources to feed the hungry, but fails adequately to do so. In the absence of campaign finance reform, poor people in the US will continue to lack meaningful political power.

While these approaches linking the right to food to civil and political rights represent important attempts to address the indivisibility and interdependence of rights, they do not fully capture the value of an economic right (such as the right to food) standing on its own. Due largely to the Cold War, human rights have been bifurcated into civil and political rights on the one hand, and economic, social and cultural rights on the other. Despite the collapse of the Cold War, the US continues to resist domestic incorporation of economic rights or recognise their value in their own right.

The US particular practice of providing limited procedural (rather than substantive) protections as regards economic rights[47] and its complex relationship to these rights reflect three countervailing values deeply embedded in the national culture. The following three values are indicated in the legislative history surrounding congressional consideration of the ICESCR and Executive branch treatment of economic rights in the aftermath of congressional consideration of the Covenant.[48] First, US resistance to recognising economic rights as authentic rights can be traced to philosophical beliefs underpinning the US constitutional regime, which include adherence to a system of limited federal government – a notion that is more consistent with the concept of negative rights rather than affirmative rights.[49] While the notion of negative rights could address one level of state obligations within the human rights paradigm (ie the duty to *respect* the rights of individuals through restraint of power), it does not speak to the other

---

45 See *San Antonio Independent School District v Rodriguez* 411 US 959 (1973).
46 See eg Sen (1990).
47 While the right to food is often described as an economic right, the practice within the US of providing a voucher or in-kind contribution of actual food rather than cash assistance may reflect a discomfort with viewing economic rights in monetary terms. Ironically, this may stem from the paternalistic belief that decision-making about resource allocation is more responsibly achieved at the government level than at the individual household level, despite the political shift toward downsizing the role of government.
48 For a fuller discussion of the legislative history, see Alston (1990).
49 See Monaghan (1978) (discussing attempts by Professors Laurence Tribe and Frank Michelman to challenge the traditional night-watchman/negative conception of federal government).

two levels of obligations (ie the duties to *protect* and *fulfil* rights), which are particularly relevant in the economic rights context. Relying on the negative/ affirmative rights dichotomy, Elliott Abrams, President Reagan's Assistant Secretary of State for the Bureau of Human Rights and Humanitarian Affairs, concluded that: 'the rights that no government can violate [ie civil and political rights] should not be watered down to the status of rights that governments should do their best to secure [ie economic, social and cultural rights].'[50] The logic underlying this dichotomy is challenged by Cass Sunstein and Stephen Holmes and separately by Henry Shue, who point out that beyond involving restraint of government authority, effectuating negative rights also requires affirmative government outlays.[51] For example, securing the right to liberty requires government support to cover the cost of trained police officers and a judicial system capable of respecting the rights of those arrested and detained;[52] securing the right to equality in the courts requires government support to cover the costs of counsel for indigent defendants.[53]

A second and closely related strain in the US psyche that reinforces resistance to economic rights is the nation's deep belief in individualism. 'American society has found symbols and values different from social solidarity and family policy around which to construct its unity ... [T]his country has chosen individualism as a central value.'[54] An internal State Department memorandum that was apparently approved by President Reagan's Secretary of State, Alexander Haig, rejected economic 'rights' as rights on this basis.[55] For the purposes of future US policy, the memorandum urged adoption of a narrower definition of human rights, limited to 'political rights and civil liberties'. In fact, the memo urged the administration to 'move away from "human rights" as a term, and begin to speak of "individual rights", "political rights" and "civil liberties"'. Henry Shue provides

---

50 Alston (1990) at 373 (quoting Review of State Department Country Reports on Human Rights Practices for 1981: Hearing Before the Subcommittee on Human Rights and International Organizations of the House Committee On Foreign Affairs, 97th Congress, 2nd Session 7 (1982) (statement of Elliott Abrams)).

  According to Alston, in addition to ideological arguments, Abrams also made a number of 'pragmatic' arguments for deleting the 'economic and social rights' sections in the first of the State Department's annual Country Reports on Human Rights Practices submitted by the Reagan Administration in February 1982. Abrams contended that recognition of economic and social rights 'tends to create a growing confusion about priorities in the human rights area and a growing dispersion of energy in ending human rights violation', and that the rights in question were 'easily exploited to excuse violations of civil and political rights'.

51 Holmes and Sunstein (1999) pp 199–203; Shue, (1980) pp 35–40; Shue, (1996) pp 113, 127 (all suggesting there is no principled basis for distinguishing between positive and negative rights). For a contrary view, see eg Bork (1979); Winter (1979); Epstein (1985).

52 Shue (1980) pp 35–40. The right to liberty, contained in ICCPR, art 9, requires that anyone who is arrested 'shall be informed, at the time of the arrest, of the reasons for the arrest and shall be promptly informed of any charges against him'; 'shall be brought promptly before a judge' where arrested or detained on a criminal charge; and 'shall be entitled to take proceedings before a court' where deprived of his liberty by arrest or detention: ICCPR, art 9(2), (3) and (4) respectively.

53 The right to equality before the courts, contained in ICCPR, art 14, entitles everyone 'to have legal assistance assigned to him, in any case where the interests of justice so require, and without payment by him in any such case if he does not have sufficient means to pay for it[.]': ICCPR, art 14(3)(d).

54 Alston (1990) p 384 (quoting Kamerman and Kahn (1988) pp 351, 375).

55 Alston (1990) p 372 (quoting New York Times, 5 November 1981, at 1, 29 and citing Jacoby (1986)).

a response that relocates the concept of individualism within the broader context of the situated self.[56] Since humans generally live as part of a social order, rather than as atomistic individuals, "one needs an adequate analysis of the critical social forces and institutions" that can protect and fulfil individual rights.[57] Viewing the right to food as an individual right that requires a social response, Shue points out that civil and political rights also require social responses, and, therefore, dichotomizing the two sets of rights on this basis fails. Because individual arrangements (such as 'an Uzi in every home'[58] to secure liberty) are not workable, a civil or political right, such as the right to liberty, requires institutional arrangements and therefore expenditure of resources:

> 'What is abundantly clear either way is that positive duties will have to be performed. Police will have to be on the streets, judges will have to be in criminal courts ... On the other hand, not everyone needs to join the police force, the criminal justice system, or the prison system.'[59]

Even in an individualist society, social responses are required to take advantage of efficiencies that result from such division of labour.

Third, some in the US have associated economic rights with a communist or socialist-style economy and the politics that go along with that. For example, in hearings before the US Senate in 1979, conservative activist, Phyllis Schlafly, warned that the ICESCR 'would constitute a giant step toward a socialist state'.[60] Other witnesses at the hearings argued that the Covenant 'is largely a document of collectivist inspiration, alien in spirit and philosophy to the principles of a free economy' and a 'socialist blueprint that encourages open-ended unlimited government meddling of the sort on which dictatorships thrive on'.[61] While the Reagan Administration official, Assistant Secretary of State Richard Schifter, pointed out that economic rights 'fit more readily within the program of Franklin D. Roosevelt than into that of Marx or Lenin',[62] paradoxically, he placed the issue of economic rights squarely in the context of the Cold War, claiming that:

> 'Critics of the Western democracies used to contend that, while emphasizing free speech and a free press, the democracies ignored such basic needs as food, jobs, housing and medical care. These critics, particularly those affiliated with the Soviet bloc, stressed that their governments guaranteed citizens the right to obtain basic needs. Supporters in democracies responded that people needed not guarantees of food, jobs, housing and medical care, but delivery of these benefits.'[63]

Rebuffing Schifter's argument, Philip Alston points out:

56 Shue (1996) p 125. See also Sandel (1984).
57 Shue (1996) p 125.
58 Shue (1996) pp 127–128.
59 Shue (1996) pp 127–128.
60 Alston (1990) p 378 (quoting International Human Rights Treaties: Hearing Before the Senate Committee on Foreign Relations, 96th Congress, 1st Session 35 (1979) (statement of Phyllis Schlafly)).
61 Alston (1990) pp 383–384 (quoting, respectively, International Human Rights Treaties: Hearing Before the Senate Committee on Foreign Relations, 96th Congress, 1st Session 35 (1979) and R Lee (1981) *The United Nations Conspiracy* p 108).
62 Alston (1990) p 375 (citing R Schifter (1998) 'The Semantics of Human Rights', Department of State, Bureau of Public Affairs, Current Policy, No 1041, at 1).
63 Alston (1990) p 375 (quoting R Schifter (1989) 'Building Firm Foundations: The Institutionalization of United States Human Rights Policy in the Reagan Years', 2 Harv Hum Rts YB 3 at 16, fn 64).

'But the "critics" of whom [Schifter] speaks have not assailed "the western democracies" in general, since, with the sole exception of the United States, all the Western democracies have accepted the validity and equal importance of economic, social and cultural human rights, at least in principle ... . If, for reasons that are unclear, the debate needs to be pursued in geopolitical terms, it is between the United States on the one hand, and most of the rest of the world on the other.'[64]

Any suggestion that economic rights are an exclusively 'Soviet-Third World' concept is misguided and ignores the fact that in addition to numerous Western European states, many western religions, including the Catholic Church, have long championed these rights.[65] The endurance of US reluctance to recognise and respect economic rights following the collapse of the Soviet Union suggests that failure to take these rights seriously in the US goes beyond Cold War politics. Moreover, the US intervenes in the market in numerous ways, including by affecting the food supply through provision of subsidies to farmers and quotas on imports of food products, such as sugar. In the post-Cold War era, the ideologies of individualism and limited government may be more central to the persistent neglect of economic rights in the United States.

CYCLICAL NATURE OF US RECOGNITION OF ECONOMIC RIGHTS

While complacency or even hostility toward economic rights has been the norm in the US (in contrast to other industrialised Western states), there have also been moments of heightened national awareness and responsiveness to the twin problems of hunger and poverty. Periodic ideological aversion to economic rights as un-American has alternated with periods of ideological embrace of substantive economic rights. Far from viewing economic rights as a foreign concept, some American political leaders have championed the need to protect humans from hunger and economic deprivation. As with Bruce Ackerman's constitutional moments,[66] these moments of heightened consciousness concerning the problem of hunger have not necessarily been acknowledged through the formal constitutional amendment process (although President Franklin D Roosevelt did call for an 'Economic Bill of Rights'). Instead, support for a substantive guarantee to ensure freedom from hunger has been reflected in congressional and executive branch leadership during these heightened moments.

The concept of hunger as a national problem did not exist in the American imagination until the New Deal period, when Congress and President Roosevelt supported the birth of the modern Welfare State in the US through the enactment of sweeping welfare legislation. '[O]ccupying a political space somewhere between Locke and Marx, exploring the possibility of a 'third way' between capitalism and socialism',[67] New Deal legislation providing protections for the poor reflected recognition of the federal government's responsibility to aid the poor. This heightened moment extended into the 1940s, when President Roosevelt described 'freedom from want' as an 'essential' freedom in the 'Four Freedoms' speech he delivered in his annual message to Congress

---

64 Alston (1990) pp 375–376.
65 Alston (1990) pp 387–388.
66 Ackerman (1998).
67 Ackerman (1998) p 347.

in 1941.[68] He saw economic rights as central to securing democracy at home as well as spreading it throughout the world. In his 1944 State of the Union Message, President Roosevelt called for an 'Economic Bill of Rights', contending: 'We have come to a clear realization of the fact that true individual freedom cannot exist without economic security and independence.'[69] Moreover, as chair of the drafting committee for the UDHR, Eleanor Roosevelt oversaw the inclusion of economic rights – including the right to food – into the document.

Attention to hunger surged again in the 1960s when Martin Luther King's Poor People's Campaign was launched. The Executive Branch took the initiative in the 1960s under Lyndon B Johnson's War on Poverty, in which he launched a set of anti-poverty programs.

Congress also demonstrated leadership in the 1960s, with Senator Robert Kennedy's much publicised trip to Appalachia, the Mississippi Delta, and other poor communities around the nation, which built support for national food assistance programs and a congressional resolution declaring the right to food.[70] Senator Kennedy's trip helped publicise the existence of a national hunger epidemic[71] and gave the problems of hunger and malnutrition visibility. By pulling the curtain back and exposing the extent of the problem, Senator Kennedy's trip helped build support to expand federal food assistance programs, such as the Food Stamp Program, the Women Infants and Children (WIC) Program, and the School Lunch Program. In 1975, the US Congress adopted a joint 'resolution declaring as national policy the right to food'.[72] While the problem of hunger was largely eliminated by the late 1970s (in large part because of expansion of federal food-assistance programs), hunger reappeared with a vengeance by the 1980s, due to cuts in these and other welfare programs.[73] According to the US Department of Agriculture, approximately ten million people in the US live in households that suffer from hunger.[74]

The Roosevelt-Johnson-Kennedy commitment to economic rights fits squarely within the US' long (albeit evolving) tradition of providing social safety net protections for the elderly, the sick and the poor. As has been the case with other affluent, Western democracies, the US has provided food assistance primarily

68 President Roosevelt spoke of freedom of speech, freedom of worship, freedom from want and freedom from fear as four fundamental freedoms in his Annual Message to Congress, delivered on 6 January 1941.
69 90 Cong Rec 55, 57 (1944).
70 Physicians Task Force on Hunger in America (1985) (cited in Urban Justice Center (2000)).
71 Physicians Task Force on Hunger in America (1985) (cited in Urban Justice Center (2000)).
72 It resolved, inter alia, that '(1) every person in this country and throughout the world has the right to food – the right to a nutritionally adequate diet – and that this right is henceforth to be recognized as a cornerstone of United States policy; and (2) this policy has become a fundamental point of reference in the formation of legislation and administrative decisions; and (3) concerning hunger in the United States[,] we seek to enroll on food assistance programs all who are in need ...': The Right to Food Resolution, Hearings Before the Subcommittee on International Resources, Food, and Energy of the Committee on International Relations, House of Representatives, 94th Congress, 2d Session (1976) (cited in part in Alston (1984) pp 9, 58).
73 Physicians Task Force on Hunger in America (1985) p xx (cited in Urban Justice Center (2000) p 49).
74 US Department of Agriculture, Food and Nutrition Service (1999).

through taxation and redistribution programs. However, this tradition has shifted over time and is subject to the political whims of the day.[75]

The cyclical nature with which the US alternates between moments of heightened consciousness about hunger within its borders on the one hand, and complacency or even hostility to the hungry and poor on the other, reflects a tension. This tension has emerged because the US espouses the universality of human rights on a rhetorical level, even while it rejects domestic incorporation of certain rights on a practical level. Reflected in the fact that the US has signed, but not ratified, several human rights treaties, this tension is recurrent because the US approach to hunger within its own borders historically has had elements of both procedural and substantive protection.[76]

Moments of heightened consciousness about both the prevalence of hunger in the US and the need for substantive protections emerge only during times of crisis, when it is clear that the systems that are in place to address poverty and hunger are broken or inadequate in important ways. With the assassinations of Senator Robert Kennedy and Martin Luther King in the late 1960s, the federal government's commitment to poverty died shortly thereafter, resulting, perhaps, in a failed 'constitutional moment'.[77] Cleansed of its earlier substantive commitments, the current national approach to hunger in the US is a minimalist and proceduralist one.

While some degree of particularity is permissible, and even desirable, in incorporating international standards at the local level to ensure responsiveness to local needs, vitiating the minimum core content of a right or retrogressing in achieving the right falls outside the permissible range of particularity. Despite the availability of procedural protections and an abundance of resources, the US has not satisfied the obligations to ensure the minimum core content of the right to food and to progressively realise this right. The US has not achieved the minimum core content of the right (ie freedom from hunger), and the number of people in the US who lack adequate food has grown.[78] Under a theory of progressive realisation, once the US had achieved a certain level of eliminating hunger, it had an obligation to continue to move progressively toward fulfilling the right to food, rather than retrogressing. However, cuts in federal funding and poor implementation of the Food Stamp Program have been exacerbated by presidential pledges to 'end welfare as we know it'.[79]

While the US failure to implement effective substantive or even procedural protections for the nation's hungry falls outside the permissible range of particularity, particularity need not inherently undercut universality. In fact, particularity and universality can be mutually supporting, so long as there is a genuine commitment to the universal and respect for the particular.

---

75 With the passage of the Personal Responsibility and Work Opportunity Act Pub L No 104-193, 110 Stat 2105 (1996), the US experienced a retrenchment in welfare rights during the 1990s – largely in response to the changing racial composition of the welfare recipient population: see Crooms (1995).

76 In addition to the Roosevelt-Johnson-Kennedy substantive embrace of economic rights, see also discussion of New York State Constitution below for another example of a substantive approach.

77 Ackerman (1998).

78 See fnn 73, 74 and accompanying text.

79 Berke (1992) (reporting on then-presidential candidate Bill Clinton's campaign pledge).

THE DIALECTIC OF UNIVERSALITY AND PARTICULARITY

That the dialectic of particularity and universality is reflected in a powerful and paradoxical interdependence of the two is well-known. Benjamin Barber artfully describes this phenomenon as 'Jihad vs McWorld'.[80] For Barber, Jihad represents the particular,[81] while McWorld represents the universal.[82] As with Barber, the present writer uses the term 'Jihad' as a metaphor for the particular.[83] The use of Barber's metaphor here is limited to the complex, dynamic relationship he describes between the particular and the universal. While Jihad and McWorld are tendencies that appear to be at odds with each other,[84] curiously they support and reinforce each other. 'Jihad not only revolts against but abets McWorld, while McWorld not only imperils but re-creates and reinforces Jihad. They produce their contraries and need one another.'[85] McWorld 'needs cultural parochialism to feed its endless appetite[,]'[86] just as Jihad's favoured weapons are McWorld's satellite dishes and other instruments of the information revolution.[87] With the Internet, television and commodification of culture, global culture provides local culture a medium, audience and set of aspirations. Transnational flows of culture, capital and labour also ensure that the Western and the non-Western, the global and the local, the universal and the particular are continuously intermingled and recombined, with the Third World present in the First and the First World visible within the Third.

In an analogous way, universal human rights norms and the growing power of the international human rights movement help fuel local claims and constructions

---

80 Barber (1996).
81 Rooted in race and nation, Barber's representation of Jihad is based on particularity, atomisation, tribalism and balkanisation. It represents a tendency toward separate imagined communities that have distinct cultures or faiths, or are defined by other aspects of identity experienced as discrete and insular. With its commitment to the insular, Jihad rebels against social co-operation and mutuality, against technology, against integrated markets and against modernity: Barber (1996) p 4.
82 By contrast, Barber's representation of McWorld is a picture of 'universalizing markets and technology that demand integration and uniformity and that mesmerize peoples everywhere with fast music, fast computers, and fast food – MTV, Macintosh, and McDonald's – pressing nations into one homogenous global theme park, one McWorld tied together by communications, information, entertainment, and commerce': Barber (1996) p 4.
83 Barber (1996) dislocates 'Jihad' from its literal meaning (ie Islamic holy war): Barber (1996) p 299 (making clear 'how little [his] argument has to do with Islam ... or with resistance to McWorld as a singular property of radical Muslims'). Barber is careful to acknowledge that he uses the term 'Jihad' as a generic term, metaphor or set of tendencies 'quite independently from its Islamic theological origins', (p 299) as his representation of Jihad can just as easily be used to describe the '"American Jihad" being waged by the radical Right' in the US: p 9. In fact, the present writer's representation of Jihad locates the phenomenon in the context of the 'American Jihad' that crusades for open markets, triumphs in less government and celebrates individualism.
84 'Caught between Babel and Disneyland, the planet is falling precipitously apart and coming reluctantly together at the very same moment': Barber (1996) p 4.
85 Barber (1996) p 5.
86 Barber (1996) p 155. McDonald's uses local foods marketed through its 'universal' fast food menu to cater to local tastes: New York Times (1999) ('its Vienna franchises also contain "McCafes" ... In Jakarta, the McDonald's menu includes rice as well as french fries. And in Seoul, the burger chain sells roast pork on a bun with ... soy sauce').
87 Recall, for example, how within the context of recent internal conflicts, while Hutu or Bosnian Serb identity was constructed through historical memory, these particularistic identities were exploited and exaggerated through 'media propaganda by a leadership set on liquidating rival clans': Barber (1996) p 17.

of rights, and these local claims can feed back and nourish a more vibrant and multifaceted universalism. Having multiple voices sing different chords of the human rights song, so to speak, supports universal norms in culturally relevant ways and, in so doing, strengthens human rights culture.[88] However, rather than find ways to incorporate universal rights, such as the right to food, in locally relevant ways, the US hides behind convenient banners, such as 'the free market', 'individualism' or 'government downsizing', limiting its approach in the economic rights area to a procedural one, which in practice falls outside the acceptable range of particularity, even as it criticises other states on human rights grounds.

While Barber's representation of McWorld is an allegory of 'universalizing markets',[89] it is suggested here that the US commitment to unfettered free trade, rugged individualism and government downsizing, as well as its interest in exporting these ideologies, are examples of Jihad (the particular), while human rights, including the right to food, is an example of McWorld (the universal). The fervour with which the free market, rugged individualism and limited government are embraced as belief systems and the extent to which they are defining features of the nation, are particular to the US and its identity. The inversion of Barber's metaphor here, therefore, has two elements. First, while Barber describes 'Jihad [as] a bloody politics of identity, [and] McWorld [as] a bloodless economics of profit[,]',[90] the US experience demonstrates that the bloodless economics of profit can be also associated with Jihad.

Second, while Barber's representation of 'McWorld' implies a universality achieved through global saturation with US exports and franchises (such as the McDonald's Corporation), the universalisation of human rights is not achieved through export of exclusively American or even Western ideas. The human rights idea draws inspiration from John Locke and from revolutionary moments in both America and France, but these eighteenth-century ideas concerning individual autonomy were eventually combined with nineteenth and twentieth-century ideas about socialism, the welfare state, decolonisation and the proliferation of modern constitutions and bills of rights.[91] Therefore, backlash against the idea of human rights is not expressed in exclusively anti-American terms.[92] In fact, the US is a resister of human rights within its own borders, even while it promotes the idea of rights overseas. The right to food provides a case in point.

Current US policy notwithstanding, a commitment to the right to food is not necessarily inconsistent with a system of negative government, the notion of individualism or free market principles, as discussed above.[93] Furthermore, the globalisation of both markets and human rights is enabled through similar mechanisms, including the proliferation of technology and communications. However, the failure of the US to deliver fully on the right to food pits its particular approach against a universal right. While the US engages in debates about food

---

88 Karen Knop uses the term 'multivocality' in arguing that the diversity that results from local incorporation of international standards in different contexts does not undermine universality: Knop (2000).

89 Barber (1996) p 4.

90 Barber (1996) p 8.

91 Henkin (1990) p 1; Henkin (1981b) p 2.

92 By contrast, the backlash against the proliferation of McDonald's is expressed in anti-US terms, as reflected by the French farmers who vandalised a McDonald's restaurant in France to protest against the growing economic and cultural global influence of the US: Souchard (2000); The Economist (2000); Agence France Presse (2000); Meunier, (2000).

93 See the text accompanying fnn 43–46, 51–53, 56–59, 62, 64–72, above.

with relative ease in the context of international trade law,[94] food does not appear on the US radar screen in the field of international human rights.

The US Department of Agriculture and federal courts have, however, intervened to address procedural irregularities in the Food Stamp Program that the federal government insists are unintended consequences of the Personal Responsibility and Work Opportunity Act (PRWOA) – federal 'welfare reform' legislation enacted in 1996 which gave state and local governments more discretion in the administration of welfare programs. While the federal government has stepped in to monitor state and local government compliance with the Food Stamp Program, it is also part of the problem. The Food Stamp Program is under-funded and the federal government excludes entire classes of people from the program, depending on the politics of the day, regardless of need.[95] Moreover, the PRWOA contains incentives for states to reduce their welfare rolls, so that the US can 'end welfare as we know it'.[96] The federal government's refusal adequately to fund and administer the Food Stamp Program violates international human rights standards.

RETHINKING THE STRUCTURE OF RIGHTS AND RESPONSIBILITIES IN THE TRANSNATIONAL CONTEXT

Several economists have observed that everyday hunger, malnourishment and famine are largely the result of economic choices and policies.[97] In an increasingly interdependent world, where states are being replaced by markets as sites for such decisions, who is the state and where lies the responsibility? Rights and responsibilities can usefully be examined through a transnational legal process approach that recognizes the erosion of borders and boundaries. The intermingling of global and local, public and private, the state and the market invite a transnational legal process approach, which acknowledges these interactions, in contrast to the more classic international legal process approach, which primarily address state to state interaction.[98]

In their critique of the ways in which the charity paradigm fails adequately to describe the state's responsibility to address hunger and poverty, Radhika Balakrishnan and Uma Narayan investigate ways in which rights and responsibilities flow transnationally.[99] Balakrishnan and Narayan challenge assumptions that underlay 'lifeboat ethics', which frequently inform philosophical discussions of world hunger.[100] They critique the 'two lifeboats' metaphor, which assumes that affluent nations of the North occupy a well-stocked and uncrowded lifeboat, while poor nations of the South occupy an under-stocked lifeboat, on

---

94 See eg Sciolino (2000).
95 For example, the PRWOA placed prohibitions on legal immigrants from receiving Food Stamps. Food Stamps were restored to some immigrants (eg eligible documented aliens) on 1 November 1998 through the Agricultural Research, Extension, and Education Reform Act of 1998, Pub. L No 105–185, ss 503–504, 112 Stat 523, 578 (1998).
96 For discussion of the new incentive structure under PRWOA, see Cashin (1999) p 560.
97 See eg Sen (1990); Balakrishnan and Narayan (1996) p 232.
98 For discussion of transnational legal process approach, see Koh (1996). See also H Koh's opening remarks to this part of the present work.
99 Balakrishnan and Narayan (1996).
100 Compare Balakrishnan and Narayan (1996) pp 234–235 (critique of 'lifeboat ethics'), with Hardin (1996) p 5 (classic defence of 'lifeboat ethics', whereby nations are analogised to lifeboats with limited carrying capacity, which must be protected from overcrowding).

the verge of capsizing because it is overwhelmed by out-of-control rates of reproduction. Now, what is wrong with this picture?

Part of the problem is that this picture assumes that one lifeboat just happens to be rich and the other poor, without any acknowledgment of the ways in which elites in both the global North and the South contributed to the causes and maintenance of hunger and poverty.[101] The responsibility of these elites is not limited to mere *charity* to those who just *happen* to be hungry and poor.

> 'Since poverty and chronic hunger often *result* from the economic and political decisions of national governments, foreign governments and international development agencies, the *responsibility* for alleviating these problems must be accepted by a number of countries and institutions.'[102]

On the one hand, then, the two-lifeboats metaphor is flawed because it dichotomizes the North and South as unrelated spheres between whom no rights and responsibilities flow, in ways that mask responsibility that the global North may share with the global South[103] for the creation and maintenance of hunger.[104] Balakrishnan and Narayan contend that states of the global North are responsible for hunger in the global South through the continuing economic effects of colonialism (such as continued reliance on single-crop economies that are vulnerable to shifting global prices); displacement of self-sufficient farming (through export promotion policies and the promotion of large-scale mechanised farming); and shrinking government assistance to the poor (through support of structural adjustment and other policies of the World Bank and IMF that require privatisation and government downsizing).[105] However, support from richer

---

101   Balakrishnan and Narayan (1996) p 235.
102   Balakrishnan and Narayan (1996) p 235 (emphasis in original).
103   The terms 'North' and 'South' are used here not to refer to geography in a literal sense, but rather as placeholders from which to consider the division of resources between wealthy, industrialised countries (which are largely located in the global North) and poor, developing countries (which are largely located in the global South).
104   Indeed, art 2 of the ICESCR supports the idea of shared responsibility and co-operation in requiring States Parties to 'take steps, individually *and through international cooperation* ... with a view to achieving progressively the full realization of the rights recognised' in the Covenant. See also ICESCR, art 11, in which the right to food appears (stressing 'the essential importance of international cooperation based on free consent' though this co-operation is 'based on free consent'). The Carter administration proposed a reservation to art 2 as well as similar language in art 11, stating that these two provisions 'import no legally binding obligation to provide aide to foreign countries': message from the President of the US, transmitting four treaties pertaining to human rights, Sen Exec C, D, E and F, 95th Congress, 2d Session vii (1978). Conceivably, this reservation would not limit the US' obligation to remedy a wrong that the US shares responsibility in creating (in contrast to providing 'aide' or charity).
105   Balakrishnan and Narayan (1996) pp 234–238. The account Balakrishnan and Narayan offer to explain the causes behind world hunger and poverty is quite different from the one that underlies the two lifeboats narrative, which is based on Malthusian assumptions that one of the lifeboats is too crowded. For an example of the latter, see Hardin (1996). Targeting women's bodies as sites for solving this 'problem' through overzealous population control measures remain central to development policies at both international and national levels which, in addition to being gendered, are also raced and classed in that they tend to focus on Third-World women, poor women, as well as women of colour in the North.

        Rather than attributing population control measures or initiatives geared toward raising per capita income as *the* solutions to curbing population growth, Balakrishnan and Narayan instead argue for literacy training, improved maternal-child health care, voluntary access to birth control and increased recognition of women's rights. They cite the success of Kerala (the state in South India famous for its zero population growth even though per capita incomes are very low), which relied on these alternative strategies.

countries to poorer ones need not be seen as a zero-sum game or as requiring reallocation of additional resources from addressing poverty in the global North to addressing poverty in the global South.[106]

On the other hand, the two-lifeboats narrative obscures the inequality that exists *within* the boats. Besides failing to take into account responsibility of Third-World elites who make military, economic and political decisions that create, exacerbate, or fail to address hunger and poverty in the global South,[107] the two-lifeboats theory is also flawed because it 'distances hunger' as a phenomenon that only occurs within the Global South. The centrality of the inquiry – what do affluent nations owe the starving masses of the Third World – serves to distance hunger by suggesting that *all* hungry people of the world live in Third-World countries.[108] This characterisation conceals the existence of hunger and malnutrition in the North and reinforces stereotypes of Third-World poverty. '"*World* hunger",' write Balakrishnan and Narayan, 'is distinctly a *global* problem, and . . . "Third World hunger" is only one of its facets.'[109]

The relative invisibility of hunger in the North in conversations about world hunger might stem from a belief that such countries provide for the needs of the poor through social safety nets. Of course, the recent experience with welfare reform in the US is but one example of how public attitudes and political responses to the poor in the global North can be informed by political apathy and even antipathy, where 'blaming the victim' often substitutes for concern with structural causes of poverty. This distancing of hunger through failure to acknowledge its presence in the North is reinforced by the geographical distance between haves and have-nots in affluent societies, where various forms of segregation place poor, marginalised groups 'out of the literal and imaginative sight of their privileged fellow citizens'.[110]

The US provides a case-study of how government policies actively create and maintain hunger. At its core, hunger results from poverty and economic insecurity that is intensified by forces of globalisation. Improvements in technology, communication and transport have led to replacement of US workers through mechanisation, immigration and the movement of jobs offshore. This outsourcing of labour is facilitated through the emergence of parallel labour forces that involve transnational employer-employee labour arrangements, which lead to job losses for (and undercut prevailing wages and standards of) US workers. Such transnational labour arrangements include US companies that outsource low-wage work to assembly plants in export processing zones overseas, as well as special immigration programs that enable low-wage workers from other countries to come to the US (such as the H2 program for agricultural workers in the US).[111] These arrangements often push workers outside the scope of formal domestic

---

106 Debt-relief and increased trade are two examples of measures that rich countries can undertake to address poverty in poor countries that do not necessarily involve expenditure of additional resources.

107 Balakrishnan and Narayan (1996) p 234 (noting that failure to acknowledge *their* agency also masks the role played by states in the North, development agencies and, increasingly, corporations in providing forms of assistance, training and support to Third-World elites).

108 Balakrishnan and Nayaran (1996) p 232.

109 Balakrishnan and Nayaran (1996) p 232.

110 Balakrishnan and Nayaran (1996) p 233.

111 Parallel labour forces also operate domestically to undercut prevailing wages and standards, such as those facilitated through temp agencies and work programs for the poor, such as workfare.

legal regimes governing labour standards.[112] Privatisation and government downsizing have also led to massive lay-offs in public sector employment in the US. Moreover, the US Federal Reserve is committed to a monetary policy that guarantees a certain percentage of unemployment, which Federal Reserve Chairman, Alan Greenspan, believes is necessary to keep inflation down.[113] The federal government has failed to respond to or cushion individuals against the adverse effects of globalisation and other fundamental shifts in the economy.

Even where work is available, income and wealth disparities cause hunger. Half of those who are hungry in the US live in households where at least one member works.[114] It is frequently difficult for unskilled workers, particularly women, to support a household of average size under current economic and labour market conditions.[115] The US Department of Agriculture estimates that 6.6 million adults and 3.4 million children live in households that suffer from hunger.[116] An additional twenty-six million do not know from where their next meal will come.[117]

FEDERALISM AND THE RIGHT TO FOOD

Because administrative responsibility for the Food Stamp Program is shared by federal, state and local governments, a brief case-study is provided here to demonstrate the US government's failure to oversee implementation of economic rights at the state and local level. The federal government provides block grants to state and local governments, which, in the case of Food Stamps, requires states and municipalities to follow certain guidelines, but also provides them with discretion to implement policies that respond to local needs.

The focus of this case-study is New York City because, in addition to being a city with a large number of people affected by hunger, it is also in a state that actually goes further than the federal government in the welfare area by ensuring substantive economic rights.[118] New York State's Constitution includes a provision requiring aid to the needy.[119] However, despite this substantive guarantee at the state level and procedural guarantees at the federal level, the state's largest city, New York City, actively prevented hungry individuals from receiving Food Stamps until a recent federal court injunction.

---

112 Export processing zones often exempt employers from labour regulations, and immigrant workers are often too intimidated to enforce their labour rights, for fear of being retaliated against by employers who may try to report workers with questionable immigration status.

113 Silverstein (2000) ('what's especially troubling for some Fed watchers ... is the central bank's apparent conviction that low unemployment and rising wages are sure signs that inflation lies ahead').

114 Urban Justice Center (2000) p 47 (citing K Alaimo et al *Food Insufficiency Exists in the United States*).

115 Edin and Lein (1997).

116 US Department of Agriculture, Food and Nutrition Service (1999).

117 US Department of Agriculture, Food and Nutrition Service (1999).

118 See Hershkoff (1999); (contending that state courts need not model their interpretations of state constitutional welfare rights provisions on the US Supreme Courts' interpretation of the federal Constitution).

119 New York State Constitution, art XVIII; *Tucker v Toia* 43 NY 2d 1, 12 (NY, 1977). ('In New York State, the provision for assistance for the needy is not a matter of legislative grace; rather it is specifically mandated by our constitution'.)

The City had diverted Food Stamp applicants away from needed assistance through a number of administrative hoops put in place during the conversion of welfare centers to 'job centers'. At the job centers, the City required welfare and Food Stamp applicants to go through a series of steps, including multiple interviews with agency staff; a repeat visit to the center before receiving an application; an extensive job search during the application process; and participation in workfare (in which welfare applicants fill city jobs in exchange for their benefits, but at lower wages than the city workers they replaced).

New York City officials appeared determined to eliminate access to Food Stamps as part of the larger effort to eliminate welfare. Human Resources Administration Commissioner Jason Turner (the head of the city agency that administers the program) contended: 'I count Food Stamps as being part of welfare. You're better off without either one.'[120] By contrast, Under-Secretary of the US Department of Agriculture, Shirley Watkins, insisted: 'There was a misreading of what the food stamp program was all about. It's a *nutrition assistance* program, not a welfare program.'[121]

A class action suit challenged the diversion of needy people away from receiving Food Stamps and other aid, in violation of federal and state law.[122] While homeless and pregnant with twins, Lou Garlick, a named plaintiff in the suit, had to wait over a month to get Food Stamps and went entirely without food more than once during that period, having been denied the right to apply for emergency Food Stamps. A federal court in New York enjoined the City from continuing to convert welfare offices to job centers, until the City developed a plan to comply with the law.

Human Resources Administration Commissioner, Jason Turner, described the city's approach stating: '[w]e didn't do a lengthy planning followed by implementation, instead we acted first and worried about the consequences later. And that seems to have worked for us'.[123] The court found, however, that this did not work for hungry citizens, like Lue Garlick, who possess enforceable procedural rights under federal Food Stamp and Medicaid law, based on an 'overarching property interest' in receiving these benefits and viable due process claims. Moreover, the US Department of Agriculture released a report which identified a range of practices in New York that violate Food Stamp application processing requirements. The report concluded that the City denied these benefits based on eligibility requirements not permitted by federal law.[124] Despite the federal government's attempts to clarify and monitor the situation by 2000, 400,000 individuals continued to suffer from moderate or severe hunger in New York City, including 118,000 children.[125]

While steps taken by the federal court and the US Department of Agriculture were important attempts to address procedural irregularities in the nation's food assistance program for the poor, it is not clear these steps have been sufficient to

120   New York Times (2000).
121   Urban Justice Center (2000) p 10 (citing Norman (1999) 'States Mistakenly Cut Back on Food Stamps, Officials Say', JS Online Milwaukee Journal Sentinel, 18 November, available at www.jsonline.com).
122   *Reynolds v Giuliani*, 35 F Supp 2d 331 (SDNY, 1991).
123   Urban Justice Center (2000) p 35 (quoting Jason Turner, 'Welfare Reform in New York State', speech given at a policy forum at the Nelson A Rockefeller Institute of Government, Albany, New York, 17 November 1998).
124   US Department of Agriculture, Food and Nutrition Service, Northeast Region Food Stamp Program (1999).
125   Urban Justice Center (2000) p 4.

meet international obligations to realise the right to food. Having set in place economic and political incentives 'to end welfare as we know it' through drastic reductions in welfare enrolment, procedural guarantees alone are not likely to reverse the growing number of those who lack adequate food nor realise, at a minimum, freedom from hunger within US borders.

CONCLUDING OBSERVATIONS

This chapter opened with a discussion of ways in which the limited proceduralist approach taken to address hunger in the US falls short of international standards concerning the right to food. Except during moments of heightened consciousness about poverty and hunger, the US has largely rejected substantive commitments to the right to food or other economic rights. President Franklin D Roosevelt's New Deal programs and his commitment to guarantee 'freedom from want' represents one of these moments. President Lyndon B Johnson's War on Poverty represents another. Senator Robert Kennedy's ability to help Americans see hunger not only as a distant phenomenon, but also as a serious health problem in the booming post-war American economy represents yet another moment of heightened awareness about hunger. Despite progress made due to expansion of food assistance programs in the aftermath of Robert Kennedy's work, the weakening of commitments to food aid in the 1980s caused widespread hunger to reappear.

The fact that the US provides nothing more than a procedural safety net to address questions of hunger and malnutrition denies the major structural problems that exist and ensures that hunger and poverty will be permanent features of the American landscape. Hunger is only publicly acknowledged as a structural problem during moments of heightened consciousness triggered by times of crisis. Otherwise, those who are hungry are seen as isolated, individual cases whose circumstances result from their own morally 'bad' behaviour.

Embracing a human rights approach to hunger would require the US to shift from its parochial approach to a transnational one. A transnational approach to hunger acknowledges the context of globalisation whose powerful forces ensure that hunger in one site is rarely a geographically isolated phenomenon. Such an approach also insists that there are certain basic standards that a state must respect, protect and fulfil to be a full member of the community of nations that have assumed duties under human rights law.

If the US were to ratify the ICESCR, there are practical ways in which economic rights could be implemented. In analyzing the right to food as an example, Philip Alston posits that:

> '... an immediate and feasible step that the United States could take would be to adopt legislation requiring all levels of government to collaborate periodically on a detailed survey of the nutritional status of the American people, [which] could constitute the basis for carefully targeted legislative, administrative and practical measures aimed at enhancing realization of the right.'[126]

At the same time, ratification alone is not the answer, particularly if ratification results from the stealth strategy of the past, in which 'inside-the-beltway' groups convince the Senate to ratify a treaty by contending that it will not significantly

---

126 Alston (1990) pp 379–380.

alter US law. Such a strategy fails to educate and mobilise those who would be the treaties ultimate beneficiaries, leaving treaties' as dead letters of the law that are under-utilised.[127]

Perhaps the most promising development that may assist in advancing the human right to food comes not from lawyers or attempts at legal enforcement, but rather from activists. Activists have developed organising strategies that present alternatives to formal legal strategies, although their advocacy is frequently informed by a legal analysis of how to articulate a human right to food. Organising strategies may also be supplemented and amplified by formal legal strategies. For example, the Kensington Welfare Rights Union, which leads a national Economic Human Rights Campaign to document and publicise welfare reform policies that violate human rights, has participated in a challenge in the Inter-American Human Rights Commission as a way to both win relief and highlight their organising campaign.[128] Borrowing tactics that the US civil rights movement used in the 1960s, Kensington organized a Freedom Bus tour that involved numerous anti-poverty organisations around the nation, in an effort to build a poor peoples' movement, using the UDHR as a vehicle for organising. The Women's Economic Agenda Project is organising a similar Freedom Bus tour in California. Yet another organisation, the Urban Justice Center, has trained human rights monitors to document violations to the right to food and other rights in New York City.

As Philip Alston has pointed out:

'... an emphasis on the role of law must not be permitted to obscure the importance of viewing the concept of the right to food essentially as a mobilizing force, as a rallying point, through which people themselves are encouraged to assert their rights by making use of all appropriate legal and extra-legal means.'[129]

Using the human rights paradigm, activists in cities across the country have been exploring non-traditional strategies to either supplement or replace formal legal strategies. Human rights activists have convinced city councils in San Francisco, Oakland and Berkeley in California to sign resolutions supporting the ICESCR.[130] The New York City Council has also embraced the basic right to food in its adoption in 1989 of a resolution supporting the Convention on the Rights of the Child. The resolution called on city agencies 'to ensure that their activities and funding processes comply with the Convention' and specifically acknowledged that children have inalienable human rights, such as the 'right to food, shelter, health care, protection from abuse, education, and the right to develop in a safe environment free from discrimination'.[131] While these city council resolutions are not binding, they create a dialogue about the meaning of rights.[132]

The emergence of these grassroots initiatives in the US is part of a broader pattern in which local communities around the globe are struggling for change through the lens of human rights. These initiatives reflect the human rights framework's powerful appeal:

127 Powell (2001).
128 Lombardi (2000).
129 Alston (1984) p 62.
130 Telephone interview with Krishanti Dharmaraj, 2 August 2000 (while non-binding, these resolutions place these cities on record as supporting national ratification of the ICESCR).
131 New York City Council Resolution No 1891, 21 November 1989 (cited in Urban Justice Center (2000) p 18).
132 See Powell (2001).

'Acknowledging that the international community has set a higher standard of government responsibility for meeting the needs of its people allows us to transcend the limited domestic debate that questions the morals of poor people [and views food assistance as a form of charity, rather than as a right] ... A human rights analysis articulates a set of norms [that] enable advocates to push for a more humane standard of government accountability and policies that work toward eliminating poverty – not public assistance.'[133]

Transnational issue networks[134] connect human rights activists across the world and enable them to plug into the global human rights movement to support each other's local struggles.[135] This linking of the international and the local demonstrates that despite the particular ways in which governments fail adequately to respect, protect and fulfil rights, the human rights idea remains a powerful idea.

Select bibliography

Ackerman, B, (1998) *We the People: Transformations.*

Agence France Presse, (2000) 'Greens Organize Anti-McDonald's Protests in Paris', 29 July.

Alston, P, (1984) 'International Law and the Human Right to Food' in P Alston and K Tomasevski (eds), *The Right to Food.*

—(1990) 'U.S. Ratification of the Covenant on Economic, Social and Cultural Rights: The Need for an Entirely New Strategy', 84 AJIL 365.

Amar, A, (1990) 'Forty Acres and a Mule: A Republican Theory of Minimal Entitlements', 13 Harv JL & Pub Policy 37.

Balakrishnan, R, and Narayan, U, (1996) 'Combining Justice with Development: Rethinking Rights and Responsibilities in the Context of World Hunger and Poverty' in W Aiken and H LaFollette (eds), *World Hunger and Morality* (2nd edn).

Barber, B R, (1996) *Jihad vs. McWorld: How Globalism and Tribalism are Reshaping the World.*

Berke, R L, (1992) 'Clinton: Getting People Off Welfare', New York Times, 10 September, at A20.

Bork, R H, (1979) 'The Impossibility of Finding Welfare Rights in the Constitution', 1979 Wash U LQ 695.

Bread for the World, (2000) 'A Program to End Hunger – Hunger 2000', Annual Report, February, cited in Bread for the World press release, 10 February, www.bread.org/media/archives/pr000210.html.

Cashin, S D, (1999) 'Federalism, Welfare Reform, and the Minority Poor: Accounting for the Tyranny of State Majorities', 99 Col LR 552 at 560.

133 Urban Justice Center (2000) p 2.
135 Keck and Sikkink (1998).
136 Human rights activists from other countries joined the Kensington Welfare Rights Union in the last leg of their Freedom Bus tour in New York at a church rally near the UN headquarters: www.libertynet.org/kwru/kwru/kwru.htm.

Crooms, L A, (1995) 'Don't Believe the Hype: Black Women, Patriarchy and the New Welfarism', 38 How LJ 611 at 625.

Economist, The, (2000) 'The French Farmers' Anti-Global Hero', 8 July (US edn).

Edelman, P, (1998) 'The United Nations Convention on the Rights of the Child: Implications for Welfare Reform in the United States', 5 Geo J On Fighting Poverty 285.

Edin, K, and Lein, L, (1997) *Making Ends Meet.*

Eide, A, (1998) 'The Human Right to Food and Freedom from Hunger' in The Food and Agricultural Organization of the United Nations (ed), *The Right to Food: In Theory and Practice,* available at www.fao.org/docrep/w9990e/w9990e03.htm.

Epstein, R, (1985) 'The Uncertain Quest for Welfare Rights', Brigham Young U LR 201.

Hardin, G, (1996) 'Lifeboat Ethics: The Case Against Helping the Poor' in W Aiken and H LaFollette (eds), *World Hunger and Morality* (2nd edn).

Henkin, L, (1981) *The International Bill of Rights: The Covenant on Civil and Political Rights.*

—(1990) *Age of Rights.*

Hershkoff, H, (1999) 'Positive Rights and State Constitutions: The Limits of Federal Rationality Review', 112 Harv LR 1131.

—(1999) 'Welfare Devolution and State Constitutions', 67 Fordham LR 1403.

Holmes, S, and Sunstein, C R, (1999) *The Cost of Rights: Why Liberty Depends on Taxes.*

Jacoby, T, (1986) 'The Reagan Turnaround on Human Rights', 64 Foreign Affairs 1066.

Kammerman, S B, and Kahn, A J, (1988) 'Social Policy and Children in the United States and Europe' in J L Palmer, T M Smeeding and B B Torrey (eds), *The Vulnerable.*

Keck, M, and Sikkink, K, (1998) *Activists Beyond Borders: Advocacy Networks in International Politics.*

Kennedy, D, (1999) 'The Disciplines of International Law and Policy', 12 Leiden JIL 9 at 25.

Knop, K, (2000) 'Here and There: International Law in Domestic Courts', 32 NYUJIL & Pol 501.

Koh, H, (1996) 'Transnational Legal Process', 75 Neb LR 181 at 183–184.

Lombardi, K, (2000) 'Welfare Outrage Goes Global', The Boston Pheonix, 1–8 June.

Meunier, S, (2000) 'The French Exception', 79 Foreign Affairs 104 (July/Aug).

Michelman, F, (1969) 'The Supreme Court, 1968 Term – Forward: On Protecting the Poor Through the Fourteenth Amendment', 83 Harv LR 7, Supreme Court Forward.

Monaghan, H P, (1978) 'The Constitution Goes to Harvard', 13 Harv CR-CL 117.

New York Times, (1999) 'Pluralism Under Golden Arches: From Abroad, McDonald's Finds Value in Local Control', 12 February, at 7.

—(2000) 'Turning the Needy Away', Editorial, 31 July, at A22.

Office of the United Nations High Commissioner for Human Rights, (2000) 'Status of Ratifications of the Principal International Human Rights Treaties', 15 May.

Physicians Task Force on Hunger in America, (1985) *Hunger in America: The Growing Epidemic.*

Powell, C, (1999) 'Introduction: Locating Culture, Identity and Human Rights', 30 Col Human Rights LR 201, Spring, Symposium Issue in Celebration of the Fiftieth Anniversary of the Universal Declaration of Human Rights.

—(2001) 'Dialogic Federalism: Constitutional Possibilities for Incorporation of Human Rights Law in the United States', 150 U Penn LRev 245.

Sandal, M, (1984) *Morality and the Liberal Idea.*

Sciolono, E, (2000) 'A Wall of Trade Between U.S. and Europe', New York Times, 1 June.

Sen, A, (1984) 'The right not be hungry' in P Alston and K Tomasevski (eds), *The Right to Food*, p 69.

—(1990) 'Individual Freedom as a Social Commitment', New York Review of Books, 14 June, p 49.

Shue, H, (1980) *Basic Rights: Subsistence, Affluence, and U.S. Foreign Policy.*

—(1996) 'Solidarity among Strangers and the Right to Food' in W Aiken and H LaFollette (eds), *World Hunger and Morality* (2nd edn).

Silverstein, S, (2000) 'Risk of Too Much Success Weighs on Fed Rate Policy', Los Angeles Times, 28 June, at A1.

Souchard, P A, (2000) 'Small Fry vs. McDonald's: 10 Farmers Go To Trial', Chicago-Tribune, 1 July.

Tomasevski, K (ed), (1987) *The Right to Food: Guide Through Applicable International Law.*

US Department of Agriculture, Food and Nutrition Service, (1999) *Household Food Security in the United States: 1995–1998.*

US Department of Agriculture, Food and Nutrition Service, Northeast Region Food Stamp Program, (1999) 'New York Program Access Review, November-December 1998', 5 February.

Urban Justice Center, (2000) *Hunger is No Accident: New York and Federal Welfare Policies Violate the Human Right to Food.*

Winter, R K Jr, (1979) 'Changing Concepts of Equality: From Equality Before the Law to the Welfare State', 1979 Wash U LQ 741.

Index